Children, Adolescents, and the MEDIA

Second Edition

To the late Dr. Michael Rothenberg: pediatrician, child psychiatrist, and teacher extraordinaire, who knew most of this a long time ago. And to my children, Max and Katya, who have taught me a lot about the impact of the media.

—Victor C. Strasburger

To my bright and beautiful daughters, Isabel and Grace, who came all the way from China to change my life and inspire my work. And to my patient and caring husband, John, who is always there for me.

—Barbara J. Wilson

To my children, who are always in my heart and mind, even when they are not physically present. And to my husband, my biggest fan, for his love and support.

—Amy B. Jordan

Children, Adolescents, and the MEDIA

Second Edition

WILLOW INTERNATIONAL LIBRARY

Victor C. Strasburger
University of New Mexico School of Medicine

Barbara J. Wilson
Department of Communication at the
University of Illinois at Urbana–Champaign

Amy B. Jordan
Annenberg School for Communication
of the University of Pennsylvania

Los Angeles • London • New Delhi • Singapore

For information:

SAGE Publications, Inc.
2455 Teller Road
Thousand Oaks, California 91320
E-mail: order@sagepub.com

SAGE Publications India Pvt. Ltd.
B 1/I 1 Mohan Cooperative Industrial Area
Mathura Road, New Delhi 110 044
India

SAGE Publications Ltd.
1 Oliver's Yard
55 City Road
London EC1Y 1SP
United Kingdom

SAGE Publications Asia-Pacific Pte. Ltd.
33 Pekin Street #02-01
Far East Square
Singapore 048763

Printed in the United States of America

Library of Congress Cataloging-in-Publication Data

Strasburger, Victor C., 1949-
Children, adolescents, and the media / Victor C. Strasburger, Barbara J. Wilson, Amy B. Jordan. — 2nd ed.
    p. cm.
Includes bibliographical references and index.
ISBN 978-1-4129-4467-0 (pbk.)
    1. Mass media and children—United States. 2. Mass media and teenagers—United States. I. Wilson, Barbara J. II. Jordan, Amy B. (Amy Beth) III. Title.

HQ784.M3S78 2009
302.23083′0973—dc22   007047618

This book is printed on acid-free paper.

08   09   10   11   12   10   9   8   7   6   5   4   3   2   1

Acquisitions Editor:	Cheri Dellelo/Erik Evans
Editorial Assistant:	Lara Grambling
Production Editor:	Astrid Virding
Copy Editor:	Gillian Dickens
Typesetter:	C&M Digitals (P) Ltd.
Proofreader:	Gail Naron Chalew
Indexer:	Jeanne R. Busemeyer
Cover Designer:	Bryan Fishman
Marketing Manager:	Stephanie Adams

Contents

Preface

Amerrican youth spend inordinate amounts of time with the media. They laugh with characters who are funny; they viciously attack and destroy evil creatures as they play their favorite video games; they see advertising for candy, makeup, and even liquor; they listen to rap lyrics about sex and violence; and they interact with people all over the world online. Needless to say, it is a very different social world than the one their parents and grandparents faced during childhood.

The purpose of this book is to provide an overview of what is known about the impact of the media on youth in the 21st century. The goal is to provide a comprehensive, research-oriented treatment of how children and adolescents interact with the media. In each chapter, we review the latest findings as well as seminal studies that have helped frame the issues. Because research alone can often be dry and difficult to follow, we have generously sprinkled each chapter with illustrations, examples from the media, policy debates, and real-life instances of media impact. Our intent is to show the relevance of social science research to media-related issues involving youth.

One of the unique features of this book is its developmental focus. In Chapter 1, we begin with a discussion of how children and teens are unique audiences of the media, and we outline developmental differences in how young people process and make sense of media content and form. This developmental framework is used throughout the remainder of the book to help readers appreciate how, for example, a 5-year-old might respond differently to a media message than a 10-year-old or a 15-year-old would. In subsequent chapters, we discuss advertising (Chapter 2), educational content (Chapter 3), prosocial content (Chapter 4), media violence (Chapter 5), sexuality and the media (Chapter 6), drugs and the media (Chapter 7), rock music and music videos (Chapter 8), obesity and the media (Chapter 9), and media and the family (Chapter 12). In addition, we asked several experts to author particular chapters on the cutting-edge topics of electronic games (Chapter 10), the Internet (Chapter 11), and media literacy (Chapter 13).

Two other features make this book unique. First, the book covers the entire developmental period of childhood and adolescence. Other media-related books have been limited to addressing only children or only teens, but to our knowledge, this is the first media book of its kind that deals with the entire age span that characterizes youth. Second, the three authors bring very different backgrounds to the issues at hand. Victor C. Strasburger is a Professor of Pediatrics who has spent most of his career looking at the impact of the mass media on children's health. Barbara J. Wilson is a Professor of Communication who conducts research on child development and the media. Amy B. Jordan is the Director of the Media and the Developing Child sector of the Annenberg Public Policy Center at the University of Pennsylvania, where she studies the impact of media policy on children and families. Together, we have identified the media topics that are most pressing to parents, health care practitioners, educators, and policymakers today. As coauthors, we bring our rich and diverse experiences in medicine, social science, child development, public policy, and media to those topics. We also all have families, which of course gives us firsthand experience with many of the issues we raise.

The approach we have taken is certainly grounded in the media effects tradition. Where appropriate, we have highlighted other perspectives and readings that take a more cultural or critical approach to the study of media and youth. Those perspectives sensitize us to the importance of considering children and teens as active and powerful agents of their media experiences. We agree with the idea that youth cannot be shielded from the media, nor should they be. Clearly, children use the media to learn about their culture as well as about childhood itself. In fact, two new chapters in this second edition of our book focus exclusively on the positive effects of exposure to the media on children's development (Chapters 3 and 4). Still, we can do much to help children and teens approach the media as critical consumers, a topic that is touched on throughout the book but covered extensively in the chapter on media literacy. Readers will notice that we have selected some of the most controversial topics about the media for several chapters of this book. Our aim is not to be one-sided but instead to target the areas that are most controversial and at the heart of debates in the United States about the media and public health. We hope we have highlighted the importance of considering the content of the messages to which children are exposed. For today's young people, there are tremendous benefits as well as serious hazards of spending time with media.

This book is designed to serve as a core text for courses in communication or psychology on children and the media. It could also serve as supplemental reading in courses on child and adolescent development, issues in child development, or issues in the media. The book is most appropriate for an upper-level or advanced undergraduate course or even a beginning graduate seminar in the area. We assume some basic knowledge of research methods in social science, but we also provide background to help readers distinguish and compare different research traditions and methodologies. As a way to engage students, we provide a series of exercises at the end of each chapter. The exercises are meant to stimulate debate and can serve as paper assignments or as small-group discussion activities. To our minds, the exercises illustrate just how complex and engaging the media environment is for today's youth.

Acknowledgments

Dr. Strasburger would like to thank his colleagues in the American Academy of Pediatrics who have supported his interest in the media and his colleagues at the University of New Mexico School of Medicine who have allowed him time to write this book, especially Dr. Loretta Cordova de Ortega, Interim Chair of the Department of Pediatrics, and Dr. Paul Roth, Executive Vice President of the UNM Health Sciences Center.

Dr. Wilson would like to thank Kristin Drogos (M.A., University of Illinois at Urbana-Champaign) and Amy Holland (M.A., University of Illinois at Urbana-Champaign) for their persistent efforts to track down journal articles and online references, as well as Robert D. Day for his help in organizing comics, figures, and images.

Dr. Jordan would like to thank Michael Delli Carpini, Dean of the Annenberg School for Communication, and Kathleen Hall Jamieson, Director of the Annenberg School for Communication, for their unfailing support in her teaching and research in the field of children and media.

Victor C. Strasburger
Barbara J. Wilson
Amy B. Jordan

Sage Publications and the authors gratefully acknowledge the contributions of the following reviewers:

Craig A. Anderson, Ph.D., Iowa State University

Brad J. Bushman, Ph.D., University of Michigan and Vrije Universiteit, Amsterdam, the Netherlands

Margaret Cassidy, Ph.D., Communications Department, Adelphi University

James A. Graham, Ph.D., Department of Psychology, The College of New Jersey

Elizabeth D. Hutchinson, Ph.D., School of Social Work, Virginia Commonwealth University

Introduction

Dorothy G. Singer

I n 1974, a 9-year-old girl was attacked by three girls and a boy and raped with a soda bottle. The children later admitted that they got the idea of the rape from a TV movie, *Born Innocent,* that had been aired on NBC. In 1977, a 15-year-old boy was put on trial for the burglary and murder of an elderly woman. The boy claimed that he was merely copying an episode from *Kojak,* one of his favorite TV programs, where a woman had been shot by intruders. The boy had even wanted to shave his head so he could look more like his hero, Kojak.

In 2001, a 13-year-old boy inadvertently killed a much younger girl as he wrestled with her. He was a fan of wrestling programs on television and did not understand that the wrestling acts are carefully staged. In 2001, a young boy who watched *Jackass* on MTV set fire to himself in his backyard after he had started a fire and fanned the flame with his hands. In the ensuing pain, he put his hands to his chest and ran wildly around the yard, suffering severe burns. He admitted that he was emulating the star of the program who had set fire to himself during one of the shows.

Nearly 30 years have passed between the first two and the latter two incidents, yet television producers still continue to offer viewers much violence, whether in dramatic programs or on reality programs. In fact, 50% of the crimes based in reality-based TV programs are murder, while in reality, only 0.2% of the crimes reported by the Federal Bureau of Investigation are murder (Bushman & Huesmann, 2001). Well aware of the problem of violence on television, Victor Strasburger, Barbara Wilson, and Amy Jordan, authors and editors of this excellent book, *Children, Adolescents, and the Media,* present a cogent argument for more reduction of violence on TV and for more vigilance on the part of parents and other caregivers. Not only are TV programs playing a role in instigating violence but also the authors note that particular video games, music videos, and rock music contribute to the climate of violence and aggression. To counteract such violence, a chapter on media literacy offers possible solutions by discussing various curricula that teach young people and adults how to decipher the media messages and how to be more critical of what they watch on television. In addition, exercises based on the content of each chapter include topics for discussion and ideas for active media involvement. If followed by educators, parents, and industry personnel, we would see some significant changes not only in the *content* of the media but also in how our youth *use* and *process* the electronic sources of information and entertainment.

Strasburger, Wilson, and Jordan selected particular topics relating to the most pressing issues on television. These chapters should appeal to college audiences and to the general public. Not only is TV violence discussed but there are also new chapters on educational media, the family and the media, and the prosocial effects of the media, and updated chapters on commercials, sexuality, nutrition, and the Internet. I am impressed by the extent of research the authors bring to this book, but I have some additional comments to add to their fine reviews of the literature.

Video games are of particular interest to young people, and that topic is well covered in this book. Recently, a young boy age 9 years has become the world's youngest professional video game circuit winner. His favorite game is *Halo,* a violent "shoot-'em-up game." The boy's father claims that the youngster has good grades, plays the violin, swims, rides his bike every day, and is a good student (Lambert, 2007). Perhaps he is an exception, but certainly the parental mediation in this case has prevented him from imitating any violent acts. We know that the teenage shooters in Paducah (Kentucky), Jonesboro (Arkansas), and Littleton (Colorado) were students who habitually played video games. Games such as *Doom* were favorites of the boys involved in the Columbine High School murders. Although the fact that these boys were addicted to such games is not enough evidence to insist that violent video games are the cause of such behavior, surely they contribute to some degree.

Young people between the ages of 8 and 18 spend more than 40 hours per week using some form of media, and among boys ages 8 to 13, the average amount of time spent with console and computer video games is 7.5 hours per week. College students play at least 6 hours per week. Indeed, one of the most tragic school shootings took place on the campus of Virginia Tech in Blacksburg, Virginia, in April 2007 when a student shot and killed 32 people and wounded many more before he committed suicide. He had sent photographs of himself to a news program on that very day showing himself dressed like a character in a video game, wearing a black hat, jacket, and gloves and posed with arms outstretched holding two guns. Thus, it behooves us to pay attention to new studies on video game playing (C. A. Anderson, Gentile, & Buckley, 2007) and to an early meta-analysis of the research involving video games. One significant finding is that exposure to violent video games is negatively associated with prosocial behavior and positively related to aggressive affect and physiological arousal (C. A. Anderson & Bushman, 2001). Playing such games reduces the likelihood of youths evidencing empathy or helping others.

Commercials are also affecting young people's lives as the chapter on this topic asserts. Kuczynski (2001) reported on the popularity of teenage magazines. Not only are the ads on TV influencing purchases for girls, such as the styles of clothes worn by actresses on nighttime situation comedies or by the stars on MTV, but also ads and articles in the magazines themselves contribute to teenage consumerism.

CosmoGIRL!, Teen People, and *Teen Vogue* are just a few of the magazines that hype makeup and fashions but also feature articles about relationships and, when daring, even AIDS, as in *Teen People.*

When war-related toys are advertised on TV, children coax their parents to buy these, and when using such toys, they act out their aggressive scripts on the playground imitating Power Rangers, Ninja Turtles, or any of the characters who use fists, karate kicks, or laser weapons. In a study of toy gun play and aggression, for example, Watson and Peng (1992) found that toy gun play and parental punishment were positively associated with a higher level of *real* aggression, not pretend aggression, by the children.

Commercials not only affect children's desires for the purchase of toys but also their food habits. More Americans are becoming obese, and indeed, the authors present a strong chapter with much evidence concerning how the media affect nutrition and our eating habits. Food and toy advertisements on TV are the two largest categories targeted to children. Two thirds of ads on Saturday morning deal with ads for fats, oils, sweets, and high-sugar cereals.

Two significant new studies have been released about food advertising to children on television: one in March 2007 from the Kaiser Family Foundation and the other in June 2007 from the Federal Trade Commission (FTC). While the average findings in the two studies are similar, there are differences when it comes to findings for specific age groups. The FTC study found that young children (ages 2–5) are exposed to approximately 1,000 more food ads per year, or 23% higher than the Kaiser estimate, and it also found that older children are exposed to substantially fewer food ads than the Kaiser study found (approximately 2,000 fewer food ads per year, or 26% less). The FTC report attempts to explore trends over time through a comparison with similar data from 1977, whereas the Kaiser study is limited to an analysis of advertising in 2005 and draws no conclusions about trends (Federal Trade Commission, 2007; Kaiser Family Foundation, 2007). In an earlier monograph, it was found that one effect of television viewing is obesity in girls who are heavy viewers of TV. It is possible that obese girls may feel less popular than others and, therefore, they spend more time at home using TV as a substitution for social relationships (D. R. Anderson, Huston, Schmnitt, Linebarger, & Wright, 2001).

The chapter on the Internet is valuable in terms of the electronic boom in our society. We find that adolescents between ages 12 and 17 represent the highest number of Internet users, and even children between the ages of 3 and 5 are now online. In addition, numerous videos and CDs are now targeted to children younger than age 2. The Children's Online Privacy Protection Act of 1998 requires parental permission for a commercial Web site to collect personal information from a child younger than age 13. But there are no laws protecting children from chat rooms or from Web sites that offer pornography or hate information.

Teenagers are becoming "multitaskers," the practice named for the computer term describing a machine's ability to run several programs at once. Many teenagers are able to use their computer, talk on the phone, and listen to the radio at the same time. Hafner (2001) describes one teenager who worked on a class paper, searched the Web for information, checked her e-mail, kept up to eight messenger screens running, engaged in online conversation with friends, and listened to her MP3 player and a CD with songs. Some studies suggest that excessive use of computers has been linked to increased risk of obesity, repetitive-strain injuries, impaired vision, declines in social involvement, and feelings of loneliness and depression. Given the fact of multitasking among many teenagers, the social involvement issue for this group, at least, seems moot.

Although the authors touch on many vital issues dealing with the media, some topics have been omitted, such as multicultural factors, morality, stereotypes, and the economics of the television industry, to name just a few. For more information on these and other topics, the reader is referred to two handbooks (Dowd, Singer, & Wilson, 2006; Singer & Singer, 2001). As both those books and this present volume assert, it is important to stress the fact that the *content* of television is the issue and not the technology itself. Television can be a powerful teacher if it is used wisely and if parental mediation and guidance are offered to children and to adolescents.

References

Anderson, C. A., & Bushman, B. J. (2001). Effects of violent video games on aggressive behavior, aggressive cognition, aggressive affect, physiological arousal and prosocial behavior: A meta-analytic review of scientific literature. *Psychological Science, 12,* 353–359.

Anderson, C. A., Gentile, D.A., & Buckley, K. E. (2007). *Violent video games effects on children.* New York: Oxford University Press.

Anderson, D. R., Huston, A. C., Schmnitt, K. L., Linebarger, D. L., & Wright, J. C. (2001). *Early childhood television viewing and adolescent behavior.* Boston: Blackwell.

Bushman, B. J., & Huesmann, L. R. (2001). Effects of televised violence on aggression. In D. G. Singer & J. L. Singer (Eds.), *Handbook of children and the media* (pp. 223–254). Thousand Oaks, CA: Sage.

Dowd, N., Singer, D. G., & Wilson, R. F. (Eds.). (2006). *Handbook of children, culture, and violence.* Thousand Oaks, CA: Sage.

Federal Trade Commission. (2007, June 1). *Food for thought: Television food advertising to children in the United States.* Washington, DC: Author.

Hafner, K. (2001, April 12). Teenage overload, or digital dexterity? *The New York Times,* pp. G1, G5.

Kaiser Family Foundation. (2007, March 28). *Children's exposure to TV advertising in 1977 and 2004: Information for the obesity debate.* Menlo Park, CA: Author.

Kuczynski, A. (2001, April 2). The age of diminishing innocence. *The New York Times,* pp. C1, C6.

Lambert, B. (2007, June 7). He's 9 years old and 56 pounds, and a video-game circuit star. *The New York Times,* pp. 1, B6.

Singer, D. G., & Singer, J. L. (Eds.). (2001). *Handbook of children and the media.* Thousand Oaks, CA: Sage.

Watson, M. W., & Peng, Y. (1992). The relation between toy gun play and children's aggressive behavior. *Early Education & Development, 3,* 370–389.

CHAPTER 1

Children and Adolescents

Unique Audiences

Sometimes wise and disconcertingly like adults, children are nonetheless children. To the wonder, joy, and vexation of adults, they are different. As they grow older, they become increasingly like us and therefore intelligible to us, but at each age or stage of development there is something for adults to learn more about, to be amused by, and to adjust to.

—Professor Aimee Dorr,
*Television and Children: A Special
Medium for a Special Audience* (1986, p. 12)

Over the past twenty or thirty years, the status of childhood and our assumptions about it have become more and more unstable. The distinctions between children and other categories—"youth" or "adults"—have become ever more difficult to sustain.

—Professor David Buckingham,
*After the Death of Childhood: Growing
Up in the Age of Electronic Media* (2000, p. 77)

Children and young people are a distinctive and significant cultural grouping in their own right—a sizeable market share, a subculture even, and one which often "leads the way" in the use of new media.

—Professor Sonia Livingstone,
*Young People and New Media: Childhood and
the Changing Media Environment* (2002, p. 3)

Parents could once easily mold their young children's upbringing by speaking and reading to children only about those things they wished their children to be exposed to, but today's parents must battle with thousands of competing images and ideas over which they have little direct control.

—Professor Joshua Meyrowitz,
No Sense of Place: The Impact of Electronic Media on Social Behavior (1985, p. 238)

Because it was one of her favorite movies, Louise decided to rent a DVD of the film *E.T. —The Extra-Terrestrial* to share with her two children, a 4-year-old and a 10-year-old. The 10-year-old immediately liked the alien character, laughing at the creature's peculiar appearance and eating habits. The 4-year-old, on the other hand, tensed up the first time she saw E.T.'s strangely shaped hand with its two slender, protruding fingers. The young child asked several nervous questions: "What is that?" "Why is he hiding?" "What's wrong with his fingers?" Shortly thereafter, the 4-year-old announced that she did not like this "show" and that she wanted to turn the channel. When E.T.'s face was finally revealed on screen, the 4-year-old let out a yelp and buried her face into her blanket. Louise was dismayed at her young child's reaction, wondering how anyone could be frightened by such a benevolent creature.

Although this example involves a fictitious family, the incident is likely to resonate with parents who are often perplexed by their children's responses to the media. Indeed, a great many parents have reported that their preschool children were unpredictably frightened by the gentle but strange-looking alien called E.T. (Cantor, 1998). Likewise, G-rated movies such as *Bambi* and *Beauty and the Beast* have provoked fear in younger children (Hoekstra, Harris, & Helmick, 1999). One study even found that younger children were frightened by Michael Jackson's music video "Thriller," which featured the popular singer transforming into a werewolf (Sparks, 1986).

These reactions are not unique to a few films or videos. Research has documented strong differences in the types of media themes that frighten people across age (Harrison & Cantor, 1999). The types of stories that most often upset children younger than 7 involve animals or distorted-looking characters such as ghosts and witches (see Figure 1.1). Such themes greatly diminish in impact by the time people reach adolescence and adulthood. Instead, portrayals involving blood and physical injury are most likely to trigger negative emotions in older viewers.

From an adult perspective, a young child's fears of monsters and ghosts are difficult to explain. But they signal the importance of considering children's unique orientation to the world in trying to understand how the media can affect younger audiences (see Figure 1.2). In this chapter, we will explore how children and adolescents interact with the media, concentrating on the crucial role that human development plays in this process. As background, we will first give an overview of the media environment and media habits of today's youth. Next, we will explore several major principles or ideas that can be gleaned from child development

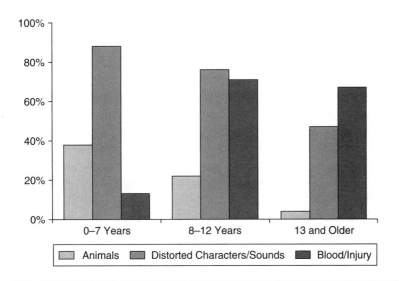

Figure 1.1   Percentage of Respondents Reporting Fright Responses to Media
Themes as a Function of Age at Time of Exposure

SOURCE: Adapted from Harrison and Cantor (1999).

research: Children are different from adults, children are different from each other, and adolescents are different from children. We will conclude the chapter with a focused look at specific cognitive skills that emerge during childhood and adolescence that are relevant to making sense of the mass media.

Figure 1.2   Media Violence Cartoon

SOURCE: Copyright ©John Branch, *San Antonio Express-News*. Used with permission.

Media Environment and Habits of Today's Youth

A recent headline in the *New York Times* warned that "28 Arrested in Florida Online Sex Sting" (Newman, 2007). Several of the predators worked for the Walt Disney Company and were caught when they arrived at a suburban house purportedly to meet with an underage girl. According to research cited in the article, 1 in 7 children (14%) say they have received an online solicitation, and 1 in 11 children (9%) have received a solicitation characterized as aggressively sexual in nature. Such statistics help to stir a sense of panic about the impact of media technologies on youth. But even more traditional forms of media can raise concerns. Reality programs on television feature couples who are tempted sexually in remote locations. Rap artists such as Eminem and 50 Cent celebrate hatred, revenge, and violence in their music. And video games have become increasingly violent. A popular video game series called *Grand Theft Auto* allows the player to take on the role of a criminal in a large city, engaging in numerous illegal activities, including killing police and military personnel.

There is no doubt that today's youth are confronted with a media environment that is very different from the one faced by their grandparents or even their parents (see Figure 1.3). Terms such as *digital television, gangsta rap,* and *Google* did not even exist 20 or 30 years ago. One of the most profound changes concerns the sheer proliferation of media outlets and technologies. Children today live in a "multidevice, multiplatform, multichannel world" (Carr, 2007). The advent of cable and satellite television has dramatically increased the number of channels available in most homes today. Digital cable is multiplying this capacity. Many homes in the United States also are equipped with CD players, DVD players, personal computers, wireless Internet access, and digital cameras. At a very young age, then, children are learning about keypads, CD-ROMs, mouses, and remote controls.

As these technologies proliferate, they are changing the nature of more traditional media. The TV screen, which once provided a way to watch broadcast television, is now being used for a much wider range of activities, including online

Figure 1.3

SOURCE: Baby Blues by Rick Kirkman and Jerry Scott. Reprinted with permission of King Features Syndicate.

shopping, video-on-demand, and viewing digitally recorded photographs and home movies. Newspapers can still be delivered to the doorstep or they can be received online. In other words, old distinctions between the television screen and the computer screen or between print and broadcast are becoming less meaningful.

And as media technologies converge, so too are the corporations that own them. In January 2001, America Online, the largest Internet service provider, and Time Warner, the world's biggest entertainment company, joined to become the largest media merger in history. Together, these two media giants own four film studios; CNN, HBO, Cinemax, and the WB networks; several book publishers; three major record companies; a large cable television system; and more than two dozen popular magazines. All of this, plus the merger, means access to more than 24 million Internet subscribers. The deal represents a powerful integration of content and delivery, meaning that programming can be created, promoted, and delivered by a single corporation. This $165 billion megamerger is one of many examples of corporate synergy and partnership.

Such mergers have sparked heated debates in the United States about the dangers of monopolistic growth (Bagdikian, 2000; Noam & Freeman, 1997). Furthermore, media corporations that were once primarily American based now have major stakes in the international market. So our capitalistic, privately owned media system and the cultural messages we produce are being exported worldwide. And as these media industries grow, they are becoming increasingly commercial in nature. For example, advertising is now a regular part of the Internet (see Chapters 2 and 11) and is creeping into cable television and even movie theaters.

In the relentless search for new markets, media corporations are increasingly recognizing and targeting youth as a profitable group of consumers (see Chapter 2). Television networks such as Nickelodeon and the Cartoon Network are designed for young viewers; magazines such as *Sports Illustrated for Kids, CosmoGIRL!, Skateboarding,* and *Teen Voices* are a growing phenomenon; and even Web sites are aimed specifically at children and adolescents. Nicktropolis, a new site developed by Nickelodeon, allows young children to enter an immersive 3-D virtual world where they can design their own rooms, interact with characters, and chat with other kids in real time. Even technologies are being marketed to youth. Colored iPods and child-friendly cell phones are in high demand, even among elementary schoolers (see Figure 1.4). By the end of 2006, some 6.6 million of the 20 million American children between the ages of 8 and 12 had their own cell phone (Foderaro, 2007). The proliferation of such handheld devices, which now allow access to the Internet, means that children can experience media around the clock, 7 days a week.

Finally, digital technology is altering the very nature of media experiences. Images and sounds are more realistic than ever, further blurring the distinction between real-world and media events. Children can enter virtual worlds in arcades and even in their bedrooms, traveling to different places, encountering strange creatures, and playing adventurous and often violent games. And these new media are far more interactive, allowing youth to become participants in their quest for information, action, and storytelling.

How are youth of today responding to this modern and complex media environment? A recent national study took an in-depth look at the media habits of

Figure 1.4

SOURCE: Baby Blues by Rick Kirkman and Jerry Scott. Reprinted with permission of King Features Syndicate.

American children (Roberts, Foehr, & Rideout, 2005). Surveying more than 2,000 children ages 8 to 18, the study documented that youth today are surrounded by media. The average child in the United States lives in a home with three TVs, four CD or tape players, three radios, three VCR/DVD players, two video game consoles, and one computer. More telling, the media have penetrated young people's bedrooms. A full 68% of American children between the ages of 8 and 18 have a television in their room. Moreover, 54% have their own VCR/DVD player, and 49% have a video game console that connects to their bedroom TV (see Figure 1.5). Having a TV as well as a video game console in the bedroom is more common

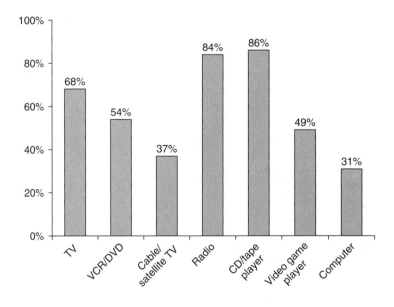

Figure 1.5   Proportion of Children (8–18 Years of Age) Having Various Media in Their Bedroom

SOURCE: Adapted from Roberts et al. (2005).

among African American than Caucasian youth. Hispanic youth fall in between the other two groups in the proportion having television equipment in the bedroom.

In terms of exposure, the average U.S. child between the ages of 8 and 18 spends 6½ hours a day using media (Roberts et al., 2005). Yet, despite all the technologies available, most of this time is spent watching television (see Figure 1.6). On average, American children watch 3 hours of TV per day. Notably, one out of five children in the national study by Roberts et al. (2005) reported that they had watched 5 or more hours of TV on the previous day. The study also revealed that parents typically do not exercise much control over their children's media experiences (see Figure 1.7). More than half (53%) of the children reported that there are no rules in their home about how often and what they can watch on TV, and an additional 23% said there were rules but they were seldom enforced. Of course, when parents themselves are queried, many more report supervising their children's media exposure (Gentile & Walsh, 2002). Underscoring how important parental oversight is, children who have a TV set in their bedroom spend substantially more time watching television than do those without a set in their room (Robinson, Winiewicz, Fuerch, Roemmich, & Epstein, 2006).

Although computers are rapidly spreading in American homes, access to this technology continues to be tied to income. Roughly three fourths (78%) of children in families with annual incomes of less than $35,000 have access to a home computer, compared with nearly all (93%) of those in families with incomes greater than $50,000 (Roberts et al., 2005). Even when they have a computer, children in low-income families are less likely to have an Internet connection.

More recently, a national study looked closely at the media habits of infants and preschoolers (Vandewater et al., 2007), age groups that many assume are too young to be involved much with media. Contrary to this assumption, the average American child between the ages of 6 months and 6 years spends about 1½ hours a day using media. Again, most of this time is spent watching television or videos/DVDs (see Figure 1.8). In fact, children younger than age 6 spend more time

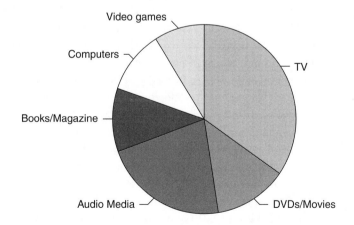

Figure 1.6   Average Time Children (8–18 Years of Age) Spend With Different Media Each Day

SOURCE: Adapted from Roberts et al. (2005).

Figure 1.7

SOURCE: Patrick O'Connor/*The Kent-Ravenna,* Ohio Record Courier. Reprinted by permission.

watching TV and videos than they do reading (or being read to) or playing outside. Perhaps most surprising, 20% of children younger than age 3 have a TV set in their bedroom; roughly 40% of 3- to 6-year-olds have a TV in their room.

American children are not so different from some of their counterparts abroad. One study of more than 5,000 children living in 23 different countries found that the average 12-year-old spent 3 hours a day watching television (Groebel, 1999), a figure remarkably comparable to that found in the United States. Another study of 12 European countries found that televisions and video recorders are in nearly every home, but having such technology in a child's bedroom varies considerably by country (d'Haenens, 2001). For example, more than 60% of children in the United Kingdom have a TV in their bedroom, whereas less than 20% of children in Switzerland do. As in the United States, those children who have technological equipment in their bedrooms also spend more time with the media each day.

To summarize, youth today are confronted with a media environment that is rapidly changing. Technologies are proliferating, merging, and becoming more interactive. And the content featured in these technologies is increasingly graphic, realistic, and commercial in nature. At the same time, media use is at an all-time high. Youth today spend anywhere from one third to one half of their waking hours with some form of media (see Figure 1.9). Preteens and teens frequently are engaging in more than one media activity at a time, called "media multitasking" (Foehr, 2006). And much of this media use is becoming more private as children retreat to their bedrooms to watch TV, play video games, or listen to music. We will now highlight several developmental principles that underscore the need to consider youth as a special audience in today's media environment.

Figure 1.8

SOURCE: Baby Blues by Rick Kirkman and Jerry Scott. Reprinted with permission of King Features Syndicate.

BABY BLUES By Rick Kirkman and Jerry Scott

Figure 1.9

SOURCE: Baby Blues by Rick Kirkman and Jerry Scott. Reprinted with permission of King Features Syndicate.

Children Are Different From Adults

Most adults believe that they personally are not affected much by the mass media. In a well-documented phenomenon called the "third-person effect," people routinely report that others are more strongly influenced by the mass media than they themselves are (Hoffner & Buchanan, 2002; Perloff, 2002). This difference in perceived impact gets larger as the age of the "other" person decreases. In other words, adults perceive that the younger the other person is, the stronger the effect of the media will be (Eveland, Nathanson, Detenber, & McLeod, 1999). Interestingly, even children endorse a kind of third-person effect, claiming that only "little kids" imitate what they see on TV (Buckingham, 2000).

Are children more susceptible to media influence than adults are? At the extremes, there are two radically different positions on this issue (see Buckingham, 2000). One view is that children are naive and vulnerable and thus in need of adult protection. This stance sees the media as inherently problematic and in some cases evil because they feature material that children are simply not yet ready to confront. Buckingham (2000) points out that "media panics" have been with us a long time, especially those concerning the impact of sex and violence on children. Such panics gain steam any time a public crisis occurs, such as the massacre at Columbine High School, or any time a new and unknown form of media technology is developed (Wartella & Reeves, 1985).

A contrasting view is that children are increasingly sophisticated, mature, and media savvy (Livingstone, 2002). According to this position, efforts to shield youth from media are too protectionist in nature, smack of paternalism, and construe children as acted upon instead of actors. Instead, children should be empowered to take control of their own media experiences, negotiating and learning along the way. Buckingham (2000) argues that this position is widely shared among those who see children as independent consumers who should be able to spend their own money and buy what they want.

These very different perspectives illustrate that notions of childhood are constantly being defined, debated, and renegotiated over the course of history (James, Allison, Jenks, & Prout, 1998). In truth, neither of these extreme positions seems very satisfying. Children are not entirely passive in the face of the mass media, nor are they extremely worldly and discriminating. The reality is probably somewhere in between. Nevertheless, most parents, developmental psychologists, policymakers, and educators would agree that children are not the same as adults (see Figure 1.10).

Several features of childhood support this distinction. First, children bring less real-world knowledge and experience to the media environment (Dorr, 1986). Every aspect of the physical and social world is relatively new to a young child who is busy discovering what people are like, how plants grow, what animals eat, and where one neighborhood is located relative to another. As they get older, children explore increasingly abstract concepts and ideas such as the social norms of their culture, what prejudice is, and how life begins. In almost every arena, though, children possess a more limited knowledge base compared with adults.

One implication of this is that children can fail to understand a media message if they lack the background knowledge needed to make sense of the information.

Figure 1.10

SOURCE: Baby Blues by Rick Kirkman and Jerry Scott. Reprinted with permission of King Features Syndicate.

As an illustration, in 1996, researchers at the Children's Television Workshop (now called Sesame Workshop) wanted to produce a *Sesame Street* segment about visiting the doctor. On the basis of preliminary interviews, the researchers discovered that preschoolers mostly associated doctor visits with getting shots and that they had little knowledge of the importance of such vaccinations ("Feeling Good," 1996). Had the producers not discovered this, they might have created a script that focused too much on getting shots, inadvertently reinforcing children's negative and limited impressions of the purpose of going to a physician.

As another example, researchers working on the *Sesame Street* Web site wanted to create an activity that would help preschoolers learn about e-mail. In developing the "*Sesame Street* Post Office," the researchers discovered that preschool children have little, if any, experience with e-mail or with composing letters (Revelle, Medoff, & Strommen, 2001). In other words, the children's background knowledge was quite limited. Taking this into account, the post office activity was designed to be very concrete by having the child choose a Muppet to e-mail from a set of pictures of Muppets and then choose questions to ask from a set tailored to each Muppet (see www.sesameworkshop.org/sesamestreet/mail/sspo/). The child's message is displayed on the screen before it is sent so that children can see how their choices influence the composed letter. Researchers also determined that adding a "Dear [name of Muppet]" to the beginning of the e-mail and a "Your friend, [name of child]" to the end of it helped children understand the conventions of letter writing.

The lack of real-world knowledge also can make children more willing to believe the information they receive in the media. It is difficult to evaluate a story for accuracy or truthfulness in the face of no alternative data. An adult watching a TV advertisement is able to evaluate that message in the context of knowledge about the television industry as well as a vast array of personal experiences with purchasing products. A child, on the other hand, rarely has this rich set of knowledge structures on which to rely. As an illustration, Figure 1.11 presents children's perceptions of how truthful advertisements are (Wilson & Weiss, 1995). In a sample of nearly 100 girls ages 4 to 11, a full 45% reported that ads tell the truth "most of the time" or "always." Given this level of trust, a young child seems fairly defenseless when

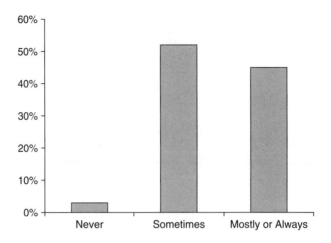

Figure 1.11   Children's (4–11 Years of Age) Perceptions of How Often TV
Advertisements Tell the Truth

SOURCE: Adapted from Wilson and Weiss (1995).

confronted with a slick TV ad that costs thousands of dollars to produce and may yield millions of dollars in sales profit.

A second feature that distinguishes childhood from adulthood is the strong eagerness to learn that marks the early years (Dorr, 1986). Parents experience this with exhaustion sometimes, as their infant daughter puts one more object in her mouth or their preschool son asks for the twentieth time, "What's that?" or "Why?" Such curiosity is a hallmark of childhood and is celebrated by educators. But it means that children are as open to learn from the mass media as from other sources, particularly in situations when firsthand experience is not possible. For example, most American children are not able to visit Japan, but they can learn about the country by reading a book or viewing a TV documentary. A preschooler can even watch *Big Bird in Japan,* a Sesame Workshop production available on DVD. These examples show the educational benefits of the media. Unfortunately, a child could also learn about Japan by visiting a Web site created by a hate group that disparages people of Asian descent.

A third feature that characterizes childhood is a relative lack of experience with the media. Admittedly, these days some children are actually more media savvy than their parents. Indeed, many children know how to surf the Web or program the digital video recorder while their parents still fumble with these technologies. One study found that 19% of children younger than age 6 were able to turn on the computer by themselves (Rideout & Hamel, 2006). But it is still the case that with most media, adults simply have spent more time with the technology. Adults readily appreciate, for example, that the placement of a story in a newspaper signals something about its importance, that public television is a noncommercial channel in contrast to the broadcast networks, and that there are different genres and subgenres of movies. In contrast, children often show an incomplete understanding of production techniques such as dissolves and split screens (Beentjes, deKoning, & Huysmans, 2001), have difficulty distinguishing nightly news programs from shows such as *Hard Copy* and *Current Affair* (Wilson & Smith, 1995), and do not fully appreciate the commercial nature of most media in the United States (Dorr, 1980).

This lack of familiarity with the technical forms and structure of the media makes a child less able to critically evaluate the content presented.

To summarize, children differ from adults in a number of ways that have implications for responding to the media. Younger age groups have less experience with the real world and at the same time possess a strong readiness to learn about those things with which they are unfamiliar. They also tend to be less savvy about the nature, the intricacies, and the potential distortions of the mass media. Such naïveté makes a preschooler and even an elementary schooler more likely to believe, learn from, and respond emotionally to media messages than is a more mature and discriminating adult.

Children Are Different From Each Other

It may be easier to recognize that children are different from adults than it is to appreciate how much children differ from one another. In some ways, the label *children* itself is misleading because it encourages us to think of a fairly homogeneous group of human beings. As the E.T. example at the start of this chapter illustrates, a 4-year-old thinks and responds to the world very differently than a 12-year-old does. But even a group of 4-year-olds will exhibit marked differences in how they respond to the same situation. In fact, sometimes it is difficult to believe that two children are the same age or in the same grade level.

On any elementary school playground, kindergartners can be readily distinguished from sixth graders—they are shorter in height and normally weigh less. Their heads are smaller, they dress differently, and they tend to be more physically active. But even more profound differences exist in their cognitive functioning. Younger children attend to and interpret information in different ways than do their older counterparts. Several influential perspectives on children's development support this idea, including Piaget's (1930, 1950) theory of cognitive development as well more recent models of information processing (Flavell, Miller, & Miller, 2002; Siegler, 2005).

Age is often used as a marker of these differences in cognitive abilities, although there is tremendous variation in how and when children develop. Still, most research reveals major differences between preschoolers and early elementary schoolers (3–7 years of age), on the one hand, and older elementary school children (8–12 years of age), on the other, in terms of the strategies that are used to make sense of the world (Flavell et al., 2002). These strategies have important implications for how children respond to mass media, as will be discussed below in the section titled "Developmental Differences in Processing the Mass Media."

Cognitive development is not the only factor that distinguishes children from each other. Personality differences also set children apart. For instance, some children are withdrawn or inhibited in unfamiliar situations whereas others are not (Kagan, 1997). Children also differ in the degree to which they possess prosocial dispositions toward others (Eisenberg, Fabes, & Spinrad, 2006), the degree to which they are capable of regulating their emotions (Stegge & Terwogt, 2007), and the degree to which they enjoy novel or stimulating situations (Zuckerman, 1994).

Research consistently shows sex differences among children too. For example, girls tend to prefer activities that are less vigorous than boys do (Eaton & Enns, 1986), and

Figure 1.12

SOURCE: Baby Blues by Rick Kirkman and Jerry Scott. Reprinted with permission of King Features Syndicate.

boys typically are more physically aggressive (Baillargeon et al., 2007). In terms of cognitive skills, girls generally obtain higher grades in school and do better on tests involving writing, whereas boys do better on visual-spatial tasks (Halpern, 2004).

The fact is that children, even those who share biological parents and are raised in the same environment, differ on many dimensions (Scarr, 1992). And children themselves recognize these differences early in development. For example, children become aware of their own gender by around age 2 (Berk, 2000). During the preschool years, they begin formulating mental conceptions of activities, norms, attributes, and scripts that are associated with being male or female (Bem, 1981). Young children's initial understanding of gender as a social category is often based on superficial qualities such as hair length and dress (see Figure 1.12). As they enter elementary school, children's conceptions grow to be more sophisticated, and they become keenly interested in gender-role information in the culture. They actively search for cultural meanings about gender in their homes, on the playground, and in the media (see Bussey & Bandura, 1999). In other words, the unique characteristics that differentiate children in turn get represented and reinforced in the culture.

All of these unique characteristics make it difficult to come up with a single prototype for what a child is like. Therefore, when we make generalizations about children and the media, we must be careful to take into account the developmental, personality, and gender characteristics of the individuals involved.

Adolescents Are Different From Children

Adolescence is often characterized as a time of challenge and turbulence (Roth & Brooks-Gunn, 2000). Along with bodily changes that can be quite dramatic, teens are faced with increased independence and growing self-discovery. Scholars of adolescent development refer to these changes as developmental transitions or passages between childhood and adulthood (Arnett, 1992a). In other words, the sometimes stormy periods are a necessary and normal part of growing up (Gondoli, 1999).

Unfortunately, parents and even the general public often view the teenage years with some trepidation. One national poll revealed that 71% of adults describe today's teenagers negatively, using terms such as *irresponsible* and *wild* (Public Agenda, 1999). Some of this public opinion is likely fueled by the media's preoccupation with high-profile cases of troubled teens who become violent. Contrary to public opinion, though, most teens are able to navigate adolescence in a socially responsible way, learning new competencies and new roles on the path to adulthood (Graber, Brooks-Gunn, & Petersen, 1996; Petersen, 1988).

What are some of the developmental hallmarks of adolescence? One of the main challenges a teen faces is identity formation (Schwartz & Pantin, 2006). During the teenage years, boys and girls alike begin to ask questions about who they are and how they differ from their parents. This emerging sense of the self is fragile and malleable as teens "try on" different appearances and behaviors. An article in *Newsweek* magazine described the teen years like this: "From who's in which clique to where you sit in the cafeteria, every day can be a struggle to fit in" (Adler, 1999, p. 56). There is growing evidence that adolescents use the Internet to experiment with their identities. For example, one study found that 50% of 9- to 18-year-olds who use the Internet had pretended to be somebody else while communicating by e-mail, instant messaging (IM), or chat (Valkenburg, Schouten, & Peter, 2005). Teens also spend a great deal of time posting photographs, videos, and personal information on popular Web sites such as YouTube, MySpace, and Facebook. As they experiment with ways of expressing themselves online, some have argued that the Internet is changing the way that teens communicate with each other about their identities (Eagle, 2007).

A second challenge of adolescence is increased independence. Parents naturally feel less need to supervise a 13-year-old who, compared with a 5-year-old, can dress, study, and even go places alone. Teens often have jobs outside the home and by age 16 can typically drive a car, furthering their autonomy. In one study, the percentage of waking hours that teens spent with their families fell from 33% to 14% between the 5th and 12th grade (Larson, Richards, Moneta, Holmbeck, & Duckett, 1996).

Time away from parents can provide teens with opportunities to make independent decisions. It also can allow for experimentation with a variety of behaviors, some of which are not very healthy. A large national study involving more than 90,000 adolescents in Grades 6 to 12 found strong differences between those teens who regularly ate dinner with a parent and those who did not (Fulkerson et al., 2006). In particular, teens who spent less dinner time with parents showed significantly higher rates of smoking, drinking, depression, violence, and school problems, even after controlling for family support and family communication. The direction of causality is difficult to pinpoint here because it may be that troubled teens simply choose to spend less time at home. However, other studies have also documented the importance of parent involvement as a buffer against unhealthy behaviors during the teenage years (Cookston & Finlay, 2006).

This point leads us to a third feature of adolescence—risk taking. Today's teens face tough decisions regarding a number of dangerous behaviors such as smoking, drug use, and sexual activity. And there is no doubt that adolescence is a time of experimentation with reckless activities (Gullone & Moore, 2000). For example, recent estimates suggest that every day, more than 6,000 American youth start smoking cigarettes (American Lung Association, 2003). Furthermore, a recent national survey revealed that 47% of 9th through 12th graders reportedly have had sexual intercourse (Centers for Disease Control and Prevention, 2006). The same study found that 18% of the teens had carried a weapon during the 30 days preceding the survey, 43% had drunk alcohol, 20% had used marijuana, and 37% of sexually active students had not used a condom.

Some of this risk taking may be a function of what scholars have labeled "adolescent egocentrism" (Dolcini et al., 1989; Elkind, 1967, 1985). In particular, teenagers often seem preoccupied with their own thoughts and appearance and assume others are equally interested in their adolescent experiences. This view of the self as unique and exceptional can in turn lead to a feeling of invulnerability to negative consequences (Greene, Krcmar, Walters, Rubin, & Hale, 2000). In other words, self-focused teens think they are different from everyone else and that tragedies occurring to others "won't happen to me." Indeed, studies show that teens routinely underestimate their own personal chances of getting into a car accident compared with the risks they assume others face (Finn & Bragg, 1986). Similar misjudgments have been found among sexually active young girls who underestimate the likelihood that they themselves might get pregnant (Gerrard, McCann, & Fortini, 1983). One study linked this type of optimistic bias to teen smoking. Arnett (2000) surveyed 200 adolescents and found that a majority agreed that smoking is addictive and causes death for "most people." Yet compared to nonsmokers, adolescent smokers were more likely to doubt that they themselves would die from smoking even if they engaged in such behavior for 30 or 40 years.

Risk taking also can be viewed as an adolescent's effort to assert independence from parents and to achieve adult status (Jessor, 1992). However, not all teens engage in reckless behaviors, and even the ones who do seldom limit their activities to those legally sanctioned for adults. Arnett (1992b) argues that risk taking must be viewed in the larger context of an adolescent's socialization. Some teens experience *narrow socialization,* which he characterizes as involving strong allegiance to the family and community, clear expectations and responsibilities, unambiguous standards of conduct, and swift sanctions for any deviation from those standards. Other teens are raised in an environment of *broad socialization,* where independence and autonomy are encouraged, standards of conduct are loose or even self-determined, and enforcement of standards is lenient and uneven. Arnett argues that in addition to parents, the schools, the legal system, and even the media contribute to these overarching patterns of socialization. As might be expected, risk taking is more prevalent in cultures in which socialization is broad rather than narrow (see Arnett, 1999, for review).

A fourth feature of adolescence is the importance of peers. Teens spend a great deal of time with friends and place a high value on these relationships (Berndt, 1996). On average, teens spend up to one third of their waking hours with friends (Hartup & Stevens, 1997). In her controversial book *The Nurture Assumption: Why Children Turn Out the Way They Do,* Judith Harris argued that parents have a minimal influence on their child's development other than to nurture and shape the child's peer group (Harris, 1998). Peer groups certainly do make a difference during adolescence. Studies have documented the role of peers in the initiation of behaviors such as cigarette smoking (Chassin, 1985), drug use (Halebsky, 1987), and sexual intercourse (Whitbeck, Yoder, Hoyt, & Conger, 1999). Engaging in reckless behavior often helps a teen become a member of a peer group, and the group itself can foster a sense of collective rather than individual invincibility (Arnett, 1992a).

But peer influence is not as straightforward and not necessarily as negative as some might assume. Friends actually can be a source of support for teens and also can increase self-esteem (Hartup & Stevens, 1999). Generally, adolescents are more susceptible to *antisocial* peer pressure when they have more delinquent than non-delinquent friendships (Haynie, 2002), when they have poorer relationships with parents (Dishion, 1990), and when they are alienated from community support structures such as schools (Arnett, 1992b; Resnick et al., 1997).

Last but not least, puberty and sexual development are hallmarks of adolescence. Body hair, acne, muscle growth, and weight gain are only a few manifestations of the dramatic physical changes that occur during the teenage years. Puberty typically begins during early adolescence, around age 9 or 10 for girls and roughly 1 to 2 years later for boys (Archibald, Graber, & Brooks-Gunn, 2003), although there are large individual variations. At the same time as their bodies are changing, many teens experience an increased energy level as a function of significant changes in their endocrine system (Petersen & Taylor, 1980). Furthermore, increased hormonal production of androgens and estrogens stimulates the growth of reproductive organs (see Rekers, 1992).

As might be expected, the hormonal and physical changes associated with puberty are accompanied by an increased interest in sexuality. In one study, for example, 12- to 15-year-old girls who were more physically mature (i.e., earlier pubertal timing) reported a greater interest in seeing sexual content in the movies, television, and magazines than did those who were less mature (J. D. Brown, Halpern, & L'Engle, 2005). Thus, at some point during adolescence, most teens will become intensely curious about sex and will seek information about sexual norms, attitudes, and practices in their culture. It is no accident, then, that popular teen magazines devote a great deal of space to sexual issues and relationships (Walsh-Childers, 1997).

Whether the teenage years are characterized as tempestuous or transitional, there is no doubt that significant developmental changes occur during this period. Adolescents spend more time alone or with friends and less time with parents. This growing independence comes at the same time that teens are exploring their own identities and their sexuality. The challenge is to provide these young people with enough latitude as well as guidance so that the decisions they make will result in a healthy rather than risky lifestyle.

Developmental Differences in Processing the Mass Media

So far, we have focused on broad developmental features that characterize childhood and adolescence and that differentiate these periods from adulthood. Now we will turn our attention more directly to young people's interactions with the media. Any individual who confronts a mediated message must make sense of and interpret the information that is presented. Like adults, children and adolescents construct stories or readings of media messages that they encounter (Dorr, 1980).

Given some of the pronounced differences in experience and maturation described above, we can expect that interpretations of the same content will vary across the life span. That is, a young child is likely to construct a different story from a TV program than is an older child or a teenager.

These different interpretations may seem "incorrect" or incomplete to an adult viewer (see Figure 1.13). But even among mature adult viewers, there are differences in how people make sense of stories. For example, one study looked at people's reactions to a 1970s TV sitcom called *All in the Family,* which featured a bigoted character named Archie Bunker (Vidmar & Rokeach, 1974). The research revealed that interpretations of the program varied widely based on individual attitudes about race. Those viewers who held prejudiced attitudes identified with Archie Bunker and saw nothing wrong with his racial and ethnic slurs (see Figure 1.14). In contrast, viewers who were less prejudiced evaluated Archie in negative ways and perceived the program to be a satire on bigotry.

What cognitive activities are involved when a young person watches a television program, enjoys a movie, or plays a video game? In general, five mental tasks are involved (Calvert, 1999; Collins, 1983). First, the child needs to select important information for processing. When viewing television, for example, a multitude of auditory and visual signals are presented in a particular program or advertisement. Moreover, there are cues in the environment that often compete with the television, such as family members talking in the background or loud music from another room. A viewer must allocate attention to these myriad cues, consciously or unconsciously filtering out what is not essential and instead focusing on what is important in the situation.

Second, the child needs to sequence the major events or actions into some kind of story. Most media messages feature a narrative or storyline (Grossberg, Wartella, & Whitney, 1998). Television plots are the easiest example of this, but even an advertisement, a video game, a song, and a radio program convey stories.

Third, the child needs to draw inferences from implicit cues in the message. The media do not have the space or the time to explicitly present all aspects of a story. Television programs jump from one location to another, characters in movies have dreams or experience flashbacks, and even in video games characters travel in ways that are not always orderly or linear. A sophisticated consumer recognizes the need to "read between the lines" to fill in the missing information. But a young child may fail to recognize that time has passed between scenes (R. Smith, Anderson, & Fischer, 1985) or that the events depicted are only part of a dream (Wilson, 1991).

Fourth, to make sense of both explicit and implicit cues in the message, a child must draw on the rich database of information he or she has stored in memory that relates to the media content. For instance, a child who lives in a rural community will have an easier time making sense of a movie about a family that loses a farm to bank foreclosure than will a child who lives in an apartment complex in New York City. The rich set of past experiences and acquired knowledge forms a mental database that helps a child interpret new messages.

Fifth, the child typically will evaluate the message in some way. The simplest evaluation pertains to liking or not liking the message. Children as young as 2 years of age already show preferences for certain types of TV programs, such as those

BABY BLUES By Rick Kirkman and Jerry Scott

Figure 1.13

SOURCE: Baby Blues by Rick Kirkman and Jerry Scott. Reprinted with permission of King Features Syndicate.

featuring puppets and young characters (Lemish, 1987; Rideout & Hamel, 2006). As they grow older, children become increasingly sophisticated and critical of media messages (Potter, 2005). Not only are they capable of evaluating the content but they also begin to appreciate the forms, economic structure, and institutional constraints that characterize different media (Dorr, 1980). An adolescent, for example, may reject all mainstream American television programming because of its inherent commercialism.

Given this set of tasks, we can expect that children will process media messages in different ways across development. We now describe some of the major shifts in

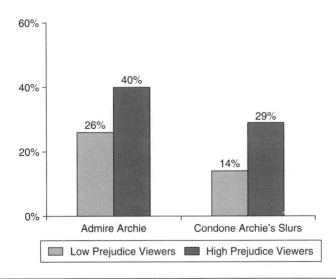

Figure 1.14   Adults' Reactions to the TV Show *All in the Family* as a Function of Viewer Prejudice

SOURCE: Adapted from Vidmar and Rokeach (1974).

cognitive processing that occur during the transition from early to middle childhood and during the transition from late childhood to adolescence. This is by no means an exhaustive list but instead reflects some of the skills most relevant to interacting with the media (for further reading, see Dorr, 1980; Flavell et al., 2002; Valkenburg & Cantor, 2000).

Two caveats need to be made here. First, most of the changes highlighted below occur gradually rather than abruptly during development (Flavell et al., 2002). Piaget (1950, 1952) argued that younger children's thinking is qualitatively different from that of older children, such that their cognitive systems progress through distinct stages (i.e., sensorimotor, approximately 0–2 years of age; preoperational, 2–7 years; concrete operational, 7–11 years; formal operational, 11 years and older). However, recent research indicates that cognitive performance can be uneven across different types of tasks and that children exhibit varied skill levels even within a particular domain (Siegler, 2005). Thus, it is widely believed that development is far less stagelike or abrupt than Piaget's theory would have us believe.

Second, the ages during which these shifts occur vary markedly across children. For rough approximations, we define younger children as those between 2 and 7, older children as those between 8 and 12, and adolescents as those between 13 and 18.

Younger Children Versus Older Children

From Perceptual to Conceptual Processing. Preschoolers pay close attention to how things look and sound. This focus on salient features has been referred to as *perceptual boundedness* (Bruner, 1966). Perceptual boundedness is defined as an overreliance on perceptual information at the expense of using nonobvious or unobservable information that may be more relevant (Springer, 2001). For example, preschoolers frequently group objects together based on shared perceptual features such as color or shape (Bruner, Olver, & Greenfield, 1966; Melkman, Tversky, & Baratz, 1981). In contrast, by age 6 or 7, children begin sorting objects based on conceptual properties such as the functions they share (Tversky, 1985). With regard to television, studies show that younger children pay strong visual attention to perceptually salient features such as animation, sound effects, and lively music (Anderson & Levin, 1976; Calvert & Gersh, 1987; Schmitt, Anderson, & Collins, 1999). On the other hand, older children tend to be more selective in their attention, searching for cues that are meaningful to the plot rather than those that are merely salient (Calvert, Huston, Watkins, & Wright, 1982).

One creative experiment involving television reveals this distinction quite clearly. Hoffner and Cantor (1985) exposed children to a television character who was either attractive or ugly and who acted kind toward others or was cruel (see Figure 1.15). Preschoolers generally rated the ugly character as mean and the attractive character as nice, independent of the character's actual behavior. In other words, their evaluations were strongly affected by the character's physical appearance. Older children's judgments, in contrast, were influenced more by the character's behavior than her looks.

Figure 1.15   Four Old Ladies Holding Cats

SOURCE: From Hoffner and Cantor (1985). Copyright ©American Psychological Association. Reprinted with permission.

Why are younger children so perceptual in their focus? Tversky (1985) has argued that all children can be swayed by strong perceptual cues in a situation, but that with development children come to suppress immediate, salient responses in favor of slower, more thoughtful ones. This shift undoubtedly is fostered by the acquisition of knowledge that is conceptual in nature, such as the idea that motives are an important predictor of behavior. Children of all ages, and even adults, also are less likely to be swayed by perceptual cues when they are dealing with situations and tasks that are familiar (Springer, 2001)

We can apply this developmental trend in perceptual boundedness to the example at the beginning of this chapter. The preschool child is transfixed by E.T.'s strange physical appearance, reacting with fright when she sees its distorted form. In contrast, the older child is able to minimize the character's looks and instead focus on the creature's behavior and motivation.

From Centration to Decentration. As noted above, children and even adults can respond strongly to salient features in a message. But another characteristic of younger children's thinking is that they often focus on a single striking feature to the exclusion of other, less striking features. This tendency has been called *centration* and is illustrated in some of Piaget's classic liquid conservation tasks (see Ginsburg & Opper, 1979). In these tasks, a child is shown two glasses containing identical amounts of water. Once the child agrees that the amounts are identical, the experimenter pours the water from one glass into a third glass, which is taller and thinner (see Figure 1.16). The experimenter then asks the child whether the two amounts of liquid are still identical or whether one glass now contains more water. The typical preschooler concludes that the taller glass has more liquid in it. Why? Because the taller glass *looks* like it has more in it. In other words, the differential height of the liquids captures most of the preschooler's attention.

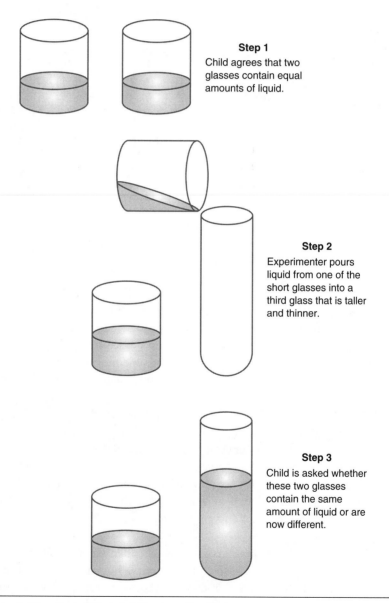

Step 1
Child agrees that two glasses contain equal amounts of liquid.

Step 2
Experimenter pours liquid from one of the short glasses into a third glass that is taller and thinner.

Step 3
Child is asked whether these two glasses contain the same amount of liquid or are now different.

Figure 1.16   Typical Piagetian Conservation Task

In contrast, older children are increasingly able to "decenter" their attention and take into account the full array of perceptual cues. The liquid in one glass is higher but that glass also has a different shape to it. It is taller and thinner. Also, pouring the liquid from one container to another does not change the quantity. The "amount" of the liquid stays the same. By recognizing that the liquid is the same, the older child is able to *conserve* continuous quantities.

The same developmental differences are found with other types of conservation tasks. For example, two rows of six pennies can be laid out next to one another, in a one-to-one correspondence. If one row is then compressed, a younger child is likely to perceive it as containing fewer coins because it is now shorter (Ginsberg & Opper, 1979). In contrast, the older child notes all the perceptual data in the situation and recognizes that the number of pennies is conserved or unchanged despite appearances.

O'Bryan and Boersma (1971) documented these differences further by examining children's eye movements during conservation tasks. They found that younger children who are unable to conserve or master the task correctly tend to fixate on a single dimension, such as the height of the liquid in a glass. Older children who are able to conserve show more varied eye movements, shifting their gaze over many parts of the testing display.

Applying the idea of centration to the media, younger children are likely to respond strongly to a single feature in a television or movie scene, such as a character's red dress or a hero's shiny weapon. The prominence of the cues as well as the child's own interests will help determine what is most salient. Other perceptual cues such as the character's hair color, name, physical size, and even certain overt behaviors may go unnoticed. In emotional stories, for example, a character's feelings are often conveyed through facial expressions as well as situational information in the plot. Younger children will be more likely to fixate on one or the other of these sets of cues, even when they conflict (Wiggers & van Lieshout, 1985). Thus, in some cases, we can expect that this centration will interfere with a young child's comprehension of the storyline (see Figure 1.17).

From Perceived Appearance to Reality. Another important cognitive skill during childhood concerns the ability to distinguish fantasy from reality. Much to a

Figure 1.17

SOURCE: PEANUTS reprinted by permission of United Features Syndicate, Inc.

BABY BLUES By Rick Kirkman and Jerry Scott

Figure 1.18

SOURCE: Baby Blues by Rick Kirkman and Jerry Scott. Reprinted with permission of King Features Syndicate.

parent's amazement, a 3-year-old child may attribute life to an inanimate object such as a rock, have an invisible friend, and want Barney the dinosaur to come over to the house for a play date (see Figure 1.18). All of these tendencies reflect a fuzzy separation between what is real and what is not.

Numerous studies have found strong developmental differences in children's perceived reality of television (see Dorr, 1983; Wright, Huston, Reitz, & Piemyat, 1994). Very young 2- and 3-year-olds show little understanding of the boundary between television and the real world (Jaglom & Gardner, 1981). In fact, at this age, children routinely talk to the television set and wave at the characters (Noble, 1975). For example, in one study, many 3-year-olds reported that a bowl of popcorn shown on TV would spill if the television set were turned upside down (Flavell, Flavell, Green, & Korfmacher, 1990).

By around age 4, the young child begins to appreciate the representational nature of television but still tends to assume that anything that *looks* real is real (M. H. Brown, Skeen, & Osborn, 1979). This literal interpretation has been called the "magic window" perspective, reflecting the idea that young children naively assume that television provides a view of the real world (see Figure 1.19). Gradually, children come to appreciate that some of what is shown on television is not real, although most of this centers first on perceptual cues. For example, 5-year-olds typically judge cartoons as not real because they feature physically impossible events and characters (Wright et al., 1994). In other words, the young child assesses content by looking for striking violations of physical reality (Dorr, 1983). It is important to note, though, that these emerging distinctions are initially quite fragile. Young children may be able to report that an animated character is "not real" yet still become quite frightened of it (Cantor, 1998). In one recent study (Wooley, Boerger, & Markman, 2004), preschoolers were introduced to a novel fantasy creature named the "Candy Witch," and even 5-year-olds believed she was real and not "pretend," particularly if the witch purportedly visited their homes at night and left candy.

As children mature, they begin to use multiple criteria for judging reality on television (Hawkins, 1977). Not only do they notice marked perceptual cues but they also take into account the genre of the program, production cues, and even the

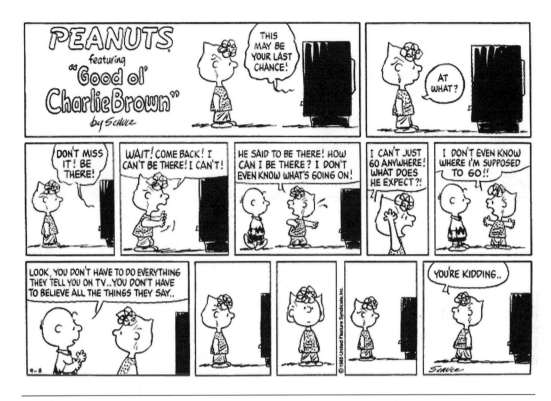

Figure 1.19

SOURCE: PEANUTS reprinted by permission of United Features Syndicate, Inc.

purpose of the program. Most important, older children begin to judge content based on how similar it is to real life (M. H. Brown et al., 1979). Although they recognize that much of television is scripted, older children are likely to judge a scene or a program as realistic if it depicts characters and events that are *possible* in the real world (Dorr, 1983; Hawkins, 1977). In one survey, 28% of second and third graders and 47% of sixth graders spontaneously referred to "possibility" criteria in judging whether a series of characters and events on television were realistic (Dorr, 1983). In contrast, only 17% of kindergartners used this type of criteria. These trends are congruent with research on language comprehension, which suggests that the concept of possibility is not fully understood until around 8 years of age (Hoffner, Cantor, & Badzinski, 1990; Piaget & Inhelder, 1975).

Obviously, a child's personal experiences will place a limit on how sophisticated these reality judgments can be. As an illustration, Weiss and Wilson (1998) found that elementary schoolers rated the TV sitcom *Full House* as very realistic, indicating on average that "most" to "all" real-life families are like the family featured in this program. These perceptions seem a bit naive given that the program is about a widowed father raising his three daughters with live-in help from his brother-in-law and his best friend.

From Concrete to Inferential Thinking. A final cognitive trend during childhood that has implications for the media is the shift from concrete to inferential thinking.

As we have mentioned above, a young child's thinking is very tangible, focusing closely on what can be seen and heard (Bruner, 1966). For a 2- or 3-year-old, this means that attention can be swayed by highly salient cues that might actually be extraneous to the plot (Schmitt et al., 1999). For example, a purple costume might get more attention than the actions of the character who is wearing this garment.

By age 4, children can begin to focus more on information that is central to the plot than on incidental details (Lorch, Bellack, & Augsbach, 1987). Of course, younger children do best with age-appropriate content, programs that are relatively short in duration, and comprehension tests that assess forced-choice recognition rather than spontaneous recall (Campbell, Wright, & Huston, 1987). With development, children become increasingly able to extract events that are central to the storyline in a program (Collins, 1983). Yet the information younger children focus on is still likely to be fairly explicit in nature. For example, one study found that 4- and 6-year-olds most often recalled actions after watching televised stories, whereas adults most often recalled information about characters' goals and motives (van den Broek, Lorch, & Thurlow, 1996). Actions typically are concrete and fairly vivid in television programming, making them easy to understand and represent in memory.

As discussed above, however, full comprehension involves apprehending not only explicit content but also implicit information in the unfolding narrative. For instance, in one scene, a protagonist might discover that a "friend" is trying to steal his money. In a later scene, the protagonist might hit the friend. The viewer must deduce that the protagonist's aggression, which in isolation might appear unprovoked, is actually motivated by a desire to protect personal property. In other words, the viewer must link scenes together and draw causal inferences about content that is not explicitly presented. Studies show that older children are better able than their younger counterparts to draw different types of inferences from verbally presented passages (Ackerman, 1988; Thompson & Myers, 1985). The same pattern emerges in the context of television. By roughly age 8 or 9, children show dramatic improvements in their ability to link scenes together and draw connections between characters' motives, behaviors, and consequences (Collins, Berndt, & Hess, 1974; Collins, Wellman, Keniston, & Westby, 1978). This shift from concrete to inferential processing has implications for other forms of media as well. A video game and even a Web site require the user to make connections across space and time.

To summarize, a number of important cognitive shifts occur between early and middle childhood. A preschooler watching television is likely to focus on the most striking perceptual features in a program. This child may comprehend some of the plot, especially when the program is brief and age appropriate. Yet comprehension will be closely tied to concrete actions and behaviors in the storyline. In addition, the preschooler is likely to have difficulty distinguishing reality from fantasy in the portrayals. As this same child enters elementary school, she will begin to focus more on conceptual aspects of the content such as the characters' goals and motives. She increasingly will be able to link scenes together, drawing causal connections in the narrative. And her judgments of reality will become more accurate and discriminating as she compares television content with that which could possibly occur in the real world. Clearly, her overall understanding of a media message is quite advanced compared with what she was capable of as a preschooler. Nevertheless, her skills are continuing to develop even during her later elementary school years. Next, we will explore some of the cognitive shifts that occur between late childhood and adolescence.

Older Children Versus Adolescentss

From Real to Plausible. As described above, older children use a variety of cues to judge the reality of media content. One of the most important yardsticks for them is whether the characters or events depicted in the media are possible in real life (Morison, Kelly, & Gardner, 1981). Adolescents become even more discriminating on this dimension, judging content as realistic if it is *probable* or likely to occur in real life (Dorr, 1983; Morrison et al., 1981). In Dorr's (1983) research, almost half of adolescents defined real television events as those that were probable or plausible in real life. In contrast, probability rationales were seldom used by older elementary school children. To illustrate this distinction, a movie featuring an evil stepfather who is trying to poison his stepchildren might be very upsetting to a 9- or 10-year-old because this scenario *could* happen in real life. A teenager, on the other hand, is less likely to be disturbed by such content, reasoning that the vast majority of stepfathers in the world are not murderers. The movement to probabilistic thinking is consistent with studies of language comprehension that indicate that the ability to differentiate probability from possibility crystallizes during early adolescence (Piaget & Inhelder, 1975; Scholz & Waller, 1983).

From Empirical to Hypothetical Reasoning. A related development that occurs between late childhood and early adolescence is the shift from empirical to hypothetical reasoning (Flavell et al., 2002). Adolescents become increasingly able to understand abstract concepts, use formal logic, and think hypothetically (Byrnes, 2003). Along with this abstract thinking comes an ability to engage in inductive and deductive reasoning (Keating, 2004). An older child is able to reason conceptually too, but much of this process is based on collecting empirical evidence. A fifth or sixth grader, for example, may watch a person's behavior across several situations and infer from these actions what the person's motives are. In contrast, an adolescent might begin with a theory or hypothetical set of motives for a person and then observe behaviors to see if the theory is correct. In other words, the teenager is capable of more abstract thinking that need not be tied too closely to observable data.

Adolescents also are increasingly capable of suspending their own beliefs to evaluate the reasoning of someone else (Moshman, 1998). Put another way, teens can sometimes reason about arguments at an objective level.

The ability to think hypothetically means that a teenager can anticipate different plot events and predict logical outcomes as a storyline unfolds. The teen also is able to critique the logic and causal structure of different media messages. As abstract thought flourishes, the adolescent also may consider the meaning behind the message—who is the source and why is the message constructed this way? How would the message differ if it were designed by someone else with different motives?

Metacognitive Thinking. Metacognition refers to the ability to understand and manipulate one's own thought processes (Metcalfe & Shimamura, 1994). It is called *meta*cognition because it refers to second-order mental activities: A person thinks about his or her own thinking. Adults routinely reflect on their own cognitive processing, especially during situations that highlight the need to do so. For instance, studying for a test or actually taking one requires a person to concentrate carefully on cognitive enterprises such as attention, comprehension, and memory.

Flavell and his colleagues (2002) have distinguished between two types of metacognition: metacognitive *knowledge* and metacognitive *monitoring and self-regulation*. Metacognitive knowledge refers to a person's knowledge and beliefs about the human mind and how it works. For example, most adults realize that short-term memory is of limited capacity (see section below on processing capacity), that it is generally easier to recognize something when you see it than to recall it outright, and that certain tasks are more difficult and demanding of the human mind than are others. But young children do not necessarily possess such metacognitive knowledge. In one study, for example, Lovett and Flavell (1990) presented first graders, third graders, and undergraduates with three tasks: a list of words to be memorized, a list of words to match up with a picture, and a list of words to memorize and match. Unlike the first graders, the third graders and the undergraduates were able to select what type of strategy—rehearsal, word definition, or both—would work best for each task. Yet only the undergraduates understood that the tasks would be more difficult with longer lists and unfamiliar words. Thus, as children develop, they become increasingly aware that the mind engages in a range of activities, including memory, comprehension, and inference (Flavell et al., 2002).

The second type of metacognition involves monitoring and readjusting one's ongoing thinking. Consider the test-taking instance, for example. An adult who is having difficulty with a certain section on a test might decide to jump ahead to an easier part for efficiency's sake and to build confidence before returning to the harder material. Research suggests that this type of self-monitoring is difficult during early childhood (see Flavell et al., 2002). In one study, preschoolers and elementary schoolers were instructed to examine a set of objects until they were sure they could recall them (Flavell, Friedrichs, & Hoyt, 1970). Older children examined them for a period of time, determined they were ready, and typically recalled all the items correctly. In contrast, the preschoolers examined the items, thought they were ready, and generally failed on the recall test. In other words, the preschoolers were not capable of monitoring their memory processes very accurately.

How do metacognitive knowledge and monitoring relate to the media? We can expect that as children approach adolescence, they will be better able to analyze the cognitive demands of different media and even different messages within a particular medium. According to Salomon (1983), some media require more nonautomatic mental elaborations or more AIME (amount of invested mental effort) than do others. In general, television requires less effort and concentration than reading, for example, because the former is highly visual and relies less on language skills (Salomon & Leigh, 1984). Thus, a teenager is more likely than a young child to recognize that a difficult book or a television documentary requires higher concentration than does watching MTV. Their awareness of different media will affect the depth of processing they will use, which in turn will enhance comprehension and learning. Interestingly, when children are instructed to pay attention and to learn from TV, their mental effort and performance increase compared with what they do without such instruction (Salomon, 1983).

Also, as children reach the teenage years, they increasingly should be able to monitor their own reactions to the media, slowing down when they do not understand a book passage or reminding themselves it is only a movie when they feel scared. In one illustration of this, preschoolers and 9- to 11-year-olds were given different types of instructions for how to think about a frightening program they were about to watch on television (Cantor & Wilson, 1984). Children were told either to imagine themselves as the protagonist (role-taking set) or to remember that the story and the characters were make-believe (unreality set). The cognitive-set instructions had no appreciable effect on the preschoolers' emotional reactions to the program. In other words, they showed little ability to use the information to alter how they perceived the program. In contrast, older children in the role-taking condition were more frightened by the program, and those in the unreality condition were less frightened compared with a control group that received no instructions at all (see Figure 1.20). The findings are consistent with the idea that as children develop, they increasingly are able to modify their thought processes while watching television.

Regulatory Competence. Adults have long assumed that much of cognitive growth occurs during the childhood years. Recent research on the brain contradicts this view. With better measurement tools such as magnetic resonance imaging (MRI), we are beginning to realize that there are substantial changes in brain development during adolescence (Kuhn, 2006). Much of this development occurs in the frontal

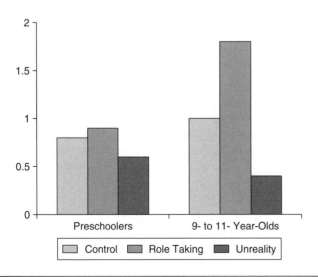

Figure 1.20   Children's Self-Reported Fear Reactions to a Scary Program as a
Function of Instructional Set

SOURCE: Adapted from Cantor and Wilson (1984).

cortex regions of the brain, which are crucial to the regulation of behavior and emotion (Sowell, Trauner, Gamst, & Jernigan, 2002). Thus, during the teen years, young people become increasingly able to regulate and control their moods and responses to different situations, including those mediated by technologies. This development of an "executive suite" or executive control function takes time, however (Steinberg, 2005). Therefore, younger adolescents typically will show less maturity and more risk taking when they confront various dilemmas in life. For example, younger teens are more likely than older ones to play with their identity in Internet communications (Valkenburg et al., 2005). Younger teens are also more likely than older teens to talk with strangers on the Internet (Jochen, Valkenburg, & Schouten, 2006).

Two Overall Developmental Trends

Two other important trends occur continuously throughout childhood and adolescence and are not specific to particular age groups: increasing knowledge about the social, physical, and mediated world in which we live and increasing processing capacity.

Increase in Domain-Specific Knowledge. It may seem obvious to state that children gain increasing amounts of knowledge across different domains as they grow. But the point is still worth making because it has such important implications for interacting with the media. With each new experience, a child stores more and more information in highly organized ways in memory. The resulting knowledge structures, sometimes called mental templates or *schemas,* are powerful organizers that help children anticipate and assimilate new information (Fiske & Taylor, 1991). Research suggests that children as young as 3 years of age possess well-developed schemas or scripts for familiar events such as getting ready for bed and taking a bath (Hudson, Sosa, & Shapiro, 1997). As evidence of the power of these mental organizers, a young child is likely to protest quite strongly if someone tries to alter these routines.

Young children also develop schemas for stories that include information about the typical structure and components of a narrative (Mandler, 1998). Research suggests that a well-developed story schema can help a child to organize and interpret television programming (Meadowcroft & Reeves, 1989). In addition, children can form schemas about the social and physical world in which they live. In the social realm, for example, children develop templates for emotions that include information about expressive signals, situational causes, and display rules associated with each affect (e.g., Campos & Barret, 1984). These schemas undoubtedly assist a child in making sense of an emotional scene on television. Such schemas, in turn, can be shaped and modified by exposure to the media (see Wilson & Smith, 1998).

Not surprisingly, children develop schemas about the media as well (Calvert, 1999). Each form of the media has its own special audiovisual techniques and codes, which at least in the case of television have been referred to as "formal features" (Bickham, Wright, & Huston, 2001; Huston & Wright, 1983). Television and film, for example, use production techniques such as cuts, zooms, fades, and special effects to signal shifts in time and changes in setting. Video games and computers have their own technological conventions. A user of the World Wide Web, for example, needs some understanding of search engines and hypertext. Knowing what to expect from each medium greatly increases a child's sophistication with it (Calvert, 1999; R. Smith et al., 1985). For this reason, efforts to teach youth to become critical consumers of the media often include instruction about the conventions of different technologies (see Chapter 13).

In addition to developing schemas *about* the media, spending time with certain technologies can actually enhance cognitive thinking (see Subrahmanyam & Greenfield, 2008). For example, studies show that practicing certain types of video games can improve dynamic spatial skills in both children (Subrahmanyam & Greenfield, 1996) and adults (Feng, Spence, & Pratt, 2007). There is also evidence that video game playing improves strategies for dividing visual attention, presumably because players must cope with events that occur simultaneously at different places on the screen (Greenfield, deWinstanley, Kilpatrick, & Kaye, 1996). In addition, listening to a song seems to stimulate imagination more so than watching a music video of the same song does (Greenfield et al., 1987). All of these studies suggest a kind of interactive relationship between media exposure and schematic processing and development.

To summarize here, children can call on larger stores of remembered information across a variety of domains as they grow. In addition, they can integrate and combine information in more complex ways, forming more elaborate connections with what they already know (Siegler, 2005). In other words, their schemas become more elaborate and differentiated. Hence, their interpretations of media content will be richer and more complex.

Having a great deal of knowledge and experience in a given area has all kinds of benefits for cognitive processing. Compared to a beginner, the veteran has familiar concepts and ready-made strategies to apply to a problem (Siegler, 2005). Given that the terrain is familiar, the expert expends less cognitive energy and is free to apply mental workspace to high-order activities such as metacognition (Flavell et al., 2002). Consider for a moment how a 6-year-old might respond to a cigarette advertisement in a magazine compared with how a 16-year-old would process the same message. The 6-year-old presumably has never smoked, has little knowledge of how the lungs work, is unaware of the legal battles ensuing against the tobacco industry, is not cognizant of who paid for the placement of the ad in the magazine, and has little experience with the cost of various products in a grocery store. The teenager certainly has less experience than an adult would have in this domain, but compared with the grade schooler, the adolescent brings a much broader knowledge base from which to draw in interpreting and evaluating such an ad.

Increase in Processing Capacity. Regardless of age or level of development, all humans experience limits in the capacity of their working memory (Fougnie & Marois, 2006). In other words, certain situations and tasks are so demanding that they exceed a person's available cognitive resources. One way to demonstrate this has been through reaction time studies that show that people perform slowly or poorly on secondary tasks when their mental energies are consumed by a primary task (Kail, 1991; Lang, 2000).

Developmental research demonstrates that as children mature, they are able to hold increasing amounts of information in working memory (Cowan, Nugent, Elliott, Ponomarev, & Saults, 1999; Kail, 1990). For example, a 5-year-old typically is able to deal with only four or five bits of information at once (e.g., digits, letters), whereas the average adult can handle seven (Dempster, 1981). There are differing theoretical accounts for this increased processing capacity. Some have argued that the structure or size of one's memory space actually increases with development (Cowan et al., 1999). Others have argued that the size remains fixed, but the functional use or efficiency of the space increases (Kail, 1991). As certain tasks become familiar, they are easily categorized into preexisting schemas. This categorization and routinization mean that fewer demands are placed on the cognitive system, and hence space is freed up for other cognitive processing.

Regardless of which view is correct, the implications are the same. Younger children have difficulty considering multiple pieces of information in working memory (see Figure 1.21). In addition, their capacities may be taxed quickly by a single cognitive activity that is somewhat novel and thus cannot be easily schematized. As children mature and gain experience in certain arenas, they can quickly classify new information into preexisting schemas. This schematization allows them to consider and interrelate more bits of information at once and to engage in concurrent cognitive tasks. In other words, they become more efficient information processors.

How does processing capacity affect children's interactions with the media? Research suggests that older children are better able than younger children to consider multiple cues within a scene or across several scenes when interpreting a television portrayal (Collins et al., 1974; Hoffner, Cantor, & Thorson, 1989). Likewise, older children are able to track the main plot of a television story even

Figure 1.21

SOURCE: Baby Blues by Rick Kirkman and Jerry Scott. Reprinted with permission of King Features Syndicate.

when there is a subplot interspersed throughout, whereas younger children's comprehension suffers in the face of a distracting subplot (Weiss & Wilson, 1998). Older children also are better equipped to handle fast-paced programming that involves the integration of information across rapid changes in time and place (Wright et al., 1984). As discussed above, older children also are better able to consider their own thought processes while attending to a television program (Cantor & Wilson, 1984).

Any time a media message is complex, lengthy, fast-paced, or delivered in a distracting environment, it is likely to present a cognitive challenge to younger children because of their more limited processing capacities. Extending these ideas to newer technologies, we might also expect that interactive media such as computer games will quickly tax the mental resources of a young child because of the need to simultaneously comprehend content and respond cognitively and physically to it. As processing capacity increases throughout childhood and adolescence, these once very difficult types of media interactions will become increasingly routinized.

Conclusion

The purpose of this chapter has been to underscore the fact that children are very different from adults and from each other when they interact with the media. Children are eager to learn, have less real-world experience, and have less developed cognitive skills, making them ultimately more vulnerable to media messages. The remainder of this book will explore how children and teens respond to different types of media content such as violence and sexual messages as well as to different media technologies such as video games and the Internet. We will continually draw on the concepts and developmental trends presented in this chapter to explain how children deal with the stimulating media world that confronts them. Clearly, there are robust developmental differences in children's attention to and comprehension of media messages. These cognitive processes in turn have implications for emotional responding as well as behavioral reactions to the media.

Exercises

1. Think about your childhood. What is the first experience you remember having with the media? How old were you? What medium was involved? What type of content was involved? What was your reaction or response to the experience? Did your parents know about it? Could a child today have a similar experience? Why or why not?

2. For one day, chart the time you spend with the media (e.g., television, radio, books, Internet). Note which media you are using and what type of content you are experiencing. Also note when you are "media multitasking" or using two or more media at once (i.e., reading a book and listening to music). How much of your day did you spend with the media? Is your media use similar to that of the typical American child (see the Roberts et al. [2005] study described in this chapter)? How is it similar and how is it different?

3. Watch an episode of a TV sitcom that is popular with children. Think about the main theme of the program, the sequence of events in the storyline, and the nature of the characters. Based on developmental differences in cognitive processing, describe three ways in which a 4-year-old's interpretation of the episode would differ from that of a 10-year-old. How would a 10-year-old's interpretation differ from that of a teenager? What type of viewer do you think the program is targeted toward? Think about the program itself as well as the commercial breaks in addressing this question.

4. Some scholars argue that childhood is disappearing in today's modern society. They maintain that children are dressing more like adults, talking like them, and experiencing adult activities and even adult media content. Can you think of examples to support this thesis? Can you think of examples that challenge it? How is childhood changing in the 21st century? Do you agree that childhood is vanishing? How crucial are the media in debates about these issues?

5. When you were a child, did your parents have rules about what you could do with the mass media? Did they have rules when you were a teenager? Did you have a TV set in your bedroom? Do you think parents should exercise control over their children's media experiences? Why or why not?

6. Compare and contrast three rating systems designed to inform parents about media content: (a) the Motion Picture Association of America's ratings for movies (see www.mpaa.org/FlmRat_Ratings.asp), (b) the TV Parental Guidelines for television shows (see www.tvguidelines.org/ratings.asp), and (c) the Entertainment Software Rating Board's ratings for computer and video games (www.esrb.org/ratings/ratings_guide.jsp). Evaluate the three systems in terms of what we know about child development, as discussed in this chapter. Do the systems seem accurate? Are they likely to be helpful to parents? How could they be improved? Can you think of a movie, TV show, or video game that you think is rated inappropriately?

7. Watch a program targeted to children that airs on public broadcasting (e.g., *Sesame Street, Dragon Tales, Maya & Miguel*). Now compare it with a cartoon that airs on Cartoon Network, ABC Kids, or Kids' WB. Compare and contrast the two programs in terms of plot, characters, formal features, and degree of realism. Which program seems better suited to the developmental capabilities of a 4- or 5-year-old? Why?

8. Find the lyrics to a song from a genre of music that is popular among young people today (e.g., hip-hop, rap). Now compare the lyrics to those from a Beatles' song of the 1960s or 1970s. What do the songs say about adolescence? How are the songs similar in their representation of adolescent themes such as risk taking, social identity, peer relations, and sexuality? How are they different? Think about the social and political context in which these songs were written in addressing these issues.

References

Ackerman, B. P. (1988). Reason inferences in the story comprehension of children and adults. *Child Development, 59,* 1426–1442.

Adler, J. (1999, May 10). Beyond Littleton: The truth about high school. *Newsweek,* pp. 56–58.

American Lung Association. (2003). *Adolescent smoking statistics.* Retrieved April 5, 2007, from http://www.lungusa.org/site/pp.asp?c=dvLUK9O0E&b=39868

Anderson, D. R., & Levin, S. R. (1976). Young children's attention to "Sesame Street." *Child Development, 47,* 806–811.

Archibald, A. B., Graber, J. A., & Brooks-Gunn, J. (2003). Pubertal processes and physiological growth in adolescence. In G. R. Adams & M. D. Berzonsky (Eds.), *Blackwell handbook of adolescence* (pp. 24–47). Malden, MA: Blackwell.

Arnett, J. J. (1992a). Reckless behavior in adolescence: A developmental perspective. *Developmental Review, 12,* 339–373.

Arnett, J. J. (1992b). Socialization and adolescent reckless behavior: A reply to Jessor. *Developmental Review, 12,* 391–409.

Arnett, J. J. (1999). Adolescent storm and stress, reconsidered. *American Psychologist, 54*(5), 317–326.

Arnett, J. J. (2000). Optimistic bias in adolescent and adult smokers and nonsmokers. *Addictive Behaviors, 25*(4), 625–632.

Bagdikian, B. H. (2000). *The media monopoly* (6th ed.). Boston: Beacon.

Baillargeon, R. H., Zoccolillo, M., Keenan, K., Cote, S., Perusse, D., Wu, H., et al. (2007). Gender differences in physical aggression: A prospective population-based survey of children before and after 2 years of age. *Developmental Psychology, 43*(1), 13–26.

Beentjes, J., deKoning, E., & Huysmans, F. (2001). Children's comprehension of visual formal features in television programs. *Journal of Applied Developmental Psychology, 22*(6), 623–638.

Bem, S. L. (1981). Gender schema theory: A cognitive account of sex typing. *Psychological Review, 88,* 354–364.

Berk, L. E. (2000). *Child development* (5th ed.). Boston: Allyn & Bacon.

Berndt, T. J. (1996). Transitions in friendship and friends' influence. In J. A. Graber, J. Brooks-Gunn, & A. C. Petersen (Eds.), *Transitions through adolescence: Interpersonal domains and context* (pp. 57–85). Mahwah, NJ: Lawrence Erlbaum.

Bickham, D. S., Wright, J. C., & Huston, A. C. (2001). Attention, comprehension, and the educational influences of television. In D. G. Singer & J. L. Singer (Eds.), *Handbook of children and the media* (pp. 101–119). Thousand Oaks, CA: Sage.

Brown, J. D., Halpern, C. T., & L'Engle, K. L. (2005). Mass media as a sexual super peer for early maturing girls. *Journal of Adolescent Health, 36,* 420–427.

Brown, M. H., Skeen, P., & Osborn, D. K. (1979). Young children's perception of the reality of television. *Contemporary Education, 50,* 129–133.

Bruner, J. S. (1966). On cognitive growth I & II. In J. S. Bruner, R. R. Olver, & P. M. Greenfield (Eds.), *Studies in cognitive growth* (pp. 1–67). New York: John Wiley.

Bruner, J. S., Olver, R., & Greenfield, P. (1966). *Studies in cognitive growth.* New York: John Wiley.

Buckingham, D. (2000). *After the death of childhood: Growing up in the age of electronic media.* Cambridge, UK: Polity.

Bussey, K., & Bandura, A. (1999). Social cognitive theory of gender development and differentiation. *Psychological Review, 106,* 676–713.

Byrnes, J. P. (2003). Cognitive development during adolescence. In G. R. Adams & M. D. Berzonsky (Eds.), *Blackwell handbook of adolescence* (pp. 227–246). Malden, MA: Blackwell.

Calvert, S. L. (1999). *Children's journeys through the information age.* Boston: McGraw-Hill.

Calvert, S. L., & Gersh, T. L. (1987). The selective use of sound effects and visual inserts for children's story comprehension. *Journal of Applied Developmental Psychology, 8,* 363–374.

Calvert, S. L., Huston, A. C., Watkins, B. A., & Wright, J. C. (1982). The relations between selective attention to television forms and children's comprehension of content. *Child Development, 53,* 601–610.

Campbell, T. A., Wright, J. C., & Huston, A. C. (1987). Form cues and content difficulty as determinants of children's cognitive processing of televised educational messages. *Journal of Experimental Child Psychology, 43,* 311–327.

Campos, L. A., & Barret, K. C. (1984). Toward a new understanding of emotions and their development. In C. E. Izard & R. B. Zajonc (Eds.), *Emotion, cognition, and behavior* (pp. 229–263). Cambridge, UK: Cambridge University Press.

Cantor, J. (1998). *"Mommy, I'm scared": How TV and movies frighten children and what we can do to protect them.* San Diego: Harcourt Brace & Company.

Cantor, J., & Wilson, B. J. (1984). Modifying fear responses to mass media in preschool and elementary school children. *Journal of Broadcasting, 28,* 431–443.

Carr, D. (2007, March 29). Do they still want their MTV? *New York Times.* Retrieved April 3, 2007, from http://www.nytimes.com/2007/02/19/business/media/19carr.html

Centers for Disease Control and Prevention. (2006). Youth risk behavior surveillance—United States, 2005. *Morbidity and Mortality Weekly Report, 55*(SS-5). Retrieved January 15, 2008, from http://www.cdc.gov/mmwr/PDF/SS/SS5505.pdf

Chassin, L. (1985). Changes in peer and parent influence during adolescence: Longitudinal versus cross-sectional perspectives on smoking initiation. *Developmental Psychology, 22,* 327–334.

Collins, W. A. (1983). Interpretation and inference in children's television viewing. In J. Bryant & D. R. Anderson (Eds.), *Children's understanding of television* (pp. 125–150). New York: Academic Press.

Collins, W. A., Berndt, T. J., & Hess, V. L. (1974). Observational learning of motives and consequences for television aggression: A developmental study. *Child Development, 45,* 799–802.

Collins, W. A., Wellman, H., Keniston, A., & Westby, S. (1978). Age-related aspects of comprehension and inference from a televised dramatic narrative. *Child Development, 49,* 389–399.

Cookston, J. T., & Finlay, A. K. (2006). Father involvement and adolescent adjustment: Longitudinal findings from Add Health. *Fathering: A Journal of Theory, Research, and Practice About Men as Fathers, 4*(2), 137–158.

Cowan, N., Nugent, L. D., Elliott, E. M., Ponomarev, I., & Saults, J. S. (1999). The role of attention in the development of short-term memory: Age differences in the verbal span of apprehension. *Child Development, 70,* 1082–1097.

Dempster, F. N. (1981). Memory span: Sources of individual and developmental differences. *Psychological Bulletin, 89,* 63–100.

d'Haenens, L. (2001). Old and new media: Access and ownership in the home. In S. Livingstone & M. Bovill (Eds.), *Children and the changing media environment: A European comparative study* (pp. 53–84). Mahwah, NJ: Lawrence Erlbaum.

Dishion, T. J. (1990). The family ecology of boys' peer relations in middle childhood. *Child Development, 61,* 874–892.

Dolcini, M. M., Cohn, L. D., Adler, N. E., Millstein, S. G., Irwin, C. E., Jr., Kegeles, S. M., et al. (1989). Adolescent egocentrism and feelings of invulnerability: Are they related? *Journal of Early Adolescence, 9*(4), 409–418.

Dorr, A. (1980). When I was a child, I thought as a child. In S. B. Withey & P. P. Abeles (Eds.), *Television and social behavior: Beyond violence and children* (pp. 191–230). Hillsdale, NJ: Lawrence Erlbaum.

Dorr, A. (1983). No shortcuts to judging reality. In J. Bryant & D. R. Anderson (Eds.), *Children's understanding of television* (pp. 199–220). New York: Academic Press.

Dorr, A. (1986). *Television and children: A special medium for a special audience.* Thousand Oaks, CA: Sage.

Eagle, G. (2007, May 3). Facebook changes the way teens are communicating. *Peterborough Examiner.* Retrieved May 8, 2007, from http://www.thepeterboroughexaminer.com

Eaton, W. O., & Enns, L. R. (1986). Sex differences in human motor activity level. *Psychological Bulletin, 100,* 19–28.

Eisenberg, N., Fabes, R. A., & Spinrad, T. L. (2006). Prosocial development. In N. Eisenberg, W. Damon, & R. M. Lerner (Eds.), *Handbook of child psychology: Vol. 3. Social, emotional, and personality development* (pp. 646–718). Hoboken, NJ: John Wiley.

Elkind, D. (1967). Egocentrism in adolescence. *Child Development, 38,* 1025–1034.

Elkind, D. (1985). Egocentrism redux. *Developmental Review, 5,* 218–226.

Eveland, W. P., Nathanson, A. I., Detenber, A. I., & McLeod, D. M. (1999). Rethinking the social distance corollary: Perceived likelihood of exposure and the third-person perception. *Communication Research, 26,* 275–302.

Feeling good about visiting the doctor. (1996). *Research Roundup, 5,* 1.

Feng, J., Spence, I., & Pratt, J. (2007). Playing an action video game reduces gender difference in spatial cognition. *Psychological Science, 18,* 850–855.

Finn, P., & Bragg, B. W. (1986). Perception of risk of an accident by young and older drivers. *Accident Analysis and Prevention, 18,* 289–298.

Fiske, S. T., & Taylor, S. E. (1991). *Social cognition* (2nd ed.). New York: McGraw-Hill.

Flavell, J. H., Flavell, E. R., Green, F. L., & Korfmacher, J. E. (1990). Do young children think of television images as pictures or real objects? *Journal of Broadcasting & Electronic Media, 34,* 399–417.

Flavell, J. H., Friedrichs, A. G., & Hoyt, J. (1970). Developmental changes in memorization processes. *Cognitive Psychology, 1,* 324–340.

Flavell, J. H., Miller, P. H., & Miller, S. A. (2002). *Cognitive development* (4th ed.). Englewood Cliffs, NJ: Prentice Hall.

Foderaro, L. W. (2007, March 29). Child wants cellphone; reception is mixed. *New York Times.* Retrieved March 30, 2007, from http://www.nytimes.com/2007/03/29/fashion/29cell.html

Foehr, U. G. (2006). *Media multitasking among American youth: Prevalence, predictors and pairings.* Menlo Park, CA: Henry J. Kaiser Family Foundation.

Fougnie, D., & Marois, R. (2006). Distinct capacity limits for attention and working memory: Evidence from attentive tracking and visual working memory paradigms. *Psychological Science, 17,* 526–534.

Fulkerson, J. A., Story, M., Mellin, A., Leffert, N., Neumark-Sztainer, D., & French, S. A. (2006). Family dinner meal frequency and adolescent development: Relationships with developmental assets and high-risk behaviors. *Journal of Adolescent Health, 39,* 337–345.

Gentile, D. A., & Walsh, D. A. (2002). A normative study of family media habits. *Applied Developmental Psychology, 23,* 157–178.

Gerrard, M., McCann, L., & Fortini, M. (1983). Prevention of unwanted pregnancy. *American Journal of Community Psychology, 11,* 153–167.

Ginsburg, H., & Opper, S. (1979). *Piaget's theory of intellectual development* (2nd ed.). Englewood Cliffs, NJ: Prentice Hall.

Gondoli, D. M. (1999). Adolescent development and health. In T. L. Whitman, T. V. Merluzzi, & R. D. White (Eds.), *Life-span perspectives on health and illness* (pp. 147–163). Mahwah, NJ: Lawrence Erlbaum.

Graber, J. A., Brooks-Gunn, J., & Petersen, A. C. (Eds.). (1996). *Transitions through adolescence: Interpersonal domains and context.* Mahwah, NJ: Lawrence Erlbaum.

Greene, K., Krcmar, M., Walters, L. H., Rubin, D. L., & Hale, J. (2000). Targeting adolescent risk-taking behaviors: The contributions of egocentrism and sensation-seeking. *Journal of Adolescence, 23,* 439–461.

Greenfield, P. M., Bruzzone, L., Koyamatsu, K., Satuloff, W., Nixon, K., Brodie, M., et al. (1987). What is rock music doing to the minds of our youth? A first experimental look at the effects of rock music lyrics and music videos. *Journal of Early Adolescence, 7,* 315–329.

Greenfield, P. M., deWinstanley, P., Kilpatrick, H., & Kaye, D. (1996). Action video games and informal education: Effects on strategies for dividing visual attention. In P. M. Greenfield & R. R. Cocking (Eds.), *Interacting with video* (pp. 187–205). Norwood, NJ: Ablex.

Groebel, J. (1999). Media access and media use among 12-year-olds in the world. In C. von Feilitzen & U. Carlsson (Eds.), *Children and media: Image, education, participation* (pp. 61–68). Goteborg, Sweden: UNESCO International Clearinghouse on Children and Violence on the Screen.

Grossberg, L., Wartella, E., & Whitney, D. C. (1998). *Media making: Mass media in a popular culture.* Thousand Oaks, CA: Sage.

Gullone, E., & Moore, S. (2000). Adolescent risk-taking and the five-factor model of personality. *Journal of Adolescence, 23,* 393–407.

Halebsky, M. (1987). Adolescent alcohol and substance abuse: Parent and peer effects. *Adolescence, 22,* 961–967.

Halpern, D. F. (2004). A cognitive-process taxonomy for sex differences in cognitive abilities. *Current Directions in Psychological Science, 13*(4), 135–139.

Harris, J. R. (1998). *The nurture assumption: Why children turn out the way they do.* New York: The Free Press.

Harrison, K., & Cantor, J. (1999). Tales from the screen: Enduring fright reactions to scary media. *Media Psychology, 1,* 97–116.

Hartup, W. W., & Stevens, N. (1997). Friendships and adaptation in the life course. *Psychological Bulletin, 121,* 355–370.

Hartup, W. W., & Stevens, N. (1999). Friendships and adaptation across the lifespan. *Current Directions in Psychological Science, 8*(3), 76–79.

Hawkins, R. P. (1977). The dimensional structure of children's perceptions of television reality. *Communication Research, 7,* 193–226.

Haynie, D. L. (2002). Friendship networks and delinquency: The relative nature of peer delinquency. *Journal of Quantitative Criminology, 18*(2), 99–134.

Hoekstra, S. J., Harris, R. J., & Helmick, A. L. (1999). Autobiographical memories about the experience of seeing frightening movies in childhood. *Media Psychology, 1,* 117–140.

Hoffner, C., & Buchanan, M. (2002). Parents' responses to television violence: The third-person perception, parental mediation and support for censorship. *Media Psychology, 4*(3), 231–252.

Hoffner, C., & Cantor, J. (1985). Developmental difference in responses to a television character's appearance and behavior. *Developmental Psychology, 21,* 1065–1074.

Hoffner, C., Cantor, J., & Badzinski, D. M. (1990). Children's understanding of adverbs denoting degree of likelihood. *Journal of Child Language, 17,* 217–231.

Hoffner, C., Cantor, J., & Thorson, E. (1989). Children's responses to conflicting auditory and visual features of a televised narrative. *Human Communication Research, 16,* 256–278.

Hudson, J. A., Sosa, B. B., & Shapiro, L. R. (1997). Scripts and plans: The development of preschool children's event knowledge and event planning. In S. L. Friedman & E. K. Scholnick (Eds.), *The developmental psychology of planning: Why, how, and when do we plan?* (pp. 77–102). Mahwah, NJ: Lawrence Erlbaum.

Huston, A. C., & Wright, J. C. (1983). Children's processing of television: The informative functions of formal features. In J. Bryant & D. R. Anderson (Eds.), *Children's understanding of television: Research on attention and comprehension* (pp. 35–68). New York: Academic Press.

Jaglom, L. M., & Gardner, H. (1981). The preschool television viewer as anthropologist. In H. Kelly & H. Gardner (Eds.), *New directions for child development: Viewing children through television* (pp. 9–30). San Francisco: Jossey-Bass.

James, A., Allison, J., Jenks, C., & Prout, A. (1998). *Theorizing childhood.* New York: Teachers College Press.

Jessor, R. (1992). Risk behavior in adolescence: A psychosocial framework for understanding and action. *Developmental Review, 12,* 374–390.

Jochen, P., Valkenburg, P. M., & Schouten, A. P. (2006). Characteristics and motives of adolescents talking with strangers on the internet. *CyberPsychology & Behavior, 9*(5), 526–530.

Kagan, J. (1997). Temperament and the reactions to unfamiliarity. *Child Development, 68,* 139–143.

Kail, R. (1990). *The development of memory in children* (3rd ed.). New York: W. H. Freeman.

Kail, R. (1991). Developmental changes in speed of processing during childhood and adolescence. *Psychological Bulletin, 109,* 490–501.

Keating, D. P. (2004). Cognitive and brain development. In R. M. Lerner & L. Steinberg (Eds.), *Handbook of adolescent psychology* (2nd ed., pp. 45–84). Hoboken, NJ: John Wiley.

Kuhn, D. (2006). Do cognitive changes accompany developments in the adolescent brain? *Perspectives on Psychological Science, 1*(1), 59–67.

Lang, A. (2000). The limited capacity model of mediated message processing. *Journal of Communication, 50*(1), 46–70.

Larson, R., Richards, M. H., Moneta, G., Holmbeck, G., & Duckett, E. (1996). Changes in adolescents' daily interactions with their families from ages 10 to 18: Disengagement and transformation. *Developmental Psychology, 32,* 744–754.

Lemish, D. (1987). Viewers in diapers: The early development of television viewing. In T. R. Lindlof (Ed.), *Natural audiences: Qualitative research of media uses and effects* (pp. 33–57). Norwood, NJ: Ablex.

Livingstone, S. (2002). *Young people and new media: Childhood and the changing media environment.* Thousand Oaks, CA: Sage.

Lorch, E. P., Bellack, D. R., & Augsbach, L. H. (1987). Young children's memory for televised stories: Effects of importance. *Child Development, 58,* 453–463.

Lovett, S. B., & Flavell, J. H. (1990). Understanding and remembering: Children's knowledge about the differential effects of strategy and task variables on comprehension and memorization. *Child Development, 61,* 1842–1858.

Mandler, J. M. (1998). Representation. In D. Kuhn & R. Siegler (Eds.), *Cognition, perception, and language,* Vol. 2 of W. Damon (Series Ed.), *Handbook of child psychology* (pp. 255–308). New York: John Wiley.

Meadowcroft, J. M., & Reeves, B. (1989). Influence of story scheme development on children's attention to television. *Communication Research, 16,* 352–374.

Melkman, R., Tversky, B., & Baratz, D. (1981). Developmental trends in the use of perceptual and conceptual attributes in grouping, clustering, and retrieval. *Journal of Experimental Child Development, 31,* 470–486.

Metcalfe, J., & Shimamura, A. P. (Eds.). (1994). *Metacognition: Knowing about knowing.* Cambridge: MIT Press.

Meyrowitz, J. (1985). *No sense of place: The impact of electronic media on social behavior.* New York: Oxford University Press.

Morison, P., Kelly, H., & Gardner, H. (1981). Reasoning about the realities of television: A developmental study. *Journal of Broadcasting, 25,* 229–242.

Moshman, D. (1998). Cognitive development beyond childhood. In W. Damon (Series Ed.), D. Kuhn & R. Siegler (Vol. Eds.), *Handbook of child psychology: Vol. 2. Cognition, perception, and language* (5th ed., pp. 947–978). New York: John Wiley.

Newman, M. (2007, April 2). 28 arrested in Florida online sex sting. *New York Times.* Retrieved April 3, 2007, from http://www.nytimes.com/2007/04/02/us/02cnd-sting.html

Noam, E. M., & Freeman, R. N. (1997). The media monopoly and other myths. *Television Quarterly, 29*(1), 18–23.

Noble, G. (1975). *Children in front of the small screen.* Thousand Oaks, CA: Sage.

O'Bryan, K. G., & Boersma, F. J. (1971). Eye movements, perceptual activity, and conservation development. *Journal of Experimental Child Psychology, 12,* 157–169.

Perloff, R. M. (2002). The third-person effect. In J. Bryant & D. Zillman (Eds.), *Media effects: Advances in theory and research* (pp. 489–506). Mahwah, NJ: Lawrence Erlbaum.

Petersen, A. C. (1988). Adolescent development. *Annual Reviews in Psychology, 39,* 583–607.

Petersen, A. C., & Taylor, B. (1980). The biological approach to adolescence: Biological change and psychological adaptation. In J. Adelson (Ed.), *Handbook of adolescent psychology* (pp. 117–155). New York: John Wiley.

Piaget, J. (1930). *The child's conception of the world.* New York: Harcourt, Brace & World.

Piaget, J. (1950). *The psychology of intelligence.* New York: International Universities Press.

Piaget, J. (1952). *The origins of intelligence in children.* New York: International Universities Press.

Piaget, J., & Inhelder, B. (1975). *The origin of the idea of chance in children.* New York: Norton.

Potter, W. J. (2005). *Media literacy.* Thousand Oaks, CA: Sage.

Public Agenda. (1999). *Kids these days '99: What Americans really think about the next generation.* Retrieved January 15, 2008, from http://www.publicagenda.org/specials/kids/kids.htm

Rekers, G. A. (1992). Development of problems of puberty and sex roles in adolescence. In C. E. Walker & M. C. Roberts (Eds.), *Handbook of clinical child psychology* (pp. 607–622). New York: John Wiley.

Resnick, M. D., Bearman, P. S., Blum, R. W., Bauman, K. E., Harris, K. M., Jones, J., et al. (1997). Protecting adolescents from harm: Findings from the national longitudinal study on adolescent health. *Journal of American Medical Association, 278,* 823–832.

Revelle, G. L., Medoff, L., & Strommen, E. F. (2001). Interactive technologies research at the Children's Television Workshop. In S. M. Fisch & R. T. Truglio (Eds.), *"G" is for growing: Thirty years of research on* Sesame Street (pp. 215–230). Mahwah, NJ: Lawrence Erlbaum.

Rideout, V., & Hamel, E. (2006). *The media family: Electronic media in the lives of infants, toddlers, preschoolers and their parents.* Menlo Park, CA: Henry J. Kaiser Family Foundation.

Roberts, D. F., Foehr, U. G., & Rideout, V. (2005). *Generation M: Media in the lives of 8–18 year-olds.* Menlo Park, CA: Henry J. Kaiser Family Foundation.

Robinson, J. L., Winiewicz, D. D., Fuerch, J. H., Roemmich, J. N., & Epstein, L. H. (2006). Relationship between parental estimate and an objective measure of child television watching. *International Journal of Behavioral Nutrition and Physical Activity, 3,* 43.

Roth, J., & Brooks-Gunn, J. (2000). What do adolescents need for healthy development? Implications for youth policy. *Social Policy Report, 14,* 3–19.

Salomon, G. (1983). Television watching and mental effort: A social psychological view. In J. Bryant & D. R. Anderson (Eds.), *Children's understanding of television: Research on attention and comprehension* (pp. 181–198). New York: Academic Press.

Salomon, G., & Leigh, T. (1984). Predispositions about learning from print and television. *Journal of Communication, 34*(2), 119–135.

Scarr, S. (1992). Developmental theories for the 1990s: Development and individual differences. *Child Development, 63,* 1–19.

Schmitt, K. L., Anderson, D. R., & Collins, P. A. (1999). Form and content: Looking at visual features of television. *Developmental Psychology, 35,* 1156–1167.

Scholz, R. W., & Waller, M. (1983). Conceptual and theoretical issues in developmental research on the acquisition of the probability concept. In R. W. Scholz (Ed.), *Decision making under uncertainty* (pp. 291–311). New York: North Holland.

Schwartz, S. J., & Pantin, H. (2006). Identity development in adolescence and emerging adulthood: The interface of self, context, and culture. In A. Columbus (Ed.), *Advances in psychology research* (pp. 1–40). Hauppauge, NY: Nova Science Publishers.

Siegler, R. S. (2005). Children's learning. *American Psychologist, 60,* 769–778.

Smith, R., Anderson, D. R., & Fischer, C. (1985). Young children's comprehension of montage. *Child Development, 56,* 962–971.

Sowell, E. R., Trauner, D. A., Gamst, A., & Jernigan, T. L. (2002). Development of cortical and subcortical brain structures in childhood and adolescence: A structural MRI study. *Developmental Medicine & Child Neurology, 44*(1), 4–16.

Sparks, G. G. (1986). Developmental difference in children's reports of fear induced by the mass media. *Child Study Journal, 16,* 55–66.

Springer, K. (2001). Perceptual boundedness and perceptual support in conceptual development. *Psychological Review, 108*(4), 691–708.

Stegge, H., & Terwogt, M. M. (2007). Awareness and regulation of emotion in typical and atypical development. In J. J. Gross (Ed.), *Handbook of emotion regulation* (pp. 269–286). New York: Guilford.

Steinberg, L. (2005). Cognitive and affective development in adolescence. *Trends in Cognitive Sciences, 9*(2), 69–74.

Subrahmanyam, K., & Greenfield, P. (1996). Effect of video game practice on spatial skills in girls and boys. In P. M. Greenfield & R. R. Cocking (Eds.), *Interacting with video* (pp. 95–218). Westport, CT: Ablex.

Subrahmanyam, K., & Greenfield, P. (2008). Media symbol systems and cognitive processes. In S. Calvert & B. J. Wilson (Eds.), *The Blackwell handbook of children, media, and development.* London: Blackwell.

Thompson, J. G., & Myers, N. A. (1985). Inferences and recall at ages four and seven. *Child Development, 56,* 1134–1144.

Tversky, B. (1985). Development of taxonomic organization of named and pictured categories. *Developmental Psychology, 21,* 1111–1119.

Valkenburg, P., & Cantor, J. (2000). Children's likes and dislikes of entertainment programs. In D. Zillmann & P. Vorderer (Eds.), *Media entertainment: The psychology of its appeal* (pp. 135–152). Mahwah, NJ: Lawrence Erlbaum.

Valkenburg, P., Schouten, A., & Peter, J. (2005). Adolescents' identity experiments on the internet. *New Media and Society, 7*(3), 383–402.

van den Broek, P., Lorch, E. P., & Thurlow, R. (1996). Children's and adults' memory for television stories: The role of causal factors, story-grammar categories, and hierarchical level. *Child Development, 67,* 3010–3028.

Vandewater, E. A., Rideout, V. J., Wartella, E. A., Huang, X., Lee, J. H., & Shim, M. (2007). Digital childhood: Electronic media and technology use among infants, toddlers and preschoolers. *Pediatrics, 119,* e1006–e1015. Retrieved May 7, 2007, from www.pediatrics.org

Vidmar, N., & Rokeach, M. (1974). Archie Bunker's bigotry: A study in selective perception and exposure. *Journal of Communication, 24*(1), 36–47.

Walsh-Childers, K. (1997). *A content analysis: Sexual coverage in women's, men's, teen and other specialty magazines.* Menlo Park, CA: Kaiser Family Foundation.

Wartella, E., & Reeves, B. (1985). Historical trends in research on children and the media: 1900–1960. *Journal of Communication, 35*(2), 118–132.

Weiss, A. J., & Wilson, B. J. (1998). Children's cognitive and emotional responses to the portrayal of negative emotions in family-formatted situation comedies. *Human Communication Research, 24,* 584–609.

Whitbeck, L., Yoder, K. A., Hoyt, D. R., & Conger, R. D. (1999). Early adolescent sexual activity: A developmental study. *Journal of Marriage & the Family, 61,* 934–946.

Wiggers, M., & van Lieshout, C. F. (1985). Development of recognition of emotions: Children's reliance on situational and facial expressive cues. *Developmental Psychology, 21*(2), 338–349.

Wilson, B. J. (1991). Children's reactions to dreams conveyed in mass media programming. *Communication Research, 18,* 283–305.

Wilson, B. J., & Smith, S. L. (1995, May). *Children's comprehension of and emotional reactions to TV news.* Paper presented at the annual conference of the International Communication Association, Albuquerque, NM.

Wilson, B. J., & Smith, S. L. (1998). Children's responses to emotional portrayals on television. In P. Anderson & L. Guerrero (Eds.), *Handbook of communication and emotion: Research, theory, applications, and contexts* (pp. 533–569). New York: Academic Press.

Wilson, B. J., & Weiss, A. J. (1995, May). *Children's reactions to a toy-based cartoon: Entertainment or commercial message?* Paper presented to the International Communication Association, Albuquerque, NM.

Wooley, J. D., Boerger, E. A., & Markman, A. B. (2004). A visit from the candy witch: Factors influencing young children's belief in a novel fantastical being. *Developmental Science, 7*(4), 456–468.

Wright, J. C., Huston, A. C., Reitz, A. L., & Piemyat, S. (1994). Young children's perceptions of television reality: Determinants and developmental differences. *Developmental Psychology, 30,* 229–239.

Wright, J. C., Huston, A. C., Ross, R. P., Calvert, S. L., Rolandelli, D., Weeks, L. A., et al. (1984). Pace and continuity of television programs: Effects on children's attention and comprehension. *Developmental Psychology, 20,* 653–666.

Zuckerman, M. (1994). *Behavioral expressions and biosocial bases of sensation seeking.* New York: Cambridge University Press.

CHAPTER 2

Advertising

Children's social worlds are increasingly constructed around consuming, as brands and products have come to determine who is "in" or "out," who is hot or not, who deserves to have friends or social status.

—Juliet B. Schor, *Born to Buy:*
The Commercialized Child and the
New Commercial Culture (2004, p. 11)

Keeping brands young is critical for the long-term health of the brands. Businesses need to plan ahead and nurture the brands and customers of the future.

—Anne Autherland and Beth Thompson,
Kidfluence: The Marketer's Guide to Understanding and
Reaching Generation Y—Kids, Tweens, and Teens (2003, p. 149)

Children are seen by some as commodities—as products to be sold to advertisers.

—Federal Communications Commissioner
Michael J. Copps, Children NOW conference on
The Future of Children's Media: Advertising (2006, p. 5)

In certain categories kids are perhaps the most fickle of consumers. They can tire very quickly of certain kinds of products and programs. The implication is to constantly "freshen" your product lines and program lineups to cater to this desire for the new.

—Dan S. Acuff, *What Kids Buy and Why* (1997, p. 190)

Five-year-old Isabel came home from kindergarten one day and announced to her mother, "I need a Powerpuff Girl, Mom." Her mother was a bit surprised given that, to her knowledge, Isabel had never even seen a TV episode of *The Powerpuff Girls* cartoon, which featured three female superheroes with oversized heads.

"What's a Powerpuff Girl?" her mother asked.

"Their names are Blossom, Bubbles, and Buttercup," replied Isabel.

"How do you know about them?" her mother continued.

"My friends told me. We play them during recess."

"What do the Powerpuff Girls do?" probed her mother.

"They save people and stuff," Isabel replied.

On the next trip to Walgreens, Isabel spotted a display of small, plush Powerpuff Girl dolls in one of the aisles and shrieked, "Mom, can I have one, PLEEEESE!"

Isabel's mom checked the price, weighed this struggle against all others she might encounter that day, and reluctantly tossed one of the $4.99 dolls into the shopping cart. Along with millions of other parents, she caved in to what has been called the "nag factor" in the world of television advertising. Just to be clear, Isabel's mom is one of the authors of this book. In other words, even researchers who study children and the media can feel the pressure of commercialism. As it turns out, Isabel's mom got away pretty cheaply that day. Anyone searching the eBay.com Web site can find 469 different toy products and apparel items associated with this successful cartoon. Children and their parents can purchase, for example, a Powerpuff Girl lunch bag, a key chain, a bank, a wristwatch, costumes, girls' bedding, a backpack, socks, and even a hair dryer (see Figure 2.1). And the cartoon series went off the air in 2004! As a comparison, eBay offers 5,933 products associated with the very popular cartoon series *SpongeBob SquarePants*.

It is estimated that more than $15 billion a year is now spent on advertising and marketing to children, representing almost three times the amount spent just 15 years ago (McNeal, 1999). Marketers are paying more attention to young consumers these days for at least three reasons (McNeal, 1998). First, American children today have a great deal of their own money to spend. Consumers younger than age 12 spent $2.2 billion in 1968; roughly 35 years later, this amount rose dramatically to $42 billion (McNeal, 2007). As seen in Figure 2.2, children's spending power has steadily risen over the years. Much of this increase comes from children earning more money for household chores and receiving more money from relatives on holidays (McNeal, 1998). As might be expected, teens spend even more than children—roughly $175 billion in the year 2003 alone (Teenage Research Unlimited, 2004a). In fact, the average American teenager spends nearly $100 a week on such products as clothes, candy, soft drinks, and music (Teenage Research Unlimited, 2004b).

Figure 2.1   Merchandise Related to the TV Cartoon *Powerpuff Girls*
SOURCE: © 2008 TW & Cartoon Network, Powerpuff Girls.

Second, in addition to spending their own money, young people influence their parents' consumer behaviors. At an early age, children give direction to daily household purchases such as snacks, cereals, toothpaste, and even shampoos. As they get older, teens often voice opinions about what type of car to buy, what new media equipment is needed, and even where to go on vacation (Gunter & Furnham, 1998). And this influence has grown over the years. In the 1960s, children influenced about $5 billion of their parents' purchases. By 1984, that figure increased to $50 billion, and by 2005, it had leaped to $700 billion (McNeal, 2007). Relaxed parenting styles, increased family incomes, higher divorce rates, and more parents working outside the home are some of the historical changes that may account for children's increased economic influence in the family (see Valkenburg & Cantor, 2001).

Third, marketers recognize that the children of today represent adult consumers of tomorrow. Children develop loyalties to particular brands of products at an early age, and these preferences often persist into adulthood (Moschis & Moore, 1982).

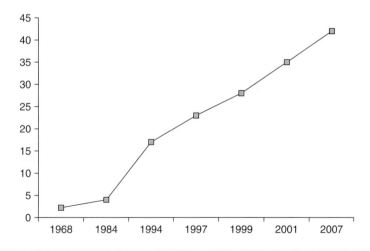

Figure 2.2   Annual Spending Power of Children Younger Than 12 Years of Age
SOURCE: Adapted from McNeal (1998, 2007).

Many companies today such as McDonald's and Coca-Cola engage in what is called "cradle-to-grave" marketing in an effort to cultivate consumer allegiance at a very early age (McNeal, 1998).

Marketers have developed sophisticated strategies for targeting young consumers. Magazines such as *Teen Vogue* and *Sports Illustrated for Kids* contain glossy full-page ads promoting clothes, shoes, and beauty products. Web sites targeted to children feature all types of advertising, and even schools are marketing products to children. By far, the easiest way to reach young people is through television. Recent estimates suggest that the average American child sees more than 25,000 television ads per year (Gantz, Schwartz, Angelini, & Rideout, 2007), although the amount varies depending on the age of the viewer (see Figure 2.3). But marketers are exploring new ways to reach young consumers through online sources and through personal, handheld technologies such as iPods and cell phones.

In this chapter, we will explore advertising messages targeted to children and teens. First, we will examine how marketing to children has changed over the years, focusing primarily on television advertising. Then we will look at the amount and nature of television advertising targeted to youth. Next we will give an overview of how children cognitively process and make sense of advertising. Then we will examine the persuasive impact of advertising on youth. The chapter will then turn to more recent marketing efforts targeted to children, including viral marketing, marketing in schools, product placement, and online advertising. We will close with a discussion of the regulation of advertising in the United States as well as in other countries and with an overview of efforts to teach advertising literacy. It should be noted that two other chapters in this book deal with advertising as it relates to specific health hazards. Chapter 7 examines advertising of cigarettes and alcohol, and Chapter 9 looks at the impact of food advertising on nutrition. The focus here is primarily on advertising of toys, clothes, and other consumer goods, although food products will be referenced occasionally as well.

Historical Changes in Advertising to Children

Efforts to advertise products to children date back to the 1930s, the early days of radio. Companies such as General Mills, Kellogg's, and Ovaltine routinely pitched food products during child-oriented radio shows such as *Little Orphan Annie* and *Story Time* (Pecora, 1998). Household products such as toothpaste and aspirin also were marketed during children's programming. In these earliest endeavors, children were considered important primarily because they were capable of influencing their parents' consumer behavior.

In the 1950s, children gradually became recognized as consumers in their own right (Pecora, 1998). During this decade, the sheer number of children increased so dramatically that it is now referred to as the baby boomer period. In addition, parents who had lived through the Depression and World War II experienced a new level of economic prosperity that they wanted to share with their offspring (Alexander, Benjamin, Hoerrner, & Roe, 1998). As noted by Kline (1993), "the 1950s' family

Figure 2.3

SOURCE: Reprinted with permission of Tribune Media Services.

became preoccupied with possession and consumption and the satisfaction that goods can bring" (p. 67). And of course, the advent of television offered new ways to demonstrate products to captive audiences of parents and children (Pecora, 1998).

The earliest television advertising looked very different than it does today. At first, programmers were more interested in getting people to buy television sets than in attracting advertisers (Adler, 1980). Some programs were offered by the broadcast networks themselves with no commercial sponsorship at all. Other programs had a single sponsor that would underwrite the entire cost of the 30-minute or 60-minute time slot. Consequently, there were fewer interruptions, and the sponsors sometimes pitched the company rather than any specific product. As more and more American homes purchased sets, the focus shifted toward attracting this large potential audience to one program or network over others. Programs also became more expensive to produce, thereby increasing the cost of advertising time so that more sponsors were necessary to share the burden.

In one of the only systematic studies of early TV advertising, Alexander and colleagues (1998) assessed 75 commercials that aired during children's shows in the 1950s. The researchers found that the average length of a commercial was 60 seconds, considerably longer than the 15-and 30-second ads of today. In addition, less over-all time was devoted to advertising—only 5 minutes per hour in the 1950s compared with roughly 11 minutes per hour today (Gantz et al., 2007). Reflecting the fact that ads were directed more at families than specifically at children, household products such as appliances, dog food, and even staples such as peanut butter were commonly pitched. The vast majority of ads were live action rather than animated. And the practice of host selling, using a character from the interrupted program to endorse a product in the commercial segment, was quite common. In fact, 62% of the ads featured some form of host selling, which has since been banned.

In his book *Out of the Garden: Toys, TV, and Children's Culture in the Age of Marketing,* Kline (1993) argues that 1955 was a turning point in television adver-tising to children. That year marked the debut of the highly successful TV show *The Mickey Mouse Club.* In great numbers, children rushed out to buy Mickey Mouse ears, guitars, and other paraphernalia, demonstrating their own purchasing power. Shortly thereafter, the toy industry moved aggressively into television.

In the 1960s, the broadcast networks too recognized the revenue potential of targeting children. However, adults continued to be the most profitable consumers to reach. So those children's programs still airing in the valuable prime-time period were shifted to Saturday morning, when large numbers of children could be reached efficiently and cost-effectively with cartoons. Throughout the 1970s, the networks increased the number of Saturday morning hours devoted to children's programming in response to marketers' increasing interest in young consumers.

The 1980s saw the birth of toy-based programs (Pecora, 1998). Creating spin-off toys based on popular children's shows is a practice that dates back to the early days of radio. Toy-based programs are slightly different, however, because they are *orig-inally* conceived for the sole purpose of promoting new toys. Hence, critics have charged that the shows themselves are actually half-hour commercials. In an unusual twist, toy manufacturers and producers come together at the earliest stage of program development. Shows are created with the consultation and often the financial backing of a toy company. In her book *The Business of Children's Entertainment,* Pecora (1998) argued that in the 1980s,

> the line between sponsorship and program became blurred as producers, looking to spread the risk of program production costs, turned to toy manu-facturers, and toy manufacturers, wanting to stabilize a market subject to children's whim and fancy, turned to the media. (p. 34)

The first example of such a partnership occurred in 1983, when Mattel toy com-pany joined together with Filmation production house to create *He-Man and the Masters of the Universe.* In the deregulated era of the 1980s, these mutually benefi-cial arrangements proliferated. In 1980, there were no toy-based programs; by 1984, there were 40 of them on the air (Wilke, Therrien, Dunkin, & Vamos, 1985). According to Pecora (1998), the success of toy-based shows such as the *Smurfs* meant that "neither toy nor story is now considered without thought of its market potential" (p. 61). She went on to argue that today, "Programming evolves not from the rituals of storytelling but rather the imperative of the marketplace" (p. 59).

In the 1990s, the proliferation of cable and independent channels opened up new avenues for reaching children. Disney created its own television network, and others such as Nickelodeon and Cartoon Network have been tremendously successful in targeting the child audience. Recognizing the economic benefits, marketers are now segmenting the child audience into different age groups. Teenage consumers are widely recognized for their spending power, as evidenced by the creation of MTV, Black Entertainment Network (BET), the CW Network (a merger of the WB and UPN networks), and other specialized channels devoted to attracting adolescents and young adults. And advertisers are responsible for coining the term *tweens,* referring to 8- to 12-year-olds who are on the cusp of adolescence, are deeply interested in brand names and fashion, and spend a lot of time at shopping malls (de Mesa, 2005). Even the youngest age groups are being targeted. In 2006, a 24-hour cable channel called BabyFirstTV was launched to provide television programming for babies and toddlers. The network airs no commercials, but there is a link on its Web site that allows parents to buy BabyFirst T-shirts, as well as Baby Einstein and Baby Mozart DVDs. Infant videos and DVDs accrue more than $100 million in sales a year (Shin, 2007).

Thus, the current market is far different than in the 1950s when the broadcast networks dominated television and there were only a few other media options. Today, licensed characters such as Dora the Explorer and SpongeBob SquarePants routinely cross over from television to other media such as books, home videos, CDs, film, and computer software. And numerous media outlets actually specialize in child- and teen-oriented content in an effort to attract affluent young consumers.

Content Analyses of Television Advertising

What do ads that are targeted to children look like? Most of the research has focused on television advertising, in part because children continue to spend so much time with this medium. In one early content analysis, Barcus (1980) looked at advertising during children's shows in 1971 and in later samples of programming from 1975 and 1978. In 1971, roughly 12 minutes of each broadcast hour were devoted to commercials, a marked jump from the 5 minutes documented in the 1950s (Alexander et al., 1998). Given that the typical ad had shrunk to 30 seconds, children on average were exposed to 26 different commercials each hour. The time devoted to advertising dropped in 1975 to roughly 9 minutes per hour (Barcus, 1980). This shift reflects pressure on the industry in the mid-1970s from child advocacy groups and the federal government to reduce advertising to children (see section on regulation below).

What products were being pitched? In the 1978 sample, Barcus (1980) found that most advertisements were for cereal, candy, toys, and fast-food restaurants. In fact, food ads generally accounted for nearly 60% of all commercials targeted to children (cereal, 24%; candy, 21%; fast foods, 12%). Barcus also found that the appeals used in children's ads were mostly psychological rather than rational. Instead of giving price, ingredient, or quality information, ads typically focused on how fun the product is or how good it tastes.

By the 1980s, commercials were shortened even more so that many lasted only 15 seconds (Condry, Bence, & Scheibe, 1988). Although the total time devoted to ads remained somewhat constant, the briefer messages meant that children were exposed to a greater number of ads during any given hour of broadcast television.

Using a more comprehensive sample than in earlier research, Kunkel and Gantz (1992) examined a composite week of child-oriented programming during February and March 1990. Programming was sampled from seven different channels: the three major broadcast networks, two independent stations, and two cable channels (Nickelodeon and USA). The researchers found more advertising on the networks (10 minutes/hour) than on independents (9 minutes/hour) or cable (6 minutes/hour). Consistent with earlier research, the same types of products dominated commercials during children's programming. Roughly 80% of all ads were for toys, cereals, snacks, and fast-food restaurants (see Figure 2.4). Interestingly, only 3% of all ads were for healthy foods. When the researchers compared channel types, they found that toy ads were most prevalent on independent channels, whereas cereals and snacks were most common on the broadcast networks. Cable channels offered the most diverse range of products, with 35% of the ads falling into the "other" category. Kunkel and Gantz (1992) reasoned that toy ads, which have been consistently criticized for deceptive practices, may show up less often on the broadcast networks because of their more rigorous self-regulatory standards.

The researchers also coded the primary persuasive appeal used in each ad. The most prevalent theme was fun/happiness, which accounted for 27% of all ads. Two other common appeals were taste/flavor (19%) and product performance (18%). In contrast, appeals based on price, quality of materials, nutrition, and safety each accounted for less than 1% of the ads.

Rather than focusing just on programs targeted to children, the Kaiser Family Foundation sponsored a comprehensive study of all advertising content on the

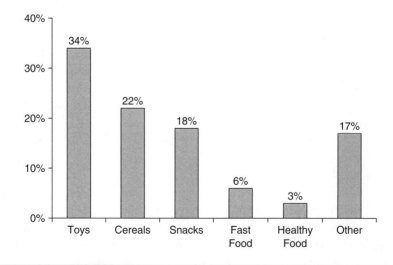

Figure 2.4   Types of Products Advertised During Children's TV Programming

SOURCE: Adapted from Kunkel and Gantz (1992).

channels that children watch most (Gantz et al., 2007). The study looked at a composite week of programming airing in 2005 across 13 networks channels, including Nickelodeon, Disney, Cartoon Network, the four major broadcast networks (ABC, NBC, CBS, and Fox), PBS, BET, and MTV. There was considerable variation in the amount of advertising and promotional messages across the channels; PBS (1 minute/hour) and Disney (20 seconds/hour) had the least amount of such content, whereas ABC, CBS, and Fox had the most (roughly 14 minutes/hour). On average, the broadcast networks devote more time to advertising than do the cable networks, a finding consistent with the earlier Kunkel and Gantz (1992) study.

The study looked closely at food advertising, in particular. Although food commercials are common on television, food is marketed even more to children than to adults. Food ads constituted 13% of the ads on the four major broadcast networks, but they constituted 32% of the ads on three of the top children's networks (ABC Family, Nickelodeon, Cartoon Network). In fact, half of all advertising time during children's shows was devoted to food commercials. And most of these food ads were for cereal (31%), candy and snacks (30%), and fast food (11%). Commercials for healthy foods were very rare in the 2005 sample. Of the 8,854 food commercials analyzed in the Kaiser Family Foundation study, there were no ads for fruits or vegetables targeted at children or teens. Consistent with the low nutritional value of the products, most food ads emphasized taste and fun as the main persuasive appeals (see Figure 2.5). All of these patterns are very comparable to what Kunkel and Gantz (1992) found 15 years ago.

Therefore, despite the proliferation of channels on television, it seems that advertising to children has not changed much over the years. The same products dominate commercials, and the selling appeals continue to focus more on fun, happiness, and taste than on actual information about the product.

Content analyses also have looked at other qualities inherent in children's advertising, such as how gender is portrayed. In a study of nearly 600 commercials targeted to children, Larson (2001) compared ads that feature only girls or only boys with those that feature both girls and boys in them. She found that girls-only ads were far more likely to feature a domestic setting such as a bedroom or a backyard

CALVIN AND HOBBES By Bill Watterson

Figure 2.5

SOURCE: Reprinted with permission of Universal Press Syndicate.

than were boys-only or mixed-gender ads. Boys-only ads seldom occurred around the house and instead featured settings such as restaurants, video arcades, and baseball fields. The types of interactions that occurred also differed across ads. More than 80% of the girls-only ads portrayed cooperation, whereas less than 30% of the boys-only ads did. Consistent with gender stereotypes, nearly 30% of the boys-only ads featured competitive interactions, but none of the girls-only ads did. Finally, there were gender differences across the types of products being pitched. Food commercials were most likely to feature girls and boys together, whereas toy ads typically were single gender in nature. Commercials targeted to boys were frequently for video games or action figures, and those targeted to girls often were for Barbie dolls.

Gender stereotypes exist in commercials targeted toward teens as well. In one study, ads targeted to males teens emphasized competition, having the best, and achievement in the persuasive appeals, whereas ads targeted to female teens emphasized romance, sexuality, and belonging to a group (Buijzen & Valkenburg, 2002).

Single-gender commercials can convey stereotypes in more subtle ways as well. One study examined the production techniques used in toy ads directed to boys versus girls (Welch, Huston-Stein, Wright, & Plehal, 1979). Toy ads for boys were faster in pace, used more abrupt transitions such as cuts, and had more sound effects and other types of noise. In contrast, toy ads directed at girls used smoother transitions such as fades and dissolves between scenes and had more background music. In a follow-up study (Huston, Greer, Wright, Welch, & Ross, 1984), elementary schoolers readily identified these different production techniques as being associated with a "boy's toy" or a "girl's toy" even when the toy itself was gender neutral (e.g., a mobile).

There are also stereotypes about race and ethnicity in commercial messages targeted to children. Advertisements featuring only White children are far more common than ads featuring only children of color (Larson, 2001). Furthermore, ads featuring Black children are more likely to sell convenience foods, especially fast foods, than are ads featuring no Black children (Harrison, 2006). Indeed, marketers target African American consumers with ads for high-calorie and low-nutrient foods and beverages (Institute of Medicine, 2006).

Commercials for children also have been analyzed for violence. Palmerton and Judas (1994) looked at ads featured during the 21 top-rated children's cartoons in 1993. One third of the ads contained overt displays of physical aggression, most commonly found in toy commercials. Furthermore, ads that were clearly targeted to boys were far more likely to feature violence than were ads targeted to girls. Literally every commercial for action figures in the sample contained violence. This link between violence and ads directed at boys has been documented in more recent research (Larson, 2001).

In summary, the typical hour of television features anywhere from 10 to 14 minutes of advertising on the channels that youth watch most (Gantz et al., 2007). Most of the commercial messages targeted to children market toys or food products that are not particularly healthy. In fact, the average tween (8–12 years of age) in this country sees 21 food ads a day on TV (Gantz et al., 2007), most of which feature candy, snacks, and fast foods. The commercials designed for youth do not offer much in the way of "hard" information about products such as what they are made of or how much they cost. Instead, the appeals are largely emotional ones based on fun or good taste. Toy ads in particular are fairly stereotyped in terms of gender. Ads targeted to boys typically sell violent toys that are demonstrated through action, force, and noise. Ads for girls, in contrast, are for dolls that are featured in a quieter, slower, and more domestic environment. Commercials targeted to teens show similar gender stereotypes; ads for males tend to focus on competition, whereas ads for females focus more on relationships. The next section addresses how young people respond cognitively to these messages.

Cognitive Processing of Advertising

In the United States, policies dating back to the Communications Act of 1934 stipulate that advertising must be clearly identifiable to its intended audience (Wilcox & Kunkel, 1996). In other words, commercials should be recognized by the target audience as obvious attempts to persuade. If a viewer is unaware of or incapable of recognizing an ad, then he or she is presumably more vulnerable to its persuasive appeals. Under these circumstances, commercial messages are thought to be inherently unfair and even deceptive. Because of the potential for unfairness, researchers as well as policymakers have focused on how children of different ages make sense of advertising.

Attention to Advertising

One of the first questions to ask is whether children pay any attention to advertising. Marketers use sound effects, bright colors, jingles, animated characters, and a variety of other production techniques to attract consumers. In fact, ads are typically louder in volume than accompanying programs. All of these techniques are perceptually salient and, as we learned in Chapter 1, likely to capture the attention of younger children in particular.

Certainly many adults use commercial time to leave the room, engage in other activities, or even to change the channel. With digital video recording devices such as TiVo, consumers can record their favorite programs and skip over the advertising. Based on in-home observation, one study found that adults pay visual attention to programming 62% of the time and to ads only 33% of the time (Krugman, Cameron, & White, 1995). As it turns out, children's attention depends on the age of the viewer. In one early study, mothers of 5- to 12-year-olds were trained to observe their children's attention to commercials aired during different types of TV programming (Ward, Levinson, & Wackman, 1972). All children exhibited a drop in attention when a commercial was shown, and attention also decreased over the course of several ads shown in a series. However, the youngest children (5–7 years) generally displayed higher levels of attention to both commercials and programs, whereas the 11- and 12-year-olds were most likely to stop looking when an ad came on. A more recent study that videotaped families while they watched television found that 2-year-olds paid just as much attention to ads as to programs (Schmitt, Woolf, & Anderson, 2003). In contrast, 5-, 8-, and 12-year-olds looked more at programs than ads, with the difference increasing by age (see Figure 2.6). These findings suggest that older children, like adults, screen out advertisements. The data also suggest that very young children may not be making clear distinctions between program and nonprogram content, an issue we will turn to in the next section.

Similar age differences have been found in laboratory research. Zuckerman, Ziegler, and Stevenson (1978) videotaped second through fourth graders while they watched a brief program with eight cereal commercials embedded in it. Overall, children paid less attention to the ads than to the program, but once again, attention to the commercials decreased with age.

Younger children's greater attention to ads may be due in part to attention-getting techniques such as jingles, animation, and slogans used to pull in the audience. Greer, Potts, Wright, and Huston (1982) found, for example, that preschoolers paid more attention to advertisements that contained high action, frequent scene changes, and numerous cuts than to ads without these production features. Likewise, Wartella and Ettema (1974) found that compared with kindergarten and second-grade children, preschoolers' level of attention to ads varied more as a function of visual and auditory attributes of the message. Such patterns are consistent with younger children's tendency to focus on and be swayed by perceptually salient cues in the media, as discussed in Chapter 1.

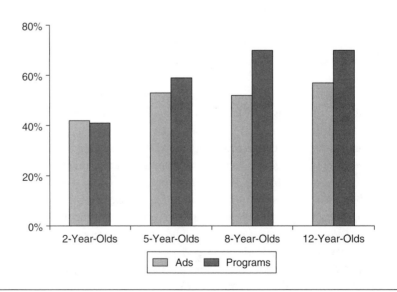

Figure 2.6   Percentage of Time Looking at TV Screen During Commercials and Programs as a Function of Age of Child

SOURCE: Adapted from Schmitt et al. (2003).

Overall, then, preschoolers and early elementary schoolers pay more attention to television advertising than do older children. In part, this may be due to the strong perceptual attributes commonly found in commercials. However, the relatively steady attention patterns during transitions from programming to advertising also suggest that younger children may not be distinguishing these two types of messages very clearly.

Discrimination of Ads From Programming

Discrimination can be tested by showing different types of television content and asking children to identify what they are watching. For example, Palmer and McDowell (1979) stopped a videotape of Saturday morning content at preselected points and asked kindergartners and first graders whether they had just seen "part of the show" or a "commercial." The young elementary schoolers were able to accurately identify commercials only 53% of the time, which is roughly equivalent to chance guessing.

In other studies employing similar techniques, young children's discrimination skills sometimes have been better and often are above chance levels (Butter, Popovich, Stackhouse, & Garner, 1981; Levin, Petros, & Petrella, 1982). Nevertheless, age differences are consistently found through the preschool years; 3- and 4-year-olds are less able to make these distinctions than are 5-year-olds (Butter et al., 1981; Levin et al., 1982).

Once children learn to discriminate a TV ad from a program, they often do so on the basis of perceptual features rather than more conceptual properties of the two messages. For instance, when Palmer and McDowell (1979) asked kindergartners and first graders how they knew a particular segment was a commercial, the predominant reason cited was the length of the message ("because commercials are short"). Other studies that have interviewed children about ads versus programs without showing television content support this finding (Blatt, Spencer, & Ward, 1972; Ward, Wackman, & Wartella, 1977).

We should point out that the television industry employs separation devices to help signal to child viewers that a commercial break is occurring. These devices vary considerably in degree, from the simple insertion of several seconds of blank screen between a program and an ad to a more complex audiovisual message indicating that a program "will be right back after these messages." As it turns out, these types of separators do not help young children much. Studies comparing blank screens, audio-only messages, visual-only messages, and audiovisual separators have found little improvement in young children's discrimination abilities with any of these devices (Butter et al., 1981; Palmer & McDowell, 1979; Stutts, Vance, & Hudleson, 1981). One possible reason for the ineffectiveness of such separators is that they may be too brief to be noticed. Another possibility is that they look too much like adjacent programming. In many cases, visuals of the characters or part of the soundtrack from the show are actually featured in the separators. A more effective device may be one that is far more obvious. For example, a child or adult spokesperson who has no affiliation with programming could state, "We are taking a break from the program now in order to show you a commercial."

To summarize, the research shows that a substantial number of preschoolers do not recognize a commercial message on TV as distinctly different from programming. By age 5, most children are capable of making this distinction, although it is typically based on somewhat superficial qualities of the messages such as how long they are. Still, being able to identify and accurately label a commercial does not necessarily mean that a child fully comprehends the nature of advertising, a topic we turn to next.

Comprehension of Advertising

Adult consumers realize that advertisements exist to sell product and services. This realization helps a person to interpret a commercial as a persuasive form of communication. According to D. F. Roberts (1982), an "adult" understanding of advertising entails four ideas: (a) the source has a different perspective (and thus other interests) than that of the receiver, (b) the source intends to persuade, (c) persuasive messages are biased, and (d) biased messages demand different interpretive strategies than do informational messages. Most research dealing with children has focused on the first two ideas, encompassed in studies of how and when young viewers understand the selling intent of ads. Less attention has been given to children's recognition of bias in advertising, relating to the last two ideas. Not reflected in Roberts' list is the notion that other facets of advertising require understanding too, such as disclaimers. This section will consider all three topics: children's comprehension of selling intent, of advertiser bias, and of disclaimers such as "parts sold separately."

Understanding Selling Intent. Recognizing the selling motive that underlies advertising is not a simple task. For one thing, the actual source of a commercial is rarely identified explicitly. A television commercial, for example, might show children playing with a toy or eating a type of cereal and yet the company that manufacturers these products is invisible. It is easy to assume that the "source" of the message is the child, the celebrity, or the animated character who in fact is merely demonstrating a new product that is available.

Research suggests that younger children's views are just this naive. In one early study, Robertson and Rossiter (1974) asked first-, third-, and fifth-grade boys a series of open-ended questions such as, "What is a commercial?" and "What do commercials try to get you to do?" First graders often described commercials as informational messages that "tell you about things." Although older children did this too, they were far more likely to describe advertising as persuasive in nature (i.e., "commercials try to make you buy something"). In fact, the attribution of selling intent increased dramatically with age: Only 53% of the first graders mentioned persuasive intent, whereas 87% of third graders and 99% of fifth graders did so.

A more recent study found a very similar pattern (Wilson & Weiss, 1992). When asked what commercials "want you to do," only 32% of 4- to 6-year-olds mentioned the selling intent of ads. Instead, this youngest age group was far more likely to cite an entertainment (e.g., "they want you to watch them," "make you laugh") or informational ("show you stuff") function for commercials. In contrast, 73% of 7- to 8-year-olds and a full 94% of 9- to 11-year-olds spontaneously mentioned the selling intent of commercials. A host of other studies using similar interviewing techniques support these age trends (Blatt et al., 1972; Ward, Reale, & Levinson, 1972; Ward et al., 1977).

Given variations in development, it is difficult to pinpoint the specific age at which the idea of selling intent is mastered. Nevertheless, most studies suggest that children begin to develop an understanding of the persuasive purpose of advertising around the age of 8 (for reviews, see Kunkel et al., 2004; Smith & Atkin, 2003).

Some scholars have argued that the reliance on verbal measures can mask younger children's true abilities, which may be hampered by language difficulties (Macklin, 1987; Martin, 1997). To test this notion, Donohue, Henke, and Donohue (1980) devised a nonverbal measure to assess 2- to 6-year-olds' understanding of selling intent. After watching a Froot Loops commercial, children were asked to choose which of two pictures—one of a mother and child picking out a box of cereal at a supermarket and the other of a child watching television—illustrated what the commercial wanted them to do. A full 80% of the young children selected the correct picture, well above chance level with two options. However, as seen in Table 2.1, several efforts to replicate this finding with younger children have been unsuccessful (Macklin, 1985, 1987). For example, Macklin (1985) used a set of four pictures, reasoning that the two used by Donohue et al. were too easy (i.e., only one of the pictures featured cereal, which made it obviously more relevant). When four pictures were shown, 80% of 3- to 5-year-olds could *not* select the correct one.

Table 2.1   Comparison of Preschoolers' Correct Responses Across Studies Using Different Nonverbal Measures of Comprehension of Selling Intent (in Percentages)

Nature of Nonverbal Task	Incorrect	Correct
Select from 2 pictures (Donohue, Henke, & Donohue, 1980)	20	80
Select from 4 pictures (Macklin, 1985)	80	20
Select from 10 sketches in a game (Macklin, 1987)	91	9
Enact selling intent in creative play (Macklin, 1987)	87	13

SOURCE: Adapted from Macklin (1985, 1987).

Theoretically, it makes sense that comprehension of selling intent might be difficult for younger children. Certain cognitive skills seem to be required first, such as the ability to recognize the differing perspectives of the seller and receiver. In support of this idea, one study found that the ability to role-take was a strong and significant predictor of elementary schoolers' understanding of the purpose of advertising (Faber, Perloff, & Hawkins, 1982). Interestingly, exposure to television did not correlate with comprehension of selling intent, suggesting that viewing numerous television ads is not enough to help a child recognize the purpose of commercials.

In addition to role taking, comprehension of selling intent also seems to depend on the ability to think abstractly about what persuasion is and who the true source of the message is. Consistent with this idea, one study found that the ability to identify the source of advertising and the awareness of the symbolic nature of commercials were two skills that helped differentiate children who understood the purpose of ads from those who did not (Robertson & Rossiter, 1974).

To summarize, a large body of research suggests that very young children do not comprehend the purpose of advertising and often view it as informational in nature. The ability to role-take and the ability to think conceptually have been identified as important precursors to being able to appreciate advertising as a form of persuasion. Given that such skills do not emerge until the later elementary school years (see Chapter 1), it stands to reason that understanding the selling intent of commercials does not occur much before the age of 8.

As a final issue, we might ask why comprehending the purpose of advertising is so important. Perhaps the naive view of a young child is just that—a naive view, with little or no consequence. Several studies suggest otherwise. Comprehension of selling intent seems to alter a child's reactions to advertising (Robertson & Rossiter, 1974; Ward & Wackman, 1973). For example, Robertson and Rossiter (1974) found that elementary schoolers who understood the persuasive intent of commercials were less likely to trust ads, more likely to dislike them, and less likely to want advertised products. In other words, recognizing the motives behind commercials may help trigger a cognitive defense or shield against such messages. Interestingly, the opposite pattern was found among children who viewed ads as informational—they expressed higher trust and more liking of such messages. The next section will explore skepticism toward advertising more fully.

Recognition of Bias. Appreciating that advertising is inherently one-sided and therefore biased is another facet of sophisticated consumerism (Roberts, 1982). This realization also is age related in its development. In interview situations, younger children are more likely to report that they believe what commercials say than older children are (Bever, Smith, Bengen, & Johnson, 1975; Robertson & Rossiter, 1974). For instance, Ward and his colleagues (1977) found that 50% of kindergartners said yes when asked, "Do commercials always tell the truth?" Only 12% of third graders and 3% of sixth graders responded affirmatively to this question.

Similarly, Wilson and Weiss (1995) asked 4- to 11-year-olds a series of questions about advertising, including how much commercials tell you about a toy and how often commercials tell the truth. As seen in Figure 2.7, strong age trends were found on three different measures, all indicating growing skepticism of advertising across

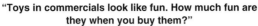

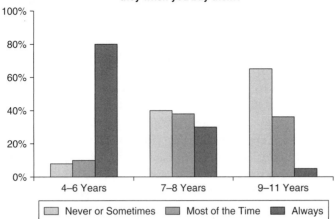

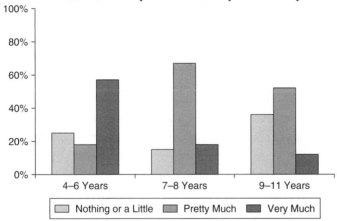

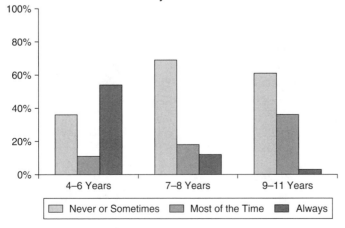

Figure 2.7   Age Differences in Children's Trust in Advertising

SOURCE: Adapted from Wilson and Weiss (1995).

the childhood years. Even while watching television, older children spontaneously express more negative comments and criticisms of ads than do younger children (Ward, Levinson, & Wackman, 1972).

Several factors contribute to younger children's trust in advertising. First, younger children have more difficulty differentiating appearance from reality, as discussed in Chapter 1 (see Figure 2.8). They rely heavily on perceptual cues in judging an ad (Ward & Wackman, 1973) and thus are likely to believe that products look and perform the way they are depicted in commercials. Second, younger children have less experience as consumers. One way to learn expeditiously that ads can be deceptive is to experience disappointment over a purchase. By sixth grade, the vast majority of children can describe a product they bought that turned out to be worse than what was depicted in an ad (Ward et al., 1977). As children grow older, they are more likely to cite their own consumer experiences as reasons for not trusting ads (Ward & Wackman, 1973). Third, the failure to understand selling intent makes a young child more trusting. In one study, a full 100% of older, cognitively mature children referred to advertisers' motives when asked to explain why commercials do not always tell the truth (Ward & Wackman, 1973). For example, older children based their assessments of bias on the fact that advertisers "want you to buy their product," and "they want you to think their product is good."

It makes sense that skepticism would help children to be less gullible when they confront commercial messages. One study found that 8- to 12-year-olds who felt distrustful and negative toward advertising evaluated particular commercials less favorably than did those who were more trusting of advertising (Derbaix & Pecheux, 2003). Unfortunately, the study did not measure how much children wanted to buy the products in the commercials. Some scholars have speculated, though, that even the most savvy child consumer can be temporarily misled by powerful or seductive persuasive tactics (Derbaix & Pecheux, 2003).

Skepticism toward advertising continues to develop into early adolescence. One longitudinal study found relatively high levels of mistrust in commercial claims as well as advertiser motives in a large sample of middle schoolers (Boush, Friestad, &

CALVIN AND HOBBES By Bill Watterson

Figure 2.8

SOURCE: ©1995 Universal Press Syndicate.

Rose, 1994). On a 5-point scale, the students' average ratings were all around 4. 0, indicating strong agreement with statements such as "Advertisers care more about getting you to buy things than what is good for you," and "TV commercials tell only the good things about a product; they don't tell you the bad things." Yet skepticism did not increase much within a single school year, nor were there any significant differences between 6th and 8th graders in these beliefs.

As a child reaches the teen years, then, factors other than cognitive development may be important in predicting who is most critical of advertising. One study found that skepticism toward advertising is higher among teens who watch more television, who come from families that stress independent thinking, and who rely on peers for information about products (Mangleburg & Bristol, 1999). In contrast, skepticism is lower among teens who report trying to impress peers with product purchases. This research suggests that once a young person is cognitively capable of recognizing the motives and tactics of advertisers, socializing forces such as parents and peers may be needed to make such information salient on a regular basis.

Comprehension of Disclaimers. Disclaimers are warnings or disclosures about a product, intended to prevent possible deception caused by an ad. "Batteries not included," "parts sold separately," and "part of a balanced breakfast" are examples of disclaimers that are quite common in advertising to children. Kunkel and Gantz (1992) found that more than half of the commercials targeted to children contained at least one disclaimer, and 9% featured two or more.

Disclaimers are very common in commercials for cereal. Nearly three fourths of all cereal ads feature such a message (Gantz et al., 2007)—typically, indicating that the advertised product is only "part of a nutritious/balanced breakfast." Disclaimers are also frequently included in ads for pastries and bread (Gantz et al., 2007). Interestingly, food ads targeted to children and teens are more likely to contain disclaimers than are food ads targeted to adults (Gantz et al., 2007).

Typically, disclaimers are conveyed by an adult voiceover or by inserting the words in small print at the bottom of the screen (Muehling & Kolbe, 1999). It is rare for a disclaimer to be presented both auditorily and visually (Kunkel & Gantz, 1992).

Disclosures exist because of consumer pressure to ensure that advertisements give accurate information about products (Barcus, 1980). Yet disclaimers have been criticized as "jargon" because the wording is often fairly obscure (Atkin, 1980). In fact, research indicates that young children do not comprehend disclaimers very well. One study found that preschoolers exposed to a disclaimer in a toy ad were no better able to understand the workings of the toy than were those who saw the same ad with no disclaimer (Stern & Resnik, 1978). Another study revealed that kindergarten and first-grade children had little understanding of what a "balanced breakfast" means and were far more likely to remember the Rice Krispies cereal in an ad than the milk, orange juice, or strawberries that accompanied it on the table (Palmer & McDowell, 1981). Cognitive as well as language development should help to make these disclaimers more accessible with age. One study found that 85% of 10-year-olds understood "partial assembly required" in a toy ad, whereas only 40% of 5-year-olds did (Liebert, Sprafkin, Liebert, & Rubinstein, 1977).

Yet disclaimers could be designed in a more straightforward way even for younger children. In an innovative experiment, Liebert and colleagues (1977) exposed kindergartners and second graders to a toy commercial under one of three conditions: no disclaimer at all, a standard disclaimer ("partial assembly required"), or a modified disclaimer that contained simpler wording ("you have to put it together"). Regardless of age, children who heard the simplified disclaimer were significantly more likely to understand that the toy required assembly than were those who heard the standard disclaimer (see Figure 2.9). Interestingly, the standard wording was no more effective in helping children understand that the toy needed assembly than was having no disclaimer at all; less than 25% of children in either condition understood this idea.

To recap how children process advertising, most preschoolers have difficulty differentiating a television commercial from programming, and they do not comprehend the standard wording used in disclaimers in advertising. Thus, for this age group in particular, advertising may be unfair given the legal principle that the audience must be capable of recognizing such content. By age 5 or 6, most children have mastered the distinction between a TV ad and a program, although it is based primarily on perceptual cues such as the length of the messages. As commercials get shorter and as they increasingly resemble adjacent programming, a kindergartner or first grader may have more difficulty making this distinction. Further complicating matters for younger children is the nature of advertising in newer media. Web sites flash ads and banners, for example, that are mixed in seamlessly with content. In fact, some Web sites are entirely commercial in nature, as we will discuss below, although

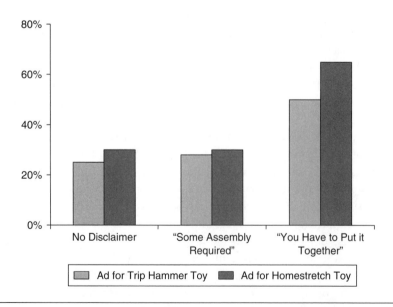

Figure 2.9   Percentage of Children Who Understood That Toy Required Assembly as a Function of Type of Disclaimer in Ad

SOURCE: Adapted from Liebert et al. (1977).

they may appear to be informational in nature. The Internet requires even higher levels of cognitive sophistication to disentangle what is commercial from what is not.

Nevertheless, being able to identify an ad still does not mean that a young child comprehends its purpose. Initially, ads are viewed as informational or entertaining in nature, and young children express a high degree of trust in such messages. It is not until roughly 8 years of age that a child begins to understand the selling intent of such messages. This transition is facilitated by the development of role-taking skills and conceptual thinking. By age 12 or so, most children are able to recognize the source of the message, the advertisers' motives, and typical strategies that are used to persuade. This level of awareness, coupled with a rich base of consumer experience, means that by the teenage years, most youth are fairly critical and skeptical of advertising. The only caveat here is that all of this research has been done with television and not with newer media. Even so, children of all ages, like many adults, can still be persuaded by commercials, as we will discover next.

Persuasive Impact of Advertising

The most direct effect of an advertisement is to convince a consumer to purchase a new product. Advertisers and companies alike believe in the power of advertising to do just that. There is no other way to explain the fact that companies paid $2.7 million for a 30-second commercial during the 2008 Super Bowl. But there are more subtle consequences of advertising too. For example, commercials can influence family interactions. Whenever a child tries to get a parent to buy something or a parent tries to resist that effort, conflict can occur. Researchers have looked at how often this occurs and with what consequence. In addition, extensive exposure to advertising may affect more general attitudes or values that youth hold regarding consumption, money, and even physical appearance. We discuss each of these potential influences in this section.

Brand Loyalty

One of the goals of advertising is to create brand loyalty. Creating branded characters that appeal to children is a crucial component of successful marketing (Institute of Medicine, 2006). Tony the Tiger was created in 1951 to promote Kellogg's Frosted Flakes, and although he has become slimmer and more muscular, he is still used in advertising today. Ronald McDonald is recognized by nearly 96% of American children and is used to sell fast food internationally in more than 25 languages (Enrico, 1999). Through licensing agreements, popular television characters such as SpongeBob SquarePants are used to sell products as well.

It is not surprising that children are highly aware of brand names, jingles, and slogans associated with specific commercials and of the celebrities who endorse certain products (Burr & Burr, 1977; Fox, 1996). One study revealed that children between the ages of 8 and 12 could name five brands of beer but only four

American presidents (Center for Science in the Public Interest, 1988). Another study found that teens remember brand names and recognize ad content better than adults do (Dubow, 1995).

Even preschoolers show awareness of brands and brand loyalty. One study asked 3- to 6-year-olds to match 22 brand logos to 12 different products pictured on a game board (Fischer, Schwartz, Richards, Goldstein, & Rojas, 1991). The children showed high rates of logo recognition (see Figure 2.10). More than 90% recognized the logo for the Disney Channel, but children even recognized logos for many adult products. More than 90% of the 6-year-olds in particular were able to match Old Joe (the cartoon character promoting Camel cigarettes) to a picture of a cigarette. Another study found that children as young as 2 years of age can recognize many brand logos for products (Valkenburg & Buijzen, 2005). In this same study, preschoolers who watched a great deal of television were more familiar with brand names than were preschoolers who watched little television.

Brand recognition seems to breed brand preference. One study had preschool children select which product they preferred from a series of eight choices

Figure 2.10   Popular Brand Logos

involving a branded option and a carefully chosen nonbranded one (Pine & Nash, 2003). The nonbranded options were pretested to ensure that they matched the branded ones in size, color, and other perceptual qualities. Children chose the branded products 68% of the time. Preschool girls showed stronger brand loyalty than preschool boys did. Among the eight types of products presented (e.g., a toy, cereal, chocolate bar, a T-shirt), the only product that did not generate brand loyalty was training/running shoes. More recently, Robinson, Borzekowski, Matheson, and Kramer (2007) presented preschoolers with two samples each of five different fast-food items (e.g., hamburger, French fries, milk). For each pair of items, one was packaged in McDonald's wrapping, and the other was packaged in plain paper. The foods or drinks inside the wrappings were identical, however. Children were asked to taste each sample and decide if the two were the same or if one tasted better. The preschoolers showed a strong preference for the foods and drinks that they thought were from McDonald's. In other words, the simple branding of the food items significantly influenced children's taste perceptions.

Desire for Products

Asking whether advertising creates a desire for products may seem like a ridiculous question to some. American children wear T-shirts emblazoned with Pokémon characters, carry lunch boxes decorated with Disney images, wear designer jeans and Nike athletic shoes, and love anything with the word *Abercrombie* on it (see Figure 2.11). Adolescents seem even more conscious of brand names as well as the

Figure 2.11

SOURCE: Reprinted with permission of Copley News Service.

latest fads in clothing and technology. Where does all this consumer desire come from? When asked, most children report that they bought something because "you see it a lot" or "everybody has one" (Fox, 1996). As noted above, advertising often conveys the idea that a product will bring fun and happiness to a youngster's life. Images of other children playing with a toy or eating at a fast-food restaurant reinforce the notion that everyone else is doing it too.

But does exposure to advertising create desires? A number of surveys show that children who watch a lot of television want more advertised toys and actually consume more advertised foods than do children with lighter TV habits (Atkin, 1976, 1982; Goldberg, 1990; Goldberg, Gorn, & Gibson, 1978; Robertson & Rossiter, 1977; Robertson, Ward, Gatignon, & Klees, 1989). As an example, one recent study asked 250 children in the Netherlands to list their Christmas wishes and then compared them with the commercials that were aired on TV at the time (Buijzen & Valkenburg, 2000). More than half the children requested at least one advertised product. Moreover, heavy exposure to television significantly predicted requests for more advertised products, even after controlling for age and gender of the child (see Figure 2.12). Another recent study of more than 900 fifth and sixth graders found that those who watched a great deal of television had more positive attitudes toward junk food, such a sugared cereals and fast-food items, than did light viewers (Dixon, Scully, Wakefield, White, & Crawford, 2007). Heavy TV viewers also perceived that other children ate junk food more often, and they perceived junk food to be healthier and reportedly ate more junk food themselves. These patterns held up even after controlling for gender, grade level, and socioeconomic status of the family.

Among adolescents too, exposure to television has been linked to increased desire for products and brand names (Moschis, 1978; Moschis & Moore, 1979). However, evidence suggests that the strength of this relationship may decrease somewhat with age (Buijzen & Valkenburg, 2000; Robertson & Rossiter, 1977), consistent with children's growing awareness of the purpose of advertising as well as increased skepticism about such messages.

BABY BLUES By Rick Kirkman and Jerry Scott

Figure 2.12

SOURCE: Baby Blues by Rick Kirkman and Jerry Scott. Reprinted with permission of King Features Syndicate.

Clearly, correlational evidence reveals that there is a relationship between TV advertising and product desires, but it is difficult to establish causality in such studies. It is possible that youth who are eager to buy toys, games, clothes, and snacks actually seek out television more often to find out about new products, a reverse direction in this relationship. Thus, researchers have turned to experiments to more firmly establish the impact of advertising.

In the typical experiment, children are randomly assigned to either view or not view an advertisement for a particular product. Afterward, children are allowed to select the advertised product from a range of other choices, or they are asked a series of questions about how much they like or want that product compared to others. Experiments generally show that commercials are indeed effective. In one study, preschoolers exposed to a single ad for a toy were more likely than those not exposed to (a) choose the toy over the favorite activity at the school, (b) select the toy even if it meant playing with a "not so nice boy," and (c) choose the toy despite their mother's preference for a different toy (Goldberg & Gorn, 1978). In a study of older children, exposure to a single ad for acne cream caused fourth and fifth graders to worry more about skin blemishes and to want to buy the cream (Atkin, 1976).

Although one ad can increase desire for a product, multiple exposures may be even more influential. Gorn and Goldberg (1977) found that viewing one versus three commercials was equally effective in increasing positive attitudes toward a new toy compared to a no-exposure control group, but only the three-exposure condition made children try harder to win the toy. Other research supports the idea that a single ad can increase awareness and liking of a product, but multiple exposures to varied commercials are most effective in changing consumer behavior (Gorn & Goldberg, 1980; Resnik & Stern, 1977).

Beyond repetition, there are other ways to enhance the impact of an advertisement. One tactic is to include a premium or prize with the product, as is done in boxes of cereal. In 1975, premiums were offered in nearly 50% of cereal ads targeted to children (Barcus, 1980). This practice is less common today in cereal ads, but fast-food commercials routinely entice children with small toys that come with kids' meals (Kunkel & Gantz, 1992). In 1997, McDonald's had difficulty keeping Teenie Beanie Babies in stock once it began offering them as premiums in kids' Happy Meals. Research suggests that premiums in commercials can significantly increase children's desire for a product (Miller & Busch, 1979) and actually can affect children's requests for cereals in a supermarket (Atkin, 1978).

Another strategy involves the use of a celebrity or a popular character to endorse a product in an ad. Professional athlete Michael Jordan has long been associated with Nike and even has a pair of athletic shoes (Air Jordans) named after him. There are countless other examples. Teen pop star Hilary Duff has her own Barbie doll and used to endorse Candie's fashions through Kohl's department stores (see Figure 2.13). Golf star Tiger Woods is a spokesperson for American Express and pitches Macintosh computers, among other products. And Bart Simpson claims to love Butterfinger candy bars.

Research supports the idea that popular figures can be effective sources of persuasion. One study found that teens perceived celebrities as more trustworthy,

Figure 2.13   Sample Celebrity Ads

SOURCE: ©2007–2008 Kohl's Illinois, Inc. and ©2006 Iconix Brand Group, Inc.; ©Sony Computer Entertainment, Inc.

competent, and attractive than noncelebrity endorsers featured in nearly identical ads (Atkin & Block, 1983). Furthermore, the celebrities resulted in more favorable evaluations of a product. In a controlled experiment, Ross and her colleagues (1984) exposed 8- to 14-year-old boys to a commercial for a racecar set but systematically varied whether a celebrity endorser was included in the ad. The researchers found that exposure to the celebrity significantly enhanced boys' liking of the racing set and increased their belief that the celebrity was an expert about the toy.

Taken as a whole, the research demonstrates that commercials can have quite powerful effects on children's desires. Even a single ad can change the way a child perceives a toy or a game. Ads also can persuade young viewers to eat foods that are not very nutritional (see Chapter 9) and to try certain drugs such as tobacco (see Chapter 7). As it turns out, even a bland ad can make a product appealing (Resnik & Stern, 1977), but incorporating tactics such as premiums and celebrity endorsers can make a pitch even more effective. Next we will consider effects of advertising that are more indirect and not necessarily intentional on the part of advertisers: increased family conflict and changes in youth values.

Parent-Child Conflict

Most advertising agency executives believe that TV commercials do not contribute to family conflict (Culley, Lazer, & Atkin, 1976). Yet research suggests otherwise (see Figure 2.14). One study presented stories to elementary schoolers about a child who sees a TV commercial for an attractive product (Sheikh & Moleski, 1977). When asked if the child in the story would ask a parent to buy the product, nearly 60% of the children responded affirmatively. When asked what would happen if the parent said no, 33% of the children said the child in the story would feel sad, 23% said the child would be angry or hostile, and 16% said the child would persist in requesting the product. Only 23% indicated the child would be accepting of the decision.

According to mothers, children's efforts to influence purchasing occur most often for food items, especially cereals, snacks, and candy (Ward & Wackman, 1972). Coincidentally, those same products are among the most heavily advertised to children. Requesting a parent to purchase something does seem to decrease with age (Ward & Wackman, 1972), in part because as children get older, they have more of their own money to make independent decisions. Yet for expensive items, even adolescents can pester parents. One national survey found that 40% of 12- to 17-year-olds had asked for an advertised product they thought their parents would disapprove of, and most of these young people said they were persistent (New American Dream, 2002). In fact, the teens estimated that they had to ask an average of nine times before their parents gave in and made the purchase.

Several studies actually have observed parents and children as they shop together in an effort to assess conflict more directly. In an early study, Galst and White (1976) observed 41 preschoolers with their mothers in a grocery store. The researchers documented an average of 15 purchase influence attempts (PIAs) by the

Figure 2.14

SOURCE: Tribune Media Services, *Boston Globe,* Dan Wasserman, 2000.

child in a typical shopping trip, or one every 2 minutes! Most of the PIAs were for cereals and candy, and 45% of them were successful. In other words, the mother acquiesced to nearly half of the children's requests. In another observational study, Atkin (1978) found that open conflict occurred 65% of the time that a parent denied a child's request for a cereal in a supermarket.

One experiment creatively linked PIAs directly to advertising. Stoneman and Brody (1981) randomly assigned preschoolers to view a cartoon that contained six food commercials or no commercials at all. Immediately afterward, mothers were told to take their preschoolers to a nearby grocery store to buy a typical week's worth of groceries, purportedly as part of another study. Posing as clerks in the store, research assistants surreptitiously coded the interactions that occurred. Children who had been exposed to the food commercials engaged in significantly more purchase influence attempts than did children in the control group. Children exposed to the commercials also made more requests for those foods that were featured in the ads. In addition, the mothers' behavior was influenced by the commercials. Mothers of children who had seen the ads engaged in significantly more control strategies during the shopping trip, such as putting the item back on the shelf and telling the child no.

In sum, advertising can produce pressure on parents to buy products, which in turn can cause family conflict when such requests are denied. Younger children who confront parental resistance are likely to whine, become angry, and even cry (Williams & Burns, 2000). Older children, in contrast, tend to use more sophisticated persuasion tactics, such as negotiation and white lies. There is some evidence of gender differences in this nag factor (Buijzen & Valkenburg, 2003a). Boys are more forceful and demanding in their requests than girls are, and boys also tend to be less compliant. Finally, research suggests that parent-child discord is not just an American phenomenon. One cross-cultural study found that heavy television viewing among children is linked to higher parent-child conflict about purchases in Japan and Great Britain as well as in the United States (Robertson et al., 1989).

Materialism and Value Orientations

Critics worry that in addition to creating demand for certain products, advertising may contribute more generally to materialistic attitudes in our youth. Materialism refers to the idea that money and possessions are important and that certain qualities such as beauty and success can be obtained from having material property (see Figure 2.15). Fox (1996) claims that "when kids are saturated in advertising, their appetites for products are stimulated. At the same time, kids desire the values that have been associated with those products—intangible values that, like sex appeal, are impossible to buy" (p. 20). The popular Bratz dolls, for example, are marketed to tween girls as a "lifestyle brand" that revolves around makeup, sexualized clothing, and communal shopping and congregating at the mall (McAllister, 2007). In support of this idea of materialism or hyperconsumption, one national poll found that 53% of teens said that buying certain products makes them feel better about themselves (New American Dream, 2002). Other critics argue that advertising should not be singled out for attack and that youthful consumerism is part of children's participation in a larger culture that has become rooted in commodities (Seiter, 1993).

Calvin and Hobbes

Figure 2.15

SOURCE: Reprinted with permission from Universal Press Syndicate.

Disentangling advertising from all the other forces that might foster materialism is difficult, especially because nearly all children are exposed to a world filled with toy stores, fast-food restaurants, movies, peer groups, and even schools, all of which promote consumer goods. Several correlational studies have looked to see if there is a relationship between media habits and materialism in youth. To measure materialism, students are typically asked to agree or disagree with statements such as "It is really true that money can buy happiness," and "My dream in life is to be able to own expensive things." One large survey of more than 800 adolescents found that heavy exposure to television was positively correlated with buying products for social acceptance, even after controlling for age, sex, socioeconomic status, and amount of family communication about consumption (Churchill & Moschis, 1979). In this same study, teens who reported watching a lot of TV also were more likely to associate possessions and money with happiness. Another survey found a similar pattern for tweens (Buijzen & Valkenburg, 2003b). That is, 8- to 12-year-olds who frequently watched television commercials were more materialistic than were their peers who seldom watched commercials. This was true regardless of the child's age, gender, or socioeconomic status.

These patterns are certainly suggestive, but they do not permit firm causal conclusions. Materialistic youth could seek out advertising, advertising might cause materialism, or both. Clearly, longitudinal research is needed to ascertain whether heavy exposure to advertising during early childhood leads to more materialistic attitudes over time. One such study exists in the published literature. Moschis and Moore (1982) surveyed 6th through 12th graders twice, across 14 months, about their exposure to television commercials and their materialistic attitudes. At Time 1, there was a significant association between exposure to ads and materialism, as has been found in other studies. Looking over time, exposure to advertising at Time 1 also predicted higher scores on materialism 14 months later at Time 2, but *only* among those youth who were initially low in materialism. In other words, television seemed to have its greatest impact on those who were not already highly materialistic. More longitudinal research of this sort is needed, particularly with younger children whose values are still developing. Obviously, studies need to control for other relevant socialization factors, such as the parents' own values regarding material goods.

Another concern is whether advertising contributes to a preoccupation with physical appearance, especially among female adolescents. Teen magazines, in particular, are rife with ads featuring thin, attractive models (see Figure 2.16). Studies have found that female adolescents and college students do compare their physical attractiveness to models featured in advertising (Martin & Kennedy, 1993; Richins, 1991). Moreover, looking at ads of highly attractive models can temporarily affect self-esteem and even body image (Stice & Shaw, 1994), especially among girls who are encouraged to evaluate themselves (Martin & Gentry, 1997). In one experiment, adolescent girls who were exposed to a heavy dose of commercials emphasizing physical appearance were more likely to believe that being beautiful is an important characteristic and is necessary to attract men than were those in a control group exposed to other types of ads (Tan, 1979).

Longitudinal evidence is also beginning to emerge, suggesting that early television and magazine exposure increases young girls' desire to have a thin body (Harrison & Hefner, 2006) and young boys' desire to have a muscular body (Harrison & Bond, 2007) when they grow up.

Figure 2.16   Ads Taken From *CosmoGIRL!* (May 2007) and *Teen* (Spring 2007)

Phases of Consumer Behavior During Childhood

Valkenburg and Cantor (2001) outlined four phases of consumer development in childhood, which provide a nice overview of much of the material covered in this chapter so far. The first phase, which they call "Feeling Wants and Preferences," characterizes infants and toddlers. During this phase, young children show distinct preferences for smells, colors, sounds, and objects, an important component of consumer behavior. Still, at this young age, children are primarily reactive rather than goal directed, so they are not capable of acting like true consumers.

The second phase, "Nagging and Negotiating," captures the preschool years. As we have noted above, preschoolers have difficulty distinguishing ads from programs and do not fully comprehend the intent of commercials. Consequently, Valkenburg and Cantor (2001) argue that marketing efforts have a strong impact on this age group. Because of the idea of centration (see Chapter 1), preschoolers are likely to gravitate toward products that are visually striking. They also want what they see immediately, so this age group is most likely to pester parents and to exhibit noncompliant and emotional behavior when they are denied something.

Phase 3, "Adventure and the First Purchase," characterizes the early elementary school years, between the ages of 5 and 8. Cognitive abilities are in transition here as children gradually consider more conceptual information, become more responsive to verbally presented information, and increase their attention span. But this age group can still be confused about the purpose of ads and can still respond strongly to perceptual cues. Children typically make their first solo purchase during this phase, becoming a bona fide consumer independent of a parent.

Phase 4, "Conformity and Fastidiousness," marks the tween years, from 8 to 12. The ability to critically evaluate information, compare products, and appreciate the selling intent of ads develops during this time. Because of their attention to detail and quality, many children become serious collectors of objects during this period. Tweens show a strong sensitivity to the norms and values of their peers, as well as to what older adolescents are buying and doing. Most tweens regularly visit different types of stores, making independent purchases and influencing household buying practices. Valkenburg and Cantor (2001) argue that consumer skills continue to develop during adolescence, but by late elementary school, all the fundamentals of consumer behavior are in place (i.e., child shows preferences, can evaluate options, and can choose and purchase a product).

Marketing Strategies in the 21st Century

As children's and teens' spending power continues to increase, marketers are continuously experimenting with new ways to reach young consumers. In this section, we will examine five techniques that are burgeoning as we enter the 21st century: character merchandising, product placement, viral marketing, online marketing, and marketing in schools.

Character Merchandising

Character merchandising refers to the licensing of popular characters to promote many types of products (Institute of Medicine, 2006). Using characters to build brand loyalty is not a new phenomenon. Mickey Mouse was created in 1928 by Walt Disney, and today the anthropomorphized creature is an international icon. Similarly, the promotion of toys that are based on popular programs is a marketing strategy that has been around for a while, as discussed earlier in this chapter. As early as 1969, the cartoon *Hot Wheels* was criticized as nothing more than a 30-minute commercial for Hot Wheels toys (Colby, 1993). Roughly 20 years later, the *Teenage Mutant Ninja Turtles* cartoon helped to sell more than $500 million worth of toy merchandise in 1990 alone (Rosenberg, 1992).

Nowadays, however, characters are being used in a more integrated fashion across media platforms. Consider the Pokémon craze. The cute pocket-sized monsters originated in 1996 in Japan as characters in a Nintendo video game. In 1998, U.S. marketers simultaneously launched a TV cartoon series, trading cards, a video game, and toy merchandise. Later came party products, a Warner Brothers motion picture, a CD, children's apparel sold at J. C. Penney, kids' meal premiums at Burger King, and even Pokémon tournament leagues that met weekly at Toys 'R' Us to play the video game (Annicelli, 1999; Brass, 1999; Jones, 2000). The Pokémon franchise explicitly reinforces the idea that the best way to become cool is to collect as many monsters as possible. Apparently, children are convinced. Since its 1996 launch, the franchise has generated $26 billion in retail sales, more than 155 million Pokémon video games have sold worldwide, and 14 billion trading cards have been sold (Graft, 2007). And there is no end in sight to the pocket monsters' popularity. In 2007, 107 new characters were unveiled as Nintendo released its newest handheld games, "Pokémon Diamond" and "Pokémon Pearl," plus a new movie, *Pokémon Ranger and the Temple of the Sea*, on DVD.

Such tactics do seem to blur the differences between advertising and entertainment content. Toy-based cartoons, for example, have been criticized as "animated sales catalogs masquerading as entertainment" (Waters & Uehling, 1985, p. 85). One of the challenges for young viewers is that toy-based cartoons feature the same popular characters, slogans, and sound effects that are employed in related commercials for the toys. Several studies reveal that the combination of a cartoon and related advertising can be very confusing for young children (Hoy, Young, & Mowen, 1986; Kunkel, 1988). For example, Wilson and Weiss (1992) found that 4- to 6-year-olds were less able to recognize an ad for a Beetlejuice toy or comprehend its selling intent when it was shown with a *Beetlejuice* cartoon than with an unrelated *Popeye* cartoon. Moreover, the confusion occurred regardless of whether the related *Beetlejuice* cartoon was immediately adjacent to the ad or separated from it by 5 minutes of filler material. This finding is consistent with younger children's perceptual dependence, as discussed in Chapter 1.

Interestingly, the evidence is mixed on whether airing ads together with related programming is a good marketing strategy. Some studies have found that this technique enhances children's desire for a product (Kunkel, 1988; Miller & Busch, 1979), whereas others have not (Hoy et al., 1986; Wilson & Weiss, 1992). Success presumably depends in part on the nature of the product as well as the popularity of the related character.

Thus, as commercials increasingly resemble TV programs and popular characters appear in movies, on cereal boxes, as toys, on Web sites, in CDs, and in video games, the young child is likely to become even more confused about what advertising actually is. On occasion, even sophisticated consumers may feel bewildered or perhaps overwhelmed by these multimedia character merchandising endeavors.

Product Placement

Product placement is a promotional tactic used by marketers whereby a commercial product is placed in a visible setting outside a typical marketing context. The most common product placement occurs in movies, where a corporation will typically pay to have its product used by the characters. Candy sales shot up by 66%, for example, when Spielberg's movie character E. T. was shown eating Hershey's Reese's Pieces (Mazur, 1996). Product placement on television has become popular in recent years too, especially because consumers are using newer digital recording technologies such as TiVo to skip over commercials. Reality TV shows in particular have become known for their use of brand-name products in helping people to redesign their homes, their gardens, and even their love lives. For example, the Coca-Cola Company paid $10 million in 2002 to have coke served to the judges on *American Idol* (Howard, 2002).

Unlike reality shows, children's programs have avoided product placement so far, presumably because of the separation principle. This principle, established by the Federal Communications Commission (FCC) in 1974, mandates that there must be a clear distinction between program and advertising content during shows targeted to children (see discussion below on regulation).

The idea behind product placement is to have a product fit seamlessly into the context of a story or program. This subtle technique is an effort to build brand loyalty without calling attention to the persuasive intent of the strategy. Some have referred to these types of tactics as "stealth marketing" because the consumer is unaware that it is an attempt to influence purchasing behaviors (Institute of Medicine, 2006).

Product placement also occurs when Web sites have sponsors that place their logos on the page. The Nickelodeon Web site (Nick.com), for example, has links on its homepage to Holiday Inn family suites and to Nick Mobile, a site where children can purchase special ring sounds and wallpapers for their cell phones. The links are marked as "ads" but in a very small font size.

Advertisers also have developed "advergames," which are online video games with a subtle or overt commercial message. For example, Candystand.com, a Web site hosted by various candy companies, features dozens of games, including one called Gummi Grab involving Gummi Bears and another called Match Maker involving Life Savers. While playing these games, the user is exposed to multiple images of such candy, purportedly helping to build brand loyalty. One recent study of 77 food-related Web sites targeted to children found a total of 546 different games containing food brands on these sites (E. S. Moore, 2006).

Like character merchandising, product placement blurs the traditional distinction between commercial content and entertainment content. As we have discussed above, these covert strategies are likely to make it even more challenging for young children who already struggle to identify and comprehend advertising. Because such tactics are subtle, they may go unnoticed even by older children and teens who could ordinarily muster their cognitive defenses in the face of overt commercial persuasion.

Viral Marketing

Viral marketing is another form of "under-the-radar" or stealth marketing (Institute of Medicine, 2006). This term refers to the "buzz" or "word of mouth" about a product that occurs when people talk about it. Marketers use various techniques to stimulate buzz about a product, from paying trendsetters to use a product and talk about it to creating a blog (i.e., a user-generated Web site where entries are made in journal style and posted in reverse chronological order) to encourage online chat about a product (Calvert, 2008). For example, music industry marketers have used this approach by sending attractive young consumers into music stores to talk about a new CD to each other, knowing that unsuspecting customers will overhear such conservation (Kaikati & Kaikati, 2004).

Stimulating buzz is not an accident—such campaigns are meticulously engineered and the results are carefully measured (Khermouch & Green, 2001). In fact, Webbed Marketing, an agency specializing in viral marketing, recently announced the release of the Webbed-O-Meter ("Viral Marketing Agency," 2007). The tool is designed to measure the amount of buzz surrounding any Web site, which consists of all the online references made to that site by Internet consumers, bloggers, analysts, reviewers, and reporters.

Viral marketing is thought to be particularly effective with young, trend-conscious consumers who want to be first among their peers to have new products and fashion (Khermouch & Green, 2001). Finding the right individuals, then, to stimulate the buzz is part of the challenge. Companies often recruit popular teens, called "connectors," through the Internet, either through their own Web sites or by monitoring online chat rooms related to teen culture (Dunnewind, 2004). This type of viral marketing is frequently one component of an integrated media marketing campaign. But many believe it will only become more common as marketers struggle to reach consumers in a media landscape composed of hundreds of television channels that increasingly segment audiences into smaller groups. In addition, marketers recognize that young people use the Internet a great deal, are often cynical about 30-second TV ads, and are greatly influenced by peers.

Yet viral marketing is also controversial. Critics charge that it is an insidious form of commercialism because marketers are working at the grassroots level, manipulating people's social relationships with these relatively inexpensive ploys (Khermouch & Green, 2001; Minow, 2004). There is also concern that these techniques may come under regulatory scrutiny because consumers can be misled about the commercial relationship that often exists between the connectors and the corporations sponsoring their activities (Creamer, 2005). According to the basic principle of advertising, people should know they are being solicited for commercial purposes.

Online Marketing to Youth

Millions of American children and teens go online each week, and there are countless Web sites to attract them (see Chapter 11). In fact, several lists exist to help parents and children identify Web sites designed just for young people. Berit's Best Sites for Children names 1,000 sites for kids, and among them are ones for favorite TV television shows, movies, and magazines.

As anyone who goes online knows, the Internet is filled with advertising. In fact, Internet ad spending worldwide was projected at $31 billion in 2007 (Aun, 2007). Online advertising still has a ways to go to catch up with other media—it is estimated that $168 billion was spent globally on television advertising in 2007 (Aun, 2007). Nevertheless, ad spending on the Internet is expected to surpass that spent on radio by 2008 (Aun, 2007).

Many online commercial messages are targeted directly to children. Banners lure children to commercial Web sites to advertise and sell products. And some Web sites for children blend commercialism with content in ways that make them indistinguishable (Center for Media Education, 1996). Many branded products targeted to youth have Web sites that are created to supplement traditional forms of advertising. These "branded environments" are relatively cheap to maintain and typically feature a range of activities such as games, polls, quizzes, and guestbooks. All of these activities are designed to entice children and teens, but they also provide marketers with data on youth consumers. For example, the Crayola Web site offers the child user a variety of games to play, crafts to make, e-cards to send, and an option to join the Crayola Community by registering. Of course, the site also sells Crayola products.

Several Web sites entice children to enter virtual worlds that involve products. The Webkinz World Web site is a recent example of this craze (www.webkinz.com). One journalist likened it to "Beanie Beanies in cyberspace" (Hawn, 2007). The company sells Webkinz plush animals for $10 to $12 apiece. Each animal comes with a "secret code" that allows the child to enter the Webkinz Web site where the animal comes to life and can be named and adopted (see Figure 2.17). The child can also play games to earn "KinzCash," which can be used to buy the animal food, clothes, and furniture. Retailers have had difficulty keeping the toys in stock—the company has sold more than 2 million pets since 2005, and more than 1 million users have registered online (Hawn, 2007).

Unlike other media, the Internet also allows marketers to collect personal information from individuals to be used in promotional efforts, market research, and electronic commerce. And this makes parents worried. According to a national survey, 73% of parents with home Internet connections are nervous about Web sites having their personal information, and 95% believe that teenagers should have to get their parents' consent before giving out information online (Turow, 2003). Research suggests parents need to be vigilant. One study of 162 Web sites popular

Figure 2.17   Webkinz

SOURCE: ©2005–2007 GANZ. All rights reserved.

with children found that nearly 70% collected personal information from the user such as name, e-mail address, birth date, and postal address (Cai, Gantz, Schwartz, & Wang, 2003). Roughly 15% of those sites requesting information asked for a credit card number. Most alarming, two thirds of the sites requesting information made no effort to obtain parental permission first.

Recognizing these problems, in 1998, Congress passed the Children's Online Privacy Protection Act (COPPA). To be enforced by the Federal Trade Commission (FTC), the law requires that all Web sites targeted to children younger than 13 must have a prominent link to a privacy policy that clearly identifies how personal information is collected and used. Despite this ruling, some children's Web sites still do not post a privacy policy, and many that have one do not make the link very prominent or the policy itself very accessible or readable for parents (Center for Media Education, 2001; Turow, 2001). In the content analysis of popular children's Web sites described above (Cai et al., 2003), only 4 of the 162 Web sites were in full compliance with COPPA. It should be noted that COPPA does not apply to Web sites targeted to those 13 years of age and older, even though parents are concerned about privacy protection for this age group as well (Turow, 2003).

Even still, a privacy policy may not be enough to protect families. In a national survey of 10- to 17-year-olds, 31% reported that they had given out personal information to a Web site (Turow & Nir, 2000). Moreover, 45% of the youngsters said they would exchange personal information on the Web for a free gift, and 25%

reported never having read a site's privacy policy. It is also the case that adolescent boys are more willing to give out personal information online than adolescent girls are (Youn, 2005). Thus, it seems reasonable to conclude that as long as marketers are free to collect information about users regardless of age, the Internet will be a relatively easy way to discover and try to influence the consumer preferences of youth.

Marketing in Schools

Commercialism in schools has soared in recent years, spurring much public debate about the ethics of such practices (Aidman, 1995; Richards, Wartella, Morton, & Thompson, 1998). Corporations are eager to partner with schools as a way to reach young consumers, who spend almost 20% of their time in the classroom. In turn, public schools often feel desperate to augment tight budgets, and corporate support offers one way to do so.

Four types of commercial practices can be found in various degrees across American schools (Consumers Union Education Services, 1995; Wartella & Jennings, 2001). First, marketers often advertise directly to students by placing ads on school billboards, buses, athletic scoreboards, and even in student newspapers and yearbooks. Second, corporations occasionally give away products or coupons to expose children to different brand names. For example, Minute Maid, McDonald's, and Pizza Hut have offered food coupons to students who meet their teachers' reading goals.

Third, corporations frequently sponsor fund-raisers to help schools afford new equipment, uniforms, or class trips. Students themselves become marketers in these efforts, approaching aunts and uncles, neighbors, and even parents' work colleagues. Pitching anything from poinsettia plants to gift wrap to frozen pizzas, students can earn prizes for themselves and money for their school. Fourth, marketers often create educational materials such as workbooks, brochures, and videos on specific curriculum topics. For instance, Kellogg's publishes nutrition posters that give health information and also display the corporate logo and several Kellogg's cereals. Unfortunately, one study found that nearly 80% of these corporate-sponsored materials contain biased or incomplete information (Consumers Union Education Services, 1995).

A fifth and more controversial form of commercialism in schools is Channel One, a 12-minute daily news program designed for middle and high school students. Introduced in 1990 by Whittle Communications, the program includes 10 minutes of originally produced news for teens and 2 minutes of advertising. Schools sign a 3-year contract that provides them with a dedicated satellite dish, two centralized VCRs, television sets for each classroom, and all wiring and maintenance for the equipment. In exchange, a school agrees to have 90% of its students watch the program daily. Roughly 11,000 American middle and high schools have entered into this contractual arrangement (Atkinson, 2007).

Channel One has been challenged on several fronts (see Figure 2.18). Critics charge that the arrangement cedes control of the curriculum to outside parties, requires students to be a captive audience to ads, and exposes students to messages

Figure 2.18

SOURCE: Reprinted by permission from Tribune Media Services, *Boston Globe,* Dan Wasserman, 2000.

that run counter to nutritional lessons taught in school (Consumers Union Education Services, 1995). Amid the controversy, several advertisers such as Pepsi Cola Co. and Cingular decided to pull their advertising from the newscast, and the network has struggled financially in recent years (Atkinson, 2007).

Research supports some of the criticisms that have been lodged against Channel One. A study by Brand and Greenberg (1994) found that compared with nonviewers, students exposed to Channel One gave more favorable ratings to products that were advertised during the newscast. Viewers also expressed more materialistic attitudes than nonviewers did. On the positive side, viewers do seem to learn more about news, particularly those events covered in the daily programs (Greenberg & Brand, 1993).

A similar initiative in Canada, called Youth News Network (YNN), has had minimal success. This corporate initiative promised audiovisual and computer equipment to schools in exchange for showing a 12½-minute newscast that included 2½ minutes of ads. The service was banned in every Catholic school in Canada and in 6 of the 13 provinces. A report by the Canadian Centre for Policy Alternatives concluded that

> having a corporate presence in the classroom is tantamount to giving such companies school time—and the public money which pays for that time—in which to advertise their products to kids. Our taxes are literally paying for the commercial targeting of our students, and diverting time and money from their education. (Shaker, 2000, p. 19)

Today, more than 7 million American teens watch advertising on television each day in the classroom (Atkinson, 2007). Other students enter contests, receive curriculum materials, and are exposed to hallway ads that promote products. Some believe these arrangements represent innovative ways to support struggling schools (see Richards et al., 1998). Others view this growing trend as a violation of "the integrity of education" (Consumers Union Education Services, 1995). Regardless of which view is taken, such practices are likely to continue as marketers search for creative ways to reach youth.

Regulation of Advertising Targeted to Youth

As described above, the Children's Online Privacy Protection Act illustrates that the federal government is indeed willing to set policies to protect young children from marketing. This willingness dates back to the early 1970s, when questions first arose concerning the fairness of advertising to young children. In this section, we give an overview of major efforts by the government as well as by the industry itself to regulate advertising to youth.

Government Regulation

In 1974, the first U.S. policy regarding children and advertising was issued by the FCC. The FCC, which is responsible for allocating and renewing licenses to broadcasters, explicitly acknowledged younger children's vulnerability to commercial messages and issued two guidelines that year. First, the overall amount of time that could be devoted to ads during children's programming was limited to 9.5 minutes per hour on weekends and 12 minutes per hour on weekdays (FCC, 1974). Second, stations were required to maintain a clear separation between program content and commercial messages during shows targeted to children. Three aspects of this separation principle were outlined: (a) separation devices, known as "bumpers," were mandated to clearly signal the beginning and end of a commercial break during children's shows; (b) host selling was prohibited, meaning that no program characters were allowed to sell products during commercials embedded in or directly adjacent to their show; and (c) program-length commercials, or the promotion of products within the body of a program, were forbidden.

Led by a group called Action for Children's Television (ACT), several public interest groups felt that the 1974 policy did not go far enough in protecting children. Out of frustration, they turned to the FTC and pushed for a complete ban of all ads targeted to children too young to recognize commercial intent (FTC, 1978). The FTC considered the petition for several years, proposing rulings, holding hearings, and reviewing evidence. During this time, the broadcasting and advertising industries along with several major corporations lobbied heavily against such a ban (Kunkel & Watkins, 1987). In 1981, the FTC issued a final ruling acknowledging that children younger than age 7 "do not possess the cognitive ability to evaluate adequately child-oriented television advertising" and that because of this, such content represents a "legitimate cause for public concern" (FTC, 1981, pp. 2–4). Yet the FTC ultimately decided against a ban, asserting that it would economically threaten the very existence of children's programming.

The Reagan presidency helped turn the 1980s into a decade of deregulation. Responding to this trend, in 1984, the FCC relaxed its policies toward children's advertising in two ways. First, it revoked its earlier restrictions on the amount of advertising permissible during children's shows (FCC, 1984). In doing so, the FCC asserted that marketplace forces should be left alone to determine the appropriate levels of advertising. Critics have pointed out that if very young children are unable to recognize or be critical of ads, it is doubtful whether they as consumers can register complaints over too many commercials (Wilcox & Kunkel, 1996). Second, the FCC rescinded its earlier ban on program-length commercials, asserting instead that they represented an innovative means of financing children's programming (FCC, 1984). Shortly after, toy-based programming flooded the broadcast schedule (Colby, 1993).

Out of increasing concern about children's television, Congress stepped in and passed the Children's Television Act (CTA) in 1990. The law mainly dealt with educational programming, but it also reinstated time limits on advertising to children. The new limits are still in effect today and apply to broadcasting as well as cable, permitting no more than 10.5 minutes of advertising per hour on weekends and 12 minutes per hour on weekdays during children's programming. Some stations have violated these limits over the years. For example, in 2004, the FCC levied a fine of $1,000,000 to Viacom and $500,000 to Disney for exceeding the CTA commercial advertising limits (de Moraes, 2004).

As part of the law, Congress also ordered the FCC to reconsider its lenient stance on program-length commercials. One year later, the FCC decided to reinstate its earlier ban on such content, but in doing so, it more narrowly defined a program-length commercial as "a program associated with a product in which commercials for that product are aired" (FCC, 1991, p. 2117). Readers may recognize that this new definition is essentially the same as host selling, a practice that has been prohibited since 1974. In other words, the FCC's ban imposes nothing new; it continues to allow for toy-based programs to promote products within the body of the show so long as related commercials are not aired directly within or adjacent to that show.

More recently, the FCC has taken up the issue of host selling in online marketing (FCC, 2004). To help children discriminate program from commercial content, the FCC (2004) ruled that characters that appear in television programs cannot also be featured on related Web sites selling products if the Web address is displayed on the screen during the program.

Although the FTC and the FCC have openly recognized the vulnerability of younger children, their policies reflect political compromises that also satisfy the broadcasters and advertisers involved. In contrast to the United States, other industrialized nations have much stronger laws to protect children from marketing. For example, Sweden does not allow any television advertising that directly targets children younger than age 12 (Valkenburg, 2000). In Greece, commercials for toys are banned until 10 p.m. on television, and in Belgium, commercials are not allowed during children's programming. Countries such as Australia, Canada, and England forbid any advertising targeted to preschoolers (Kunkel, 2001). Given the strong political forces that oppose such measures in the United States, a ban of any type would be difficult to implement here. Yet as recently as 2004, the American Psychological Association (APA) formed a Task Force on Advertising and Children that reviewed all the empirical evidence to date and issued a number of policy recommendations (Kunkel et al., 2004). Included among the recommendations were the following:

- Legally restrict television advertising as well as advertising in the schools directed to children 8 years and younger
- Use advertising disclaimers for children's programs in language that children can easily understand
- Educate parents and professionals who work with children and youth on the effects of advertising

Likewise, the American Academy of Pediatrics issued a policy statement in 2006 that also recommended tighter legal control of TV advertising, especially junk-food ads, to young children (Committee on Communications, 2006).

Industry Self-Regulation

Public criticism and threats of government action have forced the industries involved to engage in efforts to self-regulate. As early as 1961, the National Association of Broadcasters (NAB), a trade association representing the industry, adopted its own code of guidelines that included provisions about advertising to children. However, the code was eliminated for legal reasons in the early 1980s as part of a federal antitrust case.

Today, the main effort to self-regulate comes from the advertising industry itself. In 1974, the Children's Advertising Review Unit (CARU) was created by the Council of Better Business Bureaus. It is probably no accident that CARU came into being around the same time that the FCC issued its first policy regarding children's advertising. CARU's job is to review advertising and marketing material directed to children in all media. As part of this review process, CARU (2006) has established an extensive set of guidelines for advertising in any medium targeted to those younger than 12 years of age (www.caru.org/guidelines/index.asp). It also offers guidelines for online data collection by Web sites targeting children younger than 13 years of age. The guidelines offer recommendations on topics such as the presentation of products, disclaimers and disclosures, premiums and contests, the use of celebrities as endorsers, the blurring of advertising and program content, and online privacy protection (CARU, 2006). Some of the guidelines explicitly recognize developmental considerations, such as children's limited vocabulary and difficulty evaluating the truthfulness of information (see Figure 2.19).

Figure 2.19

SOURCE: Baby Blues by Rick Kirkman and Jerry Scott. Reprinted with permission of King Features Syndicate.

CARU is financed by the business community, and it receives support from the various organizations that advertise to children, such as advertising agencies, toy manufacturers, food companies, and Internet providers. CARU actively monitors a certain number of ads each year, but it relies heavily on voluntary compliance by advertisers. When it finds a violation, it seeks change through the voluntary cooperation of advertisers and Web site operators.

One study in the early 1990s of more than 10,000 ads directed at children found a high rate of overall adherence to the CARU guidelines (Kunkel & Gantz, 1993). Still, some of the guidelines are rather vague, and none of them question the overall legitimacy of targeting young children with advertisements (Kunkel, 2001). Furthermore, CARU does not address issues such as the volume of advertising to children or the newer, more integrated marketing strategies that are being targeted to youth (Institute of Medicine, 2006). In other words, CARU is still primarily a political effort to ward off more formal government regulation, and it is fundamentally supportive of the major manufacturing firms that underwrite this organization. Recognizing some of these limitations, the APA Task Force on Advertising and Children included in its 2004 policy recommendations a call for more rigorous industry self-regulation (Kunkel et al., 2004). One specific proposal the APA task force made is that the CARU guidelines should be publicized to parents.

Teaching Advertising Literacy

Recognizing the difficulty of changing the advertising environment in the United States, some have called for efforts to teach children how to be more critical consumers. As it turns out, even older children who clearly recognize the selling intent of ads do not typically critique commercials spontaneously while viewing them (Brucks, Armstrong, & Goldberg, 1988; Derbaix & Bree, 1997). In other words, their general skepticism toward advertising is not always activated when they actually encounter commercial messages. One study suggests that a simple cue or reminder can trigger a viewer's cognitive defenses, raising the number of counterarguments that older children produce during exposure to commercials (Brucks et al., 1988).

Other studies have explored more formal training procedures to help children deal with advertising. Roberts, Christenson, Gibson, Mooser, and Goldberg (1980) compared two 15-minute instructional films designed to teach children about commercials: *The Six Billion $$$ Sell,* which focused on tricks and appeals used in ads, and *Seeing Through Commercials,* which focused on how ads are made. Second, third, and fifth graders were randomly assigned to view one of the two films or a control film unrelated to advertising. Results revealed that the treatment films increased children's general skepticism toward advertising as well as their ability to be critical of specific ads. The strongest effects were observed for *The Six Billion $$$ Sell,* the film that detailed specific strategies and showed ad examples. Moreover, the youngest participants learned the most from the films, the same children who initially were far more accepting of advertising.

Christenson (1982) used excerpts from *The Six Billion $$$ Sell* to create a 3-minute public service announcement (PSA) about the nature of advertising. One group of children saw the PSA before watching cartoons embedded with ads, whereas another group simply watched the content without the PSA. The insertion of the PSA increased first and second graders' comprehension of the selling intent of ads, and it enhanced skepticism about ads among this younger age group as well as among fifth and sixth graders. Furthermore, the PSA actually lowered children's taste ratings of two food products advertised during the cartoons.

Instruction that is more traditional can teach children about advertising as well. One study found that half-hour training sessions over the course of several days were effective in teaching children as young as 6 how to detect persuasive tricks and strategies in ads (Peterson & Lewis, 1988). In another study, Donohue, Henke, and Meyer (1983) compared two types of instruction: role-playing, which had children assume the role of an advertiser to create a commercial, and traditional, which had children watch TV ads and discuss the purpose and nature of commercials. Compared with a control group, both treatments helped first graders to better discriminate ads from programs and to be more skeptical of commercials. However, only the traditional instruction increased children's understanding of the persuasive intent of advertising.

It would be a mistake to conclude, however, that formal instruction is the only way to help children become more resistant to advertising (see Figure 2.20). Parents can help in a number of ways. One experiment found that simply reducing grade school children's television and video game use for 6 months decreased their toy purchase requests compared to a control group that did not change media habits (Robinson, Saphir, Kraemer, Varady, & Haydel, 2001). Parents also can talk to their children about the nature of commercials and how to evaluate them. Such discussion can improve younger children's understanding of the purpose of advertising (Ward et al., 1977). Critically discussing commercials with a parent can also reduce children's desire for an advertised product (Prasad, Rao, & Sheikh, 1978) and is associated with fewer purchase requests and less materialism in elementary schoolers (Buijzen & Valkenburg, 2005). Parental discussion even seems to benefit adolescents. Teens who talk with their parents about consumption show a higher knowledge of prices (R. L. Moore & Stephens, 1975) and more discriminating

"...No, he can't really fly...no, the bad guys don't really
have a ray gun...no, this cereal really isn't the best food
in the whole world...no, it won't make you as
strong as a giant..."

Figure 2.20

SOURCE: Reprinted with permission from Tribune Media Services.

behavior when making purchases (Moschis & Churchill, 1978). Teens whose parents encourage critical thinking also show more concern about divulging privacy information on the Internet (Moscardelli& Divine, 2007). As with other types of media content (see Chapter 12), parental mediation can play an important role in preparing youth for daily encounters with commercial messages.

Conclusion

Children are literally born to become consumers in the United States. They typically visit their first store at the tender age of 2 months, and by the time they reach 2 years, most have made a request for a product (McNeal, 2007). Their bedrooms are filled with Disney characters, designer crib sheets, and BabyGap clothes, and their playrooms are stuffed with all kinds of toys. By the time children reach preschool, they are watching their favorite toy-based cartoons, seeing several hours' worth of TV advertising each week, and making regular trips with a parent to the grocery store, fast-food restaurants, and Toys 'R' Us. All of this exposure comes at a time when children are very naive about commercial messages and trusting of their content.

As children reach the early elementary school years, they gradually learn about the motives behind advertising and the tactics used in commercials. Some of this knowledge helps them to be more skeptical of such messages. Yet keeping these cognitive defenses in mind is not always easy when confronted by a slick and highly entertaining commercial suggesting that everyone else has a particular new toy. Certainly, television is not the only source of these desires. School-aged children may be most vulnerable when commercialism invades their classroom, becoming part of the decor or even the curriculum itself. And spending time online may confuse children even more as marketing becomes intimately intertwined with content.

In the face of all this commercialism, some critics have argued that advertising is inherently unfair to young children and ought to be eliminated from content targeted to those younger than age 8. An opposite position holds that children will never learn to be consumers unless they are exposed to commercial messages. A third intermediary position is that parents and educators need to develop ways to help youth become more critical consumers. As children's discretionary income grows and they spend more time surfing the Web, wandering in shopping malls, and watching TV alone in their bedrooms, early training in critical consumer skills seems vital.

Exercises

1. Find a magazine advertisement targeted to children. What type of product is being advertised? Does it fit into one of the top four categories of children's ads found on television (see the Kunkel & Gantz, 1992, study above)? What is the main appeal used in this ad to persuade children? Is there any disclaimer offered in the ad? If so, is it likely to be noticed or understood by a child? Is there anything in the ad that might be misleading or confusing for a 5-year-old child? For a 10-year-old child?

2. Find a magazine ad targeted to teens. What type of product is being advertised? Do you see evidence of gender or racial stereotyping in the ad? What is the main appeal used in the ad? Is there anything about the ad that might make teens feel self-conscious about their own physical appearance?

3. Think about your childhood. What is the first toy purchase you remember feeling disappointed about? How old were you? Did you buy the toy with your own money? Did advertising have anything to do with your disappointment? How did your mother or father respond to your disappointment? Did your parents discuss advertising with you?

4. Go to the Children's Advertising Review Unit (CARU) Web site. Examine the guidelines for advertising to children (www.caru.org/guidelines/index.asp). Find two guidelines that are clearly worded and easy for an advertiser to follow. Now find two guidelines that are vague and difficult to follow. Of the ones listed, which guideline do you think is violated most often in children's advertising?

5. In 2001, Sweden launched a movement to ban television advertising aimed at children in all member states of the European Union. Sweden itself has had such a ban in place for the past 10 years, yet other countries in Europe are not so supportive of the idea. Do you think such a ban is a good idea in the United States? Why or why not? Instead of an all-out ban, can you think of any other types of regulation of children's advertising that might be easier to enact in the United States?

6. Find two popular Web sites for children, one that is commercial and one that is not (check Berit's Best Sites for Children: www.beritsbest.com). For example, you could compare the Bratz Web site (www.bratz.com) with a site called AAA Math (www.aaamath.com), which is designed to teach children math lessons. How much advertising is on each Web site? Are there features of the Web sites that look like content but are actually advertising? Do the sites ask children for personal information? If so, is there a privacy policy? Critique the marketing strategies used in each site, thinking about a 9-year-old user without a parent in the room.

7. Harry Potter is an example of a remarkably successful brand story. To date, seven books have been published about the boy wizard and four live-action movies have been made. In addition, there are more than 400 tie-in products available for purchase, everything from candy to computer games (Brown, 2005). List as many examples as you can that reflect how this book series has been commercialized across different media. Did you spend any money on Harry Potter products? When you were a child, was there any movie you can remember that was similarly successful? What has changed in the past 20 years regarding the promotion of media stories and their characters?

8. You are a principal of a large high school in a rural area. Your school band has been invited to perform in Washington, D.C., and your basketball team is ranked highly in the state. But the band desperately needs new uniforms, and the basketball team needs new athletic equipment, both of which are not in your budget. You are approached by the head of B&W Marketing, who offers you $100,000 in exchange for placing a select number of advertisements in school hallways. What would you do? What factors should you consider in making your decision?

References

Acuff, D. S. (1997). *What kids buy and why: The psychology of marketing to kids.* New York: Free Press.

Adler, R. (1980). Children's television advertising: History of the issue. In E. L. Palmer & A. Dorr (Eds.), *Children and the faces of television: Teaching, violence, selling* (pp. 237–248). New York: Academic Press.

Aidman, A. (1995, December). *Advertising in the schools.* Urbana, IL: ERIC Clearinghouse on Elementary and Early Childhood Education. (ERIC Document Reproduction Service No. ED389473)

Alexander, A., Benjamin, L. M., Hoerrner, K., & Roe, D. (1998). "We'll be back in a moment": A content analysis of advertisements in children's television in the 1950s. *Journal of Advertising, 27*(3), 1–9.

Annicelli, C. (1999, June). *Monster cash; Pokémon has made a fortune; Prepare for the second wave.* Retrieved May 25, 2001, from http://www.findarticles.com/cf_0/m3196/6_97/55084237/p1/article.jhtml

Atkin, C. (1980). Effects of television advertising on children. In E. L. Palmer & A. Dorr (Eds.), *Children and the faces of television: Teaching, violence, selling* (pp. 287–305). New York: Academic Press.

Atkin, C. (1982). Television advertising and socialization to consumer roles. In D. Pearl, L. Bouthilet, & J. Lazar (Eds.), *Television and behavior: Ten years of scientific progress and implications for the eighties* (Vol. 2, pp. 191–200). Washington, DC: Government Printing Office.

Atkin, C., & Block, M. (1983). Effectiveness of celebrity endorsers. *Journal of Advertising Research, 23*(1), 57–61.

Atkin, C. K. (1976). Children's social learning from television advertising: Research evidence on observational modeling of product consumption. *Advances in Consumer Research, 3,* 513–519.

Atkin, C. K. (1978). Observation of parent-child interaction in supermarket decision-making. *Journal of Marketing, 42*(4), 41–45.

Atkinson, C. (2007, April 23). *Kicked out of class: Primedia sheds in-school net.* Retrieved April 25, 2007, from http://www.commercialalert.org/news

Aun, F. (2007, April 3). *ZenithOptimedia: Internet ad spending will overtake radio next year.* Retrieved April 25, 2007, from http://www.clickz.com

Autherland, A., & Thompson, B. (2003). *Kidfluence: The marketer's guide to understanding and reaching Generation Y—kids, tweens, and teens.* New York: McGraw-Hill.

Barcus, F. E. (1980). The nature of television advertising to children. In E. L. Palmer & A. Dorr (Eds.), *Children and the faces of television: Teaching, violence, selling* (pp. 273–285). New York: Academic Press.

Bever, T. G., Smith, M. L., Bengen, B., & Johnson, T. G. (1975). Young viewers' troubling response to TV ads. *Harvard Business Review, 53,* 109–120.

Blatt, J., Spencer, L., & Ward, S. (1972). A cognitive development study of children's reactions to television advertising. In G. Comstock, J. Murry, & E. A. Rubinstein (Eds.), *Television and social behavior* (Vol. 4, pp. 452–467). Washington, DC: Government Printing Office.

Boush, D. M., Friestad, M., & Rose, G. M. (1994). Adolescent skepticism toward TV advertising and knowledge of advertiser tactics. *Journal of Consumer Research, 21*(1), 165–175.

Brand, J. E., & Greenberg, B. S. (1994). Commercials in the classroom: The impact of Channel One advertising. *Journal of Advertising Research, 34*(1), 18–27.

Brass, K. (1999, November 21). *'Pokemon' fad at a fever pitch—and what a pitch indeed.* Retrieved May 25, 2001, from http://www.findarticles.com/cf_0/m0VPW/47_27/58047459/p1/article.html

Brown, S. (2005, July 21). Harry Potter brand wizard. *BusinessWeek.* Retrieved April 25, 2007, from http://www.businessweek.com/innovate/content/ju12005/di20050721_060250.htm

Brucks, M., Armstrong, G. M., & Goldberg, M. (1988). Children's use of cognitive defenses against television advertising: A cognitive response approach. *Journal of Consumer Research, 14,* 471–482.

Buijzen, M., & Valkenburg, P. (2000). The impact of television advertising on children's Christmas wishes. *Journal of Broadcasting & Electronic Media, 44,* 456–470.

Buijzen, M., & Valkenburg, P. M. (2002). Appeals in television advertising: A content analysis of commercials aimed at children and teenagers. *Communications, 27,* 349–364.

Buijzen, M., & Valkenburg, P. M. (2003a). The effects of television advertising on materialism, parent-child conflict, and unhappiness: A review of research. *Applied Developmental Psychology, 24,* 437–456.

Buijzen, M., & Valkenburg, P. M. (2003b). The unintended effects of television advertising. *Communication Research, 30,* 483–503.

Buijzen, M., & Valkenburg, P. M. (2005). Parental mediation of undesired advertising effects. *Journal of Broadcasting & Electronic Media, 49,* 153–165.

Burr, P., & Burr, R. M. (1977). Product recognition and premium appeal. *Journal of Communication, 27,* 115–117.

Butter, E. J., Popovich, P. M., Stackhouse, R. H., & Garner, R. K. (1981). Discrimination of television programs and commercials by preschool children. *Journal of Advertising Research, 21*(2), 53–56.

Cai, X., Gantz, W., Schwartz, N., & Wang, X. (2003). Children's website adherence to the FTC's online privacy protection rule. *Journal of Applied Communication Research, 31,* 346–362.

Calvert, S. L. (2008). The children's television act. In S. L. Calvert & B. J. Wilson (Eds.), *Blackwell handbook of child development and the media.* New York: Blackwell.

Center for Media Education. (1996). *Web of deception: Threats to children from online marketing.* Washington, DC: Author. Retrieved June 1, 2001, from http://www.cme .org/children/marketing/deception.pdf

Center for Media Education. (2001). *Children's Online Privacy Protection Act (COPPA)—The first year: A survey of sites.* Washington, DC: Author. Retrieved June 1, 2001, from http:// www.cme.org/children/privacy/coppa_rept.pdf

Center for Science in the Public Interest. (1988, September 4). *Kids are aware of booze as presidents, survey finds* [Press release]. Washington, DC: Author.

Children Now. (2006). *The future of children's media: Advertising* [Conference report]. Oakland, CA: Author.

Children's Advertising Review Unit (CARU). (2006). *Self regulatory program for children's advertising.* Retrieved April 24, 2007, from http://www.caru.org/guidelines/guidelines.pdf

Christenson, P. G. (1982). Children's perceptions of TV commercials and products: The effects of PSA's. *Communication Research, 9,* 491–524.

Churchill, G., Jr., & Moschis, G. P. (1979). Television and interpersonal influences on adolescent consumer learning. *Journal of Consumer Research, 5*(1), 23–35.

Colby, P. A. (1993, April). *From Hot Wheels to Teenage Mutant Ninja Turtles: The evolution of the definition of program length commercials on children's television.* Paper presented at the annual meeting of the Broadcast Education Association Las Vegas, NV.

Committee on Communications. (2006). Children, adolescents, and advertising. *Pediatrics, 118,* 2563–2569.

Condry, J. C., Bence, P. J., & Scheibe, C. L. (1988). Nonprogram content of children's television. *Journal of Broadcasting & Electronic Media, 32,* 255–270.

Consumers Union Education Services. (1995). *Captive kids: A report on commercial pressures on kids at school.* Yonkers, NY: Author.

Creamer, M. (2005). Foul mouth: Stealth marketers flirt with law. *Advertising Age, 76*(40), 6.

Culley, J., Lazer, W., & Atkin, C. (1976). The experts look at children's television. *Journal of Broadcasting, 20,* 3–20.

de Mesa, A. (2005, October 12). Marketing and tweens: Children in their middle years keep evolving into savvier consumers: With the girls' market saturated, brands are looking to boys as well. *BusinessWeek.* Retrieved April 18, 2007, from http://www.businessweek.com

de Moraes, L. (2004, October 22). FCC fines 2 networks for violating limits on kids' show ads. *The Washington Post,* p. C01.

Derbaix, C., & Bree, J. (1997). The impact of children's affective reactions elicited by commercials on attitudes toward the advertisement and the brand. *International Journal of Research in Marketing, 14,* 207–229.

Derbaix, C., & Pecheux, C. (2003). A new scale to assess children's attitude toward TV advertising. *Journal of Advertising Research, 43,* 390–399.

Dixon, H. G., Scully, M. L., Wakefield, M. A., White, V. M., & Crawford, D. A. (2007). The effects of television advertisements for junk food versus nutritious food on children's food attitudes and preferences. *Social Science & Medicine, 65,* 1311–1323.

Donohue, T. R., Henke, L. L., & Donohue, W. A. (1980). Do kids know what TV commercials intend? *Journal of Advertising Research, 20*(5), 51–57.

Donohue, T. R., Henke, L. L., & Meyer, T. P. (1983). Learning about television commercials: The impact of instructional units on children's perceptions of motive and intent. *Journal of Broadcasting, 27,* 251–261.

Dubow, J. S. (1995). Advertising recognition and recall by age—including teens. *Journal of Advertising Research, 35*(5), 55–60.

Dunnewind, S. (2004, November 20). Teen recruits create word-of-mouth "buzz" to hook peers on products. *Seattle Times.* Retrieved April 24, 2007, from http://www.seattle times.nwsource.com

Enrico, D. (1999). Top 10 advertising icons. *Advertising Age, 70*(14), 42–46.

Faber, R. J., Perloff, R. M., & Hawkins, R. P. (1982). Antecedents of children's comprehension of television advertising. *Journal of Broadcasting, 26,* 575–584.

Federal Communications Commission (FCC). (1974). Children's television programs: Report and policy statement. *Federal Register, 39,* 39396–39409.

Federal Communications Commission (FCC). (1984). Children's television programming and advertising practices. *Federal Register, 49,* 1704–1727.

Federal Communications Commission (FCC). (1991). Report and order: Policies and rules concerning children's television programming. *Federal Communications Commission Record, 6,* 2111–2127.

Federal Communications Commission (FCC). (2004). *In the matter of children's television obligations of digital television broadcasters: Report and order and further notice of proposed rule making* (MM Docket No. 00-167). Retrieved May 11, 2007, from http://www.fcc.gov/omd/pra/docs/3060-0750/3060-0750-07.doc

Federal Trade Commission (FTC). (1978). *FTC staff report on television advertising to children.* Washington, DC: Government Printing Office.

Federal Trade Commission (FTC). (1981). *In the matter of children's advertising: FTC final staff report and recommendation.* Washington, DC: Government Printing Office.

Fischer, P. M., Schwarts, M. P., Richards, J. W., Goldstein, A. O., & Rojas, T. H. (1991). Brand logo recognition by children aged 3 to 6 years: Mickey Mouse and Old Joe the Camel. *Journal of the American Medical Association, 266,* 3145–3148.

Fox, R. F. (1996). *Harvesting minds: How TV commercials control kids.* Westport, CT: Praeger/Greenwood.

Galst, J. P., & White, M. A. (1976). The unhealthy persuader: The reinforcing value of television and children's purchase-influencing attempts at the supermarket. *Child Development, 47,* 1089–1096.

Gantz, W., Schwartz, N., Angelini, J. R., & Rideout, V. (2007). *Food for thought: Television food advertising to children in the United States.* Menlo Park, CA: Henry J. Kaiser Family Foundation.

Goldberg, M. E. (1990). A quasi-experiment assessing the effectiveness of TV advertising directed to children. *Journal of Marketing Research, 27,* 445–454.

Goldberg, M. E., & Gorn, G. J. (1978). Some unintended consequences of TV advertising to children. *Journal of Consumer Research, 5*(1), 22–29.

Goldberg, M. E., Gorn, G. J., & Gibson, W. (1978). TV messages for snack and breakfast foods: Do they influence children's preferences? *Journal of Consumer Research, 5*(2), 73–81.

Gorn, G. J., & Goldberg, M. E. (1977). The impact of television advertising on children from low income families. *Journal of Consumer Research, 4*(2), 86–88.

Gorn, G. J., & Goldberg, M. E. (1980). Children's responses to repetitive television commercials. *Journal of Consumer Research, 6,* 421–424.

Graft, K. (2007, April 22). *This week: The real Pokemon hits US.* Retrieved April 24, 2007, from http://www.next-gen.biz.com

Greenberg, B. S., & Brand, J. E. (1993). Television news and advertising in schools: The "Channel One" controversy. *Journal of Communication, 43,* 143–151.

Greer, D., Potts, R., Wright, J. C., & Huston, A. C. (1982). The effects of television commercial form and commercial placement on children's social behavior and attention. *Child Development, 53,* 611–619.

Gunter, B., & Furnham, A. (1998). *Children as consumers: A psychological analysis of young people's market.* London: Routledge.

Harrison, K. (2006). Fast and sweet: Nutritional attributes to television food advertisements with and without Black characters. *Howard Journal of Communication, 17,* 249–264.

Harrison, K., & Bond, B. J. (2007). Gaming magazines and the drive for muscularity in preadolescent boys: A longitudinal examination. *Body Image, 4,* 269–277.

Harrison, K., & Hefner, V. (2006). Media exposure, current and future body ideals, and disordered eating among preadolescent girls: A longitudinal panel study. *Journal of Youth and Adolescence, 35,* 153–163.

Hawn, C. (2007, March 23). *Time to play, money to spend.* Retrieved April 18, 2007, from http://money.cnn.com/magazines/business2

Howard, T. (2002, September 9). Real winner of "American Idol": Coke. *USA Today,* p. 6B.

Hoy, M. G., Young, C. E., & Mowen, J. C. (1986). Animated host-selling advertisements: Their impacts on young children's recognition, attitudes, and behavior. *Journal of Public Policy & Marketing, 5,* 171–184.

Huston, A. C., Greer, D., Wright, J. C., Welch, R., & Ross, R. (1984). Children's comprehension of televised formal features with masculine and feminine connotations. *Developmental Psychology, 20,* 707–716.

Institute of Medicine. (2006). *Food marketing to children and youth: Threat or opportunity?* Washington, DC: National Academy of Sciences.

Jones, R. (2000). *Kids are target of Pokemon's shrewd marketing effort.* Retrieved May 25, 2001, from http://abcnews.go.com/sections/business/thestreet/pokemon_991117.html

Kaikati, A. M., & Kaikati, J. G. (2004). Stealth marketing: How to reach consumers surreptitiously. *California Management Review, 98,* 48–58.

Khermouch, G., & Green, J. (2001, July 30). Buzz marketing: Suddenly this stealth strategy is hot—but it's still fraught with risk. *BusinessWeek.* Retrieved from http://www.businessweek.com

Kline, S. (1993). *Out of the garden: Toys, TV, and children's culture in the age of marketing.* New York: Verso.

Krugman, D. M., Cameron, G. T., & White, C. M. (1995). Visual attention to programming and commercials: The use of in-home observations. *Journal of Advertising, 24*(1), 1–12.

Kunkel, D. (1988). Children and host-selling television commercials. *Communication Research, 15,* 71–92.

Kunkel, D. (2001). Children and television advertising. In D. G. Singer & J. L. Singer (Eds.), *Handbook of children and the media* (pp. 375–393). Thousand Oaks, CA: Sage.

Kunkel, D., & Gantz, W. (1992). Children's television advertising in the multichannel environment. *Journal of Communication, 42*(3), 134–152.

Kunkel, D., & Gantz, W. (1993). Assessing compliance with industry self-regulation of television advertising to children. *Journal of Applied Communication Research, 21,* 148–162.

Kunkel, D., & Watkins, B. (1987). Evolution of children's television regulatory policy. *Journal of Broadcasting & Electronic Media, 31,* 367–389.

Kunkel, D., Wilcox, B. L., Cantor, J., Palmer, E., Linn, S., & Dowrick, P. (2004). *Report of the APA Task Force on Advertising and Children.* Washington, DC: American Psychological Association. Retrieved May 11, 2007, from http://www.apa.org/releases/childrenads.pdf

Larson, M. S. (2001). Interactions, activities and gender in children's television commercials: A content analysis. *Journal of Broadcasting & Electronic Media, 45,* 41–56.

Levin, S. R., Petros, T. V., & Petrella, F. W. (1982). Preschoolers' awareness of television advertising. *Child Development, 53,* 933–937.

Liebert, D. E., Sprafkin, J. N., Liebert, R. M., & Rubinstein, E. A. (1977). Effects of television commercial disclaimers on the product expectations of children. *Journal of Communication, 27,* 118–124.

Macklin, M. C. (1985). Do young children understand the selling intent of commercials? *Journal of Consumer Affairs, 19,* 293–304.

Macklin, M. C. (1987). Preschoolers' understanding of the informational function of television advertising. *Journal of Consumer Research, 14,* 229–239.

Mangleburg, T. F., & Bristol, T. (1999). Socialization and adolescents' skepticism toward advertising. In M. C. Macklin & L. Carlson (Eds.), *Advertising to children: Concepts and controversies* (pp. 27–48). Thousand Oaks, CA: Sage.

Martin, M. C. (1997). Children's understanding of the intent of advertising: A meta-analysis. *Journal of Public Policy & Marketing, 16,* 205–216.

Martin, M. C., & Gentry, J. W. (1997). Stuck in the model trap: The effects of beautiful models in ads on female pre-adolescents and adolescents. *Journal of Advertising, 26*(2), 19–33.

Martin, M. C., & Kennedy, P. F. (1993). Advertising and social comparison: Consequences for female pre-adolescents and adolescents. *Psychology & Marketing, 10,* 513–530.

Mazur, L. A. (1996, May–June). Marketing madness. *E Magazine: The Environmental Magazine, 7*(3), 36–42.

McAllister, M. P. (2007). "Girls with a passion for fashion": The Bratz brand as integrated spectacular consumption. *Journal of Children and Media, 1,* 244–258.

McNeal, J. U. (1998). Tapping the three kids' markets. *American Demographics, 20*(4), 36–41.

McNeal, J. U. (1999). *The kids' market: Myths and realities.* Ithaca, NY: Paramount Market.

McNeal, J. U. (2007). *On becoming a consumer: Development of consumer behavior patterns in childhood.* Burlington, MA: Butterworth-Heinemann.

Miller, J. H., & Busch, P. (1979). Host selling vs. premium TV commercials: An experimental evaluation of their influence on children. *Journal of Marketing Research, 16,* 323–332.

Minow, N. (2004, September 21). 'Have you heard?' Stealth advertising puts products and pitches everywhere . . . and you may never know. *Chicago Tribune.* Retrieved April 24, 2007, from http://proquest.umi.com

Moore, R. L., & Stephens, L. F. (1975). Some communication and demographic determinants of adolescent consumer learning. *Journal of Communication, 29,* 197–201.

Moore, E. S. (2006). *It's child's play: Advergaming and the online marketing of food to children.* Menlo Park, CA: Henry J. Kaiser Family Foundation.

Moscardelli, D. M., & Divine, R. (2007). Adolescents' concern for privacy when using the Internet: An empirical analysis of predictors and relationships with privacy-protecting behaviors. *Family and Consumer Sciences Research Behavior, 35,* 232–252.

Moschis, G. P. (1978). Teenagers' responses to retailing stimuli. *Journal of Retailing, 54,* 80–93.

Moschis, G. P., & Churchill, G. A. (1978). Consumer socialization: A theoretical and empirical analysis. *Journal of Marketing Research, 15,* 599–609.

Moschis, G. P., & Moore, R. L. (1979). Decision making among the young: A socialization perspective. *Journal of Consumer Research, 6,* 101–112.

Moschis, G. P., & Moore, R. L. (1982). A longitudinal study of television advertising effects. *Journal of Consumer Research, 9,* 279–286.

Muehling, D. D., & Kolbe, R. H. (1999). A comparison of children's and prime-time fine-print advertising disclosure practices. In M. C. Macklin & L. Carlson (Eds.), *Advertising to children: Concepts and controversies* (pp. 143–164). Thousand Oaks, CA: Sage.

New American Dream. (2002). *Thanks to ads, kids won't take no, no, no, no, no, no, no, no, no for an answer.* Retrieved April 18, 2007, from http://www.newdream.org/kids/poll.php

Palmer, E. L., & McDowell, C. N. (1979). Program/commercial separators in children's television programming. *Journal of Communication, 29,* 197–201.

Palmer, E. L., & McDowell, C. N. (1981). Children's understanding of nutritional information presented in breakfast cereal commercials. *Journal of Broadcasting, 25,* 295–301.

Palmerton, P. R., & Judas, J. (1994, July). *Selling violence: Television commercials targeted to children.* Paper presented at the annual meeting of the International Communication Association, Sydney, Australia.

Pecora, N. O. (1998). *The business of children's entertainment.* New York: Guilford.

Peterson, L., & Lewis, K. E. (1988). Preventive intervention to improve children's discriminating of the persuasive tactics in televised advertising. *Journal of Pediatric Psychology, 3,* 163–170.

Pine, K. J., & Nash, A. (2003). Barbie or Betty? Preschool children's preference for branded products and evidence for gender-linked differences. *Developmental and Behavioral Pediatrics, 24,* 219–224.

Prasad, V. K., Rao, T. R., & Sheikh, A. A. (1978). Mother vs. commercial. *Journal of Communication, 28*(4), 91–96.

Resnik, A., & Stern, B. L. (1977). Children's television advertising and brand choice: A laboratory experiment. *Journal of Advertising, 6*(3), 11–17.

Richards, J. I., Wartella, E. A., Morton, C., & Thompson, L. (1998). The growing commercialization of schools: Issues and practices. *Annals of the American Academy of Political and Social Science, 557,* 148–163.

Richins, M. L. (1991). Social comparison and the idealized images of advertising. *Journal of Consumer Research, 18,* 71–83.

Roberts, D. F. (1982). Children and commercials: Issues, evidence, interventions. *Prevention in Human Services, 2*(1–2), 19–35.

Roberts, D. F., Christenson, P., Gibson, W. A., Mooser, L., & Goldberg, M. E. (1980). Developing discriminating consumers. *Journal of Communication, 30*(3), 94–105.

Robertson, T. S., & Rossiter, J. R. (1974). Children and commercial persuasion: An attribution theory analysis. *Journal of Consumer Research, 1,* 13–20.

Robertson, T. S., & Rossiter, J. R. (1977). Children's responsiveness to commercials. *Journal of Communication, 27,* 101–106.

Robertson, T. S., Ward, S., Gatignon, H., & Klees, D. M. (1989). Advertising and children: A cross-cultural study. *Communication Research, 16,* 459–485.

Robinson, T. N., Borzekowski, D. L., Matheson, D. M., & Kramer, H. C. (2007). Effects of fast food branding on young children's taste preferences. *Archives of Pediatrics & Adolescent Medicine, 161,* 792–797.

Robinson, T. N., Saphir, M. N., Kraemer, H. C., Varady, A., & Haydel, K. F. (2001). Effects of reducing television viewing on children's requests for toys: A randomized controlled trial. *Journal of Developmental and Behavioral Pediatrics, 22*(3), 185–187.

Rosenberg, J. M. (1992, February 18). Toymaker upbeat about coming year. *Santa Barbara News Press,* p. C4.

Ross, R. P., Campbell, T. A., Wright, J. C., Huston, A. C., Rice, M. L., & Turk, P. (1984). When celebrities talk, children listen: An experimental analysis of children's responses to TV ads with celebrity endorsement. *Journal of Applied Developmental Psychology, 5*(3), 185–202.

Schmitt, K. L., Woolf, K. D., & Anderson, D. K. (2003). Viewing the viewers: Viewing behaviors by children and adults during television programs and commercials. *Journal of Communication, 53,* 265–281.

Schor, J. B. (2004). *Born to buy: The commercialized child and the new commercial culture.* New York: Scribners.

Seiter, E. (1993). *Sold separately: Children and parents in consumer culture.* New Brunswick, NJ: Rutgers University Press.

Shaker, E. (Ed.). (2000, July). *In the corporate interest: The YNN experience in Canadian schools.* Ottawa: Canadian Centre for Policy Alternatives. Retrieved May 11, 2007, from http://policyalternatives.ca/documents/National_Office_Pubs/ynnexperience.pdf

Sheikh, A. A., & Moleski, L. M. (1977). Conflict in the family over commercials. *Journal of Communication, 27,* 152–157.

Shin, A. (2007, April 8). TV shows targeting the diaper demographic. *The Washington Post.* Retrieved April 10, 2007, from http://www.nashuatelegraph.com

Smith, S. L., & Atkin, C. (2003). Television advertising and children: Examining the intended and unintended effects. In E. L. Palmer & B. M. Young (Eds.), *The faces of televisual media: Teaching, violence, selling to children* (pp. 301–326). Mahwah, NJ: Lawrence Erlbaum.

Stern, B. L., & Resnik, A. J. (1978). Children's understanding of a televised commercial disclaimer. In S. C. Jain (Ed.), *Research frontiers in marketing: Dialogues and directions* (pp. 332–336). Chicago: American Marketing Association.

Stice, E., & Shaw, H. E. (1994). Adverse effects of the media portrayed thin-ideal on women and linkages to bulimic symptomatology. *Journal of Social and Clinical Psychology, 13,* 288–308.

Stoneman, Z., & Brody, G. H. (1981). The indirect impact of child-oriented advertisement on mother-child interactions. *Journal of Applied Developmental Psychology, 2,* 369–376.

Stutts, M. A., Vance, D., & Hudleson, S. (1981). Program-commercial separators in children's television: Do they help a child tell the difference between Bugs Bunny and the Quik Rabbit? *Journal of Advertising, 10*(2), 16–25.

Tan, A. S. (1979). TV beauty ads and role expectations of adolescent female viewers. *Journalism Quarterly, 56,* 283–288.

Teenage Research Unlimited. (2004a). *Teens spent $175 billion in 2003.* Retrieved May 11, 2007, from http://www.teenresearch.com/PRview.cfm?edit_id=168

Teenage Research Unlimited. (2004b). *TRU projects teens will spend $169 billion in 2004.* Retrieved May 11, 2007, from http://www.teenresearch.com/PRview.cfm?edit_id=378

Turow, J. (2001). *Privacy policies on children's Websites: Do they play by the rule?* Washington, DC: Annenberg Public Policy Center of the University of Pennsylvania.

Turow, J. (2003). *Americans & online privacy: The system is broken.* Washington, DC: Annenberg Public Policy Center of the University of Pennsylvania.

Turow, J., & Nir, L. (2000). *The Internet and the family 2000: The view from parents; the view from kids.* Washington, DC: Annenberg Public Policy Center of the University of Pennsylvania.

Valkenburg, P. M. (2000). Media and youth consumerism. *Journal of Adolescent Health, 27*(Suppl.), 52–56.

Valkenburg, P. M., & Buijzen, M. (2005). Identifying determinants of young children's brand awareness: Television, parents and peers. *Journal of Applied Developmental Psychology, 4*, 456–468.

Valkenburg, P. M., & Cantor, J. (2001). The development of a child into a consumer. *Journal of Applied Developmental Psychology, 22*(1), 61–72.

Viral marketing agency releases tool to track online buzz. (2007, April 14). Retrieved April 24, 2007, from http://www.promotionworld.com/news/press/070416Webbed Marketing.html

Ward, S., Levinson, D., & Wackman, D. (1972). Children's attention to advertising. In E. A. Rubinstein, G. A. Comstock, & J. P. Murray (Eds.), *Television and social behavior* (Vol. 4, pp. 491–515). Washington, DC: Government Printing Office.

Ward, S., Reale, S., & Levinson, D. (1972). Children's perceptions, explanations, and judgments of television advertising: A further explanation. In E. A. Rubinstein, G. A. Comstock, & J. P. Murray (Eds.), *Television and social behavior* (Vol. 4, pp. 468–490). Washington, DC: Government Printing Office.

Ward, S., & Wackman, D. (1972). Family and media influences on adolescent consumer learning. In E. A. Rubinstein, A. Comstock, & J. P. Murray (Eds.), *Television and social behavior* (Vol. 4, pp. 554–565). Washington, DC: Government Printing Office.

Ward, S., & Wackman, D. B. (1973). Children's information processing of television advertising. In P. Clarke (Ed.), *New models for mass communication research* (pp. 119–146). Beverly Hills, CA: Sage.

Ward, S., Wackman, D. B., & Wartella, E. (1977). *How children learn to buy: The development of consumer information-processing skills.* Beverly Hills, CA: Sage.

Wartella, E., & Ettema, J. S. (1974). A cognitive developmental study of children's attention to television commercials. *Communication Research, 1*, 69–88.

Wartella, E., & Jennings, N. (2001). Hazards and possibilities of commercial TV in the schools. In D. G. Singer & J. L. Singer (Eds.), *Handbook of children and the media* (pp. 557–570). Thousand Oaks, CA: Sage.

Waters, H. F., & Uehling, M. D. (1985, May 13). Toying with kids' TV. *Newsweek, 105*, 85.

Welch, R. L., Huston-Stein, A., Wright, J. C., & Plehal, R. (1979). Subtle sex-role cues in children's commercials. *Journal of Communication, 29*, 202–209.

Wilcox, B. L., & Kunkel, D. (1996). Taking television seriously: Children and television policy. In E. F. Zigler & S. L. Kagan (Eds.), *Children, families, and government: Preparing for the twenty-first century* (pp. 333–352). New York: Cambridge University Press.

Wilke, J., Therrien, L., Dunkin, A., & Vamos, M. N. (1985, March 25). Are the programs your kids watch simply commercials? *BusinessWeek,* p. 53.

Williams, L. A., & Burns, A. C. (2000). Exploring the dimensionality of children's direct influence attempts. *Advances in Consumer Research, 27*, 64–71.

Wilson, B. J., & Weiss, A. J. (1992). Developmental differences in children's reactions to a toy advertisement linked to a toy-based cartoon. *Journal of Broadcasting & Electronic Media, 36*, 371–394.

Wilson, B. J., & Weiss, A. J. (1995, May). *Children's reactions to a toy-based cartoon: Entertainment or commercial message?* Paper presented to the International Communication Association, Albuquerque, NM.

Youn, S. (2005). Teenagers' perceptions of online privacy and coping behaviors: A risk-benefit appraisal approach. *Journal of Broadcasting & Electronic Media, 49*, 86–110.

Zuckerman, P., Ziegler, M., & Stevenson, H. W. (1978). Children's viewing of television and recognition memory of commercials. *Child Development, 49*, 96–104.

CHAPTER 3

Educational Media

Children spend more time engaged with media than they do with any other activity besides sleeping. Over the course of their childhood, they will also spend more time watching television than they will in the classroom (Hearold, 1986).[1] We know from several chapters of this book that there are many potential negative effects of watching television shows and movies, playing video and computer games, reading magazines, and surfing the Web. But is there anything positive that can come from the important and extensive role of media in children's lives? Can media use be intellectually and cognitively beneficial? Dan Anderson, a professor of developmental psychology at the University of Massachusetts who has been studying television's potential as a teacher for four decades, has come to the conclusion that "educational television is *not* an oxymoron" (Anderson, 1998).

In this chapter, we consider the economic and regulatory forces that shape the availability of educational media for children today. Next, we examine different ways in which media have been found to be "educational" for children—specifically, the media's contribution to academic knowledge, creativity, and language development. From there, we consider whether there are contextual or medium-related differences in *how* children learn from media and *what* they can learn. The focus of this chapter is on the educational benefits of television, in part because this tends to be the medium of choice for most children and in part because this is the most thoroughly explored medium. When possible, we also consider the growing body of research on newer media, including computer use and video game playing.

Economic and Regulatory Forces That Affect Educational Media

Most companies that make media, including educational media for children, are part of mega-conglomerates that often own numerous media types (including magazines, movie production houses, television networks, music recording studios, Web sites) and sometimes numerous nonmedia companies. As of this writing, the Walt Disney Company, for example, has the Disney Channel, the ABC television network as well as Buena Vista Motion Pictures Group, Pixar Animation, and Hyperion books. Its many Web sites include Disney.com, ESPN.com, ABCNews.com, and Movies.com. As well, it owns many popular video game titles, theme parks, and kids' TV properties, including *Schoolhouse Rock*. The driving force behind all of media companies is the economic bottom line and accountability to the company shareholders. As such, the marketplace economy does not always work in the best interests of the developing child.

Regulation

Turow (1981) writes that the early days of television saw plenty of programs geared to children with the hope that child viewers would badger their parents into buying TV sets. Over the years, child-oriented programs were slowly replaced with programs for adults, in the expectation that adult audiences could lure more adverting dollars. By the 1970s, the lack of quality and quantity in children's programming led the public and advocacy groups such as the Action for Children's Television (ACT) to pressure the Federal Communications Commission (FCC) to step in (Kunkel & Wilcox, 2001). The FCC responded in 1974 by issuing guidelines calling upon broadcasters to make a "meaningful effort" to provide a "reasonable amount" of educational programming for children (Kunkel & Canepa, 1994). Regulators hoped that broadcasters would improve the quantity and quality of children's programming voluntarily, though the FCC warned broadcasters that if they did not do so, stricter rules would be forthcoming.

The result? By 1978, children's programming had not improved. ACT petitioned the FCC to conduct an inquiry into compliance with the 1974 Policy Statement, and within the year, the FCC had concluded that broadcasters had not met their obligations and recommended regulatory action. The commission proposed a minimum weekly requirement of children's programming (5 hours of educational programming for preschoolers and 2½ hours of educational programming for school-aged children). It also proposed defining "educational" as programs that addressed "history, science, literature, the environment, drama, music, fine arts, human relations, other cultures and languages, and basic skills such as reading and mathematics." The proposal languished.

Undeterred, advocates took up the cause with congressional leaders and ultimately gained passage of a piece of legislation known as the Children's Television Act (CTA) of 1990. Unlike other efforts at regulation, this bill emerged from Congress as an amendment to the Communications Act (implementation was left to the Federal Communications Commission), though the language was significantly modified (and watered down) from what the advocates were pressing for (Kunkel, 1998). Essentially, the CTA mandated that broadcasters serve the "educational/informational needs of children through the licensee's overall programming, including programming specifically designed to serve such needs."

Educational/informational programming was broadly defined as content that will "further the positive development of the child in any respect, including the child's cognitive/intellectual or emotional/social needs." Left undefined, however, were issues such as how much programming is enough, how age specific the programming needs to be, when the programming needs to air, and how the programming should be identified.

The Children's Television Act of 1990 did not dramatically change the landscape of children's television. Kunkel and Canepa (1994, p. 406) found inconsistencies in how licensees submitted their applications and dubious claims of "educational value" for programs such as *Teenage Mutant Ninja Turtles* and *G. I. Joe*. Lawmakers were ready to tighten the loopholes. By 1997, the FCC adopted a processing guideline wherein broadcasters would be fined for making false claims about their educational efforts on behalf of children (FCC, 1996).[2] In addition, the FCC processing guideline specified how much, when, and to whom such "core" educational programming must be directed to qualify for an expedited license renewal. See Figure 3.1 for a summary of the Three-Hour Rule guidelines for educational programming.

Has education as a significant purpose

Specifically addresses the needs of a child audience wherein children are defined as 16 and under

Is labeled as educational on the air and in printed listings

Airs between the hours of 7 a.m. and 10 p.m.

Is regularly scheduled

Is at least 30 minutes in length

Figure 3.1   Core Educational Programming Requirements

SOURCE: Federal Communications Commission MM Docket No. 93-48.

Despite a government mandate to provide informational/educational material to children over the public airwaves, some complain that it remains difficult to find shows that are enriching and beneficial (Jordan, 2004). Why are there not more high-quality programs available, and why are those that are available widely seen as less profitable for the networks than the lower-quality programs? Clearly, these concerns go hand in hand. If broadcasters could make more money on the high-quality, educational programs, they would be more likely to air them.

Economics

Television programs have traditionally received the bulk of their profits from advertising revenue (Jordan, 2004). Historically, companies that advertised to children through the medium of television were most interested in reaching the largest possible number of children between the ages of 2 and 12. Competition for advertisers' dollars in an ever crowded field led broadcasters to keep a close eye on the ratings. Advertisers buy blocks of time in children's programs "upfront," or before the new season actually begins, to get discount rates. For their part, the networks guarantee a certain level of ratings. If the programs don't reach expectations, networks must "make good" by providing free airtime elsewhere in their schedule (Jordan, 1996). Prior to the widespread proliferation of cable access, most broadcast networks aimed for the largest possible audience of 6- to 11-year-olds. Recent years have seen the adoption of the "niche programming" model, where narrower slices of the audience allow for a more focused tailoring of advertising messages. One example of this is the Disney Channel's discovery of the "tween" audience—children (primarily girls) who are not yet teenagers but no longer interested in cartoons.

The Disney Channel, unlike most commercial broadcast channels directed at young audiences, does not derive revenue from an advertising base, however. Their programs, such as the hugely popular *Hannah Montana,* find a second life on the sister station, ABC (which does receive ad dollars), and through product licensing and merchandising. In addition, many children's programs—particularly those geared to younger children—garner profits from DVD sales. Most often, a program, such as PBS' *Thomas the Tank Engine* series, develops loyal audiences who collect both the programs and the products that are licensed. Rarely will a program begin on DVD or VHS and later find a broadcast home. This was the case with Big Idea Productions' *VeggieTales,* based on biblical stories. The series had a firm audience base (established partly through Sunday school screenings) and was picked up by NBC to satisfy the FCC's "core educational programming" mandate (see Figure 3.2).

A final way in which children's programs make money is through international distribution (Jordan, 2004; Pecora, 1998). This presents challenges for educational TV producers. Though animated cartoons with a lot of action sequences dub easily and have storylines that are universally understandable, educational content may be less appealing to worldwide audiences. The WB's program *Histeria!,* which focused on teaching history lessons through humor and animation, did not contain content (e.g., details about the American Revolutionary War) that would be of much interest abroad. This program only lasted a few seasons.

Children's Learning From Media

As we see in the next chapter, most programs airing to fulfill the FCC requirements are what we might consider "prosocial"—programs that address children's ability to feel good about themselves and get along well with others (Jordan, 2004). In this chapter, however, we explore the relationship between children's media use and

Figure 3.2   NBC's *VeggieTales*
SOURCE: ©1999–2006 Big Idea, Inc.

their cognitive, intellectual, and academic skills. Though many have argued that entertainment media use is antithetical to learning (because it displaces time spent in more intellectually stimulating activities; see Healy, 1990), many have also linked children's media use to creativity, language development, school-related learning, and more (Anderson, Huston, Schmitt, Linebarger, & Wright, 2001).

The Lessons of *Sesame Street* and Educational Preschool Programming

Far and away, the majority of studies on preschool children's learning from television have involved *Sesame Street* (Fisch, Truglio, & Cole, 1999; see Figure 3.3). The program, launched in 1969, was designed by producer and founder Joan Ganz Cooney to address the gap between children who had access to preschool and other economic advantages and those who did not (Fisch & Truglio, 2001). In Cooney's words, "It's not whether children learn from television, it's what they learn" (Knowlton & Costigan, 2006). From the beginning, a research team was in place to ensure that children not only liked the characters and the programs but also learned from them. The data suggest that the program did then—and still does today—achieve its mission of making children more "ready-to-learn" (Fisch & Bernstein, 2001).

Through his research on *Sesame Street* and other programs such as *Gullah Gullah Island* and *Blue's Clues,* Anderson has provided convincing evidence that children are active and engaged viewers. In one clever study, Anderson and his colleagues replaced the *Sesame Street* soundtrack with Greek (Anderson, Lorch, Field,

Figure 3.3   PBS' *Sesame Street*

SOURCE: ©2005 Sesame Workshop.

& Sanders, 1981). They found that children paid less attention when they couldn't understand what they were watching. In another, he mixed up the narratives so that the bits did not make sense. Again, children paid less attention (Anderson et al., 1981). Anderson argues that children bring their learning skills to bear when they watch television, and if they determine that a program is nonsensical, they stop attending. This is a far different argument from social critics who have argued that television's fast cuts and funny voices are solely responsible for driving children's attention (Healy, 1990). Children want to understand television, and if they don't, they stop watching.

Sesame Street research has also indicated that children learn most when a parent is involved in the viewing. In fact, even if a mother is simply in the room coviewing and not saying anything, children learn more than if she is not present (though they learn most when the mother is actively engaged, talking and pointing things out) (Wright, St. Peters, & Huston, 1990). For this reason, the creators of *Sesame Street* put in content that only adults would understand or would find funny, such as the take-off on the opera singer Placido Domingo (on the show he is Placido Flamingo) or the inclusion of adult celebrities (such movie stars as Glenn Close or rock band REM). Despite this, parents' coviewing of *Sesame Street* has declined significantly over the years, to the point where producers determined that the adult-oriented portions of the program were providing few benefits to the majority of the audience watching along. Most of the adult-oriented content has therefore been stripped from the program (Fisch & Truglio, 2001).

Research on preschoolers' viewing of educational programming beyond *Sesame Street* also suggests learning benefits. Multiple viewing of the program *Blue's Clues*, in which a host encourages child viewers to help solve puzzles posed by his sidekick dog Blue, led to a greater increase in engagement with the program, an increase in specific attention skills, and the use of problem-solving strategies when compared to single viewing (Crawley, Anderson, Wilder, Williams, & Santomero, 1999) or the viewing of a noninteractive children's educational program (Crawley et al., 2002; see Figure 3.4).

Media and Make-Believe

Television and other entertainment media use—such as video game playing—is sometimes blamed for stifling children's creativity, imagination, and make-believe (or pretend) play. Since these are cognitive activities that are linked to language development, critical thinking, and abstract thinking, such an accusation should be taken seriously (Bellin & Singer, 2006). Certainly, children's imaginative play is influenced by their environment, including the presence or absence of electronic media, as well as their developmental stages. Valkenburg (2001) suggests that there are contradictory opinions about the influence of media, in particular television, on play and creativity. One line of thinking, which Valkenburg labels the "stimulation hypothesis," suggests that media enrich the store of ideas from which children can draw when engaged in imaginative play or creative tasks (p. 123). TV content

Figure 3.4   Nickelodeon's *Blue's Clues*

may be incorporated into pretend play, computer game settings may spark curiosity about other people and places, and music may set off images and emotions that might otherwise lay dormant. At least two preschool educational programs have been linked with increased imaginative play and creative thinking: *Mister Rogers' Neighborhood* (which includes a clear transition from the real-world setting for Fred Rogers' home to the Land of Make-Believe via trolley) (Anderson et al., 2001; Singer & Singer, 1976) and *Barney & Friends* (which has imagination—led by a big purple dinosaur—as a central tenet of the core curriculum) (Singer & Singer, 1998). Research on the viewing of these programs shows significant gains in creative and imaginative play when compared with the viewing of other children's programs. Importantly, however, gains are greatest when viewing is facilitated by adults, either parents or teachers (Singer & Singer, 1976).

An alternative hypothesis, which Valkenburg (2001) calls the "reduction hypothesis," suggests that media stifle children's creative capacities by replacing more cognitively stimulating activities (such as reading or playing with friends) with passive viewing and mindless surfing. In addition, some media (particularly those that have both audio and visual components) might be seen as supplanting children's imaginings with prefabricated pictures from which children have trouble disassociating (Runco & Pezdek, 1984; Valkenburg & Beentjes, 1997). Researchers looking specifically at the content of media have also argued that media violence adversely affects imaginative play, though it is not clear whether this is because children become more impulsive (Singer, Singer & Rapaczynski, 1984), or more anxious (Fein, 1981), or whether some other mechanism is at work.

Though there is little evidence that screen media use stimulates children's imaginative play and creativity (with the exception of a few preschool programs), there

Figure 3.5   PBS' *Barney & Friends*

is some suggestion that audio-visual media interventions can be designed to encourage play. *My Magic Story Car,* a video-based series designed to enhance children's play with the goal of building their early literacy skills, found quite positive effects when used in a classroom setting (Bellin & Singer, 2006). In this series, low-income, at-risk children and their caregivers were given explicit ideas for engaging in make-believe play. For example, adults help children assemble their own "magic story cars" (chairs, cushions, or cardboard boxes decorated with alphabet letters) with a "license plate" on which children are assisted in writing their names or initials. Child viewers drive their magic story cars to play learning games with make-believe narratives designed to strengthen specific emergent literacy and socioemotional skills (p. 107). Bellin and Singer found that, when compared to a control group, children who were exposed to the intervention showed significant gains in virtually all aspects of emergent literacy. The brilliance of this program is in the recognition that parents and caregivers have, in many ways, forgotten how to "play" in ways that are developmentally constructive. In addition, *My Magic Story Car* capitalizes on the ubiquity of the medium and children's affinity for it. Though similar claims have been made about the potential for video and computer games to stimulate creativity and imagination (Johnson, 2005), and though many of the games themselves claim to boost children's make-believe skills (Valkenburg, 2001), research in this area is lacking.

Media and Language Learning

Another way in which media may contribute to children's academic achievement is by acting as an "incidental language teacher" (Naigles & Mayeux, 2001). In the course of a recent study of families' use of television, researchers at the Annenberg Public Policy Center employed the Peabody Picture Vocabulary Test (PPVT) to assess vocabulary (Scantlin & Jordan, 2006). One 9-year-old boy was given the word *cascade* and asked to point to the picture that represented the word. The boy immediately did so correctly, asserting that he had learned the word from his favorite video game! Indeed, for decades, researchers (Rice, 1984, 1990) have asserted that television programs have the potential to encourage children to understand and use new words, though it is unclear whether media can effectively teach more complex language acquisition skills such as grammar (Naigles & Mayeux, 2001).

Program complexity and age appropriateness of the verbal content of media play an important role in language development. Linebarger and Walker (2004) examined the relationship between children's television viewing and their expressive language and vocabulary. Unlike most studies, which look cross-sectionally at children's cognitive abilities and their viewing patterns (making it difficult to establish causality), this study collected data on children's viewing every 3 months, beginning at 6 months of age and ending at about 30 months of age. Even when parent's education, child's home environment, and child's cognitive performance were statistically controlled, watching *Dora the Explorer, Blue's Clues, Arthur, Clifford,* or *Dragon Tales* resulted in greater vocabularies and higher expressive language scores; watching *Teletubbies* was related to fewer vocabulary words and smaller expressive language scores; watching *Sesame Street* was related only to smaller expressive language scores; and viewing *Barney* was related to fewer vocabulary words and more expressive language. What is interesting about this study is the notion that what kind of educational program children watched resulted in different cognitive outcomes. *Blue's Clues* and *Dora* are "interactive" shows, where children are encouraged to talk to the screen. *Sesame Street* is not (potentially explaining less gains in expressive language). *Barney* aims to engage children in creative and imaginative play but keeps its language fairly simple and straightforward (potentially explaining the gap in vocabulary word gain).

Lasting Effects of Exposure to Educational Media

In a 10-year longitudinal study of children from the time they were preschoolers to the time they were in high school, researchers in Massachusetts and Kansas found that children who watch educational television in the early years perform better some 10 years later, even when other important variables (such as family socioeconomic and the availability of books) are factored in. The researchers found that viewing educational versus entertainment programs was associated with greater gains, but some programs encouraged the development of some skills more than others. A similar study, which tracked two cohorts of German children over a 4-year period, also found that although educational program viewing was positively correlated with reading achievement, relations between entertainment program viewing and reading performance were negative (Ennemoser & Schneider, 2007). These important and groundbreaking studies ultimately concluded that McLuhan (1964) was wrong when he wrote, "The medium is the message." Rather, they argue, "the message is the message" (Anderson et al., 2001, p. 134).

When the Medium Is the Message

Despite what Anderson et al. (2001) argue, however, there are properties of media that seem to encourage the use of some cognitive skills or academic pursuits more than others. Studies of computer and video games suggest that visual attention,

Figure 3.6   Nickelodeon's *Dora the Explorer* and PBS' *Clifford the Big Red Dog*

peripheral vision, and spatial reasoning can be improved by game play (see, e.g., Okagaki & Frensch, 1994; Subrahmanyam & Greenfield, 1994). Jackson et al. (2006) found that children who were struggling as readers were helped by at-home use of the Internet (presumably because it encouraged the use of text-based information). Beal and Arroyo (2001) provided evidence that a user-driven computer game could effectively encourage the integration of math and science concepts above and beyond what a teacher alone can do with a classroom.

Time Spent With Media and Academic Achievement

In addition to tracking the kind of media and media content to which young viewers are exposed, it is also clear that it is critical to track the amount of time they spend with media. Several studies have shown that, over time, heavy media use is negatively associated with educational achievement (Fetler, 1984; Sharif & Sargent, 2007) and attention (Christakis, Zimmerman, DiGiuseppe, & McCarty, 2004). Of course, a key question is this: What constitutes "heavy" media use? Most researchers have found that less than 2 hours a day is optimum. In fact, the relationship between television time and academic achievement might be characterized as curvilinear—with the greatest benefits seen between 1 and 2 hours per day (Fetler, 1984; Williams, Haertel, Haertel, & Walberg, 1982). The relationship between media use and academic achievement is complicated by socioeconomic status, however. In an early study of California students' academic achievement and high school grades, Fetler (1984) found television viewing to be the most beneficial for students who had fewer economic resources and the least beneficial for students who were the most affluent. He hypothesizes that television can function as an educational resource if there is a dearth of educational opportunity, but for those who grow up in a relatively "rich" environment (with plenty of books, museum visits, etc.), viewing displaces more intellectually stimulating alternatives.

Though some might argue that the entrance of new media into the homes of children would displace children's television viewing, Rideout, Roberts, and Foehr (2005) have found that new media have supplemented it. Thus, children today watch as much television as children two decades ago. In fact, it appears that children who are heavy TV users are often heavy video game players, computer users, and music listeners (p. 21). In addition, many youth have become master multi-taskers. Most youth say that they use media when they do their homework "some" or "most of the time." Researchers have yet to determine if multitasking with media has a negative affect on academic achievement, however.

Learning to Learn From Media

Few scholars have recognized the fact that children are not born using media—indeed, as much as children are socialized by media, they are socialized to use media in particular ways. Social psychologist Gavriel Salomon systematically explored how children's preconceptions about a medium—for example, that print is "hard" and television is "easy"—shapes the amount of mental effort they will invest in processing the medium. This amount of invested mental effort, or AIME, is defined as "the number of non-automatic mental elaborations applied to the material" (Salomon, 1984). AIME, in turn, shapes how much children will take away from the medium; that is, how much they might learn. The contexts of a child's life will contribute to how "shallowly" or how "deeply" viewers process mediated information (Cohen & Salomon, 1979). For example, comparisons of Israeli children and American children during the 1970s showed that, even when IQ was accounted for, Israeli children learned more from television programming than their American counterparts. He reasoned that this was because at the time of his studies, Israelis used television primarily as a news source. Salomon also found that the perceived demand characteristics (PDCs) of a medium could be altered. Children who were told that they would be asked questions about what they viewed, or who were told to pay attention because the material was hard, did in fact pay more attention and did in fact learn more (Salomon, 1983).

AIME theory begs the question of how children come to think about media as fulfilling particular uses or gratifying particular needs. Van Evra (1998) suggests that since much of television is entertainment, children develop a particular schema for how much processing is required—a schema that will drive viewing of even educational programming. While preschool programming, particularly that which airs on PBS, has historically had a mission to educate, the past decade has seen a virtual explosion of educational offerings for children—and novel approaches for getting children engaged with the material. Research with the program *Blue's Clues* has been an interesting case study. The producers of the program designed the series to be "interactive," mimicking Mr. Rogers' (*Mister Rogers' Neighborhood*) style of speaking and pausing as though he were talking with the young viewers themselves. Assessments of viewers' reactions to the series indicate that the program encouraged a novel style of TV watching—one in which

Figure 3.7

preschoolers talk to characters, shout out solutions to problems, and generally "interact" with what is on the screen. These *Blue's Clues*–induced viewing styles, moreover, translated to the viewing of other programs, including noninteractive ones such as Cartoon Network's *Big Bag* (Crawley et al., 2002).

We know very little about how children learn to use nontelevision media during the first 5 years of life, though research by the Kaiser Family Foundation suggests that media are plentiful in the homes of preschoolers and that, in a typical day, 83% of 6-month-old to 6-year-old children watch television, 32% watch videos or DVDs, 16% use computers, and 11% play video games (Rideout & Hamel, 2006). Lessons about when and how to use media may come from parents, siblings, day care providers, and teachers. An observational study of a child care center serving low-income urban minority youth found that though television was used often and for several hours during the course of a typical day, teachers did not attempt to use it as a medium of instruction (Jordan, 2005). Rather, videotapes of educational programs were put on to help teachers transition children from one activity to another or for "quiet time." Unlike the use of books in the center, the educational potential of these videotapes was neither extended nor explored in other settings.

Conclusion

In one version of an ideal world, children would spend their time with more high-quality, enriching media products and less time with entertainment-only content that, at best, wastes their time and, at worst, is detrimental to their cognitive development. Of course, in an ideal world, adults would do the same—forsaking the fluff and the junk for media designed to improve their knowledge of the world and culture. But the fact of the matter is that neither children nor adults always (or even usually) watch television, play video games, or go online with such lofty goals. It would be unrealistic, if not unfair, to condemn the pure entertainment value the media play in our lives. Unfortunately, much of what is in the "pure entertainment" is potentially deleterious for children. One report found that the majority of TV programs for children were "low quality" (primarily entertainment-oriented programs with heavy doses of violence) (Jordan, 1996). This study also found that the "high-quality" (educational, age-appropriate) programs were not getting the kinds of high ratings that the low-quality programs received (Jordan, 1996).

Media makers have a belief that if children think that something is good for them, they will reject it. (This is known in industry circles, as well as in parenting circles, as the "spinach syndrome" [Jordan, 2004].) This is partly why so much educational media matter is devoted to preschoolers—to them, all learning is fun! One very important job in the "work" of childhood, however, is developing a sense of how one should spend time—how much of it should be devoted to goofing off and how much of it should be focused on getting bigger, stronger, and smarter. Children don't always make the "healthiest" choices when it comes to media. But they shouldn't be expected to automatically do so or be expected to figure it out for themselves. Imagine, for example, if it was left to the child to determine what he or she would eat for breakfast, lunch, and dinner (French fries, candy bars, and milkshakes?). We don't let them make such choices because we know their choices wouldn't be the best ones. Responsible parents (and media makers) offer children a variety of foods (which may include the occasional Happy Meal with the regular chicken, broccoli, and milk), encourage them to make healthy choices, and teach them the benefits of consuming a balanced diet—whether it is a diet of food or a diet of media. Eventually, we hope, children develop a taste for the "good stuff" so that they can grow up to be smart and active adults.

Exercises

1. Watch television on Saturday mornings and see if you can find the educational shows that commercial broadcast stations are offering to children. You can tell by the "e/i" symbol that is on the screen throughout the show. Can you tell what the "lesson" of the show is?

2. Think back to some of the make-believe games that you played as a child. Did your parents play pretend games with you? Ask them!

3. *Sesame Street* is the most researched show on television—and also the most enduring. If you haven't watched it for a while, tune in and see if you can figure out the ways that it has changed.

4. Even though *Barney & Friends* has been found to be a truly educational program for children, parents complain loudly about it. What is it about the program that makes it so endearing to kids and so maddening to parents?

5. Go to a store that sells computer games for children and look at the back of the box to see what kind of "educational" claims they are making about the product. Think about how you, as a researcher, would test whether there is any substance to back the claims.

6. One study found that children who were below grade level in reading significantly improved their reading skills by having access to the Internet at home. Think about your own Internet use. How much of the time would you say you spend reading (vs. watching television episodes or movie trailers!)?

7. Design an educational media product for children that you think fills the gap in the current landscape of offerings for children. The product should be theoretically driven and empirically justified. What would it look like?

Notes

1. On average, children spend nearly 4 hours (3:51) watching television (including videos and DVDs); 1¾ hours (1:44) listening to the radio or to CDs, tapes, or MP3 players; just over 1 hour (1:02) on the computer outside of schoolwork; and just under 1 hour (:49) playing video games. By contrast, children say they read for pleasure 43 minutes a day (books, magazines, newspapers). These data, collected in 2005 by the Kaiser Family Foundation and based on a national sample of 3rd to 12th graders, suggest the vast potential media have for contributing to children's cognitive development. This seems particularly

true when one contrasts children's media time with the amount spent hanging out with parents (2:17), doing homework (:50), or doing chores (:32) (Rideout et al., 2005).

2. In 2007, Univision received a fine of over a million dollars for labeling a telenovela (Spanish-language soap opera for adults) as educational for children (Ahrens, 2007).

References

Ahrens, F. (2007, February 25). FCC expected to impose record $24 million fine against Univision. *The Washington Post*, Sunday Final Edition.

Anderson, D. (1998). Educational television is not an oxymoron. *Annals of the American Academy of Political and Social Science, 557,* 24–38.

Anderson, D., Huston, A., Schmitt, K., Linebarger, D., & Wright, J. (2001). Early childhood television viewing and adolescent behavior. *Monographs of the Society for Research in Child Development, 68*(Serial No. 264), 1–143.

Anderson, D. R., Lorch, E. P., Field, D. E., & Sanders, J. (1981). The effects of TV program comprehensibility on preschool children's visual attention to television. *Child Development, 52,* 151–157.

Beal, C., & Arroyo, I. (2002). The AnimalWatch project: Creating an intelligent computer mathematics tutor. In S. Calvert, A. Jordan, & R. Cocking (Eds.), *Children in the digital age: Influences of electronic media on development* (pp. 183–198). Westport, CT: Praeger.

Bellin, H., & Singer, D. (2006). My Magic Story Car: Video-based play intervention to strengthen emergent literacy of at-risk preschoolers. In D. Singer, R. Golinkoff, & K. Hirsh-Pasek (Eds.), *Play = learning: How play motivates and enhances children's cognitive and social-emotional growth* (pp. 101–123). Oxford, UK: Oxford University Press.

Christakis, D. A., Zimmerman, F. J., DiGiuseppe, D. L., & McCarty, C. A. (2004). Early television exposure and subsequent attentional problems in children. *Pediatrics, 113,* 708–713.

Cohen, A., & Salomon, G. (1979). Children's literate television viewing: Surprises and possible explanations. *Journal of Communication, 29*(3), 156–163.

Crawley, A., Anderson, D., Santomero, A., Wilder, A., Williams, M., Evans, M., et al. (2002). Do children learn how to watch television? The impact of extensive experience with *Blue's Clues* on preschool children's television viewing behavior. *Journal of Communication, 52*(2), 264–279.

Crawley, A., Anderson, D., Wilder, A., Williams, M., & Santomero, A. (1999). Effects of repeated exposures to a single episode of the television program *Blue's Clues* on the viewing behaviors and comprehension of preschool children. *Journal of Educational Psychology, 91,* 630–637.

Ennemoser, M., & Schneider, W. (2007). Relations of television viewing and reading: Findings from a 4-year longitudinal study. *Journal of Educational Psychology, 99*(2), 349–368.

Federal Communications Commission (FCC). (1996). In the matter of policies and rules concerning children's television programming: Report and order. *Federal Communications Commission Record, 11,* 10660–10778.

Fetler, M. (1984). Television viewing and school achievement. *Journal of Communication, 34*(2), 104–118.

Fein, G. G. (1981). Pretend play in childhood: An integrative review. *Child Development, 52,* 1095–1118.

Fisch, S., & Bernstein, L. (2001). Formative research revealed: Methodological and process issues in formative research. In S. Fisch & R. Truglio (Eds.), *"G" is for growing* (pp. 39–60). Mahwah, NJ: Lawrence Erlbaum.

Fisch, S., & Truglio, R. (Eds.). (2001). *"G" is for growing.* Mahwah, NJ: Lawrence Erlbaum.

Fisch, S., Truglio, R., & Cole, C. (1999). The impact of *Sesame Street* on preschool children: A review and synthesis of 30 years' research. *Media Psychology, 1,* 165–190.

Healy, J. (1990). *Endangered minds: Why our children don't think.* New York: Simon & Schuster.

Hearold, S. (1986). A synthesis of 1043 effects of television on social behavior. In G. Comstock (Ed.), *Public communication and behavior* (Vol. 1, pp. 65–133). Orlando, FL: Academic Press.

Jackson, L. A., von Ey, A., Biocca, F., Barbatsis, G., Zhao, Y., & Fitzgerald, H. (2006). Does home Internet use influence the academic performance of low-income children? *Developmental Psychology, 42,* 429–435.

Johnson, S. (2005). *Everything bad is good for you: How today's popular culture is actually making us smarter.* New York: Riverhead.

Jordan, A. (1996). *The state of children's television: An examination of quantity, quality and industry beliefs* (Report No. 2, the Annenberg Public Policy Center). Philadelphia: University of Pennsylvania Press.

Jordan, A. (2004). The three-hour rule and educational television for children. *Popular Communication, 2*(2), 103–119.

Jordan, A. (2005). Learning to use books and television: An exploratory study in the ecological perspective. *American Behavioral Scientist, 48*(5), 523–538.

Knowlton, L., & Costigan, L. (Producers/Directors). (2006). *The world according to* Sesame Street [Documentary]. (2006). United States: Participant Productions.

Kunkel, D. (1998). Policy battles over defining children's educational television. *Annals of the American Academy of Political and Social Sciences, 557,* 39–53.

Kunkel, D., & Canepa, J. (1994). Broadcasters' license renewal claims regarding children's educational programming. *Journal of Broadcasting and Electronic Media, 38,* 397–416.

Kunkel, D., & Wilcox, B. (2001). Children and media policy. In D. Singer & J. Singer (Eds.), *The handbook of children and media* (pp. 589–604). Thousand Oaks, CA: Sage.

Linebarger, D., & Walker, D. (2004). Infants' and toddlers' television viewing and language outcomes. *American Behavioral Scientist, 46,* 1–22.

McLuhan, M. (1964). *Understanding media: The extension of man.* New York: McGraw-Hill.

Naigles, L., & Mayeux, L. (2001). Television as incidental language teacher. In D. Singer & J. Singer (Eds.), *The handbook of children and media* (pp. 135–152). Thousand Oaks, CA: Sage.

Okagaki, L., & Frensch, P. (1994). Effects of video game playing on measures of spatial performance: Gender effects in late adolescence. *Journal of Applied Developmental Psychology, 15,* 33–58.

Pecora, N. (1998). *The business of children's entertainment.* New York: Guilford.

Rice, M. (1984). The words of children's television. *Journal of Broadcasting, 28,* 445–461.

Rice, M. (1990). Preschoolers' QUIL: Quick incidental learning of words. In G. Conti-Ransden & C. Snow (Eds.), *Children's language* (Vol. 7). Hillsdale, NJ: Lawrence Erlbaum.

Rideout, V., & Hamel, E. (2006, May). *The media family: Electronic media in the lives of infants, toddlers, preschoolers and their parents* (Report No. 7500). Menlo Park, CA: Kaiser Family Foundation.

Rideout, V., Roberts, D., & Foehr, U. (2005). *Generation M: Media in the lives of 8–18 year-olds.* Menlo Park, CA: Kaiser Family Foundation.

Runco, M. A., & Pezdek, K. (1984). The effect of television and radio on children's creativity. *Human Communication Research, 11,* 109–120.

Salomon, G. (1983). Television watching and mental effort: A social psychological view. In D. Anderson & J. Bryant (Eds.), *Children's understanding of television: Research on attention and comprehension* (pp. 181–198). New York: Academic Press.

Salomon, G. (1984). Television is "easy" and print is "tough": The differential investment of mental effort as a function of perceptions and attributions. *Journal of Educational Psychology, 76,* 647–658.

Scantlin, R., & Jordan, A (2006). Families' experiences with the V-chip: An exploratory study. *Journal of Family Communication, 6*(2), 139–159.

Sharif, I., & Sargent, J. (2007). Association between television, movie, and video game exposure and school performance. *Pediatrics, 118,* e1061–e1070.

Singer, J. L., & Singer, D. G. (1976). Can TV stimulate imaginative play? *Journal of Communication, 26*(3), 74–80.

Singer, J. L., & Singer, D. G. (1998). Barney & Friends as entertainment and education: Evaluating the quality and effectiveness of a television series for preschool children. In J. K. Asamen & G. Berry (Eds.), *Research paradigms, television, and social behavior* (pp. 305–367). Beverly Hills, CA: Sage.

Singer, J. L., Singer, D. G., & Rapaczynski, W. S. (1984). Family patterns and television viewing as predictors of children's beliefs and aggression. *Journal of Communication, 34*(2), 73–89.

Subrahmanyam, K., & Greenfield, P. (1994). Effect of video game practice on spatial skills in girls and boys. *Journal of Applied Developmental Psychology, 15,* 13–32.

Turow, J. (1981). *Entertainment, education and the hard sell: Three decades of network children's television.* New York: Praeger.

Valkenburg, P. (2001). Television and the child's developing imagination. In D. Singer & J. Singer (Eds.), *Handbook of children and media* (pp. 121–134). Thousand Oaks, CA: Sage.

Valkenburg, P., & Beentjes, J. (1997). Children's creative imagination in response to radio and television stories. *Journal of Communication, 47*(2), 21–38.

Van Evra, J. (1998). *Television and child development.* Mahwah, NJ: Lawrence Erlbaum.

Williams, P. A., Haertel, E. H., Haertel, G. D., & Walberg, H. J. (1982). The impact of leisure time television on school learning: A research synthesis. *American Educational Research Journal, 19*(1), 19–50.

Wright, J., St. Peters, M., & Huston, A. (1990). Family television use and its relation to children's cognitive skills and social behavior. In J. Bryant (Ed.), *Television and the American family* (pp. 227–251). Hillsdale, NJ: Lawrence Erlbaum.

CHAPTER 4

Prosocial Effects of Media

Though the term *prosocial* is often bandied about by the media industry, federal regulators, academics, and advocates, there is not necessarily a shared definition within or between groups. Most writers suggest that prosocial media content is somehow socially helpful (such as that which promotes altruism, friendliness, acceptance of diversity, and cooperation). Others would include content that is more personally helpful (calming fears, engaging in safer sex practices, eating healthfully). In this chapter, we use the definition provided in one of the first comprehensive reports of the positive effects of the media written in the 1970s, titled "Television and Behavior." The author defines *prosocial* as that which is "socially desirable and which in some way benefits other persons or society at large" (quoted in Lowery & DeFleur, 1995, p. 354).

Any definition of *prosocial* involves some level of value judgment. Some might argue that a program that emphasizes "looking out for #1" prepares a child better for a competitive world than one that instills values of "cooperation." Despite this caveat, we examine studies that have explored the benefits of prosocial media in its traditional sense. Most of the landmark studies were conducted in the 1970s, in response to increased federal funding to investigate the positive role of television in children's lives (this, on the heels of the Surgeon General's report outlining the negative role of television—particularly the deleterious consequences of TV violence) (Lowery & DeFleur, 1995). The studies reviewed in this chapter are mainly focused on television content, though by extension, many of the findings would hold true for DVD and videotape viewing of the programs. Less clear is the impact of other electronic media—including computer and video games, Internet social Web sites (including networking sites), music, or magazines.

Many studies have found that children's emotional and social skills are linked to their early academic standing (e.g., Wentzel & Asher, 1995). Children who have difficulty paying attention in class, getting along with their peers, and controlling their own negative emotions of anger and distress do less well in school (Arnold et al., 1999; McLelland, Morrison, & Holmes, 2000). What's more, longitudinal studies suggest that this link may be causal: "For many children, academic achievement in their first few years of schooling appears to be built on a firm foundation of children's emotional and social skills" (Raver, 2002, p. 3). Specifically, research on early schooling suggests that the relationships that children build with peers and teachers are (a) based on children's ability to regulate emotions in prosocial versus antisocial ways, and (b) a "source of provisions" that either help or hurt children's chances of doing well, academically, in school (Ladd, Birch, & Buhs, 1999, p. 1375).

Developmental psychologists believe that children have a set of "emotional competencies" that determine how they think about and handle their own and others' emotions (Saarni, 1990). For example, a child's ability to recognize and label different emotions gives him or her powerful social tools. Children's emotional styles are thought to be influenced not only by their temperament but also by their environments. Certainly, parents' uses of warmth, control, and harshness in the home matter (see Chapter 12). Media may matter too. As we shall see in a moment, media have been shown to be effective at developing skills such as altruism and cooperation in young viewers.

Prosocial Media for Children

In the early days of television, the limited offerings of the networks featured many "family-friendly" prosocial programs such as *Lassie, Captain Kangaroo,* and *The Waltons.* Through the 1970s and early 1980s, content analyses revealed that children's favorite programs often featured portrayals of empathy, altruism, and an exploration of feelings (Palmer, 1988). Networks soon discovered, however, that more money could be made on so-called program-length commercials—cartoons that were mainly vehicles for selling toys such as action figures (Kunkel, 1988). As a consequence, prosocial television declined through the 1980s and mid-1990s (Calvert & Kotler, 2003). The Children's Television Act of 1990 aimed to reverse that trend, but it really wasn't until the Federal Communications Commission (FCC) processing guideline went into effect—explicitly stating a minimum requirement of 3 hours per week of educational television—that the landscape of children's television began to include more prosocial television. Today, more than three quarters of the commercial broadcasters' educational offerings are "prosocial" shows (Jordan, 2004).

How Do Prosocial Media Affect Youth?

Researchers who study children's prosocial learning from media typically work under the assumption that characters who behave kindly, cooperatively, responsibly, and altruistically are providing models that children can learn from and subsequently imitate. Much of this research is grounded in Bandura's social cognitive theory, which originally explored how televised aggression might be imitated under certain conditions (see Chapter 5), but has also looked at prosocial behavior that might result from media exposure. Generally speaking, the mechanism goes like this: Children observe a character behave in a positive manner. That behavior is more likely to be imitated if the character (a) is realistic, (b) is similar to the child (for example, in age or gender), (c) receives positive reinforcement, and (d) carries out an action that is imitable by the child (Thomas, 2005).

Prosocial content may also be providing children with skills for dealing with their emotions and managing their moods. As noted at the beginning of the chapter, children are born with temperament but look to their environments to learn emotional competencies—for example, ways to feel better about themselves or get through a bad day. *Sesame Street* has, in its three decades on the air, taught children about emotional coping in its curricular goals. It has addressed the scariness of hurricanes, the jealousy that arrives with a new sibling, and even the uncertainty that came after the 2001 terrorist attacks. However, we know very little about the efficacy of these storylines. Similarly, *Mister Rogers' Neighborhood* produced many episodes for children on topics that scared them or made them uncomfortable. (Indeed, there is a large body of research on children's management of their fright reactions to media. See, for example, Cantor, 2001.)

A third potential mechanism underlying the relationship between media content and prosocial behavior may be that prosocial content offers children "scripts" for dealing with unfamiliar situations. According to schema or script theory, a schema is an organized structure of knowledge about a topic or event that is stored in memory and helps a person assimilate new information (Mandler, 1984). Schema theory suggests that people possess schemas for emotions, which include information about facial expressions, the cause of feelings, and the appropriate ways of expressing feelings. Children use schemas to help them interpret what they encounter in the media. In turn, media content can contribute to a child's schemas. Cultivation theory, described in Chapter 5, has found that, over time, heavy TV viewers tend to adopt beliefs about the world that are consistent with television's portrayal of the world. In other words, children who watch a lot of TV featuring crime or hospitals may come to see the world as a mean and scary place (Gerbner, Gross, Signorielli, & Morgan, 1986).

The Research Evidence

Empathy

Social learning theory, emotional competency theory, and schema theory might all be used to understand children's development of empathy, or the ability of children to understand and relate to another's feelings by taking his or her perspective. Many would argue that the ability of humans to empathize with others is both hardwired and learned. Developmental psychologists who follow the Piagetian tradition would argue that it is not until children are 6 or 7 years old that they are "sociocentric" enough to understand that not everyone sees the world or events as they do. In one famous experiment, children were put in front of a constructed three-dimensional mountain with different objects placed on it. Piaget asked the child to choose from four pictures which view the experimenter would see (the experimenter was standing on the opposite side of the mountain). Younger children selected the picture of the view that they themselves saw (Thomas, 2005). From this experiment and others, Piaget argued that children have difficulty under-standing others' perspectives, including understanding how they might feel. By the time children reach school age, they become more tuned into the feelings and needs of others.

Research suggests that child audiences can recognize the feelings of media char-acters, though it appears that younger children are less likely to experience the character's feelings (that is, empathize with them) than older children. In one study, 3- to 5-year-olds and 9- to 11-year-olds watched a scary movie clip. For one clip, a threatening "stimulus" was shown. For the other, a character's fear in response to the threatening stimulus was shown. Older children were more fright-ened and physiologically aroused than the younger children, though all children recognized the character as frightened (Wilson & Cantor, 1985).

Calvert and Kotler (2003) examined a more recent crop of prosocial programs for elementary school-age youth airing on commercial broadcast, cable, and public television. Their two-pronged study involved second to sixth graders in both a nat-uralistic reporting methodology (in which children logged onto a Web site and reported on what they were watching and what they learned) as well as an experi-mental methodology (in which children were shown programs in the classroom and asked about them afterwards). Their research suggests that school-age children learn from prosocial programs even more so than from traditional, school-related educa-tional shows. Moreover, much of what the children seemed to be learning is how to identify the emotions of characters and apply what they learn to their own lives. As this sixth-grade girl in the experimental condition wrote about the program *Anatole*, "This program was about a little mouse who tried her hardest in singing but just couldn't do it. The mouse gave up and ripped her opera notes up because of her frustration. When her dad (Papa) met an Opera singer named Renee, he knew that if his daughter heard her singing, she would have kept her confidence. And she did. She learned that just because you are not good at something doesn't mean you have to give up. And that is the lesson that I will keep in mind when I get frustrated with something I am not good at" (quoted in Calvert & Kotler, 2003, p. 316).

Altruism/Helping

One of the first studies of the impact of prosocial television came with the program *Lassie*, which ran from 1954 to 1974 on commercial broadcast TV. The show featured an extraordinary collie, who was devoted to his family and, in par-ticular, the boy owner (Jeff). Because of his devotion and intelligence, Lassie often helped them out of dangerous situations. In the Sprafkin, Liebert, and Poulos (1975) experiment, first-grade children saw one of three TV shows. In one condi-tion, they saw a prosocial episode of *Lassie* in which Jeff rescues a puppy. In the second, they viewed a "neutral" episode of Jeff trying to avoid taking violin lessons.

In the third, the children watched a "competitive" episode of the *Brady Bunch*. After viewing the television program, children were told to play a game to win points and prizes. They were also told that if they needed assistance, they could press a "help" button, though that would mean they would need to stop playing the game and presumably be less likely to win a prize. Children could hear dogs barking with increasing intensity and distress through the experimental period (the barking was, of course, prerecorded). Children who saw the prosocial episode of *Lassie* condition were nearly twice as likely to seek help as children in the neutral condition. Children in the competitive condition were the least likely to seek help.

Social Interaction

In a 1979 study of *Mister Rogers' Neighborhood*, Friedrich-Cofer, Huston-Stein, Kipnis, Susman, and Clewett explored the effects of daily exposure to different kinds of television over a 2-month period on preschool children's social interactions with one another. All of the children were enrolled in Head Start programs. In one classroom, children watched *Mister Rogers*, and teachers were trained and relevant play material was provided. In a second classroom, children watched *Mister Rogers*, but teachers had no training. Relevant play material was provided. In the third, children viewed *Mister Rogers*, but there was neither teacher training nor program-related play material. In the final condition, children watched "neutral" films, with irrelevant play material in the classroom. Researchers observed children's natural social behaviors in the classroom and on the playground before

Figure 4.1   PBS' *Mister Rogers' Neighborhood*

SOURCE: ©2001 Family Communications, Inc. and PBS.

and after the 2 months' worth of viewing. They found that positive interactions with peers increased the most in the condition where children had exposure to prosocial programming, teachers were trained, and relevant play material was provided. Prosocial television alone, however, led to few differences in children's behavior, at least in this early study.

A second program that has been extensively studied is *Barney & Friends*. This program, which features a big purple dinosaur and emphasizes kindness and good manners, has been found to have a positive effect on children from diverse regions in the United States. Similar to the *Mister Rogers* study described above, day care centers were assigned to either a viewing or a viewing plus lessons condition or a no-viewing control group. Even without the accompanying lessons, children who viewed *Barney* were rated as more civil and having better manners.

Acceptance of Others/Acceptance of Diversity

A major goal of the program *Sesame Street* has been to highlight the diversity of American life and to model racial harmony. Program characters are African Americans, Latino Americans, White Americans, American Indians, and Asian Americans. Even its Muppets are different colors! In 1989, in response to increasing racial unrest, the producers and researchers at Sesame Workshop (the nonprofit production company that makes the program) designed a curriculum to encourage friendship among people of different races and cultures. Preschool viewers were encouraged to perceive people who look different from themselves as possible friends and to bring a child who has been rejected because of physical and/or cultural differences into the group. Truglio, Lovelace, Segui, and Schneider (2001) write that initially, there was some doubt as to whether race relations was truly an issue for preschoolers. However, a review of the literature, along with meetings with experts, revealed that preschoolers were aware of racial differences. Their formative research suggested that ethnic minority children felt less good about themselves and that White children were more likely to segregate African American children in an imaginary neighborhood they were asked to create. However, most of the children were open to the idea of being friends with children of different races.

One very interesting study analyzed two segments for *Sesame Street* that were created to address racial harmony and interaction. In one, "Visiting Ieshia," a White girl visits an African American girl in her home. The other, "Play Date," shows a similar family visit with an African American boy in his home and his White friend. Researchers at Sesame Workshop found that children liked the segments and identified with and remembered them. Most of the children who viewed the episodes stated that the visiting White child felt positive about being at Ieshia's home (70%) and Jamal's home (58%). However, less than one half of the children who viewed "Play Date" felt that the African American mother in the film (48%) and the White mother of the visiting boy (39%) felt happy about the visit. Why? Preschoolers perceived their own mothers as not feeling positively about other-race friendships, even after viewing friendly and inviting images of parents in "Play Date." From these findings, the researchers recommended that in future segments, mothers and

Figure 4.2   PBS' *Sesame Street*
SOURCE: ©2005 Sesame Workshop.

fathers needed to have a more prominent role in expressing support about the child character's friendships with children of different races before, during, and after these visits. They also suggested that the segments show the parents of the different-race children interacting and expressing the positive value of making good friends (Truglio et al., 2001).

The Limitations of Research on Prosocial Content for Children

It is unfortunate that so few studies have investigated the potential benefits of prosocial programming for children, particularly when there are so many programs now being offered by commercial broadcasters to satisfy the 3-hour rule. As Mares and Woodard (2001) point out, there are still many unanswered questions about how best to design prosocial content for children. First, does children's exposure to specific prosocial models (such as donating money) translate into more "general kindness" or "goodness"? They argue that such a link has been found in exposure to antisocial models (with, of course, the opposite effect) and that despite the fact that the research could be carried out fairly easily, it never has. The popular series *American Idol,* for example, televised a double episode called "Idol Gives Back" in which the judges spotlighted the ravages of poverty, including the desperate plight of AIDS-afflicted mothers and children in Africa. By modeling charitable behavior (one of the episode's hosts, Ellen DeGeneres, donated $100,000 and the program's host, Ryan Seacrest, went to Africa and cared for dying women and children), they raised a total of $60 million. Children watching the program asked their parents to give and pledged their own allowances. But is this generosity fleeting, or have children's beliefs and behaviors been affected in the longer term?

There is also a question about what kind of prosocial portrayal is most effective for different ages. For example, Mares and Woodard (2001) argue that "the combination of aggression and a prosocial theme is particularly pernicious. That is, showing violence and mayhem in the cause of social justice or followed by a rapid conclusion in which the villains are punished for their aggression may be more deleterious to children's prosocial interactions than showing violence unadulterated by any prosocial theme" (p. 195). One study by Krcmar and Valkenberg (1999) found that 6- to 12-year-olds could easily reason that "unjustified violence" is wrong in an abstract, hypothetical situation. However, those children who were heavy viewers of the fantasy violence program *Power Rangers* were more likely to judge "justified" aggression in the hypothetical scenarios as morally correct, while those who seldom watched the program did not. One might argue that children who see the world in this way (that is, that justified violence is morally right) are drawn to superhero-type shows such as *Power Rangers.* Krcmar and Curtis (2003) conducted an experiment in which 5- to 14-year-olds were randomly assigned to one of three conditions: One watched an action cartoon that featured characters arguing and eventually engaging in violence, another watched a similar clip involving an argument but the characters walked away instead of fighting, and a control group did not watch television. Afterward, the subjects listened to and judged four hypothetical stories involving violence. Children who had watched the violent program were subsequently more likely than those in the control group to judge the violence as morally acceptable. They also exhibited less sophisticated moral reasoning in their responses (for example, they relied on punishment as rationale—"don't hit or you'll get in trouble").

Not only is much of children's superhero programming portrayed with conflicting pro- and antisocial messages, so too is the adult programming that is popular with young audiences. The Fox program *24* has been roundly criticized for having its hero, Jack Bauer, use torture against his enemies (including his bad-guy brother) to save the world from disaster (Moritz, 2007). Similarly, if one aim is to have children imitate constructive, prosocial behavior, what is the best way to promote that? Should the reward be intrinsic or extrinsic? Should children be shown how to carry this behavior over into their own lives? The program *Captain Planet* highlighted the ecological problems facing the world—problems that were solved by superheroes called "planeteers." At the end of the program, however, children were shown exactly what they could do in their own homes and communities to be a "planeteer" too. Behaviors included recycling newspapers, making birdhouses, and picking up litter.

One of the few studies to examine the impact of production values on the takeaway value of a prosocial program tracked elementary school children's reaction to a popular family sitcom, *Full House,* in which a young character was trying to cope with anxiety about earthquakes or taking a fall while trying to learn how to ride a bicycle. In addition, half of the children were exposed to a humorous subplot that was interspersed with the main plot (the other half saw no subplot). The study revealed that while the subplot reduced the younger children's (5- to 7-year-olds) comprehension of the emotional event in the storyline, it had no impact on older children's comprehension. Thus, it is clear that research needs to account for the developmental differences of audiences when examining the potential benefits of prosocial content. As described earlier, Georgetown researchers Calvert and Kotler (2003) argued that at least for school-age children, prosocial program content is even more "educational" than academic-oriented shows that feature science, literature, or math. As Jordan (2003) points out, however, it is difficult to know whether the children remember the lessons better because they have been ingrained in them since they were toddlers (share, be nice, etc.) or whether it is because the narrative structure is more entertaining and engaging.

Prosocial Media for Adolescents

The great majority of research on prosocial effects of media has involved children, especially very young children (Hogan & Strasburger, 2008). Only a handful of studies and experiments have specifically examined the possibility of prosocial effects of media on adolescents (Mares & Woodard, 2001, 2005). A recent meta-analysis of 35 prosocial studies found that the impact of prosocial content seems to peak at age 7 and fall off rapidly after that (Mares & Woodard, 2005), so that teenagers may be relatively "immune" to such influences or simply too egocentric to be affected. One of the earliest and classic experiments involved assigning 60 young people, ages 9, 13, and 16, to view one of two versions of *The Mod Squad*. In the violent version, a police captain who is framed for bribery gets even with the villain. In the prosocial version, everything is worked out through negotiation. The subjects were then placed in front of a "help/hurt" machine in a mock experimental situation. Those who had viewed the prosocial version spent more time pressing the help button and less time pressing the hurt button (Collins & Getz, 1976). In an intriguing use of prosocial TV, Elias (1983) used a 5-week series of 10 prosocial videos about dealing with teasing, bullying, and peer pressure to help treat a group of 109 boys, ages 7 to 15 years, who had serious emotional disturbances. Compared with control subjects, the boys were rated as less isolated and less troubled, and this effect lasted as long as 2 months after the videos were seen. Media popular with teens can also be used to teach them about important subjects. For example, Singer and Singer (1994) developed and tested an effective adolescent health education mini-curriculum using five episodes of *Degrassi Junior High* with teens and preteens in Grades 5 to 8.

Content analyses have also found that prosocial content is relatively rare. An analysis of the top 20 shows for children and teens ages 2 to 17 found that only two contained themes of altruism, antiviolence, or friendliness in the episodes analyzed (Mares & Woodard, 2005). An older analysis of the most popular shows among fourth, sixth, and eighth graders found that there were as many antisocial acts as prosocial acts depicted (Greenberg, Atkin, Edison, & Korzenny, 1980). However, the most recent analysis of 2,227 programs on 18 different channels found that 73% of the programs featured altruistic acts, with a rate of 2.92 incidents per hour (Smith et al., 2006).

Both video games and the Internet have been used recently and creatively to try to reach teens and young adults (Baranowski, Buday, Thompson, & Baranowski, 2008).

Recently, a 16-week online intervention succeeded in producing weight loss and a reduction in binge eating for a small group of adolescents (Jones et al., 2008). A new video game titled *Re-Mission* (HopeLab, Palo Alto, CA) has been developed for cancer patients and features a "nanobot" named Roxxi, an attractive brunette who travels through the body blasting away at cancer cells. In a study of 375 cancer patients, ages 13 to 29 years, at 34 different medical centers, those who played the game were more compliant with chemotherapy and antibiotic treatments (Beale, Kato, Marin-Bowling, Guthrie, & Cole, 2007). *Dance Dance Revolution* is a popular video game that encourages exercise at home and can double energy expenditure (Lanningham-Foster et al., 2006). However, a 6-month follow-up of 30 children who used it at least 150 minutes a week found no reduction in body mass index (Madsen, Yen, Wlasiuk, Newman, & Lustig, 2007). Another new video game, *Body Mechanics,* tries to teach children to avoid becoming obese by allying themselves with a team of superheroes to battle villains such as Col Estorol and Betes II (Ellis, 2007). TV has also been used successfully to distract children having blood drawn (Bellieni et al., 2006). Finally, a computer-delivered HIV/AIDS program resulted in increased condom use in a recent randomized trial with 157 college students (Kiene & Barta, 2006).

National and International Prosocial Efforts

Evidence is increasing that well-conceived health campaigns involving mass media can have a demonstrable impact (Noar, 2006). One of the earliest prosocial experiments was conducted in Mexico by Miguel Sabido. His telenovela, *Acompaname (Accompany Me)*, featured a young woman with two children who decided that she didn't want any more pregnancies and therefore needed contraception. The show was immensely popular, and sales of contraceptives increased 23% in the first year the show aired, compared with 7% the year before the show began (Brink, 2006). Subsequently, the use of soap operas to convey public health messages spread to India, China, and Africa, where radio characters would discuss the problems of dealing with the risk of AIDS (Singhal & Rogers, 1999). In Zambia, a media campaign to reduce the risk of HIV resulted in a doubling of condom use among those teenagers who viewed at least three TV ads from the campaign (Underwood, Hachonda, Serlemitsos, & Bharath-Kumar, 2006). In 2006, the African Broadcast Media Partnership Against HIV/AIDS began a 3- to 5-year campaign involving a series of public service announcements (PSAs) on radio and TV in 25 African countries (Kaiser Family Foundation, 2006). The goal of the "An HIV-Free Generation. . . . It Begins With You" campaign is to educate people in Africa about what they can do to stop the spread of HIV. And in China, students have been successfully taught sex education via the Internet (Lou, Zhao, Gao, & Shah, 2006).

In the United States, the Kaiser Family Foundation began partnering with MTV in 1997 and has produced a total of 62 different PSAs and 19 full-length shows that deal with HIV/AIDS (Rideout, 2003). In 2003, Kaiser joined with Viacom to get HIV/AIDS storylines incorporated into shows such as *Becker, Touched by an Angel,* and *Queer as Folk* (Kaiser Family Foundation, 2004). A RAND study of 506 regular viewers of the hit sitcom *Friends* found that more than one fourth could recall seeing one particular episode in which Rachel became pregnant despite the use of condoms. Of those, 40% watched the episode with an adult, and 10% talked with an adult about condom use as a direct result of the show (Collins, Elliott, Berry, Kanouse, & Hunter, 2003). Similarly, a Kaiser survey of more than five hundred 15- to 17-year-olds found that one third had a conversation with a parent about a sexual matter because of something they saw on television (Figure 4.3). In the same survey, 60% of teens said that they learned how to say no to sex by seeing something on TV, and nearly half said that TV helped them talk to a partner about safe sex (Kaiser Family Foundation, 2002). Two Centers for Disease Control and Prevention (CDC) surveys in the past 7 years have found that half of regular viewers of daytime soap operas in the United States say that they have learned important health information, and one fourth of prime-time viewers say that TV is one of their top three sources of health information (Brink, 2006). And an innovative campaign in North Carolina used TV and radio PSAs and billboards to encourage parents to talk to their teenagers about sex. "Talk to your kids about sex. Everyone else is," was the primary message, and a subsequent survey of 1,132 parents found that the campaign had indeed been effective (DuRant, Wolfson, LaFrance,

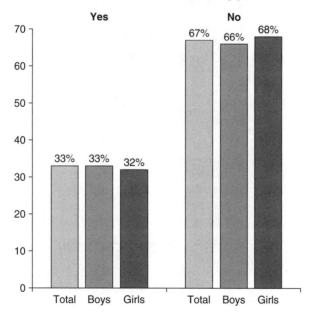

Figure 4.3

SOURCE: Kaiser Family Foundation (2002). This information was reprinted with permission from the Henry J. Kaiser Family Foundation. The Kaiser Family Foundation, based in Menlo Park, California, is a nonprofit, private operating foundation focusing on the major health care issues facing the nation and is not associated with Kaiser Permanente or Kaiser Industries.

Balkrishnan, & Altman, 2006). Both the National Campaign to Prevent Teen and Unplanned Pregnancy and Advocates for Youth have run similar campaigns (see Figure 4.4). In San Francisco, the Department of Public Health has become the first in the country to begin sending safer sex text messages to young people who request them (Allday, 2006).

Ratings

One of the most important noncontroversial possibilities for improving the quality of children's media experiences would be to create a uniform rating system for all media. This would end the current confusion of the "alphabet soup" of different ratings for different media and would yield a system that is far more "user-friendly" and content based (Gentile, Humphrey, & Walsh, 2005; Greenberg & Rampoldi-Hnilo, 2001). Every available study shows that parents and public health organizations are overwhelmingly in favor of a content-based ratings system, not an age-based one (Cantor, 1998a, 1998b; Gentile et al., 2005; Greenberg

Figure 4.4   Advocates for Youth Ad

SOURCE: Advocates for Youth (www. advocatesforyouth.org). Reprinted with permission.

& Rampoldi-Hnilo, 2001; Hogan, 2001). Yet, to date, every media industry has resisted such a change.

The first ratings system, of movies, was created in 1968 as a joint venture between the Motion Picture Association of America (MPAA) and the National Association of Theatre Owners (see Figure 4.5). Interestingly, it quickly followed two Supreme Court decisions that upheld the power of states to regulate children's access to media otherwise protected by the First Amendment (*Ginsberg v. New York,* 1968; *Interstate Circuit v. Dallas,* 1968). Although the system is voluntary, most films are rated. Ninety percent of parents are aware of the ratings system, and more than half approve of it (Federman, 1996). However, a significant percentage of parents disagree with the ratings for particular movies (Walsh & Gentile, 2001), and a recent survey of more than 1,000 parents found that only 53% find the ratings "very" useful (see Figures 4.6 and 4.7) (Rideout, 2007). The current movie ratings are as follows (see also Figure 4.8) (Federman, 1996; FTC, 2000):

Motion Picture Association of America (MPAA)

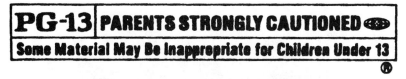

Figure 4.5   MPAA Movie Ratings

SOURCE: From Kaiser Family Foundation (2000b). Reprinted with permission.

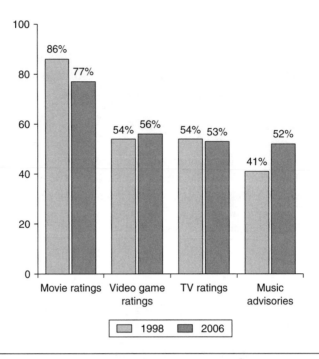

Figure 4.6   Percentage of Parents Who Say They Have Ever Used Movie Ratings, Video Game Ratings, and Music Advisories

SOURCE: Rideout (2007). Used with permission.

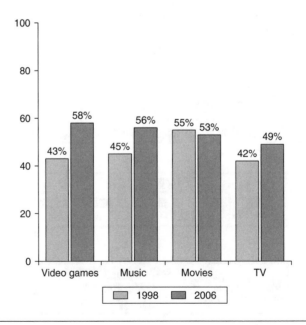

Figure 4.7   Percentage of Parents Who Have Used Each Rating or Advisory System and Found Them "Very" Useful

SOURCE: Rideout (2007). Used with permission.

G: General audiences—all ages admitted.

- Signifies that the film contains nothing that most parents will consider offensive, even for their youngest children. No nudity, sex scenes, or scenes depicting drug use.

- Recent examples: *Finding Nemo, Wallace & Gromit—The Curse of the Were-Rabbit, Garfield, Cars, Ratatouille.*

PG: Parental guidance suggested—some material may not be suitable for children.

- May contain some material that parents might not like their young children exposed to, but explicit sex scenes or scenes of drug use are absent. However, nudity may be briefly seen, and horror and violence may be present at "moderate levels."

- Recent examples: *The Chronicles of Narnia, Charlie and the Chocolate Factory, Nanny McPhee, Dreamer: Inspired by a True Story, Alvin and the Chipmunks.*

PG-13: Parents strongly cautioned—some material may be inappropriate for children under 13.

- "Rough or persistent violence" is absent, as is sexually oriented nudity. There may be some scenes of drug use but one use (only) of a common sexually derived expletive.

- Recent examples: *Mission Impossible 3, Harry Potter and the Goblet of Fire, Star Wars III—The Revenge of the Sith, Flags of Our Fathers, Pirates of the Caribbean: Dead Man's Chest, I Am Legend, Juno.*

R: Restricted, under 17 requires accompanying parent or adult guardian.

- May contain some adult material. May contain "hard" language, "tough violence," sex or nudity, or drug use. Consequently, parents are urged to learn more about the film before taking their children to see it.

- Recent examples: *Saw III, The Wedding Crashers, Snakes on a Plane, Crash, Brokeback Mountain, Hostel: Part II, Knocked-Up, Super-Bad, American Gangster.*

NC-17: No one under 17 admitted.

- May contain material that the ratings board feels is "patently adult," and therefore children 17 and younger should not be viewing it. May contain explicit sex scenes, considerable sexually oriented language, and/or scenes of excessive violence.

- Recent examples: *Where the Truth Lies; This Film Is Not Yet Rated; Lust, Caution.* (Older examples: *Showgirls, Kids*)

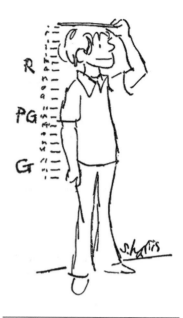

Figure 4.8

SOURCE: Copyright Sidney Harris. Reprinted with permission.

There are several problems with the MPAA system. Initially, the ratings were evaluative only, not descriptive (see Table 4.1). Parents would be given only the "PG" or "PG-13" symbol without being told exactly what content was problematic (Harris, 2007).

For certain parents, offensive language could be more of an issue than scenes with brief nudity, for example. Recently, however, and with very little public fanfare, the MPAA added descriptive information below the symbols (e.g., the 2007 film *Hostel: Part II* is rated R for "sadistic scenes of torture and bloody violence, terror, nudity, sexual content, language, and some drug content"). But the descriptions do not always accompany the rating, nor is the print always large enough to be deciphered by the average parent with average eyesight.

Sometimes, decisions by the ratings board defy explanation. The movie *Billy Elliot* was a fine film for children and teenagers, except for repeated use of the "f" word. Despite the fact that the word was spoken in a northern English accent so thick that it was barely decipherable, the film received an R rating, putting it out of reach of many teens who would have enjoyed seeing it. *Hannibal,* a gory sequel to *Silence of the Lambs,* was rated R, not NC-17. As critic Roger Ebert noted in his review, "If it proves nothing else, it proves that if a man cutting off his face and feeding it to the dogs doesn't get the NC-17 rating for violence, nothing ever will" (Ebert, 2001, p. 4). Similarly, *Hostel: Part II* shows grisly scenes of blood and torture, "which means it's perfectly okay to take a 5-year-old to see it if you can't get a sitter" (Harris, 2007, p. 76). The board is also notoriously susceptible to negotiation with the industry (Dick, 2006). Thus, the movie *South Park: Bigger, Longer & Uncut* received an R rating only after it was rated five times as NC-17. "God's the biggest bitch of them all" qualified the film for an R rating, whereas "God f—ing me up the a—" would have merited an NC-17 (Hochman, 1999). Even the makers of the film were surprised that their film escaped with just an R rating (Hochman, 1999).

Many observers have felt that the MPAA rates more harshly for sex than for violence, which is the exact reverse of what European countries do (see Figure 4.9) (Federman, 1996). Any depiction of sexual activity is likely to earn a picture an R

Table 4.1   Examples of Descriptive and Evaluative Ratings

Descriptive	Evaluative
Contains some violence	Parental discretion advised
Nudity/sex level 3	Teen: ages 13+
Violence: blood and gore	R: restricted
Language: mild expletives	Adults only
Contains extreme violence	Mature: ages 17+
BN: brief nudity	PG: parental guidance

SOURCE: Federman (1996). Reprinted with permission.

rating, whereas a PG-13 movie can contain an appreciable amount of violence. Films that were extremely violent, such as *Natural Born Killers* and *Pulp Fiction,* received R ratings, whereas *Showgirls,* which had graphic sexuality and some nudity but only brief violence, received an NC-17 rating (Federman, 1996). Even former members of the MPAA ratings board have serious problems with how this is decided (Waxman, 2001a).

Other problems with the MPAA system are that, through the years, the industry has tolerated significant drug and violent content in G- and PG-rated movies, despite its own guidelines (see Figure 4.10) (Associated Press, 2005). Of all the animated feature films produced in the United States between 1937 and 1999, 100% contained violence, and the portrayal of intentional violence increased during this 60-year period (Yokota & Thompson, 2000). Two studies of G-rated children's films released between 1937 and 1997 have found that nearly half displayed at least one scene of tobacco or alcohol use (Goldstein, Sobel, & Newman, 1999; Thompson & Yokota, 2001).

Figure 4.9

SOURCE: Reprinted with permission from King Features.

Figure 4.10

SOURCE: Reprinted with special permission of King Features Syndicate.

Another significant problem is what has been labeled "ratings creep." Between 1992 and 2003, for example, the PG rating seemed to be turning into a G rating, the PG-13 rating into a PG rating, and the R rating into a PG-13 rating for many films (Thompson & Yokota, 2004). In particular, the amount of violence (PG and PG-13 films), sex (PG, PG-13, and R films), and profanity (PG-13 and R films) seems to be ratcheted up in the past decade. As always, the MPAA rates more severely for sex or nudity than it does for violence, despite what the research says.

Several studies have noticed that the age-based ratings simply encourage children, especially boys, to seek "older" fare (see Figure 4.11) (Cantor, 1998b). When ratings are based on age rather than content, the "forbidden fruit theory" seems to become operational (Bushman & Stack, 1996).

There is also the problem of "enforcing" the ratings system. Half of movie theater operators surveyed confessed that they admit teens younger than 17 to R-rated movies without an accompanying parent or guardian (FTC, 2000). Even if theater owners were more conscientious, today's multiplex theaters allow children and teens to pay for a PG movie and switch to an R movie with minimal chances of being caught. There is some evidence that this trend may be changing, however. A 2001 study by an industry research firm found that films may lose as much as 40% of their potential opening-weekend earnings if they are rated R (Waxman, 2001b). Researchers who polled 1,500 people per week found that increasingly teens were being turned away at R-rated movies (Waxman, 2001b). In addition, of the top 20 films in 2002, 13 were rated PG-13 and none were R rated (Weinraub, 2003).

The television industry has lagged far behind the motion picture industry in developing a ratings system. Nearly 30 years after the MPAA system was introduced, the networks began rating their shows but only after considerable pressure from parents, advocacy groups, and the federal government (Broder, 1997; Hogan,

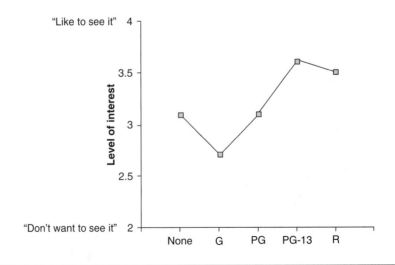

Figure 4.11   Effect of MPAA Ratings on Older Children's Interest in a Movie

SOURCE: Cantor (1998b, p. 64). Used with permission.

2001). In fact, it took congressional legislation to accomplish it. In 1996, the Telecommunications Act mandated that new television sets be manufactured with a V-chip and that television programs be rated so that the chip could be programmed accordingly (see Figure 4.12). Like the MPAA ratings, the TV ratings system also has many flaws (see Figure 4.13). News and sports programs are not rated. Initial age-based ratings had to be supplemented with content descriptors (see Table 4.2). Many public health groups suggested that the system should have been modeled after the premium cable channels' practice of indicating the level of sex, violence, and coarse language in each program (Cantor, 1998b; Mediascope, 2000).

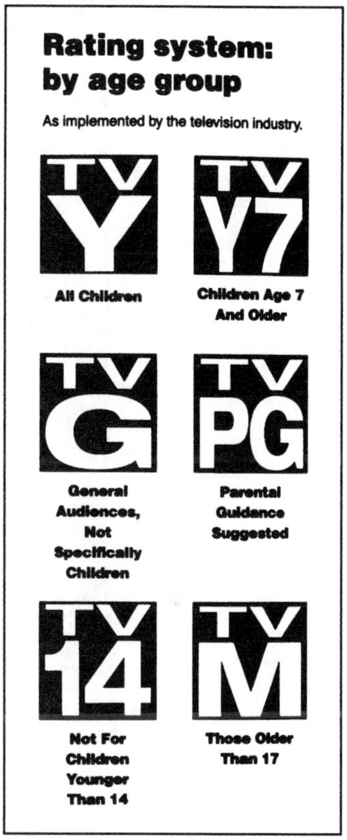

However, even after descriptors were added, studies show that the system is still not working properly. For several years, NBC refused to use the content descriptors in its ratings. The current categories are not specific enough regarding content, and the contextual impact of violent or sexual references is completely ignored. For example, certain content becomes lost to the highest rating: A TV-MA program with an "S" for sexual content may contain violence at a TV-14 level but is not given a "V" for violent content. In addition, parents may be tempted to place inappropriate faith in the rating "FV" for fantasy violence, even though research shows that this represents some of the most potentially detrimental programming for young children (Cantor, 1998a; Federman, 1998). In fact, in a recent study of more than 1,000 parents, only 11% knew what "FV" stands for, and 9% actually thought it meant "Family Viewing" (Rideout, 2007). Finally, the ratings are completely voluntary, and two studies reveal that producers are not always conscientious about rating their own programs (Greenberg, Rampoldi-Hnilo, & Mastro, 2000; Kunkel et al., 1998). Nearly 80% of shows with violence and more than 90% of shows with sex do not receive the V or S content descriptors (Kunkel et al., 1998) (see Figure 4.14). For example, an episode of *Walker, Texas Ranger* featured the stabbing of two guards on a bus, an assault on a church by escaped convicts threatening to rape a nun, and a fight scene in which one escapee is shot and another is beaten unconscious. It did not receive a V descriptor. In addition, 80% of children's programs with violence do not receive the FV descriptor (see Figure 4.15) (Kunkel et al., 1998).

To add to all of this confusion for parents, the gaming industry began by using two different systems, one for video games and the other for computer games. The former won out, but it bears little resemblance to the movie and TV ratings systems (Gentile et al., 2005): a new EC rating (ages 3 and older), E (everyone), a new E 10+ rating (everyone 10 and older), T (teen), M (mature), and AO (adults only) (see Figure 4.16). A recent study of the Entertainment Software Rating Board (ESRB) ratings found that more than half of all games are rated as containing violence, including more than 90% of games rated as appropriate for children

Rating system: by age group

As implemented by the television industry.

TV-Y — All Children

TV-Y7 — Children Age 7 And Older

TV-G — General Audiences, Not Specifically Children

TV-PG — Parental Guidance Suggested

TV-14 — Not For Children Younger Than 14

TV-M — Those Older Than 17

Figure 4.12 Current National TV Ratings System

SOURCE: From Kaiser Family Foundation (2000b). Reprinted with permission.

NOTE: These ratings are voluntary and self-administered. FV (for fantasy violence) is rarely used.

Figure 4.13

SOURCE: Reprinted with special permission of Universal Press Syndicate.

Table 4.2   Current TV Ratings System

TV-Y (appropriate for all children)
TV Y7 (directed to older children)
FV (fantasy violence—intense violence in children's programming)
TV-G (general audience)
TV-PG (parental guidance suggested)
   V (moderate violence)
   S (some sexual situations)
   L (infrequent coarse language)
   D (some suggestive dialogue)
TV-14 (parents strongly cautioned)
   V (intense violence)
   S (intense sexual situations)
   L (strong coarse language)
   D (intensely suggestive dialogue)
TV-MA (mature audiences only)
   V (graphic violence)
   S (explicit sexual activity)

SOURCE: Hogan (2001). Reprinted with permission.

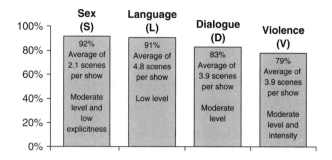

Figure 4.14   Percentage of Shows With Sex, Violence, or Adult Language That Did Not Receive a Content Descriptor

SOURCE: Kunkel et al. (1998). Reprinted with permission.

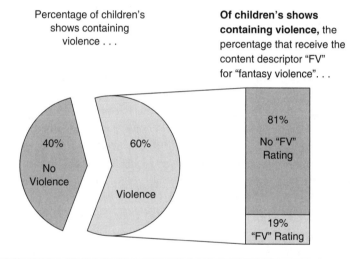

Figure 4.15   Percentage of Children's Shows Containing Violence

SOURCE: Kunkel et al. (1998). Reprinted with permission.

Entertainment Software Rating Board (ESRB)

Figure 4.16   Original Video Game Ratings

SOURCE: ©2006 Entertainment Software Association. All rights reserved. The ESRB rating icons are registered trademarks of the Entertainment Software Association.

NOTE: Now "E" (for "Everyone") and "E10+" categories have been added.

10 years and older (Gentile, 2008). Finally, the music industry uses a single rating system, "Parental Advisory: Explicit Lyrics." It, too, is voluntary and does not distinguish among lyrics that are explicitly violent, sexual, or profane (Federman, 1996).

All of these disparate systems rely on the integrity, honesty, and judgment of the producers of the program, except for the MPAA system, which has an independent board, composed of parents, that confers the rating. However, even then, the independence of the board is sometimes questionable, and the lack of expert membership is often apparent (Federman, 1996; Waxman, 2001a, 2001b). These separate and noncompatible systems have been developed with very little input from the public, the medical community, or the academic community (Gentile et al., 2005). One recent "test" of the ratings systems found that parents frequently disagree with the industry about the ratings applied to different media, particularly when violent content is involved. Only half of parents surveyed agreed with the G rating given to popular movies, and more than a third disagreed with PG ratings (see Table 4.3) (Walsh & Gentile, 2001).

The solution here should be readily apparent: a single, uniform, content-based ratings system that could be applied to all media that children and teenagers use (Gentile et al., 2005; Greenberg & Rampoldi-Hnilo, 2001; Hogan, 2001). The current "alphabet soup" of ratings systems is too confusing for parents to learn and apply and is even difficult for researchers to study (Greenberg et al., 2000). In addition, the voluntary nature of the current ratings systems is too easy for producers to exploit. The temptations are ever present to downcode a product to capture a larger audience (or, ironically, upcode it) or to depict increasingly edgy sexual, violent, or drug-taking behavior (Gentile et al., 2005). An external ratings board, with representation from the various industries, along with parents, health professionals, and academics, would put the United States on par with many other Western countries (Federman, 1996). In addition, such a move would inevitably lead to a societal discussion of cultural values: What should we rate most heavily against? How do we define quality and educational? That, in itself, would be useful.

Table 4.3   Should This Movie Have Been Rated PG? (no, according to many parents)

Austin Powers: The Spy Who Shagged Me
Charlie's Angels
Little Nicky
Nutty Professor II: The Klumps
She's All That
The Wedding Singer

SOURCE: Walsh and Gentile (2001).

Exercises

1. Where do you draw the line between prosocial messages and what George Orwell described as "mind control" in his novel, *1984?* For example, most people agree that, in general, war is bad. Should primetime shows contain messages about the recent war in Iraq, or would that be "crossing the line"? Should children's shows such as *Sesame Street* contain antiwar messages? Messages about terrorism? Where do you draw the line between public health and moralizing?

2. Imagine a version of *Sesame Street* designed and produced by (a) the Chinese government, (b) Al-Jazeera TV, (c) the former Soviet Union, and (d) the state of California. Who would the main characters be? What would some of the main themes be? Try watching *The World According to Sesame Street*, a documentary where co-productions from China, Israel/Palestine, and Russia are shown. Are there differences between these shows and the American version?

3. As regular viewers of *The Simpsons* know, *The Itchy & Scratchy Show* is a parody of violent children's cartoons. Like Wile E. Coyote and the Roadrunner, Itchy and Scratchy do little more than pummel each other constantly. After Marge writes a letter to the producer of the show, however, the tone becomes much more prosocial—and dull. Kids began turning off their TV sets and heading outdoors. Can prosocial programming be entertaining as well as educational? Or do most prosocial shows come off sounding like they've been directed and produced by a consortium of religious organizations?

4. Should shows and entertainment acts that are antisocial be banned? In 2006, an infamous videophone clip posted on the Internet showed Michael Richards, of Kramer and *Seinfeld* fame, in Los Angeles' Comedy Club repeatedly using the "n" word (Heffernan, 2006). Does he have the right to use whatever language he wants in his act? Richard Pryor repeatedly used the "n" word in his stand-up routines, to very powerful effect. Can only African Americans use the word? Conversely, should the White supremacist teenage twins, Prussian Blue, be censored? They call non-Whites "muds," play a video game called *Ethnic Cleansing*, and sing songs that glorify the Third Reich. A feature story about Prussian Blue in the magazine *Teen People* was recently killed by parent company Time Inc. (Hammond & Dillon, 2005). If you are in favor of censorship—for whatever reason—*who decides* what should be censored? Should prosocial media explicitly deal with issues of diversity and racism?

5. The MPAA recently announced that it would allow filmmakers to appeal ratings based on what other films had been rated in the past (Halbfinger, 2007). This move came after the success of the movie, *This Film Is Not Yet Rated*, which is extremely critical of the MPAA. Should the MPAA ratings members be kept secret from the public? Should ratings be a negotiation between the MPAA and the filmmaker? What about the recent MPAA decision to consider scenes of smoking in movies in determining the rating (MPAA, 2007, May 10)? Do you think the MPAA will follow through on its decision? What improvements could be made to the current ratings system?

Figure 4.17   Examples of Two Opposing Public Health-Related Media Campaigns

SOURCE: ©2008 The National Rifle Association and Ceasefire, School of Public Health.

6. Public health campaigns can be "pro" or "con" on certain issues, such as firearms. Look at the two opposing ads in Figure 4.17. Which ad do you think is more effective? What emotions are the ads trying to elicit? A 2008 study found that TV stations donate an average of 17 seconds an hour to PSAs, usually broadcasting them between midnight and 6 a.m. (Gantz, Schwartz, Angelini, & Rideout, 2008). Is this acceptable? If not, how could stations be encouraged to show more PSAs at popular viewing times?

7. Why do you think parents take young children to see violent movies that are rated PG-13 or R and are clearly inappropriate for them? Is it because they cannot afford a babysitter? Or is it because they think such movies are harmless or will not affect *their* children? Should movie theaters bar young children from seeing such movies, even if their parents are accompanying them, or is that too Big-Brotherish?

References

Allday, E. (2006, April 26). Safer sex info goes high-tech. *San Francisco Chronicle*, p. B-1.

Arnold, D. H., Ortiz, C., Curry, J. C., Stowe, R. M., Goldstein, N. E., Fisher, P. H., et al. (1999). Promoting academic success and preventing disruptive behavior disorders through community partnership. *Journal of Community Psychology, 5*, 589–598.

Associated Press. (2005, November 22). Are G-rated films going too far? Retrieved January 7, 2008, from http://www.commonsensemedia.org/news/press-coverage.php?id=83

Baranowski, T., Buday, R., Thompson, D. I., & Baranowski, J. (2008). Playing for real: Video games and stories for health-related behavior change. *American Journal of Preventive Medicine, 34*, 74–82.

Beale, I. L., Kato, P. M., Marin-Bowling, V. M., Guthrie, N., & Cole, S. W. (2007). Improvement in cancer-related knowledge following use of a psychoeducational video game for adolescents and young adults with cancer. *Journal of Adolescent Health, 41,* 263–270.

Bellieni, C. V., Cordelli, D. M., Raffaelli, M., Ricci, B., Morgese, G., & Buonocore, G. (2006). Analgesic effect of watching TV during venipuncture. *Archives of Disease in Childhood, 91,* 1015–1017.

Brink, S. (2006, November 13). Prime time to learn. *Los Angeles Times.* Retrieved January 10, 2007, from http://www.latimes.com/features/health/la-he-media13nov13,1,5874234 .story

Broder, J. M. (1997, February 28). Broadcast industry defends TV ratings system. *New York Times,* p. A1.

Calvert, S., & Kotler, J. (2003). Lessons from children's television: The impact of the Children's Television Act on children's learning. *Applied Developmental Psychology, 24,* 275–335.

Cantor, J. (1998a). *"Mommy, I'm scared": How TV and movies frighten children and what we can do to protect them.* San Diego: Harcourt Brace.

Cantor, J. (1998b). Ratings for program content: The role of research findings. *Annals of the American Academy of Political and Social Science, 557,* 54–69.

Cantor, J. (2001). The media and children's fears, anxieties, and perceptions of danger. In D. Singer & J. Singer (Eds.), *The handbook of children & media.* Thousand Oaks, CA: Sage.

Collins, R. L., Elliott, M. N., Berry, S. H., Kanouse, D. E., & Hunter, S. B. (2003). Entertainment television as a healthy sex educator: The impact of condom-efficacy information in an episode of *Friends. Pediatrics, 112,* 1115–1121.

Collins, W. A., & Getz, S. K. (1976). Children's social responses following modeled reactions to provocation: Prosocial effects of a television drama. *Journal of Personality, 44,* 488–500.

Dick, K. (2006). *America's film rating system is a sham.* Retrieved September 15, 2006, from http://www.abcnews.go.com/Entertainment/print?id=2448557

DuRant, R. H., Wolfson, M., LaFrance, B., Balkrishnan, R., & Altman, D. (2006). An evaluation of a mass media campaign to encourage parents of adolescents to talk to their children about sex. *Journal of Adolescent Health, 38,* 298.e1–299.e9.

Ebert, R. (2001, February 9). A loose "Hannibal" loses power. *Albuquerque Journal,* p. 4.

Elias, M. J. (1983). Improving coping skills of emotionally disturbed boys through television-based social problem solving. *American Journal of Orthopsychiatry, 53,* 61–72.

Ellis, J. (2007, February 21). *New DVD game battles childhood obesity.* Retrieved February 21, 2007, from http://abcnews.go.com/Business/print?id=2892244.

Federal Trade Commission (FTC). (2000). *Marketing violent entertainment to children: A review of self-regulation and industry practices in the motion picture, music recording, and electronic game industries.* (Available from FTC Consumer Reponse Center, Room 130, 600 Pennsylvania Avenue, N.W., Washington, DC 20580)

Federman, J. (1996). *Media ratings: Design, use and consequences.* Studio City, CA: Mediascope.

Federman, J. (Ed.). (1998). *National television violence study* (Vol. 3). Thousand Oaks, CA: Sage.

Friedrich-Cofer, L. K., Huston-Stein, A., Kipnis, D. M., Susman, E. J., & Clewett, A. S. (1979). Environmental enhancement of prosocial television content: Effect on interpersonal behavior, imaginative play, and self-regulation in a natural setting. *Developmental Psychology, 15,* 637–646.

Gantz, W., Schwartz, N., Angelini, J. R., & Rideout, V. (2008). *Shouting to be heard (2): Public service advertising in a changing television world.* Menlo Park, CA: Kaiser Family Foundation.

Gentile, D. A. (2008). The rating systems for media products. In S. Calvert & B. Wilson (Eds.), *Handbook on children and media*. Boston: Blackwell.

Gentile, D. A., Humphrey, J., & Walsh, D. A. (2005). Media ratings for movies, music, video games, and television: A review of the research and recommendations for improvements. *Adolescent Medicine Clinics, 16*, 427–446.

Gerbner, G., Gross, L., Signorielli, N., & Morgan, M. (1986). *Television's mean world: Violence profile no. 14–15*. Philadelphia: University of Pennsylvania, Annenberg School of Communications.

Ginsburg v. New York, 390 U.S. 629 (1968).

Goldstein, A. O., Sobel, R. A., & Newman, G. R. (1999). Tobacco and alcohol use in G-rated children's animated films. *Journal of the American Medical Association, 281*, 1131–1136.

Greenberg, B. S., Atkin, C. K., Edison, N. G., & Korzenny, F. (1980). Antisocial and prosocial behaviors on television. In B. S. Greenberg (Ed.), *Life on television: Content analysis of U.S. TV drama*. Norwood, NJ: Ablex.

Greenberg, B. S., & Rampoldi-Hnilo, L. (2001). Child and parent responses to the age-based and content-based television ratings. In D. G. Siner & J. L. Singer (Eds.), *Handbook of children and the media* (pp. 621–634). Thousand Oaks, CA: Sage.

Greenberg, B. S., Rampoldi-Hnilo, L., & Mastro, D. (2000). *The alphabet soup of television program ratings*. Cresskill, NJ: Hampton.

Halbfinger, D. M. (2007, January 18). Hollywood rethinks its ratings process. *New York Times*, p. E1.

Hammond, B., & Dillon, N. (2005, November 23). Mag tells 'Nazi' singers: Heil, no! *New York Daily News*. Retrieved January 12, 2007, from http://www.nydailynews.com/front/v-pfriendly/story/368373p-313337c.html

Harris, M. (2007, June 22). Hating the ratings. *Entertainment Weekly*, p. 76.

Heffernan, V. (2006, November 22). Television: Bewildering-sounding man and bewildering words. *The New York Times*, p. E6.

Hochman, D. (1999, July 9). Putting the "R" in "Park." *Entertainment Weekly*, pp. 15–16.

Hogan, M. (2001). Parents and older adults: Models and monitors of healthy media habits. In D. G. Singer & J. L. Singer (Eds.), *Handbook of children and the media* (pp. 663–680). Thousand Oaks, CA: Sage.

Hogan, M. J., & Strasburger, V. C. (2008). Media and prosocial behavior in children and adolescents. In L. Nucci & D. Narvaez (Eds.), *Handbook of moral and character education*. Mahwah, NJ: Lawrence Erlbaum.

Interstate Circuit v. Dallas, 390 U.S. 676 (1968).

Jones, M., Luce, K. H., Osborne, M. I. et al. (2008). Randomized, controlled trial of an Internet-facilitated intervention for reducing binge eating and overweight in adolescents. *Pediatrics, 121*, 453–462.

Jordan, A. B. (2003). Children remember prosocial program lessons but how much are they learning? *Applied Developmental Psychology, 24*, 341–345.

Jordan, A. B. (2004). The three-hour rule and educational television for children. *Popular Communication, 2*(2), 103–118.

Kaiser Family Foundation. (2002). *Teens, sex and TV*. Menlo Park, CA: Author.

Kaiser Family Foundation. (2004). *Entertainment education and health in the United States*. Menlo Park, CA: Author.

Kaiser Family Foundation. (2006, November 30). *African Broadcast Media Partnership Against HIV/AIDS launches coordinated, multi-year media campaign in 25 countries* [News release]. Menlo Park, CA: Author.

Kiene, S. M., & Barta, W. D. (2006). A brief individualized computer-delivered sexual risk reduction intervention increases HIV/AIDS preventive behavior. *Journal of Adolescent Health, 39,* 404–410.

Krcmar, M., & Curtis, S. (2003). Mental models: Understanding the impact of fantasy violence on children's moral reasoning. *Journal of Communication, 53*(3), 460–478.

Krcmar, M., & Valkenberg, P. (1999). A scale to assess children's moral interpretations of justified and unjustified violence and its relationship to television viewing. *Communication Research, 26,* 608–634.

Kunkel, D. (1988). From a raised eyebrow to a turned back: The FCC and children's product-related programming. *Journal of Communication, 38*(4), 90–108.

Kunkel, D., Farinola, W. J. M., Cope, K. M., Donnerstein, E., Biely, E., & Zwarun, L. (1998). *Rating the TV ratings: One year out.* Menlo Park, CA: Kaiser Family Foundation.

Ladd, G. W., Birch, S. H., & Buhs, E. S. (1999). Children's social and scholastic lives in kindergarten: Related spheres of influence? *Child Development, 70,* 1373–1400.

Lanningham-Foster, L., Jensen, T. B., Foster, R. C., Redmond, A. B., Walker, B. A., Heinz, D., et al. (2006). Energy expenditure of sedentary screen time compared with active screen time for children. *Pediatrics, 118,* e1831–e1835.

Lou, C.-H., Zhao, Q., Gao, E.-S., & Shah, I. H. (2006). Can the Internet be used effectively to provide sex education to young people in China? *Journal of Adolescent Health, 39,* 720–728.

Lowery, S. A., & DeFleur, M. L. (1995). *Milestones in mass communication research.* White Plains, NY: Longman.

Madsen, K. A., Yen, S., Wlasiuk, L., Newman, T. B., & Lustig, R. (2007). Feasibility of a dance videogame to promote weight loss among overweight children and adolescents. *Archives of Pediatrics & Adolescent Medicine, 161,* 105–107.

Mandler, J. M. (1984). *Stories, scripts and scenes: Aspects of schema theory.* Hillsdale, NJ: Lawrence Erlbaum.

Mares, M.-L., & Woodard, E. (2001). Prosocial effects on children's social interactions. In D. G. Singer & J. L. Singer (Eds.), *Handbook of children and the media* (pp. 183–203). Thousand Oaks, CA: Sage.

Mares, M.-L., & Woodard, E. (2005). Positive effects of television on children's social interactions: A meta-analysis. *Media Psychology, 7,* 301–322.

McLelland, M. M., Morrison, F. J., & Holmes, D. L. (2000). Children at risk for early academic problems: The role of learning-related social skills. *Early Childhood Research Quarterly, 15,* 307–329.

Mediascope. (2000). *Violence, women, and the media.* Studio City, CA: Author.

Moritz, O. (2007, February 10). Defense bigs ask "24" to cool it on torture. *New York Daily News,* Sports Final Edition, p. 3.

Motion Picture Association of America (MPAA). (2007, May 10). *Film rating board to consider smoking as a factor* [Press release]. Washington, DC: Author.

Noar, S. M. (2006). A 10-year retrospective of research in health mass media campaigns: Where do we go from here? *Journal of Communication, 11,* 21–42.

Palmer, E. L. (1988). *Television and America's children: A crisis of neglect.* New York: Oxford University Press.

Raver, C. C. (2002). Emotions matter: Making the case for the role of young children's emotional development for early school readiness. *Social Policy Report, 16*(3), 1–18.

Rideout, V. J. (2003). *Reaching the MTV generation: Recent research on the impact of the Kaiser Family Foundation/MTV Public Education Campaign on Sexual Health.* Menlo Park, CA: Kaiser Family Foundation.

Rideout, V. J. (2007). *Parents, children & media*. Menlo Park, CA: Kaiser Family Foundation.

Saarni, C. (1990). Emotional competence: How emotions and relationships become integrated. In R. Thompson (Ed.), *Nebraska Symposium on Motivation 1988: Socioemotional Development* (pp. 115–182). Lincoln: University of Nebraska Press.

Singer, D. G., & Singer, J. L. (1994). Evaluating the classroom viewing of a television series, "Degrassi Junior High." In D. Zillmann, J. Bryant, & A. C. Huston (Eds.), *Media, children, and the family: Social scientific, psychodynamic, and clinical perspectives* (pp. 97–115). Hillsdale, NJ: Lawrence Erlbaum.

Singhal, A., & Rogers, E. M. (1999). *Entertainment-education: A communication strategy for social change*. Mahwah, NJ: Lawrence Erlbaum.

Smith, S. W., Smith, S. L., Pieper, K. M., Yoo, J. H., Ferris, A. L., Downs, E., et al. (2006). Altruism on American television: Examining the amount of, and context surrounding, acts of helping and sharing. *Journal of Communication, 56,* 707–727.

Sprafkin, J. N., Liebert, R. M., & Poulos, R. W. (1975). Effects of a prosocial televised example on children's helping. *Journal of Experimental Child Psychology, 20,* 119–126.

Thomas, R. M. (2005). *Comparing theories of child development* (6th ed.). Belmont, CA: Wadsworth/Thomson.

Thompson, K. M., & Yokota, F. (2001). Depiction of alcohol, tobacco, and other substances in G-rated animated films. *Pediatrics, 107,* 1369–1374.

Thompson, K. M., & Yokota, F. (2004). *Violence, sex, and profanity in films: Correlation of movie ratings with content*. Retrieved November 1, 2006, from http://www.medscape.com/viewarticle/480900

Truglio, R. T., Lovelace, V. O., Segui, I., & Schneider, S. (2001). The varied role of formative research: Case studies from 30 years. In R. Truglio & S. Fisch (Eds.), *G is for growing*. Mahwah, NJ: Lawrence Erlbaum.

Underwood, C., Hachonda, H., Serlemitsos, E., & Bharath-Kumar, U. (2006). Reducing the risk of HIV transmission among adolescents in Zambia: Psychosocial and behavioral correlates of viewing a risk-reduction media campaign. *Journal of Adolescent Health, 38,* 55e1–55e13.

Walsh, D. A., & Gentile, D. A. (2001). A validity test of movie, television, and video game ratings. *Pediatrics, 107,* 1302–1308.

Waxman, S. (2001a, April 8). Rated S, for secret. *Washington Post,* p. G1.

Wasman, S. (2001b, May 31). Rating enforcement changes Hollywood's picture. *Washington Post,* p. C1.

Weinraub, B. (2003, August 17). This story is not rated R. Everybody please read it. *New York Times,* p. WK5.

Wentzel, K. R., & Asher, S. R. (1995). The academic lives of neglected, rejected, popular, and controversial children. *Child Development, 66,* 754–763.

Wilson, B. J., & Cantor, J. (1985). Developmental differences in empathy with a television protagonist's fear. *Journal of Experimental Child Psychology, 39,* 284–299.

Yakota, F., & Thompson, K. M. (2000). Violence in G-rated animated films. *Journal of the American Medical Association, 283,* 1504–1506.

CHAPTER 5

Media Violence

True, media violence is not likely to turn an otherwise fine child into a violent criminal. But, just as every cigarette one smokes increases a little bit the likelihood of a lung tumor someday, every violent show one watches increases just a little bit the likelihood of behaving more aggressively in some situation.

—Psychologists Brad J. Bushman
and L. Rowell Huesmann (2001, p. 248)

Television is not a schoolhouse for criminal behavior. . . . Viewers turn to this light entertainment for relief, not for instruction. Video action exists, and is resorted to, to get material out of minds rather than to put things into them. . . . Television violence is good for people.

—Jib Fowles, *The Case for
Television Violence* (1999, pp. 53, 118)

Obviously, the preference would be to have the industry police itself when it comes to excessive violence. However, if they can't or won't do it, then Congress must step in and address this growing societal problem.

—Sen. John D. Rockefeller IV (D–W. Va.),
quoted in the *Los Angeles Times* (Puzzanghera, 2007)

Media violence isn't going to disappear and most current efforts to stop it are unlikely to succeed. Like displays of material excess and gratuitous sex, violence exists within a commercial structure predicated on a powerful system of fantasies.

—David Trend, *The Myth of Media Violence:
A Critical Introduction* (2007, p. 10)

Violence in America threatens the very fabric of contemporary society. More than 2 million people are victims of violent injury each year (Vyrostek, Annest, & Ryan, 2004), and homicide is the second leading cause of death among 6- to 19-year-olds (Centers for Disease Control and Prevention [CDC], 2006). Every day, 16 children in this country are murdered, and 82% of these youth are killed with firearms (CDC, 2006). Despite a drop in violent crime in the 1990s, the United States still ranks first among industrialized nations in youth homicides (Snyder & Sickmund, 1999). Moreover, violent crime has actually risen in cities across the United States in the past 2 years, suggesting a reversal of the declines of the mid-1990s (Zernike, 2007). The statistics are certainly troubling but so too are the national tragedies involving homicide. The massacre at Virginia Polytechnic Institute and State University is only one recent case in a deluge of shootings in American schools over the past decade (Toppo, 2007). Responding to these school tragedies, former Attorney General John Ashcroft argued that there is an "ethic of violence" among America's youth ("Ashcroft Blames 'Culture,'" 2001).

As violence permeates our society, government officials, health professionals, educators, and scientists struggle to understand the complex causes of human aggression. To be sure, no single factor propels a person to become violent. Neurological and hormonal abnormalities (Berman, Gladue, & Taylor, 1993; Miles & Carey, 1997), deficiencies in cognitive functioning (Dodge & Frame, 1982), and even parental violence (Moretti, Obsuth, Odgers, & Reebye, 2006) have been linked to aggression. So too have social forces such as poverty, drugs, and the availability of guns (Archer, 1994; Guerra, Huesmann, Tolan, VanAcker, & Eron, 1995). Another factor that continually emerges in public debates about violence is the role of the mass media. Public opinion polls indicate that 75% of American adults believe that televised violence contributes to real-world crime and aggression (Lacayo, 1995), and a comparable proportion feels that Hollywood should do more to reduce violence in entertainment programming (Lowry, 1997). Being a parent seems to heighten these concerns. In one recent poll, 90% of parents with children younger than age 7 believed that TV violence has a serious negative impact on their children ("New Poll Finds," 2005).

Are the mass media part of the problem, or do they merely reflect the violence that is occurring in society (see Figure 5.1)? Is media violence chiefly a form of entertainment that dates back to the ancient Greeks, or is it a cultural tool that serves to legitimate violent means of power and social control? There are many opinions about the topic of media violence, and we cannot possibly resolve all of the issues in a single chapter. Consistent with the approach taken throughout this book, we will focus primarily on social scientific research regarding media violence and youth.

There are literally hundreds of published studies on the impact of media violence. Researchers who have comprehensively reviewed these studies argue quite conclusively that media violence can have antisocial effects (Anderson et al., 2003; Huesmann, 2007). In recent years, several professional organizations also have examined the evidence and concurred that TV violence is harmful to children (e.g., American Academy of Pediatrics, 2001; American Medical Association, 1996).

Figure 5.1

SOURCE: Reprinted with permission from KAL, the cartoonist & writer syndicate.

In fact, a 2001 report on youth violence by the Surgeon General states that "research to date justifies sustained efforts to curb the adverse effects of media violence on youths" (*Youth Violence*, 2001).

This chapter will begin by addressing the issue of how much violence exists in American media. Then we turn to the question of whether media violence appeals to young people. Next we will give an overview of the research regarding three potential harmful effects of exposure to media violence: (a) the learning of aggressive attitudes and behaviors, (b) desensitization, and (c) fear. As an important contrast, we will present some of the views of critics who disagree with this research. We will conclude with brief sections on guns and the media, suicide and the media, a cross-cultural look at violence in Japan, and prosocial effects of media violence on youth.

How Violent Are American Media?

American television and movies provide young people with a relentless diet of violent content. Conservative estimates indicate that the average child or teenager in this country views 1,000 murders, rapes, and aggravated assaults per year on television alone (Rothenberg, 1975). A review by the American Psychological Association puts this figure at 10,000 per year—or approximately 200,000 by the time a child reaches the teenage years (Huston et al., 1992). This statistic is likely to be even higher if a child concentrates his or her viewing on certain channels and types of programming, as we will see below.

In one of the earliest efforts to quantify violence on television, George Gerbner and his colleagues analyzed a week of programming each year from 1967 until the late 1980s (e.g., Gerbner, Gross, Morgan, & Signorielli, 1980; Gerbner, Signorielli, Morgan, & Jackson-Beeck, 1979). Looking at the three major broadcast networks, the researchers found a great deal of consistency over time, with roughly 70% of prime-time programs and 90% of children's programs containing some violence (see Signorielli, 1990). The rate of violence was fairly steady too, with 5 violent actions per hour featured in prime time and 20 actions per hour in children's shows (see Figure 5.2).

More recently, the National Television Violence Study assessed violence on broadcast as well as cable television (Smith et al., 1998; Wilson et al., 1997, 1998). In this large-scale content analysis, researchers randomly selected programming during a 9-month period across 23 channels from 6:00 a.m. to 11:00 p.m., 7 days a week. This method produced a composite week of television consisting of more than 2,500 hours of content each year. For 3 consecutive years (1996–1998), the researchers found that a steady 60% of all programs contained some violence. However, violence varied a great deal by channel type. More than 80% of the programs on premium cable channels featured violence, whereas fewer than 20% of the programs on public broadcasting did (see Figure 5.3).

But violence in the media is not all the same. To illustrate, compare a film such as *Schindler's List,* about the brutality of the Holocaust, with a movie such as *Kill Bill,* which features a an attractive former assassin played by Uma Thurman who goes on a revenge-inspired killing spree. One movie shows the tragic consequences

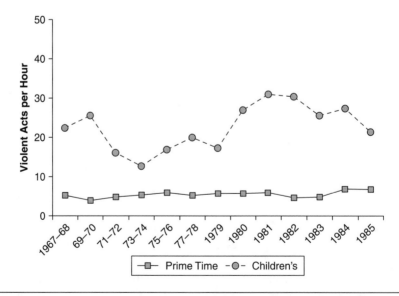

Figure 5.2   Violence in Prime-Time and Children's Programming Based on Annual Content Analyses by George Gerbner and Colleagues

SOURCE: Adapted from Signorielli (1990).

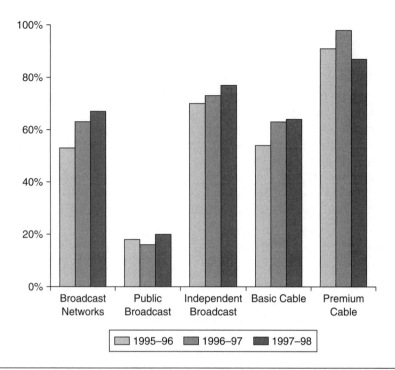

Figure 5.3   Proportion of Programs Containing Violence by Channel Type

SOURCE: Adapted from Smith et al. (1998).

of brutality, whereas the other seems to celebrate or at least condone violence. The National Television Violence Study assessed how often violence is shown in a way that can be educational to viewers. Despite the overall pervasiveness of violence, less than 5% of violent programs featured an antiviolence theme across the 3 years of the study (Smith et al., 1998).

The researchers also examined contextual features of violence such as who commits the aggression, whether the violence is rewarded or punished, and whether it results in negative consequences. The study drew several conclusions from the findings:

Violence on television is frequently glamorized. Nearly 40% of the violent incidents were perpetrated by "good" characters who can serve as role models for viewers. In addition, a full 71% of violent scenes contained no remorse, criticism, or penalty for violence.

Violence on television is frequently sanitized. Close to half of the violent incidents on television showed no physical harm or pain to the victim. Furthermore, less than 20% of the violent programs portrayed the long-term negative repercussions of violence for family and friends of the victim.

Violence on television is often trivialized. More than half of the violent incidents featured intense forms of aggression that would be deadly if they were to occur in real life. Yet despite such serious aggression, 40% of the violent scenes on television included some type of humor.

As we will see below, all of these contextual features increase the chances that media violence will have a harmful effect on the audience.

Of course, the patterns outlined here characterize all programming taken together, not necessarily the shows that young people spend most of their time viewing. In subsequent analyses of the National Television Violence Study sample, researchers looked specifically at two genres that are popular among youth: programs targeted specifically to children younger than 12 (Wilson, Smith, et al., 2002) and music videos (Smith & Boyson, 2002).

In programs targeted to children, nearly all of which are cartoons, violence is far more prevalent. For example, roughly 7 out of 10 children's shows contained some violence, whereas 6 out of 10 nonchildren's shows did (Wilson, Smith, et al., 2002). Furthermore, a typical hour of children's programming contained 14 different violent incidents, or 1 incident every 4 minutes. In contrast, nonchildren's programming featured about 6 violent incidents per hour, or 1 every 12 minutes. The researchers also found that children's programs were substantially more likely than other types of programming to depict unrealistically low levels of harm to victims compared with what would happen in real life. This pattern is particularly problematic for children younger than age 7, who have difficulty distinguishing reality from fantasy (see below) and may assume such aggression is harmless. Finally, when children's shows were divided into categories, superhero cartoons such as *Exosquad* and *Spiderman* as well as slapstick cartoons such as *Animaniacs* and *Road Runner* were far more saturated with violence than were social relationship cartoons such as *Care Bears* and *Rugrats* (Wilson, Smith, et al., 2002). Magazine-formatted shows such as *Barney, Blue's Clues,* and *Bill Nye the Science Guy* rarely contained any violence at all.

Looking at music videos, which are popular with preteens and teens, the overall prevalence of violence is quite low (Smith & Boyson, 2002). In fact, in a typical week of television, only 15% of all videos featured on BET, MTV, and VH1 contained violence. However, violence varied by music genre. As seen in Figure 5.4, rap and heavy metal videos were more likely to contain violence than other genres were. In fact, nearly one in three rap videos featured physical aggression. The violence in rap videos also was more likely to involve repeated acts of aggression against the same target. Finally, the researchers found more violence on BET than on the other two channels, in part because BET features more rap.

What about violence in other screen media? Chapter 10 focuses on video games, so we will not include that medium here. Two fairly recent studies examined movies that are marketed to children. Yokota and Thompson (2000) analyzed G-rated animated films released between 1937 and 1999. All 74 movies in the sample contained at least one act of physical aggression. Furthermore, there was a significant increase in the duration of screen violence over the 40-year period. One classic theme featured in many of the movies was the good guy triumphing over the bad guy by using physical force. A subsequent study by the same authors revealed that G-rated films that were animated actually contained more violence than did those that were not

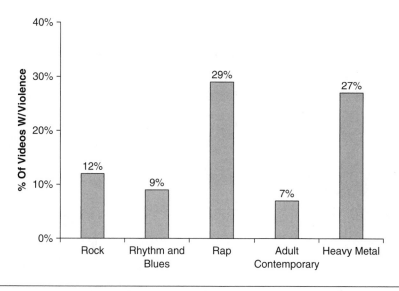

Figure 5.4   Prevalence of Violence in Different Genres of Music Videos

SOURCE: Adapted from Smith and Boyson (2002).

animated (Thompson & Yokota, 2004). For both television and movies, then, animated content is some of the most violent fare in the market.

The statistics presented here demonstrate what many adults increasingly recognize—there is a great deal of violence in screen entertainment (see Figure 5.5). And today, there are more television channels and other screen-based technologies (e.g., computers, iPods) available for young people to find and experience such content. Furthermore, much of this violence is portrayed in formulaic ways that glamorize, sanitize, and trivialize aggression. Finally, violence is particularly prevalent in many of the very products that are targeted to younger viewers.

Does Media Violence Attract Youth?

Writers and producers often claim that there would be less violence in the media if people would stop being attracted to it. Certainly we can think of many films and television shows that have drawn huge audiences and are brimming with violence. Slasher films such as *Scream* and the sequels of *Halloween* are examples of violent content that has been extremely popular among teenagers. And the success of *Mighty Morphin Power Rangers,* the *Powerpuff Girls,* and even *Pokémon* demonstrates that violent programming can be popular with children too.

But does violence ensure that a movie or TV show will be appealing? One way to answer this question is to look at viewership statistics. Hamilton (1998) analyzed Nielsen ratings for more than 2,000 prime-time TV movies airing on the four major broadcast networks between 1987 and 1993. Controlling for factors such as the channel and time the movie aired, the popularity of the program preceding the movie, and the amount of advertising in *TV Guide,* he found that movies about

"Let's wait. Maybe he kills her or something."

Figure 5.5

SOURCE: Reprinted with permission from the *New Yorker*.

murder or about family crime did in fact have higher household ratings. He also found that films explicitly described in *TV Guide* as "violent" attracted higher viewership as measured by household ratings. Yet despite all the factors Hamilton controlled for, there are still many differences among movies that could account for their varying popularity.

Other researchers have exposed viewers to different programs to determine whether those with violence are rated as more appealing (Diener & Woody, 1981; Greenberg & Gordon, 1972). Even with this methodology, it is difficult to tease out the role that violence plays in enhancing appeal given that programs differ on so many other dimensions. What is needed is a controlled study that varies the level of violence while holding all other program features constant. Berry, Gray, and Donnerstein (1999) did just that. In a series of three experiments, the researchers left a movie intact or cut specific scenes of graphic violence from it. Across all three studies, undergraduates rated the cut versions as less violent than the uncut versions. The presence of violence also influenced enjoyment, but the findings differed by the sex of the student. Cutting violence from a full-length movie actually increased women's enjoyment of the content, but it decreased men's ratings of enjoyment.

Yet a recent study involving television programming contradicts this pattern. In a large-scale experiment, Weaver and Wilson (2005) edited an episode from five different television series (e.g., *The Sopranos, OZ, 24*) to create three versions of each: a version with graphic violence, a version with sanitized violence, and a version with no violence. Across all five episodes, undergraduates enjoyed the nonviolent version more than the violent ones. This pattern held true for both males and females, regardless of the graphicness of the content.

Table 5.1   Top Broadcast Programs Among Children Ages 2–11: 2003–2004 Season

Rank	Program	Channel	Genre
Saturday morning			
1	Ozzy & Drix	WB	cartoon
2	Batman	WB	cartoon
3	X-Men	WB	cartoon
4	Yu-Gi-Oh! (11 a.m.)	WB	cartoon
5	Pokémon	WB	cartoon
6	Pokémon 2	WB	cartoon
7	Xiaolin Showdown	WB	cartoon
8	Yu-Gi-Oh! (11:30 a.m.)	WB	cartoon
9	Teen Titans	WB	cartoon
10	Static Shock	WB	cartoon
Prime time			
1	American Idol (Tuesday)	Fox	reality
2	American Idol (Wednesday)	Fox	reality
3	Survivor: All Stars	CBS	reality
4	Survivor: Pearl Islands	CBS	reality
5	Fear Factor	NBC	reality
6	The Simpsons	Fox	animated sitcom
7	Big Fat Obnoxious Fiancé	Fox	reality
8	Wonderful World of Disney	ABC	family-oriented movie
9	Apprentice	NBC	reality
10	King of the Hill 2	Fox	animated sitcom

NOTE: Rankings are based on national ratings from Nielsen Media Research for the 2003–2004 season.

The evidence is similarly mixed for children. In one random survey of parents in Madison, Wisconsin, nearly 30% named the *Mighty Morphin Power Rangers* as their elementary schoolers' favorite TV show (Cantor & Nathanson, 1997). Nevertheless, the family situation comedy *Full House* was cited as a favorite more often. A look at Nielsen ratings reveals that violent cartoons such as *Yu-Gi-Oh!* and

X-Men are quite popular among 2- to 11-year-olds, especially during the Saturday morning time block (see Table 5.1). However, family programming such as *The Wonderful World of Disney* and reality shows such as *American Idol* and *Survivor* rank high when the prime-time hours are considered.

These types of divergent patterns have led several researchers to conclude that violence is not necessarily always attractive (Cantor, 1998; Goldstein, 1999; Zillmann, 1998). Instead, the appeal of violence seems to depend on several factors, including the nature of the aggression involved. For example, undergraduates who were exposed to a graphic documentary-style film portraying the bludgeoning of a monkey's head or the slaughtering of steer uniformly found the content disgusting, and most chose to turn the television off before the program ended (Haidt, McCauley, & Rozin, 1994). On the other hand, brutal violence against a vicious villain who deserves to be punished can be enjoyable (see Zillmann, 1998).

The appeal of violence not only depends on its form but also on the type of viewer involved. A large body of research documents that there are sex differences in attraction to violence (see Cantor, 1998). Compared with girls, boys are more likely to enjoy violent cartoons (Cantor & Nathanson, 1997), select violent fairytale books (Collins-Standley, Gan, Yu, & Zillmann, 1996), seek out violent movies at the theater (Sargent et al., 2002), play violent video games (Funk, Buchman, & Germann, 2000), and play with violent toys (Servin, Bohlin, & Berlin, 1999). Various theories have been posited for these patterns, some focusing on gender-role socialization and others on biological differences between the sexes (see Oliver, 2000). Nevertheless, greater attraction to media violence among males is not merely a childhood phenomenon—it persists into adolescence and adulthood (Hamilton, 1998; Johnston, 1995).

Certain viewers possess personalities that seem to draw them to media violence as well. Zuckerman (1979) has argued that individuals vary in their need for arousal and that those high on "sensation seeking" will generally seek out novel and stimulating activities. Indeed, studies show that sensation seeking does predict exposure to violent television shows, movies, and even violent Web sites among adolescents and adults (Aluja-Fabregat, 2000; Krcmar & Greene, 1999; Slater, 2003). Moreover, sensation seeking is positively related to the enjoyment of graphic horror films (Tamborini & Stiff, 1987; Zuckerman & Litle, 1986). High sensation seeking among teens has even been linked to a preference for listening to heavy metal music (Arnett, 1995).

Finally, children who are more aggressive themselves seem to prefer violent television (see Figure 5.6). In one survey, parents who rated their children as aggressive also rated them as more interested in violent cartoons (Cantor & Nathanson, 1997). A similar pattern has been documented among adolescents (Selah-Shayovits, 2006). In a study of eighth graders, for example, boys who were rated as more aggressive by teachers also watched more violent films (Aluja-Fabregat, 2000). Huesmann, Moise-Titus, Podolski, and Eron (2003) have found longitudinal evidence showing that aggressive children seek out more violent television programs over time. Fenigstein (1979) and others (Cantor & Nathanson, 1997) speculate that aggressive people use violent scenes in the media to understand and justify their own behaviors.

"I loved the way you beat the pulp out of that guy after my game, Dad. It was better than those video games and movies you don't want me to see."

Figure 5.6

SOURCE: Reprinted with permission of Copley News Service.

One final caveat concerns conceptual confusion about the term *attraction*. Several scholars have begun to recognize that there may be a distinction between being drawn to content that is violent, often called "selective exposure," and actually enjoying that experience (Cantor, 1998; Weaver, 2006). There seems to be more empirical support for the idea that people may select violent over nonviolent material, but afterward they do not always like it better (Weaver, 2006). Unpacking these two concepts will help us to better understand the role that violence plays in media entertainment.

To summarize, there is a fair amount of evidence supporting the idea that violence sells. But a closer look at the data suggests that it is not that simple. Nonviolent themes in programming can attract large audiences too. However, the sheer prevalence of violence on television and in movies means that there are simply fewer options available if someone is seeking nonviolent content. Still, it may not be accurate to think of violence in a unidimensional way as either present or absent. Certain forms of violence seem to be more popular than others. In addition, particular individuals enjoy aggressive portrayals more than others do. To complicate matters further, Cantor (1998) speculates that there may be a relationship between an individual's personality and the types of violence that are most appealing. For example, highly anxious children may seek out portrayals in which good wins over evil, whereas an aggressive bully may enjoy a good TV battle regardless of the characters involved or the outcome. In other words, more research is needed on the types of violent messages that are most appealing, on the types of youth who seek out this content, and on the distinction between selective exposure and enjoyment of violent entertainment.

Can Media Violence Lead to Aggression?

Undoubtedly, the single issue that has received most attention with regard to the media is whether violent content can lead to aggressive behavior. No researcher today would argue that the media are the sole or even the most important cause of aggressive behavior in youth (see Figure 5.7). Yet there is strong agreement among social scientists that extensive exposure to media violence can *contribute* to aggressiveness in individuals (see Huesmann & Taylor, 2006; Smith & Donnerstein, 1998). This section will begin with an overview of the research evidence that has been brought to bear on this issue. Next we will present three theoretical perspectives that can help explain the relationship between media violence and aggression. The section will conclude with a discussion of who is most at risk for learning aggressive attitudes and behaviors from the media.

Experimental Studies

Some of the earliest evidence linking media violence to aggression comes from laboratory studies of children in controlled settings. In a series of classic experiments, Bandura and his colleagues exposed nursery school children to a filmed model who engaged in violent behaviors, often directed against a plastic, inflatable Bobo doll or punching bag (Bandura, Ross, & Ross, 1961, 1963a, 1963b). Afterward, children were taken to a playroom that contained a number of toys, including a Bobo doll, and their own behaviors were observed from behind a one-way mirror.

Figure 5.7

SOURCE: Reprinted with permission of John Branch.

The purpose of such research was to investigate the circumstances under which children would learn and imitate novel aggressive acts they had seen on film. The researchers consistently found that children who were exposed to a violent model were more likely to act aggressively than were children in control groups who had not viewed such violence (Bandura et al., 1961, 1963b). Furthermore, children were more likely to imitate a violent model who had been rewarded with cookies than one who had been punished. In fact, children generally imitated the model so long as no punishment occurred, suggesting that the absence of punishment can serve as a tacit reward or sanction for such behavior (Bandura, 1965).

Bandura and his colleagues also found that children could learn novel aggressive responses as easily from a cartoon-like figure, a "Cat Lady," for example, as from a human adult (Bandura et al., 1963a). This finding clearly implicates Saturday morning TV as an unhealthy reservoir of violence. Subsequent studies using similar procedures revealed other aspects of imitation. For example, children exposed to televised aggressive sequences could reproduce the behaviors they had seen up to 6 to 8 months later (Hicks, 1965). In addition, preschoolers would aggress against a human adult dressed as a clown just as readily as they would a Bobo doll (Hanratty, O'Neal, & Sulzer, 1972; Savitsky, Rogers, Izard, & Liebert, 1971). This finding helped to undercut the criticism that attacking an inflatable doll is merely play behavior and not akin to real aggression.

Experimental studies have looked at older age groups too. For instance, research shows that older adolescents and even adults who are exposed to television violence in laboratory settings will engage in increased aggression (Berkowitz & Geen, 1967; Scharrer, 2005).

However, the experimental evidence has been criticized on several methodological grounds (Fowles, 1999; Freedman, 1986, 2002). Laboratory studies often (a) employ unrealistic or "play" measures of aggression, (b) are conducted in artificial viewing situations, (c) involve adult experimenters who willingly show violence on TV in a way that may seem to be condoning aggression, and (d) are able to assess only short-term effects of exposure. According to Fowles (1999), "Viewing in the laboratory setting is involuntary, public, choiceless, intense, uncomfortable, and single-minded. . . . Laboratory research has taken the viewing experience and turned it inside out so that the viewer is no longer in charge" (p. 27).

To overcome some of these limitations, researchers have conducted field experiments in nonlaboratory settings with more realistic measures of aggression (Friedrich & Stein, 1973; Josephson, 1987). In one early study, 3- to 5-year-old children were randomly assigned to watch violent or nonviolent TV shows for 11 days at their school (Steuer, Applefield, & Smith, 1971). Children in the violent viewing condition displayed significantly more physical aggression against their peers (e.g., hitting, kicking, throwing objects) during play periods than did children in the nonviolent TV group.

More recently, researchers exposed elementary schoolers to a single episode of the *Mighty Morphin Power Rangers* and then observed verbal and physical aggression in the classroom (Boyatzis, Matillo, & Nesbitt, 1995). Compared with a control group, children and particularly boys who had watched the violent TV program committed significantly more intentional acts of aggression inside the classroom, such as hitting, kicking, shoving, and insulting a peer. In fact, for every aggressive act perpetrated by children in the control group, there were seven aggressive acts committed by children who had seen the *Power Rangers*. Notably, these types of bullying behaviors are no longer seen as part of normal development and have been linked to high levels of psychological distress, poor social and emotional adjustment, failure in school, and even long-term health difficulties among victims (Nansel et al., 2001; Rigby, 2003).

With regard to the *Power Rangers*, the Boyatzis et al. (1995) study reveals that the prosocial message delivered at the end of each episode in this TV series is not nearly as salient to children as the perpetual violence that the superheroes commit. At least one other study has demonstrated that moral lessons on television are relatively ineffective when they are couched in violence (Liss, Reinhardt, & Fredriksen, 1983).

In general, controlled experiments dating back to the 1960s clearly demonstrate that media violence can *cause* short-term increases in aggression in some children (see Figure 5.8). Moreover, this effect has been found with various age groups and in laboratory as well as more naturalistic studies. But such evidence is still limited in that it points only to immediate effects that may not persist much beyond the viewing situation. In addition, most experiments involve small samples of children or teens who may or may not be representative of young people in general.

Figure 5.8

SOURCE: Reprinted with permission of the Creators Syndicate.

Correlational Studies

In the 1970s, a number of investigators surveyed large populations of children and teenagers to determine if those who were heavy viewers of TV violence also were more aggressive. As an example, one study surveyed 2,300 junior and senior high school students in Maryland and asked them to list their four favorite programs, which were then analyzed for violent content (McIntyre & Teevan, 1972). Measures of aggression were compiled from a self-reported checklist of activities, using five scales that ranged from aggressive acts (e.g., fighting at school) to serious delinquency (involvement with the law). Results revealed that children whose favorite programs were more violent also were higher in overall aggressive and delinquent behavior.

Other studies used slightly different measures of aggression, including peer ratings (McLeod, Atkin, & Chaffee, 1972a, 1972b) and self-reports of willingness to use violence in hypothetical situations (Dominick & Greenberg, 1972). Across different samples in different regions of the country, the findings were remarkably consistent. Higher exposure to TV violence was positively associated with higher levels of aggressive behavior (Belson, 1978; Dominick & Greenberg, 1972; McLeod et al., 1972a, 1972b; Robinson & Bachman, 1972). Furthermore, the relationship held up even after controlling for factors such as parental education, school achievement, socioeconomic status, and overall amount of television viewing (McLeod et al., 1972a, 1972b; Robinson & Bachman, 1972). In a recent survey of more than 30,000 adolescents from eight different countries (Kuntsche et al., 2006), heavy television viewing was significantly associated with increased verbal aggression and verbal bullying. This finding held up in all eight countries, even after controlling for gender and age. In three of the countries in which teens spent a lot of time watching TV on weekends (i.e., the United States, Poland, Portugal), there was also a significant relationship between television viewing and physical forms of bullying (e.g., kicking, pushing).

The large and often representative samples in these studies suggest that the causal effects documented in experimental studies can be generalized to the real world. However, the problem with correlational studies is that we cannot be certain about which variable came first. TV violence could be causing an increase in aggression. Alternatively, youth who are already aggressive could be seeking out violent content. To disentangle the direction of causality, longitudinal studies are needed.

Longitudinal Studies

In the past several decades, social scientists have increasingly moved toward longitudinal studies, which involve surveying the same group of individuals at repeated intervals over time. This type of design permits a researcher to test the cumulative effects of exposure to the media. It also provides a test of the "chicken and egg" quandary: Does violence in the media lead to aggression, or do aggressive people seek out such content?

In one of the most impressive longitudinal studies, Leonard Eron, Rowell Huesmann, and their colleagues tested the same sample of children, originally from upstate New York, over a 22-year period (Eron, Huesmann, Lefkowitz, & Walder, 1972; Huesmann, 1986; Huesmann, Eron, Lefkowitz, & Walder, 1984; Lefkowitz, Eron, Walder, & Huesmann, 1972). The researchers measured television viewing habits and aggressive behavior at three different points in time: when the participants were 8, 19, and 30 years of age. As seen in Figure 5.9, the results revealed that among boys, the relationship between viewing TV violence in the third grade and aggressive behavior 10 years later was positive and highly significant. In other words, exposure to TV violence during early childhood was predictive of higher levels of aggression at age 19. This relationship persisted even after controlling for IQ, socioeconomic status (SES), and overall exposure to television. In contrast, aggressive behavior in the third grade was *not* predictive of violent TV consumption at age 19. Thus, the idea that being aggressive can lead a child to watch more TV violence did not receive support. Interestingly, neither of the cross-lagged correlations from Time 1 to Time 2 was significant for girls.

The researchers followed up on these same individuals another 10 years later, most of them now age 30 (Huesmann, 1986). In some of the most compelling evidence to date, the data revealed a link between exposure to TV violence at age 8 and self-reported aggression at age 30 among males (Huesmann & Miller, 1994). Moreover, violent TV habits in childhood were a significant predictor of the seriousness of criminal acts performed at age 30 (see Figure 5.10). Once again, this relationship held up even when childhood aggression, IQ, SES, and several parenting variables were controlled. Huesmann (1986) concluded that "early childhood television habits are correlated with adult criminality independent of other likely causal factors" (p. 139).

Using a similar longitudinal approach, these same researchers conducted a 3-year study of more than 1,000 children in five countries: Australia, Finland, Israel, Poland, and the United States (Huesmann & Eron, 1986a). Despite very

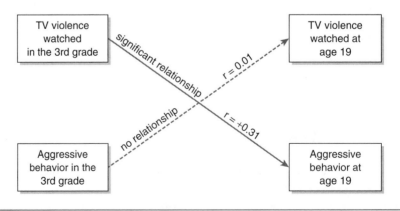

Figure 5.9   TV Violence Watched in Third Grade Correlates With Aggressive Behavior at Age 19 For Boys

SOURCE: Reproduced from Liebert and Sprafkin (1988).

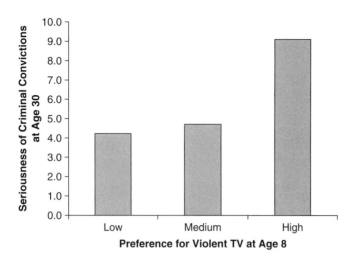

Figure 5.10   The Relationship Between Boys' Viewing of TV Violence at Age 8 and Their Violent Criminal Behavior 22 Years Later

SOURCE: Adapted from Huesmann (1986).

different crime rates and television programming in these nations, early childhood exposure to television violence significantly predicted subsequent aggression in every country except Australia. Furthermore, the relationship was found just as often for girls as for boys in three of the countries, including the United States. Finally, although the relationship between early TV habits and later aggression was always stronger, there was some evidence for the reverse direction: Early aggression led to higher levels of violent viewing. Based on this pattern, Huesmann and his colleagues now argue that pinning down the precise direction of causality between TV violence and aggression is not so crucial because the relationship is probably reciprocal: Early violent viewing stimulates aggression, and behaving aggressively then leads to a heightened interest in violent TV content (Huesmann, Lagerspetz, & Eron, 1984). Likewise, Slater (2003) has posited that the relationship between TV violence and aggressive behavior becomes mutually reinforcing over time, resulting in what he calls a "downward spiral model."

The most recent longitudinal research by Huesmann and his colleagues continues to support the idea that both boys and girls are influenced by television violence (Huesmann et al., 2003). In this study, the researchers interviewed more than 500 elementary school children and then surveyed them again 15 years later. Again, they found that heavy exposure to television violence in childhood predicted increased aggressive behavior in adulthood. Unlike their earliest work, their more current evidence reveals the same pattern for both boys and girls. The researchers speculated that the shift in findings pertaining to girls is due to increased societal acceptance of assertive behavior for females as well as an increase in aggressive female characters on television.

With one exception (Milavsky, Kessler, Stipp, & Rubens, 1982), other longitudinal evidence corroborates these patterns. For example, in one 5-year study, children who had watched the most television during preschool, particularly action adventure shows, were also the most aggressive at age 9 (Singer, Singer, & Rapaczynski, 1984). Early viewing of violence in the preschool years also predicted more behavioral problems in school. These relationships remained just as strong after the effects of parenting style, IQ, and initial aggressiveness were statistically removed.

To summarize, longitudinal studies provide powerful evidence that television violence can have a cumulative effect on aggression over time. Childhood exposure to such content has been shown to predict aggression in later years and even serious forms of criminal behavior in adulthood. Some of the earliest research indicated that these effects held true only for boys, but more recent studies have found significant relationships over time for girls too. Finally, the relationship between TV violence and aggressive behavior may be cyclical in nature, such that each reinforces and encourages more of the other.

Meta-Analyses

When researchers conclude that media violence can increase aggressive attitudes and behaviors, they typically look at all the evidence collectively. Lab experiments provide convincing evidence of causal effects, but they may be detecting outcomes that would not occur in everyday life, and they assess short-term effects only. Field experiments increase our confidence that real aggression is involved, correlational studies show that there is a positive relationship between TV violence and aggression in large samples of youth, and longitudinal studies suggest a cumulative effect of TV violence over time, even after controlling for other potential causal variables. In other words, each method has its strengths and weaknesses, but collectively the research shows a consistent pattern.

Another way to detect patterns is to conduct a meta-analysis. A meta-analysis is the statistical analysis of a large collection of results from individual studies. In this case, each study becomes a data point in a new, combined "super-study" (Mullen, 1989). The goal of a meta-analysis is to synthesize findings from a large body of studies but to do so in a statistical rather than a descriptive way (Cooper & Hedges, 1994). Meta-analyses produce numerical estimates of the size of an effect across all studies on a particular topic.

Several meta-analyses have been conducted on the research regarding media violence and aggression. In the earliest one, Hearold (1986) looked at 230 studies of the impact of TV on both prosocial and antisocial behavior. Antisocial behavior consisted mostly of physical aggression but also included other outcomes such as theft and rule breaking. Hearold found an average effect size of .30 (similar to a correlation) between violent TV content and the broad category of antisocial behavior. According to scientific conventions, any effect around .10 is considered to be "small," around .3 to be "medium," and around .5 to be "large" in magnitude (Cohen, 1988).

In a much smaller meta-analysis, Wood, Wong, and Chachere (1991) examined only those experiments that actually observed children's aggressive behavior after viewing violence. The goal was to isolate the studies that used the most realistic measures of aggression in order to respond to the criticism that laboratory studies are artificial. Across a total of 23 experiments, the researchers found a significant aggregate effect of media violence on aggression. They concluded that "media violence enhances children's and adolescents' aggression in interactions with strangers, classmates, and friends" (p. 380).

Updating the Hearold (1986) study, Paik and Comstock (1994) analyzed 217 studies of the impact of television violence on antisocial behavior (the researchers did not include studies of prosocial behavior, as Hearold did). Paik and Comstock found that the overall effect size between TV violence and antisocial behavior was .31, surprisingly consistent with that found by Hearold. Another way to interpret this statistic is that roughly 10% of the individual variation ($.31^2$) in antisocial behavior can be accounted for by exposure to TV violence.

More recently, Bushman and Anderson (2001) limited their meta-analysis to studies looking at aggression as an outcome rather than the broader category of antisocial behavior. Across 212 different samples, the researchers found a positive and significant relationship between media violence and aggression. In addition, the study found that since 1975, the effect sizes in media violence research have increased in magnitude, suggesting that the media are becoming more violent and/or that people are consuming more of this type of content.

Bushman and Anderson (2001) also compared the overall effect of media violence with other types of effects found in scientific research. As it turns out, the link between media violence and aggression is much stronger than several effects that today go unquestioned, such as the link between ingesting calcium and increased bone mass or the link between exposure to asbestos and laryngeal cancer (see Figure 5.11). Furthermore, the correlation between media violence and aggression (.31) is only slightly smaller than that between smoking and lung cancer (nearly .40). Obviously, not everyone who smokes will develop lung cancer, but the risk is

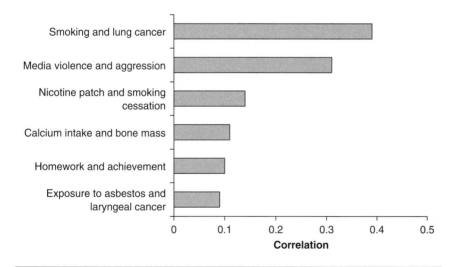

Figure 5.11   A Comparison of the Media Violence-Aggression Link With Other Public Health Relationships That Have Been Established Scientifically

SOURCE: Adapted from Bushman and Huesmann (2001).

real and significant. The analogy to media violence is clear; not every child or teen who watches a heavy dose of violent programming will become aggressive, but some young people are certainly at risk to do so.

Why Does Exposure to Violence Encourage Aggression?

Many theories have been offered to account for the relationship between media violence and aggression. Catharsis theory was first proposed by Aristotle, who argued that good drama offers audience members a way to purge their negative feelings of emotion. Extended to media violence, the idea is that exposure to such content can cleanse one's feelings of anger and frustration, resulting in a therapeutic *reduction* in aggression. There is very little empirical support for catharsis theory. In fact, most data suggest an opposite, instigational effect of media violence on aggression (see the review above). Yet catharsis theory continues to be cited today, especially by some members of the media industry. Another theory called excitation transfer posits that any type of media content can enhance aggression so long as the material is arousing (Zillmann, 1991). According to excitation transfer theory, an erotic film is more likely to enhance aggression in an angered individual than a violent film is, so long as the erotic material is more arousing (Zillmann, 1971).

In this section, we will review three major perspectives, all of which focus on the content of media portrayals rather than their arousal properties. Each perspective has generated much research and made significant contributions to our understanding of how media violence might facilitate aggression.

Cognitive Priming. Cognitive priming is a perspective developed by Berkowitz and his colleagues to explain short-term reactions to media violence (Berkowitz, 1984; Jo & Berkowitz, 1994). According to the theory, violent stimuli in the media can activate or elicit aggressive thoughts in a viewer. These thoughts can then "prime" other closely related thoughts, feelings, and even motor tendencies stored in memory. For a short time after exposure, then, a person is in a state of activation whereby hostile thoughts and action tendencies are at the forefront of the mind. Research supports the idea that violent media content can "prime" aggressive thoughts in people (Bushman & Geen, 1990). For example, in a study by Berkowitz, Parker, and West (cited in Berkowitz, 1973, pp. 125–126), children who read a war comic book were more likely to select aggressive words when asked to complete a series of sentences than were children who read a neutral comic book.

Several conditions can encourage these aggressive thoughts and feelings to unfold into aggressive behavior. One such condition is the person's emotional state. Berkowitz (1990) has argued that individuals who are experiencing negative affect, particularly anger or frustration, are more likely to be primed to act aggressively by the media because they are in a state of readiness to respond in a fight-or-flight manner. Indeed, angered individuals do seem to be more strongly influenced by media violence (Paik & Comstock, 1994).

Another condition that helps encourage individuals to act out their aggressive thoughts is justification (Jo & Berkowitz, 1994). If media violence is portrayed as morally proper, it can help to reduce a person's inhibitions against aggression for a short time afterward, making it easier to act out such behavior. Justified violence in the media may even help a person rationalize his or her own aggression (Jo & Berkowitz, 1994). There is a great deal of evidence indicating that justified violence can facilitate aggression (Paik & Comstock, 1994).

Finally, cues in the environment that remind people of the media violence they have just seen can trigger aggressive behavior (Jo & Berkowitz, 1994). Such cues help to reactivate and sustain the previously primed aggressive thoughts and tendencies, thereby prolonging the influence of the violent media content. In a classic study that demonstrates such cuing, second-and third-grade boys were exposed to either a violent or a nonviolent TV show (Josephson, 1987). The violent program prominently featured walkie-talkies in the plot. Immediately afterward, the boys were taken to a school gymnasium to play a game of floor hockey. At the start of the game, an adult referee interviewed each boy using a walkie-talkie or a microphone. Results revealed that aggression-prone boys who had viewed the violent program and then saw the real walkie-talkie were more aggressive during the hockey game than were those in any other condition, including boys who had seen the violent show but no real walkie-talkie. According to priming theory, the walkie-talkie served as a cue to reactivate aggressive thoughts and ideas that had been primed by the earlier violent program.

Cognitive priming theory helps to explain how media violence can have short-term effects by triggering already learned aggressive thoughts and behaviors. But where do these aggressive tendencies come from originally? Social learning theory focuses on how the media can help children acquire aggressive attitudes and behaviors in the first place.

Social Learning. Developed by Bandura (1965, 1977), social learning theory posits that children can learn new behaviors in one of two ways: by direct experience through trial and error or by observing and imitating others in their social environment. Bandura (1994) has pointed out that observational learning ultimately is more efficient than trying to discover everything on your own. Children can and do learn from other people in their environment, including parents, siblings, peers, and teachers. Children also can learn from characters and people featured in the mass media (see Figure 5.12).

According to social learning theory, a child observes a model enact a behavior and also witnesses the reinforcements that the model receives. In a sense, the child experiences those reinforcements vicariously. If the model is rewarded, the child too feels reinforced and will imitate or perform the same behavior. If the model is punished, the child is unlikely to perform the behavior, although the actions may still be stored in memory and performed at a later date (Bandura, 1965).

Early experiments supported social learning theory and demonstrated that children could learn just as easily from a filmed model as from a real person (Bandura, 1965; Bandura et al., 1963a, 1963b; Walters & Parke, 1964). In addition

"I don't place much credence in the effects of TV violence on children."

Figure 5.12

SOURCE: King Features. Reprinted with permission.

to imitation, early research showed that the media could encourage children to act aggressively in ways that differed from the precise behaviors seen in a portrayal. In one study, nursery school children viewed either a violent or a nonviolent cartoon and then were given two toys with which to play (Lovaas, 1961). One toy had a lever that caused a doll to hit another doll over the head with a stick; the other toy consisted of a wooden ball that maneuvered through obstacles inside a cage. Compared with those in the nonviolent condition, children who had seen the violent cartoon used the hitting doll more frequently. Bandura and his colleagues (1963b) called this process "disinhibition," whereby exposure to media violence can weaken a child's normal inhibitions or restraints against behaving aggressively, resulting in acts of violence that are similar but not identical to what was seen in a program.

Today, certain models in the media can have remarkable effects on young people. Consider the thousands of preteen and teen girls who donned chains and skimpy clothes in an effort to emulate Madonna during her Material Girl phase. More recently, Paris Hilton, Lindsay Lohan, and Britney Spears seem to be captivating youth, despite some of their destructive behaviors (Deveny & Kelley, 2007). One survey of Los Angeles teens found that nearly 40% of the 12- to 17-year-olds named a media figure as their role model—roughly the same percentage (42%) that named a parent or relative (Yancey, Siegel, & McDaniel, 2002). As a well-known Hollywood producer once stated,

I'd be lying if I said that people don't imitate what they see on the screen. I would be a moron to say they don't, because look how dress styles change. We have people who want to look like Julia Roberts and Michelle Pfeiffer and Madonna. Of course we imitate. It would be impossible for me to think they would imitate our dress, our music, our look, but not imitate any of our violence or our other actions. (qtd. in Auletta, 1993, p. 45)

In the 1980s, Bandura (1986) reformulated his theory because it had been criticized as too behavioristic, focusing mostly on reinforcements and how people act. Now called social cognitive theory, the newer perspective acknowledges that cognitive processes such as attention and retention are involved in observational learning. These mental activities place more emphasis on how children symbolically construe or make sense of a model's behavior. Children selectively pay attention to different features of a model's behavior, they bring forth different experiences to interpret and evaluate the model's actions, and they store different information in memory. These types of cognitive processes can be used to help explain why some children might imitate a model but others do not.

Social learning and social cognitive theory are useful frameworks for understanding how children can learn new behaviors from media violence. But they tend to focus most on short-term learning. The final theory we will discuss takes observational learning a bit further and provides a perspective to account for cumulative or long-term effects of media violence on a child's behavior.

Social Informational Processing Theory. Huesmann (1998) has developed an information-processing model that deals with how aggressive behaviors are both developed and maintained over time. The model focuses on scripts, which are mental routines for familiar events that are stored in memory (Abelson, 1976). A script typically includes information about what events are likely to happen, how a person should behave in response to these events, and what the likely outcome of these behaviors will be. Consequently, scripts are used to guide behavior and social problem solving. For example, young children possess scripts for common activities such as going to the doctor and getting ready for bed.

Scripts can be acquired through personal experience as well as through exposure to mass media (Krcmar & Hight, 2007). Huesmann (1998) has argued that a child's early learning experiences play a critical role in the development of scripts. According to the theory, a child who is exposed to a great deal of violence, either in real life or through the media, is likely to develop scripts that encourage aggression as a way of dealing with problems (Huesmann, 1986, 1988).

Once scripts are learned, they can be retrieved from memory and tried out in social situations. Some scripts are easier to retrieve than others. Those that are rehearsed by the child, through simple recall, through fantasizing, or even through playacting, will be more accessible in memory. In addition, cues in the environment that are similar to those present when the script was first developed can encourage retrieval of that script (Tulving & Thomson, 1973). Similar to priming, then, a situational cue can prompt an aggressive memory based on a previously seen violent TV show or film.

Regardless of how a script is retrieved, once an aggressive strategy is employed, it can be reinforced and elaborated by new information in a given situation, and eventually the script becomes applicable to a wider set of circumstances (Geen, 1994). According to this perspective, the aggressive child is one who has developed from an early age a network of stable and enduring cognitive scripts that emphasize aggression as a response to social situations. Consistent and repeated exposure to violent messages in the media can contribute to the creation of these scripts and to the retrieval of already learned ones (see Figure 5.13).

Huesmann's theory incorporates ideas from observational learning and from priming but takes a broader view of how the media can contribute to aggression over time. The perspective reminds us that media violence is only one of many environmental influences that can foster habitual forms of aggression in some children. Next, we turn to the types of media portrayals that are most likely to teach aggressive patterns of behavior and the types of individuals who are most at risk for this learning.

Types of Portrayals That Encourage the Learning of Aggression

As discussed earlier, violence can be portrayed in a variety of ways. For instance, the same act of aggression looks very different when it is perpetrated by a law officer

Figure 5.13

SOURCE: Reprinted with permission of Copley News Service.

trying to save lives than by a thief trying to steal something. As it turns out, the way in which violence is portrayed may be even more important than the sheer amount of it when trying to assess its likely impact on a viewer. Research has identified seven contextual features of violence that affect the likelihood that a viewer will learn aggressive attitudes and behaviors from a portrayal (see Wilson et al., 1997).

First, an *attractive perpetrator* increases the risk of learning aggression. In accord with social learning theory, children as well as adults are more likely to attend to, identify with, and learn from attractive role models than unattractive ones (Bandura, 1986, 1994). The most obvious way to make a perpetrator appealing is to make him or her a hero (Liss et al., 1983). But even characters who act in benevolent ways can be attractive to young people (Hoffner & Cantor, 1985). Moreover, characters who are similar to the self can be potent role models. Research suggests that children, for example, pay more attention to younger than older characters when watching television (Schmitt, Anderson, & Collins, 1999) and are more likely to imitate peer than adult models (Hicks, 1965). Viewers also pay attention to and identify more with same-sex characters than opposite-sex ones (Bandura, 1986; Jose & Brewer, 1984).

Second, the motive or *reason for violence* is important. Consistent with cognitive priming, violent actions that seem justified or morally defensible can facilitate viewer aggression, whereas unjustified violence can actually diminish the risk of learning aggression (Berkowitz & Powers, 1979; Hogben, 1998). Third, the *presence of weapons* in a portrayal, particularly conventional ones such as guns and knives, can enhance aggressive responding among viewers (Berkowitz, 1990; Carlson, Marcus-Newhall, & Miller, 1990). Weapons are assumed to function as a violent cue that can prime aggressive thoughts in a viewer (Berkowitz, 1990).

Fourth, violence that seems *realistic* can promote the learning of aggressive attitudes and behaviors among viewers (Atkin, 1983; Feshbach, 1972). From this finding, it is tempting to conclude that cartoon or fantasy violence in the media is relatively harmless. However, research with very young children, to be discussed below, challenges such an assumption.

Fifth, we know from social learning theory that violence that is explicitly *rewarded* or that simply goes *unpunished* increases the risk of imitative aggression, whereas violence that is condemned decreases that risk (Bandura, 1965; Carnagey & Anderson, 2005). Sixth, the *consequences* of violence for the victim are an important contextual cue; explicit portrayals of a victim's physical injury and pain actually can decrease or inhibit the learning of aggression among viewers (R. A. Baron, 1971a, 1971b; Wotring & Greenberg, 1973). Finally, violence that is portrayed as *humorous* can increase aggression in viewers (R. A. Baron, 1978; Berkowitz, 1970). Part of the reason for this effect is that humor can trivialize the seriousness of violence (Gunter & Furnham, 1984). Researchers have speculated that humor also may serve as a positive reinforcement or reward for violence (Berkowitz, 1970).

Taken as a whole, the research clearly suggests that there are risky and not-so-risky ways of portraying violence. If a parent is concerned about a child learning aggressive behaviors from the media, then programs that feature heroes or good characters engaging in justified violence that is not punished and results in minimal consequences should be avoided (see Table 5.2). As it turns out, this formula is very common in animated programming, especially superhero and slapstick

Table 5.2   Risky Versus Educational Depictions of Violence

Media themes that *encourage* the learning of aggression

✓ "Good guys" or superheroes as perpetrators
✓ Violence that is celebrated or rewarded
✓ Violence that goes unpunished
✓ Violence that is portrayed as defensible or justified
✓ Violence that results in no serious harm to the victim
✓ Violence that is made to look funny

Media themes that *discourage* the learning of aggression

✓ Evil or bad characters as perpetrators
✓ Violence that is criticized or penalized
✓ Violence that is portrayed as unfair or morally unjust
✓ Violence that causes obvious injury and pain to the victim
✓ Violence that results in anguish and suffering for the victim's loved ones

cartoons (Wilson, Smith, et al., 2002). On the other hand, portrayals that feature less attractive perpetrators who are punished in the plot and whose violence results in serious negative consequences can actually teach youth that aggression is not necessarily a good way to solve problems.

Types of Youth Most at Risk

Not only do certain messages pose more risk, but certain young people are more susceptible to violent content. In their meta-analysis, Paik and Comstock (1994) found that viewers of all age groups can be influenced by television violence but that preschoolers show the strongest effect size. This is consistent with Huesmann's (1998) argument that early childhood learning is critical. It also reflects the fact that younger children are least likely to have developed and internalized strong social norms against aggression. As will be discussed later, younger children also have difficulties in distinguishing reality from fantasy on television (see Chapter 1), making them prone to imitating even the most fantastic presentations.

The heightened vulnerability that characterizes the preschool years means that parents should be especially cautious about mindlessly using television as a babysitter for their young children. Indeed, studies indicate that even infants as young as 12 months old are capable of imitating what they see on television (Barr, Muentener, Garcia, Fujimoto, & Chavez, 2007). Fortunately, when busy parents need a break, public broadcast channels contain very little violence and feature educational programs such as *Sesame Street* that are truly enriching for children (Fisch & Truglio, 2001).

Research also indicates that at any age, children who perceive television as realistic and who identify strongly with violent characters are most likely to learn from violent content (Huesmann et al., 2003; Konijn, Nije Bijvank, & Bushman, 2007). In a tragic case in 1999, a 12-year-old fan of TV wrestling claimed he was simply imitating his favorite heroes when he threw a 6-year-old playmate into a metal staircase, killing her (see box below). It seems that even some older children can be confused by highly scripted and unrealistic portrayals of violence.

Being in a particular emotional state also can make a child more vulnerable. Numerous studies reveal that viewers who are made to feel angry or frustrated are more likely to behave aggressively after exposure to media violence than are nonangered persons (see Paik & Comstock, 1994). According to priming, angered individuals are in a state of readiness to respond that facilitates aggressive actions (Berkowitz, 1990). It is important to note, however, that a child does not have to be angry to learn aggression from the media (see Hearold, 1986).

Being unpopular with peers and doing poorly in school also place a child at greater risk for learning aggression from media violence (see Huesmann, 1986). Social and academic failures can be frustrating experiences that instigate aggression (Huesmann, 1988). Such experiences can in turn lead to more social withdrawal and more television viewing, making the process a vicious cycle. Finally, children

TELEVISION ON TRIAL FOR MURDER?
Lionel Tate at age 14

On July 28, 1999, a 12-year-old boy named Lionel Tate beat to death his 6-year-old playmate, Tiffany Eunick. The two were playing in the Florida home that Lionel shared with his mother, who was babysitting for the girl. The mother was asleep at the time.

An autopsy showed that Tiffany suffered a fractured skull, lacerated liver, internal hemorrhaging, and more than 30 other injuries. The 170-pound boy allegedly had punched, kicked, and thrown the 48-pound girl around the room. When questioned by authorities, Lionel claimed to have accidentally thrown Tiffany into a metal staircase and a wall while trying to toss her onto a sofa.

During the murder trial, defense attorney Jim Lewis argued that Lionel was an avid fan of pro wrestling who was imitating moves he had seen on TV without realizing the damage that could occur. He claimed that Lionel was too immature to understand that pro wrestlers are not actually hurting one another. "He wanted to emulate them," Attorney Jim Lewis said (Spencer, 2001). "Like Batman and Superman, they were his heroes. He loved to play." Earlier, Lewis had tried unsuccessfully to subpoena professional wrestlers to testify at the trial.

Prosecutor Ken Padowitz argued that television violence was not on trial and that the boy knew he was savagely beating Tiffany.

After only 3 hours of deliberation, a Florida jury found Lionel guilty of first-degree murder. Pointing to the cruelty and callousness of Lionel's acts, Judge Joel T. Lazarus sentenced the boy to life in prison without the possibility of parole. Tate was one of the youngest defendants in the United States to be sentenced to spend the rest of his life in prison.

In 2004, a state appeals court overturned Tate's conviction. The appeals court ruled that it was not clear whether Tate had understood the charges against him. He was freed from prison after he agreed to plead guilty to second-degree murder and was sentenced to time already served and 10 years' probation.

Tate has been in and out of court since then. In 2005, he was arrested and accused of robbing a pizza delivery person at gunpoint. He recently pleaded no contest to the robbery charge and is serving a 30-year sentence for violating his probation in the murder case.

raised in homes characterized by parental rejection and parental aggression show stronger effects of media violence (Bauer et al., 2006; Singer & Singer, 1986).

It is important to remember that no single factor will propel a child from non-violence to violence. Instead, each risk factor increases the chances that a child will internalize and act out the violence that he or she witnesses in the media. Huesmann and Eron (1986b) summarize risk in the following way:

> For most children, aggressiveness seems to be determined mostly by the extent to which their environment reinforces aggression, provides aggressive role models, frustrates and victimizes the child, and instigates aggression. (p. 4)

Developmental Differences in Processing Media Violence

Chapter 1 describes several ways in which younger and older children differ in their processing of media messages. At least three of these have important implications for how young people are likely to interpret media violence. First, children differ markedly in their cognitive ability to distinguish reality from fantasy (see Dorr, 1983; Wright, Huston, Reitz, & Piemyat, 1994). Preschoolers often assume that anything that looks or sounds real *is* real (Brown, Skeen, & Osborn, 1979). Consistent with this tendency, studies show that preschoolers and even young elementary schoolers will readily imitate violent cartoon characters such as the Ninja Turtles and even Bugs Bunny (Bandura et al., 1963a; Friedrich & Stein, 1973; Steuer et al., 1971). Such portrayals are likely to be discounted as fantasy by older, more sophisticated viewers who are far more responsive to portrayals of violence involving events and characters that are possible in the real world (Atkin, 1983; Scharrer, 2005; Thomas & Tell, 1974).

The television rating system takes this developmental consideration into account with its "TVY7" label. Programs rated TVY7 are designed for children 7 years of age and older who have "acquired the developmental skills needed to distinguish between make-believe and reality" (*TV Parental Guidelines*, n.d.).

A second relevant cognitive skill concerns the shift from perceptual to conceptual processing. Younger children pay close attention to perceptually salient features in a program, such as what characters look like and what they do (Gibbons, Anderson, Smith, Field, & Fischer, 1986; Hoffner & Cantor, 1985; van den Broek, Lorch, & Thurlow, 1996). Older children and teens, on the other hand, can consider more conceptual or abstract information in a plot (Collins, 1975; van den Broek et al., 1996). In the realm of violence, this means that younger children are most likely to comprehend and learn from those violent behaviors and consequences that are explicitly portrayed on screen in concrete ways. When events are implied or not visually depicted, they will be more difficult for a young child. In support of this idea, Krcmar and Cooke (2001) found that younger children focused more on the punishments that a character received in judging whether an aggressive behavior was right or wrong, whereas older children focused more on the character's motives, which are typically depicted in more subtle ways.

A third important skill is the ability to draw inferences. As seen in Chapter 1, younger children are less able than their older counterparts to link scenes together, integrate information, and draw causal conclusions from the plot (Collins, 1983). Therefore, contextual cues that are separated from the violence itself will be more difficult for younger children to appreciate. Collins (1973) demonstrated this in an intriguing study involving 3rd, 6th, and 10th graders. Children viewed a violent scene in which the perpetrator was punished either immediately after engaging in violence or after a 4-minute commercial break. The results revealed that 3rd graders gave more aggressive responses themselves in the separation than in the no-separation condition (see Figure 5.14). In other words, the commercial break interfered with younger children's ability to connect the punishment to the violence—the violence stood alone as a model for behavior. In contrast, older children's responses were unaffected by the separation manipulation, suggesting that they appreciated the punishment even when it occurred at a different point in the storyline.

Unfortunately, television supplies numerous instances in which aggressive behavior goes unpunished, at least in the short run; if punishment is delivered, it typically happens toward the end of the plot (Wilson, Smith, et al., 2002). A child younger than age 7 or 8 is not capable of connecting this delayed consequence back to an earlier transgression. Therefore, if punishment is temporally separated from the act, it will seem to a younger viewer like the perpetrator "got away" with violence.

One last developmental consideration is the age of the perpetrator. As discussed above, people tend to like characters in the media who are most like themselves. It stands to reason, then, that young people will be most attracted to younger

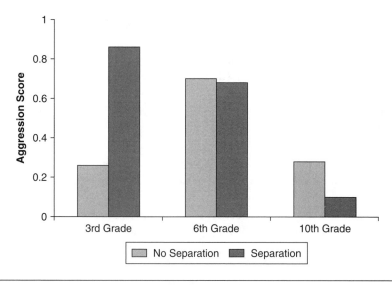

Figure 5.14   Aggression Scores as a Function of Whether the Punishment Was Separated From a Violent Act by a 4-Minute Commercial

SOURCE: Adapted from Collins (1973).

characters. Studies support this; children's visual attention to the television screen increases when a child character appears (Schmitt et al., 1999). Moreover, children typically choose characters who are similar in age as their favorites (Cohen, 1999; Hoffner, 1996). Although there are far fewer child and teen perpetrators than adult ones on television (Wilson, Colvin, & Smith, 2002), these young aggressors should be particularly salient for a younger viewer. Movies such as *Home Alone* or *Karate Kid* that feature a child engaging in justified violence are likely to be very appealing to children. Likewise, music videos, which often feature teen perpetrators (Wilson, Colvin, & Smith, 2002), can be potent messages for preadolescent and adolescent audiences.

Indirect or Social Aggression

Up to this point, we have focused primarily on physical aggression as a possible outcome of exposure to media violence. Yet in the past decade or so, developmental psychologists have come to recognize that there are other, less overt ways to engage in aggression (Underwood, 2003). Relational or social aggression involves acts that are intended to harm others emotionally rather than physically. Examples include gossiping, spreading rumors, socially isolating others, or engaging in insulting or mean talk. These types of socially aggressive behaviors can occur in face-to-face situations, and they can even be perpetrated using the Internet. In one large survey of middle school children, 11% of the youth reported that they had been electronically bullied through instant messaging, in a chat room, or by e-mail at least once in recent months (Kowalski & Limber, 2007)

Like physical aggression, social aggression emerges early in development, by age 3 or so (Crick, Ostrov, & Werner, 2006). However, unlike physical aggression, social aggression is more common among girls than boys (Ostrov, 2006). Public concern about this type of behavior has spawned a number of popular books, with titles such as *Queen Bees and Wannabes: Helping Your Daughter Survive Cliques, Gossip, Boyfriends, and Other Realities of Adolescence*. Popular movies such as *Mean Girls* also illustrate this type of behavior.

Some preliminary research suggests that the media may be contributing to social aggression. One content analysis found that 92% of programs popular among adolescents contained acts of social or indirect aggression (Coyne & Archer, 2004). Such behavior was perpetrated by female characters more often than by male characters. Research also suggests that adolescents are exposed to far more indirect and social aggression on television than they are in school (Coyne, Archer, & Eslea, 2006). Finally, one recent study of preschoolers found that media exposure was positively associated with physical aggression for boys and with relational aggression for girls (Ostrov, Gentile, & Crick, 2006). Unfortunately, the study did not cleanly assess the content of what children were watching. Clearly, more research is needed on this provocative topic. It may be that our fixation on physical aggression has caused us to overlook other types of harmful outcomes of media violence, especially those that are more prominent among girls.

Can Media Violence Desensitize Young People?

Concern about children's aggressive behavior has certainly dominated most of the public debates and the research on media violence. However, an outcome that may be far more pervasive is desensitization (see Figure 5.15). Desensitization refers to the idea that extensive exposure to a stimulus can lead to reduced emotional responsiveness to it. In clinical settings, desensitization techniques have been used to treat people's phobias (Graziano, DeGiovanni, & Garcia, 1979). For example, a person who is frightened of dogs is gradually exposed under nonthreatening circumstances to a variety of these types of animals. Eventually, the person acclimates to dogs and the fear is eliminated. Can repeated exposure to media violence be similarly therapeutic?

We do know that repeated viewing of violent materials can affect a person's arousal responses. For example, one study found that boys who were heavy viewers of television exhibited less physiological arousal during selected scenes from a violent film than did light viewers (Cline, Croft, & Courrier, 1973). Other studies have documented that even within a single program, people's heart rate and skin conductance go down over time during prolonged exposure to violence (Lazarus & Alfert, 1964; Speisman, Lazarus, Davison, & Mordkoff, 1964). Some critics have speculated that American films and television programs are becoming increasingly graphic and violent because audiences are desensitized to tamer versions of such content (Plagens, Miller, Foote, & Yoffe, 1991).

Figure 5.15

SOURCE: Reprinted with permission of the Creators Syndicate.

If repeated exposure to media violence merely resulted in decreased arousal, there might be little cause for concern. In fact, one could argue that a reduction in arousal is even functional given that being in a heightened state of arousal for too long can be taxing to the body (Ursin & Eriksen, 2001). What alarms people is the possibility that desensitization to entertainment violence might in turn affect responses to real-life violence. In their book *High Tech, High Touch: Technology and Our Search for Meaning*, Naisbitt, Naisbitt, and Philips (1999) write,

> In a culture of electronic violence, images that once caused us to empathize with the pain and trauma of another human being excite a momentary adrenaline rush. To be numb to another's pain—to be acculturated to violence—is arguably one of the worst consequences our technological advances have wrought. That indifference transfers from the screen, TV, film, Internet, and electronic games to our everyday lives through seemingly innocuous consumer technologies. (pp. 90–91)

Research suggests that there is some merit to this concern. For example, one study found that both children and adults were less physiologically aroused by a scene of real-life aggression if they had previously watched a violent drama on TV than if they had watched a nonviolent program (Thomas, Horton, Lippincott, & Drabman, 1977). In other words, the fictional portrayal produced an indifference to real-life violence. Violent video games can have a similar effect (see Chapter 10). In one study, college students who were avid violent game players were less responsive to explicit photographs of real violence than were those who seldom played such games (Bartholow, Bushman, & Sestir, 2006).

Even more troubling, can desensitization affect people's willingness to intervene or take action on behalf of a victim? In one experiment (Thomas & Drabman, 1975), first and third graders were shown either a violent or a nonviolent TV program and then placed in charge of monitoring the behavior of two preschoolers at play. Older children who viewed the violent TV show were significantly slower in seeking help when the preschoolers broke into a fight than were those who viewed the nonviolent show. In fact, more than half the older children in the violent TV condition never left the room even though they had been told to get an adult if trouble erupted. This type of callousness to real violence has been replicated in other media studies involving children (Drabman & Thomas, 1974; Molitor & Hirsch, 1994).

Research suggests that young adults can become callous too. Over a period of 1 or 2 weeks, Linz, Donnerstein, and Penrod (1984, 1988) exposed male undergraduates to five full-length "slasher" films depicting violence against women, such as *Texas Chainsaw Massacre* and *Toolbox Murders*. After each film, emotional reactions, perceptions of violence in the films, and attitudes toward the women in the films were measured. Supporting the idea of desensitization, males perceived less violence in the films and evaluated the films as less degrading to women over the course of the exposure period. At the end of the viewing period, participants were asked to evaluate a videotaped enactment of a legal trial involving a rape victim.

Compared with various control groups, males who had been exposed to a heavy dose of slasher films were less sympathetic toward a rape victim and more inclined to hold her responsible.

One critical question is whether desensitization is a transitory effect or a more permanent state that persists beyond the exposure period. That is, can people become *re*sensitized to real-world violence? Mullin and Linz (1995) tested this idea by varying the amount of time that lapsed between exposure to fictional violence and evaluations of real victims of violence. In this experiment, male college students were exposed to three slasher films over a 6-day period. In a supposedly unrelated context, they were asked either 3, 5, or 7 days later to watch a documentary about domestic abuse. The researchers found that 3 days after exposure, males expressed less sympathy for domestic violence victims and rated their injuries as less severe than did a no-exposure control group (see Figure 5.16). However, 5 and 7 days later, levels of sympathy had rebounded to the baseline level of the control group. In other words, the desensitization effect seemed to diminish after about a 3-day period.

Of course, resensitization requires that a person is no longer exposed to entertainment violence during the "recovery" period. As we have seen, most children watch between 2 and 3 hours of television per day, and many watch a great deal more. Given the pervasiveness of violence in this medium, heavy viewers are presumably exposed to a fairly constant diet of aggressive behaviors. If these same children also play violent video games, listen to violent music, and go to a violent film or two a month, there are ample occasions for desensitization to occur and not much of an opportunity to reestablish sensitivity to aggression.

Because desensitization is construed as an automatic process similar to habituation, it can happen without a person's awareness. Furthermore, unlike aggression, which is easy to see, there are fewer outward manifestations of this type of effect.

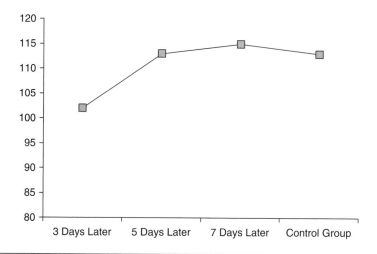

Figure 5.16   Perceptions of Domestic Violence Victim Days After Desensitization to Media Violence

SOURCE: Adapted from Mullin and Linz (1995).

Thus, large numbers of young people in our society may be gradually becoming desensitized by media violence without us ever knowing. The popularity in recent years of graphically violent movies such as *Casino Royale* and graphic television series such as *24* suggests to some that we are already experiencing a cultural shift in our tolerance for violence in the media (Hayes, 2007). The danger, of course, is in the possibility that such an effect will spill over into real life, resulting in a society that is increasingly indifferent to the plight of others.

Can Media Violence Produce Fear?

The third potential effect of media violence is to create fear in audiences (see Figure 5.17). Many of us can remember a movie or TV show that frightened us as a child. In one study, more than 90% of college students could vividly describe a film or television program that caused intense fear when they were younger (Harrison & Cantor, 1999). *Psycho, Jaws,* and *The Exorcist* were just a few of the more common movies cited. Amazingly, one fourth of these students said they were still bothered today by what they had seen.

These patterns are consistent with research involving children themselves. Surveys indicate that a majority of preschoolers and elementary schoolers have experienced fright reactions to mass media programming, much of which is

Figure 5.17

SOURCE: Jeff Stahler: ©Columbus Dispatch/Dist. by Newspaper Enterprise Association, Inc. Reprinted with permission.

violent (Cantor & Sparks, 1984; Sparks, 1986; Wilson, Hoffner, & Cantor, 1987). Furthermore, many of these reactions have endured beyond the viewing experience, resulting in nightmares, sleep disturbances, and even acute fears in some cases (see Cantor, 1998). In fact, studies have documented symptoms of posttraumatic stress disorder in young people as a result of media exposure to violent news events such as the Oklahoma City bombing and the terrorist attacks on September 11, 2001 (Otto et al., 2007; Pfefferbaum et al., 2000).

The types of images that frighten children change as a function of age or developmental level (for reviews, see Cantor, 2003; Cantor & Wilson, 1988). Preschoolers and younger elementary schoolers respond most to characters and scenes that *look* scary, consistent with the idea of perceptual dependence discussed in Chapter 1. Therefore, younger children are often frightened by programs that feature monsters, gory-looking characters, and witches. *The Wizard of Oz* and even certain Disney films are examples of upsetting content for this age group. In contrast, older elementary school children are less upset by surface features and more concerned about whether a violent portrayal could happen in real life. Again, this is consistent with the gradual understanding of reality-fantasy distinctions. Thus, more realistic programs that involve harm to human beings, especially family members, are often cited as frightening by 8- to 12-year-olds. Interestingly, this age group also is more likely to be scared by TV news stories of violent crime than their younger counterparts are (Cantor & Nathanson, 1996; Smith & Wilson, 2002). Adolescents respond to realistic depictions too, but their abstract thinking skills also allow them to imagine implausible and inconceivable events (see Chapter 1). Therefore, teens are far more susceptible than children to intangible threats in the media such as global conflict, nuclear war, and political attacks (Cantor, Wilson, & Hoffner, 1986).

Gerbner and his colleagues took the idea of fear one step further, arguing that extensive exposure to media violence can lead to a greater sense of apprehension, mistrust, and insecurity about the real world (Gerbner & Gross, 1976; Gerbner, Gross, Morgan, & Signorielli, 1994). In other words, violence in the media can cultivate a "mean world syndrome" in viewers (Signorielli, 1990). According to cultivation theory, heavy exposure to television can alter a person's perceptions of social reality in a way that matches the TV world. Given that television features so much violence, heavy viewers should come to see the world as more violent (see Figure 5.18). In numerous studies with samples of all different ages, Gerbner and his colleagues consistently found that frequent viewers of television perceive the world as a more violent place and perceive themselves as more likely to become a victim of violence than do light viewers (see Signorielli & Morgan, 1990).

Cultivation theory has been rigorously critiqued by other researchers (Hawkins & Pingree, 1981; Hirsch, 1980; Hughes, 1980; Potter, 1993). One of the most widespread concerns is that most of the findings that support the theory are correlational. The cultivation effect does typically hold up even after controlling for demographic variables as well as other factors that could explain the relationship between TV and perceptions of reality (see Morgan & Shanahan, 1996). But even after controlling for "third" variables, it is difficult to determine the direction of causality from correlational data. Does television cause fear, or are frightened

Figure 5.18

SOURCE: Reprinted with permission.

people drawn to watching more TV, in part because such content allows them to work out their fears? In support of cultivation theory, experimental evidence shows that repeated exposure to television violence, for as little as 1 week or as much as 6 weeks, under controlled conditions can heighten fear and anxiety in viewers (Bryant, Carveth, & Brown, 1981; Ogles & Hoffner, 1987). However, research also shows that crime-apprehensive people seek out violent drama, especially that which features the restoration of justice (Zillmann & Wakshlag, 1985). As with aggression, then, the relationship between entertainment violence and anxiety may be cyclical in nature.

A second criticism of the theory is that it assumes all television content is alike and that what matters most in predicting cultivation is sheer amount of exposure to TV. We have already seen that PBS features relatively little violence (Wilson et al., 1998), so it stands to reason that if a child selectively watches that particular channel, there would be less likelihood of enhanced fear. Research also suggests that cultivation is heightened among those who watch a great deal of news content (Romer, Jamieson, & Aday, 2003). Thus, a person's television habits and favorite genres seem to be important factors to consider.

A third criticism is that the theory is too simplistic because it predicts an effect for anyone who watches a lot of television. In fact, not all of the subgroups in Gerbner's studies show a cultivation effect (Gerbner et al., 1980), suggesting that intervening variables are at work. Some studies indicate that cultivation is more likely to occur among those who perceive television as realistic (e.g., Busselle, 2001). Also, research suggests that personal experience with crime as well as motivation for viewing television (i.e., to learn vs. to escape) may be important mediating factors (Gross & Aday, 2003; Perse, 1990). In addition, the cognitive abilities of the viewer may make a difference. Preschoolers, for example, lack the ability to distinguish reality and fantasy and the ability to integrate information from a program, so their perceptions may be less influenced by media content (Hawkins & Pingree, 1980). However, recent studies have found that by the elementary school years, exposure to news programming on TV is associated with exaggerated perceptions of murder and even child kidnapping (Smith & Wilson, 2002; Wilson, Martins, & Marske, 2005).

Finally, the theory has paid little attention to the cognitive processes that underlie cultivation. Shrum (2002) has argued that cultivation is a result of heuristic processing. Compared with more careful, systematic processing, heuristic processing is characterized by rapid and less careful thinking as well as the reliance on cognitive shortcuts and readily available or salient information. According to Shrum, most people engage in heuristic processing when asked to make judgments. Moreover, heavy viewers of television have numerous salient examples of violence stored in their memory. The more a person watches violent programming, the more accessible these exemplars are and the more likely they will be used in making judgments about social reality. In support of this model, one study found that college students who were encouraged to think carefully and accurately in answering questions about the incidence of crime in the world were *less* likely to show a cultivation effect than were students encouraged to make rapid judgments or students given no instructions about how to answer the questions (Shrum, 2001). Thus, cultivation may be a function of the extent to which people engage in heuristic processing and have lots of instances of media violence stored in memory.

Despite the criticisms of cultivation theory, there is still a great deal of evidence supporting the idea that media violence can make people feel more anxious about real-world crime (see Potter, 1999). As Shrum (2001) recently stated, "The notion that the viewing of television program content is related to people's perceptions of reality is virtually undisputed in the social sciences" (p. 94). The challenge for the future is to better understand how and when this cultivation effect occurs. Also, research needs to explore the relationship between fear and desensitization, which seem like contradictory outcomes. Perhaps repeated exposure to media violence frightens some and numbs others, depending on the nature of the content that is sought as well as the type of individual who seeks it.

Cultural Debates About Media Violence

Despite all the evidence presented here, there are critics who disagree that media violence is harmful (see Figure 5.19). Some of the most vocal opponents are people who work in the industry. To many of them, media violence has become a convenient scapegoat for politicians who refuse to grapple with more deep-seated causes of violence such as gun access and poverty (Schaefer, 1999). Another argument often made is that good drama requires conflict and conflict means violence (Braxton, 1991). Others in the industry argue that media violence will disappear if people simply quit watching it and paying for it (Pool, 1991). In other words, in the marketplace of American culture, consumers are ultimately responsible for the violence that surrounds us. Violence does seem to attract audiences, as we discussed above. Yet there are many examples of good storytelling with little or no physical aggression. Cartoon series such as *Arthur,* situation comedies such as *Zoey 101,* and even movies such as *Dreamer* and *Akeelah and the Bee* illustrate this point. One of the problems is that violence is relatively easy and cheap to produce and has a strong international market (Groebel, 2001). Action movies seem to translate fairly easily across cultural, national, and linguistic borders.

There also are scholars who challenge the research. Some are social scientists themselves who critique the validity and reliability of the studies. For example, Freedman (2002) points out the limitations of laboratory studies, field experiments, and correlational research and concludes that the evidence does not yet support a causal relationship between TV violence and aggression. Others argue that focusing on the "effects" of media violence on children is too simplistic and unidimensional, ignoring how young people choose, interpret, and negotiate violent media texts in their lives (Buckingham, 2000). Still others believe that social science research obfuscates larger issues such as how media violence as a cultural institution legitimates power and control in our society (Ball-Rokeach, 2000). A more radical

Figure 5.19

SOURCE: Copyright Sidney Harris. Reprinted with permission.

view is represented by Fowles (1999), who believes that media violence is therapeutic for people. At least in the social science arena, though, there is little evidence to support this position.

Obviously, there are many points of view regarding media violence. The debates are heated, and given the stakes involved, there are no easy solutions. Social scientists are increasingly joining the debates and grappling with the politics of their work (Bushman & Anderson, 2001; Huesmann & Taylor, 2003). The challenge, it seems, is to stay focused on children in the midst of these political and scholarly disputes.

Guns and the Media

Firearms play a leading role in mortality and morbidity among American youth (CDC, 2006). In fact, the death rate due to firearms among U.S. children is nearly 12 times higher than among children in 25 other industrialized countries *combined* (CDC, 1997). Moreover, gunshot wounds to American children have increased 300% in major urban areas since 1986 (Gaensbauer & Wamboldt, 2000). In 2006 alone, more than 17,000 youth younger than age 20 were victims of nonfatal gunshot injuries (CDC, 2006).

There is little doubt that the United States is "the most heavily armed nation on earth" (O. G. Davidson, 1993), with approximately 35% of homes with children younger than 18 years of age having at least one firearm (Schuster, Franke, Bastian, Sor, & Halfon, 2000). Of these, 13% or 1.4 million homes store the firearms unlocked and either loaded or with ammunition nearby. And children seem to know it. In one national survey, 24% of adolescents reported that they have "easy access" to a gun in their home (Swahn, Hammig, & Ikeda, 2002). In another national study, 22% of boys between the ages of 11 and 15 reportedly had carried a firearm or handgun in the previous 30 days (Pickett et al., 2005) and could get a gun in 24 hours. According to this same study, weapon carrying among youth was higher in the United States than in 34 other European and North American countries.

Unfortunately, guns kept at home can be more dangerous to the people who live there than to any criminal intruder (Kellermann et al., 1993; Kellermann, Somes, Rivara, Lee, & Banton, 1998). In one 5-year study of youth brought to a medical trauma center, 75% of the guns used in suicide attempts and unintentional injuries came from the victim's home or the home of a relative or friend (Grossman, Reay, & Baker, 1999). In another study in New Mexico, 25 unintentional firearm deaths and 200 woundings were identified within a 4-year period, mostly involving children playing with loaded guns at home (Martin, Sklar, & McFeeley, 1991).

Large epidemiological studies show that keeping a gun in the home increases the risk of suicide and homicide among adults who reside there (Bailey et al., 1997; Kellermann et al., 1993) and even increases the risk of suicidal tendencies and violence among teen residents (Resnick et al., 1997). One study found that the odds of a depressed teenager successfully committing suicide increase 75-fold if there is a gun kept at home (Rosenberg, Mercy, & Houk, 1991). Yet nearly 1.7 million children and youth in the United States are living in homes with loaded and unlocked firearms (Okoro et al., 2005). Furthermore, 23% of gun-owning parents believe that their child can be trusted with a loaded gun (Farah, Simon, & Kellermann, 1999).

One study graphically demonstrates just how naive children can be about firearms. Jackman, Farah, Kellermann, and Simon (2001) observed more than 60 boys between the ages of 8 and 12 as they played in a room full of toys. The room also contained an unloaded .380 caliber handgun concealed in a drawer. Within 15 minutes of play, the vast majority of boys (75%) discovered the gun. More disturbing, 63% of the boys who found the gun handled it, and 33% actually pulled the trigger. When questioned afterward, almost half of the boys who found the gun thought it was a toy or were not sure whether it was real (see Figure 5.20). Children from gun-owning families behaved no differently than children from non-gunowning families.

Despite all the risks, many Americans seem to have a longstanding love of guns, and this passion is frequently played out in the movies and on television. A study of 50 top-grossing G-and PG-rated nonanimated films revealed that 40% of the movies featured at least one main character carrying a firearm (Pelletier et al., 1999). In fact, across the films, a total of 127 persons carried firearms, resulting in a median of 4.5 armed characters per film. Nearly all of these movies were comedies or family films likely to be seen by children.

But such images are not limited to the movies (see Figure 5.21). Young children can readily witness laser guns and a variety of other types of firearms being used in cartoons such as *Men in Black* and even *Bugs Bunny*. Using data from the National

Figure 5.20

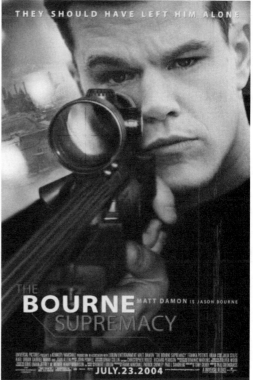

Figure 5.21   Images of Guns in Television and Film

Television Violence Study described above, Smith, Boyson, Pieper, and Wilson (2001) found that 26% of all violent incidents in a composite week of television involved the use of a gun. Three types of programming accounted for most of this gun violence: movies (54%), dramatic series (19%), and children's shows (16%). Looking at rate, a child viewer on average will see nearly two gun-related violent incidents every hour that he or she watches TV. That rate goes up if the child selectively watches gun-filled genres such as movies or children's shows.

According to cognitive priming, images of guns in the media can trigger aggressive thoughts and ideas in young viewers. In one experiment, just flashing pictures of guns and other weapons on a computer screen served to prime aggressive-related thoughts in college students (Anderson, Benjamin, & Bartholow, 1998). In other words, a gun need not even be fired to incite aggression. In support of this idea, a meta-analysis of 56 experiments found that the mere presence of weapons, either pictorially or in the natural environment, significantly enhanced aggression among angered as well as nonangered adults (Carlson et al., 1990).

Clearly, the portrayal of guns in entertainment media is a public health concern. For many young children, television will be the first place they encounter such weapons. Repeated exposure to images of heroes and other attractive role models using firearms will at the very least help to glorify these deadly devices. Even the news can now and then draw attention to gun use. Some criticized NBC's decision to release graphic photos and video clips of the Virginia Tech killer wielding guns with outstretched arms, in part because such publicity gives undue notoriety to deranged individuals (Klimkiewicz, 2007).

Suicide and the Media

Suicide is the third leading cause of death among adolescents ages 15 to 19 (Anderson & Smith, 2003). However, many teens consider suicide without attempting it or attempt it without being successful. Suicidal thoughts are alarmingly common among teenagers. In a recent national survey, 17% of all high schoolers reported having seriously considered attempting suicide in the previous 12 months, and 13% had actually made a plan about how they would do it (Youth Risk Behavior Surveillance System, 2006). Given such statistics, having firearms in the home and making firearms a common feature in the media both seem like dangerous practices.

In addition to glorifying guns, the media may contribute to adolescent suicide by highlighting such behavior in public cases (Phillips, Carstensen, & Paight, 1989). On April 5, 1994, lead singer Kurt Cobain of the popular rock group Nirvana put a shotgun to his head and pulled the trigger. The highly publicized suicide prompted a great deal of public concern about the potential of this event to spark copycat behaviors among anguished teen fans (Jobes, Berman, O'Carroll, Eastgard, & Knickmeyer, 1996). In fact, a number of studies, both in the United States and Europe, have demonstrated a link between media coverage of suicide and subsequent increases in such behavior among teens (Gould & Davidson, 1988; Gould, Shaffer, & Kleinman, 1988; Phillips & Carstensen, 1986; Romer,

Jamieson, & Jamieson, 2006). This contagion effect has been found for both local TV news coverage and newspaper coverage of stories (Romer et al., 2006). In addition, the more TV networks that feature a suicide story in the news, the greater is the increase in suicides thereafter (Phillips & Carstensen, 1986).

One key factor in this phenomenon may be the extent to which a susceptible teen identifies with the publicized suicide victim (L. E. Davidson, Rosenberg, Mercy, Franklin, & Simmons, 1989). In support of this idea, a recent meta-analysis of 55 studies on the effect of suicide stories in the news found that the risk of contagion was significantly greater when a celebrity was involved (Stack, 2005). However, because the studies to date all involve large numbers of young people, it is difficult to know precisely what influenced any particular individual. In addition, although such research typically controls for factors such as time of year and yearly trends in suicide, the data are still only correlational so they are always subject to alternative explanations. And it should be noted that a few early studies found no relationship at all between media coverage and suicide rates (J. N. Baron & Reiss, 1985; L. E. Davidson et al., 1989; Phillips & Paight, 1987).

Fictional media content can also portray suicide stories. Popular films such as *The Virgin Suicides* and *A Beautiful Mind* focus on characters struggling with mental illness and suicidal tendencies. Other films such as *Romeo and Juliet* almost seem to celebrate suicide by depicting it as a heroic act. There is some evidence to suggest that the depiction of suicidal themes in feature-length films has increased in recent years (see Gould, Jamieson, & Romer, 2003). Furthermore, exposure to such films has been linked to particular beliefs about mental illness. One recent national survey found that among adolescents and young adults identified as depressed/suicidal, frequent viewing of films with mentally disturbed characters was associated with less confidence in the effectiveness of mental health treatments (Jamieson, Romer, & Jamieson, 2006). Among nontroubled youth, however, there was no relationship between film exposure and treatment beliefs. The researchers speculated that movies that glorify suicide and fail to model successful coping techniques may be teaching young people about the futility of seeking help. Because these data are correlational, it could also be that troubled youth who are already skeptical about treatment are seeking out these types of films.

Clearly, the causes of suicidal behaviors are complex and multifold (Gould, Fisher, Parides, Flory, & Shaffer, 1996). Yet a great deal of research supports an idea known in the medical field as suicide "contagion" (Gould & Davidson, 1988), whereby exposure to the suicide of one person encourages others to attempt such behavior. The contagion effect appears to be stronger among adolescents than adults (Gould, Wallenstein, Kleinman, O'Carroll, & Mercy, 1990) and is quite consistent with the idea that suicidal tendencies might be learned and/or primed by observing the behavior of others. Given that troubled teens do seem to take notice of public suicides, the CDC and the American Association of Suicidology have issued guidelines for reporting suicide in the media (see www.suicidology.org/displaycommon.cfm?an=9). They recommend that news stories avoid sensationalizing the act, glorifying the person involved, or providing how-to details. Such suggestions can apply just as easily to entertainment programs that feature suicide in the plot.

Marketing Violence to Youth

The most graphic and intense violence is often featured in media that are targeted to adults. R-rated movies, for example, contain adult material that may include strong language, violence, nudity, and/or drug abuse and thus are not for persons younger than age 16 unless accompanied by a parent. M-rated video games may contain intense violence, blood and gore, sexual content, and/or strong language and thus are designed for persons age 17 and older. Yet many young teens and even older children find their way to such "mature" content. How do they even know about such products?

In the wake of the 1999 Columbine school shootings, public attention became focused on this very question when it was discovered that the two teen perpetrators were obsessed with graphically violent movies and video games. Then President Clinton asked the Federal Trade Commission (FTC) to investigate the extent to which media violence was being marketed to young people (see Figure 5.22). The FTC requested information from the major motion picture studios, music recording companies, and electronic game companies. Commission staff also conducted consumer surveys and visited retail stores and movie theaters. In 2000, the FTC issued its first report (*Marketing Violent Entertainment to Children: A Review of Self-Regulation and Industry Practices in the Motion Picture, Music Recording & Electronic Game Industries*). The report was critical of all three entertainment industries (movies, music, video games), pointing out that their marketing practices were inconsistent with the ratings

Figure 5.22

SOURCE: Ed Stein: ©The Rocky Mountain News/Dist. By Newspaper Enterprise Association, Inc.

and advisories they themselves assigned to many of their products. Among the findings were the following:

- Of 44 movies rated R that were examined, 80% were marketed to youngsters younger than age 17.
- Of 55 music recordings with "explicit content" labels, all or 100% were marketed to kids younger than age 17; 27% expressly identified teenagers as part of their target audience.
- Of 118 electronic games with a mature rating for violence, 70% were targeted to children younger than age 17.

The report (FTC, 2000) concluded the following:

The motion picture, music recording, and electronic game industries should stop targeting children under 17 in their marketing of products with violent content. All three industries should increase consumer outreach, both to educate parents about the meaning of the ratings and to alert them to the critical part the industries assume parents play in mediating their children's exposure to these products. (p. 53)

In follow-up reports in 2001 and 2002 (FTC, 2001, 2002), the FTC acknowledged progress made by the movie and gaming industries in restricting their advertising of violent products and in publicizing ratings for consumers. Both reports were critical, however, of the music industry, which continued to place ads for explicit-content music in TV shows and magazines popular with teens.

The FTC issued another follow-up report to Congress in 2007 (FTC, 2007). Once again, the media received a mixed review. The report found that all three industries (movie, music, and video game) generally comply with their own voluntary standards regarding the display of ratings and advisories for consumers. However, the industries continue to market some R-rated movies, M-rated video games, and explicit-content recordings on TV shows and Web sites that attract substantial teen audiences, according to the report (see Figure 5.23). The report also found that a substantial proportion of underage youth were able to rent R-rated movies on DVD and purchase music with a Parental Advisory Label. However, it was more difficult for youth to purchase M-rated video games, resulting in praise for the gaming retailers. The FTC recommended that all three industries adopt new, or tighten existing, standards for how products are marketed and sold. "Self-regulation, long a critical underpinning of U.S. advertising, is weakened if industry markets products in ways inconsistent with their ratings and parental advisories," said FTC Chair Deborah Platt Majoras (FTC, 2007).

The FTC investigations confirm what many parents and critics have long believed—the industry promotes some of its most explicitly violent materials to young consumers.

Government Regulation of Media Violence

Since the advent of television, politicians at the state and national levels have expressed concern about the impact of violent messages on youth. As early as 1954,

Figure 5.23

SOURCE: 2000 Handelsman—*Times-Picayune*. Reprinted with permission.

the U.S. Senate Subcommittee on Juvenile Delinquency held hearings on youth aggression, and at that time, television violence was identified as a possible contributory factor (U.S. Senate, 1956). In the late 1960s, Congress asked the U.S. Surgeon General to conduct a massive program of research on the effects of television violence. The resulting report concluded that exposure to television violence "may lead to increased aggressive behaviors in certain subgroups of children, who might constitute a small portion or a substantial proportion of the total population of young television viewers" (Surgeon General's Scientific Advisory Committee, 1972, p. 7). The complicated qualifications in the report led to conflicting conclusions in the popular press (Liebert & Sprafkin, 1988). Nevertheless, the report stimulated additional congressional hearings and even more research throughout the 1980s.

By the 1990s, there was considerable agreement in the scientific community about the harmful effects of television violence (Kunkel & Wilcox, 2002). Yet attempts over the years to directly regulate TV violence have faced considerable hurdles because of the First Amendment. Furthermore, any laws governing TV violence would have to define what violence is. One alternative to censorship is to pass legislation that helps consumers more effectively control their own exposure to violent content. In this vein, Congress passed the Telecommunications Act of 1996, which required all new television sets to be equipped with an electronic filtering device called a "V-chip." The V-chip can be used to screen out objectionable types of content and even entire channels, so long as there is a system in place that labels content for consumers. Toward this end, the V-chip legislation encouraged the industry to devise its own rating system. The age-based system that was created by various industry representatives mirrors the Motion Picture Association of America (MPAA) movie ratings and is called the TV Parental Guidelines. The V-chip has not been as useful as many child advocates had hoped, in part because many parents are unaware of the TV ratings and/or do not understand how to program the V-chip (see Chapter 12). There is also evidence that many programs containing violence, especially children's programs, do not get appropriately labeled with a V for violent content (Kunkel et al., 2002).

The V-chip legislation represents the first tangible policy enacted by the government regarding media violence (Kunkel & Wilcox, 2002). But recent events suggest it may not be the last. In 2007, the Federal Communications Commission (FCC) issued a major report on television violence based on hundreds of comments from parents, industry representatives, public health officials, and academic experts (FCC, 2007). The FCC (2007) report stated, "We agree with the views of the Surgeon General and find that, on balance, research provides strong evidence that exposure to violence in the media can increase aggressive behavior in children, at least in the short term" (p. 3). The report also found that "there is deep concern among many American parents and health professionals regarding harm from viewing violence in the media" (FCC, 2007, p. 3). The report argued that the V-chip and the voluntary TV ratings system are of limited effectiveness in helping parents to protect their children. Finally, the FCC concluded that Congress has the authority to regulate "excessive violence" and to extend its reach for the first time to basic cable channels that consumers pay to receive. Recommendations included the passing of legislation that would allow the FCC to regulate violent content much as it regulates sexual content and indecency, as well as providing consumers greater choice in how they purchase programming from cable and multichannel programming operators. Congress is expected to begin drafting legislation based on the conclusions of the FCC report. There is no doubt that such regulation will be controversial and hotly contested by the television industry.

Japan Versus the United States: A Cross-Cultural Comparison

The only country in the world with nearly as much entertainment violence as the United States is Japan. Yet Japanese society is less violent than American society. If media violence contributes to real-life aggression, why is Japan not more affected? There are several important differences between the two countries. First, the portrayal of violence is different in Japan. A 1981 study found that compared with American television, programming in Japan more heavily emphasizes the negative consequences of violence in the storyline (Iwao, Pool, & Hagiwara, 1981). Interestingly, in Japan, the "bad guys" commit most of the TV violence, with the "good guys" suffering the consequences—a pattern that is exactly opposite to what is found in American programming (Smith et al., 1998). As discussed earlier, featuring unattractive perpetrators and showing victim pain both reduce the risk that a portrayal will encourage aggression in viewers.

Second, children are raised in fairly traditional family structures with strong emphasis on discipline and control. Third, Japan has very strict gun control laws. Individuals are not allowed to own guns, and very few exceptions are allowed. The only type of firearm a citizen may acquire is a shotgun, for hunting purposes only, and only after a lengthy licensing procedure involving classes, a written exam, and medical certification of mental health (Kopel, 1993).

Despite these cultural differences, teen violence in Japan is on the rise. By U.S. standards, the figures are still low. But the number of minors younger than age 14 who committed violent crimes increased 47% from 2002 to 2003 (Faiola, 2004). The recent surge in youth violence has led some to point fingers at the increasingly violent nature of Japanese media (Faiola, 2004). Often quite graphic, Japanese *anime* or animation is now exported worldwide in the form of comic books, cartoons, short films, and video games (Rutenberg, 2001). Others have blamed the escalation of violence in Japan on an intensive educational system and a breakdown in traditional values (Lies, 2001). Japan can still be considered a relatively peaceful country relative to the United States, but the celebration of violence in popular culture there is giving rise to public concern.

Can Media Violence Have Positive Effects?

Much of this chapter has focused on the negative effects of exposure to media violence. However, violent portrayals can have prosocial effects as well. In June 1998, Court TV commissioned a study to assess whether television violence could help teach young people to be *less* aggressive (Wilson et al., 1999). In the study, 513 young adolescents from three different middle schools in California were randomly assigned to receive or not receive an antiviolence curriculum in school. The *Choices and Consequences* curriculum was presented by the regular teachers during normal class time (see www.courttv.com/choices/intro.html). The 3-week curriculum involved watching videotaped court cases about real teens who had engaged in risky behavior that resulted in someone dying. In one case, for example, a group of teens pushed a young boy off a railroad trestle and he drowned.

Each week, students watched portions of the videotaped trial, discussed them in class, engaged in role-playing activities, and completed homework assignments based on the trial case. Compared with the no-curriculum control group, the intervention significantly reduced middle schoolers' verbal aggression and curbed their physical aggression. The curriculum also increased empathic skills and knowledge of the legal system. In other words, exposure to programming that emphasized the lifelong negative consequences of antisocial behavior had prosocial effects on teens.

Other types of critical viewing curricula have been tested as well. For example, Huesmann, Eron, Klein, Brice, and Fischer (1983) had second and fourth graders write essays about the harmful effects of television violence and the unrealistic nature of particular violent shows. Then children were videotaped while they read their essays, and the footage purportedly was to be used to create a film about the problems of media violence. Compared with a control group that wrote essays about hobbies, the intervention group showed several positive effects. The intervention significantly altered children's attitudes about TV violence, decreased their aggressive behavior, and eliminated the relationship between TV violence and aggressive behavior. Most of these effects were measured 4 months after the intervention, suggesting that a rather simple treatment can produce lasting changes. Such efforts are consistent with larger programs designed to teach media literacy to children (see Chapter 13).

Even in the absence of instructions or structured lessons plans, programs that treat violence in a sensitive manner can have a positive impact on audience members. One large-scale experiment found that a made-for-TV movie about acquaintance rape increased adults' concern about the societal problems associated with rape and also reduced their acceptance of rape myths (Wilson, Linz, Donnerstein, & Stipp, 1992). Another study documented similar educational benefits of watching a TV movie about date rape among high schoolers (Filotas, 1993). Although no empirical tests have confirmed this, movies such as *Hotel Rwanda, Mystic River,* and *Blood Diamond* that portray the realistic consequences of violence presumably can help educate youth about the personal and societal costs associated with aggression.

Conclusion

Today there is strong consensus among social scientists that exposure to aggressive messages on television and in movies can have harmful effects on youth (Bushman & Huesmann, 2001; Smith & Donnerstein, 1998). The most well-documented effect concerns aggression. Experimental studies, correlational research, longitudinal studies, and meta-analyses of published data all point to the same conclusion: Aggression is a learned behavior that can be acquired, reinforced, and primed by media messages. Young children are particularly vulnerable, as are children who strongly identify with violent characters, who are doing poorly in school, who perceive television as realistic, and who are unpopular with peers. The evidence does not suggest that media violence is the major cause of violence in society, but it is certainly a socially significant one. The media are part of a complex web of cultural and environmental factors that can teach and reinforce aggression as a way of solving problems.

Yet aggression is not the only possible outcome. Extensive exposure to media violence also can desensitize young people and make them more callous toward real-world violence. And in others, it can lead to exaggerated concern and fear of becoming a victim of violence. None of these outcomes is straightforward and universal. Instead, certain children and teens are more vulnerable depending on cognitive development, the types of media violence they like, and the amount of exposure they have to media violence in relation to other types of messages (see Figure 5.24).

One could advocate that violence should be eliminated from the media given all these potential risks. But violence does seem to turn a profit at least with some audiences, so it is unlikely that in a free-market society it will ever go away. Nor should we necessarily advocate that it do so. Research shows quite clearly that certain

Calvin and Hobbes

Figure 5.24

SOURCE: Reprinted with permission from Universal Press Syndicate.

portrayals are less harmful than others and that some depictions actually can have educational or prosocial effects on youth. The challenge for parents and educators is to ensure that youth are exposed to these alternative messages that accurately portray the seriousness of violence in society. The challenge to the media industry is to create more of these alternative messages and to ensure that they are just as appealing as those that glorify violence.

Exercises

1. Suppose you were asked to monitor the amount of violence on television. How would you define *violence?* What types of issues need to be considered in crafting your definition? Would you include fantasy violence? Would you include slapstick violence? How might your definition differ if you were a media researcher versus an executive in the television industry? What channels would you include in your study? What challenges, if any, do technologies such as TiVo and other digital video recording (DVR) devices pose for your study?

2. What is the most violent movie or television program you have ever seen? What made it so violent? Did you enjoy the program? Why or why not? If you were a parent, would you let your 6-year-old watch this program? Your 10-year-old? Your 15-year-old? Think about cognitive development as well as the nature of the content in addressing these questions.

3. Watch a popular cartoon and an evening crime drama on television. Compare the two in terms of *how* violence is portrayed. Think about contextual features such as the nature of the perpetrators, whether violence is rewarded or punished, and the consequences of violence. According to the research cited in this chapter, which program poses more risk to a young child viewer? Why?

4. In 1999, Mario Padilla and Samuel Ramirez, two teenage cousins, said the movie *Scream* inspired them to kill one of their mothers. That same year, two troubled teens who were obsessed with violent video games walked into Columbine High School and started shooting. Media violence is often blamed in these and

many other "copycat" behaviors. Should the media be placed on trial? Who or what is responsible for violence in these cases? Should writers and producers be held to any standards regarding the violent material they create?

5. Critics charge that television news is more violent than ever, often relying on the "if it bleeds, it leads" rule of practice. Do you think TV news is too violent? Should news be treated differently than fictional content in the debates about media violence? In addressing this issue, you should consider what constitutes news versus entertainment programming. Is there a difference? Where do reality-based programs such as *Cops* and *America's Most Wanted* fit in?

6. In his provocative book *Channeling Violence: The Economic Market for Violent Television Programming*, James Hamilton (1998) argues that television violence, like pollution, generates negative externalities or costs that are shouldered by others rather than the people who produce this material. Using pollution as an analogy, he goes on to say that restrictions should be devised that place more responsibility on the TV industry while still protecting artistic freedom. For example, a violence tax could be imposed on those responsible for aggressive portrayals. How might such a tax work? Who should pay, and how should the amount be determined? Can you think of other approaches that could be implemented, using the pollution comparison? Would such efforts be constitutional?

7. Think back to your childhood. Can you remember a TV program or movie that really frightened you? How old were you? How long did your fear last? What aspect of the show frightened you? Did you change your behavior in any way as a result of seeing this show? Analyze your reaction in light of what we know about cognitive development and children's fear reactions to media, as discussed in this chapter.

8. In the debates about media violence, much less attention has been paid to desensitization as a harmful outcome than to aggression. Can you think of an occasion during which you felt desensitized to media violence? If our society gradually becomes desensitized to media violence, what are some of the possible outgrowths of this? Will it affect parenting? Will it affect the legal system? Explore some of the ways desensitization could affect individuals as well as our culture.

9. America is a violent country. Do you believe that the media have been unfairly blamed in public debates about this problem? Think about how you would respond to such a question if you worked in the media industry. Now think about how you would respond if you were a parent of a young child who had been seriously injured by a friend on the playground while imitating a cartoon superhero.

References

Abelson, R. P. (1976). Script processing in attitude formation and decision-making. In J. Carroll & J. Payne (Eds.), *Cognition and social behavior* (pp. 33–45). Hillsdale, NJ: Lawrence Erlbaum.

Aluja-Fabregat, A. (2000). Personality and curiosity about TV and films violence in adolescents. *Personality and Individual Differences, 29,* 379–392.

American Academy of Pediatrics. (2001). Media violence. *Pediatrics, 108,* 1222–1226.

American Medical Association. (1996). *Physician guide to media violence.* Chicago: Author.

Anderson, C. A., Benjamin, A. J., Jr., & Bartholow, B. D. (1998). Does the gun pull the trigger? Automatic priming effects of weapon pictures and weapon names. *American Psychological Society, 9,* 308–314.

Anderson, C. A., Berkowitz, L., Donnerstein, E., Huesmann, L. R., Johnson, J. D., Linz, D., et al. (2003). The influence of media violence on youth. *Psychological Science in the Public Interest, 4*(3), 81–110.

Anderson, R. N., & Smith, B. L. (2003). Deaths: Leading causes for 2001. *National Vital Statistics Report, 52*(9), 1–86.

Archer, D. (1994). American violence: How high and why? *Law Studies, 19,* 12–20.

Arnett, J. J. (1995). The soundtrack of recklessness: Musical preferences and reckless behavior among adolescents. *Journal of Adolescent Research, 7,* 313–331.

Ashcroft blames "culture" for school violence. (2001, March 23). Cable News Network. Retrieved April 2, 2001, from http://www.cnn.com/2001/ALLPOLITICS/03/23/ashcroft .shootings.reut/

Atkin, C. (1983). Effects of realistic TV violence vs. fictional violence on aggression. *Journalism Quarterly, 60,* 615–621.

Auletta, K. (1993, May 17). Annals of communication: What they won't do? *The New Yorker, 69,* 45–53.

Bailey, J. E., Kellermann, A. L., Somes, G. W., Banton, J. G., Rivara, F. P., & Rushforth, N. P. (1997). Risk factors for violent death of women in the home. *Archives of Internal Medicine, 157,* 777–782.

Ball-Rokeach, S. J. (2000, June). *The politics of studying media violence: Reflections thirty years after the violence commission.* Paper presented at the annual meeting of the International Communication Association, Acapulco, Mexico.

Bandura, A. (1965). Influence of models' reinforcement contingencies on the acquisition of imitative response. *Journal of Personality and Social Psychology, 1,* 589–595.

Bandura, A. (1977). *Social learning theory.* Englewood Cliffs, NJ: Prentice Hall.

Bandura, A. (1986). *Social foundations of thought and action: A social cognitive theory.* Englewood Cliffs, NJ: Prentice Hall.

Bandura, A. (1994). Social cognitive theory of mass communication. In J. Bryant & D. Zillmann (Eds.), *Media effects: Advances in theory and research* (pp. 61–90). Hillsdale, NJ: Lawrence Erlbaum.

Bandura, A., Ross, D., & Ross, S. A. (1961). Transmission of aggression through imitation of aggressive models. *Journal of Abnormal and Social Psychology, 63,* 575–582.

Bandura, A., Ross, D., & Ross, S. A. (1963a). Imitation of film-mediated aggressive models. *Journal of Abnormal and Social Psychology, 66,* 3–11.

Bandura, A., Ross, D., & Ross, S. A. (1963b). Various reinforcement and imitative learning. *Journal of Abnormal and Social Psychology, 67,* 601–607.

Baron, J. N., & Reiss, P. C. (1985). Same time, next year: Aggregate analyses of the mass media and violent behavior. *American Sociological Review, 50,* 347–363.

Baron, R. A. (1971a). Aggression as a function of magnitude of victim's pain cues, level of prior anger arousal, and aggressor-victim similarity. *Journal of Personality and Social Psychology, 18,* 48–54.

Baron, R. A. (1971b). Magnitude of victim's pain cues and level of prior anger arousal as determinants of adult aggressive behavior. *Journal of Personality and Social Psychology, 17,* 236–243.

Baron, R. A. (1978). The influence of hostile and nonhostile humor upon physical aggression. *Personality and Social Psychology Bulletin, 4,* 77–80.

Barr, R., Muentener, P., Garcia, A., Fujimoto, M., & Chavez, V. (2007). The effect on imitation from television during infancy. *Developmental Psychobiology, 49,* 196–207.

Bartholow, B. D., Bushman, B. J., & Sestir, M. A. (2006). Chronic violent video game exposure and desensitization to violence: Behavioral and event-related brain potential data. *Journal of Experimental and Social Psychology, 42,* 532–539.

Bauer, N. S., Herrenkohl, T. I., Lozano, P., Rivara, F. P., Hill, K. G., & Hawkins, J. D. (2006). Childhood bullying involvement and exposure to intimate partner violence. *Pediatrics, 118*(2), e235–e242.

Belson, W. A. (1978). *Television violence and the adolescent boy.* Westmead, UK: Saxon House, Teakfield Ltd.

Berkowitz, L. (1970). Aggressive humor as a stimulus to aggressive responses. *Journal of Personality and Social Psychology, 2,* 359–369.

Berkowitz, L. (1973). Words and symbols as stimuli to aggressive responses. In J. F. Knutson (Ed.), *Control of aggression: Implications from basic research* (pp. 113–143). Chicago: Aldine-Atherton.

Berkowitz, L. (1984). Some effects of thoughts on anti- and prosocial influences of media events: A cognitive-neoassociation analysis. *Psychological Bulletin, 95,* 410–427.

Berkowitz, L. (1990). On the formation and regulation of anger and aggression: A cognitive neoassociationistic analysis. *American Psychologist, 45,* 494–503.

Berkowitz, L., & Geen, R. G. (1967). Stimulus qualities of the target of aggression: A further study. *Journal of Personality and Social Psychology, 5,* 364–368.

Berkowitz, L., & Powers, P. C. (1979). Effects of timing and justification of witnessed aggression on the observers' punitiveness. *Journal of Research in Personality, 13,* 71–80.

Berman, M., Gladue, B., & Taylor, S. (1993). The effects of hormones, Type A behavior pattern, and provocation on aggression in men. *Motivation and Emotion, 17,* 125–138.

Berry, M., Gray, T., & Donnerstein, E. (1999). Cutting film violence: Effects on perceptions, enjoyment, and arousal. *Journal of Social Psychology, 139,* 567–582.

Boyatzis, J., Matillo, G. M., & Nesbitt, K. M. (1995). Effects of the Mighty Morphin Power Rangers on children's aggression with peers. *Child Study Journal, 25,* 45–55.

Braxton, G. (1991, July 31). Producers defend violence as honest. *Los Angeles Times,* pp. F1, F14.

Brown, M. H., Skeen, P., & Osborn, D. K. (1979). Young children's perception of the reality of television. *Contemporary Education, 50,* 129–133.

Bryant, J., Carveth, R. A., & Brown, D. (1981). Television viewing and anxiety: An experimental examination. *Journal of Communication, 31*(1), 106–109.

Buckingham, D. (2000). *After the death of childhood: Growing up in the age of electronic media.* Cambridge, UK: Polity.

Bushman, B. J., & Anderson, C. A. (2001). Media violence and the American public: Scientific facts versus media misinformation. *American Psychologist, 56,* 477–489.

Bushman, B. J., & Geen, R. G. (1990). Role of cognitive-emotional mediators and individual differences in the effects of media violence on aggression. *Journal of Personality and Social Psychology, 58,* 156–163.

Bushman, B. J., & Huesmann, L. R. (2001). Effects of televised violence on aggression. In D. G. Singer & J. L. Singer (Eds.), *Handbook of children and the media* (pp. 223–254). Thousand Oaks, CA: Sage.

Busselle, R. W. (2001). The role of exemplar accessibility in social reality judgments. *Media Psychology, 3,* 43–68.

Cantor, J. (1998). Children's attraction to violent television programming. In J. H. Goldstein (Ed.), *Why we watch: The attractions of violent entertainment* (pp. 116–143). New York: Oxford University Press.

Cantor, J. (2003). Media and fear in children and adolescents. In D. A. Gentile (Ed.), *Media violence and children: A complete guide for parents and professionals* (pp. 185–203). Westport, CT: Praeger.

Cantor, J., & Nathanson, A. I. (1996). Children's fright reactions to television news. *Journal of Communication, 46,* 139–152.

Cantor, J., & Nathanson, A. I. (1997). Predictors of children's interest in violent television programs. *Journal of Broadcasting & Electronic Media, 41,* 155–167.

Cantor, J., & Sparks, G. G. (1984). Children's fear responses to mass media: Testing some Piagetian predictions. *Journal of Communication, 34,* 90–103.

Cantor, J., & Wilson, B. J. (1988). Helping children cope with frightening media presentations. *Current Psychology: Research and Reviews, 7,* 58–75.

Cantor, J., Wilson, B. J., & Hoffner, C. (1986). Emotional responses to a televised nuclear holocaust film. *Communication Research, 13,* 257–277.

Carlson, M., Marcus-Newhall, A., & Miller, N. (1990). Effects of situational aggression cues: A quantitative review. *Journal of Personality and Social Psychology, 58,* 622–633.

Carnagey, N. L., & Anderson, C. A. (2005). The effects of reward and punishment in violent videogames on aggressive affect, cognition, and behavior. *Psychological Science, 16,* 882–889.

Centers for Disease Control and Prevention (CDC). (1997, February 7). *Rates of homicide, suicide, and firearm-related death among children—26 industrialized countries.* Atlanta, GA: Author. Retrieved February 24, 2001, from http://www.cdc.gov/epo/mmwr/pre view/mmwrhtml/00046149.htm

Centers for Disease Control and Prevention (CDC). (2006). *Understanding youth violence: Fact sheet.* Retrieved May 16, 2007, from http://www.cdc.gov/ncipc/pub-res/ YVFactSheet.pdf

Centers for Disease Control and Prevention (CDC) (2007). *Web-based injury statistics query and reporting system (WISQARS).* Retrieved January 22, 2008, from www.cdc.gov/ ncipc/wisqars

Cline, V. B., Croft, R. G., & Courrier, S. (1973). Desensitization of children to television violence. *Journal of Personality and Social Psychology, 35,* 450–458.

Cohen, J. (1988). *Statistical power analysis for the behavioral sciences* (2nd ed.). Hillsdale, NJ: Lawrence Erlbaum.

Cohen, J. (1999). Favorite characters of teenage viewers of Israeli serials. *Journal of Broadcasting & Electronic Media, 43,* 327–345.

Collins, W. A. (1973). Effect of temporal separation between motivation, aggression, and consequences: A developmental study. *Developmental Psychology, 8,* 215–221.

Collins, W. A. (1975). The developing child as viewer. *Journal of Communication, 25,* 35–44.

Collins, W. A. (1983). Interpretation and inference in children's television viewing. In J. Bryant & D. R. Anderson (Eds.), *Children's understanding of television: Research on attention and comprehension* (pp. 12–150). New York: Academic Press.

Collins-Standley, T., Gan, S., Yu, H. J., & Zillmann, D. (1996). Choice of romantic, violent, and scary fairy-tale books by preschool girls and boys. *Child Study Journal, 26,* 279–302.

Cooper, H., & Hedges, L. V. (Eds.). (1994). *The handbook of research synthesis.* New York: Russell Sage Foundation.

Coyne, S. M., & Archer, J. (2004). Indirect aggression in the media: A content analysis of British television programs. *Aggressive Behavior, 30,* 254–271.

Coyne, S. M., Archer, J., & Eslea, M. (2006). "We're not friends anymore!" Unless. . . .: The frequency and harmfulness of indirect, relational, and social aggression. *Aggressive Behavior, 32,* 294–307.

Crick, N. R., Ostrov, J. M., & Werner, N. E. (2006). A longitudinal study of relational aggression, physical aggression, and children's social-psychological attachment. *Journal of Abnormal Child Psychology, 34,* 127–138.

Davidson, L. E., Rosenberg, M. L., Mercy, J. A., Franklin, J., & Simmons, J. T. (1989). An epidemiologic study of risk factors in two teenage suicide clusters. *Journal of the American Medical Association, 262,* 2687–2692.

Davidson, O. G. (1993). *Under fire: The NRA and the battle for gun control.* New York: Holt, Rinehart, & Winston.

Deveny, K., & Kelley, R. (2007, February 12). Girls gone bad. *Newsweek.* Retrieved February 21, 2007, from http://www.msnbc.msn.com/id/16961761/site/newsweek/

Diener, E., & Woody, L. W. (1981). TV violence and viewer liking. *Communication Research, 8,* 281–306.

Dodge, K. A., & Frame, C. L. (1982). Social cognitive biases and deficits in aggressive boys. *Child Development, 53,* 620–635.

Dominick, J. R., & Greenberg, B. S. (1972). Attitudes toward violence: The interaction of television exposure, family attitudes, and social class. In G. A. Comstock & E. A. Rubinstein (Eds.), *Television and social behavior: Vol. 3. Television and adolescent aggressiveness* (pp. 314–335). Washington, DC: Government Printing Office.

Dorr, A. (1983). No shortcuts to judging reality. In J. Bryant & D. R. Anderson (Eds.), *Children's understanding of television: Research on attention and comprehension* (pp. 199–220). New York: Academic Press.

Drabman, R. S., & Thomas, M. H. (1974). Does media violence increase children's toleration of real-life aggression? *Developmental Psychology, 10,* 418–421.

Eron, L. D., Huesmann, L. R., Lefkowitz, M. M., & Walder, L. O. (1972). Does television violence cause aggression? *American Psychologist, 27,* 253–263.

Faiola, A. (2004). Youth violence has Japan struggling for answers. *Washington Post.* Retrieved February 23, 2007, from http://www.washingtonpost.com

Farah, M. M., Simon, H. K., & Kellermann, A. L. (1999). Firearms in the home: Parental perceptions. *Pediatrics, 104,* 1059–1063.

Federal Communications Commission (FCC). (2007). *Violent television programming and its impact on children.* Retrieved January 22, 2008, from www.firstamendmentcenter.org/PDF/FCC_TV_violence_2007.pdf

Federal Trade Commission (FTC). (2000). *Marketing violent entertainment to children: A review of self-regulation and industry practices in the motion picture, music recording & electronic games industries.* Retrieved February 24, 2007, from http://www.ftc.gov/reports/violence/vioreport.pdf

Federal Trade Commission (FTC). (2001). *Marketing violent entertainment to children: A six-month follow-up review of industry practices in the motion picture, music recording & electronic games industries.* Retrieved February 24, 2007, from http://www.ftc.gov/reports/violence/violence010423.pdf

Federal Trade Commission (FTC). (2002). *Marketing violent entertainment to children: A twenty-one month follow-up review of industry practices in the motion picture, music recording & electronic game industries.* Retrieved February 24, 2007, from http://www.ftc.gov/reports/violence/mvecrpt0206.pdf

Federal Trade Commission (FTC). (2007). *Marketing violent entertainment to children: A fifth follow-up review of industry practices in the motion picture, music recording, & electronic game industries.* Retrieved May 10, 2007, from http://www.ftc.gov/reports/violence/070412MarketingViolentEChildren.pdf

Fenigstein, A. (1979). Does aggression cause a preference for viewing media violence? *Journal of Personality & Social Psychology, 37,* 2307–2317.

Feshbach, S. (1972). Reality and fantasy in filmed violence. In J. P. Murray, E. A. Rubinstein, & G. Comstock (Eds.), *Television and social behavior: Television and social learning* (Vol. 2, pp. 318–345). Washington, DC: Government Printing Publication.

Filotas, D. Y. (1993). *Adolescents' rape attitudes: Effectiveness of rape prevention in high school classrooms.* Unpublished master's thesis, University of California, Santa Barbara.

Fisch, S. M., & Truglio, R. T. (2001). *"G" is for growing: Thirty years of research on children and* Sesame Street. Mahwah, NJ: Lawrence Erlbaum.

Fowles, J. (1999). *The case for television violence.* Thousand Oaks, CA: Sage.

Freedman, J. L. (1986). Television violence and aggression: A rejoinder. *Psychological Bulletin, 100,* 372–373.

Freedman, J. L. (2002). *Media violence and its effect on aggression: Assessing the scientific evidence.* Toronto: University of Toronto Press.

Friedrich, L. K., & Stein, A. H. (1973). Aggressive and prosocial television programs and the natural behavior of preschool children. *Monographs of the Society for Research in Child Development, 38*(4, Serial No. 151), 63.

Funk, J. B., Buchman, D. D., & Germann, J. N. (2000). Preference for violent electronic games, self-concept, and gender differences in young children. *American Journal of Orthopsychiatry, 70,* 233–241.

Gaensbauer, T., & Wamboldt, M. (2000, January 5). *Facts about gun violence.* Washington, DC: American Academy of Child and Adolescent Psychiatry. Retrieved February 19, 2001, from http://www.aacap.org/info_families/nationalfacts/cogunviol.htm

Geen, R. G. (1994). Television and aggression: Recent developments in research and theory. In D. Zillmann, J. Bryant, & A. C. Huston (Eds.), *Media, children, and the family: Social, scientific, psychodynamic, and clinical perspectives* (pp. 151–162). Hillsdale, NJ: Lawrence Erlbaum.

Gerbner, G., & Gross, L. (1976). Living with television: The violence profile. *Journal of Communication, 26,* 172–199.

Gerbner, G., Gross, L., Morgan, M., & Signorielli, N. (1980). The "mainstreaming" of America: Violence profile no. 11. *Journal of Communication, 30*(3), 10–29.

Gerbner, G., Gross, L., Morgan, M., & Signorielli, N. (1994). Growing up with television: The cultivation perspective. In J. Bryant & D. Zillmann (Eds.), *Media effects: Advances in theory and research* (pp. 17–41). Hillsdale, NJ: Lawrence Erlbaum.

Gerbner, G., Signorielli, N., Morgan, M., & Jackson-Beeck, M. (1979). The demonstration of power: Violence profile no. 10. *Journal of Communication, 29,* 177–196.

Gibbons, J., Anderson, D. R., Smith, R., Field, D. E., & Fischer, C. (1986). Young children's recall and reconstruction of audio and audiovisual narratives. *Child Development, 57,* 1014–1023.

Goldstein, J. (1999). The attraction of violent entertainment. *Media Psychology, 1,* 271–282.

Gould, M., Jamieson, P., & Romer, D. (2003). Media contagion and suicide among the young. *American Behavioral Scientist, 46,* 1269–1284.

Gould, M. S., & Davidson, L. (1988). Suicide contagion among adolescents. *Advances in Adolescent Mental Health, 3,* 29–59.

Gould, M. S., Fisher, P., Parides, M., Flory, M., & Shaffer, D. (1996). Psychosocial risk factors of child and adolescent completed suicide. *Archives of General Psychiatry, 53,* 1155–1162.

Gould, M. S., Shaffer, D., & Kleinman, M. (1988). The impact of suicide in television movies: Replication and commentary. *Suicide and Life-Threatening Behavior, 18,* 90–99.

Gould, M. S., Wallenstein, S., Kleinman, M. H., O'Carroll, P., & Mercy, J. (1990). Suicide cluster: An examination of age-specific effects. *American Journal of Public Health, 80,* 211–212.

Graziano, A. M., DeGiovanni, I. S., & Garcia, K. A. (1979). Behavioral treatment of children's fears: A review. *Psychological Bulletin, 86,* 804–830.

Greenberg, B. S., & Gordon, T. F. (1972). Perceptions of violence in television programs: Critics and the public. In G. A. Comstock & E. A. Rubinstein (Eds.), *Television and social behavior: Vol. 1. Media content and control* (pp. 244–258). Washington, DC: Government Printing Office.

Groebel, J. (2001). Media violence in cross-cultural perspective: A global study on children's media behaviors and some educational implications. In D. G. Singer & J. L. Singer (Eds.), *Handbook of children and the media* (pp. 255–268). Thousand Oaks, CA: Sage.

Gross, K., & Aday, S. (2003). The scary world in your living room and neighborhood: Using local broadcast news, neighborhood crime rates, and personal experience to test agenda setting and cultivation. *Journal of Communication, 53,* 411–426.

Grossman, D. C., Reay, D. T., & Baker, S. A. (1999). Self-inflicted and unintentional firearm injuries among children and adolescents: The source of firearms. *Archives of Pediatrics and Adolescent Medicine, 153,* 875–878.

Guerra, N. G., Huesmann, L. R., Tolan, P. H., VanAcker, R., & Eron, L. D. (1995). Stressful events and individual beliefs as correlates of economic disadvantage and aggression among urban children. *Consulting and Clinical Psychology, 63,* 518–528.

Gunter, B., & Furnham, A. (1984). Perceptions of television violence: Effects of programme genre and type of violence on viewers' judgements of violent portrayals. *British Journal of Social Psychology, 23,* 155–164.

Haidt, J., McCauley, C., & Rozin P. (1994). Individual differences in sensitivity to disgust: A scale sampling seven domains of disgust elicitors. *Personality & Individual Differences, 16,* 701–713.

Hamilton, J. T. (1998). *Channeling violence: The economic market for violent television programming.* Princeton, NJ: Princeton University Press.

Hanratty, M. A., O'Neal, E., & Sulzer, J. L. (1972). The effect of frustration upon imitation of aggression. *Journal of Personality and Social Psychology, 21,* 30–34.

Harrison, K., & Cantor, J. (1999). Tales from the screen: Enduring fright reactions to scary media. *Media Psychology, 1*(2), 97–116.

Hawkins, R. P., & Pingree, S. (1980). Some processes in the cultivation effect. *Communication Research, 7,* 193–226.

Hawkins, R. P., & Pingree, S. (1981). Uniform messages and habitual viewing: Unnecessary assumptions in social reality effects. *Human Communication Research, 7,* 291–301.

Hayes, J. (2007, January 19). Films and TV up the ante on graphic torture scenes. *The Post Gazette.* Retrieved February 23, 2007, from www.post-gazette.com

Hearold, S. (1986). A synthesis of 1045 effects of television on social behavior. In F. Comstock (Ed.), *Public communication and behavior* (Vol. 1, pp. 65–133). New York: Academic Press.

Hicks, D. J. (1965). Imitation and retention of film-mediated aggressive peer and models. *Journal of Personality and Social Psychology, 2,* 97–100.

Hirsch, P. (1980). The "scary world" of the nonviewer and other anomalies: A reanalysis of Gerbner et al.'s findings of cultivation analysis. Part I. *Communication Research, 7,* 403–456.

Hoffner, C. (1996). Children's wishful identification and parasocial interaction with favorite television characters. *Journal of Broadcasting & Electronic Media, 40,* 389–402.

Hoffner, C., & Cantor, J. (1985). Developmental differences in responses to a television character's appearance and behavior. *Developmental Psychology, 21,* 1065–1074.

Hogben, M. (1998). Factors moderating the effect of televised aggression on viewer behavior. *Communication Research, 25,* 220–247.

Huesmann, L. R. (1986). Psychological processes promoting the relation between exposure to media violence and aggressive behavior by the viewer. *Journal of Social Issues, 42,* 125–139.

Huesmann, L. R. (1988a). An information processing model for the development of aggression. *Aggressive Behavior, 14,* 13–24.

Huesmann, L. R. (1998b). The role of social information processing and cognitive schemas in the acquisition and maintenance of habitual aggressive behavior. In R. G. Geen & E. Donnerstein (Eds.), *Human aggression: Theories, research, and implications for social policy* (pp. 1120–1134). San Diego: Academic Press.

Huesmann, L. R. (2007). The impact of electronic media violence: Scientific theory and research. *Journal of Adolescent Health, 41*(6), S6–S13.

Huesmann, L. R., & Eron, L. D. (1986a). The development of aggression in American children as a consequence of television violence viewing. In L. R. Huesmann & L. D. Eron (Eds.), *Television and the aggressive child: A cross national comparison* (pp. 45–80). Hillsdale, NJ: Lawrence Erlbaum.

Huesmann, L. R., & Eron, L. D. (1986b). The development of aggression in children of different cultures: Psychological processes and exposure to violence. In L. R. Huesmann & L. D. Eron (Eds.), *Television and the aggressive child: A cross national comparison* (pp. 1–27). Hillsdale, NJ: Lawrence Erlbaum.

Huesmann, L. R., Eron, L. D., Klein, R., Brice, P., & Fischer, P. (1983). Mitigating the imitation of aggressive behaviors by changing children's attitudes about media violence. *Journal of Personality and Social Psychology, 44,* 899–910.

Huesmann, L. R., Eron, L. D., Lefkowitz, M. M., & Walder, L. O. (1984). Stability of aggression over time and generations. *Developmental Psychology, 20,* 1120–1134.

Huesmann, L. R., Lagerspetz, K., & Eron, L. D. (1984). Intervening variables in the TV violence-aggression relation: Evidence from two countries. *Developmental Psychology, 20,* 746–775.

Huesmann, L. R., & Miller, L. S. (1994). Long-term effects of repeated exposure to media violence in childhood. In L. R. Huesmann (Ed.), *Aggressive behavior: Current perspectives* (pp. 153–186). New York: Plenum.

Huesmann, L. R., Moise-Titus, J., Podolski, C., & Eron, L. D. (2003). Longitudinal relations between children's exposure to TV violence and their aggressive and violent behavior in young adulthood: 1977–1992. *Developmental Psychology, 39,* 2001–2021.

Huesmann, L. R., & Taylor, L. D. (2003). The case against the case against media violence. In D. A. Gentile (Ed.), *Media violence and children: A complete guide for parents and professionals* (pp. 107–130). Westport, CT: Praeger.

Huesmann, L. R., & Taylor, L. D. (2006). The role of media violence in violent behavior. *Annual Review of Public Health, 27,* 393–415.

Hughes, M. (1980). The fruits of cultivation analysis: A re-examination of television in fear of victimization, alienation, and approval of violence. *Public Opinion Quarterly, 44,* 287–302.

Huston, A. C., Donnerstein, E., Fairchild, H. H., Feshbach, N. D., Katz, P. A., Murray, J. P., et al. (1992). *Big world, small screen: The role of television in American society.* Lincoln: University of Nebraska Press.

Iwao, S., Pool, I., & Hagiwara, S. (1981). Japanese and U.S. media: Some cross-cultural insights into TV violence. *Journal of Communication, 31*(2), 29–36.

Jackman, G. A., Farah, M. M., Kellermann, A. L., & Simon, H. K. (2001). Seeing is believing: What do boys do when they find a real gun? *Pediatrics, 107,* 1247–1250.

Jamieson, P. E., Romer, D., & Jamieson, K. H. (2006). Do films about mentally disturbed characters promote ineffective coping in vulnerable youth? *Journal of Adolescence, 29,* 749–760.

Jo, E., & Berkowitz, L. (1994). A priming effect analysis of media influences: An update. In J. Bryant & D. Zillmann (Eds.), *Media effects: Advances in theory and research* (pp. 43–60). Hillsdale, NJ: Lawrence Erlbaum.

Jobes, D. A., Berman, A. L., O'Carroll, P. W., Eastgard, S., & Knickmeyer, S. (1996). The Kurt Cobain suicide crisis: Perspectives from research, public health, and the news media. *Suicide and Life Threatening Behavior, 26,* 260–269.

Johnston, D. D. (1995). Adolescents' motivations for viewing graphic horror. *Human Communication Research, 21,* 522–552.

Jose, P. E., & Brewer, W. F. (1984). Development of story liking: Character identification, suspense, and outcome resolution. *Developmental Psychology, 20,* 911–924.

Josephson, W. L. (1987). Television violence and children's aggression: Testing the priming, social script, and disinhibition predictions. *Journal of Personality and Social Psychology, 53,* 882–890.

Kellermann, A. L., Rivara, F. P., Rushforth, N. B., Banton, J. G., Reay, D. T., Francisco, J. T., et al. (1993). Gun ownership as a risk factor for homicide in the home. *New England Journal of Medicine, 329,* 1084–1091.

Kellermann, A. L., Somes, G., Rivara, F. P., Lee, R. K., & Banton, J. G. (1998). Injuries and deaths due to firearms in the home. *Journal of Trauma, Injury Infection and Critical Care, 45,* 263–267.

Klimkiewicz, J. (2007, April 20). *The making of an abhorrent icon.* Retrieved May 9, 2007, from http://www.courant.com

Konijn, E. A., Nije Bijvank, M., & Bushman, B. J. (2007). I wish I were a warrior: The role of wishful identification in the effects of violent video games on aggression in adolescent boys. *Developmental Psychology, 43,* 1038–1044.

Kopel, D. B. (1993). Japanese gun control. *Asia Pacific Law Review, 2*(2), 26–52. Retrieved June 16, 2001, from http://www.2ndlawlib.com/journals/dkjgc.html

Kowalski, R. M., & Limber, S. P. (2007). Electronic bullying among middle school students. *Journal of Adolescent Health, 41,* S22–S30.

Krcmar, M., & Cooke, M. C. (2001). Children's moral reasoning and perceptions of television violence. *Journal of Communication, 51,* 300–316.

Krcmar, M., & Greene, K. (1999). Predicting exposure to and uses of television violence. *Journal of Communication, 49,* 24–45.

Krcmar, M., & Hight, A. (2007). The development of aggressive mental models in young children. *Media Psychology, 10,* 250–269.

Kunkel, D., Farinola, W. J., Farrar, K., Donnerstein, E., Biely, E., & Zwarun, L. (2002). Deciphering the V-chip: An examination of the television industry's program rating judgments. *Journal of Communication, 52*(1), 112–138.

Kunkel, D., & Wilcox, B. (2002). Children and media policy. In D. G. Singer & J. L. Singer (Eds.), *Handbook of children and the media* (pp. 589–604). Thousand Oaks, CA: Sage.

Kuntsche, E., Pickett, W., Overpeck, M., Craig, W., Boyce, W., & deMatos, M. G. (2006). Television viewing and forms of bullying among adolescents from eight countries. *Journal of Adolescent Health, 39,* 908–915.

Lacayo, R. (1995). Violent reaction. *Time, 145,* 24–28.

Lazarus, R. S., & Alfert, E. (1964). Short-circuiting of threat by experimentally altering cognitive appraisal. *Journal of Abnormal & Social Psychology, 69,* 195–205.

Lefkowitz, M. M., Eron, L. D., Walder, L. O., & Huesmann, L. R. (1972). Television violence and child aggression: A follow-up study. In G. A. Comstock & E. A. Rubinstein (Eds.), *Television and social behavior: Vol. 3. Television and adolescent aggressiveness* (pp. 33–135). Washington, DC: Government Printing Office.

Liebert, R. M., & Sprafkin, J. (1988). *The early window: Effects of television on children and youth.* New York: Pergamon.

Lies, E. (2001, June 8). *Random violence on the rise in Japan.* Retrieved June 16, 2001, from http://cbsnews.com/now/story/0%2c1597%2c295560-412%2c00.html

Linz, D. G., Donnerstein, E., & Penrod, S. (1984). The effects of multiple exposures to filmed violence against women. *Journal of Communication, 34,* 130–147.

Linz, D. G., Donnerstein, E., & Penrod, S. (1988). Effects of long-term exposure to violent and sexually degrading depictions of women. *Journal of Personality and Social Psychology, 55,* 758–768.

Liss, M. B., Reinhardt, L. C., & Fredriksen, S. (1983). TV heroes: The impact of rhetoric and deeds. *Journal of Applied Developmental Psychology, 4,* 175–187.

Lovaas, O. I. (1961). Effect of exposure to symbolic aggression on aggressive behavior. *Child Development, 32,* 37–44.

Lowry, B. (1997, September 21). The times poll: TV on decline, but few back U.S. regulation. *Los Angeles Times,* p. A01.

Martin, J. R., Sklar, D. P., & McFeeley, P. (1991). Accidental firearm fatalities among New Mexico children. *Annals of Emergency Medicine, 20,* 58–61.

McIntyre, J. J., & Teevan, J. J., Jr. (1972). Television violence and deviant behavior. In G. A. Comstock & E. A. Rubinstein (Eds.), *Television and social behavior: Vol. 3. Television and adolescent aggressiveness* (pp. 383–435). Washington, DC: Government Printing Office.

McLeod, J. M., Atkin, C. K., & Chaffee, S. H. (1972a). Adolescents, parents, and television use: Adolescent self-report measures from Maryland and Wisconsin samples. In G. A. Comstock & E. A. Rubinstein (Eds.), *Television and social behavior: Vol. 3. Television and adolescent aggressiveness* (pp. 173–238). Washington, DC: Government Printing Office.

McLeod, J. M., Atkin, C. K., & Chaffee, S. H. (1972b). Self-report and other-report measures from the Wisconsin sample. In G. A. Comstock & E. A. Rubinstein (Eds.), *Television and social behavior: Vol. 3. Television and adolescent aggressiveness* (pp. 239–313). Washington, DC: Government Printing Office.

Milavsky, J. R., Kessler, R., Stipp, H. H., & Rubens, W. S. (1982). *Television and aggression: A panel study.* New York: Academic Press.

Miles, D. R., & Carey, G. (1997). Genetic and environmental architecture on human aggression. *Journal of Personality & Social Psychology, 72,* 207–217.

Molitor, F., & Hirsch, K. W. (1994). Children's toleration of real-life aggression after exposure to media violence: A replication of the Drabman and Thomas studies. *Child Study Journal, 24,* 191–207.

Moretti, M. M., Osbuth, C. L., Odgers, P., & Reebye, P. (2006). Exposure to maternal vs. paternal partner violence, PTSD, and aggression in adolescent girls and boys. *Aggressive Behavior, 4,* 385–395.

Morgan, M., & Shanahan, J. (1996). Two decades of cultivation research: An appraisal and meta-analysis. In B. R. Burleson (Ed.), *Communication yearbook* (Vol. 20, pp. 1–45). Newbury Park, CA: Sage.

Mullen, B. (1989). *Advanced basic meta analysis.* Hillsdale, NJ: Lawrence Erlbaum.

Mullin, C. R., & Linz, D. (1995). Desensitization and resensitization to violence against women: Effects of exposure to sexually violent films on judgments of domestic violence victims. *Journal of Personality and Social Psychology, 69,* 449–459.

Naisbitt, J., Naisbitt, N., & Philips, D. (1999). *High tech, high touch: Technology and our search for meaning.* New York: Broadway Books.

Nansel, T. R., Overpeck, M., Pilla, R. S., Ruan, W. J., Simons-Morton, B., & Scheidt, P. (2001). Bullying behaviors among US youth: Prevalence and association with psychosocial adjustment. *Journal of the American Medical Association, 285,* 2094–2100.

New poll finds escalating violence in children's TV now a crisis for parents. (2005). Retrieved May 17, 2007, from http://www.fradical.com/New_poll_finds_violence.htm

Ogles, R. M., & Hoffner, C. (1987). Film violence and perceptions of crime: The cultivation effect. In M. L. McLaughlin (Ed.), *Communication yearbook* (Vol. 10, pp. 384–394). Newbury Park, CA: Sage.

Okoro, C. A., Nelson, D. E., Mercy, J. A., Balluz, L. S., Crosby, A. E., & Mokdad, A. H. (2005). Prevalence of household firearms and firearm-storage practices in the 50 states and the District of Columbia: Findings from the behavioral risk factor surveillance system, 2002. *Pediatrics, 116*(3), e370–e376.

Oliver, M. B. (2000). The respondent gender gap. In D. Zillmann, & P. Vorderer (Eds.), *Media entertainment: The psychology of its appeal* (pp. 215–234). Mahwah, NJ: Lawrence Erlbaum.

Ostrov, J. M. (2006). Deception and subtypes of aggression during early childhood. *Journal of Experimental Child Psychology, 93,* 322–336.

Ostrov, J. M., Gentile, D. A., & Crick, N. R. (2006). Media exposure, aggression and prosocial behavior during early childhood: A longitudinal study. *Social Development, 15,* 612–627.

Otto, M. W., Henin, A., Hirshfeld-Becker, D. R., Pollack, M. H., Biederman, J., & Rosenbaum, J. F. (2007). Posttraumatic stress disorder symptoms following media exposure to tragic events: Impact of 9/11 on children at risk for anxiety disorders. *Journal of Anxiety Disorders, 21,* 888–902.

Paik, H. J., & Comstock, G. (1994). The effects of television violence on antisocial behavior: A meta-analysis. *Communication Research, 21,* 516–546.

Pelletier, A. R., Quinlan, K. P., Sacks, J. J., Van Gilder, T. J., Gulchrist, J., & Ahluwalia, H. K. (1999). Firearm use in G- and PG-rated movies. *Journal of the American Medical Association, 282,* 428.

Perse, E. M. (1990). Cultivation and involvement with local television news. In N. Signorielli & M. Morgan (Eds.), *Cultivation analysis: New directions in media effects research* (pp. 51–69). Newbury Park, CA: Sage.

Pfefferbaum, B., Seale, T. W., McDonald, N. B., Brandt, E. N., Jr., Rainwater, S. M., Maynard, B. T., et al. (2000). Posttraumatic stress two years after the Oklahoma City bombing in youths geographically distant from the explosion. *Psychiatry, 63,* 358–370.

Phillips, D. P., & Carstensen, L. L. (1986). Clustering of teenage suicides after television news stories about suicide. *New England Journal of Medicine, 315,* 685–689.

Phillips, D. P., Carstensen, L. L., & Paight, D. J. (1989). Effects of mass media news stories on suicide, with new evidence on the role of story content. In C. R. Pfeffer (Ed.), *Suicide among youth: Perspectives on risk and prevention* (pp. 101–116). Washington, DC: American Psychiatric Press.

Phillips, D. P., & Paight, D. J. (1987). The impact of televised movies about suicide: A replicative study. *New England Journal of Medicine, 317,* 809–811.

Pickett, W., Craig, W., Harel, Y., Cunningham, J., Simpson, K., Molcho, M., et al. (2005). Cross-national study of fighting and weapon carrying as determinants of adolescent injury. *Pediatrics, 116* (6), e855–e863.

Plagens, P., Miller, M., Foote, D., & Yoffe, E. (1991, April 1). Violence in our culture. *Newsweek, 117,* 46–52.

Pool, B. (1991, November 3). Screen violence would stop if it didn't sell tickets, filmmakers say. *Los Angeles Times,* pp. B1, B6.

Potter, W. J. (1993). Cultivation theory and research: A conceptual critique. *Human Communication Research, 19,* 564–601.

Potter, W. J. (1999). *On media violence.* Thousand Oaks, CA: Sage.

Puzzanghera, J. (2007, January 22). Tech's mixed message. *Los Angeles Times.* Retrieved March 16, 2007, from www.latimes.com

Resnick, M. D., Bearman, P. S., Blum, R. W., Bauman, K. E., Harris, K. M., Jones, J., et al. (1997). Protecting adolescents from harm: Findings from the national longitudinal study on adolescent health. *Journal of the American Medical Association, 278,* 823–832.

Rigby, K. (2003). Consequences of bullying in schools. *Canadian Journal of Psychiatry, 48,* 583–590.

Robinson, J. P., & Bachman, J. G. (1972). Television viewing habits and aggression. In G. A. Comstock & E. A. Rubinstein (Eds.), *Television and social behavior: Vol. 3. Television and adolescent aggressiveness* (pp. 173–238). Washington, DC: Government Printing Office.

Romer, D., Jamieson, K. H., & Aday, S. (2003). Television news and the cultivation of fear of crime. *Journal of Communication, 53,* 88–104.

Romer, D., Jamieson, P. E., & Jamieson, K. H. (2006). Are news reports of suicide contagious? A stringent test in six U.S. cities. *Journal of Communication, 56,* 253–270.

Rosenberg, M. L., Mercy, J. A., & Houk, V. N. (1991). Guns and adolescent suicides. *Journal of the American Medical Association, 266,* 3030.

Rothenberg, M. B. (1975). Effect of television violence on children and youth. *Journal of the American Medical Association, 234,* 1043–1046.

Rutenberg, J. (2001, January 28). *Violence finds a niche in children's cartoons.* Retrieved February 23, 2007, from http://www.fradical.com/violence_finds_a_niche_in_childrens_cartoons.htm

Sargent, J. D., Heatherton, T. F., Ahrens, M. B., Dalton, M. A., Tickle, J. J., & Beach, M. L. (2002). Adolescent exposure to extremely violent movies. *Journal of Adolescent Health, 31,* 449–454.

Savitsky, J. C., Rogers, R. W., Izard, C. E., & Liebert, R. M. (1971). Role of frustration and anger in the imitation of filmed aggression against a human victim. *Psychological Reports, 29,* 807–810.

Schaefer, S. (1999, June 28). Natural born scapegoats? Hollywood takes it on the chops in wake of high school shootings. *The Boston Herald,* p. 37.

Scharrer, E. (2005). Hypermasculinity, aggression, and television violence: An experiment. *Media Psychology, 7,* 353–376.

Schmitt, K. L., Anderson, D. R., & Collins, P. A. (1999). Form and content: Looking at visual features of television. *Developmental Psychology, 35,* 1156–1167.

Schuster, M. A., Franke, T. M., Bastian, A. M., Sor, S., & Halfon, N. (2000). Firearm storage patterns in US homes with children. *American Journal of Public Health, 90,* 588–594.

Selah-Shayovits, R. (2006). Adolescent preferences for violence in television shows and music video clips. *International Journal of Adolescence and Youth, 13,* 99–112.

Servin, A., Bohlin, G., & Berlin, L. (1999). Sex differences in 1-, 3-, and 5-year-olds' toy-choice in a structured play-session. *Scandinavian Journal of Psychology, 40,* 43–48.

Shrum, L. J. (2001). Processing strategy moderates the cultivation effect. *Human Communication Research, 27,* 94–120.

Shrum, L. J. (2002). Media consumption and perceptions of social reality: Effects and underlying processes. In J. Bryant & D. Zillman (Eds.), *Media effects: Advances in theory and research* (pp. 69–96). Mahwah, NJ: Lawrence Erlbaum.

Signorielli, N. (1990). Television and health: Images and impact. In C. Atkin & L. Wallack (Eds.), *Mass communication and public health: Complexities and conflicts* (pp. 96–113). Newbury Park, CA: Sage.

Signorielli, N., & Morgan, M. (Eds.). (1990). *Cultivation analysis: New directions in media effects research.* Newbury Park, CA: Sage.

Singer, J. L., & Singer, D. G. (1986). Family experiences and television viewing as predictors of children's imagination, restlessness, and aggression. *Journal of Social Issues, 42,* 107–124.

Singer, J. L., Singer, D. G., & Rapaczynski, W. (1984). Family patterns and television viewing as predictors of children's beliefs and aggression. *Journal of Communication, 34,* 73–89.

Slater, M. D. (2003). Alienation, aggression, and sensation seeking as predictors of adolescent use of violent film, computer, and website content. *Journal of Communication, 53,* 105–121.

Smith, S. L., & Boyson, A. R. (2002). Violence in music videos: Examining the prevalence and context of physical aggression. *Journal of Communication, 52,* 61–83.

Smith, S. L., Boyson, A. R., Pieper, K. M., & Wilson, B. J. (2001, May). *Brandishing guns on American television: How often do such weapons appear and in what context?* Paper presented to the annual meeting of the International Communication Association, Washington, DC.

Smith, S. L., & Donnerstein, E. (1998). Harmful effects of exposure to media violence: Learning of aggression, emotional desensitization, and fear. In R. G. Geen & E. Donnerstein (Eds.), *Human aggression: Theories, research, and implications for social policy* (pp. 167–202). San Diego: Academic Press.

Smith, S. L., & Wilson, B. J. (2002). Children's comprehension of and fright reactions to television news. *Media Psychology, 4,* 1–26.

Smith, S. L., Wilson, B. J., Kunkel, D., Linz, D., Potter, W. J., Colvin, C., et al. (1998). Violence in television programming overall: University of California, Santa Barbara study. In *National television violence study: Vol. 3* (pp. 5–220). Thousand Oaks, CA: Sage.

Snyder, H. N., & Sickmund, M. (1999). *Juvenile offenders and victims: 1999 national report* (NCJ 178257). Washington, DC: U.S. Department of Justice, Office of Juvenile Justice and Delinquency Prevention.

Sparks, G. G. (1986). Developmental differences in children's reports of fear induced by the mass media. *Child Study Journal, 16,* 55–66.

Speisman, J. C., Lazarus, R. S., Davison, L., & Mordkoff, A. M. (1964). Experimental analysis of a film used as a threatening stimulus. *Journal of Consulting Psychology, 28,* 23–33.

Spencer, T. (2001, January 25). Wrestling death case deliberated. *Los Angeles Times.* Retrieved January 25, 2001, from www.latimes.com/wires/20010125/tCB00V0225.html

Stack, S. (2005). Suicide in the media: A quantitative review of studies based on nonfictional stories. *Suicide and Life-Threatening Behavior, 35,* 121–133.

Steuer, F. B., Applefield, J. M., & Smith, R. (1971). Televised aggression and interpersonal aggression of preschool children. *Journal of Experimental Child Psychology, 11,* 442–447.

Surgeon General's Scientific Advisory Committee on Television and Social Behavior (1972). *Television and growing up: The impact of televised violence* [Report to the Surgeon General, U.S. Public Health Service]. Washington, DC: Government Printing Office.

Swahn, M. H., Hammig, B. J., & Ikeda, R. M. (2002). Prevalence of youth access to alcohol or a gun in the home. *Injury Prevention, 8,* 227–230.

Tamborini, R., & Stiff, J. (1987). Predictors of horror film attendance and appeal: An analysis of the audience for frightening films. *Communication Research, 14,* 415–436.

Thomas, M. H., & Drabman, R. S. (1975). Toleration of real life aggression as a function of exposure to televised violence and age of subject. *Merrill-Palmer Quarterly, 21,* 227–232.

Thomas, M. H., Horton, R. W., Lippincott, E. C., & Drabman, R. S. (1977). Desensitization to portrayals of real-life aggression as a function of exposure to television violence. *Journal of Personality and Social Psychology, 35,* 450–458.

Thomas, M. H., & Tell, P. M. (1974). Effects of viewing real versus fantasy violence upon interpersonal aggression. *Journal of Research in Personality, 8,* 153–160.

Thompson, K. T., & Yokota, F. (2004). Violence, sex, and profanity in films: Correlation of movie ratings with context. *MedGenMed, 6*(3), 3–11.

Toppo, G. (2007). Experts ponder patterns in school shootings. *USA Today.* Retrieved May 17, 2007, from http://www.usatoday.com/news/education/2007-04-18-school-shooters_N.htm

Trend, D. (2007). *The myth of media violence: A critical introduction.* Malden, MA: Blackwell.

Tulving, E., & Thomson, D. M. (1973). Encoding specificity and retrieval processes in episodic memory. *Psychological Review, 80,* 359–380.

TV parental guidelines. (n.d.). Washington, DC: The TV Parental Guidelines Monitoring Board. Retrieved February 21, 2001, from http://www.tvguidelines.org/guidelin.htm

Underwood, M. K. (2003). *Social aggression among girls.* New York: Guilford.

Ursin, H., & Eriksen, H. R. (2001). Sensitization, subjective health complaints, and sustained arousal. *Annals of the New York Academy of Sciences, 933,* 119–129.

U.S. Senate, Committee on the Judiciary. (1956, January 16). *Television and juvenile delinquency: Investigation of juvenile delinquency in the United States* (84th Cong., 2d Sess., Rep. No. 1466) Washington, DC: Government Printing Office.

van den Broek, P., Lorch, E. P., & Thurlow, R. (1996). Children's and adults' memory for television stories: The role of causal factors, story-grammar categories, and hierarchical level. *Child Development, 67,* 3010–3028.

Vyrostek, S. B., Annest, J. L., & Ryan, G. W. (2004, September 3). Survey for fatal and nonfatal injuries: United States, 2001. *Surveillance Summaries, 53*(SS07), 1–57.

Walters, R. H., & Parke, R. D. (1964). Influence of response consequences to a social model on resistance to deviation. *Journal of Experimental Child Psychology, 1,* 269–280.

Weaver, A. J. (2006). Reconceptualizing attraction to media violence: A meta-analysis and an experiment. *Dissertation Abstracts International, 67*(11), 4026A.

Weaver, A. J., & Wilson, B. J. (2005, November). *The enjoyment of graphic and sanitized violence in prime-time television dramas.* Paper presented at the annual meeting of the National Communication Association, Boston.

Wilson, B. J., Colvin, C. M., & Smith, S. L. (2002). Engaging in violence on American television: A comparison of child, teen, and adult perpetrators. *Journal of Communication, 52*(1), 36–60.

Wilson, B. J., Hoffner, C., & Cantor, J. (1987). Children's perceptions of the effectiveness of techniques to reduce fear from mass media. *Journal of Applied Developmental Psychology, 8,* 39–52.

Wilson, B. J., Kunkel, D., Linz, D., Potter, W. J., Donnerstein, E., Smith, S. L., et al. (1997). Violence in television programming overall: University of California, Santa Barbara study. In *National television violence study: Vol. 1* (pp. 3–268). Thousand Oaks, CA: Sage.

Wilson, B. J., Kunkel, D., Linz, D., Potter, W. J., Donnerstein, E., Smith, S. L., et al. (1998). Violence in television programming overall: University of California, Santa Barbara study. In *National television violence study: Vol. 2* (pp. 3–204). Thousand Oaks, CA: Sage.

Wilson, B. J., Linz, D., Donnerstein, E., & Stipp, H. (1992). The impact of social issue television programming on attitudes towards rape. *Human Communication Research, 19,* 179–208.

Wilson, B. J., Linz, D., Federman, J., Smith, S., Paul, B., Nathanson, A., et al. (1999). *The choices and consequences evaluation: A study of court TV's anti-violence curriculum.* Santa Barbara: Center for Communication and Social Policy, University of California, Santa Barbara.

Wilson, B. J., Martins, N., & Marske, A. L. (2005). Children's and parents' fright reactions to kidnapping stories in the news. *Communication Monographs, 72,* 46–70.

Wilson, B. J., Smith, S. L., Potter, W. J., Kunkel, D., Linz, D., Colvin, C., et al. (2002). Violence in children's television programming: Assessing the risks. *Journal of Communication, 52*(1), 5–35.

Wood, W., Wong, F., & Chachere, J. G. (1991). Effects of media violence on viewers' aggression in unconstrained social interaction. *Psychological Bulletin, 109,* 371–383.

Wotring, C. E., & Greenberg, B. S. (1973). Experiments in televised violence and verbal aggression: Two exploratory studies. *Journal of Communication, 23,* 446–460.

Wright, J. C., Huston, A. C., Reitz, A. L., & Piemyat, S. (1994). Young children's perceptions of television reality: Determinants and developmental differences. *Developmental Psychology, 30,* 229–239.

Yancey, A. K., Siegel, J. M., & McDaniel, K. L. (2002). Role models, ethnic identity, and health-risk behaviors in urban adolescents. *Archives of Pediatric and Adolescent Medicine, 156,* 55–61.

Yokota, F., & Thompson, K. M. (2000). Violence in G-rated animated films. *Journal of American Medical Association, 283,* 2716–2720.

Youth Risk Behavior Surveillance System. (2006). Youth risk behavior surveillance—United States, 2005. *Morbidity and Mortality Weekly Report, Surveillance Summaries, 55/SS-5.*

Youth violence: A report of the Surgeon General. (2001). Washington, DC: U.S. Department of Health and Human Services. Retrieved January 22, 2008, from http://www.surgeon general.gov/library/youthviolence/toc.html

Zernike, K. (2007, March 9). Violent crime in cities shows sharp surge, reversing trend. *New York Times.* Retrieved March 16, 2007, from www.nytimes.com

Zillmann, D. (1971). Excitation transfer in communication-mediated aggressive behavior. *Journal of Experimental Social Psychology, 7,* 419–434.

Zillmann, D. (1991). Television viewing and physiological arousal. In J. Bryant & D. Zillmann (Eds.), *Responding to the screen: Reception and reaction processes* (pp. 103–133). Hillsdale, NJ: Lawrence Erlbaum.

Zillmann, D. (1998). The psychology of the appeal of portrayals of violence. In J. H. Goldstein (Ed.), *Why we watch: The attractions of violent entertainment* (pp. 179–211). New York: Oxford University Press.

Zillmann, D., & Wakshlag, J. (1985). Fear of victimization and the appeal of crime drama. In D. Zillmann & J. Bryant (Eds.), *Selective exposure to communication* (pp. 141–156). Hillsdale, NJ: Lawrence Erlbaum.

Zuckerman, M. (1979). *Sensation-seeking: Beyond the optimal level of arousal.* Hillsdale, NJ: Lawrence Erlbaum.

Zuckerman, M., & Litle, P. (1986). Personality and curiosity about morbid and sexual events. *Personality and Individual Differences, 7,* 49–56.

CHAPTER 6

Sexuality and the Media

Sexually speaking, playing catch-up is what being a teenager is all about, and movies like American Pie *are, by now, an essential part of the ritual.*

—*Entertainment Weekly* critic
Owen Glieberman (1999, pp. 43–44)

By baring a single breast in a slam-dunk publicity stunt of two seconds' duration, [Janet Jackson] also exposed just how many boobs we have in this country. We owe her thanks for a genuine public service.

—*New York Times* critic Frank Rich (2004, p. 1)

One erect penis on a U.S. screen is more incendiary than a thousand guns.

—*Newsweek* critic David Ansen (1999, p. 66)

Something's in the air, and I wouldn't call it love. Like never before, our kids are being bombarded by images of oversexed, underdressed celebrities who can't seem to step out of a car without displaying their well-waxed private parts to photographers.

—Lead article, *Newsweek,* February 12, 2007
(Deveny & Kelley, 2007, p. 40)

The paradox of health values in America today is clearly illustrated by the fact that cigarettes, which are known to cause disease, are prominently advertised in the press, while condoms, which prevent disease, are not considered suitable for advertisements.

—Y. M. Felman, *Journal of the
American Medical Association* (1979, p. 2517)

n the absence of widespread, effective sex education at home or in schools, television and other media have arguably become the leading source of sex education in the United States today (Strasburger, 2005). As one noted researcher observes, "Long before many parents begin to discuss sex with their children, answers to such questions as 'When is it OK to have sex?' and 'With whom does one have sexual relations?' are provided by messages delivered on television" (Kunkel, Cope, & Biely, 1999, p. 230) (see Figure 6.1). This is a rather sad commentary, considering that American media are arguably the most sexually suggestive and irresponsible in the world. Although other countries may show more nudity, only American media titillate their viewers with countless jokes and innuendoes about all aspects of human sexuality. Yet although advertisers are using sex to sell virtually everything from hotel rooms to shampoo, the national networks remain reluctant to air advertisements for birth control products (see Figure 6.2).

Unfortunately, the body of research about how children and teenagers learn about sexuality from the media and whether it affects their behavior is slim at best (J. D. Brown, Steele, & Walsh-Childers, 2002; J. D. Brown & Strasburger, 2007; Donnerstein & Smith, 2001; Escobar-Chaves et al., 2005; Gruber & Grube, 2000;

© 1999 STAHLER—CINCINNATI POST

Figure 6.1

SOURCE: Jeff Stahler, Newspaper Enterprise Association, Inc. Reprinted with permission.

Figure 6.2

SOURCE: Jeff Stahler, Newspaper Enterprise Association, Inc. Reprinted with permission.

Huston, Wartella, & Donnerstein, 1998; Malamuth & Impett, 2001). However, three new studies indicate that the media are probably a major force to be reckoned with in considering when teens begin having sex (Ashby, Arcari, & Edmonson, 2006; J. D. Brown et al., 2006; Collins et al., 2004).

On television each year, American children and teenagers view nearly 14,000 sexual references, innuendoes, and behaviors, few of which (less than 170) involve the use of birth control, self-control, abstinence, or responsibility (L. Harris & Associates, 1988). The most recent content analysis of television found that more than 75% of prime-time shows on the major networks contain sexual content, but only 14% of incidents include any mention of the risks or responsibilities of sexual activity or the need for contraception (see Figure 6.3). This figure rises to 27% for shows depicting or implying intercourse, however (Kunkel, Eyal, Finnerty, Biely, & Donnerstein, 2005). Since the 1997–1998 season, the amount of prime-time sexual content has increased from 67% to 77%, but there has been only a slight increase in the responsible content (Eyal, Kunkel, Biely, & Finnerty, 2007; Kunkel et al., 1999). Movies and sitcoms contain the most sexual content (Kunkel et al., 2005). In fact, talk about sex or sexual behavior can occur as often as 8 to 10 times per hour of prime-time television (Kunkel, Cope, & Colvin, 1996).

Prime-time television is also very popular with teenage viewers, and much of what they see contains appreciable sexual content, according to three separate content analyses. In 19 prime-time shows viewed most often by 9th and 10th graders, just under 3 sexual references per hour occurred, usually long kisses or unmarried intercourse (Greenberg, Stanley, et al., 1993). In action adventure series, most of the sex involved either unmarried intercourse or prostitution (Greenberg, Stanley, et al., 1993). Ward (1995) found that one fourth of all verbal interactions on prime-time series watched by teens contained sexual content. Most recently, an analysis of the sexual messages in the top 15 shows according to Nielsen ratings of teenage viewers found that two thirds contain sexual talk or

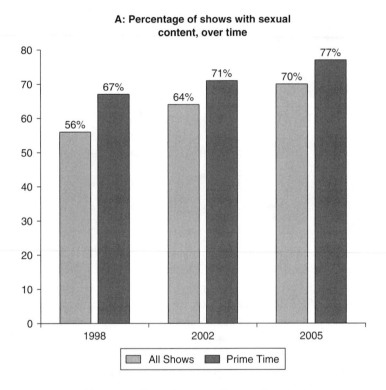

A: Percentage of shows with sexual content, over time

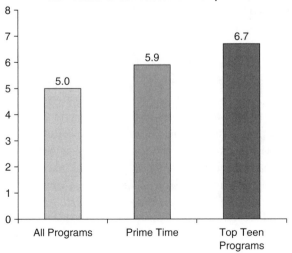

B: Among shows in 2005 with sexual content, the number of sex-related scenes per hour

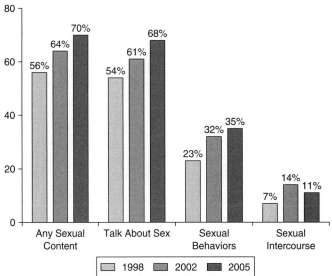

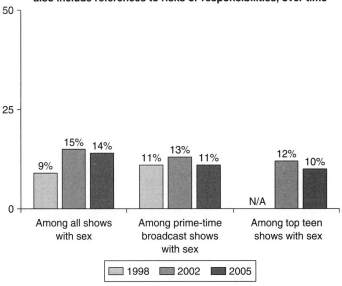

Figure 6.3   Results From the Only Ongoing Content Analysis of Sexual Content on TV

SOURCE: Kunkel et al. (2005). This information was reprinted with permission from the Henry J. Kaiser Family Foundation. The Kaiser Family Foundation, based in Menlo Park, California, is a nonprofit, private operating foundation focusing on the major health care issues facing the nation and is not associated with Kaiser Permanente or Kaiser Industries.

NOTE: Not only is there a lot of sexual content on mainstream American television, but most of it does not deal with the risks and responsibilities of sexual activity.

behavior, with intercourse depicted in 7% of the programs (see Tables 6.1–6.3) (Cope-Farrar & Kunkel, 2002).

Table 6.1 Most Popular Shows Viewed by Teens (12- to 17-Year-Olds)

1. *American Idol*
2. *Simpsons*
3. *Desperate Housewives*
4. *Survivor: Palau*
5. *CSI: Crime Scene Investigation*
6. *Extreme Makeover: Home Edition*
7. *The O.C.*
8. *Family Guy*
9. *Survivor: Vanuatu*
10. *One Tree Hill*
11. *Nanny 911*
12. *Lost*
13. *That 70s Show*
14. *WWE: Smackdown*
15. *7th Heaven*

SOURCE: Nielsen Media Research (2005). Used with permission.

Table 6.2 Sexual Content in Teens' Favorite Prime-Time Programs (*n* = 37 programs studied)

Percentage of programs with any sexual content	82
Average number of scenes per program with sexual content	4.5
Average number of scenes per hour containing sexual content	7.0

SOURCE: Data from Cope-Farrar and Kunkel (2002).

Table 6.3   Themes of Sexual Responsibility in Teens' Favorite Programs

Theme	% of All Scenes With Sexual Content
Saying no/waiting/keeping virginity	8.8
Taking "precautions"	2.5
Negative consequences of sex	2.5
Scenes without the above scenes	86.3

SOURCE: Adapted from Cope-Farrar and Kunkel (2002).

All of this talk about sex and sexual behavior on television (see Figure 6.4) contrasts dramatically with the fact that in the new millennium, adolescent sexuality and sexual activity—teen pregnancy, AIDS, other sexually transmitted diseases (STDs), and abortion—have all become battlegrounds in the public health and political arenas (R. T. Brown & Brown, 2006). With nearly 900,000 teen pregnancies a year and with the highest rate of STDs occurring among adolescents, the United States leads all Western nations in such statistics (see Figure 6.5) (Child Trends, 2006; Henshaw, 2004). Teen pregnancy costs the nation an estimated $21 billion a year, although the rate has been decreasing during the past decade (Miller, 2000). By age 17, nearly two thirds of males and one half of females have begun having sexual intercourse (see Table 6.4) (Centers for Disease Control and Prevention [CDC], 2006). Nearly one third of sexually experienced teen females have been pregnant (National Campaign to Prevent Teen Pregnancy, 2006). And a sexually active American teenager has a one in four chance of contracting an STD (Kirby, 1997).

Table 6.4   Sexual Behavior Among U.S. High School Students, 2005 (*N* = 13,953) (in Percentages)

	Ever Had Sexual Intercourse		First Sex Before Age 13		Four or More Lifetime Sex Partners		Condom Use at Last Sex	
Grade	Female	Male	Female	Male	Female	Male	Female	Male
9	29	39	5	12	6	13	72	77
10	44	42	4	8	10	13	57	74
11	52	51	3	8	14	18	58	66
12	62	64	2	6	20	23	46	66
Total	46	48	4	9	12	17	56	70

SOURCE: Data from Centers for Disease Control and Prevention (2006).

Figure 6.4

SOURCE: Copyright Chris Britt and Copley News Service. Reprinted with permission of Copley News.

So what is shown on American television is largely unrealistic, unhealthy, suggestive sexual behavior or sexual innuendoes (American Academy of Pediatrics [AAP], 2001; Hochman, 2008; Malamuth & Impett, 2001; Strasburger, 2005). It is sex as a casual pastime, a romp in the hay, with little or no consequences. What is meant by content that is sexually suggestive? A few examples will suffice:

- The famous sitcom *Seinfeld* repeated the abstinence plotline later in the 1990s, with a story about who could be "the master of his own domain" by going without masturbating for the longest period of time. *Seinfeld* also had a notorious story involving Jerry confusing a girlfriend's name for a part of the female pelvic anatomy (which later became part of a sexual harassment lawsuit in real life).

- In the late 1990s, a rash of teenage sitcoms appeared on prime-time TV. In *Popular,* a mom confronts her daughter and soon-to-be stepdaughter: "One of you is thinking of Doing It, if not already Doing It." In *That '70s Show,* one dim teenager asks, "Why cuddle when you can Do It?" These, along with several others representing the new generation of shows for teens, have been termed "Happy Days With Hormones" (K. Tucker, 1999).

- HBO's hit, *Sex and the City,* featured four single women who can never seem to get enough sex or talk enough about it. Various conversations have dealt with oral sex, anal sex, spanking, and other fetishes (Jacobs & Shaw, 1999). Nudity is not uncommon. Curiously, for a show that is so explicit, the risks of casual sex and the need for birth control are rarely mentioned. When the show switched to TBS in 2004, much of the raunchy sex language had to be cut.

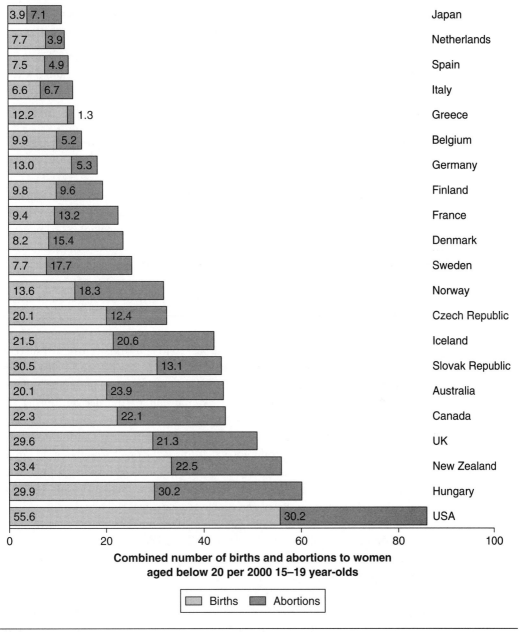

Birth and abortion rates among teenage women in selected OECD countries, expressed per 1000 women aged 15–19 (data are for 1996)

Country	Births	Abortions
Japan	3.9	7.1
Netherlands	7.7	3.9
Spain	7.5	4.9
Italy	6.6	6.7
Greece	12.2	1.3
Belgium	9.9	5.2
Germany	13.0	5.3
Finland	9.8	9.6
France	9.4	13.2
Denmark	8.2	15.4
Sweden	7.7	17.7
Norway	13.6	18.3
Czech Republic	20.1	12.4
Iceland	21.5	20.6
Slovak Republic	30.5	13.1
Australia	20.1	23.9
Canada	22.3	22.1
UK	29.6	21.3
New Zealand	33.4	22.5
Hungary	29.9	30.2
USA	55.6	30.2

Combined number of births and abortions to women aged below 20 per 2000 15–19 year-olds

Births   Abortions

Figure 6.5   The United States Continues to Have the Highest Teen Pregnancy Rate in the Western World

SOURCE: Skinner and Hickey (2003).

NOTE: Between 1990 and 2000, the teen pregnancy rate for 15- to 19-year-olds decreased 28% to 84 pregnancies per 1,000 females. This is thought to be more due to the use of contraception than the impact of abstinence-only programs. However, the teen birth rate *increased* 3% from 2005 to 2006, the first increase in 15 years (Stobbe, 2007).

- FOX's *War at Home* premiered in 2003 with an episode in which Dave, the main character, introduces his wife to the viewers by saying, "Did you check out that rack? Nice, huh?" He tells the viewing audience that he only has one rule for guys dating his teenager daughter: "If she sees your penis, I'll cut it off." Later that season, Dave buys his teenage son a lubricant because he is so sore from masturbating.

- In 2007, suggestiveness turned into explicitness for several cable shows. The HBO series *Tell Me You Love Me,* the Showtime series *Californication,* and the TNT series *Saving Grace* have all "pushed the envelope" with scenes of nudity and intercourse (Battaglio, 2007).

By contrast, consider the various messages and information presented in the following synopsis of a 1996 episode of *Malibu Shores* (Kunkel et al., 1999):

> Two teenagers are making out on the couch. Zach wants to have intercourse, but Chloe is not sure. He moves his hand underneath her shirt but she pushes it away, explaining "a month from now I don't want to be taking a pregnancy test." Zach says that he will use "protection" but Chloe says she's afraid that "protection" is not 100% effective. A friend of hers had a recent pregnancy scare. Finally, Zach says, "It's OK. I can wait. As long as it takes. I can wait. I don't want you to do something you're not ready to do." (*Malibu Shores,* NBC, March 30, 1996)

A distinct minority of TV shows in the past 10 to 15 years have wrestled successfully with sexual responsibility. Beginning with *Beverly Hills 90210,* the character of Donna (played by Tori Spelling) maintained her virginity throughout high school, when everyone else was losing theirs. At the end of the decade, during the 1999–2000 season of *Dawson's Creek,* the two major characters, Dawson and Joey, remained virgins as they approached their senior year in high school (Jacobs & Shaw, 1999). One research group notes that this is the one encouraging sign in all of the recent content analyses of mainstream television—that shows popular with teens may be more willing to address risks and responsibilities of early sex (Eyal et al., 2007). However, the actual percentage of such shows still remains surprisingly low: 14% of any shows with sexual content in 2005, but 23% of shows where teens talk about or engage in sex (see Figure 6.6) (Kunkel et al., 2005).

Sex on television is much more than sexual intercourse or sexual intimacy, however. Children and adolescents also can learn a great deal about sex roles: What does it mean to be a man or a woman? What makes someone "cool"? Attractive? Successful? How should one behave around the opposite sex (Signorielli, 2001; Steele, 1999; Strasburger, 2005)? Mainstream television is not kind to adolescent girls, for example (Pipher, 1997). A report from the National Organization for Women (NOW) found great disparities in the quality of programming for adolescent and adult women on the major networks (see Table 6.5) (Gorman, 2000). Super Bowl ads are also notorious for their questionable depiction of women (e.g., Anheuser-Busch ads showing a three-armed man grabbing a woman's rear, or two men ogling women's crotches in a yoga class) (Bennett, 2003).

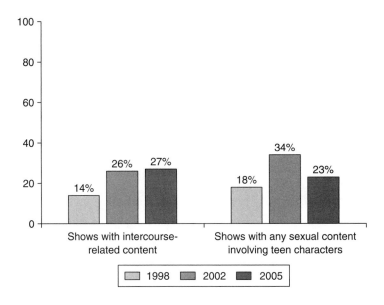

Figure 6.6   Percentage of Shows With References to Sexual Risks or Responsibilities, Over Time, of Sexual Content

SOURCE: Kaiser and Dale Kunkel, PhD, at University of Arizona.

NOTE: Programs that depict teen characters in sexual situations are more likely to include references to the risks and responsibilities of sexual intercourse.

Background

In 1976, the NBC Standards and Practices Department (the network censors) refused to let writer Dan Wakefield use the word *responsible* when *James at 15* and his girlfriend were about to have sexual intercourse for the first time and wanted to discuss birth control (Wakefield, 1987). To date, the networks still reject most public service announcements (PSAs) and advertisements about contraception, fearing that they would offend some unknown population (Strasburger, 2005). If an occasional ad for a birth control product does make it to the air, it is because of the noncontraceptive properties of the product (e.g., Ortho Tri-Cyclen is usually advertised as a treatment for acne, not a means of preventing pregnancy) (see Figure 6.7). Public service announcements that mention condoms—for example, ABC's 1994 campaign titled "America Responds to AIDS"—are largely confined to late-night TV (Painter, 1994).

Sex (the commercial networks seem to be telling us) is good for selling everything from shampoo, office machinery, hotel rooms, and beer to prime-time series and made-for-TV movies (see Figure 6.8), but a product that would prevent the tragedy of teenage pregnancy—condoms—must never darken America's

Table 6.5   Best and Worst Programs for Women, According to NOW (National Organization for Women)

Grading the Networks

NBC	B+
CBS	C+
ABC	C
FOX	D–

Best Shows: Top 10

1. *Family Law* (CBS)
2. *Chicago Hope* (CBS)
3. *Once & Again* (ABC)
4. *ER* (NBC)
5. *Sabrina the Teenage Witch* (ABC, WB)
6. *20/20* (ABC)
7. *Providence* (NBC)
8. *Becker* (CBS)
9. *Touched by an Angel* (CBS)
10. *Friends* (NBC)

Thumbs Down to

1. *Perfect Murder, Perfect Town* (made-for-TV movie about JonBenet Ramsey) (CBS)
2. *Getting Away With Murder* (another Ramsey movie) (FOX)
3. *Who Wants to Marry a Multi-Millionaire* (FOX)
4. *Norm* (ABC)
5. *The Drew Carey Show* (ABC)
6. *Spin City* (ABC)
7. *The World's Wildest Police Videos* (FOX)
8. *Walker, Texas Ranger* (CBS)
9. *Nash Bridges* (CBS)

SOURCE: Adapted from Gorman (2000).

NOTE: Eighty-one shows were analyzed during February 2000 "sweeps" weeks using four criteria: depiction of violence, gender composition and stereotypes, level of sexual exploitation, and social responsibility.

Sure, her skin is clearer.

But look deeper.

In a recent study, ORTHO TRI-CYCLEN®
caused significantly less breakthrough bleeding and spotting compared to Loestrin®* 1/20.[1]

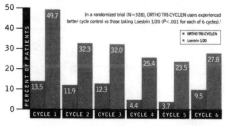

And it's still the only OC clinically proven to reduce moderate acne and maintain clearer skin.

ORTHO TRI-CYCLEN is the only OC indicated for the treatment of moderate acne vulgaris in women 15 years of age or older, with no known contraindications to oral contraceptives, who want contraception, have achieved menarche, and are unresponsive to topical antiacne medications.

Serious as well as minor side effects have been reported with the use of oral contraceptives. Serious risks include blood clots, stroke, and heart attacks. Cigarette smoking increases the risk of serious cardiovascular side effects, especially in women over 35. **The Pill does not protect against HIV or other sexually transmitted diseases.**

*Loestrin is a registered trademark of Parke-Davis.

Reference: 1. Sulak P, Lippman J, Siu C, Massaro J, Godwin A. Clinical comparison of triphasic norgestimate/ 35 μg ethinyl estradiol and monophasic norethindrone acetate /20 μg ethinyl estradiol: cycle control, lipid effects, and user satisfaction. Contraception. 1999;59:161-166.

Please see full Prescribing Information, a brief summary of which appears adjacent to this advertisement.

ORTHO-McNEIL

ORTHO-McNEIL PHARMACEUTICAL, INC.
Raritan, New Jersey 08869-0602
OOMP 1999 03J5360A Printed in U.S.A. 10/99

The Pill With Proof

Figure 6.7

television screens (Strasburger, 2005). Other media have become increasingly sexually explicit as well, particularly in the past two decades, without much regard for discussing either contraception or sexually transmitted disease. At the same time, a certain "raunchiness" has crept into mainstream American media, with four-letter words even heard on prime-time television (Rice, 2000) and celebrity role models such as Paris Hilton, Britney Spears, and Lindsay Lohan engaging in increasingly outrageous and provocative behavior (Deveny & Kelley, 2007). Only AIDS has begun to threaten the conspiracy of silence about the health consequences of

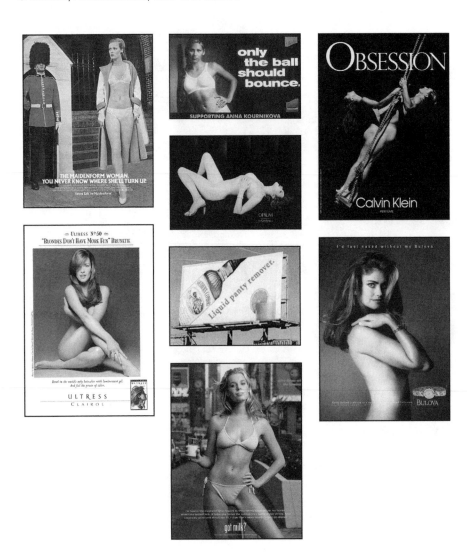

Figure 6.8

sexual activity and to free up the flow of useful and factual information to teenagers, who need it the most.

Why and how has this paradox occurred, and what effect does it have on teenage sexual activity? As with violence, the rate of sexual activity among young people has increased dramatically in the past two decades, although it has leveled off most recently (see Figure 6.9) (CDC, 2000; Strasburger et al., 2006). At the same time, the amount of sexual suggestiveness in the media has increased dramatically as well (Donnerstein & Smith, 2001; Strasburger, 2005). Although the data are not quite as convincing as with media violence, a handful of studies show that media sex still warrants considerable concern.

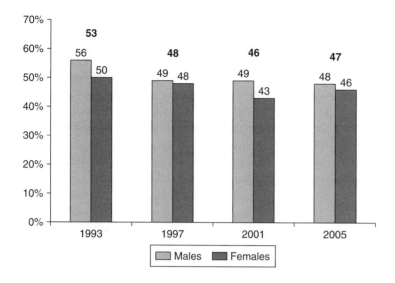

Figure 6.9   Percentage of 9th to 12th Graders, by Gender, Who Have Had Sexual
Intercourse, 1993–2005

SOURCE: Kaiser Family Foundation (2005).

Television as a Source of Sexual Information

In any given society, at any given moment in history, people become sexual the
same way they become anything else. Without much reflection, they pick up
directions from their social environment. They acquire and assemble meanings, skills, and values from the people around them. Critical choices are often
made by going along and drifting. People learn when they are quite young the
few things they are expected to be, and continue slowly to accumulate a belief
in who they are and ought to be throughout the rest of childhood, adolescence, and adulthood.

—John Gagnon, social science researcher (Roberts, 1983, p. 9)

Content analyses can determine what is being shown on television, but they do
not reveal what teenagers actually learn from these portrayals. Apart from its pervasiveness, accessibility, and content, television is an effective sex educator for many
reasons. Alternative sex educators, such as parents, may supply only restricted or
biased information (Pearl, Bouthilet, & Lazar, 1982). Parents rarely discuss sexual
activity or birth control, making a majority of teenagers dissatisfied with parents'
educational attempts (Strasburger, 2005). In a 2004 national survey of 519 teens,
ages 15 to 19, the media far outranked parents or schools as a source of information about birth control, for example (Kaiser Family Foundation/*Seventeen*

Magazine, 2004). Sex education programs in school may also have a limited impact on adolescents: Only 10% to 30% of schools offer comprehensive, high-quality programs; gains in knowledge may be small; and many curricula begin after teenagers have already begun having intercourse (Kirby, 2002, 2007; Landry, Kaeser, & Richards, 1999). The latest survey of sex education programs around the country found that 10% of schools do not teach any sex ed, 30% are abstinence-only programs, 47% are "abstinence-plus" (meaning that birth control can at least be mentioned but abstinence is stressed), and only 20% are comprehensive (National Public Radio, 2004). Yet two national polls of adults seem to indicate that parents are not in favor of abstinence-only sex ed. In 2000, a nationwide poll of adults found that 93% support sex education in high schools and 84% support it in middle schools, including contraception information as well as abstinence (Sexuality Information and Education Council of the United States [SIECUS], 2000). And more recently, a national survey of more than 1,000 adults found that 82% favor teaching teenagers about both, while 40% oppose abstinence-only sex ed. More than two thirds supported teaching teens how to use condoms properly (Bleakley, Hennessy, & Fishbein, 2006). Similarly, a recent survey of more than 1,300 parents in North Carolina found that 89% support comprehensive sex education (Ito et al., 2006). Although some people feel that abstinence only has been the key factor in the decline in U.S. teen pregnancy rates in the past decade, new research has found that better use of contraception was responsible for 86% of the decline, while abstinence contributed only 14% (Santelli, Lindberg, Finer, & Singh, 2007).

Peers, too, may play a limited role in sex education—not that their counsel is infrequently sought but because the information offered may be incomplete, misleading, distorted, and transmitted by means of jokes or boasting (and may, in fact, be influenced by the media as well) (Coles & Stokes, 1985). Two authors have hypothesized that the media may function as a "super-peer," in terms of pressuring teens into having sex earlier than expected (J. D. Brown, Halpern, & L'Engle, 2005; Strasburger, 2006a). Teenagers already overestimate the number of their peers who are engaging in sexual intercourse (National Campaign to Prevent Teen Pregnancy, 2004). Several studies document that teens who are avid consumers of media are more likely to overestimate the number of their peers and friends who are sexually active and to feel more pressure from the media to begin having sex than from friends (J. D. Brown & Newcomer, 1991; Kaiser Family Foundation/Children Now, 1999; M. E. Tucker, 2000). For example, in one survey, teenagers reported that TV was equally or more encouraging about sex than either their best male or female friends (J. D. Brown & Newcomer, 1991). In an anonymous survey of 1,015 *Seventeen* readers, ages 13 to 19, three fourths believed that most teenagers are having sex, whereas only about half actually are (M. E. Tucker, 2000). A survey of 2,100 teenage girls found that only 11-year-olds say that they do not feel pressure from the media to have sex (Haag, 1999). Early maturing girls are more likely to seek out sexual content in a variety of different media and to interpret that content as approving of teens having sex (J. D. Brown et al., 2005). Fans of music videos tend to overestimate the prevalence of sexual behaviors in the real world (Strouse, Goodwin, & Roscoe, 1994). And, finally, in one study of 314 students ages 18 to 20,

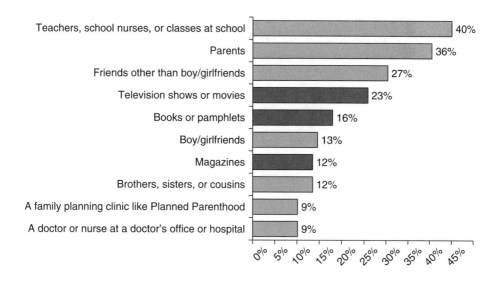

Figure 6.10   Sources From Which Teens Have Learned "A Lot" About Pregnancy and Birth Control

SOURCE: From Kaiser Family Foundation (2000). Reprinted with permission.

NOTE: Although TV and movies rank fourth in this national survey of 1,510 teens ages 12 to 18 about sources of sex information, when other media are added in (e.g., books and magazines), media become the leading source.

greater exposure to sexual content on TV led to higher expectations of the sexuality activity of one's peers and a more positive attitude toward recreational sex (Ward, Gorvine, & Cytron, 2002; Ward & Rivadeneyra, 1999). Heavy doses of television may accentuate teens' feelings that everyone is "doing it" except them and may be contributing to the steadily decreasing age at first intercourse for both males and females that has been occurring during the past two decades (Strasburger et al., 2006).

When teenagers or adults are asked about the influence of television, they acknowledge its role as an important source of sexual information but are equally quick to point out that the media have no influence on *their* behavior. This is the well-known third-person phenomenon (Eveland, Nathanson, Detenber, & McLeod, 1999): Everyone is influenced by media except oneself, and it seems particularly prevalent among teenagers. For teens, the very idea that something as simplistic and ordinary as the media could influence them is insulting; they are far more "sophisticated" than that. Yet in at least one national survey, media ranked close to first as a source of adolescents' sexual information (see Figure 6.10) (Kaiser Family Foundation, 1996). In another study, one in five teens said that they learned the most about sex from the media (J. D. Brown & Steele, 1995).

Many older studies found media ranked highly as well (L. Harris & Associates, 1986, 1987; Pearl et al., 1982; Thornburg, 1981). A 1987 Harris Report, which surveyed 1,250 adults nationwide, found that more than 80% of adults felt that TV was a major influence on teenagers' values and behavior (see Table 6.6) (L. Harris & Associates, 1987). Again, when one hypothesizes that friends and even parents may all be greatly influenced themselves by television, the cumulative effects of television may outweigh all other influences. At the same time, there seems to be a dissociation between the concerns of the general public and those in power in Hollywood (see Table 6.7) (Impoco, 1996). If anything, American parents seem

Table 6.6   Television and Birth Control (*N* = 1,250 Adults) (in Percentages)

	Yes	*No*
Should characters on TV shows be shown using birth control?	59	34
Is contraception too controversial to be mentioned on TV shows?	32	64
Are you in favor of advertising birth control on TV?	60	37
Would birth control advertising		
encourage teens to use contraceptives?	82	14
encourage teenagers to have sex?	42	52

SOURCE: Adapted from L. Harris and Associates (1987).

Table 6.7   Concerns About Sex: Hollywood Versus the American Public (in Percentages)

	American Public	*Hollywood*
Percentage who feel that TV and movies contribute to these problems		
Extramarital sex	84	43
Casual sex	83	56
Teens having sex	90	63
Violence against women	94	61
Percentage who are concerned about the following		
Verbal references to sex	82	38
Nudity or seminudity	83	42
Premarital sex	83	38

SOURCE: *U.S. News & World Report* and UCLA Center for Communication Policy polls, April 15, 1996. For details, see Impoco (1996).

more concerned about media sex than about media violence, which is the exact opposite of parents in other Western countries.

Not only are the media important generic sources of information, but particular topics may also be far more intensively discussed in the media than elsewhere (L. Harris & Associates, 1988). For instance, television may be the "medium of choice" for dissemination of information about AIDS (Goldberg, 1987). Of nearly 2,000 adults surveyed in a 1988 Roper poll, 96% said they had heard a report on AIDS in the past 3 months on TV, and 73% thought that TV was doing an effective job of educating the public (D. Jones, 1988). Media might also step in when others (i.e., schools) do not provide comprehensive information: A 1996 survey of 719 students and 13 school board members nationwide found that 93% of the students said that schools should teach about birth control and sexually transmitted diseases but that teachers are "scared" to discuss sex in the classroom (*USA Today,* July 3, 1996, p. 7D). A Kaiser study of 313 school principals nationwide found that more than half of students are not being taught how to use condoms in sex education programs (see Figure 6.11) (Kaiser Family Foundation, 1999). Yet adults increasingly want children educated about condoms. A poll by the CDC found that 86% of adults surveyed supported the airing of information about HIV and AIDS prevention, and 73% favored condoms being discussed on TV (CDC, 1994).

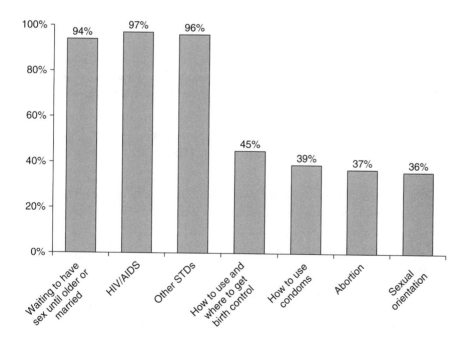

Figure 6.11   Percentage of Public Secondary School Principals Reporting Each Is Included in Their Schools' Sex Education

SOURCE: Kaiser Family Foundation (1999). Reprinted with permission.

What Do Children and Teenagers Learn From Television?

Many studies have documented television's ability to transmit information and to shape attitudes (Sutton, Brown, Wilson, & Klein, 2002). Television influences viewers' perception of social behavior and social reality (Bandura, 1977; Shrum, 2002), contributes to cultural norms (Gerbner, 1985; Greenberg, 1982), and conveys messages concerning the behaviors it portrays (Bandura, 1977; Roberts, 1982). Television may offer teenagers "scripts" for sexual behavior that they might not be able to observe anywhere else (Gagnon & Simon, 1987; Kim et al., 2007; Kunkel et al., 1999). In one experiment, exposing teens to programming with a lot of sexual content led them to rate casual sex less negatively than teens who did not view the programs (Bryant & Rockwell, 1994). In other studies, adolescents who view a lot of media are more likely to accept stereotypical sex roles (Walsh-Childers & Brown, 1993) and to believe that the unusual sexual behavior presented on talk shows is realistic (Greenberg & Smith, 2002; Strasburger & Furno-Lamude, 1997). One national survey actually found that 40% of teenagers said they have learned ideas about how to talk with their boyfriends or girlfriends about sex directly from media portrayals (Kaiser Family Foundation, 1998).

Given that the media are filled with sexual talk, behavior, and innuendoes and a lot of inaccurate information (Strasburger, 2005; Sutton et al., 2002), how do children and adolescents interpret such content? Does sexual content have the same impact on a 7-year-old as on a 17-year-old? Clearly, the answer is no. The available research concludes the following:

- Young people bring their own unique knowledge and expectations to the viewing arena (Greenberg, Linsangan, & Soderman, 1993; Truglio, 1992).

- Although young children sometimes understand the jokes and innuendoes about sex (Kaiser Family Foundation/Children Now, 1996), there is usually an age-dependent ability to interpret sexual content (Silverman-Watkins & Sprafkin, 1983).

- Interest paid to and comprehension of sexual content is probably age dependent, although the lower age limits could be decreasing. One recent study of 8- to 13-year-olds found that most of them understood the sexual messages being portrayed and tuned in because they wanted to learn something about sex (Kunkel et al., 1996).

- Sexual content is very appealing to teenagers (J. D. Brown et al., 2006; Sutton et al., 2002). Gender differences also seem to exist. Teen girls prefer more sexual content on television but often watch with their parents (Greenberg & Linsangan, 1993), whereas older adolescent boys choose more unsupervised hard-core sexual content in music lyrics and X-rated films (Buerkel-Rothfuss, Strouse, Pettey, & Shatzer, 1993; Greenberg & Linsangan, 1993). Girls who have not yet begun menstruating are much less interested in sexual content; conversely, girls who are more mature and more interested in sex seem to seek out sexual content in the media (J. D. Brown, White, & Nikopoulou, 1993).

• Many discussions about sex roles occur on television, with many focusing on the male sexual role and emphasizing a "recreational" orientation toward sex. In particular, the most frequently occurring messages depict sexual relations as a competition in which men comment on women's physical appearance and masculinity is equated with being sexual (Strasburger, 2006b; Ward, 1995).

• Viewing soap operas, which are extremely appealing to many teens, may give viewers unrealistic and unhealthy notions about single motherhood (Larson, 1996). However, not all teenagers apparently interpret the same content in the same way (Greenberg, 1993). In a study of teenagers' reactions to Madonna's video "Papa Don't Preach," J. D. Brown and Schulze (1990) found that Black teens viewed the popular music video as a father-daughter story, rather than a story about teen pregnancy (see Table 6.8). Studying individual differences among children and teens who view the same media may represent the current "cutting edge" of media research.

Studies show that subtler aspects of human sexuality may also be affected (Donnerstein & Smith, 2001; Escobar-Chaves et al., 2005; Levin & Kilbourne, 2008; Signorielli, 2001). As the National Institute of Mental Health (NIMH) report concluded, the single most significant aspect of a child's learning about sex is the set of messages that relates to "normal" male and female characteristics and roles in life (Roberts, 1982). Although television has made some progress in this area—for instance, males outnumber females 2:1 currently instead of 3:1 in the 1970s (Gerbner, 1993)—even the independent women shown in current programming frequently depend on men for advice and directions, lose control more often than men, and become more emotionally involved. This has led one critic to charge that the traditional female roles are merely being "dished up in new guises" (Canonzoneri, 1984).

Table 6.8   Teenagers' Versus Adults' Perceptions of Sex on Television (in Percentages)

Yes, TV gives a realistic picture about the following:	Teenagers (n = 1,000)	Adults (n = 1,253)
Sexually transmitted diseases	45	28
Pregnancy	41	24
Birth control	28	17
People making love	24	18

SOURCE: Adapted from Harris and Associates (1986).

Why Teenagers May Be Particularly Susceptible to Sexual Content in the Media

It is well known that teenagers sometimes seek to resemble actors and actresses as they experiment with different facets of their newly forming identities and try on different social "masks." In particular, the idiosyncrasies of adolescent psychology seem to combine to conspire against successful use of contraception during early and middle adolescence (Strasburger et al., 2006). Teenagers often see themselves egocentrically as being actors in their own "personal fable" (Elkind, 1993) in which the normal rules (e.g., having unprotected sexual intercourse may lead to pregnancy) are suspended—exactly as on television. Even though 70% of teenagers, by age 16, have reached the final level of cognitive operational thinking described by Piaget (1972)—sequential logical thinking (formal operations)—they may still suffer from what Elkind (1984) calls "pseudostupidity": "The capacity to conceive many different alternatives is not immediately coupled with the ability to assign priorities and to decide which choice is more or less appropriate than others" (p. 384).

One major conclusion of the 1985 Guttmacher Report, which found that the United States had the highest rate of teenage pregnancy in 37 developed countries (despite the fact that American teenagers were no more sexually active than French or Canadian or Belgian teens), concerned the media (E. F. Jones et al., 1985). There are only two possible hypotheses to explain these data: Either American female teens are extremely fertile, or American teens do not use birth control as effectively as teens in other countries. In fact, these data confirm that American society limits access to birth control for teenagers in three vital ways—via their physicians (who are reluctant to prescribe it), their media (which are reluctant to mention it), and their school-based sex education programs (which are reluctant to talk about it) (Strasburger, 2005). Although rates of teen sex have decreased slightly in the 1990s and early 2000s (CDC, 2006), the United States continues to have the highest teen pregnancy rate in the Western world (Abma, Martinez, Mosher, & Dawson, 2004).

Given the content of current American television, one would expect that heavy viewers would believe that premarital sex, extramarital sex, rape, and prostitution are all more common than they really are (Greenberg & Smith, 2002; Strasburger & Furno-Lamude, 1997). Although teenagers are probably not as susceptible as young children to media violence, they may be more susceptible to sexual content (Chia, 2006; Martino, Collins, Kanouse, Elliott, & Berry, 2005). Indeed, even teens may believe that what they watch on television is real (L. Harris & Associates, 1986). This belief is actually highest among those who are heavier consumers of TV and among adolescent populations with the highest teenage pregnancy rates (see Table 6.8) (L. Harris & Associates, 1986). Regular exposure to sexy TV might alter teenagers' self-perceptions as well. They might be less satisfied with their own sex lives or have higher expectations of their prospective partners (Chia, 2006; Greenberg, 1994; Martino et al., 2005).

If, as Gerbner states, "daytime serials comprise the most prolific single source of medical advice in America" (Gerbner, Morgan, & Signorielli, 1982, p. 295), then teenagers, particularly females, are getting bad advice. One of the main messages from the soaps is that adults do not use contraception and, in fact, do not plan for sex at all. Being "swept away" is the natural way to have sex (Wattleton, 1987). Unfortunately, this message dovetails with adolescents' own ambivalence about sex and helps to explain why the leading reasons sexually active teens give for not using contraception are that sex "just happens" and there was "no time to prepare" (Strasburger et al., 2006).

Several studies support these manifestations of the "cultivation hypothesis" (Strasburger, 2005). When college students were asked to identify models of responsible and irresponsible sexual behavior, they selected primarily media figures (Fabes & Strouse, 1984). And those who selected media figures as models of sexual responsibility had more permissive sexual attitudes and higher rates of sexual activity themselves (Fabes & Strouse, 1987). College students who were heavy viewers of soap operas estimated higher percentages of people in the real world who are divorced or have illegitimate children than did light viewers (Buerkel-Rothfuss & Mayes, 1981; Carveth & Alexander, 1985). In one study, pregnant teenagers were twice as likely to think that TV relationships are like real-life relationships than nonpregnant teenagers and that TV characters would not use contraception if involved in a sexual relationship (Corder-Bolz, 1981). And adolescents who identify closely with TV personalities and think that their TV role models are more proficient at sex than they are, or who think that TV sexual portrayals are accurate, report being less satisfied with their status as sexual virgins and with their own intercourse experiences (Baran, 1976a, 1976b; Courtright & Baran, 1980). Exposure to sexually explicit material online may also cultivate recreational attitudes toward sex among males (Peter & Valkenburg, 2006).

Movies

As a medium, movies are probably less significant than television because they command much less time from the average teenager and are usually viewed with friends, thus allowing the process of socialization to temper whatever potential effects may exist. If teenagers see two movies per week at their local cinema, that still represents only 10% to 15% of the time they spend watching television in an average week. This does not imply that movies are not important, however (Steele, 2002). As many as 80% of all movies later shown on network or cable TV contain sexual content (Kunkel et al., 1999), and that content may be considerably more explicit in the initial theatrical release. There has also been a consistent trend toward more sexually suggestive and sexually graphic material being presented in movies (Escobar-Chaves et al., 2005; Greenberg et al., 1987; Nashawaty, 1999). At the same time, there is a considerable gender imbalance in G-rated films: Female characters are outnumbered 3:1 by male characters (J. Kelly & Smith, 2006). The widespread prevalence of VCR and DVD players—85% of American households have one (Nielsen Media Research, 2000)—also makes the local video shop an important consideration along with the local cinema.

In a survey of 15- to 16-year-olds in three Michigan cities, more than half had seen the majority of the most popular R-rated movies between 1982 and 1984, either in movie houses or on videocassette (Greenberg et al., 1986). Compared with prime-time television, these movies have a frequency of sexual acts or references that is seven times higher, with a much franker depiction than on television (Greenberg, Siemicki, Dorfman, Heeter, & Stanley, 1993). Moreover, for a society concerned with abstinence, it seems curious that there was an average of eight acts of sexual intercourse between unmarried partners per R-rated film analyzed, or nearly half of all the sexual activity depicted. The ratio of unmarried to married intercourse was 32:1 (Greenberg, Siemicki, et al., 1993). As Greenberg (1994) notes, "What television suggests, movies and videos do" (p. 180). Content analyses of the most popular movies of 1959, 1969, and 1979 demonstrate the trend toward increasing explicitness in depictions of sexual themes, but the themes themselves have remained stable: Sex is for the young and is an "action activity" rather than a means of expressing affection (Abramson & Mechanic, 1983). And, as on TV, intercourse and contraception are distant cousins, at best.

The years 1970 through 1989 represented the era of teenage "sexploitation" films. Hollywood pandered to the adolescent population, presumably because of demographic considerations: Teenagers constitute the largest moviegoing segment of the population. Such movies as *Porky's I, II,* and *III, The Last American Virgin, Going All the Way, The First Time, Endless Love, Risky Business, Bachelor Party,* and *Fast Times at Ridgemont High* have dealt with teenage sex. Although parents may complain about their teenagers' interest in such films, it is the adults making films in Hollywood (and the adult movie house operators allowing underage teenagers in to see R-rated films) who are ultimately responsible.

With the baby boom generation and Generation Y having come of age and produced children and grandchildren of their own, Hollywood seems to have returned to targeting the teen audience. In 1999, *American Pie* updated *Porky's* for the next generation. In it, four male high school seniors all make a pact to lose their virginity by prom night. Early in the movie, the main character, Jim (Jason Biggs), masturbates with an apple pie after his friends tell him that that's what intercourse feels like. The movie also features a scene of stripping and attempted intercourse, broadcast over the Internet (D'Angelo, 1999). Talk about contraception, or the risks of intercourse, is virtually nonexistent, yet the movie still struggled to get an R rating, rather than an NC-17, primarily because of the scene the movie derives its title from (Nashawaty, 1999). As one movie critic notes, the film is "pitched to the first generation of male and female adolescents who have been taught, from birth (mostly by MTV), to act as sex objects for each other" (Glieberman, 1999, p. 43). Two more *American Pie* sequels exist. One review cites *American Pie 2* as being about "breasts, genitalia, 'potential' lesbianism, blue silicone sex toys, crude methods of seduction, 'the rule of three' (just watch the movie), a shower of 'champagne,' phone sex, tantric sex, and oh yeah. . . . superglue" ("Editorial Reviews," 2006). Other researchers feel that the distorted view of romance in contemporary movies popular with teens is at least as problematic as the overt sex (Pardun, 2002). Or that frank portrayals of adolescent sexuality are incredibly rare (C. Kelly, 2005). Even *Juno* is unrealistic (Goodman, 2008).

Nevertheless, since the 1980s, virtually every R-rated teen movie has contained at least one nude scene, and some, such as *Fast Times at Ridgemont High* and *Porky's,* contain up to 15 instances of sexual intercourse (Greenberg, Siemicki, et al., 1993). As one expert notes,

> The typical hour-long television program . . . will provide between two and three intimate sex acts, and most likely, there will be discussions/conversations about what someone is doing or has done, with the visual components quite rare. The typical 90 minute R-rated film, on the other hand, yields seven times that amount of sexual activity, with a large proportion made manifest through visual images. (Greenberg, Siemicki, et al., 1993, p. 56)

Questionable Language and Taste in Movies and Television: A New Trend?

Increasingly during the late 1990s and into the new millennium, Hollywood seems to be trying to stretch the boundaries of both the ratings and good taste. What is acceptable to the networks and the studios changes all the time, but during the past decade, the entertainment industry has seemed less inclined to fear moral watchdogs in society (see Table 6.9). A study of foul language on prime-time TV between 1998 and 2002 found an increase of nearly 95% during the so-called "Family Hour" and 109% during the 9 p.m. ET/PT timeslot (Parents Television Council, 2004). In addition, other studies have found that there is now one word of profanity uttered every 8 minutes on TV, with FOX-TV being the worst offender (Kaye & Sapolsky, 2004b). Shows rated TVPG actually have more questionable language than shows rated TV14. Similarly, more offensive language is found on shows that do not contain an "L" rating for "language" (Kaye & Sapolsky, 2004b)! Currently, George Carlin's "seven dirty words," which were once banned from broadcast media, are now heard once every 3 hours on TV (Kaye & Sapolsky, 2004a). In 2006, Congress passed legislation that increased the fines for broadcasting indecency from $32,500 to $325,000 per incident. The problem is how to define *indecency* (see Exercises) (Marcus, 2006). In addition, while broadcast TV standards may have tightened somewhat since the Super Bowl incident, cable TV continues to "push the envelope" with increasing amounts of bad language and nudity (Daly, 2005). To date, Congress has allowed the Federal Communications Commission (FCC) to have absolutely no oversight of the cable industry.

In Hollywood films, *There's Something About Mary; South Park: Bigger, Longer & Uncut; Austin Powers: The Spy Who Shagged Me; Bad Santa; Kill Bill;* and *Freddy Got Fingered* have set new standards for what can be said, shown, or discussed on screen (see Exercises for a discussion of "taste"). For example, *Freddy Got Fingered* features scenes of the star masturbating a live horse and prancing around in the skin of a gutted deer and a costar being sprayed with elephant ejaculate (Robischon, 2001). Minute for minute, *South Park* may be the crudest movie ever distributed, with 399 words that the Movie Index of Colorado Springs classified as "crude, obscene/profane or sexually suggestive" (Farhi, 1999). (Although *Pulp Fiction*

Table 6.9   A Chronology of Questionable Language on Prime-Time TV

March 18, 1979	The PBS documentary *Scared Straight* brings prison language to prime time.
February 26, 1984	Phoebe Cates' character on the miniseries *Lace* asks, "Which one of you bitches is my mother?"
January 22, 1990	Guns N' Roses let rip with four-letter words at the American Music Awards, including f—.
September 10, 1990	The first appearance of the expression, "You suck!" on prime-time TV, in the CBS comedy *Uncle Buck*.
September 21, 1993	Andy Sipowicz yells, "You pissy little bitch!" in the series premiere of *NYPD Blue*. The same episode features the terms "d—head"and "a—hole."
March 21, 1999	Whoopi Goldberg hosts the Academy Awards and uses the word "sh—" twice, as well as many double entendres.
January 19, 2003	During the live Golden Globe Awards telecast, U2 singer Bono receives an award and announces, "This is really, really [expletive] brilliant!"
December 10, 2003	Nicole Richie of the FOX reality show, *The Simple Life,* asks a simple question at the Billboard Music Awards: "Have you ever tried to get cow [expletive] out of a Prada purse? It's not so [expletive] simple."

SOURCE: Adapted from Rice (2000) and Ahrens (2003).

contained 411 such words, it ran 154 minutes in length, compared with *South Park*'s 80 minutes.) Adult films such as Spike Lee's *Summer of Sam* and Stanley Kubrick's *Eyes Wide Shut* somehow avoided the "kiss-of-death" NC-17 rating and received R ratings instead. Even PG-13 films such as *Wild Wild West* contain conversations about penis size and breast texture and sights of Salma Hayek's bare buttocks (Hershenson, 1999). Of course, any hour spent watching HBO's series, *The Sopranos,* is likely to expose a child or teenager to words that cannot even be printed in a college textbook.

One media critic feels that this has all contributed to a new "culture of disrespect" among children and adolescents, who are susceptible to the role-modeling influence of such programming (Walsh & Bennett, 2005). Another prominent critic, commenting on the summer of 2000 that produced *Me, Myself & Irene* and *Road Trip,* commented, "The stinky-poo outrages of recent Hollywood fare have no higher agenda than coaxing rowdy laughter from randy teenagers. . . . Crass is mass market" (Ansen, 2000, p. 61). To date, no research examines the impact of "raunchy" content or language on children or adolescents.

Print Media

Contemporary magazines reflect the same trend as seen in television and movies— a shift away from naive or innocent romantic love in the 1950s and 1960s to increasingly clinical concerns about sexual functioning (Planned Parenthood,

2006; Treise & Gotthoffer, 2001; Walsh-Childers, Gotthoffer, & Lepre, 2002). Content analyses demonstrate that by the 1970s, such mainstream magazines as *Ladies' Home Journal, Good Housekeeping, McCall's,* and *Time* contained a threefold increase in the number of articles that discussed sexual functioning and a sixfold increase in sexual terms used (Herold & Foster, 1975; Scott, 1986). Accompanying this change was a shift from a discussion of sexual "morality" to a concern about sexual "quality," a skepticism about virginity at marriage, and a liberalized view of extramarital sex (Silverman-Watkins, 1983).

In one of the handful of studies of print media that adolescents read, Klein et al. (1993) found that *Seventeen, Sports Illustrated, Teen, Time, Ebony, Young Miss, Jet, Newsweek,* and *Vogue* accounted for more than half of all reported reading. Adolescents who read sports or music magazines were more likely to report engaging in risky behaviors. Many teenagers, especially girls, report that they rely on magazines as an important source of information about sex, birth control, and health-related issues (Kaiser Family Foundation, 1996; Treise & Gotthoffer, 2001; Wray & Steele, 2002). A 2004 content analysis of British magazines for teens found that girls' magazines tend to focus on romance, emotions, and female responsibility for contraception, whereas boys' magazines were more visually suggestive and assumed that all males were heterosexual (Batchelor, Kitzinger, & Burtney, 2004).

Content analyses of *Seventeen* and *Sassy* have found that most of the stories in these two popular magazines contained very traditional socialization messages, including that girls depend on someone else to solve one's personal problems (Peirce, 1993), girls are obsessed with guys, girls are heterosexual, and girls are always appearance-conscious shoppers (Wray & Steele, 2002). *Sassy* initially featured content such as "Losing Your Virginity," "Getting Turned On," and "My Girlfriend Got Pregnant" (J. D. Brown & Steele, 1995). After an advertising boycott organized by the religious right, however, such content was withdrawn. *Sassy* is also no longer in print.

Kilbourne (1999) points out the trivialization of sex that occurs in women's magazines, both in their content and their advertising. For example, one print ad for jeans says, "You can learn more about anatomy after school," and shows a teenage guy groping a girl. According to Kilbourne, the print media give adolescent girls impossibly contradictory messages: be innocent, but be sexually experienced too. Teen magazines such as *Jane* are filled with articles such as "How Smart Girls Flirt," "Sex to Write Home About," "15 Ways Sex Makes You Prettier," and "Are You Good in Bed?" (Kilbourne, 1999).

In their defense, however, the print media are also far more likely to discuss contraception and advertise birth control products than broadcast media are (Walsh-Childers et al., 2002). A content analysis of teen magazines found that they devote an average of 2½ pages per issue to sexual issues (Walsh-Childers, 1997). Of sexual articles in teen magazines, nearly half (42%) concerned health issues (Walsh-Childers, 1997). In fact, the October 2005 issue of *Seventeen* featured a very frank, 2-page discussion of gynecological health, titled "Vagina 101," which won a Maggie Award from the Planned Parenthood Federation of America (Planned Parenthood, 2006). However, in general, much of the health coverage in teen magazines is in the form of advice columns, and the overarching focus seems to be on decision making about when to lose one's virginity (Huston et al., 1998; Walsh-Childers, 1997). To date, only one study has examined the possible link between sexual content in magazines and sexual attitudes and behaviors: Brown's sexual media diet included teen magazines and found that sexy media of all types decrease the age at first intercourse by approximately a year (J. D. Brown et al., 2006).

The Nature of the Research

Unlike the violence research, studies of the impact of sexy television and movies are, by necessity, considerably scarcer and more limited. Researchers cannot simply show a group of 13-year-olds several X-rated movies and then measure the attitudinal or behavioral changes that result. But a number of research modalities have yielded important data.

Content Analyses. Content analyses simply assay the amount of sexual material in current programming, lyrics, and articles without addressing its effects. From 1975 to 1988, the number of sexual behaviors on prime-time television doubled, the amount of suggestiveness increased more than fourfold, and sexual intercourse was portrayed for the first time (L. Harris & Associates, 1988). In the 1990s, mainstream television programming became even more explicit in its depiction of sexual content (see Tables 6.10 and 6.11) (Huston et al., 1998). Yet the unhealthy trends established in the 1980s also continued, with more TV sex occurring between unmarried adults than married adults and with only rare mentions of the risks of unprotected sex and teen sex (Kunkel et al., 1996). More recently, Cope-Farrar and Kunkel (2002) performed the most comprehensive analysis, examining the top 15 shows for teens ages 12 to 17 according to the Nielsen ratings (see Tables 6.1–6.3). More than 80% contained talk about sex or sexual behavior. Situation comedies featured 7 scenes per hour with sexual content, and shows with sexual material averaged 11 scenes per hour. Interestingly, for the first time in any content analysis, there was actually more sexual behavior depicted than talk about sex. All of these trends have continued into the early 2000s. Programming remains highly sexualized, according to the biennial content analyses now done at the University of Arizona (Kunkel, Cope-Farrar, Biely, Farinola, & Donnerstein, 2001; Kunkel et al., 2003, 2005) (see also Figure 6.3A–D and Figure 6.6):

- More than 75% of all prime-time shows now contain sexual content.
- Popular teen shows contain more sexual content than other, adult, prime-time shows.
- Of the most popular shows with teens, nearly half (45%) include sexual behavior.
- One of every 10 shows includes a portrayal of sexual intercourse or implied intercourse.

- Overall, only 14% of shows with sexual content mention *any* of the risks or responsibilities that go with having sex. This figure is only 10% for the top 20 teen shows. Even when risks are mentioned, they are usually inconsequential. Only 1% of all of the shows with sexual content have risks or responsibilities as the primary theme.
- Since these content analyses were first done in 1998, the total number of sexual scenes has nearly doubled. A total of nearly 5,000 TV programs have been analyzed in the four content analyses done to date.

Table 6.10   Major Issues on TV Talk Shows (*N* = 120 Shows) (in Percentages)

Issue	% of Shows
Parent-child relations	48
Dating	36
Marital relationship	35
Sexual activity	34
Abuse	23
Criminal acts	22
Sexual infidelity	18
Celebrities	10

SOURCE: Data from Greenberg et al. (1995).

Table 6.11   Sexual Content of Soap Operas (1996)

Behaviors	Frequency	Average per Hour
Passionate kissing	165	1.66
Verbal discussions about intercourse	66	0.68
Petting/caressing	30	0.31
Prostitution	27	0.28
Visual depictions of intercourse	17	0.19
Rape	13	0.14
Discussions of "safe sex," contraception, or AIDS	9	0.09

SOURCE: Adapted from Heintz-Knowles (1996).

Finally, several new studies have investigated other aspects of media in the new millennium:

- A unique content analysis of the 2001–2003 seasons found that about 15% of sexual content in programming features nonheterosexuals (Fisher, Hill, Grube, & Gruber, 2007). Another, more recent study of the 679 series characters in the 2006–2007 season found that only 1.3% of the characters are gay, lesbian, or bisexual (Moore, 2006).
- Sexual consequences in teen programming were the subject of another content analysis, examining prime-time dramas that feature characters 12 to 22 years old. The author found that the "double standard" is alive and well: Female sexual activity was more likely to have negative consequences than male sexual activity (Aubrey, 2004).

Soap Operas

As with prime-time programming, soap operas have become even more sexually oriented and sexually explicit since the 1980s. Two content analyses provide greater understanding of trends in the 1990s (Greenberg & Busselle, 1994; Heintz-Knowles, 1996). Greenberg and Busselle (1994) analyzed 10 episodes of each of the five top-rated soaps (*General Hospital, All My Children, One Life to Live, Young and the Restless,* and *Days of Our Lives*) in 1994 and found an average of 6.6 sexual incidents per hour (Greenberg & Busselle, 1994). Sex was visually depicted twice as often as it was talked about. By 1994, nearly half the sexual incidents involved intercourse, usually between unmarried partners. Surprisingly, rape was the second most frequently depicted sexual activity, with a total of 71 incidents or 1.4 per hour. Contraception or "safe sex" was mentioned only 5 times out of 333 sexual incidents. The only mention of AIDS among the 50 episodes concerned the risk associated with intravenous drug use, not sex. And there was a single episode where a parent discussed sex with her teenage daughter. By 1996, sexual behavior was three times more likely to be depicted than merely talked about. Only 10% of sexual episodes involved the use of contraception or discussions about the risks of sexual activity (Table 6.11) (Heintz-Knowles, 1996). But soap opera producers have also been more responsive to national health issues than prime-time producers (Fox, 2001; Stern, Russell, & Russell, 2005). For example, *General Hospital* (ABC) was the first to feature a character with HIV, who at one point discusses with her partner the need to use condoms if they have intercourse. On *Young and the Restless* (CBS), a woman decides to get tested for HIV after learning about her husband's affairs. Internationally, soap operas have been used prosocially to foster healthier attitudes about sex, sexuality, and particularly HIV (Howe, Owen-Smith, & Richardson, 2002; Rivadeneyra & Ward, 2005; Weinberg, 2006).

Reality TV

Despite its name, reality TV is anything but real—as any communications student, teacher, or parent well knows (Brenton & Cohen, 2003; Hill, 2005;

Murray & Ouellette, 2004). But in the early 2000s, reality TV has become immensely popular. In the Nielsen ratings for June 26 to July 2, 2006, for example, 5 of the top 20 shows were reality shows ("Nielsen Ratings," 2006). Reality shows can vary from talent shows (*American Idol, So You Think You Can Dance, Making the Band*) to adventure dramas (*Survivor, Amazing Race*) to the most common type—sexually oriented shows. These vary from all-out voyeurism (*Big Brother, Real World,* and *Are You Hot?*) to dating shows such as *The Bachelorette* and MTV's *Next* and *Parental Control*. A new BBC reality show, *The Baby Borrowers,* has parents "donating" their children to teenagers so that they can practice being parents. The announcer opens the show with the statement, "With the highest rate of teen pregnancy in Europe, Britain's teenagers are breeding like rabbits" (ABC News, 2007). The overriding message of many of the shows is that "you've got to be 'hot'" (Christenson & Ivancin, 2006). To date, only two studies have explored the impact of such shows on adolescents and young adults. A study of 197 young adults found that males and viewers who perceived the shows to be real were more likely to share the attitudes displayed in reality dating shows (Ferris, Smith, Greenberg, & Smith, 2007). And in a study of 334 college students, Zurbriggen and Morgan (2006) found that viewing such programming was correlated with beliefs in a double standard, that men are sex driven, and that men and women are sexual adversaries. But the researchers also found that those students who tended to be less sexually experienced were actually watching more of the reality dating shows, which may signify the importance of such programs in sexual socialization.

Advertisements

From the time of the Noxzema girl, who advised male viewers "to take it off, take it all off," to Brooke Shields' "nothing comes between me and my Calvins," to present-day ads for beer, wine coolers, and perfume, advertising has always used explicit visual imagery to try to make a sale (Kilbourne, 1999). In 1977, one researcher found that nearly one third of all advertisements on prime-time TV "used as selling points the desirability of sex appeal, youth, or beauty, and/or those in which sex appeal (physical attractiveness) of commercial actors or actresses was a selling point" (Tan, 1979, p. 285). A similar study 8 years later of more than 4,000 network commercials found that 1 of every 3.8 ads relied on attractiveness-based imagery (Downs & Harrison, 1985). One by-product of this kind of advertising is that women are subtly taught that their main goal in life is to attract men or serve as sexual prizes. If she is successful, can she possibly say no when he wants sex? And can he actually believe her (J. D. Brown & Steele, 1995)?

One by-product of the feminist movement of the 1970s has been that men are now being increasingly exploited for their sex appeal the way women once were (see Figure 6.12) (Svetkey, 1994). American media have become equal-opportunity exploiters.

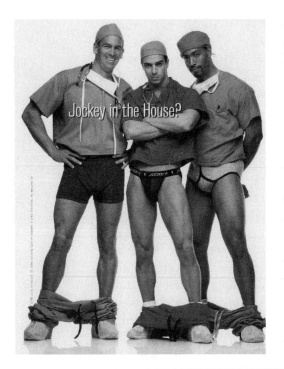 

Figure 6.12

Modern advertising often features women's bodies that have been "dismembered"—just the legs or breasts appear (see Figure 6.13) (Kilbourne, 1999). Increasingly, little girls are sexualized (e.g., a shampoo ad reads, "You're a Halston woman from the very beginning" and shows a girl of about 5) (Levin & Kilbourne, 2008). A study of fashion advertisements in popular magazines found that females are more likely than males to be shown in submissive positions, sexually displayed, or be included in violent imagery (Rudman & Verdi, 1993). As Kilbourne (1999) notes,

> When sexual jokes are used to sell everything from rice to roach-killer, from cars to carpets, it's hard to remember that sex can unite two souls, can inspire awe. Individually, these ads are harmless enough, sometimes even funny, but the cumulative effect is to degrade and devalue sex. (p. 265)

What impact does this sexualization of American advertising have on adolescents? One can only speculate, but there are data that American adults seem to be having more sexual problems than ever before. In the most recent and comprehensive study since the Kinsey Report of the 1940s, 43% of women and 31% of men reported sexual dysfunction (defined as a lack of interest in or enjoyment of sex, performance anxiety, or inability to achieve orgasm) (Laumann, Paik, & Rosen, 1999). Could it be that media images and ads for erectile dysfunction are shaping people's reality of what their sex lives should be? If so, this would again represent

Figure 6.13

the "cultivation effect" at work, which is known to be a strong factor in media influence (Gerbner, Gross, Morgan, Signorielli, & Shanahan, 2002). Is it possible to measure up to the media's apparent sexual standard, where everyone is having great (harmless) sex all the time? Considerable qualitative research with adolescents will be needed before these questions can be answered authoritatively.

Correlational Studies. Clearly, according to many content analyses, American television is both sexy and suggestive. Simple common sense would tell us that this is not healthy for children and younger adolescents. But some people want stronger evidence. Does all of this sexy content actually harm children, or is it merely fantasy and entertainment? Do teenagers who become sexually active at a younger age do so because of exposure to sexy media, or do they simply prefer to watch such programming? Unfortunately, correlational studies are rare. In stark contrast to the media violence literature, only 10 correlational studies exist in which researchers have tried to assess the relationship between early onset of sexual intercourse and amount of sexual content viewed on television, and 4 of the 10 are now more than 10 to 20 years old. However, all did demonstrate measurable effects:

- In a study of 75 adolescent girls, half pregnant and half nonpregnant, the pregnant girls watched more soap operas before becoming pregnant and were less likely to think that their favorite soap characters would use birth control (Corder-Bolz, 1981).

- A study of 391 junior high school students in North Carolina found that those who selectively viewed more sexy TV were more likely to have begun having sexual intercourse in the preceding year (J. D. Brown & Newcomer, 1991).

- A study of 326 Cleveland teenagers showed that those with a preference for MTV had increased amounts of sexual experience in their mid-teen years (R. A. Peterson & Kahn, 1984).

- Data from the National Surveys of Children revealed that males who watch more TV had the highest prevalence of sexual intercourse and that teens who watched TV apart from their family had a rate of intercourse three to six times higher than those who viewed with their family (J. L. Peterson, Moore, & Furstenberg, 1991).

- A study of 214 teens ages 13 to 18 and their families found that there appeared to be no relationship between male virginity and exposure to R-rated or X-rated films, popular music, or music videos (Strouse, Buerkel-Rothfuss, & Long, 1995). However, for females, there was a relationship between exposure to music videos and premarital sex. There was also an association between unsatisfactory home environments and premarital sex.

- A phone survey of 1,010 teens ages 14 to 19 in upstate New York found that listening to pop or hip-hop music or reading women's magazines was associated with having had sexual intercourse. It also found that adolescents spend nearly 8 hours each day with various types of media (Pazos et al., 2001).

- A study of 244 high school students' viewing habits found that viewing more talk shows and sexy prime-time shows was associated with greater sexual stereotyping and with greater levels of sexual experience (Ward & Friedman, 2006).

- An eighth, somewhat flawed study found that African American female teens with greater exposure to rap music videos or X-rated movies are more likely to have had multiple sexual partners and test positive for an STD (Wingood et al., 2001).

- Another recent study of 847 teenagers and their parents found that teens whose parents impose more restrictions on their TV viewing habits are less sexually experienced and have healthier body self-images (Schooler, Kim, & Sorsoli, 2006).

- Finally, a study of more than 1,000 teenagers from 14 middle schools in the Southeast found that exposure to sexual content in the media explained 13% of the variance in intention to have sex in the near future (L'Engle, Brown, & Kenneavy, 2006).

Longitudinal Studies. Up until recently, there were no substantial longitudinal studies that could implicate or absolve sexy media content of encouraging early teen sex. But that situation has recently changed with an influx of funding from the NIMH: Now there are three, with more in process. In the first study of its kind, California researchers found that teens who were exposed to sexy media were more likely to begin intercourse at a younger age. Nearly 1,800 teens, ages 12 to 17, were studied initially and then a year later. Exposure to sexy media doubled the risk of their initiating sexual intercourse or advancing significantly in their noncoital activity (Collins et al., 2004). Similar findings were reported using data from the National Longitudinal Study of Adolescent Health. In a study of nearly 5,000 teenagers younger than age 16 years who had not yet had sexual intercourse, researchers found that those who watched more than 2 hours of TV per day were nearly twice as likely to begin having sex within a year, compared with lighter viewers

(Ashby et al., 2006). Finally, the "gold-standard" study was done by J. D. Brown and her colleagues (2006), using a Sexual Media Diet comprising not only TV but movies, music, and print media as well. Exposure to a heavier Sexual Media Diet among one thousand 12- to 14-year-olds in North Carolina accelerated White adolescents' sexual activity and doubled their risk of early intercourse within 2 years (see Figure 6.14). The study was compelling and comprehensive in every way, except for omitting exposure to online pornography (Strasburger, 2006b). Several more longitudinal studies, funded by NIMH, are currently being conducted.

Experimental Studies. Severe constraints still exist on studying any aspect of childhood or adolescent sexuality (Huston et al., 1998). Even in the new millennium, researchers continue to fight the old shibboleth that if you ask kids about sex, they will get ideas they would not otherwise have had (Strasburger, 2005). Studies have examined the effectiveness of sex in advertising and programming: High schools girls shown 15 "beauty commercials" were more likely to believe that physical attractiveness was important for them than were girls shown neutral commercials (Tan, 1979). Male college students who viewed a single episode of *Charlie's Angels* were harsher in their evaluations of the beauty of potential dates than were males who had not seen the episode (Kenrick & Guttieres, 1980),

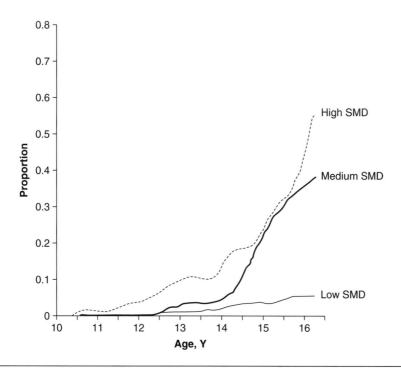

Figure 6.14   Sexual Media Diet (SMD) and Risk of Early Sexual Intercourse

SOURCE: From J. D. Brown et al. (2006).

NOTE: New research has found a doubled risk of early sexual intercourse with exposure to more sexual content in a variety of different media.

and male college students shown centerfolds from *Playboy* and *Penthouse* were more likely to find their own girlfriends less sexually attractive (Weaver, Masland, & Zillmann, 1984).

Studies have also examined the impact of sexual content on attitude formation (Greenberg & Hofschire, 2000). For example, college students shown sexually explicit films reported a greater acceptance of sexual infidelity and promiscuity than controls did (Zillmann, 1994), and adolescents viewing only 10 music videos were more likely to agree with the notion that "premarital sex is acceptable" (Greeson & Williams, 1986). In two studies, college students' disapproval of rape was lessened by exposure to only 9 minutes of scenes taken from television programs and R-rated movies or viewing 5 hours of sexually explicit films over a 6-week period (J. D. Brown, Childers, & Waszak, 1990; Zillmann & Bryant, 1982). Finally, both male and female college students exposed to hour-long nonviolent X-rated videos over a period of 6 weeks reported less satisfaction with their intimate partners (Zillmann & Bryant, 1988). The researchers concluded, "Great sexual joy and ecstasy are accessible to parties who just met, who are in no way committed to one another, and who will part shortly, never to meet again" (Zillmann & Bryant, 1988, p. 450)—certainly an ominous finding for those interested in diminishing rates of adolescent sexual intercourse.

Obviously, studying college students is considerably easier than studying younger adolescents, particularly when sexual behavior is the variable being assessed. Although about half of high school seniors have engaged in sexual intercourse (CDC, 2000) and adolescents are bombarded with sexual messages in the media, school administrators and parents are still reluctant to have their teenagers questioned about their sexual activities, even with the use of informed consent (Strasburger, 2006a).

Therefore, aside from the NIMH-funded longitudinal studies discussed above, there is currently a return to small-scale laboratory and field studies, two of which have shown intriguing results. In the first, "massive exposure" to prime-time programming that deals with pre-, extra-, or nonmarital sex desensitized young viewers to such "improprieties." However, several factors militated against this: a clearly defined value system within the family, an ability to freely discuss important issues within the family, and active, critical viewing skills (Bryant & Rockwell, 1994). In the second, a small study of adolescents' interpretations of soap operas, Walsh-Childers (1991) found that teenagers' own sexual "schemas" influenced their perceptions of the characters' relationships. Interestingly, mention of birth control did not have to be explicit to be effective. In fact, the use of the euphemism *protection* seemed to be preferable.

Prosocial Sexual Content on Television

One of the most appealing and practical approaches to address public health concerns about television has been dubbed "edutainment"—the practice of embedding socially responsible messages into mainstream programming (J. D. Brown & Strasburger, 2007; Kaiser Family Foundation, 2004). The Media Project represents a unique partnership between Advocates for Youth and the Henry J. Kaiser Family Foundation that works with the television industry in a collaborative fashion to increase the amount of accurate and prosocial sexual content on television. During the 1999 TV season, The Media Project worked with the producers of *Felicity* on a two-part episode about date rape. The Project encouraged the creation of a toll-free rape crisis hotline number to be displayed at the end of the episode, and the hotline received more than 1,000 calls directly after the show aired (Folb, 2000). In a small survey about a later episode that discussed birth control, more than one fourth of 12- to 21-year-olds surveyed felt they had learned something new about birth control and safe sex. The Project has also provided information for a *Jack & Jill* episode about an unwanted pregnancy, for a *For Your Love* episode about condom use, and for a *Get Real* episode about parent-child communication and teens becoming sexually active for the first time (Folb, 2000). In 2002, *Friends* aired an episode about condoms, and 27% of a national sample of teens saw the program. Nearly half the teens watched the episode with an adult, and 10% talked about condom efficiency as a direct result of the episode (Collins, Elliott, Berry, Kanouse, & Hunter, 2003).

Collaborative efforts between the Kaiser Foundation and the producers of the hit show *ER* also resulted in successful storylines about the risks of human papilloma virus and the usefulness of emergency contraception (see Figure 6.15)

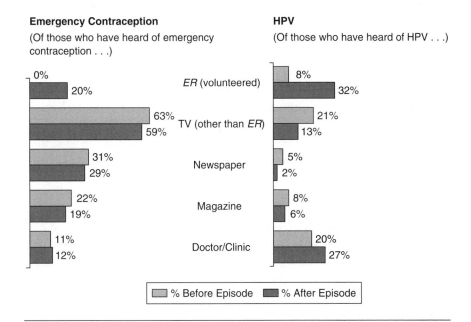

Figure 6.15 Viewers' Increased Knowledge After Storylines on the Hit Show *ER* About Emergency Contraception and about Human Papilloma Virus (HPV)

SOURCE: Brodie et al. (2001). Reprinted with permission from the Kaiser Family Foundation.

NOTE: A unique collaboration between the Kaiser Family Foundation and the producers of *ER* resulted in important health information about human papillomavirus (a sexually transmitted disease) and about emergency contraception being written into stories. This study illustrates the importance of mainstream media in disseminating information about sex and sexuality.

(Brodie et al., 2001). In England, a storyline in which one of the characters in the hit show *Coronation Street* died of cervical cancer resulted in a 21% increase in Pap smears in the 19 weeks after the show aired (Howe et al., 2002). The Soap Opera Summit in Hollywood and international efforts to embed storylines into popular soap operas are other examples of prosocial efforts. For example, media giant Viacom and the Kaiser Family Foundation launched an ambitious project in 2003 to produce $120 million worth of public service announcements and print ads concerning HIV/AIDS and to encourage Viacom producers to include storylines in their TV shows that would raise AIDS awareness (Tannen, 2003). Such efforts demonstrate that the entertainment industry can be remarkably receptive to outside input and that healthier content can be introduced into mainstream television without government pressure or the threat of censorship.

The mass media have also been used proactively to try to increase parent-child communication about sex. In North Carolina, a mass media campaign used billboards and radio and TV PSAs with the theme of "Talk to your kids about sex. Everyone else is." The impact of the campaign was assessed via a postexposure survey to 1,132 parents of adolescents living in the 32 counties covered by the campaign. Exposure to a billboard message or PSA significantly correlated with a parent talking to his or her child about sex during the following month (DuRant, Wolfson, LaFrance, Balkrishnan, & Altman, 2006).

Contraceptive Advertising

One of the key findings of the 1985 Guttmacher Report was that America's high teenage pregnancy rate partially results from inadequate access to birth control. This resulted in important health information about human papillomavirus (a sexually transmitted disease) and about emergency contraception being written into stories. This study illustrates the importance of mainstream media in disseminating information about sex and sexuality (E. F. Jones, Forrest, Henshaw, Silverman, & Torres, 1988). Despite decreases in rates of sexual activity and pregnancy among American teens in the late 1990s and early 2000s, the United States *still* leads the Western world in teen pregnancy (Abma et al., 2004; CDC, 2006). It seems odd, perhaps even hypocritical, that as the culture has become increasingly "sexualized" in the past 20 years, the one taboo remaining is the public mention of birth control. In 1985, the American College of Obstetrics and Gynecology (ACOG) made headlines when its public service announcement about teen pregnancy, titled "I Intend," was banned from all three major networks. The one offensive line that had to be removed before the networks agreed to run the PSA said, "Unintended pregnancies have risks . . . greater risks than any of today's contraceptives" (Strasburger, 1989, p. 767). Network executives claim that such PSAs or advertisements for birth control products would offend many viewers.

The situation remains the same now as it did two decades ago. However, birth control ads for nonprescription products air on many local TV stations around the United States (e.g., KABC–Los Angeles) without complaints being registered. In addition, the 1987 Harris Report shows that a majority of the American public—including 62% of the Catholics surveyed—favor birth control advertising on

Figure 6.16

television (see Table 6.6) (L. Harris & Associates, 1987). A more recent study commissioned by the Kaiser Family Foundation (2001) found similar results. Meanwhile, ads for Viagra, Cialis, and Levitra are abundant and make sex seem like a recreational sport (see Figure 6.16). In 2006, $241 million was spent advertising erectile dysfunction (ED) drugs, which helped result in sales of $1.4 billion (Agovino, 2007). The apparent "disconnect" between the networks' willingness to air ads for ED drugs and their unwillingness to air ads for birth control products seems hypocritical at best (AAP, 2006).

Would advertising of condoms and birth control pills have an impact on the rates of teen pregnancy or acquisition of HIV (see Figure 6.17)? The Guttmacher data (E. F. Jones et al., 1988) and other comparative data (Henshaw, 2004) seem to indicate that the answer is yes for teen pregnancy because European countries have far lower rates of teen pregnancy and far more widespread media discussion and advertising of birth control products. Furthermore, according to Population Services International, when Zaire began advertising condoms, there was a 20-fold increase in the number of condoms sold in just 3 years—from 900,000 in 1988 to 18 million in 1991 (Alter, 1994). In a relevant "natural experiment," Earvin "Magic" Johnson's announcement of his HIV infection was associated with a decline in "one-night stands" and sex with multiple partners in the subsequent 14 weeks in a Maryland study (CDC, 1993). It also resulted in increased awareness about AIDS (Kalichman & Hunter, 1992).

Would advertising birth control products make teenagers more sexually active than they already are? There is no evidence available indicating that allowing

Figure 6.17

SOURCE: Copyright ©John Branch, *San Antonio Express-News*. Used with permission.

freer access to birth control encourages teenagers to become sexually active at a younger age (Farrar, 2006; Mueller, Gavin, & Kulkarni, 2008; Reichelt, 1978; Strasburger et al., 2006). In fact, the data indicate the exact opposite: There are now at least eight peer-reviewed, controlled clinical trials showing that giving teens freer access to condoms does not increase their sexual activity or push virginal teenagers into having sex but does increase the use of condoms among those who are sexually active (Blake et al., 2003; Furstenberg, Geitz, Teitler, & Weiss, 1997; Guttmacher et al., 1997; Jemmott, Jemmott, & Fong, 1998; Kirby et al., 1999; Schuster, Bell, Berry, & Kanouse, 1998; Sellers, McGraw, & McKinlay, 1994; Wolk & Rosenbaum, 1995). Typically, teenage females engage in unprotected intercourse for 6 months to a year before seeking medical attention for birth control (Strasburger et. al., 2006). Organizations such as the AAP, the American College of Obstetricians & Gynecologists, and the Society for Adolescent Medicine have all called for contraceptive advertising on American television (AAP, 2001, 2007; Espey, Cosgrove, & Ogburn, 2007; Society for Adolescent Medicine, 2000). Despite the hopes of many public health officials, the fear of AIDS may not be sufficient to increase teenagers' use of contraception. In 2006, contraceptive advertising was rarely shown on national network programming (except for occasional ads for the "patch" and ads for Ortho Tri-Cyclen, which mention only improvement in acne, not pregnancy prevention; see Figure 6.7) and very much subject to the discretion of local station managers. And ads for emergency contraception are nowhere to be found, yet every year American women have 3 million unplanned pregnancies, leading to 1.3 million abortions. Advertising emergency contraceptives might be the ideal way to reduce the number of abortions in the United States (Kristof, 2006). Thus, in our opinion, a major potential solution to a significant American health problem is being thwarted by a few very powerful but fearful people (see Figure 6.17).

Pornography

The relationship of pornography to behavior remains an important health issue as well as a controversial First Amendment issue (Donnerstein & Linz, 1994; Malamuth & Huppin, 2005). Interestingly, print media are protected constitutionally by the First Amendment, whereas the broadcast media are subject to regulation under the 1934 Federal Communications Commission Charter. To date, cable television remains in a legal netherworld. For obvious reasons, there are no studies on the impact of pornography on children or adolescents.

Exposure

Pornography is a big business in the United States—nearly $13 billion a year (Bashir, 2007)—and teenagers have surprisingly ready access to a variety of R-rated and X-rated material. By age 15, 92% of males and 84% of females had seen or read

Playboy or *Playgirl* in one study; by age 18, virtually all had (D. Brown & Bryant, 1989). Exposure to more hard-core magazines begins at an average age of 13.5 years, and 92% of 13- to 15-year-olds report having seen an X-rated film (D. Brown & Bryant, 1989). Of 16 popular R-rated films, Greenberg, Siemicki, et al. (1993) found that 53% to 77% of 9th and 10th graders had seen most of them. In a study of 522 African American 14- to 18-year-olds, researchers found that 30% had seen at least one X-rated movie within the past 3 months (Wingood et al., 2001). Of course, the Internet now looms as the primary source for pornography (see Chapter 11; Kanuga & Rosenfeld, 2004). A 2001 Kaiser Foundation survey documented that 70% of teens have been exposed to pornography online, whether intentionally or unintentionally (Kaiser Family Foundation, 2001), although a newer study of 1,500 youth nationwide found that by 2006, that figure had fallen to 42% (Wolak, Mitchell, & Finkelhor, 2007).

Research

Current research involving adults seems to indicate that pornography itself is harmless unless violence is also involved (Strasburger & Donnerstein, 2000). In that situation, aggression might increase because there is a known relationship between portrayals of violence and subsequent aggressive behavior (Cline, 1994; R. J. Harris, 1994a, 1994b; Huston et al., 1992; Linz & Malamuth, 1993; Lyons, Anderson, & Larson, 1994; Malamuth & Huppin, 2005; Weaver, 1994). The term *pornography* means different things to different people. The current state-of-the-art assessment subdivides the research according to content (Huston et al., 1992; Malamuth & Huppin, 2005; Strasburger & Donnerstein, 2000).

Erotica (R- or X-rated material with implied or actual sexual contact but no violence or coercion). Probably no antisocial effect (Donnerstein, Linz, & Penrod, 1987). Wingood et al. (2001) did find an association between African American females having viewed X-rated movies and having more negative attitudes toward using condoms, having multiple sex partners, not using contraception, and having a positive test for chlamydia. This was a relatively small study that found an association, not a causal connection. It may represent a cultivation effect or its opposite: that teens who are more interested in sex tend to seek out more sexual media. Only a longitudinal correlational study will enable researchers to distinguish between the two.

X-Rated Material Degrading to Women (nonviolent XXX-rated videos in which women are the eager recipients of any and all male sexual urges). Highly controversial. Most studies find no antisocial effect (Donnerstein et al., 1987). But some researchers suggest that attitudes may be molded or changed by repeated exposure. In a study of college students, massive doses of pornographic films led to overestimates of uncommon sexual practices, decreased concern about the crime of rape, loss of sympathy for the women's liberation movement, and, among men, a more callous attitude toward sex (Zillmann & Bryant, 1982, 1988).

Violent Pornography (X-rated videos in which the woman victim is shown to be enjoying the assault or rape). Known antisocial effects. This is one of the most dangerous types of combinations—sex and violence—although it is probably the violent content that takes priority. Men exposed to such material show increased aggression against women in laboratory studies and increased callousness in their attitudes (Donnerstein, 1984; Linz & Malamuth, 1993). But men exposed to nonsexual violence can show the same effect as well (Huston et al., 1992).

Non-X-Rated Sexual Aggression Against Women (broadcast or movie programming in which women are depicted as deriving pleasure from sexual abuse or assault). Probable antisocial effects. Such content may reinforce callous attitudes toward rape and rape victims.

Wilson, Linz, Donnerstein, and Stipp (1992) performed an interesting field experiment to investigate attitudes about rape. In 1990, NBC aired a made-for-TV movie titled *She Said No,* which concerned acquaintance rape. The researchers measured audience responses to the movie to see whether it would decrease acceptance of rape myths or date rape. Using a nationally representative sample, they randomly assigned 1,038 adult viewers to watch or not watch the movie over a special closed-circuit channel. When contacted the next day, the viewers answered questions about rape myths, which demonstrated that the movie had made an impact in altering perceptions of date rape. More tolerant attitudes might affect behavior as well. Another study correlated the viewing of wrestling on TV with date violence. Researchers studied 2,228 North Carolina high school students and found that watching was associated with having started a fight with a date and with other high-risk activities such as weapon carrying and drug use (DuRant, Champion, & Wolfson, 2006).

One expert claims that much of sexy advertising is pornographic because it dehumanizes women, borrows the poses and postures of bondage and sadomasochism, and perpetuates rape myths (Kilbourne, 1999). Many ads seem to imply that women don't really mean "no" when they say it. In one ad, a woman is backing a woman against a wall. The ad says "NO" in big letters, and she is either laughing or screaming. In small letters at the bottom is the word *sweat,* and the ad is for deodorant. Another ad, for a trendy bar in Georgetown, shows a close-up of a cocktail, with the headline, "If your date won't listen to reason, try a Velvet Hammer" (Kilbourne, 1993).

Sexualized Violence Against Women (R-rated videos that are less sexually explicit but far more violent than X-rated ones, often shown on cable TV or available in video stores). Probable antisocial effects. These do not involve rape but do contain scenes of women being tortured, murdered, or mutilated in a sexual context. This may be the single most important category for teenagers because it is more "mainstream" and represents an important genre of Hollywood "slice 'em and dice 'em" movies (e.g., *Halloween I–V, Nightmare on Elm Street I–V, Friday the 13th I–VIII, Texas Chainsaw Massacre I–II, Scream I–III,* etc.). Often, the title alone tells the tale: *Hide and Go Shriek, Kiss Daddy Goodbye, Return to Horror High, Slaughter High, The Dorm That Dripped Blood, Chopping Mall, Murderlust, Deadtime Stories, Splatter University, Lady Stay Dead, I Dismember Mama, Watch Me When I Kill, Lunch Meat.*

Because sex is something that is not usually discussed or observed, except in the media, teenagers who are faithful viewers of such movies may be learning that acting aggressively toward women is expected and normal. Studies show that exposure to such material can result in desensitization to sexual violence, both for young men and women (Donnerstein et al., 1987; Mullin & Linz, 1995). However, such studies cannot always be replicated (Linz & Donnerstein, 1988; Weaver, 1994). As two prominent researchers note, "Our research suggests that you need not look any further than the family's own television set to find demeaning depictions of women available to far more viewers than pornographic material" (Linz & Donnerstein, 1988, p. 184).

Solocations

Clearly, there is a strong case to be made for the impact of sexual content in a variety of media on young, impressionable preteens and teens (J. D. Brown & Strasburger, 2007; Escobar-Chaves et. al., 2005; Strasburger, 2005). In a society that limits access to sexual information, teenagers will look to the media for answers to their questions. More important, the media may have a strong effect on teens without their even being aware of it, especially those whose parents do not inculcate in them a strong sense of "family values." Important questions get answered by the media: "When is it okay to have sex?" "How do I know if I am in love?" "Is sex fun?" "Is sex risky?" Unfortunately, as we have seen, the media answers to these questions are usually not the healthy or accurate answers.

What changes in media would give American youth a healthier view of sex and sexuality? A number of possibilities come to mind:

1. *Widespread advertising of birth control in mainstream media (e.g., TV, magazines, radio).* Advertising birth control represents one means of increasing teenagers' access to it. Such advertising needs to address the risks of pregnancy, not merely the cosmetic difference that birth control pills can make if a teenager has acne. Unless new products such as the morning-after pill are widely advertised, teenagers will not know about them or use them (see Figure 6.18). Comparative studies between the United States and Europe make it clear that countries that promote the use of birth control via advertising, sex education classes, and programming are rewarded with lower rates of teen pregnancy (Miller, 2000; Mueller et al., 2008; Strasburger et al., 2006). Most national surveys have documented that adults favor birth control advertising (Mozes, 2001), yet the media remain resistant. Given that eight studies now prove that making birth control available to teenagers does not increase the risk of early sexual intercourse, there is no longer any excuse to withhold access to it.

2. *Greater responsibility and accountability of mainstream media for producing healthy and accurate messages about sex and sexuality.* Entertainment industry executives need to realize that, like it or not, their product is educating American children and teenagers. Media have become one of the most important sources for sexual information for young people today (J. D. Brown et al., 2006; Strasburger,

Figure 6.18

SOURCE: The EC campaign is coordinated by the National Institute for Reproductive Health, the national research, education and training arm of NARAL Pro-Choice New York. Mifeprex is a registered trademark of Danco Laboratories, LLC.

2006a). Yet what they view on television and in the movies is almost counterproductive to healthy adolescence: frequent premarital sex and sex between unmarried partners, talk about infidelity on talk shows, graphic jokes and innuendoes in the movies, rape myths, and sexual violence. Where is the depiction of sexual responsibility? Where is the talk about the need for birth control or the risk of STDs? Where are the depictions of condom use when they are most needed in modern society? Why aren't topics such as abortion, date rape, and rape myths portrayed and examined in greater detail (Navarro, 2007)? In the new millennium, the answer is that we cannot go back to the "golden age" of the 1950s, when sex was rarely discussed and Laura and Rob Petrie slept in separate beds on *The Dick Van Dyke Show* despite being married. Nor should censorship be tolerated in a free society. Voluntary restraint and good judgment on the part of Hollywood and television writers, producers, and directors, however, would go far in improving the current dismal state of programming (see Table 6.12). A return to the "family hours" of protected programming between 7 p.m. and 9 p.m. would be one useful idea. *Boston Public,* which aired at 7 p.m., featured such storylines as a high school girl trading oral sex for a boy's agreement to withdraw from a student council race, a girl tossing her breast pads away in the hallway, and another high school girl's sexual affair with one of the teachers. Unfortunately, as one TV critic notes, "Almost anything goes in primetime . . . TV says get used to it" (Salamon, 2000, p. 6WK).

Yet, in 2005, *Boston Public*'s writer-producer handled the very sensitive theme of emergency contraception being refused in a Catholic hospital emergency room extremely fairly and sensitively in a *Boston Legal* episode. Another positive development is the announcement of the "Pause" public education campaign by FOX and Kaiser Family Foundation that will try to teach teenagers to make wise decisions about difficult issues, including sex and teenage pregnancy (Kaiser Family Foundation, 2006). Clearly, Hollywood is capable of dealing with the theme of adolescent sexuality in a responsible way when it wants to.

Table 6.12   Guide to Responsible Sexual Content in Media

Recognize sex as a healthy and natural part of life.
Parent and child conversations about sex are important and healthy and should be encouraged.
Demonstrate that not only the young, unmarried, and beautiful have sexual relationships.
Not all affection and touching must culminate in sex.
Portray couples having sexual relationships with feelings of affection, love, and respect for one another.
Consequences of unprotected sex should be discussed or shown.
Miscarriage should not be used as a dramatic convenience for resolving an unwanted pregnancy.
Use of contraceptives should be indicated as a normal part of a sexual relationship.
Avoid associating violence with sex or love.
Rape should be depicted as a crime of violence, not of passion.
The ability to say "no" should be recognized and respected.

SOURCE: Strasburger (1995). Modified from Haffner and Kelly (1987, pp. 9–11).

3. *Better taste in advertising* (see Exercises for a discussion of "taste"). When sex is used to sell products, it is cheapened and devalued. Manufacturers who pay for advertising and companies that produce it need to recognize that they, too, have a public health responsibility to produce ads that are not gratuitously provocative, suggestive, or demeaning (see Figure 6.19). Kilbourne (1999) should be "must" reading for all account executives.

4. *Incorporating the principles of media education into existing sex education programs.* Preliminary studies seem to indicate that a media education approach may be effective in decreasing children's aggressiveness (Huesmann, Eron, Klein, Brice, & Fischer, 1983) and teenagers' use of drugs (Austin & Johnson, 1997). There is no reason to think that helping children and teenagers decipher sexual content, the suggestiveness of advertising, and the conservatism of the broadcast industry regarding contraception would have anything but positive outcomes. In fact, a recent media literacy curriculum conducted at 22 school sites in Washington state

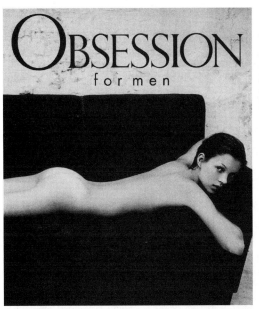

Figure 6.19

found that a five-lesson plan targeting 532 middle school students resulted in their being less likely to overestimate sexual activity among their peers and more aware of the truth about sex and sexual imagery in the media (Pinkleton, Austin, Cohen, Chen, & Fitzgerald, in press).

5. *More and better counteradvertising.* To date, only the National Campaign to Prevent Teen and Unwanted Pregnancy has engaged in long-term efforts to counterprogram through the media (see Figure 6.20A). One organization has even taken on the abstinence movement (see Figure 6.20B). Although no data exist about their success, the communications literature about drugs and media does contain several successful efforts involving counteradvertising against tobacco and illicit drugs with teens as the primary target audience (see Chapter 7). On the other hand, scare tactics that exploit the fear of HIV/AIDS to try to prevent early teenage sexual activity are unethical and probably counterproductive (DeJong, Wolf, & Austin, 2001; Strasburger, 2005).

6. *Greater sensitivity of parents to the influence of the media on children and adolescents.* Many parents often seem to be "clueless" about the impact of media on their children and teenagers (Strasburger, 2006a), although a 2007 survey of 1,008 parents nationwide found that two thirds felt that they were "closely monitoring" their children's media use (Rideout, 2007). The most important steps that parents can take are to set rules about TV viewing, monitor what shows are being watched, and keep TV sets out of the bedroom. A national study of 1,762 teenagers found that having a TV in the bedroom and having no rules about viewing correlate with viewing more sexual content (Kim et al., 2006).

Figure 6.20

SOURCE: Grant Hill.

7. *More and better research.* Three recent longitudinal studies now point to the media as one crucial factor in a teenager's decision when to have sexual intercourse (Ashby et al., 2006; J. D. Brown et al., 2006; Collins et al., 2004). More studies have been funded by NIMH and are currently under way (National Institute on Child Health and Development [NICHD], 2000). But the amount of research on sex and the media pales in comparison to the 3,500 studies done on children and media violence. Of the eight major correlational studies, four are more than 10 years old and have major defects (Huston et al., 1998; Strasburger & Donnerstein, 2000). Considerably more research needs to be funded, and such research will need to be interdisciplinary, using a variety of methods and a variety of populations, and will need to take into account developmental, gender, and ethnic differences. For example:

- How do different groups of children and teenagers view different sexual content? Do different groups use different types of media to find sexual content? Is that content interpreted differently? Are there developmental differences in how teens of different ages interpret sexual content? (A few preliminary studies of this kind have already been done [Aubrey, Harrison, Kramer, & Yellin, 2003; J. D. Brown et al., 2005; Rivadeneyra & Ward, 2005; Tolman, Kim, Schooler, & Sorsoli, 2007].)

- Do teens from different ethnic groups seek out programming unique to their own ethnic group?

- How do individuals negotiate sexual behavior in the media? What interpersonal contexts exist for sexual behavior? Do different media portray sexuality differently?

- Do media change teens' knowledge about sex and sexuality, their emotions concerning sex, or their attitudes? Regular adolescent viewers of soap operas could be recruited and be shown "future episodes" of their favorite program, which might be manipulated to show different messages, for example.

The barriers to doing this type of research are considerable (Huston et al., 1998; Strasburger, 1997). School systems and parents need to grant access to researchers, and foundations need to fund such efforts. Foundations need to recognize media research as a new and much-needed priority. In addition, society needs to accept the fact that teenagers should be able to give consent for such research on their own and that parents can be informed "passively" about ongoing studies (e.g., a letter explaining the research, along with the opportunity to withdraw the child if need be) rather than "actively" (e.g., having to send back signed permission forms) (Santelli, 1997; Strasburger, 1998).

Conclusion: Unanswered Questions

Despite this discussion, not all media are unhealthy or irresponsible for young people. Some shows have dealt responsibly with the issue of teenage sexual activity and teenage pregnancy: *Beverly Hills 90210, Dawson's Creek, Boston Legal,* and *Felicity,* at times, and several others. Made-for-TV movies such as *Babies Having Babies* and *Daddy* have used extremely frank language to good, educational effect. The 1980s cop drama *Cagney and Lacey* contained one of the first instances of a TV mother talking to her son about responsibility and birth control. On *St. Elsewhere,* the only known mention of a diaphragm on prime-time TV was aired during the 1987–1988 season, although it required that the user be the chief of obstetrics and gynecology to accomplish it. But these are the exceptions rather than the rule on American television. And, unfortunately, it has not been the tragedy of teenage pregnancy or the high rates of early adolescent sexual activity that have blunted the red pencil of the network censors but rather the appearance of AIDS as a national health emergency. But here, too, there may be much educational programming made possible that will benefit teenagers. One example is the 1987–1988 episode of *L.A. Law* that discussed the risk of AIDS in heterosexual intercourse but also included good advice on birth control and choosing sexual partners (see Strasburger, 1989). How do adolescents process the sexual content that they view? Do different ethnic groups interpret the same content differently? Can teenagers learn abstinence or the need to use birth control from what they view in the media? Until the political and funding climate changes, and until adults understand that asking children and teenagers about sex will not provoke them into early sexual activity, we will simply have to speculate about many of these crucial issues.

As one author sadly notes,

I've often wondered what it would be like if we taught young people swimming the same way we teach sexuality. If we told them that swimming was an important adult activity, one they will all have to be skilled at when they grow up, but we never talked with them about it. We never showed them the pool. We just allowed them to stand outside closed doors and listen to all the splashing. Occasionally, they might catch a glimpse of partially-clothed people going in and out of the door to the pool and maybe they'd find a hidden book on the art of swimming, but when they asked a question about how swimming felt or what it was about, they would be greeted with blank or embarrassed looks. Suddenly, when they turn 18 we would fling open the doors to the swimming pool and they would jump in. Miraculously, some might learn to tread water, but many would drown. (Roberts, 1983, p. 10)

Exercises

1. *Taste.* Several questions about "taste": Whose "taste" do we mean? Ours? Yours? Hollywood's? This is a recurring problem in discussing the media and one we do not take lightly. In this volume, we have erred on the side of public health and psychology in discussing what is questionable "taste" and what represents "good" versus "bad" programming. Although we have tried to give examples, we have left the discussion purposefully vague because we acknowledge that taste can vary considerably. But when it comes to "bad" taste or "questionable" programming that is unhealthy, we would tend to agree with a paraphrase of Supreme Court Justice Potter Stewart's definition of pornography: "We know it when we see it."

   (a) Should the media be criticized on such grounds?

   (b) If so, whose "taste" should be used as the "gold standard"? Is an objective standard possible?

   (c) In making judgments about "taste," what sociocultural factors enter into the discussion?

   (d) What about offensive and indecent language? Consider the following quote from a newspaper columnist: "A few months back, the solons of the Federal Communications Commission found that a term for bovine excrement is 'so grossly offensive' as to be 'presumptively profane.' OK, except that, according to the FCC, a certain nickname for Richard, and its two-syllable version ending in 'head,' don't violate this standard. These terms are 'understandably offensive to some viewers' but not 'sufficiently vulgar, explicit, or graphic descriptions of sexual organs or activities to support a finding of patent offensiveness.' As pretty much any 13-year-old could have told the FCC, it ordered the wrong expletive deleted" (Marcus, 2006, p. B3). Do you agree with Marcus or with the FCC? If you were a member of the FCC, how would you go about establishing rules for appropriate language on TV?

(e) During the February 1, 2004, halftime show, Janet Jackson revealed a breast for 2 seconds to 89 million viewers on national TV (see Figure 6.21). CBS was fined $500,000 for the incident. FCC Chairman Michael Powell labeled the display "classless, crass (and) deplorable." Spike Lee said, "What's going to be next? It's getting crazy, and it's all down to money. Money and fame. Somehow the whole value system has been upended" (CNN Entertainment, February 4, 2004).

(1) Did you see the halftime show? What did you think?

(2) Do you agree with Michael Powell and Spike Lee or with Frank Rich (quoted at the beginning of this chapter)?

(3) Should CBS have been fined half a million dollars?

(4) Was this positive or negative publicity for Janet Jackson? Is there such a thing as bad publicity anymore?

Figure 6.21   The Famous "Wardrobe Malfunction"

2. *Prosocial Content.* How would you go about making a prosocial soap opera that would appeal to teenagers and young adults and contain sexually responsible language, discussions, and behavior but not lose the audience with a "goody-two-shoes" program?

3. *Sex Education.* Currently, the federal government only funds abstinence-only sex education ($176 million/year in 2006). Since 1998, more than $1 billion has been spent on such sex education (SIECUS, 2006), despite any convincing evidence that abstinence-only sex education actually works (Government Accountability Office, 2006; Santelli et al., 2006). The most recent study was commissioned by the U.S. Congress and surveyed 2,057 youth from big cities and rural communities. Their average age on entering an abstinence-only program was 11 to 12, and they were followed up 4 years later and compared with students from the same communities who did not participate. There was no difference in rates of sexual intercourse, age at first sex, or numbers of sexual partners (Trenholm et al., 2007). If abstinence-only sex education is not effective, should the government be funding it? Should the government fund comprehensive sex education as well?

4. *Media Literacy.* Is there a media literacy approach to sex education that might work to decrease the impact of media on sexual attitudes and beliefs? What components would it have? How would sex education teachers be able to avoid "family values" types of issues if they discussed programming with sexual content?

5. *Doing Sexuality Research.* How could research be sensitively designed to assess what children learn from sexual content in the media?

6. *Contraceptive Ads.* Figure 6.22 shows two actual print ads for condoms. For what magazines would each be appropriate? Do the ads target different audiences? What other possibilities can you think of that might appeal specifically to all teenagers? To teenagers who are African American or Hispanic? To males? To females? Figure 6.18 shows actual print ads for emergency contraceptive pills and one for a product that produces an early medical abortion. How do these ads differ from other, "mainstream" ads? What is the target audience? Are these ads effective? In June 2007, both CBS and FOX rejected an ad for Trojans because "advertising must stress health-related uses rather than the prevention of pregnancy," according to one network executive (Newman, 2007). The ad shows women at a bar, surrounded by pigs. One pig goes to use the bathroom, returns with a condom he's purchased, and is magically transformed into an attractive man. The tagline is "Evolve: Use a condom every time." Do you think this ad is creative? Offensive? Effective?

7. *HIV/AIDS Prevention.* You are a school principal and are asked to view a sex ed video for possible inclusion in the curriculum. On it, a terminally ill AIDS patient, cachectic and stripped to the waist, stares straight at the camera and says, "Kids, if you have sex once, with the wrong person, you may die." Your brother died from AIDS a year ago, and this video affects you deeply. Should you approve it for use in the classroom?

8. *The Internet.* (1) In Shanghai, China, the government is providing sex education via the Internet (Lou, Zhao, Gao, & Shah, 2006). Is this a good idea? Can you see any drawbacks? (2) In the most recent sample of 1,500 Internet users, ages 10 to 17 years, 42% reported exposure to online pornography (two-thirds unwanted) (Wolak et al., 2007). What solutions exist to shield children and teens

"I didn't use one because I didn't have one with me."

GET REAL

If you don't have a parachute, don't jump, genius.

Helps reduce the risk

Figure 6.22

SOURCE: © 2008 Trojan Brand Condoms.

from online pornography? The Internet's oversight agency has suggested an ".xxx" domain for pornography on the Web (Jesdanun, 2007). Would that work?

9. *Celebrities.* In March 2007, the Associated Press initiated a self-imposed week-long ban on reporting anything about Paris Hilton (CNN.com, 2007). Was that a reasonable thing to do? A month earlier, *Newsweek*'s cover story was "Girls Gone Wild: What Are Celebs Teaching Kids?" (Deveny & Kelley, 2007). Find the story and discuss it. Why are Paris Hilton and Britney Spears celebrities, and should they be? How do you think that 16-year-old Jamie Lynn Spears' pregnancy will affect preteens and teens? Who determines fame in American culture, and how is it determined?

10. *Young Girls.* Recently, the American Psychological Association issued its report on the increasing sexualization of young girls (Zurbriggen et al., 2007). In covering the story, one news reporter wrote, "Ten-year-old girls can slide their low-cut jeans over 'eye-candy' panties. French maid costumes, garter belt included are available in preteen sizes. Barbie now comes in a 'bling-bling' style, replete with halter top and go-go boots. . . . American girls, say experts, are increasingly being fed a cultural catnip of products and images that promote looking and acting sexy" (Weiner, 2007, p. HE01). Is this a relatively new problem or an ongoing one? Read

the Executive Summary of the report and see if you agree with the many recommendations (www.apa.org). How easy would it be to change the portrayal of sexuality in American society, and what will it take to do so?

11. *Teen pregnancy and abortion.* In 2006 and 2007, several movies seemed to portray teen pregnancy and single motherhood in a new light. According to one prominent columnist, "By some screenwriter consensus, abortion has become the right-to-choose that's never chosen. In *Knocked Up,* it was referred to as 'shmashmortion.' In *Juno,* the abortion clinic looks like a punk-rock tattoo parlor" (Goodman, 2008, p. A8). Other observers agree (Rickey, 2007, p. B8). Do you think this is a new trend? Is it "healthy," and will it have real-life repercussions?

References

ABC News. (2007, January 12). *Teens "borrow" babies to practice parenting on reality show.* Retrieved January 12, 2007, from http://www.abcnews.go.com/GMA/print?id=2789958

Abma, J. C., Martinez, G. M., Mosher, W. D., & Dawson, B. S. (2004). *Teenagers in the United States: Sexual activity, contraceptive use, and childbearing, 2002.* National Center for Health Statistics. *Vital Health Statistics, 23.*

Abramson, P. R., & Mechanic, M. B. (1983). Sex and the media: Three decades of best selling books and major motion pictures. *Archives of Sexual Behavior, 12,* 185–206.

Agovino, T. (2007, January 24). *Levitra, Viagra running new ad campaigns.* Retrieved January 24, 2007, from http://www.washingtonpost.com/wp-dyn/content/article/2006/05/02/AR2006050200857.html

Ahrens, F. (2003, December 13). Nasty language on live TV renews old debate. *Washington Post,* p. A01.

Alter, J. (1994, January 17). The power to change what's "cool." *Newsweek,* p. 23.

American Academy of Pediatrics (AAP). (2001). Sexuality, contraception, and the media. *Pediatrics, 107,* 191–194.

American Academy of Pediatrics (AAP). (2006). Children, adolescents, and advertising. *Pediatrics, 118,* 2563–2569.

American Academy of Pediatrics (AAP). (2007). Contraception and adolescents. *Pediatrics, 120,* 1135–1148.

Ansen, D. (1999, September 13). A handful of tangos in Paris. *Newsweek,* p. 66.

Ansen, D. (2000, July 3). Gross and grosser. *Newsweek,* pp. 60–61.

Ashby, S. L., Arcari, C. M., & Edmonson, M. B. (2006). Television viewing and risk of sexual initiation by young adolescents. *Archives of Pediatric and Adolescent Medicine, 160,* 375–380.

Aubrey, J. S. (2004). Sex and punishment: An examination of sexual consequences and the sexual double standard in teen programming. *Sex Roles, 50,* 505–514.

Aubrey, J. S., Harrison, K., Kramer, L., & Yellin, J. (2003). Variety versus timing: Gender differences in college students' sexual expectations as predicted by exposure to sexually oriented television. *Communication Research, 30,* 432–460.

Austin, E. W., & Johnson, K. K. (1997). Effects of general and alcohol-specific media literacy training on children's decision making model about alcohol. *Journal of Health Communication, 2,* 17–42.

Bandura, A. (1977). *Social learning theory.* Englewood Cliffs, NJ: Prentice Hall.

Baran, S. J. (1976a). How TV and film portrayals affect sexual satisfaction in college students. *Journalism Quarterly, 53,* 468–473.

Baran, S. J. (1976b). Sex on TV and adolescent sexual self-image. *Journal of Broadcasting, 20,* 61–68.

Bashir, M. (2007, February 23). *Porn in hi-definition: Too much detail?* Retrieved February 25, 2007, from http://abcnews.go.com/Nightline/print?id=2854981

Batchelor, S. A., Kitzinger, J., & Burtney, E. (2004). Representing young people's sexuality in the "youth" media. *Health Education Research, 19,* 669–676.

Battaglio, S. (2007, August 20). Steamy shows stir controversy. *Entertainment Weekly,* pp. 8–9.

Bennett, L. (2003). *TV commercials exploit, ridicule or sideline women* [Press release]. Retrieved from http://www.now.org/nnt/spring-2003/superbowl.html

Blake, S. M., Ledsky, R., Goodenow, C., Sawyer, R., Lohrmann, D., & Windsor, R. (2003). Condom availability programs in Massachusetts high schools: Relationships with condom use and sexual behavior. *American Journal of Public Health, 93,* 955–962.

Bleakley, A., Hennessy, M., & Fishbein, M. (2006). Public opinion on sex education in US schools. *Archives of Pediatrics & Adolescent Medicine, 160,* 1151–1156.

Brenton, S., & Cohen, R. (2003). *Shooting people: Adventures in reality TV.* New York: Verso.

Brodie, M., Foehr, U., Rideout, V., Baer, N., Miller, C., Flournoy, R., et al. (2001). Communicating health information through the entertainment media. *Health Affairs, 20,* 1–8.

Brown, D., & Bryant, J. (1989). Uses of pornography. In D. Zillmann & J. Bryant (Eds.), *Pornography: Research advances and policy considerations* (pp. 3–24). Hillsdale, NJ: Lawrence Erlbaum.

Brown, J. D., Childers, K. W., & Waszak, C. S. (1990). Television and adolescent sexuality. *Journal of Adolescent Health, 11,* 62–70.

Brown, J. D., Halpern, C. T., & L'Engle, K. L. (2005). Mass media as a sexual super peer for early maturing girls. *Journal of Adolescent Health, 36,* 420–427.

Brown, J. D., L'Engle, K. L., Pardun, C. H., Guo, G., Kenneavy, K., & Jackson, C. (2006). Sexy media matter: Exposure to sexual content in music, movies, television, and magazines predicts Black and White adolescents' sexual behavior. *Pediatrics, 117,* 1018–1027.

Brown, J. D., & Newcomer, S. F. (1991). Television viewing and adolescents' sexual behavior. *Journal of Homosexuality, 21,* 77–91.

Brown, J. D., & Schulze, L. (1990). The effects of race, gender, and fandom on audience interpretations of Madonna's music videos. *Journal of Communication, 40,* 88–102.

Brown, J. D., & Steele, J. R. (1995). *Sex and the mass media.* Menlo Park, CA: Kaiser Family Foundation.

Brown, J. D., Steele, J. R., & Walsh-Childers, K. (2002). *Sexual teens, sexual media.* Mahwah, NJ: Lawrence Erlbaum.

Brown, J. D., & Strasburger, V. C. (2007). From Calvin Klein, to Paris Hilton and MySpace: Adolescents, sex & the media. *Adolescent Medicine: State of the Art Reviews, 18,* 484–507.

Brown, J. D., White, A. B., & Nikopoulou, L. (1993). Disinterest, intrigue, resistance: Early adolescent girls' use of sexual media content. In B. S. Greenberg, J. D. Brown, & N. L. Buerkel-Rothfuss (Eds.), *Media, sex and the adolescents* (pp. 177–195). Cresskill, NJ: Hampton.

Brown, R. T., & Brown, J. D. (2006). Adolescent sexuality. *Primary Care: Clinics in Office Practice, 33,* 373–390.

Bryant, J., & Rockwell, S. C. (1994). Effects of massive exposure to sexually-oriented prime-time television programming on adolescents' moral judgment. In D. Zillmann, J. Bryant, & A. C. Huston (Eds.), *Media, children, and the family: Social scientific, psychodynamic, and clinical perspectives* (pp. 183–195). Hillsdale, NJ: Lawrence Erlbaum.

Buerkel-Rothfuss, N. L., & Mayes, S. (1981). Soap opera viewing: The cultivation effect. *Journal of Communication, 31,* 108–115.

Buerkel-Rothfuss, N. L., Strouse, J. S., Pettey, G., & Shatzer, M. (1993). Adolescents' and young adults' exposure to sexually oriented and sexually explicit media. In B. S. Greenberg, J. D. Brown, & N. L. Buerkel-Rothfuss (Eds.), *Media, sex and the adolescent* (pp. 99–113). Cresskill, NJ: Hampton.

Canonzoneri, V. (1984, January 28). TV's feminine mistake. *TV Guide,* pp. 14–15.

Carveth, R., & Alexander, A. (1985). Soap opera viewing motivation and the cultivation process. *Journal of Broadcasting and Electronic Media, 29,* 259–273.

Centers for Disease Control and Prevention (CDC). (1993). Sexual risk behaviors of STD clinic patients before and after Earvin "Magic" Johnson's HIV-infection announcement—Maryland, 1991–1992. *Morbidity and Mortality Weekly Report, 42,* 45–48.

Centers for Disease Control and Prevention (CDC). (1994). Poll: HIV/AIDS prevention. *CDC HIV/AIDS Prevention Newsletter, 5,* 5–6.

Centers for Disease Control and Prevention (CDC). (2000). Youth risk behavior surveillance—United States, 1999. *Morbidity & Mortality Weekly Report, 48,* 248–253.

Centers for Disease Control and Prevention (CDC). (2006). Youth risk behavior surveillance—United States, 2005. *Morbidity & Mortality Weekly Report, 55*(SS-5), 1–108.

Chia, S. C. (2006). How peers mediate media influence on adolescents' sexual attitudes and sexual behavior. *Journal of Communication, 56,* 585–606.

Child Trends. (2006, April). *Facts at a glance.* Washington, DC: Author.

Christenson, P., & Ivancin, M. (2006). *The "reality" of health: Reality television and the public health.* Menlo Park, CA: Kaiser Family Foundation.

Cline, V. B. (1994). Pornography effects: Empirical and clinical evidence. In D. Zillmann, J. Bryant, & A. C. Huston (Eds.), *Media, children, and the family: Social scientific, psychodynamic, and clinical perspectives* (pp. 229–247). Hillsdale, NJ: Lawrence Erlbaum.

CNN.com (2007, March 4). AP: We ignored Paris Hilton. Retrieved March 4, 2007.

Coles, R., & Stokes, G. (1985). *Sex and the American teenager.* New York: Harper & Row.

Collins, R. L., Elliott, M. N., Berry, S. H., Kanouse, E., & Hunter, S. B. (2003). Entertainment television as a healthy sex educator: The impact of condom-efficacy information in an episode of *Friends. Pediatrics, 112,* 1115–1121.

Collins, R. L., Elliott, M. N., Berry, S. H., Kanouse, D. E., Kunkel, D., Hunter, S. B., et al. (2004). Watching sex on television predicts adolescent initiation of sexual behavior. *Pediatrics, 114,* e280.

Cope-Farrar, K. M., & Kunkel, D. (2002). Sexual messages in teens' favorite prime-time TV programs. In J. D. Brown, J. R. Steele, & K. Walsh-Childers (Eds.), *Sexual teens, sexual media* (pp. 59–78). Mahwah, NJ: Lawrence Erlbaum.

Corder-Bolz, C. (1981). Television and adolescents' sexual behavior. *Sex Education Coalition News, 3,* 40.

Courtright, J. A., & Baran, S. J. (1980). The acquisition of sexual information by young people. *Journalism Quarterly, 57,* 107–114.

Daly, S. (2005, September 9). Tangled up in blue. *Entertainment Weekly,* pp. 14–15.

D'Angelo, M. D. (1999, December 17). Deflower power. *Entertainment Weekly,* pp. 88–89.

DeJong, W., Wolf, R. C., & Austin, S. B. (2001). U.S. federally funded television public service announcements (PSAs) to prevent HIV/AIDS: A content analysis. *Journal of Health Communication, 6,* 249–263.

Deveny, K., & Kelley, R. (2007, February 12). Girls gone wild: What are celebs teaching kids? *Newsweek,* pp. 40–47.

Donnerstein, E. (1984). Pornography: Its effect on violence against women. In N. M. Malamuth & E. Donnerstein (Eds.), *Pornography and sexual aggression* (pp. 53–81). Orlando, FL: Academic Press.

Donnerstein, E., & Linz, D. (1994). Sexual violence in the mass media. In M. Costanzo & S. Oskamp (Eds.), *Violence and the law* (pp. 9–36). Newbury Park, CA: Sage.

Donnerstein, E., & Linz, D. (1995). The mass media: A role in injury causation and prevention. *Adolescent Medicine: State of the Art Reviews, 6,* 271–284.

Donnerstein, E., Linz, D., & Penrod, S. (1987). *The question of pornography: Research findings and policy implications.* New York: Free Press.

Donnerstein, E., & Smith, S. (2001). Sex in the media. In D. G. Singer & J. L. Singer (Eds.), *Handbook of children and the media* (pp. 289–307). Thousand Oaks, CA: Sage.

Downs, A. C., & Harrison, S. K. (1985). Embarrassing age spots or just plain ugly? Physical attractiveness stereotyping as an instrument of sexism on American television commercials. *Sex Roles, 13,* 9–19.

DuRant, R. H., Champion, H., & Wolfson, M. (2006). The relationship between watching professional wrestling on television and engaging in date fighting among high school students. *Pediatrics, 118,* e265–e272.

DuRant, R. H., Wolfson, M., LaFrance, B., Balkrishnan, R., & Altman, D. (2006). An evaluation of a mass media campaign to encourage parents of adolescents to talk to their children about sex. *Journal of Adolescent Health, 38,* 298e1–298e9.

Editorial reviews. (2006). *American Pie 2.* Retrieved May 24, 2006, from http://www.amazon.com/gp/product/B00003CY6D

Elkind, D. (1984, November/December). Teenage thinking: Implications for health care. *Pediatric Nursing,* pp. 383–385.

Elkind, D. (1993). *Parenting your teenager in the 90's.* Rosemont, NJ: Modern Learning Press.

Escobar-Chaves, S. L., Tortolero, S. R., Markham, C. M., Low, B. J., Eitel, P., & Thickstun, P. (2005). Impact of the media on adolescent sexual attitudes and behaviors. *Pediatrics, 116,* 303–326.

Espey, E., Cosgrove, E., & Ogburn, T. (2007). Family planning American style: Why it's so hard to control birth in the US. *Obstetrics & Gynecology Clinics of North America, 34,* 1–17.

Eveland, W. P., Nathanson, A. I., Detenber, A. I., & McLeod, D. M. (1999). Rethinking the social distance corollary: Perceived likelihood of exposure and the third-person perception. *Communication Research, 26,* 275–302.

Eyal, K., Kunkel, D., Biely, E. N., & Finnerty, K. L. (2007). Sexual socialization messages on television programs most popular among teens. *Journal of Broadcasting & Electronic Media, 51,* 316–336.

Fabes, R. A., & Strouse, J. S. (1984). Youth's perceptions of models of sexuality: Implications for sexuality education. *Journal of Sex Education and Therapy, 10,* 33–37.

Fabes, R. A., & Strouse, J. S. (1987). Perceptions of responsible and irresponsible models of sexuality: A correlational study. *Journal of Sex Research, 23,* 70–84.

Farhi, P. (1999, July 23). Movie index swears "South Park" is raw. *Washington Post.*

Felman, Y. M. (1979). A plea for the condom, especially for teenagers. *Journal of the American Medical Association, 241,* 2517–2518.

Farrar, K. M. (2006). Sexual intercourse on television: Do safe sex messages matter? *Journal of Broadcasting & Electronic Media, 50,* 635–650.

Ferris, A. L., Smith, S. W., Greenberg, B. S., & Smith, S. L. (2007). The content of reality dating shows and viewer perceptions of dating. *Journal of Communication, 57,* 490–510.

Fisher, D. A., Hill, D. L., Grube, J. W., & Gruber, E. L. (2007). Gay, lesbian, and bisexual content on television: A quantitative analysis across two seasons. *Journal of Homosexuality, 52,* 167–188.

Folb, K. L. (2000). "Don't touch that dial!" TV as a—what!?—positive influence. *SIECUS Report, 28,* 16–18.

Fox, S. (2001). *CDC award: Writers and producers gather to address the role of women in daytime dramas.* Retrieved July 10, 2006, from http://www.population.org/summits/soapsummit/about.htm

Furstenberg, F. F., Jr., Geitz, L. M., Teitler, J. O., & Weiss, C. C. (1997). Does condom availability make a difference? An evaluation of Philadelphia's health resource centers. *Family Planning Perspectives, 29,* 123–127.

Gagnon, J. H., & Simon, W. (1987). The sexual scripting of oral genital contacts. *Archives of Sexual Behavior, 16,* 1–25.

Gerbner, G. (1985). Children's television: A national disgrace. *Pediatric Annals, 14,* 822–827.

Gerbner, G. (1993, June). *Women and minorities on television: A study in casting and fate* [Report to the Screen Actors Guild and the American Federation of Radio and Television Artists]. Philadelphia: Annenberg School for Communication.

Gerbner, G., Gross, L., Morgan, M., Signorielli, N., & Shanahan, J. (2002). Growing up with television: Cultivation processes. In J. Bryant & D. Zillmann (Eds.), *Media effects: Advances in theory and research* (2nd ed., pp. 43–68). Hillsdale, NJ: Lawrence Erlbaum.

Gerbner, G., Morgan, M., & Signorielli, N. (1982). Programming health portrayals: What viewers see, say and do. In D. Pearl, L. Bouthilet, & J. Lazar (Eds.), *Television and behavior: Ten years of scientific progress and implications for the eighties* (Vol. 2, pp. 291–307). Rockville, MD: National Institutes of Health.

Glieberman, O. (1999, July 16). Virgin megascore. *Entertainment Weekly,* pp. 43–44.

Goldberg, M. (1987, November 28). TV has done more to contain AIDS than any other single factor. *TV Guide,* pp. 5–6.

Goodman, E. (2008, January 5). Real teen pregnancies don't have Hollywood ending. *Albuquerque Journal,* p. A8.

Gorman, S. (2000, May 22). *Feminist group frowns on FOX network.* Retrieved from http://www.now.org/issues/media/watchout/report/

Government Accountability Office (GAO). (2006, October). Efforts to assess the accuracy and effectiveness of federally funded programs. *GAO Highlights.* Retrieved February 5, 2007, from http://www.gao.gov/cgi-bin/getrpt?GAO-07–87

Greenberg, B. S. (1982). Television and role socialization: An overview. In D. Pearl, L. Bouthilet, & J. Lazar (Eds.), *Television and behavior: Ten years of scientific progress and implications for the eighties* (Vol. 2, pp. 179–190). Rockville, MD: National Institute of Mental Health.

Greenberg, B. S. (1993). Race differences in television and movie behaviors. In B. S. Greenberg, J. D. Brown, & N. L. Buerkel-Rothfuss (Eds.), *Media, sex and the adolescent* (pp. 145–152). Cresskill, NJ: Hampton.

Greenberg, B. S. (1994). Content trends in media sex. In D. Zillmann, J. Bryant, & A. C. Huston (Eds.), *Media, children, and the family: Social scientific, psychodynamic, and clinical perspectives* (pp. 165–182). Hillsdale, NJ: Lawrence Erlbaum.

Greenberg, B. S., & Busselle, R. W. (1994). *Soap operas and sexual activity.* Menlo Park, CA: Kaiser Family Foundation.

Greenberg, B. S., & Hofschire, L. (2000). Sex on entertainment television. In D. Zillmann & P. Vorderer (Eds.), *Media entertainment: The psychology of its appeal* (pp. 93–111). Mahwah, NJ: Lawrence Erlbaum.

Greenberg, B. S., & Linsangan, R. (1993). Gender differences in adolescents' media use, exposure to sexual content and parental mediation. In B. S. Greenberg, J. D. Brown, & N. L. Buerkel-Rothfuss (Eds.), *Media, sex and the adolescent* (pp. 134–144). Cresskill, NJ: Hampton.

Greenberg, B. S., Linsangan, R., Soderman, A., Heeter, C., Lin, C., Stanley, C., et al. (1987). *Adolescents and their exposure to television and movie sex* [Project CAST, Report No. 4]. East Lansing: Michigan State University, Department of Telecommunications.

Greenberg, B. S., Linsangan, R., & Soderman, A. (1993). Adolescents' reactions to television sex. In B. S. Greenberg, J. D. Brown, & N. L. Buerkel-Rothfuss (Eds.), *Media, sex and the adolescent* (pp. 196–224). Cresskill, NJ: Hampton.

Greenberg, B. S., Siemicki, M., Dorfman, S., Heeter, C., & Stanley, C. (1993). Sex content in R-rated films viewed by adolescents. In B. S. Greenberg, J. D. Brown, & N. L. Buerkel-Rothfuss (Eds.), *Media, sex, and the adolescent* (pp. 45–58). Cresskill, NJ: Hampton.

Greenberg, B. S., & Smith, S. W. (2002). Daytime talk shows: Up close and in your face. In J. D. Brown, J. R. Steele, & K. Walsh-Childers (Eds.), *Sexual teens, sexual media* (pp. 79–93). Mahwah, NJ: Lawrence Erlbaum.

Greenberg, B. S., Smith, S., Yun, J. A., Busselle, R., Hnilo, L. R., Mitchell, M., et al. (1995). *The content of television talk shows: Topics, guests and interactions.* Menlo Park, CA: Kaiser Family Foundation.

Greenberg, B. S., Stanley, C., Siemicki, M., Heeter, C., Soderman, A., & Linsangan, R. (1986). *Sex content on soaps and prime time television series viewed by adolescents* [Project CAST, Report No. 3]. East Lansing: Michigan State University, Department of Telecommunications.

Greenberg, B. S., Stanley, C., Siemicki, M., Heeter, C., Soderman, A., & Linsangan, R. (1993). Sex content on soaps and prime-time television series most viewed by adolescents. In B. S. Greenberg, J. D. Brown, & N. L. Buerkel-Rothfuss (Eds.), *Media, sex and the adolescent* (pp. 29–44). Cresskill, NJ: Hampton.

Greeson, L. E., & Williams, R. A. (1986). Social implications of music videos for youth: An analysis of the contents and effects of MTV. *Youth & Society, 18,* 177–189.

Gruber, E., & Grube, J. (2000). Adolescent sexuality and the media: A review of current knowledge and implications. *Western Journal of Medicine, 172,* 210–214.

Guttmacher, S., Lieberman, L., Ward, D., Freudenberg, N., Radosh, A., & DesJarlais, D. (1997). Condom availability in New York City public high schools: Relationships to condom use and sexual behavior. *American Journal of Public Health, 87,* 1427–1433.

Haag, P. (1999). *Voices of a generation: Teenage girls on sex, school, and self.* Washington, DC: American Association of University Women Educational Foundation.

Haffner, D. W., & Kelly, M. (1987, March/April). Adolescent sexuality in the media. *SIECUS Report,* pp. 9–12.

Harris, R. J. (1994a). *A cognitive psychology of mass communication* (2nd ed.). Hillsdale, NJ: Lawrence Erlbaum.

Harris, R. J. (1994b). The impact of sexually explicit media. In J. Bryant & D. Zillmann (Eds.), *Media effects: Advances in theory and research* (pp. 247–272). Hillsdale, NJ: Lawrence Erlbaum.

Harris, L., & Associates. (1986). *American teens speak: Sex, myths, TV and birth control.* New York: Planned Parenthood Federation of America.

Harris, L., & Associates. (1987). *Attitudes about television, sex and contraception advertising.* New York: Planned Parenthood Federation of America.

Harris, L., & Associates. (1988). *Sexual material on American network television during the 1987–88 season.* New York: Planned Parenthood Federation of America.

Heintz-Knowles, K. E. (1996). *Sexual activity on daytime soap operas: A content analysis of five weeks of television programming.* Menlo Park, CA: Kaiser Family Foundation.

Henshaw, S. K. (2004). *U.S. teenage pregnancy statistics with comparative statistics for women aged 20–24.* New York: Alan Guttmacher Institute.

Herold, E. S., & Foster, M. E. (1975). Changing sexual references in mass circulation magazines. *Family Coordinator, 24,* 21–25.

Hershenson, K. (1999, July 23). Pushing the envelope. *Albuquerque Journal,* pp. E14–E15.

Hill, A. (2005). *Reality TV: Audiences and popular factual television.* Oxford, UK: Routledge.

Hochman, D. (2008, March 24–30). Sex on TV. *TV Guide, 56* (issue #2870), pp. 18–22.

Howe, A., Owen-Smith, V., & Richardson, J. (2002). The impact of a television soap opera on the NHS Cervical Screening Programme in the North West of England. *Journal of Public Health Medicine, 24,* 299–304.

Huesmann, L. R., Eron, L. D., Klein, R., Brice, P., & Fischer, P. (1983). Mitigating the imitation of aggressive behaviors by changing children's attitudes about media violence. *Journal of Personality and Social Psychology, 44,* 899–910.

Huston, A. C., Donnerstein, E., Fairchild, H., Feshbach, N. D., Katz, P. A., Murray, J. P., et al. (1992). *Big world, small screen: The role of television in American society.* Lincoln: University of Nebraska Press.

Huston, A. C., Wartella, E., & Donnerstein, E. (1998). *Measuring the effects of sexual content in the media: A report to the Kaiser Family Foundation.* Menlo Park, CA: Kaiser Family Foundation.

Impoco, J. (1996, April 15). TV's frisky family values. *U.S. News & World Report,* pp. 58–62.

Ito, K. E., Gizlice, Z., Owen-O'Dowd, J., Foust, E., Leone, P. A., & Miller, W. C. (2006). Parent opinion of sexuality education in a state with mandated abstinence education: Does policy match parental preference? *Journal of Adolescent Health, 39,* 634–641.

Jacobs, A. J., & Shaw, J. (1999, April 2). Virgin spring. *Entertainment Weekly,* pp. 10–11.

Jemmott, J. B., III, Jemmott, L. S., & Fong, G. T. (1998). Abstinence and safer sex HIV risk-reduction interventions for African American adolescents. *Journal of the American Medical Association, 279,* 1529–1536.

Jesdanun, A. (2007, February 5). Plan would create ".xxx" Web porn domain. Associated Press/ABC News. Retrieved February 5, 2007, from http://www.abcnews.go.com/Business/print?id=2775401

Jones, D. (1988, April 13). We rely on TV for AIDS information. *USA Today.*

Jones, E. F., Forrest, J. D., Goldman, N., Henshaw, S. K., Lincoln, R., Rosoff, J. I., et al. (1985). Teenage pregnancy in developed countries: Determinants and policy implications. *Family Planning Perspectives, 17,* 53–63.

Jones, E. F., Forrest, J. D., Henshaw, S. K., Silverman, J., & Torres, A. (1988). Unintended pregnancy, contraceptive practice and family planning services in developed countries. *Family Planning Perspectives, 20,* 53–67.

Kaiser Family Foundation. (1996). *The Kaiser Family Foundation survey on teens and sex: What they say teens today need to know, and who they listen to.* Menlo Park, CA: Author.

Kaiser Family Foundation. (1998). *Kaiser Family Foundation and YM Magazine national survey of teens: Teens talk about dating, intimacy, and their sexual experiences.* Menlo Park, CA: Author.

Kaiser Family Foundation. (1999). *National survey of public secondary school principals: The politics of sex education.* Menlo Park, CA: Author.

Kaiser Family Foundation. (2000). *Teens and sex: The role of popular television* [Fact sheet]. Menlo Park, CA: Author.

Kaiser Family Foundation. (2001, June 19). *Public and networks getting comfortable with condom advertising on TV* [Press release]. Menlo Park, CA: Author.

Kaiser Family Foundation. (2004). *Entertainment education and health in the United States.* Menlo Park, CA: Author.

Kaiser Family Foundation. (2005). *U.S. teen sexual activity.* Menlo Park, CA: Author.

Kaiser Family Foundation. (2006, August 14). *FOX Networks group, Kaiser Family Foundation hit "Pause"* [Press release]. Menlo Park, CA: Author.

Kaiser Family Foundation/Children Now. (1996). *The family hour focus groups: Children's responses to sexual content on TV and their parents' reactions*. Menlo Park, CA: Kaiser Family Foundation.

Kaiser Family Foundation/Children Now. (1999). *Talking with kids about tough issues: A national survey of parents and kids*. Menlo Park, CA: Kaiser Family Foundation.

Kaiser Family Foundation/*Seventeen* Magazine. (2004). *Sex smarts: Birth control and protection*. Menlo Park, CA: Kaiser Family Foundation.

Kalichman, S. C., & Hunter, T. L. (1992). The disclosure of celebrity HIV infection: Its effects on public attitudes. *American Journal of Public Health, 82*, 1374–1376.

Kanuga, M., & Rosenfeld, W. D. (2004). Adolescent sexuality and the Internet: The good, the bad and the URL. *Journal of Pediatric and Adolescent Gynecology, 17*, 117–124.

Kaye, B. K., & Sapolsky, B. S. (2004a). Offensive language in prime time television: Four years after television age and content ratings. *Journal of Broadcasting and Electronic Media, 48*, 554–569.

Kaye, B. K., & Sapolsky, B. S. (2004b). Watch your mouth! An analysis of profanity uttered by children on prime time television. *Mass Communication and Society, 7*, 429–452.

Kelly, C. (2005, October 17). Realities of teen sex ignored in mainstream films. *Seattle Times*. Retrieved October 19, 2005, from http://www.seattletimes.nwsource.com

Kelly, J., & Smith, S. L. (2006). *Where the girls aren't: Gender disparity saturates G-rated films*. Duluth, MN: Dads & Daughters.

Kenrick, D. T., & Guttieres, S. E. (1980). Contract effects and judgments of physical attractiveness: When beauty becomes a social problem. *Journal of Personality & Social Psychology, 38*, 131–140.

Kilbourne, J. (1993). Killing us softly: Gender roles in advertising. *Adolescent Medicine: State of the Art Reviews, 4*, 635–649.

Kilbourne, J. (1999). *Deadly persuasion: Why women and girls must fight the addictive power of advertising*. New York: Free Press.

Kim, J. L., Collins, R. L., Kanouse, D. E., Elliott, M. N., Berry, S. H., Hunter, S., et al. (2006). Sexual readiness, household policies, and other predictors of adolescents' exposure to sexual content in mainstream entertainment television. *Media Psychology, 8*, 449–471.

Kim, J. L., Sorsoli, C. L., Collins, K., Zylbergold, B. A., Schooler, D., & Tolman, D. L. (2007). From sex to sexuality: Exposing the heterosexual script on primetime network television. *Journal of Sex Research, 44*, 145–157.

Kirby, D. (1997). *No easy answers: Research findings on programs to reduce teen pregnancy*. Washington, DC: National Campaign to Prevent Teen Pregnancy.

Kirby, D. (2002). The impact of schools and school programs upon adolescent sexual behavior. *Journal of Sex Research, 39*, 27–33.

Kirby, D. (2007). *Emerging answers 2007: Research findings on programs to reduce teen pregnancy*. Washington, DC: National Campaign to Prevent Teen Pregnancy.

Kirby, D., Brener, N. D., Brown, N. L., Peterfreund, N., Hillard, P., & Harrist, R. (1999). The impact of condom distribution in Seattle schools on sexual behavior and condom use. *American Journal of Public Health, 89*, 182–187.

Klein, J. D., Brown, J. D., Childers, K. W., Oliveri, J., Porter, C., & Dykers, C. (1993). Adolescents' risky behavior and mass media use. *Pediatrics, 92*, 24–31.

Kristof, N. (2006, May 2). Beyond chastity belts. *New York Times*, p. A25.

Kunkel, D., Biely E., Eyal, K., Cope-Farrar, K., Donnerstein, E., & Fandrich, R. (2003). *Sex on TV 3: A biennial report to the Kaiser Family Foundation*. Menlo Park, CA: Kaiser Family Foundation.

Kunkel, D., Cope, K. M., & Biely, E. (1999). Sexual messages on television: Comparing findings from three studies. *Journal of Sex Research, 36,* 230–236.

Kunkel, D., Cope, K. M., & Colvin, C. (1996). *Sexual messages on family hour television: Content and context.* Menlo Park, CA: Kaiser Family Foundation.

Kunkel, D., Cope-Farrar, K. M., Biely, E., Farinola, W. J. M., & Donnerstein E. (2001). *Sex on TV: A biennial report to the Kaiser Family Foundation.* Santa Barbara: University of California, Santa Barbara.

Kunkel, D., Eyal, K., Finnerty, K., Biely, E., & Donnerstein, E. (2005). *Sex on TV 4: A biennial report to the Kaiser Family Foundation.* Menlo Park, CA: Kaiser Family Foundation.

Landry, D. J., Kaeser, L., & Richards, C. L. (1999). Abstinence promotion and the provision of information about contraception in public school strict sexuality education policies. *Family Planning Perspectives, 31,* 280–286.

Larson, M. S. (1996). Sex roles and soap operas: What adolescents learn about single motherhood. *Sex Roles, 35,* 97–110.

Laumann, E. O., Paik, A., & Rosen, R. C. (1999). Sexual dysfunction in the United States. *Journal of the American Medical Association, 281,* 537–544.

L'Engle, K. L., Brown, J. D., & Kenneavy, K. (2006). The mass media are an important context for adolescents' sexual behavior. *Journal of Adolescent Health, 38,* 186–192.

Levin, D. E., & Kilbourne, J. (2008). *So sexy so soon: The new sexualized childhood, and what parents can do to protect their kids.* New York: Ballantine.

Linz, D., & Donnerstein, E. (1988). The methods and merits of pornography research. *Journal of Communication, 38,* 180–184.

Linz, D., & Malamuth, N. (1993). *Pornography.* Newbury Park, CA: Sage.

Lou, C.-H., Zhao, Q., Gao, E.-S., & Shah, I. H. (2006). Can the Internet be used effectively to provide sex education to young people in China? *Journal of Adolescent Health, 39,* 720–728.

Lyons, J. S., Anderson, R. L., & Larson, D. B. (1994). A systematic review of the effects of aggressive and nonaggressive pornography. In D. Zillmann, J. Bryant, & A. C. Huston (Eds.), *Media, children, and the family: Social scientific, psychodynamic, and clinical perspectives* (pp. 271–310). Hillsdale, NJ: Lawrence Erlbaum.

Malamuth, N., & Huppin, M. (2005). Pornography and teenagers: The importance of individual differences. *Adolescent Medicine Clinics, 16,* 315–326.

Malamuth, N., & Impett, E. A. (2001). Research on sex in the media. In D. G. Singer & J. L. Singer (Eds.), *Handbook of children and the media* (pp. 269–287). Thousand Oaks, CA: Sage.

Marcus, R. (2006, June 25). Cleaning up TV will take more than fines. *Albuquerque Journal,* p. B3.

Martino, S. C., Collins, R. L., Kanouse, D. E., Elliott, M., & Berry, S. H. (2005). Social cognitive processes mediating the relationship between exposure to television's sexual content and adolescents' sexual behavior. *Journal of Personality and Social Psychology, 89,* 914–924.

Miller, F. C. (2000). Impact of adolescent pregnancy as we approach the new millennium. *Journal of Pediatric and Adolescent Gynecology, 13,* 5–8.

Moore, F. (2006, August 22). *Study: Fewer gay television characters.* Retrieved August 22, 2006, from http://abcnews.go.com/Entertainment/print?id=2340204.

Mozes, A. (2001, June 19). US TV viewers find condom ads acceptable. *Reuters Health* [Online]. Retrieved June 20, 2001, from www.reutershealth.com

Mueller, T. E., Gavin, L. E., & Kulkarni, A. (2008). The association between sex education and youth's engagement in sexual intercourse, age at first intercourse, and birth control use at first sex. *Journal of Adolescent Health, 42,* 89–96.

Mullin, C. R., & Linz, D. (1995). Desensitization and resensitization to violence against women: Effects of exposure to sexually violent films on judgments of domestic violence victims. *Journal of Personality and Social Psychology, 69,* 449–459.

Murray, S., & Ouellette, L. (Eds.). (2004). *Reality TV: Remarking television culture.* New York: NYU Press.

Nashawaty, C. (1999, July 16). Pie in your face. *Entertainment Weekly,* pp. 26–28.

National Campaign to Prevent Teen Pregnancy. (2004). *American opinion on teen pregnancy and related issues 2003.* Washington, DC: Author.

National Campaign to Prevent Teen Pregnancy. (2006). *Pregnancy among sexually experienced teens, 2002.* Washington, DC: Author.

National Institute on Child Health and Development (NICHD). (2000, December). Workshop on Sex & the Media, Bethesda, MD.

National Public Radio/Kaiser Family Foundation/Kennedy School of Government. (2004). *Sex education in America: Principals survey.* Menlo Park, CA: Kaiser Family Foundation.

Navarro, M. (2007, June 10). On abortion, Hollywood is no-choice. *New York Times,* section 9, pp. 1, 8.

Newman, A.A. (2007, June 18). Pigs with cellphones, but no condoms. *New York Times.* Retrieved June 19, 2007, from http://www.nytimes.com/2007/06/18/business/media/18 adcol.html?_r=1&ref=media&oref=slogin

Nielsen Media Research. (2005). *2005 report on television.* New York: Author.

Nielsen ratings, June 26–July 2. (2006). *USA Today.* Retrieved July 6, 2006, from http://www.usatoday.com/life/television/nielsenhtm

Painter, K. (1994, January 5). AIDS ads get less "timid." *USA Today,* p. 1A.

Pardun, C. (2002). Romancing the script: Identifying the romantic agenda in top-grossing movies. In J. D. Brown, J. R. Steele, & K. Walsh-Childers (Eds.), *Sexual teens, sexual media* (pp. 211–225). Mahwah, NJ: Lawrence Erlbaum.

Parents Television Council. (2004). *The blue tube: Foul language on prime time network TV.* Retrieved April 26, 2006, from http://www.parentstv.org/ptc/publications/reports

Pazos, B., Fullwood, E. U., Allan, M. J., Graff, C. A., Wilson, K. M., Laneri, H., et al. (2001, March 22). *Media use and sexual behaviors among Monroe County adolescents.* Paper presented at the annual meeting of the Society for Adolescent Medicine, San Diego.

Pearl, D., Bouthilet, L., & Lazar, J. (Eds.). (1982). *Television and behavior: Ten years of scientific progress and implications for the eighties* (Vol. 1, DHHS Pub. No. ADM 82–1195). Washington, DC: Government Printing Office.

Peirce, K. (1993). Socialization of teenage girls through teen-magazine fiction: The making of a new woman or an old lady? *Sex Roles, 29,* 59–68.

Peter, J., & Valkenburg, P. M. (2006). Adolescents' exposure to sexually explicit online material and recreational attitudes toward sex. *Journal of Communication, 56,* 639–660.

Peterson, J. L., Moore, K. A., & Furstenberg, F. F., Jr. (1991). Television viewing and early initiation of sexual intercourse: Is there a link? *Journal of Homosexuality, 21,* 93–118.

Peterson, R. A., & Kahn, J. R. (1984, August 26). *Media preferences of sexually active teens.* Paper presented at American Psychological Association meeting, Toronto, Canada.

Piaget, J. (1972). Intellectual evolution from adolescence to adulthood. *Human Development, 15,* 1–12.

Pinkleton, B. E., Austin, E. W., Cohen, M., Chen, Y.-C., & Fitzgerald, E. (in press). Effects of a peer-led media literacy curriculum on adolescents' knowledge and attitudes toward sexual behavior and media portrayals of sex. *Health Communication.*

Pipher, M. (1997, February 1). Bland, beautiful, and boy-crazy. *TV Guide,* pp. 22–25.

Planned Parenthood Federation of America. (2006). *PPFA Maggie Awards: Ripped from the headlines.* Retrieved June 21, 2006, from http://www.plannedparenthood.org/pp2/portal/files

Reichelt, P. A. (1978). Changes in sexual behavior among unmarried teenage women utilizing oral contraception. *Journal of Population Behavior, 1,* 59–68.

Rice, L. (2000, April 14). Ready to swear. *Entertainment Weekly,* pp. 20–21.

Rich, F. (2004, February 15). My hero, Janet Jackson. *New York Times,* section 2, p. 1.

Rickey, C. (2007, December 7). The absent "A" word. *Albuquerque Journal,* p. B8.

Rideout, V. (2007). *Parents, children & media.* Menlo Park, CA: Kaiser Family Foundation.

Rivadeneyra, R., & Ward, L. M. (2005). From Ally McBeal to Sabado Gigante: Contributions of television viewing to the gender role attitudes of Latino adolescents. *Journal of Adolescent Research, 20,* 453–475.

Roberts, E. (1982). Television and sexual learning in childhood. In D. Pearl, L. Bouthilet, & J. Lazar (Eds.), *Television and behavior: Ten years of scientific progress and implications for the eighties* (Vol. 2, pp. 209–223). Rockville, MD: National Institute of Mental Health.

Roberts, E. (1983). Teens, sexuality and sex: Our mixed messages. *Television & Children, 6,* 9–12.

Robischon, N. (2001, April 20). Back in bleecch! *Entertainment Weekly,* pp. 24–29.

Rudman, W. J., & Verdi, P. (1993). Exploitation: Comparing sexual and violent imagery of females and males in advertising. *Women & Health, 20,* 1–14.

Salamon, J. (2000, December 10). Sex at 8: The Partridges don't live here anymore. *New York Times,* p. 6WK.

Santelli, J. (1997). Human subjects protection and parental permission in adolescent health research. *Journal of Adolescent Health, 21,* 384–387.

Santelli, J., Lindberg, L. D., Finer, L. B., & Singh, S. (2007). Explaining recent declines in adolescent pregnancy in the United States: The contribution of abstinence and improved contraceptive use. *American Journal of Public Health, 97,* 150–156.

Santelli, J., Ott, M. A., Lyon, M., Rogers, J., Summers, D., & Schleifer, R. (2006). Abstinence and abstinence-only education: A review of U.S. policies and programs. *Journal of Adolescent Health, 38,* 72–81.

Schooler, D., Kim, J. L., & Sorsoli, L. (2006). Setting rules or sitting down: Parental mediation of television consumption and adolescent self-esteem, body image, and sexuality. *Sexuality Research and Social Policy, 3,* 49–62.

Schuster, M. A., Bell, R. M., Berry, S. H., & Kanouse, D. E. (1998). Impact of a high school condom availability program on sexual attitudes and behaviors. *Family Planning Perspectives, 30,* 67–72.

Scott, J. E. (1986). An updated longitudinal content analysis of sex references in mass circulation magazines. *Journal of Sex Research, 22,* 385–392.

Sellers, D. E., McGraw, S. A., & McKinlay, J. B. (1994). Does the promotion and distribution of condoms increase sexual activity? Evidence from an HIV prevention program for Latino youth. *American Journal of Public Health, 84,* 1952–1959.

Sexuality Information and Education Council of the United States (SIECUS). (2000). *Public support for sexuality education reaches highest level* [Press release]. New York: Author.

Sexuality Information and Education Council of the United States (SIECUS). (2006, July 19). *States and communities push back against abstinence-only-until-marriage dictates from Washington while proliferation of programs continues* [Press release]. Retrieved July 19, 2006, from http://www.siecus.org/media/press/press0130.html

Shrum, L. J. (2002). Media consumption and perceptions of social reality: Effects and underlying processes. In J. Bryant & D. Zillmann (Eds.), *Media effects: Advances in theory and research* (pp. 69–95). Hillsdale, NJ: Lawrence Erlbaum.

Signorielli, N. (2001). Television's gender role images and contribution to stereotyping. In D. G. Singer & J. L. Singer (Eds.), *Handbook of children and the media* (pp. 341–358). Thousand Oaks, CA: Sage.

Silverman-Watkins, L. T. (1983). Sex in the contemporary media. In J. Q. Maddock, G. Neubeck, & M. B. Sussman (Eds.), *Human sexuality and the family* (pp. 125–140). New York: Haworth.

Silverman-Watkins, L. T., & Sprafkin, J. N. (1983). Sex in the contemporary media. In J. Q. Maddock, G. Neubeck, & M. B. Sussman (Eds.), *Human sexuality and the family* (pp. 125–140). New York: Haworth.

Skinner, S. R., & Hickey, M. (2003). Current priorities for adolescent sexual and reproductive health in Australia. *Medical Journal of Australia, 179,* 158–161.

Society for Adolescent Medicine. (2000). Media and contraception [Policy statement]. *Journal of Adolescent Health, 27,* 290–291.

Steele, J. R. (1999). Teenage sexuality and media practice: Factoring in the influence of family, friends, and school. *Journal of Sex Research, 36,* 331–341.

Steele, J. R. (2002). Teens and movies: Something to do, plenty to learn. In J. D. Brown, J. R. Steele, & K. Walsh-Childers (Eds.), *Sexual teens, sexual media* (pp. 227–251). Mahwah, NJ: Lawrence Erlbaum.

Stern, B. B., Russell, C. A., & Russell, D. W. (2005). Vulnerable women on screen and at home: Soap opera consumption. *Journal of Macromarketing, 25,* 222–225.

Stobbe, M. (2007, December 5). US teen births rise for first time in 15 years, renewing debate. Retrieved January 7, 2008, from http://www.nctimes.com/articles/2007/12/06/health/6_24_1512_5_07.txt

Strasburger, V. C. (1989). Adolescent sexuality and the media. *Pediatric Clinics of North America, 36,* 747–774.

Strasburger, V. C. (1997). "Sex, drugs, rock 'n' roll," and the media: Are the media responsible for adolescent behavior? *Adolescent Medicine: State of the Art Reviews, 8,* 403–414.

Strasburger, V. C. (1998). Parental permission in adolescent health research [Letter]. *Journal of Adolescent Health, 22,* 362.

Strasburger, V. C. (2005). Adolescents, sex, and the media: Oooo, baby, baby—a Q&A. *Adolescent Medicine Clinics, 16,* 269–288.

Strasburger, V. C. (2006a). "Clueless": Why do pediatricians underestimate the media's influence on children and adolescents? *Pediatrics, 117,* 1427–1431.

Strasburger, V. C. (2006b). Risky business: What primary care practitioners need to know about the influence of the media on adolescents. *Primary Care: Clinics in Office Practice, 33,* 317–348.

Strasburger, V. C., Brown, R. T., Braverman, P. K., Rogers, P. D., Holland-Hall, C., & Coupey, S. M. (2006). *Adolescent medicine: A handbook for primary care.* Philadelphia: Lippincott Williams & Wilkins.

Strasburger, V. C., & Donnerstein, E. (2000). Children, adolescents, and the media in the 21st century. *Adolescent Medicine: State of the Art Reviews, 11,* 51–68.

Strasburger, V. C., & Furno-Lamude, D. (1997). *The effects of media consumption on adolescents' sexual attitudes and practices: Results of a pilot study.* Unpublished manuscript.

Strouse, J. S., Buerkel-Rothfuss, N., & Long, E. C. (1995). Gender and family as moderators of the relationship between music video exposure and adolescent sexual permissiveness. *Adolescence, 30,* 505–521.

Strouse, J. S., Goodwin, M. P., & Roscoe, B. (1994). Correlates of attitudes toward sexual harassment among early adolescents. *Sex Roles, 31,* 559–577.

Sutton, M. J., Brown, J. D., Wilson, K. M., & Klein, J. D. (2002). Shaking the tree of knowledge for the forbidden fruit: Where adolescents learn about sexuality and contraception.

In J. D. Brown, J. R. Steele, & K. Walsh-Childers (Eds.), *Sexual teens, sexual media* (pp. 25–55). Mahwah, NJ: Lawrence Erlbaum.

Svetkey, B. (1994, March 18). Here's the beef. *Entertainment Weekly,* pp. 26–28.

Tan, A. (1979). TV beauty ads and role expectation of adolescent female viewers. *Journalism Quarterly, 56,* 283–288.

Tannen, T. (2003). Media giant and foundation team up to fight HIV/AIDS. *The Lancet, 361,* 1440–1441.

Thornburg, H. (1981). Adolescent sources of information on sex. *Journal of School Health, 51,* 274–277.

Tolman, D. L., Kim, J. L., Schooler, D., & Sorsoli, C. L. (2007). Rethinking the associations between television viewing and adolescent sexuality development: Bringing gender into focus. *Journal of Adolescent Health, 40,* 84e9–84e16.

Treise, D., & Gotthoffer, A. (2001). Stuff you couldn't ask your parents about: Teens talking about using magazines for sex information. In J. D. Brown, J. R. Steele, & K. Walsh-Childers (Eds.), *Sexual teens, sexual media* (pp. 173–189). Mahwah, NJ: Lawrence Erlbaum.

Trenholm, C., Devaney, B., Forston, K., Quay, L., Wheeler, J., & Clark, M. (2007). *Impacts of four Title V, Section 510 abstinence education programs.* Princeton, NJ: Mathematica Policy Research.

Truglio, R. T. (1992). *Adolescents' use of prime-time TV for sexual information: What are the risks?* Paper presented at the Society for Research on Adolescence, Washington, DC.

Tucker, K. (1999, December 17). Kids these days. *Entertainment Weekly,* pp. 62–63.

Tucker, M. E. (2000, April). Teen sex. *Pediatric News,* p. 5.

Wakefield, D. (1987, November 7). Teen sex and TV: How the medium has grown up. *TV Guide,* pp. 4–6.

Walsh, D., & Bennett, D. (2005). *WHY do they act that way? A survival guide to the adolescent brain for you and your teen.* New York: Free Press.

Walsh-Childers, K. (1991, May). *Adolescents' interpretations of the birth control behavior of a soap opera couple.* Paper presented at the annual meeting of the International Communication Association, Chicago.

Walsh-Childers, K. (1997). *A content analysis: Sexual health coverage in women's men's, teen and other specialty magazines.* Menlo Park, CA: Kaiser Family Foundation.

Walsh-Childers, K., & Brown, J. D. (1993). Adolescents' acceptance of sex-role stereotypes and television viewing. In B. S. Greenberg, J. D. Brown, & N. L. Buerkel-Rothfuss (Eds.), *Media, sex, and the adolescent* (pp. 117–133). Cresskill, NJ: Hampton.

Walsh-Childers, K., Gotthoffer, A., & Lepre, C. R. (2002). From "just the facts" to "downright salacious": Teens' and women's magazines' coverage of sex and sexual health. In J. D. Brown, J. R. Steele, & K. Walsh-Childers (Eds.), *Sexual teens, sexual media* (pp. 153–171). Mahwah, NJ: Lawrence Erlbaum.

Ward, L. M. (1995). Talking about sex: Common themes about sexuality in the prime-time television programs children and adolescents view most. *Journal of Youth and Adolescence, 24,* 595–615.

Ward, L. M., & Friedman, K. (2006). Using TV as a guide: Associations between television viewing and adolescents' sexual attitudes and behavior. *Journal of Research on Adolescence, 16,* 133–156.

Ward, L. M., Gorvine, B., & Cytron, A. (2002). Would that really happen? Adolescents' perceptions of sexual relationships according to prime-time television. In J. D. Brown, J. R. Steele, & K. Walsh-Childers (Eds.), *Sexual teens, sexual media* (pp. 95–123). Mahwah, NJ: Lawrence Erlbaum.

Ward, L. M., & Rivadeneyra, R. (1999). Contributions of entertainment television to adolescents' sexual attitudes and expectations: The role of viewing amount versus viewer involvement. *Journal of Sex Research, 36,* 237–249.

Wattleton, F. (1987). American teens: Sexually active, sexually illiterate. *Journal of School Health, 57,* 379–380.

Weaver, J. B., III. (1994). Pornography and sexual callousness: The perceptual and behavioral consequences of exposure to pornography. In D. Zillmann, J. Bryant, & A. C. Huston (Eds.), *Media, children, and the family: Social scientific, psychodynamic, and clinical perspectives* (pp. 215–228). Hillsdale, NJ: Lawrence Erlbaum.

Weaver, J. B., Masland, J. L., & Zillmann, D. (1984). Effect of erotica on young men's aesthetic perception of their female sexual partners. *Perceptual and Motor Skills, 58,* 929–930.

Weinberg, C. (2006). This is not a love story: Using soap opera to fight HIV in Nicaragua. *Gender and Development, 14,* 37–46.

Weiner, S. (2007, February 20). Goodbye to girlhood. *Washington Post,* p. HE01.

Wilson, B., Linz, D., Donnerstein, E., & Stipp, H. (1992). The impact of social issue television programming on attitudes toward rape. *Human Communication Research, 19,* 179–208.

Wingood, G. M., DiClemente, R. J., Harrington, K., Davies, S., Hook, E. W., & Oh, M. K. (2001). Exposure to X-rated movies and adolescents' sexual and contraceptive-related attitudes and behavior. *Pediatrics, 107,* 1116–1119.

Wolak, J., Mitchell, K., & Finkelhor, D. (2007). Unwanted and wanted exposure to online pornography in a national sample of youth Internet users. *Pediatrics, 119,* 247–257.

Wolk, L. I., & Rosenbaum, R. (1995). The benefits of school-based condom availability: Cross-sectional analysis of a comprehensive high school-based program. *Journal of Adolescent Health, 17,* 184–188.

Wray, J., & Steele, J. (2002). Girls in print: Figuring out what it means to be a girl. In J. D. Brown, J. R. Steele, & K. Walsh-Childers (Eds.), *Sexual teens, sexual media* (pp. 191–208). Mahwah, NJ: Lawrence Erlbaum.

Zillmann, D. (1994). Erotica and family values. In D. Zillmann, J. Bryant, & A. C. Huston (Eds.), *Media, children, and the family: Social scientific, psychodynamic, and clinical perspectives* (pp. 199–213). Hillsdale, NJ: Lawrence Erlbaum.

Zillmann, D., & Bryant, J. (1982). Pornography, sexual callousness and the trivialization of rape. *Journal of Communication, 32,* 10–21.

Zillmann, D., & Bryant, J. (1988). Pornography's impact on sexual satisfaction. *Journal of Applied Social Psychology, 18,* 438–453.

Zurbriggen, E. L., Collins, R. L., Lamb, S., Roberts, T.-A., Tolman, D. L.,Ward, L. M., et al. (2007). *Report of the APA Task Force on the sexualization of girls.* Washington, DC: American Psychological Association.

Zurbriggen, E. L., & Morgan, E. M. (2006). Who wants to marry a millionaire? Reality dating television programs, attitudes toward sex, and sexual behaviors. *Sex Roles, 54,* 1–17.

CHAPTER 7

Drugs and the Media

The Marlboro Man emanated in 1954 from the minds of Chicago admen Leo Burnett and John Benson, who were trying to devise a more macho pitch for Philip Morris' filter-tip cigarette and agreed that the "most masculine figure in America" was the cowboy. In the next 40 years, the smoking cowboy traveled the world (and 2 actors who played him died of lung cancer).

—W. Nugent (1999)

A cigarette in the hands of a Hollywood star onscreen is a gun aimed at a 12- or 14-year-old.

—Screenwriter Joe Eszterhas (2002)

How about that powerful antidrug commercial paid for by the US government? It aired right between the seventh and eighth Budweiser commercials.

—David Letterman, CBS' *Late Show*,
on the 2002 Super Bowl commercials
("Cheers & Jeers," 2002)

My 6 year-old daughter turned to me and said, "What's a 4-hour erection?" said Kelly Simmons, executive vice president at Tierney Communications in Philadelphia. "How do you explain it?"

(www.bettydodson.com/potencyads.htm)

The so-called War on Drugs has been waged by the federal government for decades in a variety of locales except in the media (see Figures 7.1 and 7.2). In fact, at the same time that parents and school programs are trying to get children and teenagers to "Just Say No" to drugs, more than $20 billion worth of cigarette, alcohol, and prescription drug advertising is very effectively working to get them to just say yes to smoking and drinking and other drugs (American Academy of Pediatrics [AAP], 2006). According to three content analyses, television programs, movies, and popular music and music videos all contain appreciable content depicting smoking, drinking, or illicit drug use (see Figure 7.3) (Christenson, Henriksen, & Roberts, 2000; Gerbner, 2001; Roberts, Henriksen, & Christenson, 1999). Although there are few data showing that drug advertising or drug content has a direct,

Figure 7.1

SOURCE: Reprinted with permission.

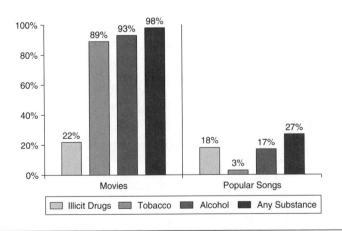

Figure 7.2   Substance Appearance in Popular Movies and Songs

SOURCE: Roberts, Henriksen, and Christenson (1999).

NOTE: The most recent and comprehensive content analysis of a variety of popular media found that tobacco, alcohol, and illicit drugs are very prevalent in movies that are popular with children and teens but considerably less prevalent in popular music. Percentages reflect the number of movies (200 total) and songs (1,000 total) in which substances appeared, whether or not they were used.

Drawn for BROADCASTING by Sidney Harris

"All right, it's a deal. The four-letter words are in, the drug lyrics are out."

Figure 7.3

SOURCE: Copyright Sidney Harris.

cause-and-effect impact on adolescents' drug use, numerous correlational studies speak to the impact of a variety of media on teenagers.

Adolescent Drug Use

Illegal drugs certainly take their toll on American society, but two legal drugs—tobacco and alcohol—pose a far greater danger to children and teenagers. Both represent significant "gateway" drugs and are among the earliest drugs used by children or teens. A child who smokes tobacco or drinks alcohol is 65 times more likely to use marijuana, for example, than a child who never smokes or drinks (National Institute on Drug Abuse [NIDA], 1995). And the effect is ongoing: A child who uses marijuana is 100 times more likely to use cocaine compared with abstaining peers (NIDA, 1995). The younger a child begins to use cigarettes, alcohol, or other drugs, the higher the risk of serious health problems and abuse carrying over into adulthood (Belcher & Shinitzky, 1998). Drug use is also one of many risky behaviors that tend to cluster: Teenagers who report that at least half of their friends are sexually active are 31 times more likely to drink, 5 times more likely to smoke, and 22 times more likely to try marijuana (National Center on Addiction and Substance Abuse, 2004).

Every year, more than 400,000 Americans die from cigarette use—more than are killed by AIDS, alcohol, automobile accidents, murder, illegal drugs, suicide, and fires combined (see Figure 7.4) (American Academy of Pediatrics, 2001; Institute of Medicine, 1994)! An estimated 3,000 teenagers begin smoking each day, and about one third of them will eventually die from a tobacco-related illness

"If you still want to belong to an organization dedicated to killing Americans, there's always the tobacco lobby."

Figure 7.4

(U.S. Department of Health and Human Services, 1994). Over the course of their lives, the high school class of 2002 will smoke an estimated 12.4 billion packs of cigarettes, generating $27.3 billion in revenue for tobacco companies, 58% to Philip Morris USA alone (Healton, Farrelly, Weitzenkamp, Lindsey, & Haviland, 2006). New evidence concerning early smoking is alarming: Damage to lung cell DNA may occur, producing physiologic changes that may persist despite quitting smoking (Wiencke et al., 1999).

Increasingly, tobacco is being marketed overseas, particularly in Third World countries, with precipitous increases in smoking rates resulting (Mackay, 1999). America is the leading producer of cigarettes, exporting three times as many cigarettes as any other country (Womach, 2003). If current smoking rates continue, 7 million people in developing countries will die of smoking-related diseases annually. One fifth of those living in industrialized countries will die of tobacco-related disorders (Peto, Lopez, Boreham, Thun, & Heath, 1992; "Tobacco's Toll," 1992), and an estimated 1 billion people may die from tobacco-related causes this century (Bridges, 2006).

Alcohol, too, is a killer, with more than 100,000 deaths annually in the United States attributed to excessive consumption (Doyle, 1996). It is the most commonly abused drug by children ages 12 to 17 years. In fact, young people younger than age 21 account for approximately 20% of all alcohol consumed (Foster, Vaughan, Foster, & Califano, 2003). Alcohol-related automobile accidents are the number one cause of death among teenagers, and alcohol consumption typically contributes to homicides and other violence, suicides, and drownings—three of the leading causes of death among 15- to 19-year-olds, together accounting for more than 75% of their mortality rate (Kulig & the Committee on Substance Abuse, 2005; National Highway Traffic Safety Administration, 2005; Thompson, Sims, Kingree, & Windle, 2008). Often, older children and preteenagers experiment with alcohol first, before other drugs. Drinking alcohol may contribute to premature sexual intercourse, lower grades, and experimentation with other drugs (Champion et al., 2004; Tapert, Aarons, Sedlar, & Brown, 2001). Youth who drink are nearly eight times more likely to use other illicit drugs than those who never drink (AAP, 1995). And people who begin drinking as teenagers are two to three times more likely to be involved in an unintentional injury while under the influence of alcohol or develop alcoholism (Hingson, Heeren, Jamanka, & Howland, 2000; Hingson, Heeren, & Winter, 2006a, 2006b; Young, Hansen, Gibson, & Ryan, 2006). Nearly half of all alcoholics are diagnosable before age 21 (Hingson, Heeren, & Winter, 2006a, 2006b). At the same time, more than one third of all revenues for the alcohol industry come from underage drinkers, nearly $50 billion in 2001 (Foster, Vaughan, Foster, & Califano, 2006).

The best data regarding adolescent drug use come from the Monitoring the Future Study. In addition, the Youth Risk Behavior Survey (YRBS), sponsored every other year by the Centers for Disease Control and Prevention (CDC), also makes an excellent contribution to the field (CDC, 2006c). But the Monitoring the Future Study is unique: Nearly 45,000 students are surveyed annually, with equal numbers of males and females in the 8th, 10th, and 12th grades, at more than 430 public and private schools across the country. Funded by the National Institute on Drug Abuse (NIDA), the study has been conducted annually since the mid-1970s by the Institute for Social Research at the University of Michigan (see Figure 7.5, Tables 7.1 and 7.2) (Johnston, O'Malley, Bachman, & Schulenberg, 2008). No data are perfect, however. The Monitoring the Future study fails to capture high school dropouts, who may be using and abusing drugs at even higher rates than their school peers. It also depends on self-reports by teenagers. But no other collection of data is so extensive over as long a period of time.

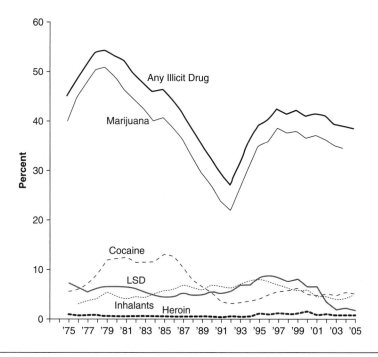

Figure 7.5   Trends in Annual Prevalence of Various Illicit Drugs Among 12th Graders, 1975–2005

SOURCE: ©University of Michigan.

Table 7.1   Adolescent Drug Use, 2007 (*N* = 14,500 12th Graders) (in Percentages)

Drug	Ever Used	Used During Past Year
Any illicit drug	47	36
Any illicit drug other than marijuana	26	19
Alcohol	72	66
Ever been drunk	55	46
Cigarettes	46	—
Marijuana	42	32
Smokeless tobacco	15	—
Amphetamines	11	8
Inhalants	11	4
Hallucinogens	8	5
Ecstasy	7	5
Tranquilizers	10	6
Cocaine	8	5
Steroids	2	1
Heroin	2	1

SOURCE: Adapted from Johnston et al. (2008).

Highlights of the research include the following:

• High but slowly decreasing levels of smoking among teenagers. More than one third of American students smoke by the time they complete high school. Half of all teenagers have tried smoking, including one quarter of all eighth graders surveyed. Nearly 22% of 12th graders have smoked within the past month. In the past 10 years, cigarette smoking among 8th and 10th graders has fallen by more than 50%. At the same time, the percentage of students saying that there is "great risk" in smoking a pack a day of cigarettes rose from 66% to 77%. Nevertheless, the decline in teen smoking may be reaching its endpoint (Johnston et al., 2008).

• Continuing high levels of alcohol use among teenagers. Although the percentage of "ever-users" decreased to 72% in 2007 from a high of 93% in 1980, 55% of high school seniors report having been drunk at least once. In the YRBS survey, 45% of high school students report drinking alcohol and 29% report binge drinking (five or more drinks in a row) during the 30 days prior to being surveyed (J. W. Miller,

Table 7.2   Trends in 12th Graders' Perception of Drugs as Harmful (in Percentages)

How Much Do You Think People Risk Harming Themselves If They . . .			
	1980	*1990*	*2007*
Try marijuana once or twice	10	23	19
Smoke marijuana occasionally	15	37	27
Smoke marijuana regularly	50	78	55
Try LSD once or twice	44	45	37
Try cocaine once or twice	31	59	51
Try MDMA once or twice	—	—	58
Try one or two drinks of an alcoholic beverage	4	8	11
Have five or more drinks once or twice each weekend	36	47	46
Smoke one or more packs of cigarettes per day	64	68	77

SOURCE: Adapted from Johnston et al. (2008).

Naimi, Brewer, & Jones, 2007). Interestingly, although athletes are ordinarily less likely to use illicit drugs other than anabolic steroids, male athletes are more likely to use alcohol (Aaron et al., 1995).

• A leveling off of illicit drug use among teenagers. Such use peaked at 66% in 1981 and declined to a low of 41% in 1992. Currently, nearly half of 12th graders report having ever used an illicit drug. More than one quarter have used an illicit drug other than marijuana.

• A leveling off in marijuana use among teenagers. Marijuana use peaked in 1979, when 60% of high school seniors reported ever having tried it. Now, about less than half of seniors have tried marijuana.

• Marijuana, cocaine, and heroin use bottomed out in the early 1990s, began rising in the mid-to-late 1990s, and now is slowly decreasing again.

• A decreasing rate of MDMA ("ecstasy") use; 6% of 12th graders report having used in 2007, compared with nearly 12% in 2001.

• For all drugs, it is important to note that young adults and older adults have higher rates of smoking and alcohol use, and young adults have the highest rates of illicit drug use. But alcohol and tobacco are first used during adolescence in the majority of cases.

The United States is not alone in experiencing increasing rates of adolescent drug use. A survey of nearly 8,000 teens ages 15 and 16 throughout the United Kingdom found that nearly all had tried alcohol and half had engaged in binge drinking, 36% had smoked cigarettes within the previous 30 days, and 42% had ever tried an illicit drug, usually marijuana (P. Miller & Plant, 1996). In a survey of 10% of all 12- to 15-year-old schoolchildren in Dundee, Scotland, two thirds reported having consumed an alcoholic drink, and by age 14, more than half reported having been drunk (McKeganey, Forsyth, Barnard, & Hay, 1996).

Determinants of Child and Adolescent Drug Use

A variety of factors have been implicated in the early use of drugs (R. T. Brown, 2002). Among adolescents, specific factors include poor self-image, low religiosity, poor school performance, alienation from parents, family dysfunction, physical abuse, and parental divorce (Belcher & Shinitzky, 1998; Briones, Wilcox, Mateus, & Boudjenah, 2006; Schydlower & Arredondo, 2006). Interestingly, two recent comprehensive reviews of substance abuse in childhood and adolescence (Belcher & Shinitzky, 1998; Briones et al., 2006) fail to mention media influence as an etiologic force among young people initiating drug use (Strasburger, 1998).

Peers. Peer pressure may play one of the most important roles in first drug use among young teens (Bahr, Hoffmann, & Yang, 2005) but may also be involved in drug abstinence as well. Teens who see their friends using drugs are more likely to partake themselves; teens who believe their friends are antidrug are more likely to abstain (Robin & Johnson, 1996). (Another alternative and as yet untested hypothesis is that teens prone to drug use are more likely to search out like-minded peers.)

Regardless, the media may function as a kind of "super-peer," making drug use seem like normative behavior for teenagers (Strasburger, 2006). Because teens are so invested in doing what is "normal" for their peer group (Olds, Thombs, & Tomasek, 2005), the media could represent one of the most powerful influences on them. Media also represent a potent source of information for teens about a variety of health issues. For example, a study of 788 African American students in Grades 5 through 12 found that television was the leading source of information about smoking (Kurtz, Kurtz, Johnson, & Cooper, 2001).

Family. Parents can be significant risk factors or protective factors, depending on the circumstances (Bahr et al., 2005; Briones et al., 2006; Halpern-Felsher & Cornell, 2005). Abused children have been found to be at increased risk for later substance abuse (Bennett & Kemper, 1994). Similarly, a "coercive" parenting style has been shown to lead to greater substance abuse and even delinquency in adolescence (McMahon, 1994). Genetically, alcoholic parents are two to nine times more likely to produce biological children who are alcoholic (Belcher & Shinitzky, 1998). The inherited risk probably also extends to other types of drug abuse as well (Comings, 1997). At the opposite end of the spectrum, growing up in a nurturing family with good communication with parents is a significant protective factor (Fisher, Miles, Austin, Camargo, & Colditz, 2007; Resnick et al., 1997).

The media have sometimes been labeled "the electronic parents," and if parents fail to give their children appropriate messages about drugs, the media may fill the void with unhealthy information or cues. For example, so-called latchkey children are more likely to use alcohol, tobacco, and marijuana, perhaps because they are unsupervised or perhaps because they have unrestrained access to a variety of unhealthy media (Chilcoat & Anthony, 1996; Richardson et al., 1989).

Personality. In general, adolescents are notorious risk takers, and new research on in development shows that the key areas of the frontal cortex (involved in judgment) do not mature until the early 20s (Walsh & Bennett, 2005). Magnetic resonance imaging (MRI) studies of teens with alcohol problems show that areas of the brain involved in drug craving and reward (e.g., the limbic system) light up more in teens when shown pictures of alcoholic beverages than in controls (Tapert et al., 2003). Areas of the brain involved in motivating behavior are also different in teenagers (Bjork et al., 2004; White & Swartzwelder, 2004). Absence of resilience may also be important at a young age because resiliency (the ability to overcome adversity) is also protective (Resnick et al., 1997). Likewise, positive self-esteem and self-image, good self-control, assertiveness, social competence, and academic success are all positive resilience factors. The role of media in encouraging or diminishing resiliency is completely unknown. Different children may respond to the same depiction completely differently (J. D. Brown & Schulze, 1990). It is possible that children who are more "media resilient" (that is, resistant to media messages) are less likely to be affected by unhealthy portrayals in the media, but only one media education study has found this to be true so far (Austin & Johnson, 1997).

Impact of Advertising on Children and Adolescents

Tobacco and alcohol represent two hugely profitable industries that require the constant recruitment of new users. With the death of 1,200 smokers a day and with thousands more trying to quit, the tobacco industry must recruit new smokers to remain profitable. Inevitably, these new smokers come from the ranks of children and adolescents, especially given the demographics of smoking (50% of smokers begin by age 13, 90% by age 19) (U.S. Department of Health and Human Services, 1994). Big Tobacco has engaged in a systematic campaign to attract underage smokers for decades and then lied to Congress about it (D. Kessler, 2001). The industry continues to resist any congressional attempts to regulate it (Nocera, 2006). Similarly, the alcohol industry has targeted minority groups and the young for years, particularly through promotion of sports and youth-oriented programming (Gerbner, 1990). Because 5% of drinkers consume 50% of all alcoholic beverages (Gerbner, 1990), new recruits are a must for the alcohol industry as well, preferably heavy drinkers.

Celebrity endorsers are commonly used, and older children and teenagers may be particularly vulnerable to such ads (AAP, 2006; Atkin & Block, 1983; Zollo, 1995). Many commercials for alcohol employ some combination of rock music, young attractive models, humor, or adventure. "Beach babes," frogs, lizards, and dogs are all commonly seen in beer commercials. Humor is particularly effective with adolescents (Salkin, 2007). Production values are extraordinary: Costs for a single 30-second commercial may easily exceed those for an entire half-hour of regular programming, and 30 seconds' worth of advertising during the Super Bowl costs well over $2 million. In 2007, Anheuser-Busch bought 5 entire minutes of advertising during the Super Bowl (Sutel, 2007). Recently, a new form of alcoholic beverage has been dubbed "learner drinks for kids"—so-called hard lemonades, which contain about 5% alcohol. They, too, use fictitious cool guys such as "Doc" Otis and One-Eyed Jack and "make a mockery of the industry's claim that it doesn't market to kids," according to one expert (Cowley & Underwood, 2001). Similarly, tobacco companies are now marketing flavored cigarettes with names like "Beach Breezer," "Kuai Kolada," "Twista Lime," and "Mandarin Mints," despite the 1998 Master Settlement Agreement that included a promise not to market to children (Harris, 2005).

A variety of studies have explored the impact of advertising on children and adolescents. Nearly all have shown advertising to be extremely effective in increasing youngsters' awareness of and emotional responses to products, their recognition of certain brands, their desire to own or use the products advertised, and their recognition of the advertisements themselves (Borzekowski & Strasburger, 2008).

Although the research is not yet considered to be scientifically "beyond a reasonable doubt," there is a preponderance of evidence that cigarette and alcohol advertising is a significant factor in adolescents' use of these two drugs (Borzekowski & Strasburger, 2008; Federal Trade Commission, 1999; Grube & Waiters, 2005; Jernigan, 2006; Pierce, Choi, Gilpin, Farkas, & Berry, 1998; Snyder, Milici, Slater, Sun, & Strizhakova, 2006). The 1999 Federal Trade Commission report on the alcohol industry concluded, "While many factors may influence an underage person's drinking decisions, including among other things parents, peers and the media, there is reason to believe that advertising also plays a role." For alcohol, advertising may account for as much as 10% to 30% of adolescents' usage (Atkin, 1993b, 1995; Gerbner, 1990). Interestingly, one study of students' use of cigarette promotional items found that a similar figure applies to cigarettes as well: Approximately one third of adolescents' cigarette use could be predicted by their purchase or ownership of tobacco promotional gear (Pierce et al., 1998). Nevertheless, as one group of researchers notes,

> To reduce the argument regarding the demonstrable effects of massive advertising campaigns to the level of individual behavior is absurdly simplistic. . . . Rather, what we are dealing with is the nature of advertising itself. Pepsi Cola, for example, could not convincingly prove, through any sort of defensible scientific study, that particular children or adolescents who consume their products do so because of exposure to any or all of their ads. (Orlandi, Lieberman, & Schinke, 1989, p. 90)

Although there is some legitimate debate about how much of an impact such advertising has on young people and their decisions whether to use cigarettes or alcohol, advertising clearly works—or else companies would not spend millions of dollars a year on it. This leaves American society with a genuine moral, economic, and public health dilemma: Should advertising of unhealthy products be allowed, when society then has to pay for the disease, disability, and death that these products cause? Tobacco companies and beer manufacturers claim that they are simply influencing "brand choice," not increasing overall demand for their products (Orlandi et al., 1989). Moreover, they claim that because it is legal to sell their products, it should be legal to advertise them as well, and any ban represents an infringement on their First Amendment rights of commercial free speech (Gostin & Brandt, 1993; Ile & Knoll, 1990; Shiffrin, 1993).

Public health advocates counter that tobacco companies and beer manufacturers are engaging in unfair and deceptive practices by specifically targeting young people, using attractive role models and youth-oriented messages in their ads, and making smoking and drinking seem like normative behavior (Atkin, 1993a, 1993b; Borzekowski & Strasburger, 2008; Grube & Waiters, 2005; Kilbourne, 1993; U.S. Department of Health & Human Services, 1994). For example, two primary studies of magazine advertising (which accounts for nearly half of all cigarette advertising expenditures) found that brands popular with teens were more likely than adult brands to be advertised in magazines with high teen readerships (King, Siegel, Celebucki, & Connolly, 1998). In fact, teen magazines have attracted an increasing number of cigarette ads since 1965 (Brown & Witherspoon, 1998). For alcohol, teens are exposed to 48% more beer advertising, 20% more advertising for hard liquor, and 92% more ads for sweet alcoholic drinks in magazines than adults of legal drinking age (Center on Alcohol Marketing and Youth [CAMY], 2005; Garfield, Chung, & Rathouz, 2003). Of the 10 most popular teen magazines, only *Seventeen*, *Teen*, and *YM* refuse alcohol advertising (Garfield et al., 2003). Teen girls are actually more likely to be exposed to alcohol advertising than women in their 20s or 30s (Jernigan, Ostroff, Ross, & O'Hara, 2004). The fact that alcohol and tobacco manufacturers are trying to get adolescents to "just say yes" to cigarettes and beer at a time when society is trying to get them to "just say no" to drugs seems like a situation straight out of *Alice in Wonderland* (Kilbourne, 1993; Strasburger, 1997). As we shall see, the available data strongly support the public health viewpoint.

Cigarettes

Impact of Cigarette Advertising

Cigarette advertising appears to increase teenagers' risk of smoking by glamorizing smoking and smokers (Borzekowski & Strasburger, 2008; CDC, 1994). Smokers are depicted as independent, healthy, youthful, and adventurous. By contrast, the adverse consequences of smoking are never shown. The weight of the evidence is such that in 1994, the U.S. Surgeon General concluded, "Cigarette advertising appears to affect young people's perceptions of the pervasiveness, image, and function of smoking. Since misperceptions in these areas constitute psychosocial risk factors for the initiation of smoking, *cigarette advertising appears to increase young people's risk of smoking*" (U.S. Department of Health & Human Services, 1994, p. 195, emphasis added).

In fact, some of the industry's advertising strategies are nearly Orwellian in their sophistication. In *The Weekly Reader,* a periodical sold in approximately 80% of all U.S. elementary schools and owned, at one time, by the same company that owned tobacco conglomerate RJR Nabisco, the following contradictory themes were seen in the early 1990s: Adults in positions of authority are trying to prevent teens from smoking (appealing to teens' sense of autonomy), laws are being enforced inconsistently, most teenagers smoke, smoking is highly pleasurable and relaxing, and teens intent on smoking will do so regardless of what adults try to do about it (DeJong, 1996). An expert in adolescent psychology could not have dreamed up a more effective "forbidden fruit" scheme to recruit new teen smokers. Legislation originally brought by the U.S. Attorney General uncovered the fact that tobacco companies have specifically targeted teenage smokers as young as age 13 in an attempt to regain market share (Weinstein, 1998), and a federal judge ruled in 2006 that the tobacco industry has been deceiving the public for five decades about the risks of smoking ("When Don't Smoke," 2006). Teenagers can even purchase cigarettes easily online (J. A. Bryant, Cody, & Murphy, 2002).

Perhaps, as a result, 40% of eighth graders do not believe that smoking a pack of cigarettes a day represents a health risk (Johnston et al., 2008). Tobacco advertising may even undermine the impact of strong parenting practices (Pierce, Distefan, Jackson, White, & Gilpin, 2002). Numerous studies show that children who pay closer attention to cigarette advertisements, who are able to recall such ads more readily, or who own promotional items are more likely to view smoking favorably and to become smokers themselves (Biener & Siegel, 2000; CDC, 1992a, 1992b; Sargent et al., 1997; Sargent, Dalton, & Beach, 2000). Teens who smoke are also more likely to believe messages in print ads for cigarettes (Hawkins & Hane, 2000). Among teenage girls, smoking rates increased dramatically around 1967, exactly the same time that women were being targeted by such new brands as Virginia Slims (see Figure 7.6) (Pierce, Lee, & Gilpin, 1994). Only a rare study can be found that concludes that tobacco advertising has no influence on children (G. Smith, 1989).

Figure 7.6

SOURCE: ©2001 Phillip Morris USA.

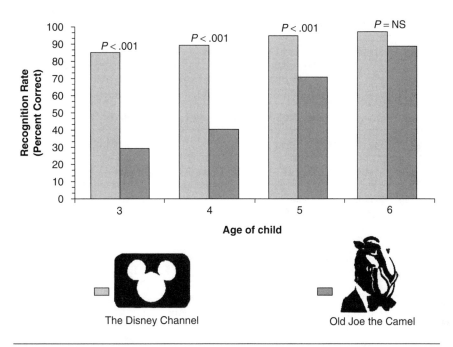

Figure 7.7   Old Joe the Camel Versus the Disney Channel

SOURCE: From the *Journal of the American Medical Association, 266,* pp. 3145–3148, 1991. Copyrighted 1991, American Medical Association.

NOTE: According to one classic study (Fischer et al., 1991), Old Joe the Camel is as recognizable to 6-year-olds as the Disney Channel logo.

Beginning in the early 1990s, some important research has more clearly delineated the impact of cigarette advertising on young people. In 1991, two studies examined the impact of the Old Joe the Camel advertising campaign. In one, 6-year-olds were as likely to recognize Old Joe as the famous mouseketeer logo for the Disney Channel (see Figure 7.7) (Fischer, Schwartz, Richards, Goldstein, & Rojas, 1991). Even at age 3, 30% of children could still make the association between the Old Joe Camel figure and a pack of cigarettes. In the second study, more than twice as many children as adults reported exposure to Old Joe. Not only were children able to recognize the association with Camel cigarettes, but they found the ads to be appealing as well (DiFranza et al., 1991). Not coincidentally, in the 3 years after the introduction of the Old Joe campaign, the preference for Camel cigarettes increased from 0.5% of adolescent smokers to 32%. During the same time period, the sale of Camels to minors increased from $6 million to $476 million, representing one quarter of all Camel sales and one third of all illegal cigarette sales to minors (DiFranza et al., 1991).

Other studies have provided important evidence as well. A California study documented that the most heavily advertised brands of cigarettes—Marlboro and Camel—are the most popular among teenage smokers (Pierce et al., 1991). A similar national study by the CDC found that 84% of teenagers purchase either Marlboros, Camels, or Newports—the three most highly advertised brands in the

Table 7.3   Is Cigarette Advertising Effective?

Advertising in $ Millions	Adolescent Brand Preference	Adult Brand Preference
1. Marlboro ($75)	1. Marlboro (60.0%)	1. Marlboro (23.5%)
2. Camel ($43)	2. Camel (13.3%)	2. Winston (6.7%)
3. Newport ($35)	3. Newport (12.7%)	3. Newport (4.8%)

SOURCE: Data from CDC (1994) and Pollay et al. (1996). From Strasburger and Donnerstein (1999). Copyright American Academy of Pediatrics. Reprinted with permission.

United States in 1990 (see Table 7.3) (CDC, 1992a, 1992b). In England, the most popular brands of cigarettes (Benson & Hedges, Silk Cut, Embassy, and Marlboro) are likewise the mostly heavily advertised (Vickers, 1992).

Cross-sectional studies in the mid-1990s found that teenagers exposed to promotional items or advertising were far more likely to become smokers. A study of 571 seventh graders in San Jose, California, found that 88% of 13-year-olds reported exposure to cigarette marketing and that experimenting with smoking was 2.2 times greater among those who owned promotional items (Schooler, Feighery, & Flora, 1996). In a national sample of 1,047 adolescents ages 12 to 17 years, Altman, Levine, Coeytaux, Slade, and Jaffe (1996) drew a similar conclusion. Sargent et al. (2000) actually found a dose-response relationship between the number of cigarette promotional items owned by adolescents and their smoking behavior. Finally, a recent meta-analysis of 51 separate studies found that exposure to tobacco marketing and advertising more than doubled the risk of a teenager beginning to smoke (Wellman, Sugarman, DiFranza, & Winickoff, 2006).

This is hardly an American phenomenon, however. In the United Kingdom, a survey of 1,450 students ages 11 and 12 years found that awareness of cigarette advertising correlated with smoking (While, Kelly, Huang, & Charlton, 1996), as did a survey of nearly 2,000 students who were exposed to so-called passive cigarette advertising during an India–New Zealand cricket series televised in India (Vaidya, Naik, & Vaidya, 1996). Unlike the United States, other countries have been more aggressive in banning cigarette advertising. In New Zealand, consumption fell after a complete ban on cigarette advertising (Vickers, 1992). In Norway, the prevalence of 13- to 15-year-old smokers decreased from 17% in 1975 to 10% in 1990 after an advertising ban was imposed (Vickers, 1992). In fact, an analysis of factors influencing tobacco consumption in 22 countries revealed that since 1973, advertising restrictions have resulted in lower rates of smoking (Laugesen & Meads, 1991).

Finally, a comprehensive 3-year longitudinal study of 1,752 California adolescents who never smoked found that one third of all smoking experimentation in California between 1993 and 1996 could be attributed to tobacco advertising and promotions (Pierce et al., 1998). This was the first study of its kind to use longitudinal correlational data that could yield cause-and-effect conclusions.

Several studies have documented that as the amount of cigarette advertising in a magazine increases, the amount of coverage of health risks associated with smoking decreases dramatically (Amos, Jacobson, & White, 1991; DeJong, 1996; L. Kessler, 1989; Warner, Goldenhar, & McLaughlin, 1992). For example, researchers using a logistic regression analysis to examine 99 U.S. magazines published over a 25-year span (between 1959–1969 and 1973–1986) found that the probability of publishing an article on the risks of smoking decreased 38% for magazines that derived significant revenue from tobacco companies (see Table 7.4) (Warner et al., 1992). Women's magazines are particularly guilty. A study of *Cosmopolitan, Good Housekeeping, Mademoiselle, McCall's,* and *Women's Day* found that between 1983 and 1987, not one of them published a single column or feature on the dangers of smoking (L. Kessler, 1989). All but *Good Housekeeping* have accepted cigarette advertising. This occurred during the same 5-year period that lung cancer was surpassing breast cancer as the number one killer of women (Moog, 1991).

Table 7.4   Does Cigarette Advertising Influence Editorial Content?

Magazine	Number of Magazine-Years	Probability of Coverage of Health Care Risks (%)
All magazines		
No cigarette ads	403	11.9
Any cigarette ads	900	8.3
Women's magazines		
No cigarette ads	104	11.7
Any cigarette ads	212	5.0

SOURCE: Adapted from Warner, Goldenhar, and McLaughlin. (1992). Copyright Massachusetts Medical Society.

Why is tobacco advertising so effective? Aside from the sheer amount of money spent on it, creating a density of such advertising that is difficult to counteract, cigarette advertising may act as a "super-peer" in influencing teenagers that everyone smokes but them (smoking is normative behavior) and that they will instantly become more attractive to their peers if they do smoke (Strasburger, 2006). Indeed, one group of researchers (Goldman & Glantz, 1998) has found that the only two strategies that are highly effective for preventing adolescents from smoking are showing the lengths to which the tobacco industry will go to recruit new smokers ("industry manipulation") and sensitizing teenagers to the risk of secondhand smoke. Both strategies involve "denormalizing" smoking (i.e., counteracting the myth that smoking is normative behavior for teens).

In 1998, the U.S. Attorney General negotiated what may be a remarkable settlement with the tobacco industry, calling for the payout of more than $206 billion to the states over the next 25 years, along with severe restrictions on marketing and advertising to children (see Table 7.5). Critics point to the fact that this figure represents a mere 8% of the $2.5 trillion that the federal government will lose over the same 25 years in health care costs related to smoking (D. Z. Jackson, 1998). In addition, according to the Federal Trade Commission (FTC), the tobacco industry actually spent more money on advertising and promotions after the lawsuits were settled: $8.2 billion in 1999, a 22% increase from 1998 ("Advertising Rose," 2001). Nevertheless, the now-substantial cigarette advertising research is hardly "moot" and may certainly have implications for alcohol advertising as well. For example, will there be future lawsuits against beer manufacturers by victims of drunk drivers or by the Attorney General to recover health care costs? In addition, the research may come back into play if the Attorney General settlement is overturned by a Congress that has traditionally been heavily influenced by tobacco money or by a federal court decision. What may replace the concerns about advertising and promotion is increasing alarm over the depictions of tobacco use in movies, music videos, and television programs—in a sense, the new "advertising" arena for tobacco companies.

Cigarettes in Television Programming, Music and Music Videos, and Movies

Smoking seems to be making a major comeback in the movies and, to a lesser extent, on television (see Figures 7.8 and 7.9).

The most recent content analysis of prime-time television found that 19% of programming portrayed tobacco use, with about one fourth of those depicting negative statements about smoking (Christenson et al., 2000). In music videos, one fourth of all Music Television (MTV) videos portrayed tobacco use, with the lead

Table 7.5   Some Features of the 1998 Tobacco Master Settlement Agreement

Payment of $206.4 billion from the tobacco industry to the states over the next 5 years, including $1.5 billion to fund research to reduce teen smoking
A ban on the use of cartoon characters in the advertising, promotion, or labeling of tobacco products
A prohibition on targeting youth in advertising, promotions, or marketing
A ban on all outdoor advertising, including billboards and signs in stadiums
A ban on the sale of merchandise with brand-name logos, such as T-shirts or backpacks
A ban on payments to producers of TV and movies for product placements

SOURCE: Adapted from *AAP News, 15*(1): 4, January 1999.

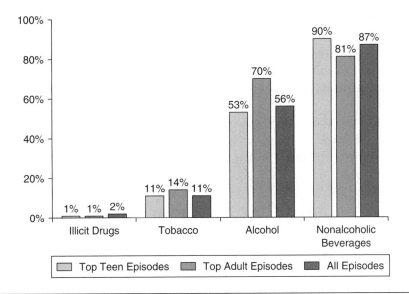

Figure 7.8   Substance Use in Television

SOURCE: Christenson et al. (2000).

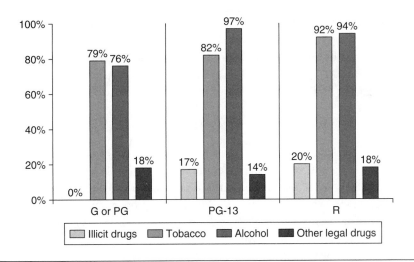

Figure 7.9   Substance Use in G- or PG-, PG-13-, and R-Rated Movies

SOURCE: DuRant et al., 1997.

performer usually the one shown as smoking (DuRant et al., 1997). By 2001, tobacco was appearing an average of 4 times per hour on TV, an increase from 2.7 times per hour in 1999 (J. Armstrong, 2002). Unlike the movies, on TV it is frequently the attractive main characters who smoke—for example, Maura Tierney's nurse Abby on *ER* and Martin Sheen's President Bartlet on *The West Wing*. Even Japanese TV serial dramas—popular throughout Asia—are experiencing a surge in characters smoking (Kanda et. al., 2006). Furthermore, nearly all American teens have been exposed to tobacco use because of movie trailers on TV. A recent study found that nearly one fourth of trailers for R-rated movies and 7.5% of trailers for PG-13 and PG movies contained images of tobacco use (Healton et al., 2006).

Movies are also providing tobacco companies with increasing opportunities for featuring smoking. Use of passive advertising—so-called product placements—has been extremely lucrative, although studio chiefs currently deny that this practice continues. The Philip Morris Company reportedly paid $350,000 to place Lark cigarettes in the James Bond movie *License to Kill* and another $42,500 to place Marlboros in *Superman II* ("Selling to Children," 1990). Direct payments for product placements of cigarettes ended in 1989 (Sargent, Tickle, Beach, Ahrens, & Heatherton, 2001), when the top 13 tobacco firms adopted the following guideline to avoid federal regulation: "No payment, direct or indirect, shall be made for the placement of our cigarettes or cigarette advertisements in any film produced for viewing by the general public" (Shields, Carol, Balbach, & McGee, 1999).

Hollywood seems to use cigarette smoking as shorthand for a troubled or anti-establishment character, but the smoking or nonsmoking status of the actors themselves is also influential in whether their characters will smoke on screen (Shields et al., 1999). The list of prominent Hollywood actors and actresses puffing away on screen is quite long: Julia Roberts in *My Best Friend's Wedding,* Al Pacino in *Any Given Sunday,* Michael Douglas in *Wonder Boys,* John Travolta in *Broken Arrow,* Brad Pitt in *Sleepers,* and Leonardo DiCaprio and Kate Winslet in *Titanic* (Roberts & Christenson, 2000). In the 1990s and early 2000s, there has been a new wave of content analyses performed, all of which have found that cigarette smoking in movies is a major occurrence and a continuing problem (Charlesworth & Glantz, 2005; Sargent, 2005; Sargent et al., 2004, 2005; Titus-Ernstoff, Dalton, Adachi-Mejia, Longacre, & Beach, 2008):

• In the most recent study, 80% of children's smoking exposure actually occurred via G, PG, or PG-13 films (Titus-Ernstoff et al., 2008).

• Another recent content analysis examined the top 100 box office hits between 1996 and 2004. Tobacco was depicted in three fourths of G-, PG-, and PG-rated movies and in 90% of R-rated movies. Although the proportion of movies that featured smoking declined from 96% in 1996 to 77% in 2004, more smoking was depicted in youth-rated films (American Legacy Foundation, 2006). In another recent analysis, the top 100 box office hits from 1998 to 2004 were studied. Nearly three quarters contained smoking, and each movie had been seen by 25% of the 6,500 teenagers surveyed nationwide. That adds up to billions of smoking images overall and 665 per 10- to 14-year-old (Sargent, Tanski, & Gibson, 2007).

• R-rated movies have the highest rates of smoking (Mekemson et al., 2004; Omidvari et al., 2005; Polansky & Glantz, 2004). Leading women are as likely to smoke in movies aimed at teenage audiences (PG/PG-13) as in R-rated movies, whereas leading men smoke more often in R-rated movies. And young actresses are four times more likely to be featured smoking than older actresses (Escamilla, Cradock, & Kawachi, 2000). As the Motion Picture Association of America (MPAA) began to give PG-13 ratings to movies that would previously have been rated R

(Thompson & Yakota, 2004), younger teens have been exposed to more smoking incidents in movies (Charlesworth & Glantz, 2005). Even children's G-rated movies contain a surprising amount of smoking scenes. In fact, smoking has long been present in children's movies. Two reviews of 50 to 74 G-rated animated feature films released between 1937 and 1997 by five major production companies found that more than half portrayed one or more instances of tobacco use, including all seven films released in 1996 and 1997 (see Table 7.6) (Goldstein, Sobel, & Newman, 1999; Yakota & Thompson, 2001). In 2007, the MPAA said that it would begin factoring in smoking as it determines the ratings it gives to movies.

Table 7.6   Tobacco or Alcohol Content of G-Rated Children's Films

Film	Tobacco Use/Exposure (Seconds)	Alcohol Use/Exposure (Seconds)
The Three Caballeros	Yes (548)	Yes (8)
101 Dalmations	Yes (299)	Yes (51)
Pinocchio	Yes (22)	Yes (80)
James & the Giant Peach	Yes (206)	Yes (38)
All Dogs Go to Heaven	Yes (205)	Yes (73)
Alice in Wonderland	Yes (158)	No
Great Mouse Detective	Yes (165)	Yes (414)
The Aristocats	Yes (11)	Yes (142)
Beauty & the Beast	No	Yes (123)

SOURCE: Adapted from Goldstein, Sobel, and Newman. (1999).

• Movie smokers tend to be White, middle-class males, who are usually the heroes (Stockwell & Glantz, 1997). Smoking among males is associated with violent behavior and dangerous acts; among females, it is associated with sexual affairs, illegal activities, and reckless driving (Sargent, 2005; Sargent et al., 2000). Movie depictions also tend to be very pro-smoking, with only 14% of screen time dealing with adverse health effects (Stockwell & Glantz, 1997). Of the top 100 grossing films of 2002, only 0.4% of smoking incidents depicted the fatal consequences of smoking (Dozier, Lauzen, Day, Payne, & Tafoya, 2005). One study of the 100 most popular films in the past 50 years found that smokers are depicted as being more romantically and sexually active than nonsmokers and as being marginally more intelligent (McIntosh, Smith, Bazzini, & Mills, 1999).

All of this would not be of much concern if movies were not extremely popular with teenagers, who comprise 16% of the U.S. population but account for 26% of all movie admissions (Rauzi, 1998). Unique longitudinal research has shown that one of the most important factors in the onset of teen drug use is exposure to others who use substances (Kosterman, Hawkins, Guo, Catalano, & Abbott, 2000). Nowhere is that exposure greater than on contemporary movie screens. *A number of correlational and longitudinal studies have now confirmed that exposure to television and movie smoking is one of the key factors in teen smoking.* In fact, exposure to movie smoking may even trump parents' smoking as being the leading factor in adolescent initiation of smoking (Sargent et al., 2005; Sargent, Stoolmiller, et al., 2007; Titus-Ernstoff et al., 2008). Public health advocates estimate that smoking depicted in movies leads 390,000 adolescents to begin smoking each year, resulting in a nearly $1 billion profit to the U.S. tobacco industry (Alamar & Glantz, 2006; Charlesworth & Glantz, 2005):

- Several cross-sectional studies of middle school students in New England have found that exposure to smoking in movies significantly increases teens' positive views of smoking and the perception that most adults smoke (Sargent et al., 2001, 2002). A prospective study of more than 3,500 teens found that exposure to smoking in all rated movies tripled the risk of initiating smoking (see Figure 7.10) (Dalton et al., 2003), while exposure to R-rated movies alone doubled the risk (Dalton et al., 2002). Preteens whose parents forbid them from seeing R-rated movies are less likely to begin smoking (or drinking, for that matter) (Dalton et al., 2006). The results were recently replicated in a study of more than 1,690 middle school students in Wisconsin (Thompson & Gunther, 2007).

- In the largest cross-sectional study of its kind, Sargent et al. (2005) recently surveyed 6,522 U.S. adolescents ages 10 to 14 years and found that those who witnessed the most smoking episodes in movies were 2.6 times more likely to begin

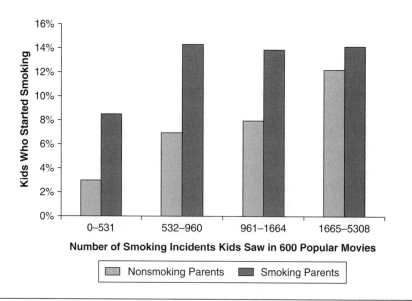

Figure 7.10   Does Smoking Depicted in Movies Increase the Risk of Teen Smoking?

SOURCE: Charlesworth and Glantz (2005). Reproduced with permission from Stanton A. Glantz.

smoking themselves, even after controlling for peer and parent smoking. A recent cross-sectional study replicated this finding in German teenagers (Hanewinkel & Sargent, 2007).

- A sample of 735 twelve- to fourteen-year-olds, with a 2-year follow-up, found that exposure to R-rated movies and having a TV set in the bedroom significantly increased the risk of smoking initiation for White teens but not for Black teens (C. Jackson, Brown, & L'Engle, 2007). This is now the third longitudinal study documenting the risk of R-rated movies (Dalton et al., 2003; C. Jackson et al., 2007; Sargent et al., 2005). Three other new longitudinal studies have documented the risk of seeing smoking in movies of all ratings (Sargent, Stoolmiller, et al., 2007), in German preteens and teens (Hanewinkel & Sargent, 2008) and for elementary schoolchildren (Titus-Ernstoff et al., 2008). In the first study, a national sample of 6,522 preteens and teens, ages 10 to 14 years, were followed for 2 years. Exposure to movie smoking doubled the risk of becoming an established smoker (Sargent, Stoolmiller, et al., 2007). In the German study, 2,711 teens and preteens were followed for a year, and the findings of a dose-response effect between viewing movie smoking and teen initiation of smoking paralleled the U.S. studies (Hanewinkel & Sargent, 2008). In the third study, a regional sample of 2,255 elementary school students, ages 9 to 12 years, was also followed for 2 years. Exposure to movie smoking accounted for at least one third of smoking initiation (Titus-Ernstoff et al., 2008).

Alcohol

Research on Alcohol Advertising

Although the research on alcohol advertising is not quite as compelling as that on tobacco advertising, children and adolescents do seem to comprise a uniquely vulnerable audience. Like cigarette advertisements, beer commercials are virtually custom-made to appeal to children and adolescents: images of fun-loving, sexy, successful young people having the time of their lives (Borzekowski & Strasburger, 2008). Who wouldn't want to indulge (see Table 7.7) (Kilbourne, 1993)? Using sexual imagery (Atkin, 1995) or celebrity endorsers (Atkin & Block, 1983) increases the impact of beer and wine ads on young people.

Content analyses show that beer ads seem to suggest that drinking is an absolutely harmless activity with no major health risks associated with it (Atkin, 1993a; Atkin, DeJong, & Wallack, 1992; Grube & Wallack, 1994; Madden & Grube, 1994; Wallack, Cassady, & Grube, 1990). Yet more than one third of ads show people driving or engaging in water sports while supposedly drinking (Madden & Grube, 1994). Alcohol ads also frequently feature sexual and social stereotypes and target teenagers (Austin & Hust, 2005).

Beer and wine ads are frequently featured on prime-time television: American children and teenagers view 1,000 to 2,000 of them annually (Jernigan, 2006; Strasburger, 2006). Australian teens are exposed to as much alcohol advertising as young adults who are of legal drinking age (Winter, Donovan, & Fielder, 2007).

Table 7.7   Seven Myths That Alcohol Advertisers Want Children and Adolescents to Believe

1. Everyone drinks alcohol.

2. Drinking has no risks.

3. Drinking helps to solve problems.

4. Alcohol is a magic potion that can transform you.

5. Sports and alcohol go together.

6. If alcohol were truly dangerous, we wouldn't be advertising it.

7. Alcoholic beverage companies promote drinking only in moderation.

SOURCE: Adapted from Kilbourne (1993).

In the United States, much of this advertising is concentrated in teen shows and in sports programming. All of the top 15 teen shows contain alcohol ads (CAMY, 2004b). In prime time, only 1 alcohol commercial appears every 4 hours, but in sports programming, 2.4 ads appear per hour (Grube, 1995; Madden & Grube, 1994). In addition, alcohol advertisements are frequently embedded in sports programming, with banners and scoreboards featuring brand logos and brief interruptions of brand sponsorship (e.g., "This half-time report is brought to you by. . . ."), at a rate of about 3 per hour (Grube, 1995). Currently, teenagers are 400 times more likely to see an alcohol ad than to see a public service ad that discourages underage drinking (Mothers Against Drunk Driving [MADD], 2004). In magazines, teenagers actually see nearly 50% more beer advertising than adults do (Garfield et al., 2003; Jernigan et al., 2004). (However, since the industry adopted a voluntary standard that restricts advertising in media where the youth audience exceeds 30%, the amount of magazine advertising has dropped significantly [CDC, 2007].) On TV, 12- to 20-year-olds also see more alcohol advertising than adults of legal drinking age (CAMY, 2004a). From 2001 to 2005, the number of alcohol ads on TV increased 33% (CAMY, 2007). And on the radio—the second most popular medium for teenagers after TV—young people hear more alcohol ads than adults in 14 of the 15 biggest markets (CAMY, 2004c). A new study by the CDC found that half of all the nearly 70,000 alcohol advertisements assessed in 104 major markets around the country were placed in radio programming whose audience was predominantly adolescent (CDC, 2006b).

Such a density of advertising seems to have a considerable impact on young people. In one survey of fifth and sixth graders, nearly 60% of them could match the brand of beer being promoted with a still photograph from a commercial (Grube, 1995). Similarly, a sample of 9- to 10-year-olds could identify the Budweiser frogs nearly as frequently as Bugs Bunny (see Table 7.8) (Leiber, 1996). In a recent study of more than 3,500 South Dakota students, 75% of fourth graders and 87% of ninth graders recognized the Budweiser ferret ad (see Figure 7.11) (Collins, Ellickson,

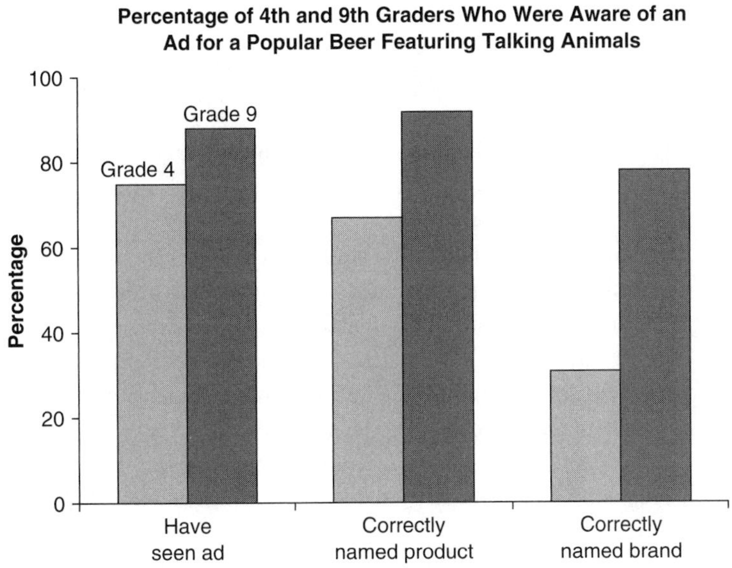
Percentage of 4th and 9th Graders Who Were Aware of an
Ad for a Popular Beer Featuring Talking Animals
Percentage
100
80
60
40
20
0
Grade 4
Grade 9
Have seen ad
Correctly named product
Correctly named brand

Figure 7.11 How Effective Are "Cute" Ads for Beer?

SOURCE: Reprinted from *Journal of Adolescent Health*, Volume 4, Ringel, Jeanne S., Collins, Rebecca L., and Ellickson, Phyllis L., "Time Trends and Demographic Differences in Youth Exposure to Alcohol Advertising on Television," p. 8, Copyright 2006, with permission from Elsevier.

Table 7.8 Are the Budweiser Frogs Effective Advertising? Commercial and Character Recall by Children 9 to 11 Years Old

Character	*Slogan or Motto*	*% Recall* (n = *221*)
Bugs Bunny	"Eh, what's up Doc?"	80
Budweiser Frogs	"Bud-weis-er"	73
Tony the Tiger	"They're grrreat!"	57
Smokey Bear	"Only you can prevent forest fires."	43
Mighty Morphin Power Rangers	"It's morphin' time!" or "Power up!"	39

SOURCE: Adapted from Leiber (1996). Copyright American Academy of Pediatrics.

NOTE: Considerable research exists that the media can make children more vulnerable to experimentation with alcohol (Fleming, Thorson, & Atkin, 2004; Grube & Waiters, 2005; Grube & Wallack, 1994; Jernigan, 2006).

McCaffrey, & Hambarsoomians, 2005). And in one well-known survey of suburban Maryland children, 8- to 12-year-olds could list more brands of beer than names of American presidents (Center for Science in the Public Interest, 1988)! Rarely do young people see ads or public service announcements urging moderation (Madden & Grube, 1994). Perhaps as a result, nearly three fourths of American adults think that such advertising encourages teenagers to drink (Lipman, 1991).

A series of survey studies by Atkin and colleagues (Atkin & Block, 1983; Atkin, Hocking, & Block, 1984; Atkin, Neuendorf, & McDermott, 1983) reveal that adolescents heavily exposed to alcohol advertising are more likely to believe that drinkers possess the qualities being displayed in the advertising (e.g., being attractive or successful), have more positive beliefs about drinking, think that getting drunk is acceptable, and are more likely to drink, drink heavily, and drink and drive.

- Other studies have found that early adolescent drinkers are more likely to have been exposed to alcohol advertising, can identify more brands of beer, and view such ads more favorably than nondrinkers (Aitken, Eadie, Leathar, McNeill, & Scott, 1988; Martino, Collins, Ellickson, Schell, & McCaffrey, 2006; Wyllie, Zhang, & Casswell, 1998). Two recent studies of 2,125 students in California middle schools found evidence of a clear association between adolescent drinking and exposure to advertising and ownership of promotional items (Henriksen, Feighery, Schleicher, & Fortmann, 2008; Hurtz, Henriksen, Wang, Feighery, & Fortmann, 2007).

- A 1990 study of 468 randomly selected fifth and sixth graders found that 88% of them could identify Spuds Mackenzie with Bud Light beer. Their ability to name brands of beer and match slogans with the brands was significantly related to their exposure and attention to beer ads. The greater the exposure and attention, the greater the likelihood that the children would think that drinking is associated with fun and good times, and not with health risks, and that the children expected to drink as adults. Their attitudes about drinking were especially conditioned by watching weekend sports programming on TV (Wallack, Cassady, & Grube, 1990).

There is also a small but demonstrable effect of exposure to advertisements on actual drinking behavior, among both teenagers (Atkin & Block, 1983; Atkin et al., 1984) and college students (Kohn & Smart, 1984, 1987). Other research is less powerful but also suggestive. For example:

- Since 1960 in the United States, a dramatic increase in advertising expenditures has been accompanied by a 50% per capita increase in alcohol consumption (Jacobson & Collins, 1985).

- In Sweden, a mid-1970s ban on all beer and wine advertising resulted in a 20% per capita drop in alcohol consumption (Romelsjo, 1987).

- In perhaps the best ecological study, Saffer (1997) studied the correlation between alcohol advertising on television, radio, and billboards in the 75 top media markets in the United States and the motor vehicle fatality rate. He found that greater density of alcohol advertising significantly increased the fatality rate, particularly for older drivers, and hypothesized that a total ban on such advertising might save 5,000 to 10,000 lives per year.

While the evidence does not support the interpretation that advertising exerts a powerful, uniform, direct influence, it seems that advertising is a significant contributing factor that increases drinking and related problems to a modest degree rather than being a major determinant (Atkin, 1993b, p. 535). Although there is always the possibility that adolescent drinkers search out or attend to alcohol advertising more than do their abstinent peers, this seems considerably less likely than advertising having a real effect (Atkin, 1990; Grube, 1993). As one advertising executive notes,

> If greater advertising over time doesn't generate greater profits, there's something seriously wrong with the fellows who make up the budgets. (Samuelson, 1991, p. 40)

What's new in the past 5 to 10 years is that several studies now exist that illuminate some of the underlying mechanisms that link alcohol ad exposure with alcohol consumption by youth.

- In an ongoing correlational study of fifth- and sixth-grade children, Grube and Wallack (1994) have found that those who are more aware of alcohol advertising have more positive beliefs about drinking and can recognize more brands and slogans. Their study is unique in that they discard a simple exposure model in favor of examining children's beliefs and behaviors only when they have processed and remembered alcohol advertisements. In their work, the finding of positive beliefs is crucial because that is what leads to an increased intention to drink, even when other important factors such as parental and peer attitudes and drinking behaviors are controlled (Grube, 1999).

- In another study by Austin and Knaus (1998) of 273 third, sixth, and ninth graders in two Washington state communities, exposure to advertising and promotional merchandise at a young age was predictive of drinking behavior during adolescence. And an 18-month-long study of more than 1,500 ninth-grade students in San Jose, California, found that the onset of drinking alcohol correlated significantly with increased viewing of both television and music videos (Robinson, Chen, & Killen, 1998). This may point to the impact of both alcohol advertising (television) and role modeling (music videos). A recent study of 1,648 Belgian teenagers also found viewing music videos to be a significant risk factor for early alcohol use (Van den Bulck & Beullens, 2005).

- A recent longitudinal study of 3,111 South Dakota teenagers found that exposure to beer ads in the seventh grade actually predicted drinking onset by ninth grade (Ellickson, Collins, Hambarsoomians, & McCaffrey, 2005).

- Another recent longitudinal study, this time of 2,250 seventh graders in Los Angeles over a 1-year period, revealed that greater exposure to alcohol ads resulted in a 44% increased risk of drinking beer, a 34% increased risk of drinking wine or hard liquor, and a 26% increased risk of binge drinking (Stacy, Zogg, Unger, & Dent, 2004). Similarly, a study of 1,786 South Dakota students found that exposure to alcohol ads in sixth grade was strongly predictive of drinking or intending to drink in seventh grade (Collins, Ellickson, McCaffrey, & Hambarsoomians, 2007).

- In another one of the latest studies, nearly two thousand 15- to 26-years-olds were surveyed repeatedly over a 21-month period. Those who saw more alcohol ads consumed more alcohol, and those young people living in media markets where more money was spent on alcohol advertising also drank more. For underage drinkers, each exposure to an alcohol ad resulted in a 1% increased risk of drinking, and each additional advertising dollar yielded a 3% increase in underage drinking (Snyder et al., 2006). This is one of the first studies that really challenges the industry's usual assertions that advertising does not increase underage drinking and that all it is trying to do is to influence brand preference (Jernigan, 2006).

No media research is perfect. Researchers cannot willfully expose children or adolescents to a barrage of alcohol ads and watch who drinks or what brand of beer they choose in a laboratory setting any more than they can assess the effects of media violence by showing children violent movies and then giving them guns and knives to play with (Austin & Knaus, 1998). Most of the data are correlational (children who drink are more likely to have seen advertisements, for example, but heavy drinkers could conceivably choose to watch more ads). But increasing numbers of longitudinal studies are beginning to confirm a cause-and-effect influence (Borzekowski & Strasburger, 2008; Jernigan, 2006).

Alcohol in Television Programming, Music and Music Videos, and Movies

During the 1970s and early 1980s, alcohol was ubiquitous on American television. It was the most popular beverage consumed, and rarely were negative consequences of drinking shown or discussed (Breed & De Foe, 1984). Especially on soap operas, alcohol was depicted as being both an excellent social lubricant and an easy means of resolving serious personal crises (Lowery, 1980). Two initiatives tried to change this: new guidelines for the industry, written by the Hollywood Caucus of Producers, Writers, and Directors (Breed & De Foe, 1982; Caucus for Producers, Writers, and Directors, 1983), and the Harvard School of Public Health Alcohol Project in the late 1980s (Rothenberg, 1988). The caucus suggested that its members avoid (a) making gratuitous use of alcohol in programming, (b) glamorizing drinking, (c) showing drinking as a macho activity, and (d) depicting drinking with no serious consequences. The Harvard Alcohol Project worked with major networks and studios to foster the notion of the "designated driver," and this device appeared in many storylines during the next few years.

Unfortunately, several content analyses demonstrate that alcohol is a problem that simply will not go away on prime-time television and in music videos. In fact, alcohol remains the most frequently portrayed food or drink on network television and in music videos (Ashby & Rich, 2005; Mathios, Avery, Bisogni, & Shanahan, 1998; Roberts, Christenson, Henriksen, & Bandy, 2002). In addition, a study by the AAP suggests that the "designated driver" concept may be failing as well. A survey of 16- to 19-year-olds by the AAP found that 80% think that drinking is acceptable as long as there is a designated driver. Unfortunately, nearly half think that designated drivers can still drink (Tanner, 1998)! These data seem to confirm the YRBS finding that in the month prior to being surveyed, nearly 30% of students had ridden in a car with a driver who had been drinking alcohol (CDC, 2006c).

A 1986 content analysis was the first to suggest that alcohol was still extremely common on TV and in the movies, despite the efforts of the Hollywood caucus: 100% of theatrical or made-for-TV movies and more than 75% of all dramatic series contained some mention of drinking (Wallack, Grube, Madden, & Breed, 1990). Of the 16 most popular R-rated movies in the mid-1980s seen frequently by teenagers, every film contained alcohol use, with an average of 16 drinking episodes per film (Greenberg, Brown, & Buerkel-Rothfuss, 1993). Much of the alcohol use portrayed in both media was unnecessary to the plot, and drinking was still presented as being problem free. In addition, adolescent drinking is often treated in a humorous fashion, and teens frequently acknowledge a desire to drink as a symbol of adulthood (De Foe & Breed, 1988). Again, the impact of "normative drinking" must always be considered when adolescents are involved.

Several more content analyses have been done in the 1990s. Compared with earlier analyses, the first found that the frequency of drinking episodes has remained relatively stable: 6 per hour in 1991 versus 10 per hour in 1984 and 5 per hour in 1976 (Grube, 1993). Prime-time drinkers are usually familiar, high-status characters, and more than 80% of the prime-time programs examined contained references to alcohol (Grube, 1993).

In the second, Gerbner (2001) found that alcohol remains the most commonly portrayed drug on American television, with one drinking scene occurring every 22 minutes, compared with one smoking scene every 57 minutes and illicit drug use every 112 minutes. On MTV, a viewer sees alcohol use every 14 minutes, compared with every 17 minutes in the movies and every 27 minutes on prime-time television. Popular movies are nearly equally rife with alcohol, with only 2 of the 40 highest grossing titles not containing alcohol depictions (Everett, Schnuth, & Tribble, 1998).

On prime-time television, 70% of program episodes depict alcohol use, according to a recent content analysis (see Figure 7.8) (Christenson et al., 2000). More than one third of the drinking episodes are associated with humor, and negative consequences are shown in only 23%. A content analysis of music videos found that alcohol is portrayed in more than one fourth of videos on MTV and VH1 (DuRant et al., 1997). In addition, alcohol is associated with increased levels of sex and sexuality—again, not a healthy association for teens pondering when and with whom to begin having sex. A 2001 analysis of 359 music videos broadcast found that drugs were present in nearly half—alcohol in 35%, tobacco in 10%, and illicit drugs in 13% (Gruber, Thau, Hill, Fisher, & Grube, 2005).

The most comprehensive study of movies examined 200 popular films from 1996 to 1997 and found that 93% of the movies contained alcohol depictions (see Figure 7.2). Even G- and PG-rated movies contained frequent references to tobacco and alcohol (see Figure 7.9) (Roberts et al., 1999; Yakota & Thompson, 2001). Although consequences of alcohol use were shown in 43% of the movies studied, only 14% depicted a refusal of an offer of alcohol, and only 9% contained anti-use sentiments (see Figure 7.12) (Roberts, Henriksen, & Christenson, 1999). These findings were almost identical to another, separate content analysis of top-grossing American films from 1985 to 1995 (Everett et al., 1998). In another analysis of films from 1996 to 2001, Bahk (2001) found that drinking alcohol is most often portrayed as normative behavior, whereas illicit drugs are often demonized. Finally, an analysis of the 601 most popular contemporary films up until 2001 found that 92% of the movies depicted some alcohol use (52% for G, 89% for PG, 93% for PG-13, and 95% for R) (Sargent, Wills, Stoolmiller, Gibson, & Gibbons, 2006).

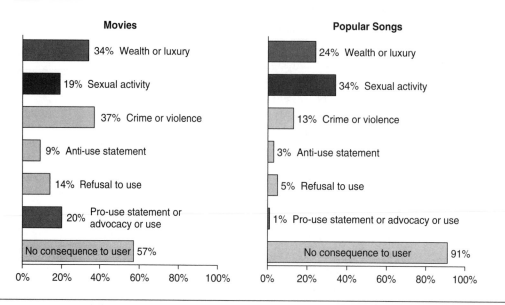

Figure 7.12 Percentage of Movies and Songs Associating Alcohol Use With Wealth, Luxury, or Sex

SOURCE: Roberts, Henriksen, and Christenson (1999).

NOTE: Based on the 183 movies and 149 songs that portrayed alcohol use. Alcohol use in movies and songs is usually associated with wealth, luxury, or sex and is rarely discouraged. In addition, the consequences of alcohol use are rarely depicted or sung about.

What impact does all of this content have? Several studies have identified certain media as a possible cause of early alcohol use. In Robinson et al. 's (1998) longitudinal study of 1,533 California ninth graders, increased television and music video viewing were found to be risk factors for the onset of alcohol use among adolescents. Odds ratios for television ranged from 1.01 to 1.18, and for music videos, they ranged from 1.17 to 1.47, both statistically significant. A recent Columbia University study found that teens who watch more than three R-rated movies per month are five times more likely to drink alcohol compared with teens who do not watch any R-rated movies (National Center on Addiction and Substance Abuse, 2005). And an intriguing study of 120 two- to six-year-olds who were asked to role-play in a make-believe store found that children were 5 times more likely to "buy" beer or wine in the store if they had been allowed to see PG-13- or R-rated movies (Dalton et al., 2005).

Drugs

Illicit Drugs in Television Programming, Music and Music Videos, and Movies

Although illicit drugs are not advertised as tobacco and alcohol are, they still make a major appearance in programming seen by children and adolescents. Here, music videos and movies are the primary culprits, the ideal venues for adolescents to be influenced. On prime-time television, illicit drugs are rarely mentioned or shown, and illicit drug use is usually associated with negative consequences (Christenson et al., 2000; Roberts & Christenson, 2000). However, there are a few notable exceptions. Shows such as Showtime's 2005 hit series *Weeds* and FOX's *That 70s Show* tend to minimize the significance of marijuana use. And the average MTV viewer sees illicit drugs once every 40 minutes, compared to once every 100 minutes in the movies and every 112 minutes on prime-time TV (Gerbner, 2001). In their study of popular movies and songs from 1996 to 1997, Roberts, Henriksen, and Christenson (1999) found that illicit drugs appeared in 22% of movies and 18% of songs (see Figure 7.2). Rap songs were far more likely to contain references to illicit drugs than were alternative rock or heavy metal. Teens may hear as many as 84 drug references daily in popular songs (Primack et al., 2008). In movies depicting illicit drugs, marijuana appeared most frequently (51%), followed by cocaine (33%) and other drugs (12%). Currently, when the top movies portray drug use, no harmful consequences are shown 52% of the time (Christenson et al., 2000; Roberts & Christenson, 2000). On the positive side, 21% of movies include a character refusing to use drugs (Roberts & Christenson, 2000).

Marijuana does seem to be making a major comeback in Hollywood movies, thanks to movies such as *There's Something About Mary* (1998) and *Bulworth* (1998) (Gordinier, 1998), *Dude, Where's My Car?* (2000), and *Harold and Kumar Go to White Castle* (2004). Cocaine is featured in *Scarface, Blow,* and *Traffic.* And heroin use is depicted quite graphically in both *Trainspotting* and *Permanent Midnight* (Ivry, 1998) and in *Ray.*

What impact these depictions have on children or adolescents is conjectural at best. Such research is difficult to accomplish, but any media portrayals that seem to legitimize or normalize drug use are likely to have an impact, at least on susceptible teens. The Columbia study mentioned above found that seeing R-rated movies was associated with a six times increased risk of trying marijuana, for example (see Figure 7.13) (National Center on Addiction and Substance Abuse, 2005). Hollywood filmmakers do not seem to understand that humor tends to undermine normal adolescent defenses against drugs and legitimizes adolescent drug use (Borzekowski & Strasburger, 2008). Clearly, far more research is needed in this crucial area.

A Word About Prescription and Nonprescription Drugs

During the past decade, there has been a virtual explosion of advertising for prescription drugs (see Figure 7.14) (Gellad & Lyles, 2007; Hollon, 2005). Perhaps not coincidentally, in a 2006 national survey, nearly 1 in 5 teens reported abusing

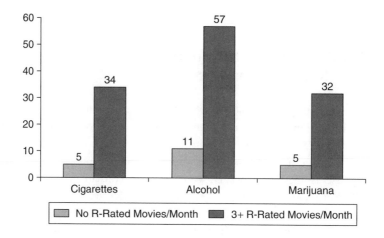

Figure 7.13 Percentage of Teens Who Have Tried Cigarettes, Alcohol, and Marijuana

Figure 7.14

prescription medications to get high, and 1 in 10 reported abusing over-the-counter drugs (Partnership for a Drug-Free America [PDFA], 2006). In 1993, prescription drug manufacturers spent $100 million on consumer-targeted advertising (Byrd-Bredbrenner & Grasso, 2000); in 2005, that figure rose to $4 billion (Rubin, 2004). Advertising of nonprescription drugs remains high, particularly for cold, flu, and headache remedies and heartburn medications (Byrd-Bredbrenner & Grasso, 2000; Tsao, 1997). In fact, drug companies now spend more than twice as much money on marketing as they do on research and development. In 2002, the top 10 drug companies made a total profit of nearly $36 billion—more than the other 490 companies in the *Fortune* 500 companies combined (Angell, 2004).

Under new guidelines issued by the Food and Drug Administration (FDA) in 1997, prescription drug ads can now mention the specific drug being advertised (rather than having to say, "see your doctor") as long as the major health risks associated with the drug are mentioned and a toll-free phone number or Internet address is given (Byrd-Bredbrenner & Grasso, 2000). As a result, ads for Meridia, Propecia, Viagra, and many other drugs are increasingly common, especially on prime-time television. In the first 10 months of 2004, drug companies spent nearly $350 million advertising Viagra, Levitra, and Cialis (Snowbeck, 2005). In 2000, prescription drug ads aired during 14% of all prime-time episodes (Christenson et al., 2000). And increasingly, prescription drugs are available to adolescents and others online, without a prescription (National Center on Addiction and Substance Abuse, 2006). Ads for nonprescription drugs are even more common during prime-time TV: Fully half of all popular adult programs and 43% of all popular teen shows contain ads for over-the-counter medicines (Christenson et al., 2000). Most of these ads emphasize the quick, easy, no-risk approach to self-medication, what one researcher calls the "magic of medicine" perspective (Byrd-Bredbrenner & Grasso, 1999, 2000). Half of the health or nutritional information in drug and food ads has been judged misleading or inaccurate (Byrd-Bredbrenner & Grasso, 1999, 2000).

Solutions

In the past two decades, when "just say no" has become a watchword for many parents and school-based drug prevention programs, unprecedented amounts of money are being spent in an effort to induce children and teenagers to "just say yes" to smoking and drinking. Perhaps, as one group of researchers suggests, the "discussion [should] be *elevated* from the scientific and legal arenas to the domain of ethics and social responsibility" (Orlandi et al., 1989, p. 92, emphasis added).

Discussed below are nine ideas that, if implemented, could very well result in significant reductions in adolescent cigarette, alcohol, and drug use.

1. *More research.* Considering how significant the impact of the media is on young people, more media research is desperately needed, including adequate funding for such efforts. Specifically, more longitudinal analyses of adolescents' drug use compared with their media use are needed, as well as studies of how teens process drug content in different media. In addition, how media affect audiences differently is critical to understand in order to better focus intervention efforts and tailor effective messages (Austin, Chen, & Grube, 2006; Ringel, Collins, & Ellickson, 2006). For example, African American youth are known to be relatively resistant to tobacco advertising, but the reasons for this are unclear (CDC, 2006a; West, Romero, & Trinidad, 2007). This research needs to be more widely disseminated as well. A new Surgeon General's report on the impact of media, for example,

would be extremely useful to researchers, health professionals, parents, and policy-makers and might provide the impetus for increased funding for media research.

2. *Development of media literacy programs.* Children and teenagers must learn how to decode the subtle and not-so-subtle messages contained in television programming, advertising, movies, and music videos (see Chapter 13 and Potter, 2008). A century ago, to be "literate" meant that you could read and write. In the year 2008, to be literate means that you can successfully understand a dizzying array of media and media messages (Rich & Bar-on, 2001). Parents need to begin this process when their children are young (ages 2–3 years), and they need to understand that a child who watches TV 4 hours or more per day has a fivefold increased risk of smoking than one who watches less than 2 hours per day (Gidwani, Sobol, DeJong, Perrin, & Gortmaker, 2002). School programs may be extremely useful as well. In particular, certain drug prevention programs have been extremely effective in reducing levels of adolescents' drug use (see Figure 7.15), but such programs must go far beyond the DARE (Drug Abuse Resistance Education) approach to include media literacy, peer resistance skills, and social skills building (Botvin & Griffin, 2005). The United States is unique among Western nations in not requiring some form of media literacy for its students (AAP, 1999; J. D. Brown, 2006). Preliminary studies indicate that successful drug prevention may be possible through this unique route (Austin & Johnson, 1997; Austin, Pinkleton, Hust, & Cohen, 2005; McCannon, 2005; Primack, Gold, Land, & Fine, 2006; Slater et al., 2006).

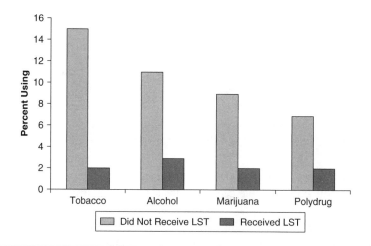

Figure 7.15 Follow-Up Results From Four Published Studies: 8th-Grade Drug Use and 12th-Grade Polydrug Use

SOURCE: Copyright Princeton Health Press. Reprinted by permission.

NOTE: An LST (life skills training) approach to drug prevention has shown dramatic decreases in adolescents' use of a variety of drugs yet has not been implemented in many communities because DARE (Drug Abuse Resistance Education) programs already exist. The LST approach is based on the work of Botvin (see Botvin & Griffin, 2005). By comparison, there is no evidence that the simplistic messages contained in the $226 million DARE program have had any impact (West & O'Neal, 2004), yet DARE is used by 80% of school systems nationwide (Kalb, 2001). Recently, the DARE curriculum underwent a revision to incorporate some of the LST principles (Kelly, 2003).

3. *A ban on cigarette advertising and a restriction on alcohol advertising in all media.* Advertising *can* be restricted, according to the U.S. Supreme Court, if there is a "compelling public health interest" (Shiffrin, 1993). Any product as harmful as tobacco should have severe restrictions placed on it (Wellman et al., 2006). An increasing number of countries are banning all tobacco advertising in all forms (Prokhorov et al., 2006). The United States as a whole remains far behind Canada, which recently legislated that more than 50% of each tobacco pack must feature a graphic representation of the hazards of smoking. The designs include photographs of cancerous lungs, damaged hearts, and stroke-clotted brains. Warning labels on American cigarette packs remain some of the weakest in the world (Newman, 2001). In alcohol advertising, tombstone ads involve showing the "purity" of the product only, not all of the qualities that the purchaser will magically gain by consuming it (see Figure 7.16). Such restrictions have already been endorsed by the FDA.

Figure 7.16

SOURCE: ©2007 Southern Comfort Company, Louisville, KY.

The Surgeon General, the AAP, and the American Medical Association would address the deceptive and alluring quality of current advertisements (AAP, 2006; Borzekowski & Strasburger, 2008). On the other hand, a total ban on alcohol advertising would be both impractical and counterproductive. Unlike cigarettes, alcohol may have some legitimate uses when consumed in moderation. Simply restricting alcohol advertising to programming with youth audiences of less than 15% would be an easily achievable and significant step (CAMY, 2007). It would result in alcohol manufacturers being able to decrease their advertising costs by 8% and teenagers' exposure to alcohol ads being reduced by 20%, but the oft-stated target audience of 21- to 34-year-olds would be unaffected (Jernigan, Ostroff, & Ross, 2005). In turn, reducing adolescents' exposure to such advertising could reduce their alcohol consumption by as much as 25% (Saffer & Dave, 2006).

4. *Higher taxes on tobacco and alcohol products.* Taxes have a direct effect on consumption of products, particularly by teenagers (CDC, 1994). Surprisingly, a recent study by the CDC suggests that the rate of gonorrhea, for example, could be decreased by nearly 10% simply by raising the beer tax by 20 cents per sixpack (CDC, 2000a, 2000b). This is because of the well-known association between drinking alcohol and unsafe sexual practices, particularly among adolescents (MacKenzie, 1993; Tapert et al., 2001). Of course, when taxes are raised and consumption goes down, revenues accruing to state and federal governments decrease, people live longer, and the costs of Social Security payments go up. Although medical costs would decrease as well, this scenario represents a very complicated financial issue of whether society can "afford" less consumption of these unhealthy products.

5. *More aggressive counteradvertising.* Counteradvertising can be effective but only if it is intensive, well planned, and coordinated and uses a variety of media

(see Figure 7.17) (Agostinelli & Grube, 2002, 2003; Flynn et al., 2007; Noar, 2006). To be truly effective, counteradvertising must approach both the occurrence rate and the attractiveness of regular advertising (Grube & Wallack, 1994). Some researchers speculate that the decrease in adolescent smoking in the mid-to-late 1970s may be attributable to a very aggressive, pre-ban counteradvertising campaign in which one public service announcement (PSA) aired for every three to five cigarette ads (J. D. Brown & Walsh-Childers, 1994; Wallack, Dorfman, Jernigan, & Themba, 1993). Currently, the density of public service announcements about alcohol has never remotely approached that of regular advertisements, nor are the production values comparable. The best-known and most sophisticated example of aggressive counteradvertising is the campaign mounted by the Partnership for a Drug-Free America. Since 1987, $3 billion has been donated to create and air 600 antidrug public service announcements (PDFA, 2000).

Figure 7.17

SOURCE: Partnership for a Drug-Free America and MADD.

In a study of nearly 1,000 public school students, ages 11 to 19, more than 80% recalled exposure to such ads, and half of the students who had tried drugs reported that the ads convinced them to decrease or stop using them (Reis, Duggan, Adger, & DeAngelis, 1992). In Kentucky, an anti-marijuana campaign specifically targeted "sensation-seeking" teenagers and resulted in a 26.7% decrease in marijuana use (Palmgreen, Donohew, Lorch, Hoyle, & Stephenson, 2001). Unfortunately, to date, not a single Partnership ad has ever aired that targets either tobacco or alcohol. Some states have used part of the tobacco settlement money to fund large and aggressive counteradvertising campaigns, with good results (see Figure 7.18) (Nelson, 2005): In Vermont, a $2 million television and radio campaign in the early 1990s cut rates of teen smoking by 35% (Flynn et al., 1994). But a 4-year media campaign to reduce alcohol use by young teenagers failed (Flynn et al., 2006). In nearby Massachusetts, a 4-year, $50 million campaign resulted in a 50% reduction in the onset of smoking by young teens (Siegel & Biener, 2000). In California, a $14.5 million state government investment in antismoking messages on billboards resulted in a decline in sales that was three times greater than anywhere else in the United States (Stein, 2005). And in Florida, a series of "Truth" ads that try to expose the tobacco industry as being manipulative and deceptive have also resulted in decreased rates of smoking among teenagers. According to a recent study, the prevalence of teen smoking declined from 25% in 1999 to 18% in 2002, and the "Truth" campaign could account for as much as 22% of that decline (Farrelly, Davis, Haviland, Messeri, & Healton, 2005). The ads are so hard-hitting that Philip Morris actually insisted that two be withdrawn. (As part of the industry's $246 billion legal settlement, the nonprofit American Legacy Foundation was established, but it is not allowed to air ads that "vilify" tobacco companies.) In one ad, two teenagers carry a lie detector into Philip Morris' New York headquarters and announce that they want to deliver it to the marketing department. In the second ad, a group of teens in a large truck pull up in front of the headquarters and begin unloading body bags. One teen shouts through a megaphone, "Do you know how many people tobacco kills every day?" (A. Bryant, 2000). The two ads can still be viewed on the American Nonsmokers' Rights Foundation's Web site (www.no-smoke.org). By contrast, ads made by Philip Morris as part of their $100 million campaign cautioning teens to "Think. Don't Smoke" are ineffectual and may be a "sham" ("Big Tobacco's Promises," 2006; Farrelly et al., 2002; Henriksen, Dauphinee, Wang, & Fortmann, 2006; Paek & Gunther, 2007; Wakefield et al., 2006).

Figure 7.18

SOURCE: Copyright © 2007 State of California.

What makes an effective counter-ad? Ads that focus on young people suffering or the deceitfulness of the tobacco industry or that elicit strong emotional reactions from teenagers are more likely to be successful (Pechmann & Reibling, 2006). Increasing interest is focusing on strong, anti-industry messages (Thrasher, Niederdeppe, Jackson, & Farrelly, 2006). Interestingly, antismoking ads may work by convincing teens that their *peers* will be influenced by the messages being aired—a unique twist on the third-person effect phenomenon (Gunther, Bolt, Borzekowski, Liebhart, & Dillard, 2006). Similar successful campaigns have also been tried in England and elsewhere (McVey & Stapleton, 2000), and teenagers in the United States, Australia, and Britain seem to respond to antismoking ads in similar ways (Wakefield, Durrant, & Terry-McElrath, 2003; Wakefield et al., 2006). On the other hand, recent cuts in many states' antismoking campaigns could result in major increases in state health care costs (Emery et al., 2005). A cheaper alternative might be Web-based smoking cessation campaigns, which have recently been shown to be effective (Klein, Havens, & Carlson, 2005).

One creative solution for an antismoking campaign would be to air antitobacco ads just before big Hollywood movies that feature a lot of smoking. There is some evidence that this could be effective (Edwards, Harris, Cook, Bedford, & Zuo, 2004), and the 15-minute period prior to the movie previews is under the control of the local theater owner, not Hollywood (Sargent, 2005).

6. *Use of MTV, BET, and shows popular with teenagers as specific media outlets for targeting older children and adolescents with prosocial health messages against smoking, drinking, and drug use.* In the late 1990s, MTV began transforming itself from a music video jukebox into what one critic calls "a programming service pandering to teens and their legions of base instincts" (Johnson, 2001). Clearly, MTV is homing in on its youth market, but the producers need to accept "the fact that with the rewards of marketing to teens come special responsibilities" (Johnson, 2001). If society is serious about trying to minimize underage drinking and decrease teen smoking, then MTV and similar channels are one of the best places to start. Rather than rely on government-produced antidrug advertising, MTV and BET could develop their own unique brand of anti-alcohol and antismoking PSAs.

7. *Increased sensitivity on the part of the entertainment industry to the health-related issues of smoking, drinking, and other drug use in television programming, music videos, and movies.* A few programs popular with teens, including the old *Beverly Hills 90210* and after-school specials, have taken the lead in this area, but soap operas, MTV and BET, and movies need to follow their example. Cigarette smoking should not be used as a shortcut to dramatize the rebelliousness of a character, nor should alcohol be used to resolve crises. *Ferris Bueller* was smoke free in the 1980s, and so was *The Devil Wears Prada* in 2006. In 2007, several national medical organizations announced a campaign to get smoking out of movies (Kluger, 2007). In Britain, old cartoons such as *Tom and Jerry, The Flintstones, The Jetsons,* and *Scooby Doo,* aired by Boomerang, a children's channel, are now being edited to eliminate smoking scenes (Associated Press, 2006). The idea that being drunk is funny needs to be seriously reexamined by the entertainment industry and could easily be contributing to the current high rates of binge drinking among teenagers (29% of high school students reported binge drinking in the most recent study) (Figure 7.19) (J. W. Miller et al., 2007). In addition, rock music lyrics should avoid glamorizing drinking or drug use (AAP, 1995). To achieve this, public health groups (e.g., American Academy of Pediatrics, American Medical Association, American Association of Family Practice, American Public Health Association) might form a coalition to convince Hollywood writers, directors, and producers that smoking in the movies has become a major public health problem.

Figure 7.19

SOURCE: ©2007 Distilled Spirits Council of the United States.

8. *Reassessment of the "designated driver" campaign.* Is it working, or do teenagers misunderstand it (Tanner, 1998)? Many public health experts question whether this campaign does not give everyone else accompanying the designated driver permission to drink excessively (Wallack, Cassady, & Grube, 1990). Despite this concern, researchers at the Harvard School of Public Health found that the "designated driver" concept appeared in 160 prime-time episodes over 4 years, and drunk driving fatalities decreased 25% (Kluger, 2007).

9. *Revision of the ratings systems for both television and movies (see Chapter 4).* The current television ratings are not specific enough regarding content (Strasburger & Donnerstein, 1999) and lack any descriptors to denote drug use. Several studies show that parents would prefer a more specific, content-based system and one universal system that would apply to movies, TV, and video games (Greenberg, Rampoldi-Hnilo, & Mastro, 2000; Walsh & Gentile, 2001). The movie ratings system, originally developed in the mid-1960s, has not been revised much since that time and tends to be inaccurate (Jenkins, Webb, Browne, & Kraus, 2005) and overly skewed toward sexual content rather than violence or depictions of drug use. A recent survey of more than 3,000 adults nationwide found that 70% support an R rating for movies that depict smoking (see Figure 7.20), and two thirds would like to see antismoking PSAs before any film that shows smoking (McMillen, Tanski, Winickoff, & Valentine, 2007). In May 2007, the MPAA announced that it would consider cigarette smoking in their ratings scheme, but how exactly this will play out is unknown at the moment (S. Smith, 2007).

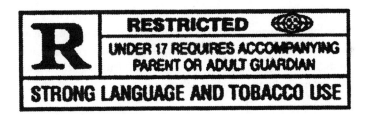

"R" FOR RESPONSIBLE. The MPAA claims the First Amendment is the reason it won't rate smoking "R." But it R-rates offensive but perfectly legal language now. Surely it doesn't consider its own age-classification system censorship? After all, the First Amendment prohibits the government from banning movies, not voluntary, responsible rating choices by the studio-controlled MPAA.

Figure 7.20

SOURCE: From http://www.smokefreemovies.org. Reprinted with permission.

NOTE: Some critics have proposed that an R rating be given by the MPAA for tobacco use in films. An alternative solution would be to have all movie sets declared smoke free because secondhand smoke is an occupational health hazard.

Exercises

1. *Product Placements.* You are the new owner of a baseball team in Milwaukee. The makers of Old Milwaukee Beer come to you, asking if they can help build you a new scoreboard out in center field. You drink Old Milwaukee Beer yourself, and you were born and raised in Milwaukee. They offer to pay for the new scoreboard ($2 million), plus give you an annual fee of $750,000. Should you accept their offer? If, instead, you were a member of the Milwaukee City Council, should you allow this to happen? Would it be legal to ban such advertising from public ballparks? Would it be ethical if you were the director of sports broadcasting for a TV station to instruct the cameramen to avoid showing advertising logos whenever possible?

2. *Drugs and the Movies #1.* You are widely considered to be the heir-apparent to Scorsese and Tarantino. A recent graduate of the USC Film School and only 24 years old, you are now being offered a plum feature film directing assignment by a major studio: a big-budget action-thriller with three major stars. But the film centers on an antihero. You, yourself, do not drink alcohol or smoke cigarettes, in part because your mother died from lung cancer and your father died from cirrhosis. How do you depict the antihero without showing him smoking or drinking and without consuming 10 extra pages of script? Will profanity alone accomplish your task?

3. *Drugs and the Movies #2.* You are a major Oscar-nominated film director in your 40s, but you have never made a film about the impact of drugs on society. You want this to be the overriding theme of your next film, which you will write, direct, and coproduce. You admired *Traffic* a great deal. You thought *Pulp Fiction* was overly violent but also made some interesting antidrug points. On the other hand, you thought that *Blow* glamorized cocaine more than it cautioned against its use (or sale), although you would still very much like to work with Johnny Depp. Is it possible to make an "issue" film that shows a lot of drug use without glamorizing that use for certain audiences, such as teenagers?

4. *Drug Advertising #1.* Over-the-counter remedies are legal, often useful, and frequently used. How should they be advertised in a way that is both fair and accurate? Try designing some sample ads.

5. *Drug Advertising #2.* How could a researcher design a study to determine if the advertising of nonprescription and prescription drugs makes teenagers more likely to use cigarettes, alcohol, or illicit drugs?

6. *Adolescents and Alcohol.* According to national studies, more than 80% of teenagers have tried alcohol by the time they graduate from high school. If you are a filmmaker interested in doing a realistic film about contemporary adolescence, how do you deal with the issue of alcohol, remain socially responsible, attract an adolescent audience, and keep your artistic soul intact?

7. *Advertising Alcohol and Cigarettes.* (a) Try to create the most outrageous print ads you can think of for advertising alcohol and cigarettes. (b) Based on what you have learned in this chapter, analyze the two cigarette ads and two alcohol ads seen in Figure 7.21. (c) Figure 7.22 shows an actual ad for a new product titled Bad Frog Beer. Does this ad target youth? If so, should restrictions be placed on where such ads can be displayed? (Note: This is based on an actual court case in New Jersey.)

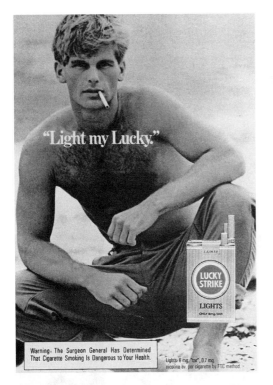

Figure 7.21

Figure 7.22

SOURCE: ©Bad Frog Brewing Co.

8. *Counteradvertising.* Think of some creative counteradvertising ads dealing with cigarettes or alcohol that might be effective in preventing children from using these drugs. Design a study that would test their impact. How would such ads have to differ if the target audience was adolescents instead? How about Hispanic adolescents versus African American or White teens? The latest ad campaign from the White House Office of National Drug Control Policy (ONDCP) is replacing the "my antidrug" tagline with a new series of ads that urge kids to "stay above the influence of drugs" (Petrecca, 2005). Are such ads likely to be effective?

9. *Tobacco Policy.* If tobacco is a legal product, how can a ban on all tobacco advertising be justified? Research the circumstances under which tobacco advertising was taken off TV by the early 1970s.

10. *Drug Control Policy #1.* In January 2000, news reports revealed that the ONDCP had been reviewing scripts from the networks' most popular shows, including *ER, Chicago Hope,* and *Beverly Hills 90210.* Under an agreement involving a little known $200 million government antidrug ad campaign, networks that accepted government PSAs had to include matching messages in their programming (Lacey, 2000). Nearly $30 million in "credit" had been given to the networks

by January 2000. The ONDCP did not ask for prior approval of scripts but did help writers and producers with information about drugs or antidrug themes.

(a) Did this agreement violate the First Amendment?

(b) Should the government be involved in screening scripts for Hollywood?

(c) Isn't there a compelling public health interest in preventing drug use among citizens, especially children and teenagers? If so, what is wrong with the government aiding writers in creating antidrug messages in mainstream programming?

(d) Does the entertainment industry have a responsibility to depict only wholesome "family values"?

11. *Drug Control Policy #2.* You are the newly appointed head of the ONDCP in the White House. Your mission is to cut the use of drugs in the United States by 20% within the next 4 years. Where do you start? With which drugs? Should you engage in discussions with the entertainment industry regarding their portrayals of alcohol and cigarettes? Should you engage in discussions with the tobacco and alcohol industries regarding their use of advertising? Does counteradvertising work? Should the government be in the business of counteradvertising? If so, which media would you target?

References

Aaron, D. J., Dearwater, S. R., Anderson, R., Olsen, T., Kriska, A. M., & LaPorte, R. E. (1995). Physical activity and the initiation of high-risk behaviors in adolescents. *Medicine and Science in Sports and Exercise, 27,* 1639–1645.

Advertising rose after tobacco suits. (2001, March 15) *Albuquerque Journal,* p. A4.

Agostinelli, G., & Grube, J. (2002). Alcohol counter-advertising and the media: A review of the recent research. *Alcohol Research & Health, 26,* 15–21.

Agostinelli, G., & Grube, J. (2003). Tobacco counter-advertising: A review of the literature and a conceptual model for understanding effects. *Journal of Health Communication, 8,* 107–127.

Aitken, P. P., Eadie, D. R., Leathar, D. S., McNeill, R. E. J., & Scott, A. C. (1988). Television advertisements for alcoholic drinks do reinforce under-age drinking. *British Journal of Addiction, 83,* 1399–1419.

Alamar, B., & Glantz, S.A. (2006). Tobacco industry profits from smoking images in the movies [Letter]. *Pediatrics, 117,* 1462.

Altman, D. G., Levine, D. W., Coeytaux, R., Slade, J., & Jaffe, R. (1996). Tobacco promotion and susceptibility to tobacco use among adolescents aged 12 through 17 years in a nationally representative sample. *American Journal of Public Health, 86,* 1590–1593.

American Academy of Pediatrics (AAP). (1995). Alcohol use and abuse: A pediatric concern [Policy statement]. *Pediatrics, 95,* 439–442.

American Academy of Pediatrics (AAP). (1999). Media literacy [Policy statement]. *Pediatrics, 104,* 341–343.

American Academy of Pediatrics (AAP). (2001). Tobacco's toll: Implications for the pediatrician. *Pediatrics, 107,* 794–798.

American Academy of Pediatrics (AAP). (2006). Children, adolescents, and advertising. *Pediatrics, 118,* 2563–2569.

American Legacy Foundation. (2006). *Trends in top box office movie tobacco use: 1996–2004.* Washington, DC: Author.

Amos, A., Jacobson, B., & White, P. (1991). Cigarette advertising and coverage of smoking and health in British women's magazines. *The Lancet, 337,* 93–96.

Angell, M. (2004). *The truth about the drug companies, how they deceive us and what to do about it.* New York: Random House.

Armstrong, J. (2002, June 7). Smoke signals. *Entertainment Weekly,* p. 9.

Ashby, S. L., & Rich, M. (2005). Video killed the radio star: The effects of music videos on adolescent health. *Adolescent Medicine Clinics, 16,* 371–393.

Associated Press. (2006, August 30). British channel bans smoking cartoons. Retrieved August 30, 2006, from http://abcnews.go.com/Entertainment/print?id=2343123

Atkin, C. K. (1990). Effects of televised alcohol messages on teenage drinking patterns. *Journal of Adolescent Health Care, 11,* 10–24.

Atkin, C. K. (1993a). Alcohol advertising and adolescents. *Adolescent Medicine: State of the Art Reviews, 4,* 527–542.

Atkin, C. K. (1993b, Winter). On regulating broadcast alcohol advertising. *Journal of Broadcasting & Electronic Media, 1993,* 107–113.

Atkin, C. K. (1995). Survey and experimental research on effects of alcohol advertising. In S. Martin (Ed.), *Mass media and the use and abuse of alcohol* (pp. 39–68). Rockville, MD: National Institute on Alcohol Abuse and Alcoholism.

Atkin, C. K., & Block, M. (1983). Effectiveness of celebrity endorsers. *Journal of Advertising Research, 23,* 57–61.

Atkin, C. K., DeJong, W., & Wallack, L. (1992). *The influence of responsible drinking TV spots and automobile commercials on young drivers.* Washington, DC: AAA Foundation for Traffic Safety.

Atkin, C. K., Hocking, J., & Block, M. (1984). Teenage drinking: Does advertising make a difference? *Journal of Communications, 28,* 71–80.

Atkin, C. K., Neuendorf, K., & McDermott, S. (1983). The role of alcohol advertising in excessive and hazardous drinking. *Journal of Drug Education, 13,* 313–325.

Austin, E. W., Chen, M. J., & Grube, J. W. (2006). How does alcohol advertising influence underage drinking? The role of desirability, identification and skepticism. *Journal of Adolescent Health, 38,* 376–384.

Austin, E. W., & Hust, S. J. T. (2005). Targeting adolescents? The content and frequency of alcoholic and nonalcoholic beverage ads in magazine and video formats November 1999–April 2000. *Journal of Health Communication, 10,* 769–785.

Austin, E. W., & Johnson, K. K. (1997). Effects of general and alcohol-specific media literacy training on children's decision making about alcohol. *Journal of Health Communication, 2,* 17–42.

Austin, E. W., & Knaus, C. (1998, August). *Predicting future risky behavior among those "too young" to drink as the result of advertising desirability.* Paper presented at the meeting of the Association for Education in Journalism & Mass Communication, Baltimore, MD.

Austin, E. W., Pinkleton, B. E., Hust, S. J. T., & Cohen, M. (2005). Evaluation of an American Legacy Foundation/Washington State Department of Health Media Literacy Study. *Health Communication, 18,* 75–95.

Bahk, C. M. (2001). Perceived realism and role attractiveness in movie portrayals of alcohol drinking. *American Journal of Health Behavior, 25,* 433–446.

Bahr, S. J., Hoffmann, J. P., & Yang, X. (2005). Parental and peer influences on the risk of adolescent drug use. *Journal of Primary Prevention, 26,* 529–551.

Belcher, H. M. E., & Shinitzky, H. E. (1998). Substance abuse in children: Prediction, protection, and prevention. *Archives of Pediatrics & Adolescent Medicine, 152,* 952–960.

Bennett, E. M., & Kemper, K. J. (1994). Is abuse during childhood a risk factor for developing substance abuse problems as an adult? *Journal of Developmental & Behavioral Pediatrics, 15,* 426–429.

Biener, L., & Siegel, M. (2000). Tobacco marketing and adolescent smoking: More support for a causal inference. *American Journal of Public Health, 90,* 407–411.

Big Tobacco's promises to reform go up in smoke [Editorial]. (2006, September 12). *USA Today,* p. 14A.

Bjork, J. M., Knutson, B., Fong, G. W., Caggiano, D. M., Bennett, S. M., & Hommer, D. W. (2004). Incentive-elicited brain activation in adolescents: Similarities and differences from young adults. *Journal of Neuroscience, 24,* 1793–1802.

Borzekowski, D. L. G., & Strasburger, V. C. (2008). Tobacco, alcohol, and drug exposure. In S. Calvert & B. J. Wilson (Eds.), *Handbook of children and the media.* Boston: Blackwell.

Botvin, G. J., & Griffin, K. W. (2005). Models of prevention: School-based programs. In J. H. Lowinson, P. Ruiz, R. B. Millman, & J. Langrod (Eds.), *Substance abuse: A comprehensive textbook* (4th ed., pp. 1211–1229). Baltimore: Lippincott Williams & Wilkins.

Breed, W., & De Foe, J. R. (1982). Effecting media change: The role of cooperative consultation on alcohol topics. *Journal of Communications, 32,* 88–99.

Breed, W., & De Foe, J. R. (1984). Drinking and smoking on television 1950–1982. *Journal of Public Health Policy, 31,* 257–270.

Bridges, A. (2006). Tobacco may kill 1 billion this century. Associated Press. Retrieved July 12, 2006, from http://www.abcnews.go.com/Health/wireStory?id=2173957

Briones, D. F., Wilcox, J. A., Mateus, B., & Boudjenah, D. (2006). Risk factors and prevention in adolescent substance abuse: A biopsychosocial approach. *Adolescent Medicine Clinics, 17,* 335–352.

Brown, J. D. (2006). Media literacy has potential to improve adolescents' health. *Journal of Adolescent Health, 39,* 459–460.

Brown, J. D., & Schulze, L. (1990). The effects of race, gender, and fandom on audience interpretations of Madonna's music videos. *Journal of Communication, 40,* 88–102.

Brown, J. D., & Walsh-Childers, K. (1994). Effects of media on personal and public health. In J. Bryant & D. Zillmann (Eds.), *Media effects: Advances in theory and research* (pp. 389–415). Hillsdale, NJ: Lawrence Erlbaum.

Brown, J. D., & Witherspoon, E. M. (1998, September). *The mass media and American adolescents' health.* Paper commissioned for Health Futures of Youth II: Pathways to Adolescent Health, U.S. Department of Health and Human Services, Annapolis, MD.

Brown, R. T. (2002). Risk factors for substance abuse in adolescents. *Pediatric Clinics of North America, 49,* 247–255.

Bryant, A. (2000, March 20). In tobacco's face. *Newsweek,* pp. 40–41.

Bryant, J. A., Cody, M. J., & Murphy, S. (2002). Online sales: Profit without question. *Tobacco Control, 11,* 226–227.

Byrd-Bredbrenner, C., & Grasso, D. (1999). Prime-time health: An analysis of health content in television commercials broadcast during programs viewed heavily by children. *International Electronic Journal of Health Education, 2,* 159–169. Retrieved February 19, 2001, from http://www.iejhe.org

Byrd-Bredbrenner, C., & Grasso, D. (2000). Health, medicine, and food messages in television commercials during 1992 and 1998. *Journal of School Health, 70,* 61–65.

Caucus for Producers, Writers, and Directors. (1983). *We've done some thinking.* Santa Monica, CA: Television Academy of Arts and Sciences.

Center for Science in the Public Interest. (1988, September 4). *Kids are as aware of booze as president, survey finds* [News release]. Washington, DC: Author.

Center on Alcohol Marketing and Youth (CAMY). (2004a). *Alcohol advertising on television 2001 to 2003: More of the same.* Washington, DC: Author.

Center on Alcohol Marketing and Youth (CAMY). (2004b, April 21). *Georgetown study finds number of alcohol ads bombarding teens rose in 2002* [Press release]. Retrieved September 30, 2005, from http://www1.georgetown.edu/explore/news/?ID=783

Center on Alcohol Marketing and Youth (CAMY). (2004c). *Youth exposure to radio advertising for alcohol—United States, summer 2003.* Washington, DC: Author.

Center on Alcohol Marketing and Youth (CAMY). (2005). *Youth overexposed: Alcohol advertising in magazines, 2001 to 2003.* Washington, DC: Author.

Center on Alcohol Marketing and Youth (CAMY). (2007). *Youth exposure to alcohol advertising on television and in national magazines, 2001 to 2006.* Washington, DC: Author.

Centers for Disease Control and Prevention (CDC). (1992a). Accessibility of cigarettes to youths aged 12–17 years—United States, 1989. *Morbidity and Mortality Weekly Report, 41,* 485–488.

Centers for Disease Control and Prevention (CDC). (1992b). Comparison of the cigarette brand preferences of adult and teenaged smokers—United States, 1989, and 10 U.S. communities, 1988 and 1990. *Morbidity and Mortality Weekly Report, 41,* 169–181.

Centers for Disease Control and Prevention (CDC). (1994). *Preventing tobacco use among young people: A report of the Surgeon General.* Atlanta, GA: U.S. Department of Health and Human Services.

Centers for Disease Control and Prevention (CDC). (2000a). Alcohol policy and sexually transmitted disease rates. *Morbidity & Mortality Weekly Reports, 49,* 346–349.

Centers for Disease Control and Prevention (CDC). (2000b). Trends in cigarette smoking among high school students—United States, 1991–1999. *Morbidity & Mortality Weekly Reports, 49,* 755–758.

Centers for Disease Control and Prevention (CDC). (2006a). Racial/ethnic differences among youths in cigarette smoking and susceptibility to start smoking—United States, 2002–2004. *Morbidity and Mortality Weekly Reports, 55,* 1275–1277.

Centers for Disease Control and Prevention (CDC). (2006b). Youth exposure to alcohol advertising on radio—United States, June–August, 2004. *Morbidity & Mortality Weekly Report, 55*(34), 937–940.

Centers for Disease Control and Prevention (CDC). (2006c). Youth risk behavior surveillance—United States, 2005. *Morbidity & Mortality Weekly Report, 55*(SS-5), 1–108.

Centers for Disease Control and Prevention (CDC). (2007). Youth exposure to alcohol advertising in magazines—United States, 2001–2005. *Morbidity & Mortality Weekly Report, 56,* 763–767.

Champion, H. L., Foley, K. L., DuRant R. H., Hensberry, R., Altman, D., & Wolfson, M. (2004). Adolescent sexual victimization, use of alcohol and other substances, and other health risk behaviors. *Journal of Adolescent Health, 35,* 321–328.

Charlesworth, A., & Glantz, S. A. (2005). Smoking in the movies increases adolescent smoking: a review. *Pediatrics, 116,* 1516–1528.

Cheers & jeers. (2002, February 23). *TV Guide.*

Chilcoat, H. D., & Anthony, J. C. (1996). Impact of parent monitoring on initiation of drug use through late childhood. *Journal of the American Academy of Child & Adolescent Psychiatry, 35,* 91–100.

Christenson, P. G., Henriksen, L., & Roberts, D. F. (2000). *Substance use in popular prime-time television.* Washington, DC: Office of National Drug Control Policy.

Collins, R. L., Ellickson, P. L., McCaffrey, D. F., & Hambarsoomians, K. (2005). Saturated in beer: Awareness of beer advertising in late childhood and adolescence. *Journal of Adolescent Health, 37,* 29–36.

Collins, R. L., Ellickson, P. L., McCaffrey, D. F., & Hambarsoomians, K. (2007). Early adolescent exposure to alcohol advertising and its relationship to underage drinking. *Journal of Adolescent Health, 40,* 527–534.

Comings, D. E. (1997). Genetic aspects of childhood behavioral disorders. *Child Psychiatry & Human Development, 27,* 139–150.

Cowley, G., & Underwood, A. (2001, February 19). Soda pop that packs a punch: Are the new alcoholic lemonades aimed at kids? *Newsweek,* p. 45.

Dalton, M. A., Adachi-Mejia, A. M., Longacre, M. R., Titus-Ernstoff, L. T., Gibson, J. J., Martin, S. K., et al. (2006). Parental rules and monitoring of children's movie viewing associated with children's risk for smoking and drinking. *Pediatrics, 118,* 1932–1942.

Dalton, M. A., Ahrens, M. B., Sargent, J. D., Mott, L. A., Beach, M. L., Tickle, J. J., et al. (2002). Correlation between use of tobacco and alcohol in adolescents and parental restrictions on movies. *Effective Clinical Practice, 1,* 1–10.

Dalton, M. A., Bernhardt, A. M., Gibson, J. J., Sargent, J. D., Beach, M. L., Adachi-Mejia, A. M., et al. (2005). Use of cigarettes and alcohol by preschoolers while role-playing as adults. *Archives of Pediatrics & Adolescent Medicine, 159,* 854–859.

Dalton, M. A., Sargent, J. D., Beach, M. L., Titus-Ernstoff, L., Gibson, J. J., Ahrens, M. B., et al. (2003). Effect of viewing smoking in movies on adolescent smoking initiation: A cohort study. *The Lancet, 362,* 281–285.

De Foe, J. R., & Breed, W. (1988). Youth and alcohol in television stories, with suggestions to the industry for alternative portrayals. *Adolescence, 23,* 533–550.

DeJong, W. (1996). When the tobacco industry controls the news: KKR, RJR Nabisco, and the Weekly Reader Corporation. *Tobacco Control, 5,* 142–148.

DiFranza, J. R., Richards, J. W., Paulman, P. M., Wolf-Gillespie, N., Fletcher, C., Jaffe, R. D., et al. (1991). RJR Nabisco's cartoon camel promotes Camel cigarettes to children. *Journal of the American Medical Association, 266,* 3149–3153.

Doyle, R. (1996, December). Deaths due to alcohol. *Scientific American, 6,* 30–31.

Dozier, D. M., Lauzen, M. M., Day, C. A., Payne, S. M., & Tafoya, M. R. (2005). Leaders and elites: Portrayals of smoking in popular films. *Tobacco Control, 14,* 7–9.

DuRant, R. H., Rome, E. S., Rich, M., Allred, E., Emans, S. J., & Woods, E. R. (1997). Tobacco and alcohol use behaviors portrayed in music videos: A content analysis. *American Journal of Public Health, 87,* 1131–1135.

Edwards, C. A., Harris, W. C., Cook, D. R., Bedford, K. F., & Zuo, Y. (2004). Out of the smoke-screen: Does an anti-smoking advertisement affect young women's perception of smoking in movies and their intention to smoke? *Tobacco Control, 13,* 277–282.

Ellickson, P. H., Collins, R. L., Hambarsoomians, K., & McCaffrey, D. F. (2005). Does alcohol advertising promote adolescent drinking? Results from a longitudinal assessment. *Addiction, 100,* 235–246.

Emery, S., Wakefield, M. A., Terry-McElrath, Y., Saffer, H., Szczypka, G., O'Malley, P. M., et al. (2005). Televised state-sponsored antitobacco advertising and youth smoking beliefs and behavior in the United States, 1999–2000. *Archives of Pediatrics & Adolescent Medicine, 159,* 639–645.

Escamilla, G., Cradock, A. L., & Kawachi, I. (2000). Women and smoking in Hollywood movies: A content analysis. *American Journal of Public Health, 90,* 412–414.

Eszterhas, J. (2002, August 9). *Hollywood's responsibility for smoking deaths.* Retrieved January 3, 2008, from http://query.nytimes.com/gst/fullpage.html?sec=health&res=9402EEDB173AF93AA3575BC0A9649C8B63

Everett, S. A., Schnuth, R. L., & Tribble, J. L. (1998). Tobacco and alcohol use in top-grossing American films. *Journal of Community Health, 23,* 317–324.

Farrelly, M. C., Davis, K. C., Haviland, M. L., Messeri, P., & Healton, C. G. (2005). Evidence of a dose-response relationship between "truth" antismoking ads and youth smoking prevalence. *American Journal of Public Health, 95,* 425–431.

Farrelly, M. C., Healton, C. G., Davis, K. C., Messeri, P., Hersey, J. C., & Haviland, M. L. (2002). Getting to the truth: Evaluating national tobacco countermarketing campaigns. *American Journal of Public Health, 92,* 901–907.

Federal Trade Commission. (1999). *Self-regulation in the alcohol industry: A review of industry efforts to avoid promoting alcohol to underage consumers.* Washington, DC: Author.

Fisher, L. B., Miles, I. W., Austin, S. B., Camargo, C. A., Jr., & Colditz, G. A. (2007). Predictors of initiation of alcohol use among US adolescents. *Archives of Pediatrics & Adolescent Medicine, 161,* 959–966.

Fischer, P. M., Schwartz, M. P., Richards, J. W., Goldstein, A. O., & Rojas, T. H. (1991). Brand logo recognition by children aged 3 to 6 years: Mickey Mouse and Old Joe the Camel. *Journal of the American Medical Association, 266,* 3145–3153.

Fleming, K., Thorson, E., & Atkin, C. K. (2004). Alcohol advertising exposure and perceptions: Links with alcohol expectancies and intentions to drink or drinking in underaged youth and young adults. *Journal of Health Communication, 9,* 3–29.

Flynn, B. S., Worden, J. K., Bunn, J. Y., Dorwaldt, A. L., Dana, G. S., & Callas, P. W. (2006). Mass media and community interventions to reduce alcohol use by early adolescents. *Journal of Studies on Alcohol, 67,* 66–74.

Flynn, B. S., Worden, J. K., Bunn, J. Y., Dorwaldt, A. L., Connolly, S. W., & Ashikaga, T. (2007). Youth audience segmentation strategies for smoking-prevention mass media campaigns based on message appeal. *Health Education & Behavior, 34,* 578–593.

Flynn, B. S., Worden, J. K., Secker-Walker, R. H., Pirie, P. L., Badger, G. J., Carpenter, J. H., et al. (1994). Mass media and school interventions for cigarette smoking prevention: Effects 2 years after completion. *American Journal of Public Health, 84,* 1148–1150.

Foster, S. E., Vaughan, R. D., Foster, W. H., & Califano, J. A., Jr. (2003). Alcohol consumption and expenditures for underage drinking and adult excessive drinking. *Journal of the American Medical Association, 289,* 989–995.

Foster, S. E., Vaughan, R. D., Foster, W. H., & Califano, J. A., Jr. (2006). Estimate of the commercial value of underage drinking and adult abusive and dependent drinking to the alcohol industry. *Archives of Pediatrics & Adolescent Medicine, 160,* 473–478.

Garfield, C. F., Chung, P. J., & Rathouz, P. J. (2003). Alcohol advertising in magazines and adolescent readership. *Journal of the American Medical Association, 289,* 2424–2429.

Gellad, Z. F., & Lyles, K. W. (2007). Direct-to-consumer advertising of pharmaceuticals. *American Journal of Medicine, 120,* 475–480.

Gerbner, G. (1990). Stories that hurt: Tobacco, alcohol, and other drugs in the mass media. In H. Resnik (Ed.), *Youth and drugs: Society's mixed messages* (OSAP Prevention Monograph No. 6, pp. 53–129). Rockville, MD: Office for Substance Abuse Prevention.

Gerbner, G. (2001). Drugs in television, movies, and music videos. In Y. R. Kamalipour & K. R. Rampal (Eds.), *Media, sex, violence, and drugs in the global village* (pp. 69–75). Lanham, MD: Rowman & Littlefield.

Gidwani, P. P., Sobol, A., DeJong, W., Perrin, J. M., & Gortmaker, S. L. (2002). Television viewing and initiation of smoking among youth. *Pediatrics, 110,* 505–508.

Goldman, L. K., & Glantz, S. A. (1998). Evaluation of antismoking advertising campaigns. *Journal of the American Medical Association, 279,* 772–777.

Goldstein, A. O., Sobel, R. A., & Newman, G. R. (1999). Tobacco and alcohol use in G-rated children's animated films. *Journal of the American Medical Association, 281,* 1131–1136.

Gordinier, J. (1998, January 30). High anxiety. *Entertainment Weekly,* p. 18.

Gostin, L. O., & Brandt, A. M. (1993). Criteria for evaluating a ban on the advertisement of cigarettes. *Journal of the American Medical Association, 269,* 904–909.

Greenberg, B. S., Brown, J. D., & Buerkel-Rothfuss, N. (1993). *Media, sex and the adolescent.* Cresskill, NJ: Hampton.

Greenberg, B. S., Rampoldi-Hnilo, L., & Mastro, D. (2000). *The alphabet soup of television program ratings.* Cresskill, NJ: Hampton.

Grube, J. W. (1993). Alcohol portrayals and alcohol advertising on television. *Alcohol Health & Research World, 17,* 61–66.

Grube, J. W. (1995). Television alcohol portrayals, alcohol advertising, and alcohol expectances among children and adolescents. In S. E. Martin (Ed.), *The effects of the mass media on use and abuse of alcohol* (pp. 105–121). Bethesda, MD: National Institute on Alcohol Abuse and Alcoholism.

Grube, J. W. (1999). *Alcohol advertising and alcohol consumption: A review of recent research* (NIAA Tenth Special Report to Congress on Alcohol and Health). Bethesda, MD: National Institute on Alcohol Abuse and Alcoholism.

Grube, J. W., & Waiters, E. (2005). Alcohol in the media: Content and effects on drinking beliefs and behaviors among youth. *Adolescent Medicine Clinics, 16,* 327–343.

Grube, J. W., & Wallack, L. (1994). Television beer advertising and drinking knowledge, beliefs, and intentions among schoolchildren. *American Journal of Public Health, 84,* 254–259.

Gruber, E. L., Thau, H. M., Hill, D. L., Fisher, D. A., & Grube, J. W. (2005). Alcohol, tobacco and illicit substances in music videos: A content analysis of prevalence and genre. *Journal of Adolescent Health, 37,* 81–83.

Gunther, A. C., Bolt, D., Borzekowski, D. L. G., Liebhart, J. L., & Dillard, J. P. (2006). Presumed influence on peer norms: How mass media indirectly affect adolescent smoking. *Journal of Communication, 56,* 52–68.

Halpern-Felsher, B. L., & Cornell, J. L. (2005). Preventing underage alcohol use: Where do we go from here? *Journal of Adolescent Health, 37,* 1–3.

Hanewinkel, R., & Sargent, J. D. (2007). Exposure to smoking in popular contemporary movies and youth smoking in Germany. *American Journal of Preventive Medicine, 32,* 466–473.

Hanewinkel, R., & Sargent, J. D. (2008). Exposure to smoking in internationally distributed American movies and youth smoking in Germany: A cross-cultural cohort study. *Pediatrics, 121,* e108–e117.

Harris, D. (2005, November 2). *Is big tobacco sweet-talking kids into smoking?* Retrieved November 3, 2005, from ABCNews.com

Hawkins, K., & Hane, A. C. (2000). Adolescents' perceptions of print cigarette advertising: A case for counteradvertising. *Journal of Health Communication, 5,* 83–96.

Healton, C., Farrelly, M. C., Weitzenkamp, D., Lindsey, D., & Haviland, M. L. (2006). Youth smoking prevention and tobacco industry revenue. *Tobacco Control, 15,* 103–106.

Healton, C. G., Watson-Stryker, E. S., Allen, J. A., Vallone, D. M., Messeri, P. A., Graham, P. R., et al. (2006). Televised movie trailers: Undermining restrictions on advertising tobacco to youth. *Archives of Pediatrics & Adolescent Medicine, 160,* 885–888.

Henriksen, L., Dauphinee, A. L., Wang, Y., & Fortmann, S. P. (2006). Industry sponsored anti-smoking ads and adolescent reactance: Test of a boomerang effect. *Tobacco Control, 15,* 13–18.

Henriksen, L., Feighery, E. C., Schleicher, N. C., & Fortmann, S. P. (2008). Receptivity to alcohol marketing predicts initiation of alcohol use. *Journal of Adolescent Health, 42,* 28–35.

Hingson, R. W., Heeren, T., Jamanka, A., & Howland, J. (2000). Age of drinking onset and unintentional injury involvement after drinking. *Journal of the American Medical Association, 284,* 1527–1533.

Hingson, R. W., Heeren, T., & Winter, M. R. (2006a). Age at drinking onset and alcohol dependence. *Archives of Pediatric and Adolescent Medicine, 160,* 739–747.

Hingson, R. W., Heeren, T., & Winter, M. R. (2006b). Age of alcohol-dependence onset: Associations with severity of dependence and seeking treatment. *Pediatrics, 118,* e755–e763.

Hollon, M. F. (2005). Direct-to-consumer advertising: A haphazard approach to health promotion. *Journal of the American Medical Association, 293,* 2030–2033.

Hurtz, S. Q., Henriksen, L., Wang, Y., Feighery, E. C., & Fortmann, S. P. (2007). The relationship between exposure to alcohol advertising in stores, owning alcohol promotional items, and adolescent alcohol use. *Alcohol and Alcoholism, 42,* 143–149.

Ile, M. L., & Knoll, L. A. (1990). Tobacco advertising and the First Amendment. *Journal of the American Medical Association, 264,* 1593–1594.

Institute of Medicine. (1994). *Growing up tobacco free: Preventing nicotine addiction in children and youths.* Washington, DC: Author.

Ivry, B. (1998, August 28). Use of drugs is rising dramatically on the big screen. *Albuquerque Journal,* p. B4.

Jackson, C., Brown, J. D., & L'Engle, K. L. (2007). R-rated movies, bedroom televisions, and initiation of smoking by White and Black adolescents. *Archives of Pediatrics & Adolescent Medicine, 161,* 260–268.

Jackson, D. Z. (1998, November 23). Big tobacco's chump change. *Liberal Opinion Week,* p. 23.

Jacobson, M. F., & Collins, R. (1985, March 10). There's too much harm to let beer, wine ads continue. *Los Angeles Times,* p. V3.

Jenkins, L., Webb, T., Browne, N., & Kraus, J. (2005). An evaluation of the Motion Picture Association of America's treatment of violence in PG-, PG-13-, and R-rated films. *Pediatrics, 115,* e512–e517.

Jernigan, D. H. (2006). Importance of reducing youth exposure to alcohol advertising. *Archives of Pediatrics & Adolescent Medicine, 160,* 100–102.

Jernigan, D. H., Ostroff, J., & Ross, C. (2005). Alcohol advertising and youth: A measured approach. *Journal of Public Health Policy, 26,* 312–325.

Jernigan, D. H., Ostroff, J., Ross, C., & O'Hara, J. A. (2004). Sex differences in adolescent exposure to alcohol advertising in magazines. *Archives of Pediatrics & Adolescent Medicine, 158,* 629–634.

Johnson, S. (2001, March 24). The new MTV: Be very afraid. *Albuquerque Journal,* p. E27.

Johnston, L. D., O'Malley, P. M., Bachman, J. G., & Schulenberg, J. E. (2008). *Monitoring the future: National results on adolescent drug use: Overview of key findings, 2007.* Bethesda, MD: National Institute on Drug Abuse.

Kalb, C. (2001, February 26). DARE checks into rehab. *Newsweek,* p. 56.

Kanda, H., Okamura, T., Turin, T. C., Hayakawa, T., Kadowaki, T., & Ueshima, H. (2006). Smoking scenes in popular Japanese serial television dramas: Descriptive analysis during the same 3-month period in two consecutive years. *Health Promotion International, 21,* 98–103.

Kelly, P. (2003, October 14). Taking a new D.A.R.E. *Charlotte Observer,* p. 1E.

Kessler, D. (2001). *A question of intent: A great American battle with a deadly industry.* New York: PublicAffairs.

Kessler, L. (1989). Women's magazines coverage of smoking related health hazards. *Journalism Quarterly, 66,* 316–323.

Kilbourne, J. (1993). Killing us softly: Gender roles in advertising. *Adolescent Medicine: State of the Art Reviews, 4,* 635–649.

King, C., III, Siegel, M., Celebucki, C., & Connolly, G. N. (1998). Adolescent exposure to cigarette advertising in magazines. *Journal of the American Medical Association, 279,* 516–520.

Klein, J. D., Havens, C. G., & Carlson, E. J. (2005). Evaluation of an adolescent smoking-cessation media campaign: GottaQuit.com. *Pediatrics, 116,* 950–956.

Kluger, J. (2007, April 12). Hollywood's smoke alarm. *Time.* Retrieved April 16, 2007, from http://www.time.com/time/magazine/article/0,9171,1609773,00.html

Kohn, P. M., & Smart, R. G. (1984). The impact of television advertising on alcohol consumption: an experiment. *Journal of Studies on Alcohol, 45,* 295–301.

Kohn, P. M., & Smart, R. G. (1987). Wine, women, suspiciousness and advertising. *Journal of Studies on Alcohol, 48,* 161–166.

Kosterman, R., Hawkins, J. D., Guo, J., Catalano, R. F., & Abbott, R. D. (2000). The dynamics of alcohol and marijuana initiation: Patterns and predictors of first use in adolescence. *American Journal of Public Health, 90,* 360–366.

Kulig, J. W., & the Committee on Substance Abuse. (2005). Tobacco, alcohol, and other drugs: The role of the pediatrician in prevention, identification, and management of substance abuse. *Pediatrics, 115,* 816–821.

Kurtz, M. E., Kurtz, J. C., Johnson, S. M., & Cooper, W. (2001). Sources of information on the health effects of environmental tobacco smoke among African-American children and adolescents. *Journal of Adolescent Health, 28,* 458–464.

Lacey, M. (2000, January 16). Federal script approval. *New York Times,* p. A1.

Laugesen, M., & Meads, C. (1991). Tobacco advertising restrictions, price, income and tobacco consumption in OECD countries, 1960–1986. *British Journal of Addiction, 86,* 1343–1354.

Leiber, L. (1996). *Commercial and character slogan recall by children aged 9 to 11 years: Budweiser frogs versus Bugs Bunny.* Berkeley, CA: Center on Alcohol Advertising.

Lipman, J. (1991, August 21). Alcohol firms put off public. *Wall Street Journal,* p. B1.

Lowery, S. A. (1980). Soap and booze in the afternoon: An analysis of the portrayal of alcohol use in daytime serials. *Journal of Studies on Alcohol, 41,* 829–838.

Mackay, J. (1999). International aspects of US Government tobacco bills. *Journal of the American Medical Association, 281,* 1849–1850.

MacKenzie, R. G. (1993). Influence of drug use on adolescent sexual activity. *Adolescent Medicine: State of the Art Reviews, 4,* 417–422.

Madden, P. A., & Grube, J. W. (1994). The frequency and nature of alcohol and tobacco advertising in televised sports, 1990 through 1992. *American Journal of Public Health, 84,* 297–299.

Martino, S. C., Collins, R. L., Ellickson, P. L., Schell, T. L., & McCaffrey, D. (2006). Socioenvironmental influences on adolescents' alcohol outcome expectancies: A prospective analysis. *Addiction, 101,* 971–983.

Mathios, A., Avery, R., Bisogni, C., & Shanahan, J. (1998). Alcohol portrayal on prime-time television: Manifest and latent messages. *Journal of Studies on Alcohol, 59,* 305–310.

McCannon, R. (2005). Adolescents and media literacy. *Adolescent Medicine Clinics, 16,* 463–480.

McIntosh, W. D., Smith, S. M., Bazzini, D. G., & Mills, P. S. (1999). Alcohol in the movies: Characteristics of drinkers and nondrinkers in films from 1940 to 1989. *Journal of Applied & Social Psychology, 29,* 1191–1199.

McKeganey, N., Forsyth, A., Barnard, M., & Hay, G. (1996). Designer drinks and drunkeness amongst a sample of Scottish school-children. *British Medical Journal, 313,* 401.

McMahon, R. L. (1994). Diagnosis, assessment and treatment of externalizing problems in children: The role of longitudinal data. *Journal of Consulting & Clinical Psychology, 62,* 901–917.

McMillen, R. C., Tanski, S., Winickoff, J., & Valentine, N. (2007). *Attitudes about smoking in the movies.* Retrieved March 8, 2007, from www.ssrc.msstate.edu/socialclimate

McVey, D., & Stapleton, J. (2000). Can anti-smoking television advertising affect smoking behaviour? Controlled trial of the Health Education Authority for England's anti-smoking TV campaign. *Tobacco Control, 9,* 273–282.

Mekemson, C., Glik, D., Titus, K., Myerson, A., Shaivitz, A., Ang, A., et al. (2004). Tobacco use in popular movies during the past decade. *Tobacco Control, 13,* 400–402.

Miller, J. W., Naimi, T. S., Brewer, R. D., & Jones, S. E. (2007). Binge drinking and associated health risk behaviors among high school students. *Pediatrics, 119,* 76–85.

Miller, P., & Plant, M. (1996). Drinking, smoking and illicit drug use among 15 and 16 year olds in the United Kingdom. *British Medical Journal, 313,* 394–397.

Moog, C. (1991). The selling of addiction to women. *Media & Values, 54/55,* 20–22.

Mothers Against Drunk Driving (MADD). (2004, May 26). *Latest CAMY study shows TV alcohol ads outnumber responsibility ads 226 to 1* [Press release]. Retrieved September 30, 2005, from http://madd.org/news/0,1056,8239,00.html

National Center on Addiction and Substance Abuse. (2004). *National Survey of American Attitudes on Substance Abuse IX: Teen dating practices and sexual activity.* New York: Author.

National Center on Addiction and Substance Abuse. (2005). *National Survey of American Attitudes on Substance Abuse X: Teens and parents.* New York: Author.

National Center on Addiction and Substance Abuse. (2006). *"You've got drugs!" Prescription drug pushers on the Internet.* New York: Author.

National Highway Traffic Safety Administration. (2005). *Traffic safety facts 2004—alcohol* (DOT HS 809–905). Washington, DC: U.S. Department of Transportation.

National Institute on Drug Abuse (NIDA). (1995). *Drug use among racial/ethnic minorities 1995* (NIH Pub. No. 95–3888). Rockville, MD: Author.

Nelson, D. E. (2005). State tobacco counteradvertising and adolescents. *Archives of Pediatrics & Adolescent Medicine, 159,* 685–687.

Newman, A. (2001, February 4). Rotten teeth and dead babies. *New York Times Magazine,* p. 16.

Noar, S. M. (2006). A 10-year retrospective of research in health mass media campaigns: Where do we go from here? *Journal of Health Communication, 11,* 21–42.

Nocera, J. (2006, June 18). If it's good for Philip Morris, can it also be good for public health? *New York Times Magazine,* pp. 46–53, 70, 76–78.

Nugent, W: (1999). *Into the West.* New York: Knopf.

Olds, R. S., Thombs, D. L., & Tomasek, J. R. (2005). Relations between normative beliefs and initiation intentions toward cigarette, alcohol and marijuana. *Journal of Adolescent Health, 37,* e75.

Omidvari, K., Lessnau, K., Kim, J., Mercante, D., Weinacker, A., & Mason, C. (2005). Smoking in contemporary American cinema. *Chest, 128,* 746–754.

Orlandi, M. A., Lieberman, L. R., & Schinke, S. P. (1989). The effects of alcohol and tobacco advertising on adolescents. In M. A. Orlandi, L. R. Lieberman, & S. P. Schinke (Eds.), *Perspectives on adolescent drug use* (pp. 77–97). Binghamton, NY: Haworth.

Paek, H.-J., & Gunther, A. C. (2007). How peer proximity moderates indirect media influence on adolescent smoking. *Communication Research, 34,* 407–432.

Palmgreen, P., Donohew, L., Lorch, E. P., Hoyle, R. H., & Stephenson, M. T. (2001). Television campaigns and adolescent marijuana use: Tests of sensation seeking targeting. *American Journal of Public Health, 91,* 292–296.

Partnership for a Drug-Free America (PDFA). (2000, November 27). *Anti-drug media campaign making inroads* [Press release]. New York: Author.

Partnership for a Drug-Free America (PDFA). (2003). *Partnership attitude tracking study, teens 2003.* New York: Author.

Partnership for a Drug-Free America (PDFA). (2006). *Generation Rx: National study confirms abuse of prescription and over-the-counter drugs.* Retrieved July 21, 2006, from http://www.drugfree.org

Pechmann, C., & Reibling, E. T. (2006). Antismoking advertisements for youth: An independent evaluation of health, counter-industry, and industry approaches. *American Journal of Public Health, 96,* 906–913.

Peto, R., Lopez, A. D., Boreham, J., Thun, M., & Heath, C., Jr. (1992). Mortality from tobacco in developed countries: Indirect estimation from national vital statistics. *The Lancet, 339,* 1268–1278.

Petrecca, L. (2005, November 1). New anti-drug spots steer away from negativity. *USA Today.* Retrieved July 21, 2006, from http://www.usatoday.com

Pierce, J. P., Choi, W. S., Gilpin, E. A., Farkas, A. J., & Berry, C. (1998). Industry promotion of cigarettes and adolescent smoking. *Journal of the American Medical Association, 279,* 511–515.

Pierce, J. P., Distefan, J. M., Jackson, C., White, M. M., & Gilpin, E. A. (2002). Does tobacco marketing undermine the influence of recommended parenting in discouraging adolescents from smoking? *American Journal of Preventive Medicine, 23,* 73–81.

Pierce, J. P., Gilpin, E., Burns, D. M., Whalen, E., Rosbrook, B., Shopland, D., et al. (1991). Does tobacco advertising target young people to start smoking? *Journal of the American Medical Association, 266,* 3154–3158.

Pierce, J. P., Lee, L., & Gilpin, E. A. (1994). Smoking initiation by adolescent girls, 1944 through 1988: An association with targeted advertising. *Journal of the American Medical Association, 271,* 608–611.

Polansky, J. R., & Glantz, S. A. (2004). *First-run smoking presentations in U.S. movies 1999–2003.* San Francisco: Center for Tobacco Control Research and Education. Retrieved September 29, 2005, from http://repositories.cdlib.org/ctcre/tcpmus/Movies2004/

Pollay, R. W., Siddarth, S., Siegel, M., Haddix, A., Merritt, R. K., Giovino, G. A., et al. (1996). The last straw! Cigarette advertising and realized market shares among youth and adults, 1979–1993. *Journal of Marketing, 50,* 1–7.

Potter, W. J. (2008). *Media literacy* (4th ed.). Thousand Oaks, CA: Sage.

Primack, B. A., Dalton, M. A., Carroll, M. V., Agarwal, A. A., & Fine, M. J. (2008). Content analysis of tobacco, alcohol, and other drugs in popular music. *Archives of Pediatrics & Adolescent Medicine, 162,* 169–175.

Primack, B. A., Gold, M. A., Land, S. R., & Fine, M. J. (2006). Association of cigarette smoking and media literacy about smoking among adolescents. *Journal of Adolescent Health, 39,* 465–472.

Prokhorov, A. V., Winickoff, J. P., Ahluwalia, J. S., Ossip-Klein, D., Tanski, S., Lando, H. A., et al. (2006). Youth tobacco use: A global perspective for child health care clinicians. *Pediatrics, 118,* 890–903.

Rauzi, R. (1998, June 9). The teen factor: Today's media-savvy youths influence what others are seeing and hearing. *Los Angeles Times,* p. F1.

Reis, E. C., Duggan, A. K., Adger, H., & DeAngelis, C. (1992). The impact of anti-drug advertising on youth substance abuse [Abstract]. *American Journal of Diseases of Children, 146,* 519.

Resnick, M. D., Bearman, P. S., Blum, R. W., Bauman, K. E., Harris, K. M., Jones, J., et al. (1997). Protecting adolescents from harm: Findings from the National Longitudinal Study on Adolescent Health. *Journal of the American Medical Association, 278,* 823–832.

Rich, M., & Bar-on, M. (2001). Child health in the information age: Media education of pediatricians. *Pediatrics, 107,* 156–162.

Richardson, J. L., Dwyer, K., McGuigan, K., Hansen, W. B., Dent, C., Johnson, C. A., et al. (1989). Substance use among eighth grade students who take care of themselves after school. *Pediatrics, 84,* 556–566.

Ringel, J. S., Collins, R. L., & Ellickson, P. L. (2006). Time trends and demographic differences in youth exposure to alcohol advertising on television. *Journal of Adolescent Health, 39,* 473–480.

Roberts, D. F., & Christenson, P. G. (2000). *"Here's looking at you, kid": Alcohol, drugs and tobacco in entertainment media.* Menlo Park, CA: Kaiser Family Foundation.

Roberts, D. F., Christenson, P. G., Henriksen, L., & Bandy, E. (2002). *Substance use in popular music videos.* Washington, DC: Office of National Drug Control Policy.

Roberts, D. F., Henriksen, L., & Christenson, P. G. (1999). *Substance use in popular movies and music.* Washington, DC: Office of National Drug Control Policy.

Robin, S. S., & Johnson, E. O. (1996). Attitude and peer cross pressure: Adolescent drug and alcohol use. *Journal of Drug Education, 26,* 69–99.

Robinson, T. N., Chen, H. L., & Killen, J. D. (1998). Television and music video exposure and risk of adolescent alcohol use. *Pediatrics, 102,* e54.

Romelsjo, A. (1987). Decline in alcohol-related problems in Sweden greatest among young people. *British Journal of Addiction, 82,* 1111–1124.

Rothenberg, G. (1988, August 31). TV industry plans fight against drunken driving. *New York Times,* p. B1.

Rubin, A. (2004, November 6). *Prescription drugs and the cost of advertising them.* Retrieved July 28, 2005, from www.therubins.com

Saffer, H. (1997). Alcohol advertising and motor vehicle fatalities. *Review of Economics and Statistics, 79,* 431–442.

Saffer, H., & Dave D. (2006). Alcohol advertising and alcohol consumption by adolescents. *Health Economics, 15,* 617–637.

Salkin, A. (2007, February 11). Noir lite: Beer's good-time humor turns black. *New York Times,* WK, p. 3.

Samuelson, R. J. (1991, August 19). The end of advertising? *Newsweek,* p. 40.

Sargent, J. D. (2005). Smoking in movies: Impact on adolescent smoking. *Adolescent Medicine Clinics, 16,* 345–370.

Sargent, J. D., Beach, M. L., Adachi-Mejia, A. M., Gibson, J. J., Titus-Ernstoff, L. T., Carusi, C. P., et al. (2005). Exposure to movie smoking: Its relation to smoking initiation among US adolescents. *Pediatrics, 116,* 1183–1191.

Sargent, J. D., Beach, M. L., Dalton, M. A., Ernstoff, L. T., Gibson, J. J., Tickle, J. J., et al. (2004). Effect of parental R-rated movie restriction on adolescent smoking initiation. *Pediatrics, 114,* 149–156.

Sargent, J. D., Dalton, M., & Beach, M. (2000). Exposure to cigarette promotions and smoking uptake in adolescents: Evidence of a dose-response relation. *Tobacco Control, 9,* 163–168.

Sargent, J. D., Dalton, M. A., Beach, M., Bernhardt, A., Pullin, D., & Stevens, M. (1997). Cigarette promotional items in public schools. *Archives of Pediatrics & Adolescent Medicine, 151,* 1189–1196.

Sargent, J. D., Dalton, M. A., Beach, M. L., Mott, L. A., Tickle, J. J., Ahrens, M. B., et al. (2002). Viewing tobacco use in movies: Does it shape attitudes that mediate adolescent smoking? *American Journal of Preventive Medicine, 22,* 137–145.

Sargent, J. D., Stoolmiller, M., Worth, K. A., Cin, S. D., Wills, T. A., Gibbons, F. X., et al. (2007). Exposure to smoking depictions in movies: Its association with established adolescent smoking. *Archives of Pediatrics & Adolescent Medicine, 161,* 849–856.

Sargent, J. D., Tanski, S. E., & Gibson, J. (2007). Exposure to movie smoking among US adolescents aged 10 to 14 years: A population estimate. *Pediatrics, 119,* e1167–e1176.

Sargent, J. D., Tickle, J. J., Beach, M. L., Ahrens, M., & Heatherton, T. (2001). Brand appearances in contemporary cinema films and contribution to global marketing of cigarettes. *The Lancet, 357,* 29–32.

Sargent, J. D., Wills, T. A., Stoolmiller, M., Gibson, J., & Gibbons, F. X. (2006). Alcohol use in motion pictures and its relation with early-onset teen drinking. *Journal of Studies on Alcohol, 67,* 54–65.

Schydlower, M., & Arredondo, R. M. (Eds.). (2006). Substance abuse among adolescents. *Adolescent Medicine Clinics, 17,* 259–504.

Schooler, C., Feighery, E., & Flora, J. (1996). Seventh graders' self-reported exposure to cigarette marketing and its relationship to their smoking behavior. *American Journal of Public Health, 86,* 1216–1221.

Selling to children. (1990, August). *Consumer Reports,* pp. 518–520.

Shields, D. L., Carol, J., Balbach, E. D., & McGee, S. (1999). Hollywood on tobacco: How the entertainment industry understands tobacco portrayal. *Tobacco Control, 8,* 378–386.

Shiffrin, S. H. (1993). Alcohol and cigarette advertising: A legal primer. *Adolescent Medicine: State of the Art Reviews, 4,* 623–634.

Siegel, M., & Biener, L. (2000). The impact of an antismoking media campaign on progression to established smoking: Results of a longitudinal youth study. *American Journal of Public Health, 90,* 380–386.

Slater, M. D., Kelly, K. J., Edwards, R. W., Thurman, P. J., Plested, B. A., Keefe, T. J., et al. (2006). Combining in-school and community-based media efforts: Reducing marijuana and alcohol uptake among younger adolescents. *Health Education Research, 21,* 157–167.

Smith, G. (1989). The effects of tobacco advertising on children. *British Journal of Addiction, 84,* 1275–1277.

Smith, S. (2007, May 12). Where's there's smoke, some see an 'R' rating. *Boston Globe,* p. A1.

Snowbeck, C. (2005, July 20). FDA tells Levitra to cool it with ad. *Business News,* Post-Gazette.com. Retrieved July 20, 2005, from http://www.post-gazette.com

Snyder, L. B., Milici, F. F., Slater, M., Sun, H., & Strizhakova, Y. (2006). Effects of alcohol advertising exposure on drinking among youth. *Archives of Pediatrics and Adolescent Medicine, 160,* 18–24.

Stacy, A. W., Zogg, J. B., Unger, J. B., & Dent, C. W. (2004). Exposure to televised alcohol ads and subsequent adolescent alcohol use. *American Journal of Health Behavior, 28,* 498–509.

Stein, L. (2005). *California's anti-tobacco media campaign.* Retrieved July 21, 2006, from http://healthresources.caremark.com/topic/casmoking

Stockwell, T. F., & Glantz, S. A. (1997). Tobacco use is increasing in popular films. *Tobacco Control, 6,* 282–284.

Strasburger, V. C. (1997). "Sex, drugs, rock 'n' roll": Are the media responsible for adolescent behavior? *Adolescent Medicine: State of the Art Reviews, 8,* 403–414.

Strasburger, V. C. (1998). Adolescents, drugs, and the media [Letter]. *Archives of Pediatrics & Adolescent Medicine, 153,* 313.

Strasburger, V. C. (2006). Risky business: What primary care practitioners need to know about the influence of the media on adolescents. *Primary Care: Clinics in Office Practice, 33,* 317–348.

Strasburger, V. C., & Donnerstein, E. (1999). Children, adolescents, and the media: Issues and solutions. *Pediatrics, 103,* 129–139.

Sutel, S. (2007, January 26). Watching the ads. *Albuquerque Journal,* p. B4.

Tanner, L. (1998, September 30). Many teens think designated drivers still can drink. *Albuquerque Journal*, p. A3.

Tapert, S. F., Aarons, G. A., Sedlar, G. R., & Brown, S. A. (2001). Adolescent substance abuse and sexual risk-taking behavior. *Journal of Adolescent Health, 28,* 181–189.

Tapert, S. F., Cheung, E. H., Brown, G. G., Frank, L. R., Paulus, M. P., Schweinsburg, A. D., et al. (2003). Neural response to alcohol stimuli in adolescents with alcohol use disorder. *Archives of General Psychiatry, 60,* 727–735.

Thompson, E. M., & Gunther, A. C. (2007). Cigarettes and cinema: Does parental restriction of R-rated movie viewing reduce adolescent smoking susceptibility? *Journal of Adolescent Health, 40,* 181.e1–181.e6.

Thompson, K. M., & Yakota, F. (2004). Violence, sex, and profanity in films: Correlation of movie ratings with content. *MedGenMed, 6,* 3. Retrieved July 13, 2006, from http://www.medscape.com/viewarticle/480900

Thompson, M. P., Sims, L., Kingree, J. B., & Windle, M. (2008). Longitudinal associations between problem alcohol use and violent victimization in a national sample of adolescents. *Journal of Adolescent Health, 42,* 21–27.

Thrasher, J. F., Niederdeppe, J. D., Jackson, C., & Farrelly, M. C. (2006). Using anti-tobacco industry messages to prevent smoking among high-risk adolescents. *Health Education Research, 21,* 325–337.

Titus-Ernstoff, L., Dalton, M. A., Adachi-Mejia, A. M., Longacre, M. R., & Beach, M. L. (2008). Longitudinal study of viewing smoking in movies and initiation of smoking by children. *Pediatrics, 121,* 15–21.

Tobacco's toll [Editorial]. (1992). *The Lancet, 339,* 1267.

Tsao, J. C. (1997). Informational and symbolic content of over-the-counter drug advertising on television. *Journal of Drug Education, 27,* 173–197.

U.S. Department of Health and Human Services. (1994). *Preventing tobacco use among young people: Report of the Surgeon General.* Washington, DC: Government Printing Office.

Vaidya, S. G., Naik, U. D., & Vaidya, J. S. (1996). Effects of sports sponsorship by tobacco companies on children's experimentation with tobacco. *British Medical Journal, 313,* 400–416.

Van den Bulck, J., & Beullens, K. (2005). Television and music video exposure and adolescent alcohol use while going out. *Alcohol and Alcoholism, 40,* 249–253.

Vickers, A. (1992). Why cigarette advertising should be banned. *British Medical Journal, 304,* 1195–1196.

Wakefield, M., Durrant, R., & Terry-McElrath, Y. (2003). Appraisal of anti-smoking advertising by youth at risk for regular smoking: A comparative study in the United States, Australia, and Britain. *Tobacco Control, 12,* 82–86.

Wakefield, M., Terry-McElrath, Y., Emery, S., Saffer, H., Chaloupka, F. J., Szczypka, G., et al. (2006). Effect of televised, tobacco company-funded smoking prevention advertising on youth smoking-related beliefs, intentions, and behavior. *American Journal of Public Health, 96,* 2154–2160.

Wallack, L., Cassady, D., & Grube, J. (1990). *TV beer commercials and children: Exposure, attention, beliefs, and expectations about drinking as an adult.* Washington, DC: AAA Foundation for Traffic Safety.

Wallack, L., Dorfman, L., Jernigan, D., & Themba, M. (1993). *Media advocacy and public health.* Newbury Park, CA: Sage.

Wallack, L., Grube, J. W., Madden, P. A., & Breed, W. (1990). Portrayals of alcohol on prime-time television. *Journal of Studies on Alcohol, 51,* 428–437.

Walsh, D., & Bennett, D. (2005). *WHY do they act that way? A survival guide to the adolescent brain for you and your teen.* New York: Free Press.

Walsh, D., & Gentile, D. A. (2001). A validity test of movie, television, and video-game ratings. *Pediatrics, 107,* 1302–1308.

Warner, K. E., Goldenhar, L. M., & McLaughlin, C. G. (1992). Cigarette advertising and magazine coverage of the hazards of smoking. *New England Journal of Medicine, 326,* 305–309.

Weinstein, H. (1998, January 15). Papers: RJR went for teens. *Los Angeles Times,* p. A1.

Wellman, R. J., Sugarman, D. B., DiFranza, J. R., & Winickoff, J. P. (2006). The extent to which tobacco marketing and tobacco use in films contribute to children's use of tobacco. *Archives of Pediatrics & Adolescent Medicine, 160,* 1285–1296.

West, J. H., Romero, R. A., & Trinidad, D. R. (2007). Adolescent receptivity to tobacco marketing by racial/ethnic groups in California. *American Journal of Preventive Medicine, 33,* 121–123.

West, S. L., & O'Neal, K. K. (2004). Project D.A.R.E. outcome effectiveness revisited. *American Journal of Public Health, 94,* 1027–1029.

When don't smoke means do [Editorial]. (2006, November 27). *The New York Times.*

While, D., Kelly, S., Huang, W., & Charlton, A. (1996). Cigarette advertising and onset of smoking in children: Questionnaire survey. *British Medical Journal, 313,* 398–399.

White, A. M., & Swartzwelder, H. S. (2004). Hippocampal function during adolescence: A unique target of ethanol effects. *Annals of the New York Academy of Sciences, 1021,* 206–220.

Wiencke, J. K., Thurston, S. W., Kelsey, K. T., Varkonyi, A., Wain, J. C., Mark, E. J., et al. (1999). Early age at smoking initiation and tobacco carcinogen DNA damage in the lung. *Journal of the National Cancer Institute, 91,* 614–619.

Winter, M. V., Donovan, R. J., & Fielder, L. J. (2007). Exposure of children and adolescents to alcohol advertising on television in Australia. *Journal of Alcohol and Drug Studies.*

Womach, J. (2003). *U.S. tobacco production, consumption, and export trends: A report to Congress.* Washington, DC: Congressional Research Service, Library of Congress.

Wyllie, A., Zhang, J. F., & Casswell, S. (1998). Positive responses to televised beer advertisements associated with drinking and problems reported by 18 to 29-year-olds. *Addiction, 93,* 749–760.

Yakota, F., & Thompson, K. M. (2001). Depiction of alcohol, tobacco, and other substances in G-rated animated films. *Pediatrics, 107,* 1369–1374.

Young, S. Y. N., Hansen, C. J., Gibson, R. L., & Ryan, M. A. K. (2006). Risky alcohol use, age at onset of drinking, and adverse childhood experiences in young men entering the US Marine Corps. *Archives of Pediatrics & Adolescent Medicine, 160,* 1207–1214.

Zollo, P. (1995). *Wise up to teens: Insights into marketing and advertising to teens.* Ithaca, NY: New Strategist.

CHAPTER 8

Rock Music and Music Videos

Sex sells in America, and as the advertising world has grown ever more risqué in pushing cars, cosmetics, jeans, and liquor to adults, pop music has been forced further past the fringes of respectability for its rebellious thrills. When Mom and Dad watch a Brut commercial in which a nude woman puts on her husband's shirt and sensuously rubs his after-shave all over herself, well, what can a young boy do? Play in a rock 'n' roll band and be a bit more outrageous than his parents want him to be. Kids' natural anti-authoritarianism is going to drive them to the frontiers of sexual fantasy in a society where most aspects of the dirty deed have been appropriated by racy advertising and titillating TV cheesecakery.

—Terence Moran, *The New Republic* (1985, p. 15)

What else can you rap about but money, sex, murder or pimping? There isn't a whole lot else going on in our world.

—Rapper Ja Rule, *Newsweek*,
October 9, 2000, quoted in
Samuels, Croal, and Gates (2000, p. 61)

When Little Richard sang, "Good golly, Miss Molly/Sure likes to bawl/When you're rockin' and rollin'/You can't hear your mama call!" in 1959, he was not singing about a young woman with hay fever and middle ear problems. Nor was the Rolling Stones' 1960s hit "Let's Spend the Night Together" about a vacationing family planning to stay at a Motel 6. In fact, the producers of *The Ed Sullivan Show* insisted that the Rolling Stones change the lyrics to "Let's spend some time together" before they could even appear on the show. And,

Figure 8.1

perhaps the most famous ambiguous rock song ever recorded—"Louie, Louie" by the Kingsmen—was played speeded up, slowed down, and backwards before the Federal Communications Commission decided in 1962 that it was "unintelligible at any speed" (Marsh, 1993; Moran, 1985). Rock lyrics and rock music have always been controversial and problematic to adult society (see Figure 8.1) (Arnett, 2002; Bennett, 2005; Christenson & Roberts, 1998; Strasburger, 2006; Strasburger & Hendren, 1995).

Of course, suggestive song lyrics did not originate with 1950s rock 'n' roll. From Cole Porter ("The Lady Is a Tramp," "Let's Do It") to 1930s country music singer Jimmy Rodgers ("If you don't wanna smell my smoke/Don't monkey with my gun") to classic blues songs such as "Hootchie Cootchie Man" and lyrics such as Mamie Smith's "You can't keep a good man down," American songwriters and singers in the 20th century have seemed obsessed with seeing how much they can get away with (Arnett, 2002). Yet, there is no question that lyrics have gotten more provocative and explicit in the past five decades (see Figure 8.2) (Fedler, Hall, & Tanzi, 1982; Robischon, Snierson, & Svetkey, 1999; Schwarzbaum, 2000; Strasburger & Hendren, 1995). Between 1980 and 1990 alone, implicit sexual references decreased 20%, whereas explicit language increased 15% (Christenson & Roberts, 1998). In other words, rock music is becoming much more graphic and much less subtle. On the other hand, to a certain extent, rock 'n' roll *must* be provocative, anti-establishment, and disliked by adults. Rock music is an important badge of identity for adolescents and an important activity for them (Hansen & Hansen, 2000).

Perhaps even more, rock 'n' roll music, music videos, and the entire MTV culture represent the latest of what could be considered an ever growing line of "media panics"—adults and society in general tend to fear each new medium as it becomes developed (Starker, 1989). Some date this tendency as far back as the banishing of storytellers from Plato's Republic. Others point to more recent historical concerns, ranging from the impact of nickelodeons, romance novels, and comic books earlier in the 1900s to the Internet, iPods, and rap music later in the century (Starker,

Figure 8.2

1989). With each new medium, similar concerns emerge: loss of control, increased sexual activity, inattention, increased aggression. Baby boom parents can remember their parents asking, "What is rock 'n' roll doing to our children?" in much the same way that parents today question what Eminem is doing to theirs (and why should he be allowed to do so?).

What is also unique in considering the effects of rock music on adolescents is that it is an aural medium and one in which exposure does not typically begin until late childhood or early adolescence. Presumably, teenagers will have developed greater critical faculties and be less susceptible to media influences at age 14 than at age 4. That is not necessarily the case with music videos, which are visual (and therefore as potent as television) and are popular with preteenagers as well (Ashby & Rich, 2005). Some critics feel that during adolescence, music becomes the preeminent medium when discussing the media's impact on young people (Christenson & Roberts, 1998). We feel that there is ample evidence that television remains important, with the addition of the powerful new element of music videos (D. F. Roberts, Foehr, & Rideout, 2005).

Rock 'n' Roll Music

The terms *rock music* and *popular music* will be used interchangeably to indicate music currently listened to by teenagers. Such music includes *hard rock, soft rock, punk rock, heavy metal, rap, grunge, salsa,* and *soul music.* Different genres of music are popular with different racial and ethnic groups, although there is considerable crossover (see Table 8.1). Teenagers' choice in music helps them to define important social and subcultural boundaries (Bennett, 2005; D. F. Roberts, Christenson, & Gentile, 2003). Although there is more crossover between music types than ever before, in the interests of simplicity, we will maintain these "older" genres rather than trying either to coin new terms or to use terms that will not last.

Table 8.1   Teenagers' Tastes in Modern Music (*N* = 2,760 Teens 14–16 Years of Age; 68% White, 32% Black) (in Percentages)

Favorite Music Type (%)	Groups Most Often Named (%)
Rock (31)	Bon Jovi (10)
	U2 (2)
Rap (18)	Run DMC (6)
	LL Cool J (4)
	Beastie Boys (4)
Soul (18)	New Edition (3)
Heavy metal (13)	Motley Crüe (2)

SOURCE: Adapted from Klein et al. (1993).

Heavy Metal Music. Of all the types of music that teenagers listen to, heavy metal and rap music have elicited the greatest concern. Once considered as only a fringe category of rock music, heavy metal is characterized by the loud, pulsating rhythm of electric bass guitar and drums and the seeming obsession with themes of violence, dominance and abuse of women, hate, the occult, satanism, and death (see Table 8.2) (Arnett, 1991). In some ways, *heavy metal* is an outdated term, but it is one that remains familiar to many (see Figure 8.3). Concerns escalated in the 1980s when themes of violence and the occult began to appear more frequently in lyrics (Gore, 1987; Hansen & Hansen, 2000). Groups such as Metallica, Black Sabbath, Megadeath, Slayer, and AC/DC gained increasing notoriety. In 1989, the group Guns N' Roses reported a 2-year income of more than $20 million ("Entertainers Have the Last Laugh," 1990). The 1980s form of heavy metal (Motley Crüe, Poison) evolved into a more stylized early 1990s form (Metallica, Tool) and finally added more rhythm from rap music (Limp Bizkit, Korn, the Deftones) to achieve mainstream status once again. Now, it could just as easily be termed *rap/metal* or *heavy rap.*

Table 8.2   Sample Death Metal Song Titles

"Staring Through the Eyes of the Dead"

"F— With a Knife"

"Stripped, Raped and Strangled"

"She Was Asking for It"

"Force Fed Broken Glass"

SOURCE: All from Cannibal Corpse CD, *The Bleeding,* copyright 1994, Maggot Music.

Figure 8.3

SOURCE: ©1983 Tribune Media Services. Reprinted with permission.

In one study, heavy metal fans were found to be higher in machismo and were more likely to overestimate the frequency of people with antisocial attitudes and behaviors and people involved in sex, drugs, and the occult in the general population. Likewise, punk rock fans were found to be less accepting of authority (Hansen & Hansen, 1991a, 2000).

One reason for the apparent upswing in popularity of heavy metal music may be that mainstream rock 'n' roll music has now been almost completely co-opted by ordinary adult society. Hardly a commercial goes by on network television that is not set to mainstream rock music. Even the Beatles have sold out to Madison Avenue (Sewell, 2007) (see Table 8.3).

Table 8.3   Madison Avenue and Mainstream Rock 'n' Roll

Artist/Group	Song	Used in Advertising for:
Bachman-Turner Overdrive	"Takin' Care of Business"	Office Depot
Beatles	"Help"	Ford Motor Company
	"Revolution"	Nike
	"Taxman"	H & R Block Tax Service
	"All You Need Is Love"	Luvs disposable diapers
Janis Joplin	"Mercedes Benz"	Mercedes Benz cars
Kool and the Gang	"Jungle Boogie"	Capitol One credit cards
Rolling Stones	"Start Me Up"	Microsoft
	"You Can't Always Get What You Want"	Coke
	"Monkey Man"	Victoria's Secret
Bob Seger	"Like a Rock"	Chevrolet trucks
Carly Simon	"Anticipation"	Heinz ketchup
Donna Summer	"Hot Stuff"	DiGiorno Pizza
Styx	"Mr. Roboto"	Volkswagen cars

The relationship between heavy metal music and violence committed by its fans has always been problematic (Cole, 2000). Consider, for example, these lyrics from "F— With a Knife" by Cannibal Corpse:

> She liked the way it felt inside her
>
> F— her, harder, harder
>
> Stick it in

Rip the skin
Carve and twist
Torn flesh
I cut her crotch
in her ass
I stick my c—
Killing as I cum
(Lyrics by Chris Barnes, ©1994 Maggot Music)

As heavy metal shades into rap, songs include provocative titles such as "S&M" by 2 Live Crew, "Stripped, Raped and Strangled" by Cannibal Corpse, and "Smack My Bitch Up" by Prodigy (Mediascope, 2000a, 2000b). Both heavy metal and rap seem to pride themselves in explicit and sexually violent themes (see Figure 8.4) (Mediascope, 2000a, 2000b). Given the enormity of the problem of domestic violence, even a slight causal connection with heavy metal or rap music would be highly significant. In the United States, domestic violence is the number one cause of injury to women (Commonwealth Fund, 1993). One woman is raped every 2 minutes in the United States, one in seven has been raped in her lifetime, and 30% of women murdered in the United States are killed by their husbands, ex-husbands, or boyfriends (U.S. Department of Justice, 1996). Because more than 40 years of research attest to the learning of aggressive attitudes and behaviors through the media (Donnerstein, Slaby, & Eron, 1994), these concerns seem warranted, although the available research may not yield many conclusions about music per se.

Figure 8.4   Cover Art for Marilyn Manson's 1998 CD, Titled *Mechanical Animals*

SOURCE: © Nothing/Interscope Records.

NOTE: The image is of "Manson as an anorexic, silver-skinned alien, with breasts and airbrushed genitals" (Browne, 1998, p. 84).

Yet a few studies are illuminating. One study of 121 high school students found that heavy metal fans had more thoughts of suicide than did nonlisteners but that the music had a positive effect on mood (Scheel & Westefeld, 1999). Another study compared data on heavy metal magazine subscriptions and suicide rates in all 50 states. The higher the subscription rate, the higher the suicide rate, and this single factor accounted for 51% of the variance in youth suicide (Stack, Gundlach, & Reeves, 1994). Other studies have found that exposure to heavy metal lyrics increases males' sex-role stereotyping and negative attitudes toward women (although classical music is more sexually arousing!) (St. Lawrence & Joyner, 1991).

All in all, the research seems divided on this issue. Heavy metal may be a "red flag," but adolescent suicide seems to be more closely related to personal and family circumstances (Scheel & Westefeld, 1999). However, the music could nurture suicidal tendencies already present in the subculture of heavy metal (Stack et al., 1994). Roe's (1995) theory of "media delinquency" is that teens gravitate toward objectionable lyrics and other media content simply because they are alienated, rather than the lyrics actually causing the alienation.

Some parents and parent groups have advocated censorship, but clearly that is not an acceptable or legal solution (American Academy of Pediatrics, 1996; Strasburger & Hendren, 1995). In October 1992, the U.S. Supreme Court let stand lower court rulings that declared that heavy metal rock star Ozzy Osbourne's free speech rights protected him against lawsuits brought by the parents of two teenagers in Georgia and South Carolina who had committed suicide after listening to his song, "Suicide Solution" (*Albuquerque Journal,* October 14, 1992). Two other suicides have been attributed to alleged subliminal messages of "do it" in Judas Priest's song, "Beyond the Realms of Death" ("Families Sue Band," 1990). In all such cases, lawsuits against the recording artists have failed.

Heavy metal fans and sympathetic critics argue that the lyrics are provocative but also symbolic and ironic (Brunner et al., 1999). Admittedly, it is sometimes difficult to understand how such lyrics as Rammstein's "Red welts on the white skin/I'm hurting you/And you are loudly whimpering/Now you are scared" should qualify for lofty literary status. Or from Insane Clown Posse: "I looked into her eyes/And she was scared as hell/I knew she was a snitch/So I cut off her tongue." *Hate rock* may be a more apt term for such music, rather than heavy metal (Brunner et al., 1999). At the same time, listeners actually misinterpret songs such as "Suicide Solution," according to one study. The song concerns the evils of alcohol, equating drinking with committing suicide, but does not advocate suicide (Hansen & Hansen, 1991b). In addition, the argument is certainly true that most Nine Inch Nails fans do not typically commit murder and mayhem. As one researcher notes,

> Not every kid that listens to a suicide song is going to commit suicide. Not every kid that listens to a song that talks about killing a policeman is going to go shoot at a policeman. On the other hand, there are kids who have done that who were inspired by a particular song. They tell me they're inspired. That the music speaks to them, to their anger and resentment, to the hate. (Cole, 2000, p. A5)

Rap/Hip-Hop Music. Rap music has its roots in Black culture and is characterized by talking to a musical beat. At times, it is angry and violent (e.g., gangsta rap—now simply referred to as rap). Many rappers, including Snoop Doggy Dogg, Tupac Shakur, and Dr. Dre have had well-publicized encounters with the law (Hirschberg, 1996; Leland, 1993), and both Shakur and Biggie Smalls were eventually gunned down in 1996 in well-publicized murders. Critics note that "hard-core rap music is now driven almost exclusively by sex, violence, and materialism" (Samuels et al., 2000, p. 62). Lyrics can be extremely sexy or just plain misogynistic and sexually violent (see Table 8.4). Many critics have expressed concern about what impact such lyrics may be having on young African American teenagers in particular (Emerson, 2002; Muñoz-Laoy, Weinstein, & Parker, 2007; Stephens & Phillips, 2003). One study of 490 rap songs found that 22% contained violent and misogynistic lyrics (Armstrong, 2001). Rap star Juvenile has a song titled "Back That Azz Up." In Eminem's "Kim," the protagonist cuts his wife's throat and locks her in the trunk of his car. Mystikal raps, "Came here with my d—k in my hand/Don't make me leave here with my foot in yo' a—" (Samuels et al., 2000). Another recent study found that the number of rebellious messages had increased from 1993 to 2003 in 260 rap/hip-hop songs analyzed (Knobloch-Westerwick, Musto, & Shaw, 2006).

As with heavy metal, rap lyrics have invited considerable controversy. Rap has drawn criticism for years (Cohen, Bell, & Ifatungji, 2005). In 1988, N. W. A. issued a song titled "F—K Tha Police." Not to be outdone, in 1992, Ice-T's song "Cop Killer" contained the lyrics, "I'm 'bout to bust some shots off/I'm 'bout to dust some cops off" and a chant of "Die, Die, Die, Pig, Die!" Ice-T's song was actually

Table 8.4   Sample Rap Music Lyrics

"I Smoke, I Drank," Lil' Boosie, 2004
I smoke (Yea!), I drank (Yea!)
I'm supposed to stop but I can't (Uh-huh)
I'm a dog (Yea!), I love hoes (Yea!)
And I'm addicted to money, cars and clothes
Do it big then
I do it big nigga [3x].

"Livin' It Up," Ja Rule, 2001
Half the ho's hate me, half them love me
The ones that hate me
Only hate me 'cause they ain't fucked me
And they say I'm lucky
Do you think I've got time
To fuck all these ho's?

SOURCE: www.lyricsandsongs.com/song/503875.html and Ja Rule, *Pain Is Love*, Def Jam Recordings, New York.

a rap/rock amalgam, with a rap performer fronting a speed metal band called Body Count. Police organizations from around the country demanded the recall of the recording (Leland, 1992). According to one version of the events, Warner Brothers Records refused to issue a recall, but Ice-T asked that the track be removed from all future productions of the album. A second version of the story is that Warner Brothers made it clear that Ice-T needed to "voluntarily" remove the song from the album. Given that Ice-T eventually left the label, the latter version is probably more accurate (Christenson & Roberts, 1998).

What separates rap from heavy metal is its newfound and widespread appeal. One study found that only 26% of rap fans were Black (Bryson, 1996). In 2000, 6 of the top 20 albums were rap records. All had parental advisory warnings (Samuels et al., 2000). The latest rap phenomenon is also the most controversial: Eminem. His album *The Marshall Mathers LP* sold 7.92 million copies in 2000 and was the number two album in America, after 'N Sync's *No Strings Attached* (Willman, 2001). The album features such lyrics as "New Kids on the Block sucked a lot of d—/Boy-girl groups make me sick/And I can't wait 'til I catch all you faggots in public/I'ma love it" (Schwarzbaum, 2000). His newfound prominence, despite some of the most racist, sexist, and homophobic lyrics ever to grace popular music, led the editors of *Entertainment Weekly* to run a cover story titled "Lewd Awakening" (Schwarzbaum, 2000). One of their lead critics notes,

> The fence that separates the decent from the indecent has so many holes in it (what is Granny Klump doing to Buddy Love in that Jacuzzi during prime time?) that homophobes, racists, misogynists, and common potty mouths step right through, unchallenged. Smirking all the way to the bank, they're indistinguishable from arts and innovators of real, if disturbing, substance. (Schwarzbaum, 2000, p. 22)

Rap music is not unidimensional, however. At times, it can also be prosocial, embracing such traditional social values as nurturing, education, and self-sufficiency (Cohen et al., 2005; Leland, 1992). One observer compares the "sexual speak" of Black women rappers to the "blues" tradition of struggling for empowerment (Perry, 1995) (although explaining what tradition violent male rappers represent may be a bit more difficult). Furthermore, no other music style has so many antidrug songs (Pareles, 1990). And rap music has contained several responsible songs about sex (e.g., "Safe Sex" by Erick Sermon, Salt 'n Pepa's "Let's Talk About Sex," and Weatoc's "I've Got AIDS") (Perry, 1995). Rap music has been used in music therapy in a residential treatment facility (Tyson, 2002, 2006). And it has formed the basis for an ambitious public health campaign. In 2003, the Kaiser Family Foundation sponsored an initiative, "Know HIV/AIDS," which has been tremendously successful in reaching African Americans by using hip-hop artists and placing public service announcements (PSAs) on Black Entertainment Television (BET). In a national survey to test the campaign's effectiveness, 94% of 18- to 24-year-olds interviewed knew about the campaign, and 83% said that they were more likely to take their sexual relationships more seriously (Kaiser Family Foundation, 2003).

How Teenagers Use Music

Consumption. As television viewing begins to wane during mid-to-late adolescence, listening to rock music increases, although television remains the predominant medium throughout childhood and adolescence (Marshall, Gorely, & Biddle, 2005; Strasburger, 2006). In one survey of 2,760 teens ages 14 to 16 in 10 different urban Southeast centers, listening to music averaged 40 hours per week (Klein et al., 1993). In a survey of California teens, consumption was lower—2½ to 3 hours per day—although the total average daily time spent with broadcast media was 7 hours (Christenson & Roberts, 1990). In a 1999 national sample of 3,155 children ages 2 to 18, older children and teens spent 6 hours and 43 minutes a day with media—56% of the total time with TV, 22% with music (Rideout, Foehr, Roberts, & Brodie, 1999). And in the most recent survey, teens and preteens exceeded 8 hours a day with a variety of different media (see Table 8.5) (D. F. Roberts et al., 2005). Of course, given that iPod and MP3 player usage seems to be skyrocketing, these surveys may severely underestimate the amount of time spent listening to music. Often, teenagers are multitasking (D. F. Roberts et al., 2005), and music is simply used as a background accompaniment to doing homework, driving, or talking with friends. There is no evidence that music media exert a displacement effect on other activities such as schoolwork (Christenson & Roberts, 1998), although there are several suggestive studies that teens who spend more time listening to music tend to do less well academically (Burke & Grinder, 1966; Larson & Kubey, 1983) and that students who study while listening to rock music exhibit lower comprehension of the material than students studying in silence or listening to classical music (LaVoie & Collins, 1975). However, with the exception of the comprehension study, these studies do not establish cause and effect, only associations. Most recently, a study of 160 eighth graders that assessed the students' homework assignments while having a soap opera, music videos, radio music, or no media on in the background found that background media did not influence homework performance (Pool, Koolstra, & van der Voort, 2003). On the other hand, when the media are in the *foreground,* the results may be different: A recent study of more than 4,500 middle school students found that weekday TV screen time did correlate with lower academic performance (Sharif & Sargent, 2006). Given the importance of popular music in adolescents' lives, the lack of research into its effects on academic performance seems rather surprising.

Why Adolescents Like Rock Music. The uses (and abuses) of popular music are myriad. Main categories include the following:

- Relaxation and mood regulation
- Social (partying, talking with friends, playing)
- Silence filling (background noise; relief from boredom)
- Expressive (identification with a particular sound, lyrics, or musical group)

Table 8.5   Preteens' and Teens' Daily Media Use

	11- to 14-Year-Olds (Hours/Minutes)	15- to 18-Year-Olds (Hours/Minutes)
Watching television	3:16	2:36
Watching DVDs and videos	0:46	0:44
Watching movies	0:23	0:21
Total TV time	4:25	3:40
Reading newspapers	0:05	0:07
Reading books & magazines	0:36	0:37
Total reading time	0:41	0:45
Listening to radio	0:57	1:15
Listening to CDs/MP3	0:45	1:09
Total music time	1:42	2:24
Total recreational computer use	0:49	1:06
Total video game time	0:52	0:33
Total media time	8:29[a]	8:29[a]

SOURCE: Adapted from Roberts, Foehr, and Rideout (2005).

a. Time estimate. Multitasking may decrease total time.

When teenagers are asked about the appeal of rock music, they respond that they are most interested in "the beat," not the lyrics. Yet even if lyric content remains unimportant to them on a conscious level, that does not exonerate provocative lyrics or dismiss the possibility that teens can learn from them. As two experts note, "We don't drive down the freeway in order to see billboards, but we see them and we acquire information from them" anyway (Christenson & Roberts, 1990, p. 28).

Music does play an important role in the socialization of adolescents. It can help them identify with a peer group (Roe, 1990) or serve as an important symbol of anti-establishment rebellion (Strasburger, 1997a, 1997b). Music with explicit lyrics about sex may give teenagers important "scripts" for future behavior, for example (Martino et al., 2006; L. M. Ward, 2003). The performers of popular music also have a significant role in adolescent development as potential role models. And with adolescent consumers estimated to have $140 billion worth of purchasing power (Span, 1999), mainstream advertising is now saturated with rock 'n' roll music. In fact, as one critic asserts, rock 'n' roll has actually become the voice of corporate America (Frith, 1992). But questions regarding the influence of popular music on adolescents need to be qualified by such information as the following: "Which music?" "Which adolescents?" "At what stage of development?" "With what coping abilities and environmental stresses?"

The anti-establishment nature of rock music and its importance in adolescent identity formation are complex issues (Arnett, 2002; D. F. Roberts et al., 2003). One view is that "young people use music to resist authority at all levels, assert their personalities, develop peer relationships and romantic entanglements, and learn about things that their parents and the schools aren't telling them" (Lull, 1987, p. 152). Another critic maintains that the critical job of music is to divide the cultural world into us versus them (Grossberg, 1992). This is similar to the "media delinquency" theory of music (Roe, 1995). Only one experimental study addresses this issue directly: a longitudinal study of Swedish youth and rock music (Roe, 1984). Early converts to rock music (age 11) were more likely to be influenced by their peers and less influenced by their parents than were older adolescents. Because this was a longitudinal study, the investigator could use statistical analyses to demonstrate that it was the early age of music involvement that predicted the increased influence of the peer group over parents.

On the other hand, most rock 'n' roll—aside from heavy metal and rap—is surprisingly mainstream in its value orientation (Christenson & Roberts, 1998). Romantic love is still the most prevalent theme, despite the fact that the lyrics have become more explicit and the treatment of love is less romantic and more physical (Fedler et al., 1982). In addition, a more modern or revisionist view of normal adolescent psychology would say that the Sturm und Drang ("storm and stress") of adolescence is inaccurate and that most teenagers never consciously identify rock music as a way of driving a rift between themselves and their parents (Christenson & Roberts, 1998).

One content issue currently being closely examined is the frequency with which drugs are mentioned in contemporary rock music. Again, the music industry's fascination with smoking, drinking, and illicit drugs is hardly new. Roger Miller sang "Chug-a-lug" back in 1964, and Jimmy Buffet made "Margaritaville" extremely popular in 1977 (Cooper, 1991). Lyrics about smoking are a bit rarer but date back at least as far as Tex Williams' 1947 song, "Smoke! Smoke! Smoke! (That Cigarette)" (D. F. Roberts & Christenson, 2000). And, of course, the 1960s and 1970s were the heyday for illicit drugs, with references sprinkled throughout popular songs by groups such as the Beatles, the Rolling Stones, and Jefferson Airplane (E. Ward, Stokes, & Tucker, 1986).

But drug-oriented lyrics seem to be making a comeback in the 1990s and early 2000s, especially in rap music (Herd, 2005). In addition, highly publicized drug use by musicians has been a continuing issue since the 1960s because of the potential role-modeling effect (Christenson & Roberts, 1998). Until recently, the only analysis of music lyrics was done in 1977, of top-rated country-and-western songs and alcohol use (cited in D. F. Roberts & Christenson, 2000). It found considerable ambivalence about drinking in country songs. Alcohol use always causes problems but also represents an important way to escape problems ("I went to hell when you left me, but heaven's just a drink away"). In 1999, D. F. Roberts, Henriksen, and Christenson examined the 1,000 most popular songs from 1996 to 1997 and found that 17% had references to alcohol (75% of all hip-hop songs) and that there was rarely a mention of the negative consequences of drinking (9%) (see Figures 8.5–8.7). Tobacco or smoking in song lyrics was even rarer: only 3% of the 1,000 songs, although rap and hip-hop songs frequently mentioned it (64%). A larger percentage of songs mentioned illicit drugs (18%). Again, there was a major difference across genres, with 63% of rap songs mentioning drugs, compared with only 1% of country songs. Marijuana was the most common illicit drug, accounting for two thirds of all the references. Unfortunately, both alcohol and illicit drug use were frequently mentioned in positive contexts, associated with sex, romance, wealth, or luxury (Figure 8.7 and Table 8.6) (D. F. Roberts et al., 1999). Other more recent studies have found that from 1979 to 1997, the number of songs with references to alcohol has increased from 8% to 44% (Herd, 2005); the majority of rap (68%) and gangsta rap (80%) songs contain at least one reference to illicit drugs (see Figure 8.8) (Brookshire, Davis, Stephens, & Bryant, 2003); and between 1996 and 2003, lyrics about ecstasy have appeared in nearly 70 rap songs (Diamond, Bermudez, & Schensul, 2006). The average teenager hears 84 drug references daily in popular songs (Primack et al., 2008).

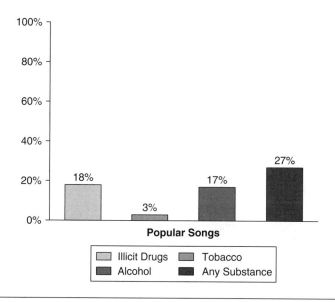

Figure 8.5   Substance Appearance in Popular Songs

SOURCE: Roberts, Henriksen, and Christenson. (1999).

NOTE: Percentages reflect the number of songs (1,000 total) from 1996 to 1997 in which substances appeared, whether or not they were used.

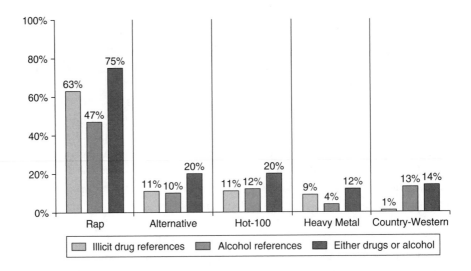

Figure 8.6 Percentage of Songs With Substance References by Genre

SOURCE: Roberts, Henriksen, and Christenson. (1999).

NOTE: Based on 212 rap songs, 211 alternative rock songs, 212 hot-100 songs, 211 heavy metal songs, and 212 country-western songs popular in 1996–1997.

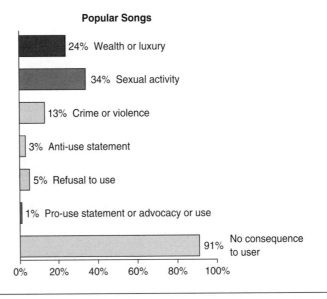

Figure 8.7 Percentage of Alcohol-Related Songs Associated With Certain Themes

SOURCE: Roberts, Henriksen, and Christenson. (1999).

NOTE: Based on 149 popular songs in 1996–1997 that portrayed alcohol use.

Table 8.6   The Context of Substance Use in Song Lyrics (in Percentages)

Context	Alcohol	Illicit Drugs
Negative effects on the community	1	8
Desire or attempt to quit	3	5
Addiction	2	7
Seeking treatment or help	1	2
Sobriety or being straight	3	3
Intoxication or being high	24	44

SOURCE: Roberts, Henriksen, and Christenson. (1999, p. 40).

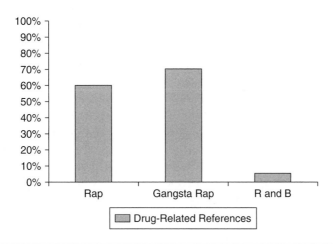

Figure 8.8   Drug-Related References in Rap and R&B Music
SOURCE: Brookshire et al. (2003).

The following case vignettes illustrate the important role rock music can play in the life of an adolescent and how one cannot talk about the effect of such music without talking about particular individuals (Strasburger & Hendren, 1995).

Case 1

Sean was a 16-year-old emotionally reserved boy whose parents ended their marriage in an acrimonious divorce 3 years earlier. Because of parental fighting, Sean saw little of his father, and when he did, they usually had a fight about the father's young girlfriend. Sean was extremely interested in the martial arts and heavy metal music. After school, he often went into his room and read martial arts books while listening to groups such as Metallica and Slayer. He reported feeling less alone and angry after this, although it upset his conservative mother. Sean has never been violent, although he continues to be emotionally reserved and socially withdrawn. Currently, he is attending law school.

Case 2

Owen was a 15-year-old boy whose parents are bright university professors, who were adolescents during the 1960s. They became concerned that Owen might be involved with drugs because he was very interested in acid rock and the music associated with the drug culture in the 1960s. Owen was bright but not doing well in school. He said he found it difficult to do as well as his successful parents. He tried recreational drugs but stopped drug use around age 17.

Currently, he is attending a liberal arts university and identifies with the "artsie liberal types" there.

Case 3

Kurt was a 17-year-old boy whose parents divorced when he was young. He had limited contact with his alcoholic father. Kurt always had trouble in school and also had some minor trouble with the law. He became involved in a satanic cult where he and others frequently listened to heavy metal rock. He was hospitalized in an adolescent psychiatric hospital after a suicide attempt. While there, he admitted to being involved in several human sacrifices as part of the satanic cult.

Adolescents' Comprehension of Song Lyrics. If there is "good" news about the increasingly explicit lyrics of popular music, it is that many teenagers do not know the lyrics or comprehend their intended meaning. For example, in one study, only 30% of teenagers knew the lyrics to their favorite songs (Desmond, 1987; Greenfield et al., 1987). Even if the students knew the lyrics, their comprehension varied greatly. For example, only 10% of fourth graders could correctly interpret a Madonna song, none could correctly interpret a Springsteen song, and nearly 50% of college students thought that "Born in the U.S.A." was a song of patriotism, not alienation (Greenfield et al., 1987). Other studies have found similarly low rates of lyric knowledge or comprehension (Denisoff & Levine, 1971; Leming, 1987; Prinsky & Rosenbaum, 1987). The impact of lyrics may be more related to their "emotional sound" than their actual meaning or content (D. F. Roberts et al., 2003). A new Rap-music Attitude and Perception (RAP) scale has been developed as a research tool (Tyson, 2006). Of course, as rap music lyrics have become more explicit, they are also more difficult to ignore (Martino et al., 2006). Consider these lyrics by rapper Lil' Kim: "When it comes to sex don't test my skills, 'cause my head game will have you head over heels. Guys wanna wife me and give me the ring. I'll do it anywhere, anyhow; I'm down for anything" (Lil' Kim, 2003).

Heavy metal music devotees seem to be the exception. In Greenfield et al.'s (1987) study, 40% knew the lyrics to their favorite songs. Other studies have found that such teenagers are more likely to listen closely to the lyrics, to feel that the music represents a very important part of their lives, and to identify with the performers (Arnett, 1991; D. F. Roberts et al., 2003; Wass et al., 1988).

Comprehension of lyrics increases with age (Strasburger & Hendren, 1995). Even so, whereas adults frequently identify such themes as sex, drugs, violence, and satanism in current rock music, teenagers tend to interpret their favorite songs as being about "love, friendship, growing up, life's struggles, having fun, cars, religion, and other topics that relate to teenage life" (Prinsky & Rosenbaum, 1987, p. 393).

Of course, these studies assess comprehension using an adult norm (Christenson & Roberts, 1998). Theoretically, the adult interpretation could be incorrect, or the incorrect interpretation could still be having significant behavioral impact. In addition, the small percentages of teens who actually do know the lyrics or comprehend their meaning might be precisely those who are at highest risk. Alternatively, those who comprehend the lyrics might then be able to reject the implied values. For example, half of a small sample of academically gifted 11- to 15-year-olds said that music had influenced how they thought about "an important topic," but 70% rejected lyrics that seemed to condone casual sex (Leming, 1987). These are teenagers who might be relatively more "media resistant." A teenager's current level of development and current level of stress could lead him or her to be more susceptible to particular lyrics—for example, a teenager contemplating her first sexual intercourse might be more interested in sexy lyrics; a depressed teen might seek out songs of alienation (Christenson & Roberts, 1998).

Behavioral Impact of Lyrics. To date, only two studies document a cause-and-effect relationship between sexy or violent lyrics and adverse behavioral effects, but they are both very recent and significant studies. The first was a unique longitudinal study of more than one thousand 12- to 14-year-olds in North Carolina, finding that exposure to sexual content in a variety of different media—including music—accelerates White teens' sexual activity and doubles their risk of early intercourse (Brown et al., 2006). Music exposure seems to be one of the most significant aspects of a teenager's Sexual Media Diet (Pardun, L'Engle, & Brown, 2005). The second study involved a national telephone survey of nearly 1,500 teenagers, ages 12 to 17, with a 1- to 3-year follow-up. Teens who listened to music with sexually degrading lyrics (see Table 8.4) were more likely to begin having sexual intercourse or advance in their noncoital activities at follow-up than teens who listened to other music (Martino et al., 2006). This was true even when 18 other determinants of early intercourse were controlled for. Degrading sexual lyrics are more likely to focus on casual sex, "boys being boys," and women only as objects for sexual pleasure (Martino et al., 2006). In addition, if teens saw the music videos of the songs, this impact would theoretically be amplified (Greenfield & Beagles-Roos, 1988). This study's finding is consistent with the notion that teens learn important cues about sexual behavior ("scripts") from media (Strasburger, 2005; L. M. Ward, 2003).

Several other studies are suggestive as well:

• Young adolescents who felt alienated from school life were more likely to prefer heavy metal music in one early study (Tanner, 1981).

• Among teenagers hospitalized for psychiatric and drug problems, 59% of those admitted for chemical dependency rated heavy metal as their musical preference. Many of them had been involved in violent activities, stealing, and sexual activity. A second group of patients with psychiatric disturbances but less substance abuse rated heavy metal as their first choice 39% of the time. By contrast, only 17% of patients with primarily a psychiatric disorder rated heavy metal as their top choice, and they were much less likely to engage in conduct-disordered behavior (King, 1988). A survey of 60 teens admitted with dysfunctional psychosocial behaviors to a different psychiatric unit found similar results (Weidinger & Demi, 1991).

- A survey of more than 2,700 teens ages 14 to 16 found that White male adolescents who reported engaging in five or more risk-taking behaviors (e.g., smoking cigarettes, drinking alcohol, cheating in school, having sex, cutting school, stealing money, smoking marijuana) were most likely to name a heavy metal group as their favorite (Klein et al., 1993). The relative risk for engaging in five or more risky behaviors was 2.1 for girls and 1.6 for boys, respectively. Discussing music preferences with teenagers—indeed, discussing preferences for a variety of different media—could serve as a useful screening tool for primary care physicians and mental health professionals (E. F. Brown & Hendee, 1989). It could also help them understand both the cultural milieu their patients live in and their patients' own unique psychology.

- In a unique set of five experiments, researchers found that songs with violent lyrics increase aggressive thoughts and feelings in college students (Anderson, Carnagey, & Eubanks, 2003). Exposure to violent lyrics may also contribute to the development of a more aggressive personality (Anderson & Huesmann, 2003) and to misogynistic attitudes and behavior (Fischer & Greitemeyer, 2006). This represents even more evidence contradicting the old shibboleth of catharsis—for example, listening to angry lyrics would make someone *less* angry by "purging" them of their feelings—at least when it comes to media effects (Anderson et al., 2003).

- In a sample of 156 community college students, ages 15 to 25, listening to rap music was associated with more alcohol and illicit drug use and aggressive behaviors, even when other variables were controlled (Chen, Miller, Grube, & Waiters, 2006).

Which comes first, adolescent alienation from mainstream society and values or a preference for heavy metal music? The answer seems to be the former (D. F. Roberts & Christenson, 2001; Roe, 1984). But, as with media violence and aggressive behavior, the relationship could be more interconnected and reciprocal than a simple, linear connection.

Effects of Parental Advisory Labels. Since 1985, recording companies have been voluntarily adding parental advisory labels to record albums, tapes, or CDs that they judge to be violent, sexually explicit, or potentially offensive (see Figure 8.9) (Gentile, Humphrey, & Walsh, 2005). Record companies are given the alternative of printing such lyrics on album jackets as consumer information for parents (Parents Music Resource Center, 1985). There has been a great deal of controversy about whether the labeling would result in the recordings becoming more or less appealing to adolescents.

As mentioned previously, several studies have found that most students cannot accurately describe the themes of their favorite songs and are usually unaware of the content or meanings of the lyrics. This raises the concern that labeling the album will call attention to the very themes that parent groups object to. Teenagers might then respond in one of two different ways: avoiding the albums (the "tainted fruit" theory) or finding them more appealing (the "forbidden fruit" theory) (Christenson, 1992a). In addition, printed lyrics on the jacket cover might make previously indecipherable lyrics easily accessible. (Imagine, for example, if the

Figure 8.9   Voluntary Label Affixed to Record Albums by Record Manufacturers

Kingsmen had published the lyrics of "Louie, Louie" on their album cover.) Only one experimental study has dealt with the issue of labeling. In it, young adolescents were asked to evaluate the same music, labeled and unlabeled (Christenson, 1992a). The adolescents liked the labeled music less well, but the impact was limited. The adolescents reacted primarily to the music per se, rather than the lyrics.

Regardless of the research, the music industry does not seem interested in complying with any restrictions on its products, including parental advisory labels. The Federal Trade Commission report of 2001 found that all five major recording companies placed advertising for explicit music on television programs and magazines with substantial under-17 audiences. In addition, ads for such music usually did not show the parental advisory label, or it was too small to be read (Federal Trade Commission, 2001).

Conclusion. Overall, the research is incomplete on rock music and music lyrics, but if any conclusion can be drawn, it is that although rock music has become increasingly more graphic in content—particularly rap and heavy metal—different teenagers respond to lyrics differently, depending on their own unique psychological, social, and developmental makeup. Very rarely, certain types of music could act as a catalyst for violence in someone who is already psychologically disposed toward it. But at the same time, there are clearly few reasons to forgive some of the increasingly sexually explicit, misogynistic, and violent lyrics in some music genres.

Music Videos and Music Television (MTV)

Things seen are mightier than things heard.

—Alfred Lord Tennyson
(cited in D. F. Roberts & Christenson, 2001)

[Pop culture] has been on a slippery slope for some time.

—Rep. Fred Upton, Chair of the House's Subcommittee
on the Internet & Telecommunications (cited in Cave, 2004)

As a visual medium, music videos are compelling. Not only do they possess the impact of ordinary television, but they could be even more powerful. Although music lyrics may be ambiguous or difficult even to hear or understand, there is no mistaking a scene of graphic violence or a couple cavorting in bed together (see Figure 8.10) (Ashby & Rich, 2005; Cave, 2004).

Music videos represent a unique form of broadcast media—impressionistic, nonlinear, and one that used to be immensely popular with teenagers and pre-teenagers but now may be fading (Christenson & Roberts, 1998; Serpick, 2002). Again as with music lyrics, although only a few cause-and-effect studies exist, music videos seem capable of influencing teenagers' ideas about adult behavior and, potentially, even modifying their own behavior. Although adolescents seem to appreciate primarily the music, the addition of sexual images seems to increase their excitement (Zillmann & Mundorf, 1987). Sexual content, in particular, seems to appeal to young people (Hansen & Hansen, 1990, 2000).

In addition, MTV and music videos have defined an entire generation (or two), the MTV generation: What's "hot," what's "cool," what's "in," and what's "out" are played out every day and night on the TV screen. Adolescent girls may use music lyrics and videos to come to grips with their own sexual identities (J. D. Brown & Steele, 1995). Many critics are concerned that the power of the music and lyrics becomes magnified when visual images are added to them, increasing the risk of deleterious effects on young people (Strasburger & Hendren, 1995). Such concern seems justified, given that numerous studies have documented television's potential

Figure 8.10

SOURCE: Copyright ©1988 King Features Syndicate. Reprinted with permission.

harmful effects in the areas of violence, smoking and drinking behavior, and risky sexual activity (Strasburger, 1993, 1997a, 1997b; Strasburger & Donnerstein, 2000).

In the 1980s and early to mid-1990s, Music Television (MTV) comprised performance videos, concept videos, and advertising. In a performance video, a musical performer or group sings the song in concert or in a studio. Roughly half of all music videos are performance videos. A concept video consists of a story that goes along with the song, which may or may not add a plot to the lyrics.

Although performance videos can occasionally be outlandish (e.g., David Lee Roth's attire or his masturbating onstage with a huge inflatable phallus in the video "Yankee Rose"), there is no evidence that such videos have demonstrable behavioral impact (American Academy of Pediatrics, 1996). Such depictions are roughly the equivalent of Elvis Presley gyrating his hips in the 1950s. Rather, it is the concept videos that have attracted much of the criticism for promoting violence, sexual promiscuity, and sexism. Concept videos are strongly male oriented, and women are frequently worshipped as upper-class sex objects (e.g., Billy Joel's "Uptown Girl" or The Thunderbirds' "Wrap It Up"). Rock stars also serve as potential role models for impressionable children and young adolescents. When Madonna sings, "Papa don't preach/I'm in trouble deep/Papa don't preach/I've been losing sleep/But I made up my mind/I'm keeping my baby" while dancing around looking like a thin Marilyn Monroe, it becomes that much more difficult to convince a pregnant 14-year-old that having a baby would be a severe hardship. One national columnist called it "a commercial for teenage pregnancy" (Goodman, 1986). George Michael's "I Want Your Sex" combines striking sexual imagery with explicit lyrics ("Sex is natural/Sex is good/Not everybody does it/But everybody should"). It also includes the disclaimer, "This song is not about casual sex. . . . Explore Monogamy. " Of course, if the equivalent ploy were tried with cigarette labeling, the disclaimer might read, "Caution: Cigarettes may be hazardous to your health, but only if you smoke them." More recently, viewers have been treated to Britney Spears in a see-through bodysuit in "Toxic," two women kissing in 182's "I Miss You," a roll in the sheets in Maroon 5's "This Love," and a lot of gyrating rear ends in Cassidy's "Hotel" and Ying Yang Twins' "Saltshaker" (Cave, 2004).

Common themes in concept videos include, in order of occurrence, the following: sex, violence or crime, visual abstraction (use of special effects to produce odd, unusual, or unexpected representations of reality), and dance (Baxter, De Riemer, Landini, Leslie, & Singletary, 1985; Escobar-Chaves et al., 2005). Music videos have also been shown to contain nihilistic images in 44% of the concept videos studied (Davis, 1985). This includes themes of destruction, death, ridicule of social institutions, and aggression against authority. As such, they seem to play on the presumably rebellious nature of the adolescent audience.

Advertising on MTV parallels prime-time advertising in that sex is used to sell every sort of product (Strasburger, 1997a, 1997b). Although birth control ads are occasionally aired on MTV (and the network was one of the first in this regard), such ads are not nearly as widespread as they should be, considering the target audience and the need. Meanwhile, alcohol advertising is particularly prevalent. Given the amount of alcohol and tobacco use in mainstream videos (DuRant, Rome, et al., 1997), some critics might say that the videos themselves have become advertisements. Speech patterns, fashion trends, and even certain behaviors have become "advertised" via music videos. Consumerism reigns supreme. Although occasional PSAs are aired, discussing drugs or AIDS or the need to vote, they are heavily outnumbered by beer commercials and ads that exploit female sexuality.

More recently, MTV has "transformed itself from a kind of video jukebox into a programming service pandering to teens," according to one critic (S. Johnson, 2001). Music videos are aired in the early morning and again on the hit afternoon show, *Total Request Live*. But much of MTV's airtime is now taken up with programming such as *Jackass*, a stunt show; *Real World*; teen soap operas like *Laguna Beach* and *The Hills*; and the annual spring break marathon (Armstrong, 2007; Serpick, 2002). Other music-oriented channels, such as VH1 and BET, have taken up the video slack. Still, MTV remains the prototype of a medium designed almost exclusively to attract teenage viewers.

Consumption. Music video has become a pervasive and influential form of consumer culture and has altered the television viewing, music listening, and record-buying habits of the young people who constitute its audience (Burnett, 1990). With 76% of American households receiving cable TV (Nielsen Media Research, 2000), most teenagers have access to MTV. Twenty percent of 16- to 24-year-olds watch MTV for at least an hour a day—the same proportion that watch NBC daily—and 60% watch every week (see Figure 8.11) (Kaiser Family Foundation, 2003). According to one study, music videos are watched more by girls than boys, more by Black teens than by Hispanic or White teens, and more by lower-income teens than by others (D. F. Roberts et al., 1999). MTV is now one of the most recognizable TV networks in the world, reaching 411 million subscribers in more than 60 countries (Ashby & Rich, 2005).

Content. From the advent of MTV, content analyses have shown that music videos are rife with sex, drugs, and violence. Surprisingly, they are relatively tame when it comes to profanity (see Tables 8.7 and 8.8) (Center for Media and Public Affairs, 1999), with perhaps the exception of recent rappers such as Dr. Dre, Lil' Kim, and Eminem.

In the mid-1980s, the first content analyses showed that the characters portrayed in concept music videos were primarily White and male (Sherman & Dominick, 1986). Episodes of violence occurred in 57% of concept videos, with White males most likely to be the aggressors. Wrestling, punching, and grabbing were the most common forms of aggression, and the outcome of the aggression was rarely shown. Sexual intimacy appeared in more than three quarters of the music videos studied and was more implied than overt. Half of all women were dressed provocatively and were often presented as upper-class sex objects. Furthermore, most of the violent videos also contained sexual imagery, usually involving violence against women.

Another 1980s content analysis found that nearly 60% of concept videos contained sexual themes, and more than half contained violence (Baxter et al., 1985). In one analysis of sexism in rock videos, more than half portrayed women in a condescending manner (Vincent, Davis, & Bronszkowski, 1987).

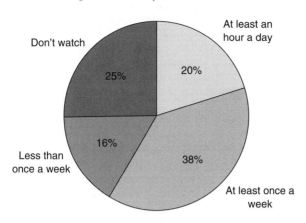

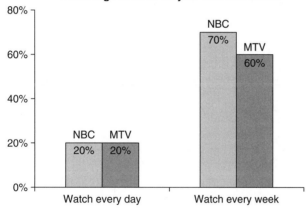

Figure 8.11   Impact of MTV

SOURCE: Rideout (2003). This information was reprinted with permission from the Henry J. Kaiser Family Foundation. The Kaiser Family Foundation, based in Menlo Park, California, is a nonprofit, private operating foundation focusing on the major health care issues facing the nation and is not associated with Kaiser Permanente or Kaiser Industries.

Women have never fared very well on MTV, and that continues into the 1990s and the present. A content analysis of 100 videos on MTV found that women are often portrayed as "bimbos" (Gow, 1993). Men are portrayed nearly twice as often as women, but women are engaged in more sexual and subservient behavior (Sommers-Flanagan, Sommers-Flanagan, & Davis, 1993). One critic feels that MTV creates a "dreamworld" in which all women are nymphomaniacs, waiting to be ravaged (Jhally, 1995). Music videos separate women into body parts (Jhally, 1995), just as mainstream advertising often does (Kilbourne, 1999). Consequently, the viewer sees erotic images, but not a whole person: sex without the humanity.

Table 8.7   Scenes With Profanity in Various Media

Medium	Hardcore Profanity	Mild Profanity	Coarse Expression
Broadcast TV	3	1,032	429
Basic cable TV	0	268	42
Premium cable TV	175	161	46
Movies	788	910	235
Music videos	0	136	24

SOURCE: Center for Media and Public Affairs (1999).

NOTE: Sample included 284 broadcast shows during the 1998–1999 season, 50 of the highest rated made-for-TV movies, 188 music videos on MTV, and the 50 top-grossing films for 1998.

Table 8.8   Dirty Dozen Music Videos

Title	Artist	Number of Scenes With Profanity
"What's So Different"	Ginuwine	7
"Wrong Way"	Sublime	3
"No Scrubs"	TLC	3
"Here We Come"	Timbaland	3
"Flagpole Sitta"	Harvey Danger	3
"Changes"	2Pac	2
"Ghetto Superstar"	Pras	2
"Gimme Some More"	Busta Rhymes	2
"Slippin'"	DMX	2
"How Do I Deal"	Jennifer Love Hewitt	2
"My Name Is"	Eminem	2
"Under the Bridge"	Red Hot Chili Peppers	2

SOURCE: Adapted from Center for Media and Public Affairs (1999).

According to one expert, "If there is such a thing as a typical music video it features one or more men performing while beautiful, scantily clad young women dance and writhe lasciviously" (Arnett, 2002, p. 256). Commercials shown on MTV tend to mimic the programming as well, so that female characters are seen less frequently than males but then are displayed as sex objects wearing skimpy clothing (Signorielli, McLeod, & Healy, 1994).

When music videos aren't overemphasizing sex and sexuality, the reality programming on MTV fills in the gap. MTV's reality shows have more than twice the sexual content of broadcast channels' reality shows (Parents Television Council, 2002) and can feature some very racy dialogue and situations (Smith, 2005, pp. 93–94):

(From *The Osbournes*): Sharon: "He started to take Viagra and we would wait and wait for it to work. I'd fall asleep, and he'd be there with a big boner. . . ." Ozzy: "I'm going, 'Sharon, I'm ready'. . . . I'm lying there like I'm camping with a tent pole. "

(From *The Real World X: Back in New York*): Lori straddles Kevin as he lies on the bed. She then puts her head in his lap, mimicking oral sex.

(From *The Real World/Road Rules: Battle of the Seasons*): Mike is nude except for a tiny piece of cloth covering his genitals.

During the past decade, rap and hip-hop music videos have moved to the forefront of parents' concerns (Kandakai, Price, Telljohann, & Wilson, 1999). Such videos contain more violence, guns, sex, alcohol, cigarettes, and profanity than any other form of music videos (e.g., rock, country, etc.) (see Table 8.9) (DuRant, Rich, et al., 1997; DuRant, Rome, et al., 1997; Jones, 1997). Of all the music video channels, BET is highest in depicting videos with sexual imagery and sex-role stereotypes, probably because it shows rap and hip-hop videos (DuRant, Rich, et al., 1997; DuRant, Rome, et al., 1997; Hansen & Hansen, 2000; Tapper, Thorson, & Black, 1994). When violence is depicted, it is usually the attractive lead singer/role model who is involved (Rich, Woods, Goodman, Emans, & DuRant, 1998). In one analysis of rap music videos, there was frequent talk about guns (59%), drug use (49%), profanity (73%), grabbing (69%), alcohol use (42%), and explicit violence (36%) (Jones, 1997). In another analysis of all forms of music videos, across several different TV channels, rap videos were by far the most violent (DuRant, Rich, et al., 1997). Even women were shown engaging in violence (41%) or carrying weapons (34%), and Black males were overrepresented in their levels of violence and weapon carrying. Interestingly, videos that had high levels of eroticism did not contain violence (the "Make Love, Not War" effect commented on by one observer) (Strasburger, 1997a). Overall, nearly one fourth of all videos across all genres contained overt violence, and a similar number depicted weapon carrying (DuRant, Rich, et al., 1997). A 2002 study of MTV, BET, and VH1 found that 15% of all the videos contained violence, usually presented realistically but sanitized (Smith & Boyson, 2002).

Table 8.9   Content of Music Video Genres (*N* = 203 Videos) (in Percentages)

Category	Rap	Hip-Hop	Rock	R&B	Country
Profanity	73	17	2	0	0
Gun talk	59	8	6	2	5
Alcohol	42	17	8	15	24
Violence	36	0	22	6	19
Female "sexdance"	25	58	8	31	8
Heavy cleavage	15	25	6	17	30
Simulated intercourse	9	42	2	13	3
Fondling	7	42	14	22	8

SOURCE: Data from Jones (1997).

What about drugs? An analysis of 518 music videos on four different channels found that MTV displayed more tobacco use (25% of all videos), with rap videos leading the way (30%) (DuRant, Rome, et al., 1997). All four channels—MTV, VH1, Country Music Television (CMT), and BET—showed videos that depicted alcohol usage between 18% and 25% of the time. Typically, the lead performer is the one shown smoking or drinking, and much of the alcohol use is combined with sexual elements. As a result, the authors conclude, even a casual observer may be exposed to substantial amounts of glamorized drug use (DuRant, Rome, et al., 1997). Most recently, a content analysis of 359 videos on MTV and BET found that two thirds of all rap videos and one third of all rock videos depicted drugs, most often alcohol, with humor more likely to be associated with drug depictions (see Table 8.10) (Gruber, Thau, Hill, Fisher, & Grube, 2005).

Table 8.10   Percentage of Music Videos Containing Substance Use, by Genre

Substance Present	Rap/Hip-Hop	Rock	R&B	Pop
Any substance	66	37	30	33
Alcohol	56	27	26	27
Tobacco	13	14	0	10
Illicit substances	31	9	4	0

SOURCE: Gruber et al. (2005).

Comprehension. Music videos are more than just television plus music. They are self-reinforcing: If viewers hear a song after having seen the video version, they immediately "flash back" to the visual imagery in the video (Greenfield & Beagles-Roos, 1988). Obviously, the impact music videos have is dependent on how the viewer interprets them. New evidence suggests that teenagers are a diverse group whose perceptions cannot always be predicted. For example, adolescent viewers of a Madonna video, "Papa Don't Preach," differed in how they interpreted the story elements based on their sex and race (see Table 8.11) (J. D. Brown & Schulze, 1990). Black viewers were almost twice as likely to say the video was a story of a father-daughter relationship, whereas White viewers were much more likely to say it was about teenage pregnancy. A similar study of Billy Ocean's video, "Get Outta My Dreams, Get Into My Car," found that children tended to be very concrete in interpreting the video (Christenson, 1992b). Some even said the video was about a man and his car, whereas slightly older 12-year-olds saw the video in more abstract terms, focusing on the relationship between the man and the woman. These studies suggest that both cognitive development and social background play a role in how teenagers and preteens process music videos.

Watching music videos—particularly MTV—may differ from watching "regular television" or listening to the radio for the average adolescent. Music videos and MTV represent an entertaining diversion, rather than a means of mood control or a social lubricant (Christenson & Roberts, 1998). If teenagers admit to learning anything from the medium, it is what's "hot," music- or fashion-wise, rather than learning social values. This is classic "social desirability bias" and "third-person effect" (i.e., the media influence everyone else but me) (Eveland, Nathanson, Detenber, & McLeod, 1999). It is also typical of normal adolescent psychology at work: After all, admitting

Table 8.11 Do Teenagers View Madonna Music Videos Differently? Reactions to "Papa Don't Preach," by Race and Sex (in Percentages)

Primary Theme	Black Males (n = 28)	Black Females (n = 40)	White Males (n = 54)	White Females (n = 64)
Teen pregnancy	21	40	56	63
Boy-girl relationship	21	5	15	5
Father-daughter relationship	43	50	22	25
Independent girl making a decision	14	5	7	8
Part of theme deals with pregnancy	43	73	85	97

SOURCE: Adapted from Brown and Schulze (1990).

that the media influence your values or ideas would mean that you are not invulnerable after all. So MTV provides pictures of attractive people and, in many ways, functions as a style show. Yet 10- to 12-year-olds recognize that some of the sexual imagery and objectionable language may not be appropriate for them (Christenson & Roberts, 1998), so some value-laden material must be getting through as well.

Behavioral Effects. As with television in general, the amount of direct imitation of music videos or MTV is rare, but when it occurs, it makes national headlines. Such was the case when MTV's infamous show *Beavis and Butthead* allegedly inspired a 5-year-old Moraine, Ohio, boy to set fire to his family's mobile home, killing his 2-year-old sister ("Mom Says MTV's *Beavis*," 1993). In response, MTV promised to delete "all references to fire" from future episodes and moved *Beavis and Butthead* to a late evening time slot (Hajari, 1993). More recently, a 15-year-old Albuquerque boy died when he jumped onto the hood of a moving car and was sucked underneath, trying to imitate a stunt he had seen on *Jackass* (Chavez, 2003). That incident occurred just after Jason Lind, a 13-year-old Connecticut boy, was hospitalized for 5 weeks with second- and third-degree burns after imitating an MTV personality who set himself on fire during *Jackass* (Associated Press, 2001). In the show, the host wore a fire-resistant suit and lay across a barbecue grill while the cast shot lighter fluid onto the flames. The teenager tried reenacting the stunt with friends in one of their backyards. Although MTV apologized to the family, it accepted no responsibility or blame for the incident (Geier, 2001).

As one observer sums it up,

> More than a week has passed since MTV's one-time-only broadcast of Madonna's new video "What It Feels Like for a Girl," but as of press time no one has stolen two cars, collided with multiple vehicles, run down street-hockey players, held up an ATM patron, torched a gas station, pointed metallic squirt guns at cops, and crashed head-on into a pole. Yet. (Geier, 2001, p. 10)

Despite the rarity of direct imitation, there is now significant evidence that even brief exposure to music videos can "prime" viewers' schemata and influence their social judgments (Hansen & Hansen, 2000). Outcomes depend on content. For example, exposing college students to videos with antisocial themes produces a greater tolerance of antisocial behavior. Showing them videos with sex-role stereotyping produces greater acceptance of such attitudes and behavior (Hansen & Hansen, 2000). Similarly, heavy exposure to MTV's reality dating programs (e.g., *Next, Date My Mom*) is associated with beliefs in a sexual double standard, that appearance is crucial in dating, and that men and women are dating "adversaries" (Zurbriggen & Morgan, 2006).

Hansen and Hansen (2000) use the following example to illustrate the impact of music videos: Imagine that Johnny, a teenager, watches a lot of MTV and BET because he enjoys rap music. Because rap videos tend to portray women as sex objects, Johnny's social schemata for women will be "primed" frequently. He enjoys the videos, so his sex object schema for women will be positively reinforced as well.

Yet if you were to ask Johnny if he thought music has influenced his attitudes or behavior, he would say no and would be giving an honest—although inaccurate—answer. In this way, music and music videos, in particular, work to prime individuals who are totally unaware of what is occurring.

Several experimental and field studies have been conducted. Music video exposure is correlated with an increase in risky behaviors among teens (Klein et al., 1993; K. R. Roberts, Dimsdale, East, & Friedman, 1998), although only two studies have been conducted longitudinally, so that a cause-and-effect relationship could be investigated (Robinson, Chen, & Killen, 1998; Wingood et al., 2003).

The largest body of research concerns violence in music videos and its possible impact on a young audience:

- Desensitization appears to occur on both a short- and long-term basis after viewing music videos (Rehman & Reilly, 1985).
- Even brief exposure to music videos with antisocial content can lead to greater acceptance of antisocial behavior (Hansen & Hansen, 1990).

In one study, 46 inner-city Black males, ages 11 to 16 years, from Wilmington were divided into three groups: The first group was exposed to a half-hour of rap videos, complete with shootings and assaults; the second viewed nonviolent rap videos; and the third saw no videos. The teens were then given two different scenarios: one to test for their propensity for violence, the other to determine their attitude about academics. Those who had viewed the violent videos were significantly more likely to condone violence in the theoretical scenario, and both groups of teens who viewed the rap videos were less likely to approve of high academic aspirations (Johnson, Jackson, & Gatto, 1995).

Several studies have documented changes in music video viewers' attitudes toward women (Johnson, Adams, Ashburn, & Reed, 1995; Peterson & Pfost, 1989; Reid & Finchilescu, 1995; L. M. Ward, Hansbrough, & Walker, 2005). A study of 144 college males found that viewing videos containing violence and eroticism resulted in less aggressive attitudes toward women than viewing videos that were violent but without eroticism (Peterson & Pfost, 1989). An alarming 40% indicated some interest in committing rape if they could be assured of not being caught and punished. A similar study found that misogynous videos facilitated sexually aggressive attitudes among college males (Barongan & Hall, 1995). Effects are not limited to males, however. In a study of African American teen females, viewing rap videos led to increased acceptance of teen dating violence (Johnson, Jackson, & Gatto, 1995). Rap videos may also foster unfavorable attitudes toward Black women among Whites, especially if the videos are sexually suggestive (Gan, Zillmann, & Mitrook, 1997; Su-Lin, Zillmann, & Mitrook, 1997).

Eliminating access to MTV in a locked treatment facility decreased significantly the number of violent acts among the adolescent and young adult inmates (Waite, Hillbrand, & Foster, 1992).

Unfortunately, fewer researchers have examined the issue of sex and sexuality in music videos. Two experiments have found that R-rated sexual images increase viewers' approval of music videos, whereas the combination of sex and violence decreases their approval (Hansen & Hansen, 2000; Zillmann & Mundorf, 1987). Cross-sectional studies of teen females seem to indicate that exposure correlates with unhealthy body image, greater sexual permissiveness, and attitudes more accepting of sexual harassment (Borzekowski, Robinson, & Killen, 2000; J. D. Brown & Newcomer, 1991; Strouse & Buerkel-Rothfuss, 1987; Strouse, Buerkel-Rothfuss, & Long, 1995; Tiggeman & Pickering, 1996). For example:

- A study of nearly 1,000 ninth-grade girls in California found that hours spent watching videos was significantly related to the girls' perceived importance of their appearance and their weight concerns (Borzekowski et al., 2000).

- In another study of 214 teenagers, ages 13 to 18 years, which surveyed the teens and their families about media use, male virginity was unrelated to viewing R- or X-rated movies, music choices, or music video exposure. However, there was a strong relationship between music video exposure and premarital permissiveness for females, which was even stronger if their home environment was unhappy (Strouse et al., 1995).

- In a different study, 7th and 10th graders who were exposed to only 1 hour of selected music videos were more likely to approve of premarital sex than were adolescents in a control group (Greeson & Williams, 1986). In addition, the 10th graders exposed to the videos showed less disapproval of violence.

- A recent study of 244 high school students found that those who viewed more music videos and had greater identification with popular figures in the media were more likely to be sexually experienced (L. M. Ward & Friedman, 2006).

- Only two longitudinal studies exist. A report of 522 African American females and their exposure to music videos found an association between heavy viewing of rap videos (up to 20 hours per week or more) and increased likelihood of high-risk behaviors a year later. Specifically, teens with greater exposure to rap videos were 3 times more likely to have hit a teacher, 2.5 times more likely to have been arrested, twice as likely to have had multiple sexual partners, and more than 1.5 times more likely to have acquired a sexually transmitted disease or used drugs or alcohol during the following year (Peterson, Wingood, DiClemente, Harrington, & Davies, 2007; Wingood et al., 2003). This study seems likely to have identified rap music as a significant marker for risky behavior in African American females—similar to the way that heavy metal has been identified in White males—rather than establishing cause-and-effect. But the second study established more of a causal connection, in this case between music videos and alcohol use. Among more than 1,500 ninth graders, the odds ratio for early alcohol use among heavy music video viewers was 1.31, exceeding network television as an influence on early adolescent drinking (Robinson et al., 1998).

Obviously, this is not a comprehensive body of research. Far more research is needed. But these studies have added to the vast body of research done on media violence in revealing important effects, even with limited amounts of exposure, of rock music and music videos.

Conclusion

Despite the fact that rock 'n' roll is practically middle-aged, and MTV just turned 28 in 2008, research on popular music and music videos is in its infancy. There has been surprisingly little research about either, despite massive public concern about violent or sexually suggestive lyrics and videos. In addition, little attention has been paid to how these immensely popular media might be harnessed to provide prosocial or health-related messages. Of course, the question would still remain, Whose prosocial or health-related messages should be dramatized? To date, only a few cause-and-effect studies exist that link either music or videos with violent or sexually promiscuous behavior, and only one links viewing music videos with an increased risk of early alcohol use during adolescence. Clearly, for a small minority of teenagers, certain music may serve as a behavioral marker for psychological distress. The most important questions to ask before drawing any conclusions about the effects of rock music or music videos on teenagers are, "Which music?" and "Which adolescents?"

Exercises

1. Go around the room and ask everyone to sing (or say) the lyrics to their favorite song. Do the results concur with the research (only 30% of you should be successful)? Discuss Bruce Springsteen's "Born in the U.S.A." What is it about? How much of the lyrics can you remember? Then read the study by Greenfield et al. (1987).

2. Why should some children and adolescents be more susceptible to the influence of rock music lyrics or music videos than others? What factors might determine vulnerability?

3. Consider the lyrics of Lil' Kim, Dr. Dre, or Eminem (or the much older lyrics of 2 Live Crew). Is there a line that has been crossed in popular music? Are there some lyrics that should—for reasons of public safety, for example—never be tolerated? Racist lyrics? Anti-Semitic lyrics? Can objectionable lyrics be made less objectionable by the artist saying that he or she is merely trying to be "ironic"?

4. You are the newest executive producer at MTV, having just been hired away from a very successful gig at *Rolling Stone* magazine. You have been hired to replace the person who produced the infamous Super Bowl halftime show for MTV that featured Janet Jackson's "wardrobe malfunction" (see Figure 6.21). You want to "make your mark" with new, insightful, controversial, and preferably very highly rated programming on the station. You are asked to devise a new half-hour show that will air during prime time. What ideas do you have? Does it make any difference that you are 23 years old and still have a 15-year-old sister back home who adores you and watches 3 hours of MTV a day?

5. Design an anti-drug PSA specifically for an MTV audience. Design a public health campaign specifically for an MTV audience.

6. You are a producer for the Big Label record company. You discover a raw new talent in Anthony, New Mexico, who has a song about killing cats because they are evil and spread disease. (You may laugh, but this is an issue that is considerably more complicated than it appears on the surface. You see, your singer lives in southeast New Mexico, where cats sometimes spread the plague. So he has something of a point, although the number of cases is limited to a handful per year, and they are easily treatable if diagnosed in time. On the other hand, hantavirus, which is spread by deer mice that could be hunted and killed off by cats, is endemic in northwest New Mexico and is much more common and far more likely to be fatal. However, your singer doesn't appreciate cats' ability to limit the rodent population.) At any rate, the song has a good beat, so you don't worry too much about the lyrics. It hits the Billboard Top 100 in early October and by the end of October, the Humane Society of America reports that thousands of cats have been killed or tortured. The Ancient Egyptian Anti-Defamation League complains that cats should be considered sacred, not evil. Both sue you, the singer, and your company. What is your defense?

7. You are a baby boom parent, a child of the 1960s. You were tear-gassed in college while marching against the war in Vietnam. You may or may not have experimented in college with illegal drugs, depending on who is doing the asking. You are now married (for the second time) and have a 13-year-old son who thinks that Eminem is "cool" and who wants to buy his latest CD. Do you let him? What do you tell him?

8. Increasingly, rock music has become mainstream music. Music by the Beatles, the Rolling Stones, James Brown, and many others has been put into the service of advertisers (Figure 8.12). Is this a good thing? Imagine advertising in 2080. What "mainstream" music will be used then?

Figure 8.12

SOURCE: Wasserman ©*Boston Globe.*

References

American Academy of Pediatrics. (1996). Rock music and music lyrics [Policy statement]. *Pediatrics, 98,* 1219–1221.

Anderson, C. A., Carnagey, N. L., & Eubanks, J. (2003). Exposure to violent media: The effects of songs with violent lyrics on aggressive thoughts and feelings. *Journal of Personality and Social Psychology, 84,* 960–971.

Anderson, C. A., & Huesmann, L. R. (2003). Human aggression: A social-cognitive view. In M. A. Hogg & J. Cooper (Eds.), *Handbook of social psychology* (pp. 296–323). Thousand Oaks, CA: Sage.

Armstrong, E. G. (2001). Gangsta misogyny: A content analysis of the portrayals of violence against women in rap music, 1987–1993. *Journal of Criminal Justice and Popular Culture, 8,* 96–126.

Armstrong, J. (2007, August 17). The hills are alive. *Entertainment Weekly,* pp. 36–38.

Arnett, J. (1991). Adolescents and heavy metal music: From the mouths of metalheads. *Youth & Society, 23,* 76–98.

Arnett, J. J. (2002). The sounds of sex: Sex in teens' music and music videos. In J. D. Brown, J. R. Steele, & K. Walsh-Childers (Eds.), *Sexual teens, sexual media* (pp. 253–264). Mahwah, NJ: Lawrence Erlbaum.

Ashby, S. L., & Rich, M. (2005). Video killed the radio star: The effects of music videos on adolescent health. *Adolescent Medicine Clinics, 16,* 371–393.

Associated Press. (2001, January 29). Jackass imitation stunt: Boy recovering after imitating MTV show stunt. *Albuquerque Journal,* p. B1.

Barongan, C., & Hall, G. C. N. (1995). The influence of misogynous rap music on sexual aggression against women. *Psychology of Women Quarterly, 19,* 195–207.

Baxter, B. L., De Riemer, C., Landini, A., Leslie, L., & Singletary, M. W. (1985). A content analysis of music videos. *Journal of Broadcasting & Electronic Media, 29,* 333–340.

Bennett, A. (2005). Editorial: Popular music and leisure. *Leisure Studies, 24,* 333–342.

Borzekowski, D. L. G., Robinson, T., & Killen, J. D. (2000). Does the camera add 10 pounds? Media use, perceived importance of appearance, and weight concerns among teenage girls. *Journal of Adolescent Health, 26,* 36–41.

Brookshire, T., Davis, C., Stephens, E., & Bryant, S. (2003). Substance use references in the lyrics of favorite songs of African-American adolescents. *Journal of Young Investigators, 8*(1). Retrieved July 25, 2006, from www.jyi.org

Brown, E. F., & Hendee, W. R. (1989). Adolescents and their music: Insights into the health of adolescents. *Journal of the American Medical Association, 262,* 1659–1663.

Brown, J. D., L'Engle, K. L., Pardun, C. J., Guo, G., Kenneavy, K., & Jackson, C. (2006). Exposure to sexual content in music, movies, television and magazines predicts Black and White adolescents' sexual behavior. *Pediatrics, 117,* e280–e289.

Brown, J. D., & Newcomer, S. F. (1991). Television viewing and adolescents' sexual behavior. *Journal of Homosexuality, 21,* 77–91.

Brown, J. D., & Schulze, L. (1990). The effects of race, gender, and fandom on audience interpretations of Madonna's music videos. *Journal of Communication, 40,* 88–102.

Brown, J. D., & Steele, J. R. (1995). *Sex and the mass media.* Menlo Park, CA: Kaiser Family Foundation.

Browne, D. (1998, September 18). Devil'd ham. *Entertainment Weekly,* pp. 84–85.

Brunner, R., Essex, A., Gordinier, J., Jacobs, A. J., Karger, D., Robischon, N., et al. (1999, June 11). A special report on violence and entertainment, part II. *Entertainment Weekly,* pp. 36–39.

Bryson, B. (1996). "Anything but heavy metal": Symbolic exclusion and musical dislikes. *American Sociological Review, 61,* 884–899.

Burke, R., & Grinder, R. (1966). Personality-oriented themes and listening patterns in teenage music and their relation to certain academic and peer variables. *School Review, 74,* 196–211.

Burnett, R. (1990). From a whisper to a scream: Music video and cultural form. In K. Roe & U. Carlsson (Eds.), *Popular music research* (pp. 21–27). Goteborg, Sweden: Nordicom-Sweden.

Cave, D. (2004, February 23). MTV under attack by FCC. *Rolling Stone.* Retrieved July 26, 2006, from http://www.rollingstone.com/news/story/5937141/mtv_under_attack-by_fcc

Center for Media and Public Affairs. (1999). *The rude and the crude: Profanity in popular entertainment.* Washington, DC: Author.

Chavez, B. (2003, January 21). Tragedies have forced teens to confront mortality. *Albuquerque Journal.* Retrieved July 30, 2006, from http://www.abqjournal.com

Chen, M.-J., Miller, B. A., Grube, J. W., & Waiters, E. D. (2006). Music, substance use and aggression. *Journal of Studies on Alcohol, 67,* 373–381.

Christenson, P. (1992a). The effects of parental advisory labels on adolescent music preferences. *Journal of Communication, 42,* 106–113.

Christenson, P. (1992b). Preadolescent perceptions and interpretations of music videos. *Popular Music and Society, 16,* 63–73.

Christenson, P. G., & Roberts, D. F. (1990). *Popular music in early adolescence.* Washington, DC: Carnegie Council on Adolescent Development.

Christenson, P. G., & Roberts, D. F. (1998). *It's not only rock 'n' roll: Popular music in the lives of adolescents.* Cresskill, NJ: Hampton.

Cohen, C. J., Bell, A., & Ifatungji, M. (2005). *Reclaiming our future: The state of AIDS among Black youth in America.* Los Angeles: Black AIDS Institute. Retrieved July 24, 2006, from www.BlackAIDS.org

Cole, T. (2000, May 1). "Into evil": Death-metal fans viciously murdered two young women, and the victims' parents blame the music. *Albuquerque Journal,* p. A1–5.

Commonwealth Fund. (1993). *First comprehensive national health survey of American women.* New York: Author.

Cooper, B. L. (1991). *Popular music perspectives: Ideas, themes and patterns in contemporary lyrics.* Bowling Green, OH: Bowling Green University Popular Press.

Davis, S. (1985, Summer). Pop lyrics: A mirror and molder of society. *Et Cetra,* pp. 167–169.

Denisoff, R. S., & Levine, M. H. (1971). The popular protest song: The case of "Eve of Destruction." *Public Opinion Quarterly, 35,* 119–124.

Desmond, R. (1987). Adolescents and music lyrics: Implications of a cognitive perspective. *Communication Quarterly, 35,* 276–284.

Diamond, S., Bermudez, R., & Schensul, J. (2006). What's the rap about ecstasy? Popular music lyrics and drug trends among American youth. *Journal of Adolescent Research, 21,* 269–298.

Donnerstein, E., Slaby, R., & Eron, L. (1994). The mass media and youth aggression. In L. D. Eron, J. H. Gentry, & P. Schlegel (Eds.), *Reason to hope: A psychological perspective on violence and youth* (pp. 219–250). Washington, DC: American Psychological Association.

DuRant, R. H., Rich, M., Emans, S. J., Rome, E. S., Allred, E., & Woods, E. R. (1997). Violence and weapon carrying in music videos: A content analysis. *Archives of Pediatrics & Adolescent Medicine, 151,* 443–448.

DuRant, R. H., Rome, E. S., Rich, M., Allred, E., Emans, S. J., & Woods, E. R. (1997). Tobacco and alcohol use behaviors portrayed in music videos. *American Journal of Public Health, 87,* 1131–1135.

Emerson, R. A. (2002). "Where my girls at?" Negotiating Black womanhood in music videos. *Gender & Society, 16,* 115–135.

Entertainers have the last laugh, pocket millions of fans' dollars. (1990, October 7). *Atlanta Journal*, p. A-3.

Escobar-Chaves, S. L., Tortolero, S. R., Markham, C. M., Low, B. J., Eitel, P., & Thickstun, P. (2005). Impact of the media on adolescent sexual attitudes and behaviors. *Pediatrics, 116*, 303–326.

Eveland, W. P., Nathanson, A. I., Detenber, A. I., & McLeod, D. M. (1999). Rethinking the social distance corollary: Perceived likelihood of exposure and the third-person perception. *Communication Research, 26*, 275–302.

Families sue band over sons' suicides. (1990, July 16). *Albuquerque Journal*, p. C12.

Federal Trade Commission. (2001, April). *Marketing violent entertainment to children: A six-month follow-up review of industry practices in the motion picture, music recording & electronic game industries: A report to Congress*. Washington, DC: Author. Retrieved from http://www.ftc.gov/opa/2001/04/youthviol.htm

Fedler, F., Hall, J., & Tanzi, L. (1982). Popular songs emphasize sex, deemphasize romance. *Mass Communication Review, 9*, 10–15.

Fischer, P., & Greitemeyer, T. (2006). Music and aggression: The impact of sexual-aggressive song lyrics on aggression-related thoughts, emotions, and behavior toward the same and opposite sex. *Personality and Social Psychology Bulletin, 32*, 1165–1176.

Frith, S. (1992). In J. Lull (Ed.), *Popular music and communication* (2nd ed., pp. 49–74). Newbury Park, CA: Sage.

Gan, S.-L., Zillmann, D., & Mitrook, M. (1997). Stereotyping effects of Black women's sexual rap on White audiences. *Basic and Applied Social Psychology, 19*, 381–399.

Geier, T. (2001, April 6). MTV's pain in the jackass. *Entertainment Weekly*, pp. 10–11.

Gentile, D. A., Humphrey, B. S., & Walsh, D. A. (2005). Media ratings for movies, music, video games, and television: A review of the research and recommendations for improvements. *Adolescent Medicine Clinics, 16*, 427–446.

Goodman, E. (1986, September 20). Commercial for teen-age pregnancy. *Washington Post*, p. A23.

Gore, T. (1987). *Raising PG kids in an X-rated society*. Nashville, TN: Abingdon.

Gow, J. (1993, April). *Gender roles in popular music videos: MTV's "top 100 of all time."* Paper presented at the 1993 Popular Culture Association/American Culture Association convention, New Orleans, LA.

Greenfield, P., & Beagles-Roos, J. (1988). Television vs. radio: The cognitive impact on different socio-economic and ethnic groups. *Journal of Communication, 38*, 71–92.

Greenfield, P., Bruzzone, L., Koyamatsu, K., Satuloff, W., Nixon, K., Brodie, M., et al. (1987). What is rock music doing to the minds of our youth? A first experimental look at the effects of rock music lyrics and music videos. *Journal of Early Adolescence, 7*, 315–329.

Greeson, L. E., & Williams, R. A. (1986). Social implications of music videos for youth: An analysis of the contents and effects of MTV. *Youth & Society, 18*, 177–189.

Grossberg, L. (1992). Rock and roll in search of an audience. In J. Lull (Ed.), *Popular music and communication* (2nd ed., pp. 152–175). Newbury Park, CA: Sage.

Gruber, E. L., Thau, H. M., Hill, D. L., Fisher, D. A., & Grube, J. W. (2005). Alcohol, tobacco and illicit substances in music videos: A content analysis of prevalence and genre. *Journal of Adolescent Health, 37*, 81–83.

Hajari, N. (1993, October 22). Playing with fire. *Entertainment Weekly*, pp. 6–7.

Hansen, C. H., & Hansen, R. D. (1990). The influence of sex and violence on the appeal of rock music videos. *Communication Research, 17*, 212–234.

Hansen, C. H., & Hansen, R. D. (1991a). Constructing personality and social reality through music: Individual differences among fans of punk and heavy metal music. *Journal of Broadcasting & Electronic Media, 35*, 335–350.

Hansen, C. H., & Hansen, R. D. (1991b). Rock music videos and antisocial behavior. *Basic and Applied Social Psychology, 11,* 357–369.

Hansen, C. H., & Hansen, R. D. (2000). Music and music videos. In D. Zillmann & P. Vorderer (Eds.), *Media entertainment: The psychology of its appeal* (pp. 175–196). Mahwah, NJ: Lawrence Erlbaum.

Herd, D. (2005). Changes in the prevalence of alcohol use in rap song lyrics, 1979–1997. *Addiction, 100,* 1258–1269.

Hirschberg, L. (1996, January 14). Does a Sugar Bear bite? *New York Times Magazine,* pp. 24–57.

Jhally, S. (1995). *Dreamworlds II.* Northhampton, MA: Media Education Foundation.

Johnson, J. D., Adams, M. S., Ashburn, L., & Reed, W. (1995). Differential gender effects of exposure to rap music in African American adolescents' acceptance of teen dating violence. *Sex Roles, 33,* 597–606.

Johnson, J. D., Jackson, L. A., & Gatto, L. (1995). Violent attitudes and deferred academic aspirations: Deleterious effects of exposure to rap music. *Basic & Applied Social Psychology, 16,* 27–41.

Johnson, S. (2001, March 24). The new MTV: Be very afraid. *Albuquerque Journal,* p. E27.

Jones, K. (1997). Are rap videos more violent? Style differences and the prevalence of sex and violence in the age of MTV. *Howard Journal of Communications, 8,* 343–356.

Kaiser Family Foundation. (2003). *Reaching the MTV generation: Recent research on the impact of the Kaiser Family Foundation/MTV public education campaign on sexual health.* Retrieved July 28, 2006, from http://www.kff.org

Kandakai, T. L., Price, J. H., Telljohann, S. K., & Wilson, C. A. (1999). Mothers' perceptions of factors influencing violence in schools. *Journal of School Health, 69,* 189–195.

Kilbourne, J. (1999). *Deadly persuasion: Why women and girls must fight the addictive power of advertising.* New York: Free Press.

King, P. (1988). Heavy metal music and drug abuse in adolescents. *Postgraduate Medicine, 83,* 295–302.

Klein, J. D., Brown, J. D., Childers, K. W., Oliveri, J., Porter, C., & Dykers, C. (1993). Adolescents' risky behavior and mass media use. *Pediatrics, 92,* 24–31.

Knobloch-Westerwick, S., Musto, P., & Shaw, K. (2006, June 19–23). *Rebellion in the top music charts: Defiant messages in rap/hip hop and rock music 1993 and 2003.* Paper presented at the International Communications Association conference, Dresden, German.

Larson, R., & Kubey, R. (1983). Television and music: Contrasting media in adolescent life. *Youth & Society, 15,* 13–31.

LaVoie, J., & Collins, B. (1975). Effects of youth culture music on high school students' academic performance. *Journal of Youth and Adolescence, 4,* 57–65.

Leland, J. (1992, June 29). Rap and rage. *Newsweek,* pp. 46–52.

Leland, J. (1993, November 29). Criminal records: Gangsta rap and the culture of violence. *Newsweek,* pp. 60–64.

Leming, J. (1987). Rock music and the socialization of moral values in early adolescence. *Youth & Society, 18,* 363–383.

Lil' Kim. (2003). Magic stick. On *La Bella Mafia* [CD]. New York: Atlantic Records.

Lull, J. (1987). Listeners' communicative uses of popular music. In J. Lull (Ed.), *Popular music and communication* (pp. 140–174). Newbury Park, CA: Sage.

Martino, S. C., Collins, R. L., Elliott, M. N., Strachman, A., Kanouse, D. E., & Berry, S. H. (2006). Exposure to degrading versus nondegrading music lyrics and sexual behavior among youth. *Pediatrics, 118,* e430–e441.

Marsh, D. (1993). *Louie Louie.* New York: Hyperion.

Marshall, S. J., Gorely, T., & Biddle, S. J. H. (2005). A descriptive epidemiology of screen-based media use in youth: A review and critique. *Journal of Adolescence, 29,* 333–349.

Mediascope. (2000a). *Violence, women, and the media: Issue brief series.* Studio City, CA: Author.

Mediascope. (2000b). *Youth and violent music: Issue brief series.* Studio City, CA: Author.

Mom says MTV's *Beavis* led son to start fatal fire. (1993, October 17). *Albuquerque Journal.*

Moran, T. (1985, August 12–19). Sounds of sex. *The New Republic,* pp. 14–16.

Muñoz-Laoy, M., Weinstein, H., & Parker, R. (2007). The hip-hop club scene: Gender, grinding and sex. *Culture, Health & Sexuality, 9,* 615–628.

Nielsen Media Research. (2000). *2000 report on television.* New York: Author.

Pardun, C. J., L'Engle, K. L., & Brown, J. D. (2005). Linking exposure to outcomes: Early adolescents' consumption of sexual content in six media. *Mass Communication & Society, 8,* 75–91.

Pareles, J. (1990, June 17). Rap: Slick, violent, nasty, and, maybe, hopeful. *New York Times,* p. 19.

Parents Music Resource Center. (1985). *PMRC, PTA, and RIAA agree on record lyrics identification* [Press release]. Arlington, VA: Author.

Parents Television Council. (2002). *Harsh reality: Unscripted TV reality shows offensive to families.* Retrieved July 30, 2006, from http://www.parentstv.org

Perry, I. (1995). It's my thang and i'll swing it the way that i feel! In J. G. Dines & J. M. Humez (Eds.), *Gender, race and class in media: A test reader* (pp. 524–530). Thousand Oaks, CA: Sage.

Peterson, D. L., & Pfost, K. S. (1989). Influence of rock videos on attitudes of violence against women. *Psychological Reports, 64,* 319–322.

Peterson, S. H., Wingood, G. M., DiClemente, R. J., Harrington, K., & Davies, S. (2007). Images of sexual stereotypes in rap videos and the health of African American female adolescents. *Journal of Women's Health, 16,* 1157–1164.

Pool, M. M., Koolstra, C. M., & van der Voort, T. H. A. (2003). The impact of background radio and television on high school students' homework performance. *Journal of Communication, 53,* 74–87.

Primack, B. A., Dalton, M. A., Carroll, M. V., Agarwal, A. A., & Fine, M. J. (2008). Content analysis of tobacco, alcohol, and other drugs in popular music. *Archives of Pediatrics & Adolescent Medicine, 162,* 169–175.

Prinsky, L. E., & Rosenbaum, J. L. (1987). "Leer-ics" or lyrics: Teenage impressions of rock 'n' roll. *Youth & Society, 8,* 384–397.

Rehman, S. N., & Reilly, S. S. (1985). Music videos: A new dimension of televised violence. *The Pennsylvania Speech Communication Annual, 41,* 61–64.

Reid, P., & Finchilescu, G. (1995). The disempowering effects of media violence against women on college women. *Psychology of Women Quarterly, 19,* 397–411.

Rich, M., Woods, E. R., Goodman, E., Emans, E. J., & DuRant, R. H. (1998). Aggressors or victims: Gender and race in music video violence. *Pediatrics, 101,* 669–674.

Rideout, V. J. (2003). *Reaching the MTV generation.* Menlo Park, CA: Kaiser Family Foundation.

Rideout, V. J., Foehr, U. G., Roberts, D. F., & Brodie, M. (1999). *Kids & media @ the new millennium.* Menlo Park, CA: Kaiser Family Foundation.

Roberts, D. F., & Christenson, P. G. (2000). *"Here's looking at you, kid": Alcohol, drugs and tobacco in entertainment media.* Menlo Park, CA: Kaiser Family Foundation.

Roberts, D. F., & Christenson, P. G. (2001). Popular music in childhood and adolescence. In D. G. Singer & J. L. Singer (Eds.), *Handbook of children and the media* (pp. 395–413). Thousand Oaks: CA, Sage.

Roberts, D. F., Christenson, P. G., & Gentile, D. A. (2003). The effects of violent music on children and adolescents. In D. A. Gentile (Ed.), *Media violence and children* (pp. 153–170). Westport, CT: Praeger.

Roberts, D. F., Foehr, U. G., & Rideout, V. (2005). *Generation M: Media in the lives of 8–18 year-olds.* Menlo Park, CA: Kaiser Family Foundation.

Roberts, D. F., Henriksen, L., & Christenson, P. G. (1999). *Substance use in popular movies and music.* Washington, DC: Office of National Drug Control Policy.

Roberts, K. R., Dimsdale, J., East, P., & Friedman, L. (1998). Adolescent emotional response to music and its relationship to risk-taking behavior. *Journal of Adolescent Health, 23,* 49–54.

Robinson, T. N., Chen, H. L., & Killen, J. D. (1998). Television and music video exposure and risk of adolescent alcohol use. *Pediatrics, 102,* e54.

Robischon, N., Snierson, D., & Svetkey, B. (1999, June 11). A special report on violence and entertainment, part II. *Entertainment Weekly,* pp. 36–39.

Roe, K. (1984). *Youth and music in Sweden: Results from a longitudinal study of teenagers' media use* [Media Panel Reports No. 32]. Lund, Sweden: Sociologiska Institutionen.

Roe, K. (1990). Adolescent music use: A structural-cultural approach. In K. Roe & U. Carlsson (Eds.), *Popular music research* (pp. 41–52). Goteborg: Nordicom-Sweden.

Roe, K. (1995). Adolescents' use of socially disvalued media: Towards a theory of media delinquency. *Journal of Youth and Adolescence, 24,* 617–631.

Samuels, A., Croal, N., & Gates, D. (2000, October 9). The rap on rap. *Newsweek,* pp. 58–65.

Scheel, K. R., & Westefeld, J. S. (1999). Heavy metal music and adolescent suicidality: An empirical investigation. *Adolescence, 34,* 253–273.

Schwarzbaum, L. (2000, August 11). Lewd awakening. *Entertainment Weekly,* pp. 20–26.

Serpick, E. (2002, November 5). MTV: Play it again. *Entertainment Weekly.* Retrieved July 29, 2006, from www.ew.com

Sewell, D. (2007, July 26). P&G's diaper ad angers Beatle fans. *Albuquerque Journal,* Business Outlook, p. 7.

Sharif, I., & Sargent, J. D. (2006). Association between television, movie, and video game exposure and school performance. *Pediatrics, 118,* 1061–1070.

Sherman, B. L., & Dominick, J. R. (1986). Violence and sex in music videos: TV and rock 'n' roll. *Journal of Communication, 36,* 79–93.

Signorielli, N., McLeod, D., & Healy, E. (1994). Gender stereotypes in MTV commercials: The beat goes on. *Journal of Broadcasting and Electronic Media, 38,* 91–101.

Smith, S. L. (2005). From Dr. Dre to Dismissed: Assessing violence, sex, and substance abuse on MTV. *Critical Studies in Media Communication, 22,* 89–98.

Smith, S. L., & Boyson, A. (2002). Violence in music videos: Examining the prevalence and context of physical aggression. *Journal of Communication, 52,* 61–83.

Sommers-Flanagan, R., Sommers-Flanagan, J., & Davis, B. (1993). What's happening on music television? A gender role content analysis. *Sex Roles, 28,* 745–753.

Span, P. (1999, June 27). Marketers hang on affluent teen-agers' every wish. *Albuquerque Journal,* p. C3.

St. Lawrence, J. S., & Joyner, D. J. (1991). The effects of sexually violent rock music on males' acceptance of violence against women. *Psychology of Women Quarterly, 15,* 49–63.

Stack, S., Gundlach, J., & Reeves, J. L. (1994). The heavy metal subculture and suicide. *Suicide and Life-Threatening Behavior, 24,* 15–23.

Starker, S. (1989). *Evil influences: Crusades against the mass media.* Brunswick, NJ: Transaction.

Stephens, D. P., & Phillips, L. D. (2003). Freaks, gold diggers, divas, and dykes: The sociohistorical development of adolescent African American women's sexual scripts. *Sexuality & Culture, 7,* 3–49.

Strasburger, V. C. (1993). Adolescents, drugs and the media. *Adolescent Medicine: State of the Art Reviews, 4,* 391–415.

Strasburger, V. C. (1997a). "Make love, not war": Violence and weapon carrying in music videos. *Archives of Pediatrics & Adolescent Medicine, 151,* 441–442.

Strasburger, V. C. (1997b). "Sex, drugs, rock 'n' roll," and the media: Are the media responsible for adolescent behavior? *Adolescent Medicine: State of the Art Reviews, 8,* 403–414.

Strasburger, V. C. (2005). Adolescents, sex, and the media: Oooo, baby, baby—a Q&A. *Adolescent Medicine Clinics, 16,* 269–288.

Strasburger, V. C. (2006). Risky business: What primary care practitioners need to know about the influence of the media on adolescents. *Primary Care: Clinics in Office Practice, 33,* 317–348.

Strasburger, V. C., & Donnerstein, E. (2000). Adolescents and the media in the 21st century. *Adolescent Medicine: State of the Art Reviews, 11,* 51–68.

Strasburger, V. C., & Hendren, R. O. (1995). Rock music and music videos. *Pediatric Annals, 24,* 97–103.

Strouse, J. S., & Buerkel-Rothfuss, N. (1987). Self-reported media exposure and sexual attitudes and behaviors of college students. *Journal of Sex Education and Therapy, 13,* 43–51.

Strouse, J. S., Buerkel-Rothfuss, N., & Long, E. C. (1995). Gender and family as moderators of the relationship between music video exposure and adolescent sexual permissiveness. *Adolescence, 30,* 505–521.

Su-Lin, G., Zillmann, D., & Mitrook, M. (1997). Stereotyping effect of Black women's sexual rap on White audiences. *Basic and Applied Social Psychology, 19,* 381–399.

Tanner, J. (1981). Pop music and peer groups: A study of Canadian high school students' responses to pop music. *Canadian Review of Sociology and Anthropology, 18,* 1–13.

Tapper, J., Thorson, E., & Black, D. (1994). Variations in music videos as a function of their musical genre. *Journal of Broadcasting & Electronic Media, 38,* 103–113.

Tiggeman, M., & Pickering, A. S. (1996). Role of television in adolescent women's body dissatisfaction and drive for thinness. *International Journal of Eating Disorders, 20,* 199–203.

Tyson, E. H. (2002). Hip hop therapy: An exploratory study of a rap music intervention with at-risk and delinquent youth. *Journal of Poetry Therapy, 15,* 131–144.

Tyson, E. H. (2006). Rap-music attitude and perception scale: A validation study. *Research on Social Work Practice, 16,* 211–223.

U.S. Department of Justice (1996). *National Crime Victimization Survey.* Washington, DC: Bureau of Justice Statistics.

Vincent, R. C., Davis, D. K., & Bronszkowski, L. A. (1987). Sexism in MTV: The portrayal of women in rock videos. *Journalism Quarterly, 64,* 750–755.

Waite, B. M., Hillbrand, M., & Foster, H. G. (1992). Reduction of aggressive behavior after removal of Music Television. *Hospital and Community Psychiatry, 43,* 173–175.

Ward, E., Stokes, G., & Tucker, K. (1986). *Rock of ages: The Rolling Stone history of rock and roll.* New York: Rolling Stone Books.

Ward, L. M. (2003). Understanding the role of entertainment media in the sexual socialization of American youth: A review of empirical research. *Developmental Reviews, 23,* 347–388.

Ward, L. M., & Friedman, K. (2006). Using TV as a guide: Associations between television viewing and adolescents' sexual attitudes and behavior. *Journal of Research on Adolescence, 16,* 133–156.

Ward, L. M., Hansbrough, E., & Walker, E. (2005). Contributions of music video exposure to Black adolescents' gender and sexual schemas. *Journal of Adolescent Research, 20,* 143–166.

Wass, H., Raup, J. L., Cerullo, K., Martel, L. G., Minglione, L. A., & Sperring, A. M. (1988). Adolescents' interest in and views of destructive themes in rock music. *Omega, 19,* 177–186.

Weidinger, C. K., & Demi, A. S. (1991). Music listening preferences and preadmission dysfunctional psychosocial behaviors of adolescents hospitalized on an in-patient psychiatric unit. *Journal of Child and Adolescent Psychiatric Mental Health Nursing, 4,* 3–8.

Willman, C. (2001, January 19). Midlife crisis? *Entertainment Weekly,* pp. 82–83.

Wingood, G. M., DiClemente, R. J., Bernhardt, J. M., Harrington, K., Davies, S. L., Robillard, A., et. al. (2003). A prospective study of exposure to rap music videos and African American female adolescents' health. *American Journal of Public Health, 93,* 437–439.

Zillmann, D., & Mundorf, N. (1987). Image effects in the appreciation of video rock. *Communication Research, 14,* 316–334.

Zurbriggen, E. L., & Morgan, E. M. (2006). Who wants to marry a millionaire? Reality dating television programs, attitudes toward sex, and sexual behaviors. *Sex Roles, 54,* 1–17.

CHAPTER 9

Eating and Eating Disorders

Television presents viewers with two sets of conflicting messages. One suggests that we eat in ways almost guaranteed to make us fat; the other suggests that we strive to remain slim.

—L. Kaufman (1980, p. 45)

Research shows that virtually all women are ashamed of their bodies. It used to be adult women, teenage girls, who were ashamed, but now you see the shame down to very young girls—10, 11 years old. Society's standard of beauty is an image that is literally just short of starvation for most women.

—Author Mary Pipher,
People magazine, June 3, 1996

They want me to look like a girl, and I'm a woman. It's very hard nowadays. I think it's hideous. I don't read articles about men working out three hours a day and eating just vegetables.

—Actress Andie MacDowell,
Albuquerque Journal, October 27, 1998

I don't think the schools have the responsibility of being the food police. And I don't think that schools should be expected to turn up their noses [at $4 million annually].

—Hillsborough County, Florida,
school board member, commenting
on a new $50 million, 12-year
contract with Pepsi—the largest contract
with schools ever signed (Mabe, 2003)

Although sex, drugs, rock 'n' roll, and violence grab the headlines and represent major health concerns during childhood and adolescence, the media have an important impact on other areas of young people's health as well. Television can serve as an important source of information for young children and teens about foods and eating habits. Television nutrition—in particular, the impact of food advertising—and the image of women in programming and advertising are coming under increasing scrutiny as pediatricians and public health officials try to understand why more American children are becoming obese and why teenagers continue to suffer from a variety of eating disorders (see Table 9.1).

Table 9.1   Some Facts About Figures

33–23–33 = average measurements of a model
36–18–33 = Barbie doll's measurements, if she were a full-sized human
5'4", 141 pounds = average American woman
5'9", 110 pounds = average model
33% = percentage of American women wearing size 16 or larger
$10 billion = revenues of the diet industry in 1970
$33 billion = revenues of the diet industry in 1996

SOURCE: Adapted from *People* magazine, June 3, 1996, p. 71.

National surveys have documented that the prevalence of obesity is increasing dramatically in the United States (see Figure 9.1) (Li, Ford, Mokdad, & Cook, 2006; National Center for Health Statistics, 2006; Ogden et al., 2006). The American food supply now furnishes 3,900 calories per day per capita, approximately twice what people actually need and 700 calories a day more than in 1980 (Nestle, 2006a, 2006b). From 1991 to 1998 alone, the prevalence of obesity (defined as a body mass index > 30) has increased from 12% to 18% (Mokdad et al., 1999). (Body mass index, or BMI, is calculated by dividing weight in kilograms by the square of the height in meters. A BMI of less than 25 is desirable, and less than 18 indicates the possibility of an eating disorder.) By 2003–2004, 17% of American children and adolescents were found to be overweight, and nearly one third were obese (Ogden et al., 2006). The latest study of 1,740 eighth graders at 12 different U.S. schools found that half were either overweight or on the verge of becoming overweight (STOPP-T2D Prevention Study Group, 2006). For children and teenagers, obesity has a whole host of negative health and psychological consequences (Dietz & Robinson, 2005; Schwimmer, Burwinkle, & Varni, 2003). Currently, about 30% of obese adolescents will develop metabolic syndrome (a combination of abnormal lipid levels, elevated blood sugar levels, and high blood pressure) (Institute of Medicine, 2006). Metabolic syndrome sometimes precedes type II diabetes, which used to be extremely rare among teenagers but is now becoming increasingly common (Duncan, 2006; Welsh & Dietz, 2005). Psychologically, obese children and teenagers tend to suffer from lower self-esteem than their peers (Franklin, Denyer, Steinbeck, Caterson, & Hill, 2006; Strasburger et al., 2006).

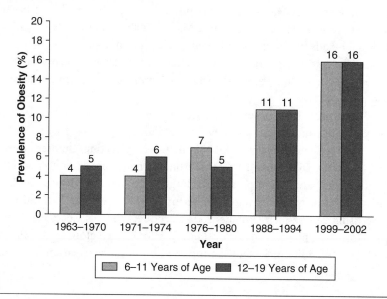

Figure 9.1   Percentages of U.S. Children and Teenagers Who Were Obese

SOURCE: From Nestle (2006a). Copyright ©2006 Massachusetts Medical Society. All rights reserved.

Obesity is not unique to the United States, however. Europe is experiencing its own epidemic, with as many as 20% to 35% of 10-year-olds in various countries now overweight (Lang & Rayner, 2005; Preidt, 2008). Globally, diets are shifting dramatically toward higher intakes of animal and partially hydrogenated fats, with concomitant increases in the prevalence of obesity (Popkin, 2006). The incidence of eating disorders among adolescents remains alarmingly high too. Anorexia nervosa occurs in as many as 1 in 100 to 200 middle-class females (Strasburger et al., 2006) and bulimia in as many as 5% of young women (British Medical Association [BMA], 2000). Eating disorders may also include symptoms that fall short of full-blown disorders. For example, a major study of nearly 2,500 middle school teens in North Carolina found that 10% of the girls and 4% of the boys reported vomiting or using laxatives to lose weight (Krowchuk, Kreiter, Woods, Sinal, & DuRant, 1998). Consequently, some researchers have looked accusingly at media portrayals of food to try to understand the underlying cause of these behaviors (Becker, 2002; Borzekowski & Bayer, 2005; Field et al., 2005; Levine & Harrison, 2003).

Food Advertisements

American children view an estimated 40,000 advertisements per year, and advertisers spend $10 billion a year trying to appeal to children (see Tables 9.2 and 9.3) (American Academy of Pediatrics [AAP], 2006; American Psychological Association, 2004; Nestle, 2006b). More than half of such ads are for food, especially sugared cereals and high-caloric snacks (Institute of Medicine, 2006; Kaiser Family Foundation, 2004a). In children's programming, 83% of all advertisements are for fast foods or snacks (Harrison & Marske, 2005). Adolescents may see relatively less food ads, about one fourth of all the TV ads they view (Powell, Szczypka, & Chaloupka, 2007a). Ads are cleverly constructed to get viewers to associate foods with happiness and fun, rather than taste or nutritional benefit (Scammon & Christopher, 1981).

Food advertising is big business. Americans spent $110 billion on fast food alone in the year 2000, more than on higher education, computers, or cars (Schlosser, 2001). Fast-food chains spend $3 billion a year targeting children with ads (Schlosser, 2001). During the 1998 fall season, the major networks averaged 8.5 to 10.3 minutes of advertising per hour (Horgen, Choate, & Brownell, 2001). But children and teens primarily watch prime-time TV, where up to 16 minutes/hour of advertising can be seen (Robins, 2002). Products such as Coke, Pepsi, potato chips, Doritos, Snickers, and Pop-tarts predominate, along with the fast-food chains. In addition, 85% of the top food brands advertised on TV also use

Table 9.2   Favorite Ads of Children and Teenagers (*N* = 800 Children Ages 6–17)

1. Budweiser
2. Pepsi
3. Nissan
4. Nike
5. American Dairy Association
6. Coke
7. Barbie
8. Snickers
9. McDonald's
10. Hostess

SOURCE: Campbell, Mithun, and Esty, *National Study Reveals Kids' Favorite TV Ads* (press release), Minneapolis, MN, June 16, 1998.

Table 9.3   What Is Advertised on TV? (*N* = 17.5 Hours; 108 Ads) (in Percentages)

Food and restaurants	37
Low-nutrient beverages	16
Desserts and snack foods	15
Breads and cereals	11
Convenience entrees	6
Fruits and vegetables	4
Dairy products	2

SOURCE: Adapted from Byrd-Bredbrenner and Grasso (2000).

corporate Web sites that market to kids online (Moore, 2006). In one study of Australian 9- to 10-year-olds, more than half believed that Ronald McDonald knows what is best for children to eat (Food Commission, 1997). But the recent upsurge in obesity rates has been associated with an equivalent increase in fast-food consumption (Niemeier, Raynor, Lloyd-Richardson, Rogers, & Wing, 2006). More than one quarter of all children's hospitals in the United States actually have a fast-food restaurant inside of the hospital (Sahud, Binns, Meadow, & Tanz, 2006).

The problem is that children rarely see a food advertisement for broccoli (see Figure 9.2) (Goodman, 2000). Healthy foods are advertised less than 3% of the time (Kunkel & Gantz, 1991). A study of 52 hours of advertising during Saturday morning programming found that two thirds of the ads were for sugared cereals, sweets, or fats and oils, but none were for fruits or vegetables (see Figure 9.3) (Kotz & Story, 1994). A separate study found that 90% of ads on Saturday morning were for sugared cereal, candy bars, salty snack food, or fast food (Center for Media Education, 1998). Researchers estimate that children see one food commercial every 5 minutes on Saturday morning TV (Kotz & Story, 1994) and that young children may see more than 500 food references per week, with almost one third for empty-calorie snacks and another one quarter for high-fat foods (Borzekowski, 2001). By 2005, 83% of foods advertised on TV shows popular with children were for fast foods or sweets (Harrison & Marske, 2005). Even PBS, Disney, and Nickelodeon now target toddlers and preschoolers with ads in the form of "sponsorships" (Connor, 2006). And two studies published in 2007 are the most incriminating:

- A sample of 50,000 ads from 2003–2004 on 170 top-rated shows found that 98% of food ads seen by children ages 2 to 11 years and nearly 90% of food ads seen by teenagers are for foods that are high in fat, sugar, or sodium (Powell, Szczypka, & Chaloupka, 2007b).

- A new Kaiser study of 1,638 hours of TV and nearly 9,000 food ads found that children and teenagers see an average of 12 to 21 food ads per day, for a total of 4,400

Figure 9.2

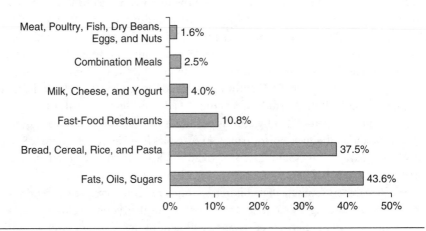

Figure 9.3   Representation of Foods in Saturday Morning Commercials

SOURCE: Bell, Berger, and Townsend (2003).

to 7,600 ads per year, yet they see less than 165 ads that promote fitness or good nutrition (see Figure 9. 4) (Gantz, Schwartz, Angelini, & Rideout, 2007). A 2007 Federal Trade Commission (FTC) study had very similar findings (FTC, 2007).

As if this weren't bad enough, food ads often contain violence (62%), conflict (41%), and trickery (20%) (Rajecki et al., 1994). Cartoon characters abound and are incredibly effective. In Leiber's (1996) study of product recall among 221 children ages 9 to 11 years, cartoon characters were extremely efficient in getting

A. *Children's Exposure to Food Advertising on TV, on Average:*			
AGE	*Number of Food Ads Seen per Day**	*Number of Food Ads Seen per Year*	*Hr: Min of Food Ads Seen per Year*
2–7	12	4,427	29:31
8–12	21	7,609	50:48
13–17	17	6,098	40:50

*This estimate of food ads seen per day has been rounded to the nearest whole number. For the calculation of the number of food ads seen per year, the more precise figure was used.

B. *Children's Exposure to Public Service Messages on Fitness or Nutrition on TV, on Average:*			
AGE	*Min: Sec of PSAs on Fitness/Nutrition Seen per Day*	*Number of PSAs on Fitness/Nutrition Seen per Year*	*Hr: Min of PSAs on Fitness/Nutrition Seen per Year*
2–7	0:14	164	1:25
8–12	0:12	158	1:15
13–17	0:04	47	0:25

Figure 9.4   What Nutritional Messages Do Children Receive on TV? (A) Children's Exposure to Food Advertising on TV and (B) Children's Exposure to Public Service Messages on Fitness or Nutrition on TV

SOURCE: Gantz et al. (2007).

children to recognize products (see Table 7.8 in Chapter 7). As an advertising icon, Ronald McDonald rates number two in the 20th century, second only to the Marlboro Man. Tony the Tiger and the Pillsbury Doughboy also made the top 10 list (Horgen et al., 2001). Worldwide, the McDonald's Corporation spends nearly $500 million a year on advertising, with approximately 40% of it targeting children (Horgen et al., 2001) (see Tables 9.4 and 9.5). Not surprisingly, such advertising works. In a remarkable study using five pairs of identical foods and beverages in packaging from McDonald's and unbranded packaging, a group of 63 children uniformly preferred the McDonald's food (Robinson, Borzekowski, Matheson, & Kraemer, 2007). Increasingly, McDonald's, Burger King, and others are engaging in toy tie-ins with major motion picture studios, trying to augment sales of fast food and attendance at children's movies (Sokol, 2000). In the only content analysis thus far to examine such advertising, Reece, Rifon, and Rodriguez (1999) found that nearly 20% of restaurant ads mentioned a toy premium in their commercials.

Table 9.4   Caloric and Fat Content of Selected Fast Food

Food	Calories	Fat (g)
McDonald's		
Big Mac	530	28
Quarter Pounder	430	21
Hamburger	270	9
Small French fries	210	10
Large French fries	450	22
Chicken McNuggets	430	26
Fajita chicken salad with lite vinaigrette dressing	250	10
Hard Rock Café		
Hamburger	660	36
Onion rings	890	65
Pizza Hut		
Cheese pizza, 2 slices	446	20
Pepperoni pizza, 2 slices	640	38
Arby's		
Roast beef sandwich	552	28
Jr. roast beef sandwich	233	11
Taco Bell		
Tacos (2)	360	22
Taco Bell salad w/o salsa	838	55
Kentucky Fried Chicken		
KFC Original Recipe, half breast	360	20
KFC Rotisserie Gold, 1/4	199	6

SOURCE: Adapted from *USA Today,* October 20, 1994, p. 7D and Hurley and Schmidt (1996). Reprinted from Strasburger (2004).

Table 9.5   Fast Food and Kids

Kids ages 12 to 17:
spend $12.7 billion per year on fast food
eat 7% of all their meals at fast-food restaurants
visit fast-food restaurants an average of 2.13 times/week
46% say their favorite food is a hamburger

SOURCE: Adapted from Preboth and Wright (1999) and Brownell (2004).

Not only are healthy foods rarely advertised on television, but public service announcements (PSAs) are not used effectively to redress the nutritional misinformation being broadcast to children. One study of 20 hours of randomly selected programming over a 3-week period found no PSAs addressing nutrition (Wallack & Dorfman, 1992). Another study of 53 hours of Saturday morning cartoons found 10 nutrition-related PSAs competing with 564 advertisements for food (Kotz & Story, 1994). In Taras and Gage's (1995) content analysis of nearly 100 hours of children's programming, only 2.5 minutes were devoted to PSAs concerning nutrition-related topics. Of these, the messages were often as simplistic (and boring for children, compared with "real" ads) as "eat well," "don't ingest too much sugar," or "brush your teeth." In the most recent study, only 8 of the 900 ads aired during 43 hours of children's programming in 1997 were PSAs, less than 1% (Reece et al., 1999).

Although the industry cites the "when eaten as part of a nutritious breakfast" voiceover as fulfilling its obligations to consumers and their children, there is little evidence that such disclaimers actually fulfill their function (Muehling & Kolbe, 1999). Some children may understand the disclaimer (Stutts & Hunnicutt, 1987), but by far the most important impact of the commercial is to intrigue the child with how "yummy" and "fun" the product is (Reece et al., 1999). Recently, General Mills announced a new "Choose breakfast" campaign that uses 10-second spots during children's shows to promote the "health benefits" of cereals like Trix, Cocoa Puffs, and Cinnamon Toast Crunch (Asch-Goodkin, 2005). Only 1% of children currently meet the U.S. Department of Agriculture's food intake guidelines set forth in the famous Food Guide Pyramid (see Figure 9.5) (Munoz, Krebs-Smith, Ballard-Barbash, & Cleveland, 1997).

New digital-age marketing techniques are targeting older children and teens as well. Cell phones can be sent advertising messages and instant electronic coupons, Web addresses are now printed on cereal packages, instant messaging Web sites contain interactive commercials, and commercials have been placed on YouTube masquerading as videos (Chester & Montgomery, 2007).

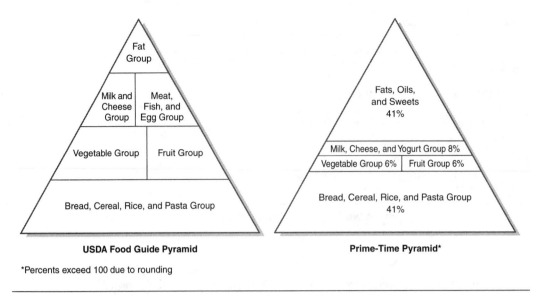

*Percents exceed 100 due to rounding

Figure 9.5   Two Conflicting Food Pyramids

SOURCE: *International Electronic Journal of Health Education* (February 1999), 2(4): 164.

The Impact of Food Advertisements on Behavior

As discussed in Chapter 2, numerous studies have documented that young children younger than ages 6 to 8 years are developmentally unable to understand the intent of advertisements and, in fact, frequently accept advertising claims as being largely true (AAP, 2006; Gunter, Oates, & Blades, 2005; Kunkel, 2001; Macklin & Carlson, 1999; Unnikrishnan & Bajpai, 1996). Preteens, between ages 8 and 10 years, possess the cognitive ability to process advertisements but do not necessarily do so unless prompted (Brucks, Armstrong, & Goldberg, 1988). Unfortunately, most research on young people's consumer behavior has been conducted by marketing researchers and remains unavailable to the academic community or to the public (Christakis, 2006; Kaiser Family Foundation, 2004a).

What research is available clearly indicates that advertising is effective in getting younger children to request more junk food and to attempt to influence their parents' purchases (see Figure 9.6) (Chamberlain, Wang, & Robinson, 2006; Institute of Medicine, 2006). In fact, in the Taras, Sallis, Patterson, Nader, and Nelson (1989) study, the amount of weekly television viewing of 3- to 8-year-olds actually correlated significantly both with children's requests for specific advertised foods and their caloric intake. A 2006 study of 827 third-grade children, followed for 20 months, also found that total TV time and total screen media time predicted future requests for advertised foods and drinks (Chamberlain et al., 2006). Even brief exposures to TV food ads can influence children as young as preschool age in their food choices (Borzekowski & Robinson, 2001), and several researchers feel that a causal connection has been established between children's exposure to food ads and their choice of foods (Chamberlain et al., 2006; Story & French, 2004). Exposure to food ads also increases young children's snacking behavior (Bolton, 1983) and correlates with unhealthy notions about nutrition (Signorielli & Staples, 1997). A study of more than 21,000 children and adolescents nationwide has found that the prevalence of snacking has increased considerably during the past 20 years. By the mid-1990s, children were consuming 25% of their daily calories by snacking, compared with 18% in 1977, and teens consume 610 calories a day by snacking (Jahns, Siega-Riz, & Popkin, 2001). Even when important variables such as reading level, ethnicity, and parents' occupation and educational level are controlled for, fourth and fifth graders' television viewing correlates with poor eating habits (Signorielli & Lears, 1992). Two recent studies found that heavier TV viewing correlates with more fast-food consumption (French, Story, Neumark-Sztainer, Fulkerson, & Hannan, 2001) and greater intake of sodas (Giammatei, Blix, Marshak, Wollitzer, & Pettit, 2003). In an intriguing study of undergraduates, Stroebele and de Castro (2004) found that on days when students watched TV, they averaged 3½ meals and 163 more calories per day versus 2¾ meals on days when they did not watch. Could it be coincidence that African American children, who are at higher risk for overweight and obesity, are exposed to more food ads on channels popular with them (BET, WB, Disney) than other children (Outley & Taddese, 2006)?

Figure 9.6

SOURCE: Jim Berry; reprinted by permission of Newspaper Enterprise Association, Inc.

Interestingly enough, the advertising industry's own "watchdog" group, the Children's Advertising Review Unit (CARU), was established in 1974 specifically to encourage the responsible advertising of children's products. CARU states that food ads should encourage good nutritional practices and show the product within the context of a balanced diet (Reece et al., 1999). As might be expected, if advertising snack foods encourages snacking, advertising healthy foods can encourage more wholesome nutritional practices, even among children as young as 3 to 6 years of age. Several studies have shown that PSAs for fruits, vegetables, or products without added sugar increase the chances that children will make wiser nutritional choices (Galst, 1980; Gorn & Goldberg, 1982). On the other hand, a recent study of 500 middle school students studied over a 19-month period found that for each additional hour of television viewed per day, consumption of fruits and vegetables actually decreases among teenagers, which may be attributable to TV advertising of snack foods (Boynton-Jarrett et al., 2003).

Cross-cultural studies show that similar problems vis-à-vis nutritional practices and advertising exist in Canada, Japan, Britain, New Zealand, and Australia (Dixon, Scully, Wakefield, White, & Crawford, 2007; Goldberg, 1990; Ishigaki, 1991; Lewis & Hill, 1998; Public Health Association of Australia, 1999; Wilson, Quigley, & Mansoor, 1999). Goldberg (1990) capitalized on the passage of a new law in Quebec that eliminated Canadian advertising to children to find that Quebec children who viewed American TV shows had more sugared cereal in their homes than those who watched only Canadian programming. In fact, there was a dose-response effect, with those who watched 1 hour per day of American programming owning 1.23 boxes of cereal but those who watched 4 hours per day owning 3.81 boxes. By the late 1970s, this body of research was convincing enough to lead the FTC to issue the following conclusion in 1981:

> The record . . . supports the following conclusions regarding child-oriented television advertising and young children six years and under: (1) they place indiscriminate trust in televised advertising messages; (2) they do not understand the persuasive bias in television advertising; and (3) the techniques, focus and themes used in child-oriented television advertising enhance the appeal of the advertising message and the advertised product. Consequently, *young children do not possess the cognitive ability to evaluate adequately child-oriented television advertising.* Despite the fact that these conclusions can be drawn from the evidence, *the record establishes that the only effective remedy would be a ban on all advertisements oriented towards young children, and such a ban, as a practical matter, cannot be implemented.* (FTC, 1981, pp. 2–4)

This was the closest that the American government has ever come to regulating advertising, specifically the advertising of sugared cereals to children. With the political landscape of the 1980s and the power of advertisers in America, however, the prospects for reform changed dramatically (Comstock, 1991). Since the late 1970s, responsibility for the regulation of advertising has been moved from the FTC to the Federal Communications Commission (FCC). This has meant that advertising is now viewed more as a broadcasting issue than an issue of corporate responsibility. Questions about advertising are now about amount and placement of ads, rather than about the meaning, representation, and public health impact that they may have.

Given the current political and social climate in the new millennium, which seems to favor business over public health, the prospects for reform remain slim. Yet many researchers (Christakis, 2006; Horgen et al., 2001; Strasburger, 2001) and public health groups such as the AAP (2006) continue to believe that advertising directed toward children younger than 8 years of age is inherently deceptive and exploitative.

Food in Television Programming and Movies

Only a handful of content analyses have been conducted to study the portrayal of food in prime-time programming or in movies (Borzekowski, 2001; Byrd-Bredbrenner, Finckenor, & Grasso, 2003; Gerbner, Gross, Morgan, & Signorielli, 1980; Jain & Tirodkar, 2001; Story & Faulkner, 1990; Sylvester, Williams, & Achterberg, 1993; Way, 1983). Perhaps this is because food advertising is such a powerful force on network and cable television and is therefore studied preferentially. Food references occur nearly 10 times per hour on prime-time TV, and 60% are for low-nutrient snacks or beverages (Story & Faulkner, 1990). Snacking in television programming occurs as frequently as eating breakfast, lunch, and dinner combined (Gerbner et al., 1980). Most of the foods eaten by characters are sweets (Gerbner et al., 1980; Story & Faulkner, 1990; Way, 1983). Borzekowski (2001) conducted a content analysis of the 30 highest rated programs among 2- to 5-year-olds. Of the top 30, 47% were on network TV, 30% were on Nickelodeon, and 23% were on PBS. Each episode had at least one reference to food, and one third of the episodes contained 16 or more references. An average child would therefore see more than 500 food references per week during programming. Nearly one third of the references were to empty-calorie foods high in fat, sugar, or salt. Another 25% of food references were to nutrient-rich foods that, however, were also high in fat, sugar, or salt. The most recent analysis of the most popular prime-time shows found that 2- to 11-year-olds see a health-related scene every 4 minutes, usually involving unhealthy foods or alcoholic beverages (Byrd-Bredbrenner et al., 2003).

Borzekowski (2001) was surprised to find that many popular children's programs contained a wide array of food choices (e.g., one episode of PBS' *Arthur* mentioned milk, cookies, apple juice, steak, corn on the cob, peanut brittle, raisins, soup, pears, watermelon, grapes, a banana, chocolate cake, pasta, lettuce, cereal, and orange juice). Of course, the amount of PBS programming "skewed" the sample somewhat, as did the choice of the youngest viewing population to study. Nevertheless, the authors of all of these content analyses concluded that the television diet is inconsistent with healthy nutritional guidelines.

One unique study examined the four most popular sitcoms among Black audiences and among general audiences and found that the former contained 27% of actors who were overweight, compared with only 2% of the latter. This is significant given that a higher percentage of African Americans are overweight than members of the general population (Jain & Tirodkar, 2001). The study also found more food items displayed and a greater number of food commercials aired during the shows popular with African Americans—nearly 5 commercials per half hour, compared with 2.89 for the shows popular with general audiences (Jain & Tirodkar, 2001).

Only three content analyses have been conducted on the portrayal of food in films. An analysis of the 71 top-grossing films of 1991 revealed that more than two thirds of the films contained two or more major food scenes. Healthier, low-fat foods were most often depicted being used by more educated characters with higher socioeconomic status; overweight characters most often were seen consuming more high-fat foods (Sylvester et al., 1993). An analysis of 100 films from 1991 through 2000 found that food and drink appear regularly in films, alcohol is the single most frequently portrayed food or drink, and fats and sweets were the most common foods depicted (see Table 9.6). In addition, product placements are shown an average of one to two times per movie, usually for a beer or soda (Bell et al., 2003). Similarly, an examination of soft drinks in the top-ten grossing movies from 1991 through 2000 found that branded soft drinks appeared in five times the number of movies as other nonalcoholic beverages (Cassady, Townsend, Bell, & Watnik, 2006).

Food Advertised in Schools

Advertisers are using any and all means possible to get messages in front of children and teens, including ads on schools buses, in gymnasiums, on book covers, on athletic teams' warm-up suits, and even on cafeteria tray liners and in bathroom stalls (AAP, 2006; Molnar, 2005). More than 80% of American schools now engage in at least one type of advertising activity (Molnar, Garcia, Boninger, & Merrill, 2006). This trend is not new, however. Trying to target schoolchildren dates back as far as the 1920s, when toothpaste samples were given away (Richards, Wartella, Morton, & Thompson, 1998).

Table 9.6   What Do Movie Characters Eat? (Frequency of Occurrence)

Food	%	Beverages	%
Fats, oils, sweets	34	Alcohol	20
Meat, fish, beans, eggs	17	Coffee/tea	14
Fruits	16	Water	8
Bread, cereal, pasta	14	Soda/juice	3
Vegetables	14	Diet soda	0.1
Milk, cheese, yogurt	4		

SOURCE: Adapted from Bell, Berger, and Townsend (2003).

According to a recent report from the U.S. General Accounting Office (GAO), 200 school districts nationwide have signed exclusive contracts with soft drink companies to sell only those companies' drinks in schools (see Figure 9.7) (Hays, 2000). Another report found that 67% of middle school students and 83% of high school students are in schools that have a contract with a bottler (Johnston, Delva, & O'Malley, 2007). In 2003, a Florida school district signed what is believed to be the largest contract ever negotiated with a bottling company—a $50-million, 12-year contract with Pepsi that will ensure that vending machines in the county's 62 middle and high schools will only sell Pepsi products (Molnar, 2005). Such agreements often specify the number, placement, and yield of soda vending machines, ironic given that schools risk losing federal subsidies for their free breakfast and lunch programs if they serve soda in their cafeterias (Williams, 2001). A 2005 GAO report found that candy, soda, and snack food were crowding out nutritious foods in 90% of schools surveyed (Quaid, 2005). When schools allow snacking and foods high in fat and calories, the BMI of their students increases, according to a study of more than 3,000 students in 16 different Minnesota middle schools (Kubik, Lytle, & Story, 2005). Another problem with this is that there is an abundance of new research that is beginning to question whether frequent consumption of soft drinks might lead to an increased risk of osteoporosis in teenage girls, obesity in children and teens, and even metabolic disorders (American Academy of Pediatrics, 2004; O'Riordan & Vega, 2007). In addition, fast food is a known risk factor for obesity, and Taco Bell sells food in at least 3,000 school cafeterias, Subway in 650, and Pizza Hut in 4,500, among others (Oleck, 1994).

Figure 9.7

SOURCE: Dan Wasserman, *The Boston Globe,* 2000. Tribune Media Services, Inc. All rights reserved.

School curricula also have been affected: One geography unit for third graders has students locating major cities according to where Tootsie Rolls are manufactured (Molnar, 2005). Even textbooks are no longer sacred. Textbook covers distributed by Philip Morris, Reebok, Ralph Lauren, and others now adorn students' textbooks. Channel One was the first to invade the noncommercial sanctity of the schoolhouse, with 10-minute news programs interlaced with 2 minutes of commercials, in exchange for $30,000 worth of TV sets, VCRs, and satellite dishes (E. W. Austin, Chen, Pinkleton, & Johnson, 2006; Bachen, 1998; Wartella & Jennings, 2001). By the end of their first year of operations, Channel One had agreements with 5,000 schools (Molnar, 1996). Currently, more than 8 million middle and high schools students watch Channel One in 12,000 schools, and advertisers pay $200,000 for ad time and the opportunity to target 40% of American teenagers for 30 seconds (Bachen, 1998; Johnston, 2001). According to the GAO report, Channel One now plays in 25% of the nation's middle and high schools and is shown in 350,000 classrooms daily (E. W. Austin et al., 2006; Hays, 2000). By 1998, it generated profits estimated at $100 million annually (Bachen, 1998), although currently it is not nearly as profitable and may be discontinued by its parent company, Primedia, Inc. (Borja, 2006). Nearly 70% of the ads for Channel One are for food—mostly gum, soda, fast food, candy, and chips (Brand & Greenberg, 1994). Considering how controversial Channel One has been, it seems odd that more research has not been conducted on its impact (Bachen, 1998). One of the leading critics of school-based advertising, Alex Molnar, heads the Commercialism in Education Research Unit at Arizona State University. He observes,

> There is a clear distinction between the purposes of marketing and education. Advertising makes no claim to telling the truth. Education attempts to tell the truth, and not because of a special interest but the interest of the entire community. The community and children don't come first in advertising. The sponsor does. (Krayeske, 1999)

Does Television Viewing Increase Childhood Obesity?

Obesity is rapidly becoming a major concern among pediatricians and public health officials, not just in the United States but internationally as well. The World Health Organization (WHO, 2003) notes that this increase in obesity is worldwide. Globally, an estimated 1 billion adults and nearly 18 million children younger than age 5 are overweight or obese (Sector, 2006; WHO, 2003). In the United Kingdom, one third of 15-year-olds are now overweight (BMI > 25), and 17% are obese (BMI > 30) (Reilly & Dorosty, 1999). These numbers have doubled among 6- to 17-year-olds during the past 20 years (Troiano & Flegal, 1998). Currently, 64% of the adult population in the United States is overweight or obese (Morrill & Chinn, 2004). Obesity is thought to be responsible for 5% to 10% of health care expenditures in the United States, costing taxpayers an estimated $92 billion a year (Finkelstein, Fiebelkorn, & Wang, 2003; Koplan & Dietz, 1999). Currently, 300,000 deaths annually can be attributed to obesity, putting it just behind smoking, with 434,000 deaths per year (Mokdad et al., 2003).

Along with aggression, obesity represents one of the two areas of television research where the medium's influence may rise to the level of cause and effect, rather than simply being contributory (AAP, 2006; Jordan & Robinson, 2008; Robinson, 2001; Strasburger, 2006b), although this point remains hotly debated (Robinson, 1998). At least six national studies, using cross-sectional data, have found a significant association between obesity and television viewing among children (see Figure 9.8). The causal arrow may run in either direction (Robinson, 1998). In other words, does television viewing cause obesity, or do obese children tend to be more sedentary and watch more television? But these six national studies seem at least to provide "food for thought" on this issue:

1. Using National Health Survey data, Dietz and Gortmaker (1985) found that hours spent watching TV proved to be a strong predictor of obesity among both 6- to 11-year-olds and 12- to 17-year-olds. For each additional hour of average television viewing above the norm, the prevalence of obesity increased 2%. To exclude the possibility that children or teens watched more television because they were

Figure 9.8

SOURCE: Reprinted with special permission of Universal Press Syndicate.

obese, the researchers studied children who were not obese at baseline (Dietz, 1993). A second study conducted at the same time failed to duplicate these findings (Robinson et al., 1993) but involved a smaller sample and did not use national data (Dietz & Gortmaker, 1993). The researchers concluded that nearly 30% of obesity cases could be prevented if children limited TV viewing to no more than 1 hour per day (Dietz & Gortmaker, 1993).

2. In the National Children and Youth Fitness Survey, parents and teachers were asked to rate a child's activity level and television viewing time (Pate & Ross, 1987). Increased amounts of television viewing were directly and independently associated with the prevalence of obesity, and increased activity was inversely related (Dietz, 1993).

3. Gortmaker et al. (1996) observed a strong dose-response relationship between the prevalence of overweight and hours of television viewed in a national sample of 746 youngsters ages 10 to 15 years. The odds of being overweight were nearly five times greater for preteens and teens who viewed 5 or more hours of television per day compared with those viewing 0 to 2 hours per day.

4. Andersen, Crespo, Bartlett, Cheskin, and Pratt (1998) analyzed data from the Third National Health and Nutrition Examination Survey (NHANES III) on more than 4,000 children ages 8 to 16 and found that those who watched 4 or more hours of television per day had greater body fat and BMIs than those who watched less than 2 hours per day.

5. Crespo et al. (2001) also analyzed data from NHANES III and found that the prevalence of obesity was lowest among children watching less than 1 hour per day of television and was highest among those watching 4 hours or more a day.

6. In a cohort of 2,343 children, ages 9 to 12 years, having a TV set in the bedroom was a significant risk factor for obesity, independent of physical activity or even total media time (Adachi-Mejia et al., 2007).

Two recent studies have also found a strong association between time spent watching TV and blood glucose control in young people with diabetes (Margeirsdottir, Larsen, Brunborg, Sandvik, & Dahl-Jørgensen, 2007) and TV viewing and hypertension (Pardee, Norman, Lustig, Preud'homme, & Schwimmer, 2007). In addition, a new group of large and intensive longitudinal studies has now added further weight to the evidence:

• A remarkable 30-year longitudinal study in the United Kingdom found that mean daily hours of TV viewed on weekends predicted a higher BMI at age 30, even when adjustments were made for socioeconomic status and parental weight status (Viner & Cole, 2005). For each additional hour of TV watched on weekends at age 5, the risk of adult obesity increased by 7%.

• In Australia, a study of nearly 1,300 children at ages 5 to 10 years, with a 3-year follow-up, found that total screen time was positively associated with measures of obesity (Hesketh, Wake, Graham, & Waters, 2007).

- A group of researchers in Dunedin, New Zealand, followed 1,000 unselected subjects from birth to 26 years of age. Average weeknight TV viewing between the ages of 5 and 15 years was strongly correlated with higher BMI (Hancox, Milne, & Poulton, 2004; Hancox & Poulton, 2006). In 26-year-olds, the following problems could have been avoided if they had been limited to no more than 2 hours of TV per day (the current AAP's recommendation) when they were children:

  17% of overweight

  15% of elevated serum cholesterols

  17% of smoking

  15% of poor fitness

- Two more international cohort studies also found significant correlations between TV viewing and obesity. In 8,234 Scottish children, more than 8 hours of TV viewing per week at age 3 was associated with an increased risk of obesity at age 7 (Reilly et al., 2005). And in 8,170 Japanese children, heavier TV viewing at age 3 resulted in higher risk of being overweight at age 6 (Sugimori et al., 2004).

- A 2003 study of 2,223 American adolescents 12 to 17 years old found that teens who watched more than 2 hours of TV a day were twice as likely to be overweight after 3 years as those who watched less than 2 hours a day (Kaur, Choi, Mayo, & Harris, 2003). A 2006 study of 1,016 preschool children followed for up to 4 years had identical findings: 2 hours of TV per day carried a two to three times increased risk of overweight (Lumeng, Rahnama, Appugliese, Kaciroti, & Bradley, 2006). The Framingham Children's Study followed a cohort of 106 children for 7 years from age 4. By age 11, children who watched 3 hours or more of TV per day had the greatest increase in body fat over time (Proctor et al., 2003). An Arkansas study that followed nearly 1,000 children from ages 2 to 12 found similar results (O'Brien et al., 2007). So did a recent study of nearly 2,400 girls, followed for up to 10 annual visits beginning at age 9 or 10 (Henderson, 2007). Finally, a study of 169 girls at ages 7, 9, and 11 years found that those who exceeded the AAP's recommendation were 13 times more likely to be overweight at age 11 and had significantly higher BMIs and percentage body fat (Davison, Marshall, & Birch, 2006).

Many cross-sectional studies, in addition to studies using smaller, regional samples, have shown similar results as well (e.g., Dennison, Erb, & Jenkins, 2002; Eisenmann, Bartee, & Wang, 2002; Schneider, Dunton, & Cooper, 2007; Utter, Neumark-Sztainer, Jeffery, & Story, 2003). Taras et al. (1989) correlated television viewing with 3- to 8-year-olds' caloric intake but did not specifically study their weights. Probably the most important of the cross-sectional studies is a study of 2,761 adults with young children in New York, which found that 40% of the 1- to 5-year-olds had a TV set in their own bedroom and that those who did were more likely to be overweight or obese (Dennison et al., 2002). At least seven international studies have shown significant results—the four cohort studies referred to above and three cross-sectional studies. In Spain, a cross-sectional study of more than 1,000 children ages 13 to 14 found that time spent watching television was significantly associated with higher BMIs in girls and with increased body fat percentages in both sexes (Moreno, Fleta, & Mur, 1998). Among Mexican children and teens, the odds ratios for obesity were 12% higher for each hour of television viewing per day in a study of 712 adolescents ages 9 to 16 (Hernandez et al., 1999). In a study of nearly 2,000 German children, TV viewing predicted being overweight (Kuepper-Nybelen et al., 2005). Furthermore, at least two studies of adults have found that television viewing is positively associated with energy intake (R. W. Jeffery & French, 1998) and with higher BMIs (Crawford, Jeffery, & French, 1999; R. W. Jeffery & French, 1998) among women (but not men). Other studies have found that number of hours of TV watched is a strong predictor for high cholesterol levels in children (Fung et al., 2001; Wong et al., 1992) and that children who watch a lot of TV are more likely to have poor eating habits and unhealthy notions about food (Signorielli & Lears, 1992). TV viewing has also been linked to the development of type II diabetes (Hu et al., 2001, 2003). Only a few studies have found no or very weak correlations between hours of TV viewed and measures of obesity (Durant, Baranowski, Johnson, & Thompson, 1994; Robinson et al., 1993; Vandewater, Shim, & Caplovitz, 2004).

So the argument linking television viewing as one *cause* of obesity is rapidly becoming persuasive. Television viewing probably contributes to overweight and obesity, but exactly *how much* it contributes remains unknown (Jordan, 2007). Interestingly, the reverse can be shown to be true: If television viewing is reduced, BMI decreases in children (Robinson, 1999, 2000). In a classic, often-cited field experiment, Robinson (1999) used a simple 18-lesson, 6-month classroom curriculum to reduce media use. He demonstrated statistically significant decreases in third- and fourth-grade students' BMIs, skinfold thicknesses, waist circumferences, and waist-to-hip ratios (all important measures of adiposity). Among the students receiving the curriculum, there was less television viewing and fewer meals eaten in front of the television set than among the control students. Gortmaker et al. (1999) achieved similar success using a health curriculum over 2 years with 1,295 sixth- and seventh-grade students that resulted in decreases in TV viewing, increased fruit and vegetable consumption, and decreases in the prevalence of obesity (Gortmaker et al., 1999). (Others have demonstrated that a family-based intervention to decrease screen media time can reduce obesity [Epstein, Valoski, Vara, & Rodefer, 1995] and that a seven-session curriculum can successfully decrease TV viewing in preschool children, although levels of obesity were not examined [Dennison, Russo, Burdick, & Jenkins, 2004].)

Why might the association between television viewing and obesity exist? Contrary to popular opinion, it only takes an excess intake of 50 kcal a day to produce a weight gain of 5 pounds per year (Dietz, 1993). In other words, obesity is probably caused by small incremental increases in daily caloric intake (or small increases in sedentary activities), not massive binges of overeating. Therefore, even if television viewing exerts only a slight effect, it may be highly significant. Because obesity is caused by an imbalance of excess intake compared with energy expenditure (Yanovski & Yanovski, 1999), TV viewing may contribute in several ways:

1. *Displacement of more active pursuits.* As the leading leisure-time activity, television constitutes the principal source of inactivity for children and adolescents (Dietz, 1993). Children spend more time watching television than in any other activity except for sleeping (Roberts, Foehr, & Rideout, 2005). Williams' (1986) naturalistic study found that children participated less in sports activities once TV was introduced into their community. In the United States, data from the National Children and Youth Fitness Survey show that parents' and teachers' ratings of a child's activity level and time spent watching TV correlated directly with children's prevalence of obesity (Pate & Ross, 1987). A study of obese 8- to 12-year-olds also found that reducing the amount of viewing and other sedentary behaviors resulted in decreased body fat and increased aerobic fitness (Epstein, Paluch, Gordy, & Dorn, 2000). Most recently, the 5-year longitudinal study, Project EAT-II, followed more than 2,500 students from early to mid-adolescence and found that moderate to vigorous exercise decreases as leisure-time computer use increases (Nelson, Neumark-Stzainer, Hannan, Sirard, & Story, 2006). The same finding was true in a 2½-year longitudinal study of 200 Australian girls ages 12 to 15 years (Hardy, Bass, & Booth, 2007). But the studies are not uniformly in agreement on the issue of displacement (Kaiser Family Foundation, 2004a; Wiecha et al., 2006). Several studies (e.g., Andersen et al., 1998; Burdette & Whitaker, 2005; Robinson et al., 1993; Taveras et al., 2007) have failed to find a relationship between decreases in television viewing and increases in physical activity. It may be that children who do not watch a lot of TV viewing may be replacing TV with *other* sedentary activities rather than vigorous exercise (Jordan, 2007; Vandewater et al., 2004). It may also be that researchers' measures of physical activity are too imprecise. Nevertheless, increasing exercise, decreasing sedentary behaviors, and changing to better nutritional practices can be shown to prevent the onset of obesity, if not decrease obesity as well (Dietz, 2006a, 2006b; Epstein et al., 2002; Goldfield et al., 2006; Haerens et al., 2006; Washington, 2005). One clever obesity researcher has developed a "TVcycle," a bicycle hooked up electrically to a television set so that the set will only work if the bicycle is being ridden. Ten overweight 8- to 12-year-olds enrolled in this study lost 1% of their total body fat in a preliminary study and decreased average TV viewing time from 21 hours to 1.6 hours per week (Faith et al., 2001). Reducing total media time may be even more effective than increasing the amount of exercise in reducing weight (Epstein et al., 1995; Robinson, 2000; Washington, 2005). Clearly, if children and adolescents devoted just 1 hour a day to physical activities of the 3 hours they spend watching TV, their risk of obesity would diminish considerably.

2. *Increased energy intake.* Today's children and teens are more likely to eat in fast-food restaurants and consume more fried and high-fat foods than young people in the 1960s and 1970s (Bowman, Gortmaker, Ebbeling, Pereira, & Ludwig, 2004; Wiecha et al., 2006). Portion sizes have also increased dramatically, by 100 to 400 kcal for the average restaurant meal (Close & Schoeller, 2006; Nielsen & Popkin, 2003;

Schwartz & Byrd-Bredbrenner, 2006). On any given day in the United States, 30% of children and teens are eating fast food and consuming an additional 187 kcal (equaling 6 extra pounds per year) (Bowman et al., 2004; Brownell, 2004). One study of 2- to 6-year-olds found a strong correlation between amount of TV viewed and fast-food consumption (Taveras et al., 2006). Not surprisingly, fast-food restaurants are clustered around schools. In Chicago, there are three to four times as many fast-food restaurants within walking distance from schools than would be expected from a normal distribution of such restaurants around the city (S. B. Austin et al., 2005). Children and teens also snack more frequently than ever before (Institute of Medicine, 2006). Teenagers who watch more television tend to eat higher fat diets (Blass et al., 2006; Robinson & Killen, 1995; Wiecha et al., 2006), drink more sodas (Giammattei et al., 2003), and eat less fruits and vegetables (Krebs-Smith et al., 1996). A study of 91 parent-child pairs found that families who watch television during mealtimes tend to eat more pizzas, snack foods, and sodas and fewer fruits and vegetables (Coon, Goldberg, Rogers, & Tucker, 2001). Another recent study of nearly 5,000 Midwest middle and high school students documented that high television use was associated with more snacking, soft drink intake, and eating more fast food (Utter et al., 2003). Similar studies of more than 162,000 preteens and teens in Europe and 10,000 Dutch teenagers found that snacking was correlated with TV viewing (Snoek, van Strien, Janssens, & Engels, 2006; Vereecken, Todd, Roberts, Mulvihill, & Maes, 2005). Even experimental studies have found that TV viewing is associated with increased snacking (Blass et al., 2006; Epstein et al., 2008; Temple, Giacomelli, Kent, Roemmich, & Epstein, 2007). In addition, older research indicates that ads for high-fat or high-calorie foods do influence children's eating habits (Gorn & Goldberg, 1982; D. B. Jeffrey, McLellarn, & Fox, 1983). Television deluges young viewers with advertisements for food products and fast-food restaurants that provide marginal nutritional value at best. In addition, prime-time and Saturday morning programming models poor nutritional behavior for children. Time spent watching TV correlates with children's attempts to influence parents' food purchases, children's choice of snacks, the frequency of snacking while watching TV, and children's total caloric intake (Dietz, 1993; Taras et al., 1989). In a study of 209 fourth- and fifth-grade students, Signorielli and Lears (1992) found that heavy TV viewing was an extremely strong predictor of poor nutritional habits and that heavy viewers were far more likely to believe that food at a "fast-food" restaurant was as nutritious as a meal prepared at home. Similarly, two studies have found that both children and adolescents tend to consume higher fat foods if they view a lot of television (Wiecha et al., 2006; Wong et al., 1992). In a recent study of 548 students in five public schools near Boston, researchers found that each hour increase in TV viewing brought an additional 167 kcal/day as the result of eating foods commonly advertised on TV (Wiecha et al., 2006).

Perhaps the leading culprits in excess energy intake are sugar-sweetened beverages, especially sodas and juices (see Table 9.7 and Figure 9.9) (Bawa, 2005; Dietz, 2006a; Jacobson, 2005; Malik, Schulze, & Hu, 2006). There seems to be little disagreement—at least among physicians, nutritionists, and public health activists (see Exercise 3)—that consumption of sugar-sweetened drinks is a major factor contributing to the new epidemic of childhood and adolescent obesity (Kaiser Family Foundation, 2004a).

Table 9.7   Sugar-Sweetened Drinks and Obesity

Sugar-sweetened drinks represent the largest single food source of calories in the American diet, providing 9% of daily calories[a,b]

Teenagers get 13% of their daily calories from soft drinks.[b]

The recent increase in type II diabetes parallels the increase in sugar-sweetened drink consumption.[c,d]

The odds of becoming obese increase 1.6 times for every drink consumed per day.[e]

Enough soda pop is produced annually in the United States to provide 557 twelve-oz. cans to every man, woman, and child.[b]

Soft drink companies spend approximately $700 million on advertising annually.[b]

One 12-oz. can of soda contains 150 kcal and 40 to 50 g of sugar. Drinking one can of soda per day will result in a 15-lb. weight gain over 1 year.[f]

There is now evidence of a causal connection between intake of sugar-sweetened beverages (soda and juice) and obesity.[f-j] A total of 30 studies have been done (15 cross-sectional, 10 prospective, 5 experimental), most of which find a significant connection.[i]

Of all beverages, soda consumption predicted BMI and poor calcium intake the best.[h]

Decreasing children's and teens' intake of sugar-sweetened beverages results in decreased measures of obesity.[k,l]

Colas contain caffeine and phosphoric acid that may also interfere with bone mineral density, according to the most recent findings of the Framingham Osteoporosis Study, which measured bone density in more than 3,000 adult subjects.[m]

---

a. Block (2004).
b. Jacobson (2005).
c. Schulze et al. (2004).
d. Bray, Nielson, and Popkin (2004).
e. Ludwig, Peterson, and Gortmaker (2001).
f. Apovian (2004).

g. Dietz (2006a).
h. Striegel-Moore et al. (2006).
i. Malik et al. (2006).
j. Berkey, Rockett, Field, Gillman, and Colditz (2004).
k. James, Thomas, Cavan, and Kerr (2004).
l. Ebbeling et al. (2006).
m. K. L. Tucker et al. (2006).

3. *Decreased energy expenditure.* Interestingly, a child's metabolic rate is actually lower while watching television than while resting quietly, according to one study (Klesges, Shelton, & Klesges, 1993), although these results have never been replicated (Cooper, Klesges, Debon, Klesges, & Shelton, 2006; Dietz, 1993; Lanningham-Foster et al., 2006). But several studies do indicate that television viewing may adversely affect physical fitness (Eisenmann et al., 2002; Motl, McAuley, Birnbaum, & Lytle, 2006; Nelson & Gordon-Larsen, 2006; Robinson et al., 1993; L. A. Tucker, 1986) and is associated with an increased caloric intake (Wiecha et al., 2006).

Recently, Horgen et al. (2001) have proposed a comprehensive theory to explain the pathway from food advertising to consumption and obesity (see Figure 9.10). Information from ads is first "coded" and then later retrieved, in some ways

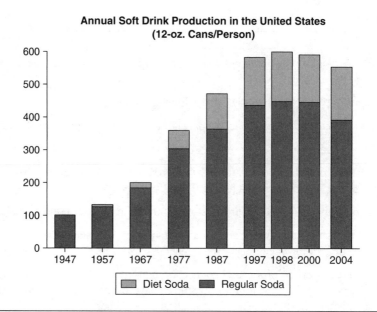

Figure 9.9   Annual Soft Drink Production in the United States (12-oz. Cans/Person)

SOURCE: Horgen et al. (2001). Reprinted with permission.

similar to the effects of music videos on teenagers: First teens see the video, and then they hear the song associated with it and "flash back" to the video (P. Greenfield & Beagles-Roos, 1988). Children viewing advertisements associate certain likeable characters and memorable slogans—triggers—with certain products. Repetitive ads increase the association. Associations are then triggered when walking down a supermarket aisle or seeing a billboard. Any of these factors could lead to either a request to the parent to purchase the product or the child purchasing the product himself or herself. Once consumed, the product leads to increased calorie levels (because products advertised are usually unhealthy and high in fat or sugar). Assuming that exercise patterns remain stable, obesity results because of the imbalance between intake and expenditure.

It should be noted that the lack of unanimity among all of the various studies should not be confusing. Given that the correlations are often small, it is not surprising that some studies' data would not reach the level of statistical significance. The other problem is that it is difficult to get accurate self-reports of TV viewing or physical activity from children and adolescents (or their parents, for that matter). Experimental studies in which the sole variable being manipulated is the amount of television viewed could be useful in the future (Robinson, 1999, 2001). The one experimental study that has been done documents that college students take in an additional 163 calories a day when they watch TV (Stroebele & de Castro, 2004). But the newer longitudinal cohort studies seem to be quite convincing all on their own, and many researchers now feel that the evidence is conclusive—excessive TV viewing is one cause of overweight and obesity (Christakis, 2006; Dietz, 2006b; Gortmaker, 2008; Jordan, 2007; Washington, 2005; Wiecha et al., 2006).

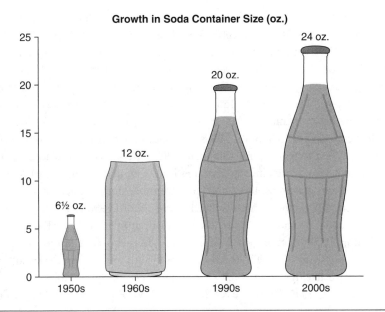

Figure 9.10   Food Pathway

SOURCE: Horgen, Choate, and Brownell (2001). Reprinted with permission.

Eating Disorders and Body Image

One of the most important developments in communication research during the past decade has been researchers' increased interest in examining the role that the media play in women's health, specifically women's self-image and eating disorders. In 2000, the British Medical Association (2000) issued a landmark report on the subject, and researchers such as Field, Kilbourne, Levine, Harrison, and many others have added considerably to our knowledge (Field et al., 2005; Kilbourne, 2000; Levine & Harrison, 2003).

One of the first researchers to take an interest in this area was Kaufman (1980), who conducted a content analysis of eating behavior on television and observed that prime-time TV characters are usually happy in the presence of food. Yet food is rarely used to satisfy hunger. Rather, it serves to bribe others or to facilitate social introductions. As with other media, television seems to have an obsession with thinness: 88% of all characters are thin or average in body build, obesity is confined to middle or old age, and being overweight provides comic ammunition (Kaufman, 1980; B. Silverstein, Perdue, Peterson, & Kelly, 1986). On shows popular with teenagers, 94% of characters are below average in weight (Levine & Smolak, 1996). Clearly, when it comes to body habitus, the world of television does not portray the real world accurately (see Table 9.8) (B. S. Greenberg, Eastin, Hofschire, Lachlan, & Brownell, 2003). Some researchers have suggested that the presence of so many TV commercials for food, combined with other ads' emphasis on female beauty, fosters the development of eating disorders (Botta, 1999; Lavine, Sweeney, & Wagner, 1999; Ogletree, Williams, Raffeld, & Mason, 1990; Tiggeman, 2005). Others have suggested that situation comedies could play a role because thin characters receive significantly more positive verbal comments from male characters than heavier female characters do (Bell et al., 2003; B. S. Greenberg et al., 2003).

Interestingly, as the number of diet food product commercials has increased dramatically on network TV between 1973 and 1991, a parallel rise has occurred in eating disorders (Wiseman, Gunning, & Gray, 1993). Similar research by B. Silverstein and Perlick (1995) found that as thin models and actresses appeared more frequently in media from 1910 to 1930 and again from 1950 to 1980, eating disorders increased as well. In the 1990s, the diet industry tripled its revenues, from $10 billion a year to $36 billion (Kilbourne, 1999). Articles about dieting and exercise in women's magazines increased dramatically around the same time (Wiseman, Gray, Mosimann, & Ahrens, 1992) and far outnumber similar articles in men's magazines (Nemeroff, Stein, Diehl, & Smilack, 1994). From 1990 to 2000, the number of teen-oriented magazines more than tripled, from 5 to 19 (Kaiser Family Foundation, 2004b). Studies have found that girls who read fashion magazines often compare themselves with the models in the ads and the articles, resulting in more negative feelings about their own appearance (Clay, Vignoles, & Dittmar, 2005; Field et al., 2005; Hofschire & Greenberg, 2001; Pinhas, Toner, Ali, Garfinkel, & Stuckless, 1999).

Whether this is cause and effect or simply correlational is arguable. As Kilbourne (1999) notes, there seems to be a very complicated connection between the diet industry and the real world. For example, a Weight Watchers ad shows a scrumptious piece of Boston cream pie, with the caption, "Feel free to act on impulse." Why would Weight Watchers want to tempt people to indulge in high-calorie desserts?

Table 9.8   How Accurately Does TV Reflect Body Types in the Real World?
(*N* = 1,018 Prime-Time TV Characters)

	On TV (%)	Real World (%)
Overweight/obese males	24	48
Overweight/obese females	14	28
Underweight females	33	5
Overweight characters	Nonrecurring	
	Fewer romances	
	Fewer friends	
	Less leadership	
	Less sex	
	Shown eating	

SOURCE: Data from B. S. Greenberg et al. (2003).

Could it be because it is actually in their best business interests for people to fatten up and then want to diet or to fail to lose weight, so that their revenues will continue to grow (Kilbourne, 1999)?

Meanwhile, the exact specifications for thinness continue to diminish, almost yearly. A classic study of body measurements of *Playboy* centerfolds and Miss America contestants over a 10-year period found that body weight averaged 13% to 19% below that expected for age (Wiseman et al., 1992). Among Miss America winners from 1922 to 1999, BMIs have declined significantly from 22 to less than 18, which signifies undernutrition (see Figure 9.11) (Rubinstein & Caballero, 2000). Two decades ago, the average American model weighed 8% less than the average American woman; today, she weighs 23% less (Kilbourne, 1999). In one study, adolescent girls described the "ideal girl" as being 5'7", 100 pounds, size 5, with long blonde hair and blue eyes (Nichter & Nichter, 1991)—clearly a body shape that is both rare and close to impossible to achieve.

Evidence is increasing that there are tremendous sociocultural pressures on today's girls and young women to try to attain body shapes that are unhealthy, unnatural, and dictated by media norms (BMA, 2000). Many researchers feel that this "internalization of the thin-ideal body image" has resulted in Western women's increasing dissatisfaction with their bodies and subsequent increase in eating disorders (see Table 9.9) (Field et al., 2001; Kilbourne, 2000; Levine & Harrison, 2003; Nishna, Ammon, Bellmore, & Graham, 2006; Stice & Whitenton, 2002; Thompson, 2003). Even young children's videos like *Cinderella* and *The Little Mermaid* have

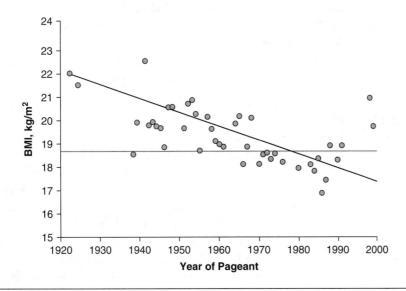

Figure 9.11   Trend in Body Mass Index (BMI) of Miss America Pageant Winners, 1922 to 1999.

SOURCE: From the *Journal of the American Medical Association, 283*, p. 1569, 2000. Copyright © AMA.

NOTE: The World Health Organization's BMI cutoff point for undernutrition is 18.5.

Table 9.9   Influence of Women's Fashion Magazines on Girls (N = 548 Girls in 5th–12th Grades)

Behavior	Infrequent Reader (%)	Frequent Reader (%)	p Value
Dieting	34	45	.03
Dieting because of a magazine article	13	22	.0
Exercising to lose weight	48	64	.004
Exercising because of a magazine article	14	29	.001
Body image influenced by pictures	59	79	.001
Pictures make them want to lose weight	41	57	.004

SOURCE: Adapted from Field, Cheung, et al. (1999).

been shown to contain body image–related themes (Herbozo, Tantleff-Dunn, Gokee-Larose, & Thompson, 2004). In one startling study of 128 five- to eight-year-olds in Australia, many of them already wanted to be thinner by age 6 (Dohnt & Tiggeman, 2006). But, as always, the research does not yield a simplistic "yes or no" answer to the question of whether media exposure *causes* eating disorders. Probably the most conservative view is that there is now considerable evidence that the media influence body image and self-dissatisfaction among young girls and women.

Disordered Body Image

Body image has become an increasingly major concern of teenagers, especially females. Dissatisfaction seems to increase among young females and decrease among males during adolescence (Bearman, Martinez, & Stice, 2006). Young African American women who are dissatisfied with their body image may be at increased risk for unintended pregnancies or sexually transmitted infections (Wingood, DiClemente, Harrington, & Davies, 2002). As many as half of normal-weight teenage girls consider themselves overweight and have tried to lose weight (Krowchuk et al., 1998; Strauss, 1999). Television, movies, magazines, and music videos all display women with impossible bodies and put pressure on adolescent females to conform (see Table 9.10 and Figure 9.12) (Field et al., 2001, 2005; Hofschire & Greenberg, 2001; Levine & Harrison, 2003; Tiggeman, 2005). Sitcoms such as *Friends* and *Ally McBeal,* soap operas, music videos, and films popular with teenagers may even expose young girls to potential role models who suffer from eating disorders themselves (Levine & Harrison, 2003). Overweight female characters on sitcoms are often criticized by male characters about their appearance (Fouts & Burggraf, 2000), whereas overweight male characters tend to make fun of themselves but receive no negative comments from female characters (Fouts & Vaughan, 2002). In music videos, one study of 837 ninth-grade girls found that the number of hours spent watching videos was related to their assessment of the importance of appearance and their weight concerns (Borzekowski, Robinson, Killen, 2000). Another recent study of nearly 100 young women viewing either a music video that emphasized the importance of appearance or a neutral music video found that the former increased comparisons and body dissatisfaction (Tiggeman & Slater, 2004). Similarly, exposing young girls to ultra-thin or even average-size magazine models lowers their body satisfaction and their self-esteem (Clay et al., 2005). Of the three recent meta-analyses performed, two have found a significant association between body dissatisfaction and exposure to media (Cafri, Yamamiya, Brannick, & Thompson, 2005; Groesz, Levine, & Murnen, 2001) and one has not (Holmstrom, 2004).

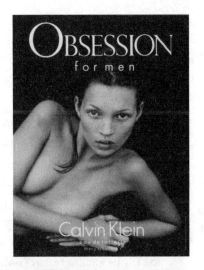

Figure 9.12

Table 9.10 How Do Men and Women Perceive the Body Weight of Media Characters? (in Percentages)

Body Weight	TV		Movies		Music Videos		Magazine Ad Models	
	Male	Female	Male	Female	Male	Female	Male	Female
Very thin	1	7	0	0	8	0	0	2
Thin	15	39	4	39	36	43	8	24
Average	65	41	76	58	44	36	58	39
Obese	6	1	4	0	0	0	0	0

SOURCE: Adapted from Signorielli (1997).

There are four key components to the theory that sociocultural factors play an important role in body image and, perhaps, eating disorders as well (see Table 9.11) (Levine, Smolak, & Hayden, 1994):

1. Although the "ideal" woman has gotten increasingly thinner since the 1990s, the real woman has actually gotten heavier (Levine & Smolak, 1996; Rubinstein & Caballero, 2000).

2. Thinness has become associated with social, personal, and professional success (Guillen & Barr, 1994; Signorielli, 1997).

3. For teen girls especially, the "thin look" has become normative (BMA, 2000; Field, Cheung, et al., 1999; Signorielli, 1997).

4. Adolescent girls and grown women have been led to believe that thinness can actually be attained easily (BMA, 2000; Field, Cheung, et al., 1999).

Advertisements on teen-oriented shows use beauty as a product appeal most of the time: 56% of the ads targeting females, compared with just 3% of the ads aimed

Table 9.11 How Media Might Contribute to Eating Disorders

Emphasis on importance of appearance
Narrow definition of physical beauty
Creation of thinness as the "gold standard"
Linking thinness to success and beauty
Abhorrence of fat and fat women
Emphasis on dieting and fashion
Establishment of gender roles based on unrealistic expectations

SOURCE: Adapted from Levine and Smolak (1996).

at males (Signorielli, 1997). In movies, 58% of female characters have their looks commented on (Signorielli, 1997). Seventy percent of girls say that they want to look like a character on television (compared with 40% of boys), and half of those say that they did something to change their appearance as a result (Signorielli, 1997). Women are often caught up in the trap of living in a culture in which they are expected to be the objects of the male gaze but then feel the need to compare favorably with ultra-thin role models (Jones, Vigfusdottir, & Lee, 2004; Martin & Gentry, 1997). American media are notorious for this, whereas non-Western media focus more on the beauty of the face rather than the body (Frith, Shaw, & Cheng, 2005). In one interesting experiment, college women concerned about their body shape judged thin celebrities as thinner than they actually were, whereas women comfortable with their body shape judged them accurately (King, Touyz, & Charles, 2000). In another series of recent studies, girls who wanted to look like media figures on television, in the movies, or in magazines were twice as likely to be very concerned with their weight, become constant dieters, and engage in purging behavior (Field, Camargo, et al., 1999; Field, Cheung, et al., 1999; Field et al., 2001). This was a large study, with a 1-year follow-up, of 6,770 girls ages 9 to 14 years in a national sample. Another recent longitudinal study of 257 preteen girls found that TV viewing predicted thinner body ideals and disordered eating a year later (Harrison & Hefner, 2006). Finally, in a large sample of nearly 11,000 male and female teens, those who wanted to look like media role models were significantly more likely to use anabolic steroids or unproven protein supplements (Field et al., 2005).

Magazines such as *Seventeen, Teen,* and *YM* were the top three teen magazines up until the late 1990s and enjoyed readerships of more than 6 million girls (Kaiser Family Foundation, 2004b). But then an explosion of teen magazines occurred, with *Teen People, CosmoGIRL!, Elle Girl, Teen Vogue,* and others entering the market. All practically dictate that thin is in, fat is out, and you are no one unless you are impossibly thin with big breasts and small hips. Or, as one 15-year-old girl put it, "Everybody feels like they are not good enough, not pretty enough, not skinny enough. . . . Every time you open a magazine you always see beautiful people . . . you have to look good to be a good person" (Wertheim, Paxton, Schutz, & Muir, 1997, p. 350). Several studies have found an association between reading popular teen or fashion magazines and the presence of weight concerns or symptoms of eating disorders in girls (Field, Cheung, et al., 1999; Hofschire & Greenberg, 2001; Jones et al., 2004; Stice & Shaw, 1994; Taylor et al., 1998). In a 1999 study of 548 girls in 5th to 12th grades, most were unhappy with their body weight and shape, and 69% reported that their ideal body was influenced by reading fashion magazines or other media (Field, Cheung, et al., 1999).

The most fascinating experiment examining teenagers and magazines was performed by Turner, Hamilton, Jacobs, Angood, and Dwyer (1997). Young college women were randomly assigned to a waiting room with two different sets of magazines before answering a survey about dieting and body image. They were exposed either to four fashion magazines or four newsmagazines. Those who chose a fashion magazine to read reported more dissatisfaction with their weight, more guilt associated with eating, and greater fear of getting fat. It is not surprising, then, that one ongoing meta-analysis of more than 20 experimental studies indicates that exposure to images of thin models causes an increase in a female's negative feelings about her body (Levine, 2000).

Many surveys have also found that adolescent females demonstrate exaggerated fears of obesity regardless of their actual body weight (Moses, Banilivy, & Lifshitz, et al., 1989; Rome et al., 2003; Story & Neumark-Sztainer, 1991). People trust the media, especially television (Horgen et al., 2001), but the image that the media display of the "ideal" woman is increasingly distorted. Aside from a few exceptions—Roseanne Barr in the 1980s and Queen Latifah more recently—there is a dearth of smart, successful, overweight female media role models. One exception was the 2002 outstanding movie portraying an overweight Hispanic teenager and her life, aptly named *Real Women Have Curves*. Another attempt to buck this trend has been the British Broadcasting Corporation's 1985 ban on televising beauty pageants, labeling them "an anachronism in this day and age of equality and verging on the offensive" ("BBC Bans Beauty Contest," 1985).

Interestingly, the media themselves have taken up this concern as well, with a nearly overbearing obsession with the fluctuation in weights of Alicia Silverstone (*Clueless*), Calista Flockhart (*Ally McBeal*), the women in *Friends,* and female supermodels. Whether this degree of publicity about actresses' body weights is healthy or harmful remains to be tested.

Anorexia Nervosa and Bulimia

Several cross-sectional studies have found an apparent link between level of media exposure and likelihood of having an eating disorder or eating disorder symptomatology (Field, Camargo, et al., 1999; Harrison, 2000a, 2000b; Levine et al., 1994; M. C. Martin & Kennedy, 1994; Murray, Touyz, & Beumont, 1996; Stice, Schupak-Neuberg, Shaw, & Stein, 1994). Body image disturbances seem to play an important role in patients with anorexia nervosa or bulimia, according to a recent meta-analysis of 66 studies (Cash & Deagle, 1997). How do such disturbances originate? Young women with eating disorders report that magazines and newspapers influence their eating habits and their concept of beauty, for example (Murray et al., 1996). They tend to overestimate body sizes in experimental situations (Verri, Verticale, Vallero, Bellone, & Nespoli, 1997; Waller, Shaw, Hamilton, & Baldwin, 1994). A study of more than 11,000 males and females, ages 9 to 14, found that those who wanted to look like figures in the media were much more likely than their peers to be concerned about their weight (Field et al., 2001). The same research group found a greater likelihood of purging behaviors among teens subscribing to a "media ideal" of beauty. Wanting to look like actresses or models on television, in movies, or in magazines doubled the risk of beginning to purge at least monthly (Field, Camargo, et al., 1999). Another recent longitudinal study of more than 2,500 middle and high school students found that the prevalence of unhealthy behaviors such as purging or using laxatives doubled after 5 years for the girls who were heavy readers of magazines with dieting and weight loss articles (van den Berg, Neumark-Sztainer, Hannan, & Haines, 2007). Elementary and middle school girls whose devotion to fashion magazines leads them to compare their bodies with fashion models report greater levels of dissatisfaction with their bodies and higher numbers of eating dis-order symptoms (Levine et al., 1994; Martin & Kennedy, 1994). Studies of college women find that those who most "internalize" the cultural bias toward thinness score higher on tests of body dissatisfaction and bulimia (Thompson, Heinberg, Altabe, & Tantleff-Dunn, 1999). And girls who decrease their exposure to television and to fashion magazines exhibit less eating disorder symptomatology over time (Vaughan & Fouts, 2003). Finally, the Internet has become a source of support for continuing unhealthy eating behaviors, with at least 20 pro-anorexia Web sites iden-tified in a recent study (Norris, Boydell, Pinhas, & Katzman, 2006).

Perhaps the most powerful link between media and eating disorders occurred in a naturalistic study (Becker, 2002). Three years after television was introduced into the Pacific isle of Fiji, 15% of teenage girls reported that they had vomited to con-trol their weight. This contrasted with only 3% reporting this behavior prior to the introduction of TV. In addition, the proportion of teen girls scoring abnormally high on a test for disordered eating doubled. Three fourths of girls reported feeling "too big or fat" after the introduction of TV, and those who watched at least 3 nights per week were 50% more likely to feel that way and 30% more likely to diet. Another recent study is intriguing as well—a study of nearly 3,000 Spanish 12- to 21-year-olds over a 19-month period. Those who read girls' magazines had a dou-bled risk of developing an eating disorder (Martinez-Gonzalez et al., 2003).

Occasionally, studies do not find a correlation between eating disorders and exposure to fashion magazines (Cusumano & Thompson, 1997), television (Harrison & Cantor, 1997), or other media (Barrett, 1997; Cash, Ancis, & Strachan, 1997; Champion & Furnham, 1999). Sometimes a study may find that one medium has no correlation with dysfunctional symptoms (e.g., television), but other media do (e.g., fashion magazines, music videos, soap operas, and movies) (Harrison & Cantor, 1997; Tiggeman & Pickering, 1996). These variable findings may result from researchers' reliance on self-reports of media exposure or from the fact that teens are notoriously susceptible to the "third-person effect" (i.e., the belief that the media affect everyone but oneself) (Eveland, Nathanson, Detenber, & McLeod, 1999). In addition, many "no effect" studies still report important findings. Harrison and Cantor's (1997) study found that reading "fitness" magazines and having an interest in dieting accounted for a significant amount of the variance on their subjects' Eating Attitudes Test (EAT) scores, but watching popular shows on television did not. Yet Harrison's (2000b) most recent study of 300 children ages 6 to 8 years at two Midwest schools did find a correlation between television viewing and symptoms of eating disorders.

So the media may play a role as a catalyst or intermediate influence, rather than as a direct and complete cause of eating problems, perhaps only in certain sub-groups of young women (Harrison, 1998). Or, it could be as simple as the media contributing to the formation of a woman's negative body image (BMA, 2000), which, if this occurs during early adolescence, makes a subsequent eating disorder more likely (Dietz, 1998). Unfortunately, little research has been done on male body images and eating disorders (Field et al., 2001; Levine, 2000). One study of boys' action figures between 1964 and 1998 found that although waist sizes have remained constant, chest and biceps measurements have ballooned (Pope, 1999).

Mostly, boys want to bulk up, not slim down (Jones et al., 2004; Tiggeman, 2005). So boys and teenage males may possess sociocultural ideals that are completely opposite from those of girls and young women.

Conclusion

Considerable data exist to justify the notion that the media have a significant impact on adolescents' eating habits, the occurrence of obesity during childhood and adolescence, and adolescents' and young women's self-images of their bodies and perhaps even contribute to the development of eating disorders. Exactly what role the media play remains open to conjecture. Clearly there is some cultivation effect at work here (Gerbner, Gross, Morgan, & Signorielli, 1994): Girls and young women view beautiful, thin characters in the media and are led to believe that these impossible ideals are "normative" and they, themselves, are inadequate. But the research is certainly complex and incomplete at the present time, and considerably more work is needed (Levine & Harrison, 2003; Strasburger, 2005).

Solutions

Solving the twin problems of obesity and eating disorders in the United States is, of course, a mission impossible. But if media images of cigarette smoking, women in athletics, drunk driving, and violence against women can change dramatically over decades, why not the "impossibly thin" body image (Levine & Harrison, 2003)? Why not reduce the unhealthy food advertisements, particularly the ones targeting young children?

Some public health groups such as the Center for Science in the Public Interest (CSPI) have been a thorn in the side of the food industry for many years and have successfully focused the public's attention on issues such as the fat content of movie popcorn and the poor nutritional choices available in fast-food restaurants (Horgen et al., 2001). Most recently, CSPI has suggested a tax on junk food (Jacobson, 2000). A national 2-cent tax on every can of soda, for example, would raise $3 billion annually (Jacobson, 2005). Michael Jacobson, the director of CSPI, notes that the food industry spends more than $33 billion a year to encourage people to buy their products, many of which are high in fat, sugar, or salt. A tax on junk foods could even the score considerably (Jacobson, 2000). Other possibilities include the following (AAP, 2006; Brownell & Horgen, 2004; Christakis & Zimmerman, 2006; Jacobson, 2005; Jordan & Robinson, 2008; Kaiser Family Foundation, 2004a; Strasburger, 2004):

- Limiting or regulating the amount of food advertising of snack food, soda, and fast food on prime-time and children's TV. Many countries (Australia, the Netherlands, Sweden) already do this and have lower rates of childhood obesity (Hawkes, 2004; Nestle, 2000a). Restrictions or a ban on the use of celebrities or cartoon characters in food advertising aimed at children could also be useful (Nestle,

2000a). In Britain, a ban on the advertising of food and beverages that are high in fat, salt, and sugar in programming for children and teens is currently being considered. Any program that attracts an average proportion of viewers younger than 16 that is higher than in the general population would be affected (International Clearinghouse on Children, Youth, & Media, 2006). Masterfoods, the maker of Snickers and Mars candy bars, recently agreed to stop advertising its candy bars to children younger than age 12 in the United States (Gold, 2007). Similarly, Kellogg's announced that it will phase out advertising to children younger than age 12 unless the foods meet specific nutritional guidelines (A. Martin, 2007). Disney has promised to limit the use of its characters in junk food marketing and, instead, will use Mickey, Minnie, Donald, and Goofy to try to sell a new line of fruits and vegetables in supermarkets around the country (CNNMoney.com, 2007). Whether these voluntary corporate concessions are sufficient or will succeed remains to be seen (Barnes, 2007; Jacobson, 2007). A recent survey of American adults found that 77% favored restricting fast food and junk food ads on children's TV (Evans, Renaud, Finkelstein, Kamerow, & Brown, 2006).

• Increasing government funding for healthy nutrition PSAs and expanding public education campaigns. The CSPI's "1% or Less" campaign to encourage people to switch from whole milk to 1% or skim milk is one example of such a campaign.

• Encouraging parents to limit their children's current 3 hours/day of screen time to 2 hours or less (AAP, 2006; Schmidt & Rich, 2006), although some recent research suggests that this may be difficult if parents are not given clear alternatives (Jordan, Hersey, McDivitt, & Heitzler, 2006). In addition, parents need to be encouraged to turn off the TV during mealtimes (Jordan & Robinson, 2008). Currently, 40% of families have a TV set in the dining room or kitchen, and several studies suggest that the set is on during dinner (Jordan et al., 2006).

• Increasing funding for research into the impact of advertising on children and adolescents, the impact of television on obesity, and creative solutions for protecting children and teens against harmful media effects. A new Beverage Guidance Panel has been convened to systematically review new research on beverages and health and provide guidance for consumers (Popkin et al., 2006). Racial and ethnic differences need to be researched (Durkin, Paxton, & Wertheim, 2005; Newman, Sontag, & Salvato, 2006; Nollen et al., 2006; Schooler, Ward, Merriwether, & Caruthers, 2004). For example, shows with a high African American viewership tend to have a higher prevalence of obese characters (27% vs. 2%) and more food commercials (4.8 per half hour vs. 2.9) (Outley & Taddese, 2006; Tirodkar & Jain, 2003). Yet adolescents' body satisfaction is highest among African American teens (Kelly, Wall, Eisenberg, Story, & Neumark-Sztainer, 2005). Are African American children and teens *more* susceptible to food advertising and therefore at higher risk for obesity, or are they more media resistant and therefore have a lower incidence of eating disorders, or both?

The American Academy of Pediatrics recently reviewed the available research and concluded that advertising directed to children younger than age 8 is inherently deceptive and unfair (AAP, 2006). Even older children and teens may still be extremely susceptible to the influence of advertising (Livingstone & Helsper, 2006). The industry itself has a regulatory unit, the Children's Advertising Review Unit (CARU), which has guidelines that advertising should not mislead children about the nutritional impact of products, should not portray snacks as substitutes for meals, and should help develop good nutritional practices in children (Kaiser Family Foundation, 2004a, 2004b). The food industry has announced plans to expand the scope of CARU and to establish a hotline for parents to offer complaints (Institute of Medicine, 2006). The top food industry advertisers have also pledged to include more "healthy lifestyle" messages directed to children. Other countries have been far more aggressive in protecting children: Sweden, Norway, and Finland do not permit commercial sponsorship of children's programs, Sweden banned all advertising directed toward children younger than age 12, and the BBC prohibits use of cartoon characters in fast-food ads (Borzekowski, Innis, & Rideout, 2007).

But the real power—to date, virtually unused—lies with the regulatory agencies of the federal government: the Federal Trade Commission, the Food and Drug Administration, and the U.S. Department of Agriculture. The FCC and the FTC have the power to ban or regulate advertising but, thus far, have chosen not to do so (FTC, 2007). Despite the Institute of Medicine (2006) report that stated that "current food and beverage marketing practices put children's long-term health at risk," the federal government has "barely noticed this problem," and the FCC "decided last year that the food industry should police itself on marketing low-nutrient foods to increasingly fat children" ("Selling Junk Food," 2006). Currently, the FTC is empowered to regulate food advertising only if it is deceptive, yet increasingly, that appears to be the case (Mello, Studdert, & Brennan, 2006). Recently, the Department of Agriculture sent a report to Congress stating that it should have the legal authority to set nutritional standards for all food and drinks sold in schools (Brasher, 2001). This would allow the Department of Agriculture to ban junk food in schools. However, it will take an act of Congress to give the department this discretionary power. According to Jacobson (1999), the food industry may be even more difficult to deal with than the tobacco industry. It contains at least 78 different lobbying groups, ready to protect the industry's interests. The entire budget for the National Cancer Institute's "5 a Day" campaign for fruit and vegetable consumption is $3.5 million a year, compared to $29 million that Pringles spends on advertising, $74 million for M&Ms, $209 million for Coke, and $1.1 billion for McDonald's (Jacobson, 2000, 2005). In a sense, this issue represents a classic public health struggle in the United States: the "rights" of free business versus the public health of certain populations in society. In the past, when children were involved, their interests took precedence, and government policy was modified accordingly (Kunkel & Roberts, 1991). But those days may have ended (Kunkel, 1998; Strasburger, 2001, 2006a).

Where does one draw the line between the free marketplace and the public health of children and adolescents? Probably, it should be drawn at the schoolhouse door. Apologists for Channel One say that schools gain valuable technological equipment they can ill afford without sacrificing anything. Others see some advantages to exposing children and teens to current events programming (E. W. Austin et al., 2006). After all, children and teenagers are already exposed to an environment that is saturated with advertising, and many of them do not even pay attention to the 2 minutes a day of advertising broadcast on Channel One (Bachen, 1998). Certainly, more research is needed (Wilcox, Cantor, Dowrick, Kunkel, Linn, & Palmer, 2004). But the line needs to be drawn somewhere, or else we will soon be selling space on our children's diapers to commercial advertisers. As with other issues such as media violence, alcohol and tobacco advertising, and inappropriate sexual content, it is extraordinarily difficult to change the producers of such media. It would be easier to change the consumers: children and teenagers. For example, children as young as 6 to 9 years can be taught to discriminate between information and selling techniques presented in commercials (Pearson & Lewis, 1988). Although prevention programs targeting diet and activity have been relatively unsuccessful at reducing obesity (Resnicow & Robinson, 1997; Robinson, 1998), many new programs are showing significant results:

- A simple program to reduce the total amount of television viewed by children has resulted in decreased measures of adiposity (Robinson, 1999, 2000).
- A 12-week program that made TV viewing contingent on pedaling a stationary bicycle resulted in both less time spent viewing TV and reductions in total body fat (Faith et al., 2001).
- A similar experimental design using a pedometer to earn children TV time was also effective in increasing physical activity, decreasing TV time, and reducing BMI (Goldfield et. al., 2006).
- As few as seven sessions of a health curriculum for preschool children and their parents can successfully decrease total TV time (Dennison et al., 2004).
- Likewise, a mass media campaign to increase physical activity among children has been shown to be effective (Huhman et al., 2005). The VERB campaign spent $59 million on slick ads that portrayed exercise as being "cool." It resulted in a 30% increase in exercise among the preteens who saw it, but the campaign was cut by the Bush administration in 2006 (Neergaard, 2006).

Currently, the American Academy of Pediatrics recommends no more than 2 hours per day of entertainment screen time for children or adolescents (AAP, 2006). There seems to be little doubt that TV and other screen media contribute significantly to obesity, especially if there is a TV or computer screen in a child's bedroom (Washington, 2005). Of course, Hollywood moguls say that any negative effects are parents' fault: They could simply control and limit their children's access to media better. But Hollywood *could* be more proactive in incorporating healthier eating styles into TV storylines without interfering with any writers' or producers' First Amendment rights. Increasing numbers of studies show that health information can be disseminated easily and effectively through TV shows (Brodie et al., 2001) or by linking plotlines to PSAs aired after the show (Kennedy, O'Leary, Beck, Pollard, & Simpson, 2004). Recently, a group of obesity experts and child advocates (including one of the authors of this textbook) asked Children's Television Workshop not to use sponsorship messages from McDonald's before or after *Sesame Street* (Commercial Alert, 2003). The producers responded that removing such messages would also remove one of the most lucrative sources of funding for children's television (Kaiser Family Foundation, 2004a, 2004b). The solution? A dedicated source of public funding for children's programming that could be derived from the general federal budget, a tax on TV sets in the United States (Britain funds the BBC with a $75 per set per year tax), or a 10% windfall profits tax on children's toy and food manufacturers who target children with their advertising (Strasburger, 2004). Unlike other Western countries and Japan, public broadcasting in the United States is woefully underfunded (Palmer, 1988).

Media education classes can encourage young people to analyze critically and decode the images they view (see Chapter 13) (AAP, 1999; Hobbs, Broder, Pope, & Rowe, 2006; Potter, 2008). If Channel One continues in schools, then a media literacy lesson about advertising could precede it (E. W. Austin et al., 2006). Media education programs could also target eating disorders as an important issue, and a few already have (Levine, Piran, & Stoddard, 1999). One such program, Student Bodies, was made available to adolescents and their parents on the Internet and was found to be effective (Brown, Winzelberg, Abascal, & Taylor, 2004). Sociocultural factors may be modifiable if they are recognized and discussed, particularly with the peer group present (Levine & Harrison, 2003; Levine & Smolak, 2001; Shaw & Waller, 1995; Story & Neumark-Sztainer, 1991). At Stanford University, a college course titled "Body Traps: Perspectives on Body Image" resulted in students significantly decreasing their body dissatisfaction and their symptoms of disordered eating (Springer, Winzelberg, Perkins, & Taylor, 1999). Other experimental work with college students has also been successful in changing notions of body image (Levine et al., 1999; Levine & Harrison, 2003; Posavac, 1998; Rabak-Wagener, Eickhoff-Shemek, & Kelly-Vance, 1998). Even at the high school level, media education courses can successfully alter students' perceptions of media images and their internalized standards of thin beauty (Irving, DuPen, & Berel, 1998; O'Dea & Abraham, 2000). To date, there are 42 different published and unpublished reports of eating disorder prevention programs in elementary, middle, and high schools. Of these, two thirds showed positive changes in at least one measure of attitude or behavioral change (Levine & Smolak, 2001).

Rather than being part of the problem, the media could become part of the solution. Media are, after all, crucial sources of important information, some of it health related (BMA, 2000; Harris, 1994). Media could be instrumental in raising awareness about eating disorders and providing information about where and when to seek help (BMA, 2000). Some American companies such as Lands' End and Dove intentionally use models who are more "plus sized," and there are experimental data that teenagers' self-images can improve with more realistic advertising (see Figures 9.13 and 9.14). In 2006, the National Eating Disorders Association enlisted celebrities such as Jamie-Lynn Sigler from *The Sopranos* and Paula Abdul from *American Idol* to encourage young girls to "be comfortable in your genes" (see www.edap.org) (Crouch & Degelman, 1998). Music videos can also buck the trend of showing beautiful women wholly subservient to men. One prime example of this is a video by TLC, "Unpretty." A young woman is shown going to a cosmetic surgery clinic at the urging of her boyfriend for a breast enlargement procedure, but at the last minute, she tears off the hospital gown, runs out, and dumps him. In a secondary storyline, a plump adolescent girl is shown gazing longingly at pictures of ultra-thin magazine models that she has pasted on her walls. She even cuts out a picture of her own face and tapes it over a model's face. But at the end of the video, she tears the pictures off the wall and decides to accept herself as she is (Arnett, 2001). This is powerful counterprogramming, indeed! Video games such as

Dance Dance Revolution are increasingly being used with overweight children and teenagers to encourage weight loss (J. Silverstein, 2005). Similarly, a Hollywood film such as *Real Women Have Curves* goes a long way toward convincing young women that their body self-images should not be determined by the media.

Figure 9.13

SOURCE: Just My Size, ©Hanesbrands Inc. All rights reserved; Gucci, ©2001–2008 Gucci Group N.V. All rights reserved.

Figure 9.14

SOURCE: Courtesy of the Dove® brand. The Dove Campaign for Real Beauty is unique in trying to present realistic images of beauty and debunk the myth that only thin is beautiful.

After the BMA report was issued, the British government held a Body Image Seminar, a summit meeting attended by heads of the fashion industry and media. Editors of the leading women's and teen magazines in Britain announced that they would adopt a new voluntary code that will prohibit pictures of ultra-thin models and celebrities in their publications (Frean, 2000). More recently, fashion houses in Spain, Brazil, and Milan have launched campaigns to ban ultra-skinny models from its shows, and the Council of Fashion Designers of America has emphasized the need for models with eating disorders to get treatment and for healthy food to be supplied backstage (Wulfhorst, 2007). Changing the way that various media portray beauty and thinness will take a true cultural shift and will not be easy to accomplish. But the rewards of healthier young women, with healthier self-images, throughout the Western world would be astounding (BMA, 2000).

Exercises

1. For 1 week, watch your normal television programs but keep a log of the commercials shown during the breaks. Try to show a link between the type of show and the type of advertising. What types of foods are being advertised? What types of body types are displayed in the advertising?

2. In 2003, the World Health Organization issued a report that concluded that obesity is a leading cause of death throughout the world and that diet and exercise were needed solutions. In addition, the report criticized the food industry for marketing unhealthy foods. As might be expected (Apovian, 2004), the food industry denounced the report as being inaccurate and unscientific. In turn, the federal government rejected the report in early 2004, saying that it was not evidence based (Dyer, 2004). Does the federal government have a responsibility to try to decrease obesity among its citizens? Should federal limits be placed on food advertising? Should warning labels be placed on heavily sugared cereals and drinks or on high-fat foods?

3. In 2006, a Harvard School of Public Health analysis of 40 years of nutrition research concluded that soda and sugary drinks are a key reason for the epidemic of obesity in the United States (Malik et al., 2006). The American Beverage Association responded, "Blaming one specific product or ingredient as the root cause of obesity defies common sense. Instead, there are many contributing factors, including regular physical activity." One of the lead authors of the study responded, "Can you imagine somebody saying we should ignore the contribution of hypertension to heart attack because there are many causes? . . . When it comes to beverage trends and obesity, it's like documenting the force of gravity" (Marchione, 2006, p. B8). What do you think?

4. If the U.S. government were to convene a Body Image Seminar as the British government did, what would the result be?

5. Name your favorite five television actors and actresses. Would you still like/watch them if they weighed 30 pounds more than they currently weigh? Does being overweight or obese ever "help" an actor or actress (hint: Renée Zellweger/ Bridget Jones, Robert DeNiro/Jake LaMotta)? Fat people are often depicted in

comical ways on television and in movies. Are there ever any good traits attached to being fat?

6. Watch *Real Women Have Curves.* From a public health point of view, there seems to be a very fine line between making people self-conscious about keeping a healthy weight and tipping them over into eating disorders. How does this movie deal with that? How should the media deal with it?

7. You are the new female editor-in-chief of *Sports Illustrated* magazine. The previous editor-in-chief (a male) was recently fired because revenues have been sagging during the past year. You know that the swimsuit issue is, by far, the leading revenue producer for your magazine, but you have two preteen daughters at home and are very familiar with the recent literature on body image and eating disorders. In fact, you had some bulimic symptoms in college for a year or two before getting counseling. How do you handle the swimsuit issue?

8. You are the president and CEO of the leading public health nonprofit association in the country. Your goal for this year is to devise a campaign that will inform parents and children about healthy nutritional practices and educate them about how unhealthy it is to eat at fast-food restaurants frequently. What sort of public campaign do you envision?

9. McDonald's is the leading producer of fast food in the world. It could be argued that McDonald's is also one of the leading causes of the new epidemic of obesity in the United States. At the same time, the Ronald McDonald Children's Charities contribute millions of dollars a year to children's hospitals around the country and provide funds for the housing of children and teens undergoing treatment for childhood cancers. Does McDonald's do more good than harm for American society? Could McDonald's do a better job of informing the public about healthier food choices it serves? Can a business that produces a product that is unhealthy compensate for it through its good deeds? What about other businesses, such as the alcohol industry? The tobacco industry? The makers of *Grand Theft Auto?*

10. If product placements are now viewed as being unethical in the movie industry, should toy placements in fast-food restaurants be allowed? What about movie advertisements on soft drink cups in fast-food restaurants?

11. If a tattoo parlor devised an agreement with a major corporation to tattoo advertisements on human bodies, with payments for the individuals being tattooed (size of payment dependent on how visible the tattoos are), what should be society's stance in allowing or forbidding such tattoos?

12. If the tobacco industry can be held liable for billions of dollars worth of damages for the health-related illnesses that tobacco causes, should the fast-food industry be held accountable as well?

13. Should fast-food restaurants be allowed in children's hospitals?

14. As of 2007, there were approximately 500 Web sites that provide advice on how to become anorexic or bulimic (Depowski & Hart, 2007). A recent study found

that more than one third of adolescents with eating disorders had visited a pro-eating disorder site on the Internet (J. L. Wilson, Peebles, Hardy, & Litt, 2006). What, if any, should be society's response to such Web sites?

15. In February 2007, 18-year-old Uruguayan model Eliana Ramos was found dead from heart failure. Her sister, Luisel, had collapsed and died at a fashion show the previous year. In November 2006, Brazilian model Ana Carolina Reston died after eating only apples and tomatoes for months and letting her weight slip to 88 pounds (Watt, 2007). Should unnaturally thin models be banned from fashion runways? If so, how would that be accomplished?

References

Adachi-Mejia, A. M., Longacre, M. R., Gibson, J. J., Beach, M. L., Titus-Ernstoff, L. T., & Dalton, M. A. (2007). Children with a TV in their bedroom at higher risk for being overweight. *International Journal of Obesity, 31,* 644–651.

American Academy of Pediatrics (AAP), Committee on Communication. (2006). Children, adolescents, and advertising. *Pediatrics, 118,* 2563–2569.

American Academy of Pediatrics (AAP), Committee on Public Education. (1999). Media literacy. *Pediatrics, 104,* 341–343.

American Academy of Pediatrics, Committee on School Health. (2004). Soft drinks in schools. *Pediatrics, 113,* 152–154.

American Psychological Association. (2004). *Report of the APA Task Force on Advertising and Children.* Washington, DC: Author. Retrieved August 10, 2006, from http://www.apa.org

Andersen, R. E., Crespo, C. J., Bartlett, S. J., Cheskin, L. J., & Pratt, M. (1998). Relationship of physical activity and television watching with body weight and level of fatness among children. *Journal of the American Medical Association, 279,* 938–942.

Apovian, C. M. (2004). Sugar-sweetened soft drinks, obesity, and type 2 diabetes. *Journal of the American Medical Association, 292,* 978–979.

Arnett, J. J. (2001). The sounds of sex: Sex in teens' music and music videos. In J. D. Brown, J. R. Steele, & K. Walsh-Childers (Eds.), *Sexual teens, sexual media* (pp. 253–264). Mahwah, NJ: Lawrence Erlbaum.

Asch-Goodkin, J. (2005). Recipe for childhood obesity: Stir in sugar, combine thoroughly with food advertising. *Contemporary Pediatrics, 22,* 14.

Austin, E. W., Chen, Y. Y., Pinkleton, B. E., & Johnson, J. Q. (2006). Benefits and costs of *Channel One* in a middle school setting and the role of media-literacy training. *Pediatrics, 117,* e423–e433.

Austin, S. B., Melly, S. J., Sanchez, B. N., Patel, A., Buka, S., & Gortmaker, S. L. (2005). Clustering of fast-food restaurants around schools: A novel application of spatial statistics to the study of food environments. *American Journal of Public Health, 95,* 1575–1581.

Bachen, C. M. (1998). Channel One and the education of American youths. *Annals of the American Academy of Political and Social Science, 557,* 132–147.

Barnes, B. (2007, July 18). Limiting ads of junk food to children. *New York Times,* p. C1.

Barrett, R. T. (1997). Making our own meanings: A critical review of media effects research in relation to the causation of aggression and social skills difficulties in children and anorexia nervosa in young women. *Journal of Psychiatric & Mental Health Nursing, 4,* 179–183.

Bawa, S. (2005). The role of the consumption of beverages in the obesity epidemic. *Journal of the Royal Society for the Promotion of Health, 125,* 124–128.

BBC bans beauty contest. (1985, June 30). *Parade Magazine.*

Bearman, S. K., Martinez, E., & Stice, E. (2006). The skinny on body dissatisfaction: A longitudinal study of adolescent girls and boys. *Journal of Youth & Adolescence, 35,* 217–229.

Becker, A. E. (2002). Eating behaviours and attitudes following prolonged exposure to television among ethnic Fijian adolescent girls. *British Journal of Psychiatry, 180,* 509–514.

Bell, R., Berger, C., & Townsend, M. (2003). *Portrayals of nutritional practices and exercise behavior in popular American films, 1991–2000.* Davis: Center for Advanced Studies of Nutrition and Social Marketing, University of California, Davis.

Berkey, C. S., Rockett, H. R. H., Field, A. E., Gillman, M. W., & Colditz, G. A. (2004). Sugar-added beverages and adolescent weight change. *Obesity Research, 12,* 778–788.

Blass, E. M., Anderson, D. R., Kirkorian, H. L., Pempek, T. A., Price, I., & Koleini, M. F. (2006). On the road to obesity: Television viewing increases intake of high-density foods. *Physiology & Behavior, 88,* 597–604.

Block, G. (2004). Foods contributing to energy intake in the US: Data from NHANES III and NHANES 1999–2000. *Journal of Food Composition and Analysis, 17,* 439–447.

Bolton, R. N. (1983). Modeling the impact of television food advertising on children's diets. *Current Issues and Research in Advertising, 6,* 173–199.

Borja, R. R. (2006, December 22). *Media conglomerate to drop Channel One.* Retrieved January 17, 2007, from http://www.commercialalert.org/news/archive/2006/12/media-conglomerate-to-drop-channel-one

Borzekowski, D. L. G. (2001). *Watching what they eat: A content analysis of televised food references reaching preschool children.* Unpublished manuscript.

Borzekowski, D. L. G., & Bayer, A. M. (2005). Body image and media use among adolescents. *Adolescent Medicine Clinics, 16,* 289–313.

Borzekowski, D. L. G., Innis, J., & Rideout, V. (2007). *A systematic review of food advertising regulatory policies and childhood obesity: A focus on Australia, Japan, Sweden, and the United Kingdom.* Manuscript under review.

Borzekowski, D. L. G., & Robinson, T. N. (2001). The 30-second effect: An experiment revealing the impact of television commercials on food preferences of preschoolers. *Journal of the American Dietetic Association, 101,* 42–46.

Borzekowski, D. L. G., Robinson, T. N., & Killen, J. D. (2000). Does the camera add 10 pounds? Media use, perceived importance of appearance, and weight concerns among teenage girls. *Journal of Adolescent Health, 26,* 36–41.

Botta, R. A. (1999). Television images and adolescent girls' body image disturbances. *Journal of Communication, 49,* 22–41.

Bowman, S. A., Gortmaker, S. L., Ebbeling, C. B., Pereira, M. A., & Ludwig, D. S. (2004). Effects of fast-food consumption on energy intake and diet quality among children in a national household survey. *Pediatrics, 113,* 112–118.

Boynton-Jarrett, R., Thomas, T., Peterson, K., Wiecha, J., Sobol, A., & Gortmaker, S. (2003). Impact of television viewing patterns on fruit and vegetable consumption among adolescents. *Pediatrics, 112,* 1321–1326.

Brand, J., & Greenberg, B. (1994). Commercials in the classroom: The impact of Channel One advertising. *Journal of Advertising Research, 34,* 18–23.

Brasher, P. (2001, February 7). *USDA: Schools send mixed message.* Retrieved February 7, 2001, from http://www.abcnews.com

Bray, G. A., Nielsen, S. J., & Popkin, B. M. (2004). Consumption of high-fructose corn syrup in beverages may play a role in the epidemic of obesity. *American Journal of Clinical Nutrition, 79,* 537–543.

British Medical Association (BMA). (2000). *Eating disorders, body image & the media*. London: Author.

Brodie, M., Foehr, U., Rideout, V., Baer, N., Miller, C., Flournoy, R., et al. (2001). Communicating health information through the entertainment media. *Health Affairs, 20,* 192–199.

Brown, J. B., Winzelberg, A. J., Abascal, L. B., & Taylor, C. B. (2004). An evaluation of an Internet-delivered eating disorder prevention program for adolescents and their parents. *Journal of Adolescent Health, 35,* 290–296.

Brownell, K. D. (2004). Fast food and obesity in children. *Pediatrics, 113,* 132.

Brownell, K. D., & Horgen, K. B. (2004). *Food fight: The inside story of the food industry, America's obesity crisis, & what we can do about it.* Chicago: Contemporary Books.

Brucks, M., Armstrong, F. M., & Goldberg, M. (1988). Children's use of cognitive defenses against television advertising: A cognitive response approach. *Journal of Consumer Research, 14,* 471–482.

Burdette, H. L., & Whitaker, R. C. (2005). A national study of neighborhood safety, outdoor play, television viewing, and obesity in preschool children. *Pediatrics, 116,* 657–662.

Byrd-Bredbrenner, C., Finckenor, M., & Grasso, D. (2003). Health related content in prime-time television programming. *Journal of Health Communication, 8,* 329–341.

Byrd-Bredbrenner, C., & Grasso, D. (2000). What is television trying to make children swallow? Content analysis of the nutrition information in prime-time advertisements. *Journal of Nutrition Education, 32,* 187–195.

Cafri, G., Yamamiya, Y., Brannick, M., & Thompson, J. K. (2005). The influence of sociocultural factors on body image: A meta-analysis. *Clinical Psychology: Science and Practice, 12,* 421–433.

Cash, T. F., Ancis, J. R., & Strachan, M. D. (1997). Gender attitudes, feminist identity, and body images among young women. *Sex Roles, 36,* 433–447.

Cash, T. F., & Deagle, E. A., III. (1997). The nature and extent of body-image disturbances in anorexia nervosa and bulimia nervosa: A meta-analysis. *International Journal of Eating Disorders, 22,* 107–125.

Cassady, D., Townsend, M., Bell, R. A., & Watnik, M. (2006). Portrayals of branded soft drinks in popular American movies: A content analysis. *International Journal of Behavioral Nutrition and Physical Activity, 3,* 4.

Center for Media Education. (1998). *The campaign for kids' TV: Children and television.* Washington, DC: Author.

Chamberlain, L. J., Wang, Y., & Robinson, T. N. (2006). Does children's screen time predict requests for advertised products? *Archives of Pediatrics & Adolescent Medicine, 160,* 363–368.

Champion, H., & Furnham, A. (1999). The effect of the media on body satisfaction in adolescent girls. *European Eating Disorders Review, 7,* 213–228.

Chester, J., & Montgomery, K. (2007). *Interactive food & beverage marketing: Targeting children and youth in the digital age.* Berkeley, CA: Berkeley Media Studies Group.

Christakis, D. A. (2006). The hidden and potent effects of television advertising. *Journal of the American Medical Association, 295,* 1698–1699.

Christakis, D. A., & Zimmerman, F. J. (2006). *The elephant in the living room.* New York: Rodale.

Clay, D., Vignoles, V. L., & Dittmar, H. (2005). Body image and self-esteem among adolescent girls: Testing the influence of sociocultural factors. *Journal of Research on Adolescence, 15,* 451–477.

Close, R. N., & Schoeller, D. A. (2006). The financial reality of overeating. *Journal of the American College of Nutrition, 25,* 203–209.

CNNMoney.com. (2007, October 12). Disney characters to push produce.

Commercial Alert. (2003, October 12). *Obesity experts, child advocates ask* Sesame Street *not to advertise for McDonald's* [Press release]. Retrieved August 25, 2006, from http://www.commercialalert.org/issues/health/childhood-obesity.

Comstock, G. (1991). *Television in America* (2nd ed.). Newbury Park, CA: Sage.

Connor, S. M. (2006). Food-related advertising on preschool television: Building brand recognition in the youngest viewers. *Pediatrics, 118,* 1478–1485.

Coon, K. A., Goldberg, J., Rogers, B. L., & Tucker, K. L. (2001). Relationships between use of television during meals and children's food consumption patterns [Abstract]. *Pediatrics, 107,* 167.

Cooper, T. V., Klesges, L. M., Debon, M., Klesges, R. C., & Shelton, M. L. (2006). An assessment of obese and non obese girls' metabolic rate during television viewing, reading, and resting. *Eating Behaviors, 7,* 105–114.

Crawford, D. A., Jeffery, R. W., & French, S. A. (1999). Television viewing, physical activity, and obesity. *International Journal of Obesity and Related Metabolic Disorders, 23,* 437–440.

Crespo, C. J., Smit, E., Troiano, R. P., Bartlett, S. J., Macera, C. A., & Andersen, R. E. (2001). Television watching, energy intake, and obesity in US children. *Archives of Pediatrics and Adolescent Medicine, 155,* 360–365.

Crouch, A., & Degelman, D. (1998). Influence of female body images in printed advertising on self-ratings of physical attractiveness by adolescent girls. *Perceptual & Motor Skills, 87,* 585–586.

Cusumano, D. L., & Thompson, J. K. (1997). Body image and body shape ideals in magazines: Exposure, awareness, and internalization. *Sex Roles, 37,* 701–721.

Davison, K. K., Marshall, S. J., & Birch, L. L. (2006). Cross-sectional and longitudinal associations between TV viewing and girls' body mass index, overweight status, and percentage of body fat. *Journal of Pediatrics, 149,* 32–37.

Dennison, B. A., Erb, T. A., & Jenkins, P. L. (2002). Television viewing and television in bedroom associated with overweight risk among low-income preschool children. *Pediatrics, 109,* 1028–1035.

Dennison, B. A., Russo, T. J., Burdick, M. A., & Jenkins, P. L. (2004). An intervention to reduce television viewing by preschool children. *Archives of Pediatrics & Adolescent Medicine, 158,* 170–176.

Depowski, K., & Hart, K. (2007, February 25). *'Pro-Ana' Web sites glorify eating disorders.* Retrieved February 25, 2007, from http://abcnews.go.com/Health/print?id=2068728

Dietz, W. H. (1998). Health consequences of obesity in youth: Childhood predictors of adult disease. *Pediatrics, 101*(Suppl.), 518–525.

Dietz, W. H. (2006a). Sugar-sweetened beverages, milk intake, and obesity in children and adolescents. *Journal of Pediatrics, 148,* 152–154.

Dietz, W. H. (2006b). What constitutes successful weight management in adolescents? *Annals of Internal Medicine, 145,* 145–146.

Dietz, W. H., Jr. (1993). Television, obesity, and eating disorders. *Adolescent Medicine: State of the Art Reviews, 4,* 543–549.

Dietz, W. H., Jr., & Gortmaker, S. L. (1985). Do we fatten our children at the television set? Obesity and television viewing in children and adolescents. *Pediatrics, 75,* 807–812.

Dietz, W. H., Jr., & Gortmaker, S. L. (1993). TV or not TV: Fat is the question. *Pediatrics, 91,* 499–501.

Dietz, W. H., & Robinson, T. N. (2005). Overweight children and adolescents. *New England Journal of Medicine, 20,* 2100–2109.

Dixon, H. G., Scully, M. L., Wakefield, M. A., White, V. M., & Crawford, D. A. (2007). The effects of television advertisements for junk food versus nutritious food on children's food attitudes and preferences. *Social Science & Medicine, 65,* 1311–1323.

Dohnt, H. K., & Tiggeman, M. (2006). Body image concerns in young girls: The role of peers and media prior to adolescence. *Journal of Youth and Adolescence, 35,* 135–145.

Duncan, G. E. (2006). Prevalence of diabetes and impaired fasting glucose levels among US adolescents. *Archives of Pediatrics & Adolescent Medicine, 160,* 523–528.

DuRant, R. H., Baranowski, T., Johnson, M., & Thompson, W. O. (1994). The relationship among television watching, physical activity, and body composition of young children. *Pediatrics, 94,* 449–455.

Durkin, S. J., Paxton, S. J., & Wertheim, E. H. (2005). How do adolescent girls evaluate body dissatisfaction prevention messages? *Journal of Adolescent Health, 37,* 381–390.

Dyer, O. (2004). US government rejects WHO's attempts to improve diet. *British Medical Journal, 328,* 185.

Ebbeling, C. B., Feldman, H. A., Osganian, S. K., Chomitz, V. R., Ellenbogen, S. J., & Ludwig, D. S. (2006). Effects of decreasing sugar-sweetened beverage consumption on body weight in adolescents: A randomized controlled pilot study. *Pediatrics, 117,* 673–680.

Eisenmann, J. C., Bartee, R. T., & Wang, M. Q. (2002). Physical activity, TV viewing, and weight in U.S. youth: 1999 Youth Risk Behavior Survey. *Obesity Research, 10,* 379–385.

Epstein, L. H., Paluch, R. A., Consalvi, A., Riordan, K., & Scholl, T. (2002). Effects of manipulating sedentary behavior on physical activity and food intake. *Journal of Pediatrics, 140,* 334–339.

Epstein, L. H., Paluch, R. A., Gordy, C. C., & Dorn, J. (2000). Decreasing sedentary behaviors in treating pediatric obesity. *Archives of Pediatrics and Adolescent Medicine, 154,* 220–226.

Epstein, L. H., Roemmich, J. N., Robinson, J. L., et al. (2008). A randomized trial of the effects of reducing television viewing and computer use on body mass index in young children. *Archives of Pediatrics & Adolescent Medicine, 162,* 239–245.

Epstein, L. H., Valoski, A. M., Vara, L. S., & Rodefer, J. S. (1995). Effects of decreasing sedentary behavior and increasing activity on weight change in obese children. *Health Psychology, 14,* 109–115.

Evans, W. D., Renaud, J. M., Finkelstein, E., Kamerow, D. B., & Brown, D. S. (2006). Changing perceptions of the childhood obesity epidemic. *American Journal of Health Behavior, 30,* 167–176.

Eveland, W. P., Nathanson, A. I., Detenber, A. I., & McLeod, D. M. (1999). Rethinking the social distance corollary: Perceived likelihood of exposure and the third-person perception. *Communication Research, 26,* 275–302.

Faith, M. S., Berman, N., Heo, M., Pietrobelli, A., Gallagher, D., Epstein, L. H., et al. (2001). Effects of contingent television on physical activity and television viewing in obese children. *Pediatrics, 107,* 1043–1048.

Federal Trade Commission (FTC). (1981, March 31). *FTC final staff report and recommendation.* Washington, DC: Author.

Federal Trade Commission (FTC). (2007, June 1). *Children's exposure to TV advertising in 1977 and 2004: Information for the obesity debate.* Washington, DC: Author.

Field, A. E., Austin, S. B., Camargo, C. A., Jr., Taylor, C. B., Striegel-Moore, R. H., Loud, K. J., et al. (2005). Exposure to the mass media, body shape concerns, and use of supplements to improve weight and shape among male and female adolescents. *Pediatrics, 116,* e214–e220.

Field, A. E., Camargo, C. A., Jr., Taylor, C. B., Berkey, C. B., & Colditz, G. A. (1999). Relation of peers and media influences to the development of purging behaviors among preadolescent and adolescent girls. *Archives of Pediatrics & Adolescent Medicine, 153,* 1184–1189.

Field, A. E., Camargo, C. A., Jr., Taylor, C. B., Berkey, C. S., Roberts, S. B., & Colditz, G. A. (2001). Peer, parent, and media influences on the development of weight concerns and frequent dieting among preadolescent and adolescent girls and boys. *Pediatrics, 107,* 54–60.

Field, A. E., Cheung, L., Wolf, A. M., Herzog, D. B., Gortmaker, S. L., & Colditz, G. A. (1999). Exposure to the mass media and weight concerns among girls. *Pediatrics, 103,* e36.

Finkelstein, E. A., Fiebelkorn, I. C., & Wang, G. (2003). National medical spending attributable to overweight and obesity: How much, and who's paying? *Health Affairs, W3-225.* Retrieved May 14, 2003, from http://www.healthaffair.org

Food Commission. (1997, January–March). Advertising to children: UK the worst in Europe. *Food Magazine.*

Fouts, G., & Burggraf, K. (2000). Television situation-comedies: Female weight, male negative comments, and audience reactions. *Sex Roles, 42,* 925–932.

Fouts, G., & Vaughan, K. (2002). Television situation comedies: Male weight, negative references, and audience reactions. *Sex Roles, 46,* 439–442.

Franklin, J., Denyer, G., Steinbeck, K. S., Caterson, I. D., & Hill, A. J. (2006). Obesity and risk of low self-esteem: A statewide survey of Australian children. *Pediatrics, 118,* 2481–2487.

Frean, A. (2000, June 22). Magazines add weight to war on superwaif models. *London Times.*

French, S., Story, M., Neumark-Sztainer, D., Fulkerson, J., & Hannan, P. (2001). Fast food restaurant use among adolescents: Associations with nutrient intake, food choices and behavioral and psychosocial variables. *Internal Journal of Obesity, 25,* 1823–1833.

Frith, K., Shaw, P., & Cheng, H. (2005). The construction of beauty: A cross-cultural analysis of women's magazine advertising. *Journal of Communication, 55,* 56–70.

Fung, T. T., Rimm, E. B., Spiegelman, D., Rifai, N., Tofler, G. H., Willett, W. C., et al. (2001). Association between dietary patterns and plasma biomarkers of obesity and cardiovascular disease risk. *American Journal of Clinical Nutrition, 73,* 61–67.

Galst, J. P. (1980). Television food commercials and pro-nutritional public service announcements as determinants of young children's snack choices. *Child Development, 51,* 935–938.

Gantz, W., Schwartz, N., Angelini, J. R., & Rideout, V. (2007). *Food for thought: Television food advertising to children in the United States.* Menlo Park, CA: Kaiser Family Foundation.

Gerbner, G., Gross, L., Morgan, M., & Signorielli, N. (1980). Health and medicine on television. *New England Journal of Medicine, 305,* 901–905.

Gerbner, G., Gross, L., Morgan, M., & Signorielli N. (1994). Growing up with television: The cultivation perspective. In J. Bryant & D. Zillmann (Eds.), *Media effects: Advances in theory and research* (pp. 17–41). Hillsdale, NJ: Lawrence Erlbaum.

Giammattei, J., Blix, G., Marshak, H. H., Wollitzer, A. O., & Pettitt, D. J. (2003). Television watching and soft drink consumption: Associations with obesity in 11- to 13-year-old schoolchildren. *Archives of Pediatrics & Adolescent Medicine, 157,* 882–886.

Gold, J. (2007, February 7). Snickers maker will aim higher. *Albuquerque Journal,* p. B4.

Goldberg, M. E. (1990). A quasi-experiment assessing the effectiveness of TV advertising directed to children. *Journal of Marketing Research, 27,* 445–454.

Goldfield, G. S., Mallory, R., Parker, T., Cunningham, T., Legg, C., Lumb, A., et al. (2006). Effects of open-loop feedback on physical activity and television viewing in overweight and obese children: A randomized, controlled trial. *Pediatrics, 118,* e157–e166.

Goodman, E. (2000, September 25). Polluted advironment is hazardous to American youth. *Albuquerque Journal,* p. A8.

Gorn, G. J., & Goldberg, M. E. (1982). Behavioral evidence of the effects of televised food messages on children. *Journal of Consumer Research, 9,* 200–205.

Gortmaker, S. L. (2008). Innovations to reduce television and computer time and obesity in childhood. *Archives of Pediatrics & Adolescent Medicine, 162,* 283–284.

Gortmaker, S. L., Must, A., Sobol, A. M., Peterson, K., Colditz, G. A., & Dietz, W. H. (1996). Television viewing as a cause of increasing obesity among children in the United States, 1986–1990. *Archives of Pediatrics and Adolescent Medicine, 150,* 356–362.

Gortmaker, S. L., Peterson, K., Wiecha, J., Sobol, A. M., Dixit, S., Fox, M. K., et al. (1999). Reducing obesity via a school-based interdisciplinary intervention among youth. *Archives of Pediatrics & Adolescent Medicine, 153,* 409–418.

Greenberg, B. S., Eastin, M., Hofschire, L., Lachlan, K., & Brownell, K. (2003). Portrayals of overweight and obese individuals on commercial television. *American Journal of Public Health, 93,* 1342–1348.

Greenfield, P., & Beagles-Roos, J. (1988). Television vs. radio: The cognitive impact on different socio-economic and ethnic groups. *Journal of Communication, 38,* 71–92.

Groesz, L. M., Levine, M. P., & Murnen, S. K. (2001). The effect of experimental presentation of thin media images on body satisfaction: A meta-analytic review. *International Journal of Eating Disorders, 31,* 1–16.

Guillen, E. O., & Barr, S. I. (1994). Nutrition, dieting, and fitness messages in a magazine for adolescent women. *Journal of Adolescent Health, 15,* 464–472.

Gunter, B., Oates, C., & Blades, M. (2005). *Advertising to children on TV: Content, impact and regulation.* Mahwah, NJ: Lawrence Erlbaum.

Haerens, L., Deforche, B., Maes, L., Stevens, V., Cardon, G., & De Bourdeaudhuij, I. (2006). Body mass effects of a physical activity and healthy food intervention in middle schools. *Obesity, 14,* 847–854.

Hancox, R. J., Milne, B. J., & Poulton, R. (2004). Association between child and adolescent television viewing and adult health: A longitudinal birth cohort study. *The Lancet, 364,* 257–262.

Hancox, R. J., & Poulton, R. (2006). Television is associated with childhood obesity: But is it clinically important? *International Journal of Obesity, 30,* 171–175.

Hardy, L. L., Bass, S. L., & Booth, M. L. (2007). Changes in sedentary behavior among adolescent girls: A 2.5-year prospective cohort study. *Journal of Adolescent Health, 40,* 158–165.

Harris, R. J. (1994). *A cognitive psychology of mass communication* (2nd ed.). Hillsdale, NJ: Lawrence Erlbaum.

Harrison, K. (1998). The role of self-discrepancies in the relationship between media exposure and eating disorders. *Dissertation Abstracts International, 59,* no. 0648.

Harrison, K. (2000a). The body electric: Thin-ideal media and eating disorders in adolescents. *Journal of Communication, 50,* 119–143.

Harrison, K. (2000b). Television viewing, fat stereotyping, body shape standards, and eating disorder symptomatology in grade school children. *Communication Research, 27,* 617–640.

Harrison, K., & Cantor J. (1997). The relationship between media consumption and eating disorders. *Journal of Communication, 47,* 40–67.

Harrison, K., & Hefner, V. (2006). Media exposure, current and future body ideals, and disordered eating among preadolescent girls: A longitudinal panel study. *Journal of Youth and Adolescence, 35,* 146–156.

Harrison, K., & Marske, A. L. (2005). Nutritional content of foods advertised during the television programs children watch most. *American Journal of Public Health, 95,* 1568–1574.

Hawkes, C. (2004). *Marketing food to children: The global regulatory environment.* Geneva, Switzerland: World Health Organization.

Hays, C. (2000, September 14). New report examines commercialism in U.S. schools. *New York Times,* p. A1.

Henderson, V. R. (2007). Longitudinal associations between television viewing and body mass index among White and Black girls. *Journal of Adolescent Health, 41,* 544–550.

Herbozo, S., Tantleff-Dunn, S., Gokee-Larose, J., & Thompson, J. (2004). Beauty and thinness messages in children's media: A content analysis. *Eating Disorders, 12,* 21–34.

Hernandez, B., Gortmaker, S. L., Colditz, G. A., Peterson, K. D., Laird, N. M., & Parra-Cabrera, S. (1999). Association of obesity with physical activity, television programs and other forms of video viewing among children in Mexico City. *International Journal of Obesity and Related Metabolic Disorders, 23,* 845–854.

Hesketh, K., Wake, M., Graham, M., & Waters, E. (2007). Stability of television viewing and electronic game/computer use in a prospective cohort study of Australian children: Relationship with body mass index. *International Journal of Behavioral Nutrition and Physical Activity, 4,* 60 [Epub ahead of print].

Hobbs, R., Broder, S., Pope, H., & Rowe, J. (2006). How adolescent girls interpret weight-loss advertising. *Health Education Research, 21,* 719–730.

Hofschire, L. J., & Greenberg, B. S. (2001). Media's impact on adolescents' body dissatisfaction. In J. D. Brown, J. R. Steele, & K. Walsh-Childers (Eds.), *Sexual teens, sexual media* (pp. 125–149). Mahwah, NJ: Lawrence Erlbaum.

Holmstrom, A. J. (2004). The effects of the media on body image: A meta-analysis. *Journal of Broadcasting & Electronic Media, 48,* 196–217.

Horgen, K. B., Choate, M., & Brownell, K. D. (2001). Television food advertising. In D. G. Singer & J. L. Singer (Eds.), *Handbook of children and media* (pp. 447–461). Thousand Oaks, CA: Sage.

Hu, F. B., Leitzmann, M. F., Stampfer, M. J., Colditz, G. A., Willett, W. C., & Rimm, E. B. (2001). Physical activity and television watching in relation to risk for type 2 diabetes mellitus in men. *Archives of Internal Medicine, 161,* 1542–1548.

Hu, F. B., Li, T. Y., Colditz, G. A., Willett, W. C., & Manson, J. E. (2003). Television watching and other sedentary behaviors in relation to risk of obesity and type 2 diabetes mellitus in women. *Journal of the American Medical Association, 289,* 1785–1791.

Huhman, M., Potter, L. D., Wong, F. L., Banspach, S. W., Duke, J. C., & Heitzler, C. D. (2005). Effects of a mass media campaign to increase physical activity among children: Year-1 results of the VERB campaign. *Pediatrics, 116,* e277–e284.

Hurley, J., & Schmidt, S. (1996). Hard artery cafe? *Nutrition Action Health Letter, 23,* 1.

Institute of Medicine. (2006). *Food marketing to children and youth: Threat or opportunity?* Washington, DC: National Academies Press.

International Clearinghouse on Children, Youth, & Media. (2006). New restrictions on television advertising of food and drink products to children. *Newsletter on Children, Youth, & Media,* no. 2. Goteborg, Sweden: Author.

Irving, L. M., Dupen, J., & Berel, S. (1998). A media literacy program for high school females. *Eating Disorders: The Journal of Treatment & Prevention, 6,* 119–132.

Ishigaki, E. H. (1991). The health and eating habits of young children in Japan. *Early Child Development & Care, 74,* 141–148.

Jacobson, M. (1999, December). Diet & disease: Time to act. *Nutrition Action Health Letter, 26,* 2.

Jacobson, M. (2000, December). Tax junk foods. *Nutrition Action Health Letter, 27,* 2.

Jacobson, M. (2005). *Liquid candy: How soft drinks are harming Americans' health.* Washington, DC: Center for Science in the Public Interest.

Jacobson, M. (2007, July/August). Kellogg's curbs ads to kids. *Nutrition Action Healthletter,* p. 2.

Jahns, L., Siega-Riz, A. M., & Popkin, B. M. (2001). The increasing prevalence of snacking among US children from 1977 to 1996. *Journal of Pediatrics, 138,* 493–498.

Jain, A., & Tirodkar, M. (2001, April 30). *Food, obesity, and advertising and the African-American audience.* Paper presented at the annual meeting of the Ambulatory Pediatric Association/Society for Pediatric Research, Baltimore, MD.

James, J., Thomas, P., Cavan, D., & Kerr, D. (2004). Preventing childhood obesity by reducing consumption of carbonated drinks: Cluster randomised controlled trial. *British Medical Journal, 328,* 1237.

Jeffrey, D. B., McLellarn, R. W., & Fox, D. T. (1983). The development of children's eating habits: The role of television commercials. *Health Education Quarterly, 9,* 78–93.

Jeffery, R. W., & French, S. A. (1998). Epidemic obesity in the United States: Are fast foods and television viewing contributing? *American Journal of Public Health, 88,* 277–280.

Johnston, C. (2001). Commercialism in classrooms. *Pediatrics, 107,* e44.

Johnston, L. D., Delva, J., & O'Malley, P. M. (2007). Soft drink availability, contracts, and revenues in American secondary schools. *American Journal of Preventive Medicine, 33,* S209–S225.

Jones, D. C., Vigfusdottir, T. H., & Lee, Y. (2004). Body image and the appearance culture among adolescent girls and boys. *Journal of Adolescent Research, 19,* 323–339.

Jordan, A. B. (2007). Heavy television viewing and childhood obesity. *Journal of Children and Media, 1,* 45–54.

Jordan, A. B., Hersey, J. C., McDivitt, J. A., & Heitzler, C. D. (2006). Reducing children's television-viewing time: A qualitative study of parents and their children. *Pediatrics, 118,* e1303–e1310.

Jordan, A. B., & Robinson, T. N. (2008). Children, television viewing, and weight status: Summary and recommendations from an expert panel meeting. *Annals of the American Academy of Political & Social Science, 615,* 119–132.

Kaiser Family Foundation. (2004a). *The role of media in childhood obesity.* Retrieved August 7, 2006, from http://www.kff.org

Kaiser Family Foundation. (2004b). *Tweens, teens, and magazines.* Retrieved August 21, 2007, from http://www.kff.org

Kaufman, L. (1980). Prime-time nutrition. *Journal of Communication, 30,* 37–45.

Kaur, H., Choi, W. S., Mayo, M. S., & Harris, K. J. (2003). Duration of television watching is associated with increased body mass index. *Journal of Pediatrics, 143,* 506–511.

Kelly, A. M., Wall, M., Eisenberg, M. E., Story, M., & Neumark-Sztainer, D. (2005). Adolescent girls with high body satisfaction: Who are they and what can they teach us? *Journal of Adolescent Health, 37,* 391–396.

Kennedy, M., O'Leary, A., Beck, V., Pollard, W., & Simpson, P. (2004). Increases in calls to the CDC National STD and AIDS Hotline following AIDS-related episodes in a soap opera. *Journal of Communication, 54,* 287–301.

Kilbourne, J. (1999). *Deadly persuasion: Why women and girls must fight the addictive power of advertising.* New York: Free Press.

Kilbourne, J. (2000). *Can't buy my love: How advertising changes the way we think and feel.* New York: Touchstone.

King, N., Touyz, S., & Charles, M. (2000). The effect of body dissatisfaction on women's perceptions of female celebrities. *International Journal of Eating Disorders, 27,* 341–347.

Klesges, R. C., Shelton, M. L., & Klesges, L. M. (1993). Effects of television on metabolic rate: Potential implications for childhood obesity. *Pediatrics, 91,* 281–286.

Koplan, J. P., & Dietz, W. H. (1999). Caloric imbalance and public health policy. *Journal of the American Medical Association, 282,* 1579–1581.

Kotz, K., & Story, M. (1994). Food advertisements during children's Saturday morning television programming: Are they consistent with dietary recommendations? *Journal of the American Dietetic Association, 94,* 1296–1300.

Krayeske, K. (1999, February 25–March 3). Branded! Americans are losing their identities to marketing mania. *Hartford Advocate*. Retrieved from www.hartfordadvocate.com/articles/branded.html

Krebs-Smith, S., Cook, A., Subar, A., Cleveland, L., Friday, J., & Kahle, L. L. (1996). Fruit and vegetable intakes of children and adolescents in the United States. *Archives of Pediatrics & Adolescent Medicine, 150,* 81–86.

Krowchuk, D. P., Kreiter, S. R., Woods, C. R., Sinal, S. H., & DuRant, R. H. (1998). Problem dieting behaviors among young adolescents. *Archives of Pediatrics & Adolescent Medicine, 152,* 884–888.

Kubik, M. Y., Lytle, L. A., & Story, M. (2005). Schoolwide food practices are associated with body mass index in middle school students. *Archives of Pediatrics & Adolescent Medicine, 159,* 1111–1114.

Kuepper-Nybelen, J., Lamerz, A., Bruning, N., Hebebrand, J., Herpertz-Dahlmann, B. H., & Brenner, H. (2005). Major differences in prevalence of overweight according to nationality in preschool children living in Germany: Determinants and public health implications. *Archives of Disease in Childhood, 90,* 359–363.

Kunkel, D. (1998). Policy battles over defining children's educational television. *Annals of the American Academy of Political and Social Science, 557,* 39–53.

Kunkel, D. (2001). Children and television advertising. In D. G. Singer & J. L. Singer (Eds.), *Handbook of children and the media* (pp. 375–393). Thousand Oaks, CA: Sage.

Kunkel, D., & Gantz, W. (1991). *Television advertising to children: Message content in 1990. Report to the Children's Advertising Review Unit of the National Advertising Division, Council of Better Business Bureaus, Inc.* Bloomington: Indiana University.

Kunkel, D., & Roberts, D. (1991). Young minds and marketplace values: Issues in children's advertising. *Journal of Social Issues, 47,* 57–72.

Lang, T., & Rayner, G. (2005). Obesity: A growing issue for European policy? *Journal of European Social Policy, 15,* 301–327.

Lanningham-Foster, L., Jensen, T. B., Foster, R. C., Redmond, A. B., Walker, B. A., Heinz, D., et al. (2006). Energy expenditure of sedentary screen time compared with active screen time for children. *Pediatrics, 118,* e1831–e1835.

Lavine, H., Sweeney, D., & Wagner, S. H. (1999). Depicting women as sex objects in television advertising: Effects on body dissatisfaction. *Personality & Social Psychology Bulletin, 25,* 1049–1058.

Leiber, L. (1996). *Commercial and character slogan recall by children aged 9 to 11 years: Budweiser frogs versus Bugs Bunny.* Berkeley, CA: Center on Alcohol Advertising.

Levine, M. P. (2000). Mass media and body image: A brief review of the research. *Health Weight Journal, 14,* 84–85, 95.

Levine, M. P., & Harrison, K. (2003). The role of mass media in the perpetuation and prevention of negative body image and disordered eating. In J. K. Thompson (Ed.), *Handbook of eating disorders and obesity* (pp. 695–717). New York: John Wiley.

Levine, M. P., Piran, N., & Stoddard, C. (1999). Mission more probable: Media literacy, activism, and advocacy as primary prevention. In N. Piran, M. P. Levine, & C. Steiner-Adair (Eds.), *Preventing eating disorders: A handbook of interventions and special challenges* (pp. 3–25). Philadelphia: Brunner/Mazel.

Levine, M. P., & Smolak, L. (1996). Media as a context for the development of disordered eating. In L. Smolak, M. P. Levine, & R. Striegel-Moore (Eds.), *The developmental psychopathology of eating disorders* (pp. 235–257). Mahwah, NJ: Lawrence Erlbaum.

Levine, M. P., & Smolak L. (2001). Primary prevention of body image disturbances and disordered eating in childhood and early adolescence. In J. K. Thompson & L. Smolak (Eds.), *Body image, eating disorders, and obesity in childhood and adolescence* (pp. 237–260). Washington, DC: American Psychological Association.

Levine, M. P., Smolak, L., & Hayden, H. (1994). The relation of sociocultural factors to eating attitudes and behaviors among middle school girls. *Journal of Early Adolescence, 14,* 471–490.

Lewis, M. K., & Hill, A. J. (1998). Food advertising on British children's television: A content analysis and experimental study with nine-year-olds. *International Journal of Obesity and Related Metabolic Disorders, 22,* 206–214.

Li, C., Ford, E. S., Mokdad, A. H., & Cook, S. (2006). Recent trends in waist circumference and waist-height ratio among US children and adolescents. *Pediatrics, 118,* e1390–e1398.

Livingstone, S., & Helsper, E. J. (2006). Does advertising literacy mediate the effects of advertising on children? A critical examination of two linked research literatures in relation to obesity and food choice. *Journal of Communication, 56,* 560–584.

Ludwig, D. S., Peterson, K. E., & Gortmaker, S. L. (2001). Relation between consumption of sugar-sweetened drinks and childhood obesity: A prospective, observational analysis. *The Lancet, 357,* 505–508.

Lumeng, J. C., Rahnama, S., Appugliese, D., Kaciroti, N., & Bradley, R. H. (2006). Television exposure and overweight risk in preschoolers. *Archives of Pediatrics & Adolescent Medicine, 160,* 417–422.

Mabe, L. (2003, August 21). Pepsi high. *St. Petersburg Times,* p. 1D.

Macklin, M. C., & Carlson L. (Eds.). (1999). *Advertising to children: Concepts and controversies.* Thousand Oaks, CA: Sage.

Malik, V. S., Schulze, M. B., & Hu, F. B. (2006). Intake of sugar-sweetened beverages and weight gain: A systematic review. *American Journal of Clinical Nutrition, 84,* 274–288.

Marchione, M. (2006, August 9). Sugared soft drinks linked to epidemic of obesity. *Albuquerque Journal,* p. B8.

Margeirsdottir, H. D., Larsen, J. R., Brunborg, C., Sandvik, L., & Dahl-Jørgensen, K. (2007). Strong association between time watching television and blood glucose control in children and adolescents with type 1 diabetes. *Diabetes Care, 30,* 1567–1570.

Martin, A. (2007, June 14). Kellogg's to curb marketing of foods to children. *New York Times,* p. C1.

Martin, M. C., & Gentry, J. W. (1997). Stuck in the model trap: The effects of beautiful models in ads on female pre-adolescents and adolescents. *Journal of Advertising, 26,* 19–33.

Martin, M. C., & Kennedy, P. F. (1994). Social comparison and the beauty of advertising models: The role of motives for comparison. *Advances in Consumer Research, 21,* 365–371.

Martinez-Gonzalez, M. A., Gual, P., Lahortiga, F., Alonso, Y., Irala-Esevez, J., & Cervera, S. (2003). Parental factors, mass media influences, and the onset of eating disorders in a prospective population-based cohort. *Pediatrics, 111,* 315–320.

Mello, M. M., Studdert, D. M., & Brennan, T. A. (2006). Obesity—the new frontier of public health law. *New England Journal of Medicine, 354,* 2601–2610.

Mokdad, A. H., Ford, E. S., Bowman, B. A., Dietz, W. H., Vinicor, F., Bales, V. S., et al. (2003). Prevalence of obesity, diabetes, and obesity-related health risk factors, 2001. *Journal of the American Medical Association, 289,* 76–79.

Mokdad, A. H., Serdula, M. K., Dietz, W. H., Bowman, B. A., Marks, J. S., & Koplan, J. P. (1999). The spread of the obesity epidemic in the United States, 1991–1998. *Journal of the American Medical Association, 282,* 1519–1522.

Molnar, A. (1996). *Giving kids the business: The commercialization of America's schools.* Boulder, CO: Westview.

Molnar, A. (2005). School commercialism and adolescent health. *Adolescent Medicine Clinics, 16,* 447–461.

Molnar, A., Garcia, D. R., Boninger, F., & Merrill, B. (2006). *A national survey of the types and extent of the marketing of foods of minimal nutritional value in schools.* Tempe, AZ: Arizona State University.

Moore, E. S. (2006). *It's child's play: Advergaming and the online marketing of food to children.* Menlo Park, CA: Kaiser Family Foundation.

Moreno, L. A., Fleta, J., & Mur, L. (1998). Television watching and fatness in children [Letter]. *Journal of the American Medical Association, 280,* 1230–1231.

Morrill, A. C., & Chinn, C. D. (2004). The obesity epidemic in the United States. *Journal of Public Health Policy, 25,* 353–366.

Moses, N., Banilivy, M. M., & Lifshitz, F. (1989). Fear of obesity among adolescent girls. *Pediatrics, 83,* 393–398.

Motl, R. W., McAuley, E., Birnbaum, A. S., & Lytle, L. A. (2006). Naturally occurring changes in time spent watching television are inversely related to frequency of physical activity during early adolescence. *Journal of Adolescence, 29,* 19–32.

Muehling, D. D., & Kolbe, R. H. (1999). A comparison of children's and prime-time fine-print advertising disclosure practices. In M. C. Macklin & L. Carlson (Eds.), *Advertising to children: Concepts and controversies* (pp. 143–164). Thousand Oaks, CA: Sage.

Munoz, K. A., Krebs-Smith, S. M., Ballard-Barbash, R., & Cleveland, G. E. (1997). Food intakes of U.S. children and adolescents compared with recommendations. *Pediatrics, 100,* 323–329.

Murray, S. H., Touyz, S. W., & Beumont, P. J. V. (1996). Awareness and perceived influence of body ideals in the media: A comparison of eating disorder patients and the general community. *Eating Disorders: The Journal of Treatment and Prevention, 4,* 33–46.

National Center for Health Statistics. (2006). *Prevalence of overweight among children and adolescents: United States, 2003–2004* [Fact sheet]. Retrieved August 4, 2006, from www.cdc.gov/nchs

Neergaard, L. (2006, September 14). Obese kids not getting right help. *Albuquerque Journal,* p. A6.

Nelson, M. C., & Gordon-Larsen, P. (2006). Physical activity and sedentary behavior patterns are associated with selected adolescent health risk behaviors. *Pediatrics, 117,* 1281–1290.

Nelson, M. C., Neumark-Stzainer, D., Hannan, P. J., Sirard, J. R., & Story, M. (2006). Longitudinal and secular trends in physical activity and sedentary behavior during adolescence. *Pediatrics, 118,* e1627–e1634.

Nemeroff, C. J., Stein, R. I., Diehl, N. S., & Smilack, K. M. (1994). From the Cleavers to the Clintons: Role choices and body orientation as reflected in magazine article content. *International Journal of Eating Disorders, 16,* 167–176.

Nestle, M. (2006a). Food marketing and childhood obesity—a matter of policy. *New England Journal of Medicine, 354,* 2527–2529.

Nestle, M. (2006b, September 11). One thing to do about food. *The Nation,* p. 14.

Newman, D. L., Sontag, L. M., & Salvato, R. (2006). Psychosocial aspects of body mass and body image among rural American Indian adolescents. *Journal of Youth and Adolescence, 35,* 265–275.

Nichter, M., & Nichter, M. (1991). Hype and weight. *Medical Anthropology, 13,* 249–284.

Nielsen, S. J., & Popkin, B. M. (2003). Patterns and trends in food portion sizes, 1977–1998. *Journal of the American Medical Association, 289,* 450–453.

Niemeier, H. M., Raynor, H. A., Lloyd-Richardson, E. E., Rogers, M. L., & Wing, R. R. (2006). Fast food consumption and breakfast skipping: Predictors of weight gain from adolescence to adulthood in a nationally representative sample. *Journal of Adolescent Health, 39,* 842–849.

Nishna, A., Ammon, N. Y., Bellmore, A. D., & Graham, S. (2006). Body dissatisfaction and physical development among ethnic minority adolescents. *Journal of Youth and Adolescence, 35,* 179–191.

Nollen, N., Kaur, H., Pulvers, K., Choi, W., Fitzgibbon, M., Li, C., et al. (2006). Correlates of ideal body size among Black and White adolescents. *Journal of Youth and Adolescence, 35,* 276–284.

Norris, M. L., Boydell, K. M., Pinhas, L., & Katzman, D. K. (2006). Ana and the Internet: A review of pro-anorexia websites. *International Journal of Eating Disorders, 39,* 443–447.

O'Brien, M., Nader, P. R., Houts, R. M., Bradley, R., Friedman, S. L., Belsky, J., et al. (2007). The ecology of childhood overweight: A 12-year longitudinal analysis. *International Journal of Obesity, 31,* 1469–1478.

O'Dea, J. A., & Abraham, S. (2000). Improving the body image, eating attitudes, and behaviors of young male and female adolescents: A new educational approach that focuses on self-esteem. *International Journal of Eating Disorders, 28,* 43–57.

Ogden, C. L., Carroll, M. D., Curtin, L. R., McDowell, M. A., Tabak, C. J., & Flegal, K. M. (2006). Prevalence of overweight and obesity in the United States, 1999–2004. *Journal of the American Medical Association, 295,* 1549–1555.

Ogletree, S. M., Williams, S. W., Raffeld, P., & Mason, B. (1990). Female attractiveness and eating disorders: Do children's television commercials play a role? *Sex Roles, 22,* 791–797.

Oleck, J. (1994, July 20). Go ahead, make my lunch: Restaurant chains vying for school media market. *Restaurant Business Magazine,* p. 54.

O'Riordan, M., & Vega, C. (2007, July 25). The choice of a metabolic syndrome generation: Soft drink consumption associated with increased metabolic risk. *Medscape Medical News.* Retrieved August 18, 2007, from http://www.medscape.com/viewarticle/560344_print

Outley, C. W., & Taddese, A. (2006). A content analysis of health and physical activity messages marketed to African American children during after-school television programming. *Archives of Pediatrics & Adolescent Medicine, 160,* 432–435.

Palmer, E. K. (1988). *Television and America's children.* New York: Oxford University Press.

Pardee, P. E., Norman, G. J., Lustig, R. H., Preud'homme, D., & Schwimmer, J. B. (2007). Television viewing and hypertension in obese children. *American Journal of Preventive Medicine, 33,* 502–504.

Pate, R. R., & Ross, J. G. (1987). The national children and youth fitness study II: Factors associated with health-related fitness. *Journal of Physical Education, Recreation, and Dance, 58,* 93–95.

Pearson, L., & Lewis, K. E. (1988). Preventive intervention to improve children's discrimination of the persuasive tactics in television advertising. *Journal of Pediatric Psychology, 13,* 163–170.

Pinhas, L., Toner, B. B., Ali, A., Garfinkel, P. E., & Stuckless, N. (1999). The effects of the ideal of female beauty on mood and body satisfaction. *International Journal of Eating Disorders, 25,* 223–226.

Pope, H. (1999, Summer). Toy muscles linked to harmful image of male body. *Harvard Medical Alumni Bulletin,* p. 13.

Popkin, B. M. (2006). Global nutrition dynamics: The world is shifting rapidly toward a diet linked with noncommunicable diseases. *American Journal of Clinical Nutrition, 84,* 289–298.

Popkin, B. M., Armstrong, L. E., Bray, G. M., Caballero, B., Frei, B., & Willett, W. C. (2006). A new proposed guidance system for beverage consumption in the United States. *American Journal of Clinical Nutrition, 83,* 529–542.

Posavac, H. D. (1998). Reducing the impact of exposure to idealized media images of feminine attractiveness on college-age women with psychoeducational interventions. *Dissertation Abstracts International, 58,* no. 4466.

Potter W. J. (2008). *Media literacy* (4th ed.). Thousand Oaks, CA: Sage.

Powell, L. M., Szczypka, G., & Chaloupka, F. J. (2007a). Adolescent exposure to food advertising on television. *American Journal of Preventive Medicine, 33,* S251–S256.

Powell, L. M., Szczypka, G., & Chaloupka, F. J. (2007b). Exposure to food advertising on television among US children. *Archives of Pediatrics & Adolescent Medicine, 161,* 553–560.

Preboth, M. A., & Wright, S. (1999). Quantum sufficit. *American Family Physician, 59,* 1729.

Preidt, R. (2008). Overweight now a global problem. Retrieved April 16, 2008, from http://abcnews.go.com/print?id=4509129

Proctor, M. H., Moore, L. L., Gao, D., Cupples, L. A., Bradlee, M. L., Hood, M. Y., et al. (2003). Television viewing and change in body fat from preschool to early adolescence: The Framingham Children's Study. *International Journal of Obesity, 27,* 827–833.

Public Health Association of Australia. (1999). *Television food advertising during children's viewing times.* Retrieved January 6, 2001, from http://www.phaa.net.au/policy/TVadv.htm

Quaid, L. (2005, September 7). Junk food more available in middle schools. Associated Press. Retrieved September 7, 2005, from http://www.abcnews.go.com/Health/print?id=1104417

Rabak-Wagener, J., Eickhoff-Shemek, J., & Kelly-Vance, L. (1998). The effect of media analysis on attitudes and behaviors regarding body image among college students. *Journal of American College Health, 47,* 29–35.

Rajecki, D. W., McTavish, D. G., Rasmussen, J. L., Schreuders, M., Byers, D. C., & Jessup, K. S. (1994). Violence, conflict, trickery, and other story themes in TV ads for food for children. *Journal of Applied Social Psychology, 24,* 1685–1700.

Reece, B. B., Rifon, N. J., & Rodriguez, K. (1999). Selling food to children: Is fun part of a balanced breakfast? In M. C. Macklin & L. Carlson (Eds.), *Advertising to children: Concepts and controversies* (pp. 189–208). Thousand Oaks, CA: Sage.

Reilly, J. J., Armstrong, J., Dorosty, A. R., Emmett, P. M., Ness, A., Rogers, I., et al. (2005). Early life risk factors for obesity in childhood: Cohort study. *British Medical Journal, 330,* 1357.

Reilly, J. J., & Dorosty, A. R. (1999). Epidemic of obesity in U.K. children. *The Lancet, 354,* 1874–1875.

Resnicow, K., & Robinson, T. N. (1997). School-based cardiovascular disease prevention studies: Review and synthesis. *Annals of Epidemiology, 7*(Suppl.), 14–31.

Richards, J. I., Wartella, E. A., Morton, C., & Thompson, L. (1998). The growing commercialization of schools: Issues and practices. *Annals of the American Academy of Political and Social Science, 557,* 148–163.

Roberts, D. F., Foehr, U. G., & Rideout, V. (2005). *Generation M: Media in the lives of 8–18 year-olds.* Menlo Park, CA: Kaiser Family Foundation.

Robins, J. M. (2002, March 30–April 5). Increasingly, TV's a mess of messages. *TV Guide,* pp. 41–42.

Robinson, T. N. (1998). Does television cause childhood obesity? *Journal of the American Medical Association, 279,* 959–960.

Robinson, T. N. (1999). Reducing children's television viewing to prevent obesity: A randomized controlled trial. *Journal of the American Medical Association, 282,* 1561–1567.

Robinson, T. N. (2000). Can a school-based intervention to reduce television use decrease adiposity in children in grades 3 and 4? *Western Journal of Medicine, 173,* 40.

Robinson, T. N. (2001). Television viewing and childhood obesity. *Pediatric Clinics of North America, 48,* 1017–1025.

Robinson, T. N., Borzekowski, D. L. G., Matheson, D. M., & Kraemer, H. C. (2007). Effects of fast food branding on young children's taste preferences. *Archives of Pediatrics & Adolescent Medicine, 161,* 792–797.

Robinson, T. N., Hammer, L. D., Wilson, D. M., Killen, J. D., Kraemer, H. C., Hayward, C., et al. (1993). Does television viewing increase obesity and reduce physical activity? Cross-sectional and longitudinal analyses among adolescent girls. *Pediatrics, 91,* 273–280.

Robinson, T. N., & Killen, J. D. (1995). Ethnic and gender differences in the relationships between television viewing and obesity, physical activity and dietary fat intake. *Journal of Health Education, 26*(Suppl.), 91–98.

Rome, E. S., Ammerman, S., Rosen, D. S., Keller, R. J., Lock, J., Mammel, K. A., et al. (2003). Children and adolescents with eating disorders: The state of the art. *Pediatrics, 111,* e98–e108.

Rubinstein, S., & Caballero, B. (2000). Is Miss America an under-nourished role model? [Letter]. *Journal of the American Medical Association, 283,* 1569.

Sahud, H. B., Binns, H. J., Meadow, W. L., & Tanz, R. R. (2006). Marketing fast food: Impact of fast food restaurants in children's hospitals. *Pediatrics, 118,* 2290–2297.

Scammon, D. L., & Christopher, C. L. (1981). Nutrition education with children via television: A review. *Journal of Advertising, 6,* 131–133.

Schlosser, E. (2001). *Fast food nation.* Boston: Houghton Mifflin.

Schmidt, M. E., & Rich, M. (2006). Media and child health: Pediatric care and anticipatory guidance for the information age. *Pediatrics in Review, 27,* 289–297.

Schneider, M., Dunton, G. F., & Cooper, D. M. (2007). Media use and obesity in adolescent females. *Obesity, 15,* 2328–2335.

Schooler, D., Ward, L. M., Merriwether, A., & Caruthers, A. (2004). Who's that girl: Television's role in the body image development of young White and Black women. *Psychology of Women Quarterly, 28,* 38–47.

Schulze, M. B., Manson, J. E., Ludwig, D. S., Colditz, G. A., Stampfer, M. J., Willett, W. C., et al. (2004). Sugar-sweetened beverages, weight gain, and incidence of type 2 diabetes in young and middle-aged women. *Journal of the American Medical Association, 292,* 927–934.

Schwartz, J., & Byrd-Bredbrenner, C. (2006). Portion distortion: Typical portion sizes selected by young adults. *Journal of the American Dietetic Association, 106,* 1412–1418.

Schwimmer, J. B., Burwinkle, T. M., & Varni, J. W. (2003). Health-related quality of life of severely obese children and adolescents. *Journal of the American Medical Association, 289,* 1813–1819.

Sector, C. (2006). *World is getting bigger, after all.* Retrieved August 15, 2006, from http://abcnews.go.com/International/print?id=2315516

Selling junk food to toddlers [Editorial]. (2006, February 23). *New York Times,* p. A26.

Shaw, J., & Waller, G. (1995). The media's impact on body image: Implications for prevention and treatment. *Eating Disorders: The Journal of Treatment & Prevention, 3,* 115–123.

Signorielli, N. (1997). A *content analysis: Reflections of girls in the media.* Menlo Park, CA: Kaiser Family Foundation.

Signorielli, N., & Lears, M. (1992). Television and children's conceptions of nutrition: Unhealthy messages. *Health Communication, 4,* 245–257.

Signorielli, N., & Staples, J. (1997). Television and children's conception of nutrition. *Health Communication, 9,* 289–301.

Silverstein, J. (2005). *Fitness: Coming to a video game near you.* Retrieved March 25, 2005, from http://www.abcnews.go.com/Technology/Health/story?id=562729&page=1

Silverstein, B., Perdue, L., Peterson, B., & Kelly, E. (1986). The role of mass media in promoting a thin standard of bodily attractiveness for women. *Sex Roles, 14,* 519–532.

Silverstein, B., & Perlick, D. (1995). *The cost of competence: Why inequality causes depression, eating disorders, and illness in women.* New York: Oxford University Press.

Snoek, H. M., van Strien, T., Janssens, J., & Engels, R. (2006). The effect of television viewing on adolescents' snacking: Individual differences explained by external, restrained and emotional eating. *Journal of Adolescent Health, 39,* 448–451.

Sokol, R. J. (2000). The chronic disease of childhood obesity: The sleeping giant has awakened. *Journal of Pediatrics, 136,* 711–713.

Springer, E. A., Winzelberg, A. J., Perkins, R., & Taylor, C. B. (1999). Effects of a body image curriculum for college students on improved body image. *International Journal of Eating Disorders, 26,* 13–20.

Stice, E., Schupak-Neuberg, E., Shaw, H. E., & Stein, R. I. (1994). Relation of media exposure to eating disorder symptomatology: An examination of mediating mechanisms. *Journal of Abnormal Psychology, 103,* 836–840.

Stice, E., & Shaw, H. E. (1994). Adverse effects of the media portrayed thin-ideal on women and linkages to bulimic symptomatology. *Journal of Social and Clinical Psychiatry, 13,* 288–308.

Stice, E., & Whitenton, K. (2002). Risk factors for body dissatisfaction in adolescent girls: A longitudinal investigation. *Developmental Psychology, 38,* 669–678.

STOPP-T2D Prevention Study Group. (2006). Presence of diabetes risk factors in a large U.S. eighth-grade cohort. *Diabetes Care, 29,* 212–217.

Story, M., & Faulkner, P. (1990). The prime time diet: A content analysis of eating behavior and food messages in television program content and commercials. *American Journal of Public Health, 80,* 738–740.

Story, M., & French, S. (2004). Food advertising and marketing directed at children and adolescents in the U.S. *International Journal of Behavior of Behavioral Nutrition and Physical Activity, 1,* 3.

Story, M., & Neumark-Sztainer, D. (1991). Promoting health eating and physical activity in adolescents. *Adolescent Medicine: State of the Art Reviews, 10,* 109–123.

Stroebele, N., & de Castro, J. M. (2004). Television viewing is associated with an increase in meal frequency in humans. *Appetite, 42,* 111–113.

Strasburger, V. C. (2001). Children and TV advertising: Nowhere to run, nowhere to hide. *Journal of Developmental & Behavioral Pediatrics, 22,* 185–187.

Strasburger, V. C. (2004). Children, adolescents, and the media. *Current Problems in Pediatric and Adolescent Health Care, 34,* 54–113.

Strasburger, V. C. (2005). Adolescents, sex, and the media: Oooo, baby, baby—a Q&A. *Adolescent Medicine Clinics, 16,* 269–288.

Strasburger, V. C. (2006a). Is there an unconscious conspiracy against teenagers in the United States? *Clinical Pediatrics, 45,* 714–717.

Strasburger, V. C. (2006b). Risky business: What primary care practitioners need to know about the influence of the media on adolescents. *Primary Care: Clinics in Office Practice, 33,* 317–348.

Strasburger, V. C., Brown, R. T., Braverman, P. K., Rogers, P. D., Holland-Hall, C., & Coupey, S. (2006). *Adolescent medicine: A handbook for primary care.* Philadelphia: Lippincott Williams & Wilkins.

Strauss, R. S. (1999). Self-reported weight status and dieting in a cross-sectional sample of young adolescents. *Archives of Pediatrics & Adolescent Medicine, 153,* 741–747.

Striegel-Moore, R. H., Thompson, D., Affenito, S. G., Franko, D. L., Obarzanek, E., Barton, B. A., et al. (2006). Correlates of beverage intake in adolescent girls: The National Heart, Lung, and Blood Institute Growth and Health Study. *Journal of Pediatrics, 148,* 183–187.

Stutts, M. A., & Hunnicutt, G. G. (1987). Can young children understand disclaimers in television commercials? *Journal of Advertising, 16,* 41–46.

Sugimori, H., Yoshida, K., Izuno, T., Miyakawa, M., Suka, M., Sekine, M., et al. (2004). Analysis of factors that influence body mass index from ages 3 to 6 years: A study based on the Toyama cohort study. *Pediatrics International, 46,* 302–310.

Sylvester, G. P., Williams, J., & Achterberg, C. (1993). Food and nutrition messages in film: A preliminary content analysis. *Annals of the New York Academy of Science, 699,* 295–297.

Taras, H. L., & Gage, M. (1995). Advertised foods on children's television. *Archives of Pediatrics and Adolescent Medicine, 149,* 649–652.

Taras, H. L., Sallis, J. F., Patterson, T. L., Nader, P. R., & Nelson, J. A. (1989). Television's influence on children's diet and physical activity. *Developmental and Behavioral Pediatrics, 10,* 176–180.

Taveras, E. M., Field, A. E., Berkey, C. S., Rifas-Shiman, S. L., Frazier, A. L., Colditz, G. A., et al. (2007). Longitudinal relationship between television viewing and leisure-time physical activity during adolescence. *Pediatrics, 119,* e314–e319.

Taveras, E. M., Sandora, T. J., Shih, M.-C., Ross-Degnan, D., Goldmann, D. A., & Gillman, M. W. (2006). The association of television and video viewing with fast food intake by preschool-age children. *Obesity, 14,* 2034–2041.

Taylor, C. B., Sharpe, T., Shisslak, C., Bryson, S., Estes, L. S., Gray, N., et al. (1998). Factors associated with weight concerns in adolescent girls. *International Journal of Eating Disorders, 24,* 31–42.

Temple, J. L., Giacomelli, A. M., Kent, K. M., Roemmich, J. N., & Epstein, L. H. (2007). Television watching increases motivated responding for food and energy intake in children. *American Journal of Clinical Nutrition, 85,* 355–361.

Thompson, J. K. (Ed.). (2003). *Handbook of eating disorders and obesity.* New York: John Wiley.

Thompson, J. K., Heinberg, L. J., Altabe, M., & Tantleff-Dunn, S. (1999). *Exacting beauty: Theory, assessment, and treatment of body image disturbance.* Washington, DC: American Psychological Association.

Tiggeman, M. (2005). Television and adolescent body image: The role of program content and viewing motivation. *Journal of Social and Clinical Psychology, 24,* 361–381.

Tiggeman, M., & Pickering, A. S. (1996). Role of television in adolescent women's body dissatisfaction and drive for thinness. *International Journal of Eating Disorders, 20,* 199–203.

Tiggeman, M., & Slater, A. (2004). Thin ideals in music television: A source of social comparison and body dissatisfaction. *International Journal of Eating Disorders, 35,* 48–58.

Tirodkar, M., & Jain, A. (2003). Food messages on African American television shows. *American Journal of Public Health, 93,* 439–441.

Troiano, R. P., & Flegal, K. M. (1998). Overweight children and adolescents: Description, epidemiology, and demographics. *Pediatrics, 101,* 497–504.

Tucker, K. L., Morita, K., Qiao, N., Hannan, M. T., Cupples, L. A., & Kiel, D. P. (2006). Colas, but not other carbonated beverages, are associated with low bone mineral density in older women: The Framingham Osteoporosis Study. *American Journal of Clinical Nutrition, 84,* 936–942.

Tucker, L. A. (1986). The relationship of television viewing to physical fitness and obesity. *Adolescence, 21,* 797–806.

Turner, S. L., Hamilton, H., Jacobs, M., Angood, L. M., & Dwyer, D. H. (1997). The influence of fashion magazines on the body image satisfaction of college women: An exploratory analysis. *Adolescence, 32,* 603–610.

Unnikrishnan, N., & Bajpai, S. (1996). *The impact of television advertising on children.* Thousand Oaks, CA: Sage.

Utter, J., Neumark-Sztainer, D., Jeffery, R., & Story, M. (2003). Couch potatoes or French fries: Are sedentary behaviors associated with body mass index, physical activity, and dietary behaviors among adolescents? *Journal of the American Dietetic Association, 103,* 1298–1305.

van den Berg, P., Neumark-Sztainer, D., Hannan, P. J., & Haines, J. (2007). Is dieting advice from magazines helpful or harmful? Associations with weight-control behaviors and psychological outcomes in adolescents. *Pediatrics, 119,* e30–e37.

Vandewater, E., Shim, M., & Caplovitz, A. (2004). Linking obesity and activity level with children's television and video game use. *Journal of Adolescence, 27,* 71–85.

Vaughan, K. K., & Fouts, G. T. (2003). Changes in television and magazine exposure and eating disorder symptomatology. *Sex Roles, 49,* 313–320.

Vereecken, C. A., Todd, J., Roberts, C., Mulvihill, C., & Maes, L. (2005). Television viewing behaviour and associations with food habits in different countries. *Public Health Nutrition, 9,* 244–250.

Verri, A. P., Verticale, M. S., Vallero, E., Bellone, S., & Nespoli, L. (1997). Television and eating disorders: Study of adolescent eating behavior. *Minerva Pediatrica, 49,* 235–243.

Viner, R. M., & Cole, T. J. (2005). Television viewing in early childhood predicts adult body mass index. *Journal of Pediatrics, 147,* 429–435.

Wallack, L., & Dorfman, L. (1992). Health messages on television commercials. *American Journal of Health Promotion, 6,* 190–196.

Waller, G., Shaw, J., Hamilton, K., & Baldwin G. (1994). Beauty is in the eye of the beholder: Media influences on the psycho-pathology of eating problems. *Appetite, 23,* 287.

Wartella, E., & Jennings, N. (2001). Hazards and possibilities of commercial TV in the schools. In D. G. Singer & J. L. Singer (Eds.), *Handbook of children and the media* (pp. 557–570). Thousand Oaks, CA: Sage.

Washington, R. (2005). One way to decrease an obesogenic environment. *Journal of Pediatrics, 147,* 417–418.

Watt, N. (2007, February 28). *Still skinny in Milan.* Retrieved February 28, 2007, from http://abcnews.go.com/Nightline/print?id=2908135

Way, W. L. (1983). Food-related behaviors on prime-time television. *Journal of Nutritional Education, 15,* 105–109.

Welsh, J., & Dietz, W. (2005). Sugar-sweetened beverage consumption is associated with weight gain and incidence of type 2 diabetes. *Clinical Diabetes, 23,* 150–152.

Wertheim, E. H., Paxton, S. J., Schutz, H. K., & Muir, S. L. (1997). Why do adolescent girls watch their weight? An interview study examining pressures to be thin. *Journal of Psychosomatic Research, 42,* 345–355.

Wiecha, J. L., Peterson, K. E., Ludwig, D. S., Kim, J., Sobol, A., & Gortmaker, S. L. (2006). When children eat what they watch: Impact of television viewing on dietary intake in youth. *Archives of Pediatrics & Adolescent Medicine, 160,* 436–442.

Wilcox, B., Cantor, J., Dowrick, P., Kunkel, D., Linn, S., & Palmer, E. (2004). *Report of the APA Task Force on Advertising and Children.* Washington, DC: American Psychological Association.

Williams, M. (2001, January 15). The soda subsidy. *Liberal Opinion Week,* p. 6.

Williams, T. B. (Ed.). (1986). *The impact of television: A natural experiment in three communities.* New York: Academic Press.

Wilson, J. L., Peebles, R., Hardy, K. K., & Litt, I. F. (2006). Surfing for thinness: A pilot study of pro-eating disorder Web site usage in adolescents with eating disorders. *Pediatrics, 118,* e1635–e1643.

Wilson, N., Quigley, R., & Mansoor, O. (1999). Food ads on TV: A health hazard for children? *Australia and New Zealand Journal of Public Health, 23,* 647–650.

Wingood, G. M., DiClemente, R. J., Harrington, K., & Davies, S. L. (2002). Body image and African American females' sexual health. *Journal of Women's Health & Gender Based Medicine, 11,* 433–439.

Wiseman, C. V., Gray, J. J., Mosimann, J. E., & Ahrens, A. H. (1992). Cultural expectations of thinness in women: An update. *International Journal of Eating Disorders, 11,* 85–89.

Wiseman, C. V., Gunning, F. M., & Gray, J. J. (1993). Increasing pressure to be thin: 19 years of diet products in television commercials. *Eating Disorders, 1,* 52–61.

Wong, N. D., Hei, T. K., Qaqundah, P. Y., Davidson, D. M., Bassin, S. L., & Gold, K. V. (1992). Television viewing and pediatric hypercholesterolemia. *Pediatrics, 90,* 75–79.

World Health Organization (WHO). (2003). *Obesity and overweight fact sheet.* Geneva, Switzerland: Author. Retrieved August 14, 2006, from http://who.int/dietphysical activity/media/en/gsfs_obesity.pdf

Wulfhorst, E. (2007, January 12). NY fashionistas weigh in on thin model flap. Reuters/ABC News. Retrieved Janaury 12, 2007, from http://abcnews.go.com/Entertainment/ print?id=2790878

Yanovski, J. A., & Yanovski, S. Z. (1999). Recent advances in basic obesity research. *Journal of the American Medical Association, 282,* 1504–1506.

CHAPTER 10

Video Games

Jeanne B. Funk

Video and computer games are no longer "new media." These games have established themselves as a permanent leisure choice for all age groups, particularly for children and adolescents. This chapter will review the history of video games and describe current research in the following areas: time commitment, including video game addiction; reasons for video game popularity; ratings; game preference; the impact of violent games; physical health risks; potential for positive applications, particularly as demonstrated in the Serious Games movement; and implications for public policy and parents.

Definitions

Video games have outgrown platform-based definitions. The term now includes games played on dedicated console-type systems, on personal computers, on hand-held systems, and via the Internet. The primary focus of the present chapter will be on games that are played alone or face-to-face with another player.

The Development of Video Games

The first video game was introduced about 30 years ago. In the early 1970s, adult consumers became fascinated with the first arcade version of Pong, which was basically a simple visual-motor exercise. Soon home systems and cartridge games became available, and video games became popular across all age groups. In the early 1980s, consumers became disenchanted with uninspiring copycat games and sales dropped precipitously. At this point, video games were dismissed as just another vanishing toy fad.

The industry recovered in the second half of the 1980s when special effects were improved, new game accessories were made available, and games with violent content were promoted. In addition, the industry introduced cross-media marketing, with game characters featured as action figures and in movies. At the same time, children became targeted consumers. Beginning with *Mortal Kombat*, violent games with ever more realistic graphics became an industry staple. The typical goal of violent games is to maim or kill one's opponent, and in many cases, players can choose the level of realism of the battle, including very graphic portrayals of injuries. Fueled by the success of multifunctional systems (PlayStation 3 from Sony) and wireless controllers (Wii from Nintendo), sales of video games now typically exceed several billion dollars annually worldwide.

Time Commitment

Video games are now well established as one of the most popular choices in the array of leisure activities available across childhood and adolescence. Even children ages 2 to 7 average about 43 minutes of video game play every day (see Figure 10.1) (Gentile & Walsh, 2002). Gender differences in time commitment to game playing are consistently reported, with boys playing more than girls at all ages. For example, in a group of first and second graders, boys played about 3½ hours per week, while girls played about 2½ hours (Funk & Buchman, 2006). Gender differences are critical to understanding the implications of some game-playing habits, so gender-specific information will be selectively highlighted throughout this chapter.

Figure 10.1

SOURCE: www.CartoonStock.com.

Two media use studies were recently completed by the Kaiser Family Foundation. One sample included children ages 6 months to 6 years (Rideout & Hamel, 2006). On a typical day, 11% of children in this sample played video games, with use, not surprisingly, increasing with age. In a study of 8- to 18-year-olds, on average, boys played about an hour and a half per day, while girls played about 40 minutes (Rideout, Roberts, & Foehr, 2005). Time commitment decreased with age in this group. Most current research suggests that playing time peaks for many in middle childhood to early adolescence. In surveys of fourth through eighth graders, Buchman and Funk (1996) found that fourth-grade girls reported playing about 4.5 hours in the home in a typical week, while eighth-grade girls reported playing only about 2 hours. Fourth-grade boys reported about 7 hours of average weekly home play, while eighth-grade boys reported less than 4 hours. Studying eighth and ninth graders, boys averaged about 13 hours of play per week, and girls averaged 5 (Gentile, Lynch, Linder, & Walsh, 2004). International studies also demonstrate the popularity of video games, as well as gender differences. For example, Wake, Hesketh, and Waters (2003) reported that most Australian children ages 5 through 11 played video games, with boys generally playing more than girls. A recent study in the United Kingdom also identified playing video games as an extremely popular activity, with 100% of 6- to 10-year-olds reporting regular play (Pratchett, 2005).

Most time use studies identify a small group of players who spend considerable time playing each week. For example, Tejeiro Salguero and Bersabe Moran (2002) reported that a group of adolescents responded to a survey assessing time spent and feelings about game play in a manner suggesting addiction. These adolescents reported that their game playing is out of their control, is used to escape from reality, and interferes with normal daily activities. Players who appear to be addicted to game playing were also identified in studies of children and adolescents in China (Yang, 2005) and Taiwan (Chiu, Lee, & Huang, 2004; Ko, Yen, Yen, Lin, & Yang, 2007). Some researchers prefer the concept of "dependency" to describe a significant but less pathological preoccupation in which game playing meets certain social and/or psychological needs to an unusual degree (K. M. Lee & Peng, 2006). Based on a survey of 12- to 16-year-olds from the 1990s, Griffiths and Hunt (1998) reported that about one in five of these adolescents could be classified as being game dependent. Electronic gambling is a newer form of gaming that has been referred to as the "crack cocaine" of gambling (Dowling, Smith, & Thomas, 2005). However, at present, there is little evidence to support this claim. There are a few published examples of tragic outcomes as a result of overinvolvement in game playing. A Korean couple left their 4-month-old daughter alone while they played an Internet game for hours (Gamespot, 2005). The infant died of suffocation.

In summary, research indicates that for most children through high school age, some time is devoted to playing video games. Across all ages, boys play much more than girls. In most cases, playing video games occupies only a relatively small percentage of total leisure time. Several studies suggest that there is an identifiable though small group of children whose excessive time commitment may interfere with other activities. More research is needed to understand the reasons for dependence or addiction to game playing and how to resolve these issues.

Why Are Video Games Popular?

The reasons for the popularity of video games are just beginning to be systematically studied. On a theoretical basis, Klug and Schell (2006) proposed five basic reasons why people play video games: to control the environment, to vicariously experience, to vicariously live in other places and times, to compete, and to safely explore fantasy relationships. Salisch, Oppl, and Kristen (2006) cite survey research from Germany that suggests that children play to enhance attainment of developmental tasks and to escape problems and manage mood. Raney, Smith, and Baker (2006) suggest that adolescents play games for entertainment, arousal, mood management, and to master a challenge.

One recent investigation used focus groups to directly examine the game-playing experience of children and young adults (Funk, Chan, Brouwer, & Curtiss, 2006). Pure entertainment value was mentioned by both groups. Children noted pride in game accomplishments as a primary motivator for play, while adults described relief from boredom and positive mood change. Interacting with others was described as a social benefit of game playing by both children and adults. Some adults reported that engaging in antisocial activities through the fantasy of video games is appealing. Both children and young adults noted becoming highly absorbed in game playing; this experience was described in both positive and negative terms, with both children and adults noting that absorption in some games could be scary.

The experience of being absorbed is an important aspect of game playing for many. It has been proposed that this complete state of immersion in video games may precipitate an altered state of consciousness (Glickson & Avnon, 1997). When positive, this may be an example of the "flow" state described by Csikszentmihalyi and Csikszentmihalyi (1988). *Flow* is a term used to describe the intense feelings of enjoyment that occur when a balance between skill and challenge is attained in an activity that is intrinsically rewarding (Csikszentmihalyi & Csikszentmihalyi, 1988; Moneta & Csikszentmihalyi, 1999). Being in a flow state may enhance learning (Moneta & Csikszentmihalyi, 1996) and make a person more susceptible to suggestion (Center for Media Education, 1996). Because of these features, the experience of absorption in video game playing deserves additional research attention. The concept of presence is related to the concepts of absorption and flow. Presence is an immersive experience that occurs when the player's subjective experience is shaped by technology (Tamborini & Skalski, 2006). There is no presumption of an altered state of consciousness for the experience of presence, thus differentiating presence from absorption and flow. However, it seems reasonable to consider the possibility that there could be a continuum from presence to absorption and/or flow.

Sherry, Lucas, Greenberg, and Lachlan (2006) conducted a series of focus groups with undergraduates to determine their reasons for playing video games. The researchers identified six primary reasons: arousal, challenge, competition, diversion (avoidance of stress or responsibilities), involvement in fantasy activities, and social interaction. Using an experimental paradigm, Chumbley and Griffiths (2006) studied specific aspects of the game-playing experience of young adults. Participants preferred a lower difficulty condition where they received more positive reinforcement. More frustration was reported in a higher difficulty condition, but this did not make them want to stop playing. Only boredom was related to less willingness to continue play.

Some consistent themes emerge from recent research on reasons for playing video games. On the most basic level, video games are purely entertaining. Most research has been done with young adults, who seem to enjoy arousal, competition, and avoidance of boredom. Children also report that the competitive quality of game playing is important. Both children and adults acknowledge the social interaction opportunities provided by video game playing and describe periods of intense absorption.

Game Preference

Early research on video games paid little attention to the kind of games children were playing. When used, systems were dichotomous, and games were either considered violent or nonviolent. The simplistic nature of early games encouraged this commonsense approach to content definition and limited interest in studying the implications of game preference. With the advent of movie-quality images and virtual reality technology, it became necessary to systematically evaluate game content from the participants' perspective. This resulted in the development of the game categories described in Table 10.1. In addition to providing more specific information about age and gender-specific preferences, these categories are useful in examining the meaning and importance of game preference. This is especially important given that research suggests that up to 90% of video games contain some type of violent content (Children Now, 2001).

Table 10.1   Revised Video Game Categories With Descriptions

Category	Description
General Entertainment	Story or game with no fighting or destruction
Educational	Learning new information or figuring out new ways to use information
Fantasy violence	Cartoon character must fight or destroy things and avoid being killed or destroyed while trying to reach a goal, rescue someone, or escape from something
Human violence	Human character must fight or destroy things and avoid being killed or destroyed while trying to reach a goal, rescue someone, or escape from something
Nonviolent sports	Sports without fighting or destruction
Sports violence	Sports with fighting or destruction

SOURCE: Adapted from Funk and Buchman (1995). Copyright 1995 by SLACK, Inc.

Game preference was assessed in the 1990s for fourth through eighth graders (Funk, Buchman, Myers, Jenks, & Hagan, 2000; see also Table 10.2). Across grade levels, girls preferred cartoon or fantasy violent games, while boys preferred more realistic, human violent games (see Figure 10.2). Few boys stated a preference for educational games. Ten years later, fifth through seventh and first and second graders were surveyed using the same categories (see Tables 10.3 and 10.4). Comparing seventh graders 10 years ago to now, boys' preferences are similar. Seventh-grade girls today report a stronger preference for educational games than 10 years ago, possibly reflecting increased choice in this game genre. Girls today are also more likely to play sports games and less likely to prefer games with fantasy violence than seventh-grade girls 10 years ago.

Examining preferences stated by first and second graders, girls in both grades most strongly prefer games with fantasy violence, though educational and general entertainment games are also favorites. First-grade boys also strongly prefer games with fantasy violence, with educational and nonviolent sports games being next most preferred. There is some change for boys from first to second grade, however. Educational games drop in popularity, and games with human violence gain (see Figure 10.3).

The gaming industry asserts that violent games account for only a small percentage of sales and that the ultra-violent games are only bought by adults. In 2000, a Federal Trade Commission (FTC) investigation found that children were targeted consumers for violent video games, as well as for other violent media. In a more

Table 10.2   Percentage of Favorite Games in Each Category by Gender and Grade

	Fourth		Fifth		Sixth		Seventh		Eighth	
	Girl (n = 289)	Boy (n = 241)	Girl (n = 197)	Boy (n = 187)	Girl (n = 157)	Boy (n = 169)	Girl (n = 126)	Boy (n = 177)	Girl (n = 166)	Boy (n = 183)
General entertainment	14.0	6.3	16.8	5.9	16.0	8.9	33.3	7.3	28.9	14.2
Educational	17.6	2.9	24.4	4.3	8.3	3.6	1.6	0.0	5.4	0.5
Fantasy violence	32.7	27.5	30.5	26.2	44.6	24.9	43.7	24.9	44.6	19.1
Human violence	11.5	25.0	10.2	26.2	16.0	26.0	7.1	29.4	7.2	20.8
Nonviolent sports[a]	9.3	17.9	12.7	19.8	10.5	20.1				
Sports violence	14.7	20.4	5.6	17.6	5.7	16.6	4.3	38.4	13.9	45.4

NOTE: *n* refers to number of games listed.

a. When seventh and eighth graders were surveyed, there was only one sports category.

Table 10.3 Percentage of Favorite Games in Each Category by Gender and Grade, Fifth Through Sixth Graders, 2006

	Fifth		Sixth		Seventh	
	Girls[a]	Boys[b]	Girls[c]	Boys[d]	Girls[e]	Boys[f]
General entertainment	38	17	31	8	30	6
Educational	25	25	26	12	24	7
Fantasy violence	13	17	16	24	11	29
Human violence	0	0	7	28	10	33
Nonviolent sports	25	42	18	16	21	19
Sports violence	0	0	1	12	3	6

a. Four girls listed 8 favorite games.
b. Four boys listed 12 favorite games.
c. Forty-six girls listed 106 favorite games.

d. Thirty-eight boys listed 106 favorite games.
e. Thirty-one girls listed 70 favorite games.
f. Forty-four boys listed 124 favorite games.

Table 10.4 Percentage of Favorite Games in Each Category by Gender and Grade, First and Second Graders, 2006

	First		Second	
	Girls[a]	Boys[b]	Girls[c]	Boys[d]
General entertainment	23	2	19	6
Educational	31	20	39	6
Fantasy violence	39	49	32	27
Human violence	8	8	3	22
Nonviolent sports	0	16	0	29
Sports violence	0	4	6	9

a. Thirteen girls listed 26 favorite games.
b. Twenty-two boys listed 49 favorite games.

c. Fifteen girls listed 31 favorite games.
d. Nineteen boys listed 45 favorite games.

Figure 10.2

SOURCE: ©Gamespot.com.

recent report, however, the FTC noted that there was progress in limiting advertisements in popular teen media for M-rated games that typically include "intense violence" (Federal Trade Commission, 2006a). It is, however, important to recognize
that the most recent research indicates that children and adolescents of all ages
choose to play games with some degree of violence.

Figure 10.3

SOURCE: ©Rpgamer.com.

Game Ratings

As video games became a common leisure choice for children and adolescents, researchers and policymakers, as well as some members of the general public, became concerned about the increasing realism and graphic violence of many popular games. As a result, pressure was placed on the industry to self-regulate by the threat of government-imposed regulation (Funk, Flores, Buchman, & Germann, 1999). Two voluntary systems were developed, one by the Entertainment Software Association, which created the Entertainment Software Rating Board (ESRB), and the other by the Software Publishers Association, whose ratings group was called the Recreational Software Advisory Council or RSAC. The content-based RSAC system is no longer being used to rate games, but a version of these ratings is now available to rate Web site content under the new association name, Internet Content Rating Association.

The ESRB's system is age based and covers console games, PC software, and Internet games (Entertainment Software Rating Board, 2006). The age-based ESRB game classifications are presented in Table 10.5. Each game is rated independently by three trained raters. Raters come from a variety of occupational and ethnic backgrounds and are paid for their work. Because a solely age-based system did not seem adequate, content descriptors were added to highlight content in the following areas: violence, sexual themes, and language. Other specific descriptors such as the presence of alcohol and tobacco use may be added at the discretion of each individual rater. Rating information appears on game packaging (see Figure 10.4).

Some researchers have found that the ratings provided by the ESRB do not correspond to content as perceived by consumers (see, e.g., Funk, Flores, et al., 1999; Gentile, Humphrey, & Walsh, 2005; Haninger & Thompson, 2004; and Walsh & Gentile, 2001). Possibly in response to these concerns, the E10+ category was added to the original categories. Games with this rating are recom-

Figure 10.4

SOURCE: ©http://www.esrb.com.

mended for consumers age 10 and older. However, significant discrepancies remain between consumer perception of game content and game ratings, particularly in the area of violence. In a recent study, first and second graders listed and rated up to three favorite video games using a ratings system developed by Funk and Buchman (1995; see Table 10.1). Using standardized definitions, children categorized their favorite games into one of the six categories. Then these games were also categorized by two college students and a psychology graduate student, and ratings provided by the ESRB were obtained. Categorizations and ratings were collapsed into those reflecting violent or nonviolent content, and the three groups of ratings were compared. Although there was good agreement between child and adult raters, agreement between consumer perception of game content as violent and ESRB ratings was

Table 10.5 Summary of Primary ESRB Rating Categories

Rating	Description
Early Childhood (EC)	Age 3 and older. No inappropriate content.
Everyone (E)	Age 6 and older. May have minimal violence and language.
Everyone 10 and older (E 10 +)	Age 10 and older. More mild violence, language, and minimal suggestive themes.
Teen (T)	Age 13 and older. Violence, suggestive themes, crude humor, minimal blood, and infrequent strong language.
Mature (M)	Ages 17 and older. Intense violence, blood and gore, sexual content, and strong language.
Adults Only (AO)	Ages 18 and older. Prolonged scenes of intense violence and/or graphic sexual content and nudity.
Rating Pending (RP)	Submitted to the ESRB, awaiting final rating.

SOURCE: Adapted from information presented at http://www.esrb.com.

tsumers and needs additional refinement (Funk, Brouwer, Curtiss, & Leininger, 2006).

Lack of compliance by both consumers and retailers also decreases the usefulness of the ESRB ratings. In 2000, the Federal Trade Commission reported that, based on undercover "sting" operations, children were usually able to purchase games with extreme violence and ratings above their age level (Federal Trade Commission, 2000). The FTC has continued to conduct undercover operations assessing enforcement of the game ratings, and compliance has steadily improved (Federal Trade Commission, 2006b; see Table 10.6). However, in 2005, children ages 13 to 16 were still able to purchase games with M ratings almost half the time. In recent congressional testimony, the FTC spokesperson noted that it is vital that parents familiarize themselves with the existing ratings system and be aware that game content can be

Table 10.6 Federal Trade Commission Nationwide Undercover Survey Results, 2000–2005

	2000	2001	2003	2005
Was the shopper able to buy the M-rated video game?	85	78	65	42
Did the store provide information about ratings or enforcement?	12	26	27	44
Did the cashier or clerk ask the child's age?	15	21	24	50

SOURCE: Adapted from information presented at http://www.ftc.gov/opa/2006/03/videogameshop.htm.

NOTE: All answers are percent "yes."

modified using widely available "mods" that can be accessed through the Internet (Federal Trade Commission, 2006a). However, a recent survey of 94 parents of children ages 5 and younger found that even well-educated parents lack familiarity with video game ratings (Funk, Brouwer, Curtiss, & McBroom, 2007).

In summary, the video game ratings provided by the ESRB do give information about game content, as well as about age appropriateness of this content from the perspective of the ESRB raters. There are continuing problems that include lack of agreement with consumer perceptions, failure to enforce ratings, and lack of consumer familiarity with ratings.

A Closer Look at Violent Video Games

The Appeal of Violent Video Games

One of the most interesting questions about violent video games is why they are so popular. In addition to previously discussed reasons for the general popularity of video games, violent content seems to add to their appeal. The reasons behind the attraction to violent media have long been a subject of professional study and debate (Funk, 2000; Goldstein, 1998). Industry spokesmen often cite catharsis or tension release as a benefit of exposure to many forms of violent media, but this claim has been disproven in a sizable body of research (see, e.g., Bushman, 2002; Geen, 2001). Others suggest that the appeal of violent media is enhanced by ratings indicating violence, but there is only mixed support for this "forbidden fruit" explanation, which seems most likely to apply to boys (Kirsh, 2006). Some have suggested that children and adolescents may seek out violent entertainment to meet their need for new experiences and for pure physiological arousal (Aluja-Fabregat, 2000; Raney et al., 2006; Slater, 2003). McCauley (1998) suggests that the entertainment context modifies the anxiety normally associated with violent images into a general state of arousal or excitement that some find enjoyable. For children and adolescents, it is most likely that media violence is appealing to different individuals for different reasons. Personal history seems to be a key variable, with callous children who have been overexposed to violence looking for continuing arousal, while anxious and emotionally reactive children are trying to master anxiety-provoking experiences (Cantor, 1998) (see Figure 10.5).

There has been minimal research directed specifically to understanding the attraction of violent video games. In focus groups described earlier, participants reported enjoying engaging in antisocial activity during game playing, such as extreme defiance of authority, and rule breaking (Funk, Chan, et al., 2006). Jansz (2005) suggests that the reason that violent video games are so appealing to adolescent males is because they provide the adolescent with the opportunity of choosing to experience different

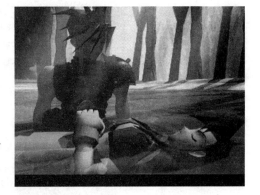

Figure 10.5

SOURCE: ©Funender.com.

emotions, some of which are gender appropriate (anger) and some not as appropriate (fear). Hind (1995) investigated the game preference of 72 juvenile offenders ages 15 to 18 and 30 nonoffenders. Participants played two computer games, one violent and one nonviolent, and then rated their satisfaction with each game. The juvenile offenders preferred the game that involved simple destruction of objects to the nonviolent game, which required planning to achieve success. This finding may provide support for arousal as the explanation of the appeal of violent games, at least in the case of juvenile offenders. Obviously, more work is needed to understand the appeal of violent video games.

The Importance of a Preference for Violent Video Games

Over the past few years, researchers have given considerable attention to the importance of the widespread preference for violent video games. Related media research suggests that there are sensitive periods when exposure to media violence can have a significant impact on the development of a behavioral predisposition to aggression in young children (Eron, Huesmann, Brice, Fischer, & Mermelstein, 1983). However, there may also be a cumulative effect of long-term exposure to violent media, affecting older children and adolescents (Johnson, Cohen, Smailes, Kasen, & Brook, 2002).

From a biological standpoint, it has long been established that early experience affects the development of neural connections. Newer imaging techniques have revealed that there are dramatic anatomical changes in the brain during adolescence (see, e.g., Dorn et al., 2003; Thompson et al., 2000). The behavioral implications of this information about brain development have not yet been established, but this finding does raise interesting questions about how vulnerable adolescents may be to negative impact from continued exposure to violent media. For some adolescents, participation in highly arousing activities such as playing violent video games may be valued because this activity meets their heightened need for stimulation. It is interesting that the pattern of video game play across adolescence mirrors the development of aggressive behaviors, with both video game play and aggression increasing from ages 11 to 14 and decreasing in later adolescence (Kirsh, 2002). In some cases, preexisting aggressive tendencies may lead youth to more actively seek out violent media, and the resulting exposure may reinforce and exacerbate aggressive tendencies (Slater, Henry, Swaim, & Anderson, 2003).

Mechanisms

Several theoretical perspectives have been used to understand the possible effects of playing violent video games. Both short-term and long-term effects must be considered. Commonly recognized mechanisms for the effect of exposure to violent video games are summarized in Table 10.7.

Table 10.7   Mechanisms to Explain the Impact of Violent Video Games

Mechanism	Description	Time Span of Impact
Observational learning	After observing the behavior of others, these behaviors are integrated into the individual's behavioral repertoire.	Both short and long term
Imitation	Learned behaviors are taken from the repertoire and exhibited.	Short term
Schema development	Knowledge structures about the typical organization of daily experience develop as a way to manage information efficiently.	Long term
Script development	Specific types of schemas for events develop to guide behavioral reactions.	
Priming	Violent media activate aggressive schemas.	Short term
Automatization of aggressive schemas	Repetitive priming of aggressive schemas makes them chronically accessible.	Long term
Arousal	Physiological arousal occurs in response to a particular stimuli; aggressive stimuli cause aggressive arousal.	Short term
Excitation transfer	Misattribution of the source of aggressive arousal could lead to aggression.	Short term
Cognitive desensitization	Belief that violence is common and mundane decreases likelihood that moral evaluation will inhibit aggression.	Long term
Emotional desensitization	Numbing of emotional response to violent actions or experiences decreases likelihood that moral evaluation will inhibit aggression.	Long term

NOTE: For a comprehensive discussion of these theoretical mechanisms, see Anderson et al. (2004).

In the short term, observational learning and imitation of game actions are possible. Increased aggressive arousal is a well-established short-term effect of playing violent video games. Misattribution of the source of aggressive arousal could lead to aggressive behavior (excitation transfer).

Over the longer term, game playing has the characteristics of a powerful learning environment. Players experience repeated demonstrations of violent behavior, coupled with the contingent reward of "winning" for choosing built-in violent strategies, which are integral to playing violent video games (Provenzo, 1991). Successful players will consistently choose the preprogrammed violent alternatives and receive cycles of positive reinforcement, increasing the likelihood that these behaviors will be internalized and accessible later.

From another perspective, it is possible that the actual structure of experience could be affected by repeated exposure to violent video games (Funk, 2006). Children learn general social rules and specific behaviors from observation, practice, and reinforcement. The development and internalization of behavioral scripts is one component of this process. A behavioral script is a set of situation-specific expectations and behavioral guidelines. A behavioral script helps an individual to predict what will happen in a certain situation and to implement a preprogrammed sequence of behaviors without really thinking about it (Huesmann & Miller, 1994). For example, most adults have driving scripts: Find the keys, walk to the car, open the door, get in the car, shut the door, put on the seat belt, turn on the ignition, and so forth. A restaurant script is another common example: Walk in the door, be seated, order, eat, pay, leave. Scripts may be triggered by internal or by situational cues, causing the individual to behave based on the previously internalized set of guidelines. Though they increase efficiency, scripts are not always entirely accurate and may cause an individual to misinterpret or disregard new information. Perceived experience may even be altered to conform to a script (Guerra, Nucci, & Huesmann, 1994; Huesmann & Miller, 1994). That explains why it can be difficult to get used to a new car: Your driving script must be altered to accommodate differences in the location of the windshield wipers and other controls.

During childhood, scripts are constantly being developed and revised in response to many different types of learning experiences. In theory, a child could develop and internalize scripts for situations that trigger aggression based in part on playing violent video games. Exposure to violent video games can also prime existing aggressive scripts; if this happens over and over, the scripts will become easily accessible to guide behavior. Games with more realistic storylines, such as *Bully*, in which the main character must defend himself from school bullies but also may "make out" with them, and *Super Columbine Massacre*, in which players play as both Harris and Klebold, moving around the school and deciding who to kill, may be even more likely to foster script development as they have an added element of pseudo-credibility (see Figure 10.6).

If behavioral scripts are derived from unreal violence with no negative consequences, then the child's response to violence in real life will be influenced accordingly: The child will be less sensitive to the true consequences of violent actions (emotional desensitization), and violence will seem to be a reasonable alternative in many interpersonal situations (cognitive desensitization) (Funk, 2005b). Although research on desensitization to violence as a result of exposure to media violence is relatively limited, this may be one of the most important unintended consequences as it could affect many social interactions, including a person's willingness to respond to others in need (Funk, 2005a; Funk & Buchman, 2006).

Craig Anderson and colleagues have proposed a model that integrates most of the existing theories to explain the occurrence of aggression: the general aggression model or GAM (Anderson & Bushman, 2002; Anderson & Huesmann, 2003; Carnagey & Anderson, 2003). They have applied this model to understand the possible effects of playing violent video games. In GAM, there is a continuous reciprocal

Figure 10.6

SOURCE: ©Teamxbox.com.

interaction between the person and the environment. Three key elements contribute to this cycle: input variables related to both what the person brings to the situation and the current environment, the person's current internal state, and outcomes that result from decision processes. Input variables can influence cognition, affect, and arousal. The research of Anderson and colleagues suggests that playing violent video games increases aggressive behavior, aggressive thoughts, and aggressive feelings (Anderson & Bushman, 2001; Anderson et al., 2004). In very simplistic terms, in GAM, this could result in learning and performing aggressive behaviors (Carnagey & Anderson, 2003).

Research on the Effects of Playing Violent Video Games

The effects attributed to exposure to violent video games range from no important measurable effects (Freedman, 2002; Scott, 1995) to minimal effects (Office of Film and Literature Classification, 1999) to desensitization, including decreased empathy and stronger proviolence attitudes (Funk, Bechtoldt-Baldacci, Pasold, & Baumgardner, 2004; Funk, Buchman, Jenks, & Bechtoldt, 2003), to increased feelings of hostility and increased aggression (Anderson & Bushman, 2001; Anderson et al., 2004; Anderson, Gentile, & Buckley, 2007). It must be recognized that most published research does report some type of negative effect. Two organizing principles were used to guide the choice of literature for the following summary. The first principle was to include only recent research because today's violent video games are very different from the "violent" games of the late 1970s, 1980s, and early 1990s. Video games are now much more realistic, with much more graphic violence, and many include the option of personalizing the images of game characters.

The second principle was to separately consider studies of short-term and long-term effects. Short-term effects are the immediate results of a specific game-playing experience, either observable behavioral change or change in some specific aspect of thinking or emotion. Short-term effects may be representative of real-life experience and may be long lasting and cumulative; however, this is not proven in the laboratory setting. Long-term effects are determined by examining relationships among certain behaviors, personality characteristics, or cognitions, and game-playing habits, such as a preference for violent games. Some studies examine both immediate (short-term) effects and longer term relationships by combining experimental manipulations and surveys.

It is worth noting that, after conducting a meta-analytic review (a reanalysis combining the results of several studies looking at the same problem), Bushman and Huesmann (2006) concluded that children are less likely than adults to demonstrate short-term effects of exposure to media violence because children's associative networks are less well developed, leading to lower priming of aggression. Children, however, may demonstrate more pronounced long-term effects than adults because they more easily encode new scripts and beliefs than adults, who must overrride and replace these established knowledge structures.

Short-Term Effects. Only a few studies published in recent years have used child participants. Funk and colleagues (2003) studied children's responses to stories about everyday situations after they played either a violent or nonviolent video game. Prior to game playing, third through fifth graders completed standardized measures of empathy and attitudes toward violence, and they listed and categorized up to three favorite games using standard definitions (Funk & Buchman, 1995). Following game playing, children responded to several questions ("You see a child sitting on the side of the playground crying. What happens next?"). Half the situations would commonly trigger empathic responses, and half would commonly trigger aggressive responses.

There were no differences in empathic or aggressive responses between children who played the violent or nonviolent game. However, children whose favorite game was violent gave more aggressive responses than those whose favorite game was nonviolent. Significant relationships were also identified for preexisting empathy and aggression: Children with more empathy before the experiment had higher vignette empathy scores. Similarly, stronger proviolence attitudes were associated with higher aggression scores on the aggression vignettes. In this study, preexisting characteristics were a more important determinant of postexperiment behavior than the short-term manipulation.

In a similar study done with first and second graders, again no effect of the violent versus nonviolent game was found, but a stronger preference for violent games was related to lower pregame empathy in girls (Funk, Buchman, Chan, & Brouwer, 2005). Consistent with Bushman and Huesmann's (2006) findings, it may not be reasonable to expect that brief periods of game playing will cause measurable change in relatively stable traits such as empathy and attitudes toward violence in young children.

In studies primarily with undergraduates, Anderson and associates have demonstrated increases in hostile cognitions and aggressive feelings and behavior after playing violent video games. There are variations, but in the typical general paradigm, undergraduates play either a violent or nonviolent video game. Then participants complete a competitive reaction time test in which their goal was to push a button faster than their opponent. The loser of the race receives a blast of noise, with the noise level supposedly set by the opponent (but actually controlled by the computer). Aggressive behavior is operationalized as the intensity and duration of the noise blast chosen by the participant. Anderson and colleagues typically find that students who play the violent game delivered more intense noise blasts than those who played the nonviolent game and therefore are considered to be more aggressive (Anderson et al., 2004; Anderson & Dill, 2000; Carnagey & Anderson, 2005). Notably, this finding held true in a more recent study of 9- to 12-year-olds (Anderson et al., 2007)

Several researchers have attempted to determine what personality or other factors may explain or change the relationship between playing violent video games and various outcomes. For example, Arriaga, Esteves, Carneiro, and Monteiro (2006) had undergraduates self-report on aggression and anxiety, then play a violent or nonviolent video game, then report again on hostility and anxiety. Playing the violent game increased self-reported feelings of hostility, but not anxiety, with more prior feelings of hostility related to more postgame hostility.

In one of the first attempts to demonstrate a short-term desensitization effect, Carnagey, Anderson, and Bushman (2006) monitored heart rate and galvanic skin response (GSR) while undergraduates viewed scenes of real-life violence. Those who had previously played a violent video game had lower heart rate and GSR than those who played nonviolent games, demonstrating physiological desensitization to violence. Combining both long-term and short-term methodology, Bartholow, Bushman, and Sestir (2006) examined participant brainwaves while viewing standardized violent and nonviolent pictures. They found that more past exposure to violent video games was associated with less brain response to violent images and with increased aggression in a competitive reaction time task. The authors suggest that these results indicate physiological evidence of desensitization to violence as a result of violent video game exposure. Both studies represent important first steps in examining the subtle, yet potentially highly significant, desensitization effect.

Long-Term Effects. Although causal relationships can be studied in the laboratory, this setting cannot take into consideration variables that may be active in the real world and influence behavior outside the game-playing situation. Surveys and longitudinal studies are needed to examine real-world relationships. For example, investigators have tried to link game preference and real-world problem behaviors, including aggression. Gentile et al. (2004) surveyed eighth and ninth graders and found that more exposure to video game violence was associated with more self-reported hostility, arguments with teachers, and physical fights. Similar findings resulted from a survey of German eighth graders, with more exposure to violent video games being associated with acceptance of physical aggression and a hostile attributional style (tendency to view ambiguous situations as hostile) (Krahe & Moller, 2004).

Associations between a preference for violent video games and adolescents' self-perceptions of various problem behaviors and emotions were examined by Funk et al. (2002). Based on past media research, it was predicted that adolescents with a preference for violent games would report more aggressive emotions and behaviors on the Youth Self-Report (YSR), a widely used measure of adolescent psychopathology (behavior and emotional problems). Although expected relationships with externalizing behaviors, including aggression, were not found, relationships were found with total number of problem behaviors and with some internalizing behaviors, including anxiety. Across all YSR subscales, children with a higher preference for violent games had more clinically significant elevations (indicating more psychopathology) than those with a low preference. This approach cannot establish a causal relationship between a preference for violent video games and psychopathology, but the associations are interesting and worthy of further study.

Several surveys with adolescent and child participants have investigated relationships between playing violent video games, empathy, and attitudes toward violence. In one early survey, older adolescents whose favorite game was violent had lower empathy scores on the "fantasy empathy" subscale of the Interpersonal Reactivity Index (Barnett et al., 1997). In a similar survey with sixth graders, it was anticipated that a stronger preference for violent games would be associated with lower empathy and stronger proviolence attitudes (Funk, Buchman, Schimming, & Hagan, 1998). Marginally significant relationships in the expected direction were identified. In addition, children with both a high preference for violent games and high time commitment to playing demonstrated the lowest empathy. In two surveys, with fourth and fifth graders and with 5- through 12-year-olds, relationships were found between long-term exposure to violent video games, lower empathy, and in some cases stronger proviolence attitudes (Funk et al., 2003, 2004). In a sample of Chinese adolescents, relationships were found between exposure to online video game violence and greater tolerance of aggression, lower empathy, and more aggressive behavior (Wei, 2007). These results are important because of their consistency and because they can be interpreted as demonstrating a link between long-term exposure to violent video games and desensitization to violence as reflected in the findings of lower empathy and stronger proviolence attitudes.

Anderson and Dill (2000) surveyed 227 undergraduates to examine links between typical time spent playing video games, game preference, personal history of aggression and delinquent behavior, and perception of the likelihood of being a victim of common crimes. Participants also completed scales measuring irritability and anger. Undergraduates whose favorite games were violent were more likely to report aggressive delinquent behavior, trait aggressiveness, and an aggressive personality style. In a more recent, similar survey, Anderson et al. (2007) confirmed these relationships and found that exposure to violent video games is associated with endorsement of physical aggression. Anderson et al. also surveyed elementary school students and teachers at two points in the school year. They found that high exposure to violent video games early in the school year was positively related to aggressive behavior later in the school year, even after controlling for prior aggression level.

The studies described above suggest that support continues to grow for the contention that exposure to violent video games is associated with less prosocial behavior in children, including increased aggression and lower empathy. In the one study found contradicting this conclusion, Williams and Skoric (2005) studied young adults playing online violent games for 1 month and concluded there was no effect of game violence. However, this study has several serious potential flaws, including the measures of aggressive behavior (self-reported "arguing in past month") and the data-analytic techniques (Anderson et al., 2007). Additional research on the effects of exposure to violent video games is still needed, particularly long-term longitudinal research.

High-Risk Players and High-Risk Content. There is still much to learn about which environmental, situational, and personality factors place children at increased risk for negative consequences from playing violent video games. A relative risk model suggests that the more risk factors that a child has, the more likely a negative outcome. Exposure to violent video games can be conceptualized as one potentially modifiable risk factor for aggressive behavior. An emerging body of research does suggest that some children are "high-risk" players (Funk, 2003; Funk & Buchman, 1996). High-risk players may be drawn to violent video games because of preexisting adjustment problems. Game playing may then have a causal role in either perpetuating preexisting problems or in contributing to the development of new problems. For example, some children with academic problems may use video games as either an escape from schoolwork or as an area in which they can excel. Although there could be temporary benefits such as an increase in self-esteem, over the long term, academic problems may worsen because of this strategy, leading to a decrease in self-esteem. Anand (2007) found a negative correlation between SAT scores and time spent playing video games in a group of college students; a negative correlation was also found between grade point average and time spent. Time commitment may provide one indicator for high-risk status. The work of various investigators hints that girls who play more than their peers may have adjustment issues (Colwell, Grady, & Rhaiti, 1995; Funk & Buchman, 2006; Roe & Muijs, 1998). Any child, boy or girl, who typically plays more than 2 hours each day and who demonstrates an extreme negative reaction if play is limited should be considered at risk for negative impact simply due to time displacement from other developmentally appropriate activities.

A strong preference for violent games may be another indicator of high-risk status (Funk, 2003; Funk et al., 2002; Roe & Muijs, 1998). However, video games with violence are popular with many children, and the level at which preference for such games becomes pathological has not yet been established. Children in focus groups have reported the urge to copy some aggressive behavior: "And sometimes I even ram into my sister, but not on accident" (Funk, Chan, et al., 2006). Children who routinely copy aggressive actions from video games may need play restriction.

Personality variables are a key factor in Anderson and colleagues' GAM. Regarding personality features that may increase susceptibility to negative influence, Anderson et al. (2004) reported that undergraduates with high trait hostility and high physical aggression were predisposed to be aggressive against others in laboratory video game experiments. Children with lower frustration tolerance and high general irritability appear to be at above-average risk for at least short-term negative impact, including unpleasant and uncooperative behavior, particularly after a prolonged period of play (Funk, 2003). Gentile et al. (2004) suggest that children with high hostility who play violent video games increase their risk of physical aggression. Bartholow, Sestir, and Davis (2005) found that trait hostility, empathy, and aggression partially account for the effects of exposure to violent video games on laboratory aggression. These studies are intriguing and suggestive, but much more research is needed to fully understand risk factors for negative outcomes from exposure to violent video games. The developing field of social neuroscience, in which the effects of a specific experience on specific neural structures are examined using neurocognitive tools such as functional magnetic resonance imaging (fMRI), holds considerable promise for better understanding the effects of violent video games (Carnagey, Anderson, & Bartholow, 2007).

A Brief Word About Online Games

A full discussion of the massively multiplayer online games (MMOGs) and massively multiplayer online role-playing games (MMORPGs) is beyond the scope of this chapter. However, these games deserve a brief mention because of their considerable popularity. For example, *World of Warcraft* (commonly abbreviated to *WoW*), the most successful online role-playing game to date, had more than 9 million active subscriptions from players around the world as of January 2008. The game is cleverly designed so that new players can build characters at their own pace, but experienced players continually face increasing challenges. Players first choose and then control a character within the gameworld, exploring, fighting monsters, and performing quests. Success results in the acquisition of money and useful items, as well as experience, skill, and power. The majority of the quests during the early and middle stages of gameplay can be completed without the help of other players. Activities in more advanced portions of the game, such as dungeons, are designed to require other players to work together as "guilds." The most complex quests are designed to take guilds months of playtime before they succeed.

Research on this game genre is quite limited (Chan & Vorderer, 2006; Jansz & Tanis, 2007). R. T. A. Wood, Griffiths, and Eatough (2004) described difficulties researching this phenomenon. These include recruiting participants and establishing the validity of responses, difficulties that are common to most social science research. One unique issue is the question of participant observation, when the researcher enters the virtual world to collect data on a specific research question. Wood et al. recommend that the researcher make this goal known to other gamers to allow for a kind of informed consent. Limited research on motivation for online play suggests that social interaction is a key feature that influences players to keep playing (Axelsson & Regan, 2006; Choi & Kim, 2004; Griffiths, Davies, & Chappell, 2007). This interaction can involve a wide range of activities from helping to hostility. Choi and Kim (2004) suggest that having an optimal experience, such as attaining a flow state, also encourages players to continue. Much more research is needed to understand this ever evolving leisure choice.

Video Games and Health

Risks: Musculoskeletal

Since video games first became popular, there have been various case reports of minor negative health impact, primarily temporary musculoskeletal injury (see, e.g., Greene & Asher, 1982). Ramos, James, and Bear-Lehman (2005) surveyed 476 children in first to eighth grade to determine whether video game playing could result in repetitive strain injury (RSI). *RSI* is a term used to cover a variety of muscular complaints resulting from prolonged repetitive movements. More than half the children reported some degree of discomfort associated with playing video games, most often neck discomfort, although the back, fingers, and hand were also mentioned. The authors conclude that playing video games may place some children at risk for RSI.

Risks: Seizures

The risk of video or computer game–related seizures in photosensitive individuals, even those without a previous seizure history, is well established (Chuang et al., 2006; Fisher, Harding, Erba, Barkley, & Wilkins, 2005; Graf, Chatrian, Glass, & Knauss, 1994; Piccioli, Vigevano, Buttinelli, & Trenite, 2005). These seizures seem to be triggered by specific features, including the display flicker of the screen, screen brightness, distance from the screen, and the specific pattern of the images. Treatment alternatives include avoidance of video games and administration of sodium valproate for those whose seizures are persistent (Chuang et al., 2006; Fisher et al., 2005). It is important to note that researchers believe that individuals with epilepsy who do not have photosensitivity (estimated at greater than 95%) may safely play video games. Regarding online multiplayer games, reports are emerging of a variety of types of seizures in a small group of players (Chuang et al., 2006). Chuang et al. (2006) suggest that factors such as anxiety, excitement, and stress may play a role in triggering seizures.

Risks: Cardiovascular Reactivity

Several studies have identified increases in the cardiovascular reactivity of children and adolescents during video game play (Ballard & Wiest, 1996; Wang & Perry, 2006). This finding is important, as it has been suggested that cardiovascular reactivity may serve as either a marker or mechanism for the development of essential hypertension or coronary disease (Murphy, Stoney, Alpert, & Walker, 1995). Matthews, Zhu, Tucker, and Whooley (2006) evaluated cardiovascular reactivity in 2,816 women ages 20 to 35 years old while playing a video game, then examined these women 13 years later for coronary calcification ("hardening of the arteries"). They found that changes in blood pressure during the video game play predicted later calcification. The clinical significance of increasing cardiovascular reactivity over extended video game playing periods has yet to be determined, but the Matthews et al. results suggest that long-term research in this area is clearly indicated.

Risks: Sleep

Only a few studies have considered the possible effects of video game play on sleep patterns in children and adolescents. Effects identified include sleep-onset delay, night-waking, sleep anxiety, and shortened sleep duration (Dworak, Schierl, Bruns, & Struder, 2007). One recent study used polysomnography (using a polygraph to make a continuous record during sleep of physiological variables such as breathing, heart rate, and muscle activity) to examine the effects of 60 minutes of video game play and an exciting video on young adolescents' sleep patterns and on visual and verbal memory (Dworak et al., 2007). Results indicated that game playing adversely affected sleep patterns. Given the widespread nature of late-night video game play, this issue needs further investigation.

Risks: Sedentary Behavior

Like all media, playing video games may contribute to a sedentary lifestyle with the accompanying health risks. Using a 24-hour recall method, Myers, Strikmiller, Webber, and Berenson (1996) assessed the activity levels of 995 nine- though fifteen-year-olds in relation to watching television and playing video games. More time was spent in these sedentary activities by girls and African Americans when compared, respectively, with boys and European Americans. The authors also reported that physical activity declined with age.

Obesity is a particular risk associated with a sedentary lifestyle. However, results of research examining relationships between playing video games and being overweight have been mixed. In American adolescents between ages 10 and 16, McMurray et al. (2000) found that low socioeconomic status and African American ethnicity were more important contributors to obesity than television viewing or video game play. Kautiainen, Koivusilta, Lintonen, Virtanen, and Rimpela (2005) surveyed a nationally representative sample of adolescents from Finland and found that video game playing was not associated with being overweight. Vandewater, Shim, and Caplovitz (2004) studied relationships between weight and video game playing in American children ages 1 through 12. For children younger than age 8, there was a relationship between more video game play and higher weight. A meta-analysis done by Marshall, Biddle, Gorely, Cameron, and Murdey (2004) identified a small but significant relationship between television viewing and video game play and being overweight in 3- to 18-year-olds. However, the authors state that the relationships between these types of sedentary behavior are complex and need to be considered in context with other contributing factors such as consumption of high-calorie snacks while watching television or playing video games. Other researchers suggest that video game play is not truly a sedentary activity, which may account for the variable relationships found between game play and obesity (Wang & Perry, 2006).

Risks: Extreme

There have been a few troubling reports of "eThrombosis" (a thrombosis is a blood clot) occurring in people who sit at a computer for long periods (Murrin, 2004; Ng, Khurana, Yeang, Hughes, & Manning, 2003). One fatality in a 24-year-old was reported following approximately 80 hours of continuous game play (H. Lee, 2004). Researchers suspect that the immobility and the sometimes odd positions associated with extensive game play could cause blood clots in susceptible individuals. They recommend regular leg exercises and intermissions during prolonged game play.

The Positive Potential of Video Games

Serious Games

There are a growing number of video games whose primary purpose goes beyond pure entertainment, moving toward promoting positive social change. These are known as "Serious Games," and this is an important and encouraging movement in the gaming industry (Schollmeyer, 2006). More than 500 such games have been identified, and more than 200 are now catalogued at http://www.socialimpactgames.com, ranging from games with health and mental health applications to educational, political, public policy, and business applications. The Serious Games Initiative began formally in 2000, launched by the Woodrow Wilson International Center for scholars in order to develop games to address policy and management issues. In 2004, subgroups of this movement were created to help develop practice standards. These included games for health, focusing on games with health care applications, and games for change, focusing on social issues.

Games for Health

Several video games have been developed specifically for children with chronic medical conditions. One of the best studied is an educational game called *Packy and Marlon* (Brown et al., 1997). This game was designed to improve self-care skills and medical compliance in children and adolescents with diabetes. Players take the role of characters who demonstrate good diabetes care practices while working to save a summer camp for children with diabetes from rats and mice who have stolen the supplies. There are also many case reports describing the use of video games for rehabilitation (see, e.g., Krichevets, Sirotkina, Yevsevicheva, & Zeldin, 1995; S. Wood, 2003). For a review of publications describing the use of video games to promote health-related behavior change, see Baranowski, Buday, Thompson, and Baranowski (2008).

Virtual reality game technology has many applications in children's health care. For example, a game called *Zora* has been used to promote coping in a pediatric hemodialysis unit (Bers, Gonzalez-Heydrich, & Demaso, 2003). Users build virtual identities and converse with other patients in real time to obtain support. Players and staff reported that the game situation was both enjoyable and safe. Sik Lanyi et al. (2004) described a research program developing virtual reality games for, among others, children with a variety of disabilities, including stroke, phobias, vision impairments, hearing problems, and mental retardation. They note that their approach is especially useful because the disabled child can experience success as well as motivating visual and audio feedback.

Some games are clearly not sedentary activities. For example, in the PlayStation-based EyeToy system, a mini-camera sits on the television and captures the image of the player dancing or engaging in various activities ranging from dancing, window washing, kung fu, or a variety of sports using motion sensors. The player then navigates through menus and interacts with the system's games by moving around. In Eye Toy's *Operation Spy,* the player's image is seen on the television as he or she moves through activities designed to result in the capture of a network of master criminals. The Xavix system is another game system that uses a peripheral device to allow the player to literally become a part of the game. For example, in the baseball game, the player uses a wireless battery-powered bat to swing at a virtual pitch. The game system senses the velocity and swing angle to judge whether the "ball" is hit out of park or whiffed. *Dance Dance Revolution* is another exercise-based game that includes software and peripherals that can be attached to several game systems. Using high-energy music, players are challenged to match dance steps with flashing arrows on the screen. Players can choose from levels of difficulty that are designed to increase fitness. Most recently, the Nintendo Wii adds to the options for active video game play. The Wii remote allows users to control the game using physical gestures as well as traditional button presses. This system has become popular with users across age groups.

Games for Change

More and more games are being developed to address social issues. Many are available without cost, primarily over the Internet, or for a small nominal fee. Although most have not been formally researched to determine the effectiveness of the message delivered, some have found a large audience, as demonstrated by the number of downloads. These games are aimed at developing critical thinking about issues where there is no one right answer and difficult choices must be made. Designers believe that the games can raise public awareness and empower youth to work for positive social change, thus the designation "Games for Change." Examples of games in this genre include *Food Force, Darfur Is Dying, Peacemaker, September 12, A Force More Powerful,* and *Squeezed.* These games are described in Table 10.8.

Table 10.8   Description of Selected Serious Games/Games for Change

Name of Game	Developers/Sponsors	Primary Content and Goal
Food Force	Deepend, Playerthree/United Nations World Food Programme	Solve a major hunger crisis by delivering food
Darfur Is Dying	Students at University of Southern California/Reebok, MTVu/ International Crisis Group	Increase awareness of the humanitarian crisis in the Sudan
Peacemaker	Carnegie Mellon students/ University of Southern California	Develop a lasting Middle East peace
A Force More Powerful	Ivan Marovic, Serbian Youth Movement/International Center on Nonviolent Conflict	Learn nonviolent ways to fight dictators and corrupt rulers
Squeezed	Students at University of Denver/MTVu, Cisco Systems	Empathize with the immigrant experience
September 12	Gonzalo Frasca, University of Copenhagen/Powerful Robot Games	Learn the unintended effects of bombing as a way to win the war on terror

NOTE: For more information, see http://www.socialimpactgames.com or search the name of the game on the Internet.

Financing the development of games directed to social issues is a challenge. Most of these games have been developed by volunteers (primarily graduate students) or with foundation support. For example, the International Center on Nonviolent Conflict invested $3 million and allied with a commercial game developer to create *A Force More Powerful*. Some believe that it is unlikely that most games with a message will be sufficiently entertaining to attract a large enough audience to ensure profitability (Mandrid, 2006). Some of these serious games have highly controversial subject matter that may discourage potential support. In *September 12,* for example, bombing terrorists kill innocent bystanders, spawning more terrorists. Amnesty International described this game as "disturbing rather than fun—but that's the point" (http://www.newsgaming.com). When *September 12* was first made available, some players sent hate mail to the designer, accusing him of being sympathetic to terrorists.

In the area of mental health, the game *Earthquake in Zipland* was developed to help children cope with divorce (see http://www.zi-ltd.com). Targeted at 7- to 14-year-olds, the player goes on a quest to reunite a divided island. The game makes skillful use of metaphor, music, and an entertaining game interface to help children examine difficult feelings within a safe, comfortable, therapeutic context. Games have also been developed (with many not fully researched) to promote AIDS prevention, to relieve stress associated with cancer, to alert children to the dangers of child predators, to treat phobias and depression, to provide pain distraction, to aid rehabilitation, to promote relaxation, and to enhance self-esteem, among others (see http://www.socialimpactgames.com for game descriptions and availability).

Video Games and Education

Educational gaming systems are available for all age groups. Sometimes called "edutainment," these games deliver instruction or other messages packaged as entertainment. For example, the V. Smile system provides a "dynamic learning platform" for 3- to 7-year-olds, with games that address skill development in the areas of language, logic, and cognition. The LeapFrog family of games and devices is designed for players from early childhood through high school, with the line of products' stated goal being to instill a "lifelong love of learning." One of their most interesting products is the FLY Pentop Computer. FLY Pentop Computer's power comes from an optical scanner that sees everything that is scanned and written on special dot-matrix FLY paper. With additional software, this miniature computer can perform a range of tasks, including playing games for entertainment.

Emerging data suggest that there may be measurable benefit to playing educational games. LeapFrog presents several studies documenting gains made by those who use their products (see http://www.leapfrogschoolhouse.com/do/listScientificStudies). A study using Sony PlayStation games found that kindergarten students who play an educational game learn spelling and decoding skills, but not math, better than those who did not play (Din & Calao, 2001). Obviously, more research on the specific educational benefits of these heavily promoted systems is needed. Plowman and Stephen (2003) reviewed international literature on the debate over the value and desirability of preschoolers' use of computers and related technology. They concluded that there is as yet little evidence for either negative or positive effects, though it is clear that these technologies are here to stay.

Within the classroom, computer-assisted instruction, including games, has been an option for many years. It has long been believed that using video games as one teaching approach strengthens student engagement in the learning environment, and some "serious games," including *Food Force*, are designed with classroom/teacher components. "Blended learning environments" is an emerging education development (Kirkley & Kirkley, 2005). These environments take advantage of the latest advances in virtual and mixed reality technologies. Virtual reality technology allows the individual to become immersed in a programmable synthetic or "virtual environment" where real-life physical limitations can be erased. Mixed reality is the experience of a blended virtual and real world; in other words, some elements of the real world, such as physical space, are blended with digital objects. Although exciting, the applicability of these environments to classroom instruction continues to be limited by the nature of most current classrooms and by funding both for game development and for hardware.

"Pervasive learning games" is a variant of the blended learning environment (Thomas, 2006). Pervasive games use all the current technologies available on which to play games, including mobile phones, computers, PDAs, fax machines, television, and newspapers. Play can occur at any time of the day. In *MAJESTIC,* one well-known pervasive role-playing game, players were contacted through a series of instant messages, e-mails, phone calls, and faxes with clues to find and stop the people behind a plot to shut down the game and kill the design team. The game takes advantage of a series of technology partnerships with companies that include America Online, voice delivery system Sentica, and Hotvoice voicemail deployment. Pervasive learning relies on the 24-hour availability of pervasive gaming. As described by Thomas (2006), "Pervasive learning is essentially a social process that connects learners to communities of devices, people, and situations so that learners can construct relevant and meaningful learning experiences, that they author themselves, in locations and times that they find meaningful and relevant" (p. 45). The exciting potential of this emerging educational application, as well as dealing with its possible problems such as invasion of privacy, is ready to be more fully developed and more widely applied.

Implications for Public Policy and for Parents

In the realm of video games, most of the public policy debate centers on violent games. Several states have proposed that the sale of violent video games to minors be banned or at least closely regulated, with harsh punishments for retailers who violate this regulation. This does not appear to be a viable option for many reasons, especially First Amendment considerations. In 2003, video games were declared a medium for artistic expression, and as such, they are considered protected speech (U.S. Court of Appeals for the Eighth Circuit, 2003). However, some argue that exceptions already exist for children. For example, children are restricted from exposure to pornography. The Supreme Court has not yet agreed to hear an appeal in order to make the definitive decision on this issue.

In February 2003, Rep. Joe Baca (D-CA) introduced H. R. 669, "The Protect Children From Video Game Sex and Violence Act of 2003." This bill sought to impose fines on anyone who sells or rents "any video game that depicts nudity, sexual conduct, or other content harmful to minors" (see http://www.house.gov/baca/hotissues/video_factsheet.htm for additional details about the bill). Introduced February 11, 2003, and assigned to the Committee on the Judiciary, the bill was then referred to the Subcommittee on Crime, Terrorism and Homeland Security. Although the bill had more than 40 sponsors, it appears to have "died in committee."

There are alternatives to imposed regulation. Children are attracted to violent games in part because of advertisements. Limiting the marketing of violent games to younger audiences has been a priority for the Federal Trade Commission. In a 2006 report to a congressional subcommittee, the Federal Trade Commission stated that, although the video game industry has made progress in developing and complying with its self-regulatory policies on the marketing of violent video games to teens and children, more improvement is needed.

Some believe that parents must take more responsibility for monitoring children's video game exposure (Gentile, Saleem, & Anderson, 2007). Many parents still do not realize that popular video games often have very violent content. In one study, most parents of third to fifth graders were unable to correctly name their child's favorite game (Funk, Hagan, & Schimming, 1999). In 70% of these incorrect matches, the child's favorite game had violent content. Parents and children also disagreed on what amount of supervision was typically provided by parents. This suggests that many parents may overestimate their knowledge of their child's game-playing experiences and underestimate their child's exposure to violence in video games. Parents need to become informed about the content of their child's favorite games, preferably by playing the games themselves at all levels as content may change dramatically through a game. If this is not possible, then they can search the name of the game on the Internet and look for game clips posted by groups of players known as clans. These groups post clips for bragging rights, and the clips often showcase the game's most violent content. Parents should become familiar with how the existing ratings system considers features such as violence and sexual material so they can use these guidelines to help them decide what games are consistent with their value system (see Figure 10.7). The presence or absence of violence against humans, and especially against women and minorities, may be one way for parents to decide if a particular game is acceptable for their child to play.

Parents can at least partially insulate their children from possible negative video game effects by sensitizing children to the embedded messages about violence so that children can think about the validity of these messages. For example, is violence really fun? Older children and adolescents can be encouraged to watch news reports about current world conflicts and local violent crime and then discuss these with parents. Parents can also counter the potentially desensitizing impact of embedded messages about violence by sharing their own ideas about conflict resolution and the use of violence to solve problems, as well as about the real-life consequences of violence.

Figure 10.7
SOURCE: © Gamespy.com.

It is clear that video games have considerable positive potential, and it is vital that this potential continue to be developed. The Serious Games movement is an important step in this direction. However, at the present time, many of the most popular games require and reward violent actions. Given currently available research, it is reasonable to be concerned about the impact of violent games on some children and adolescents. Game developers need support and encouragement to put in the additional effort necessary to develop interesting, commercially viable games whose appeal does not rely primarily on violent actions with unrealistic outcomes.

Exercises

1. Pick 10 friends, half male and half female. Ask if they play video or computer games. If they do, ask them to name their favorite game and tell you about it. Ask why this is their favorite game. Compare the responses of your male and female friends.

2. Should children have access to M (17 years or older)–rated games? According to the ESRB, titles in this category may contain intense violence, blood and gore, sexual content, and/or strong language. Why or why not?

3. Go on the Internet and find a "serious game" in the Games for Change genre. Play it and think about how it affects you.

4. Based on what you have read here, do you think that people can become addicted to video games? What is your own experience? Do you have friends who are "addicted"?

5. Can exposure to video game violence be desensitizing? Think about this based on your reading and your experience.

6. You've just been hired to create a new video game for 12-year-olds. What's the theme? Will your game be primarily targeting males, females, or both? How long will the game be? How will you hold the player's attention for that long? Will there be levels? Will there be violence in the game? If so, will it involve guns? Swords? Humans? Aliens? Animals? Are you thinking that this new game will be primarily educational or primarily entertainment? Why?

References

Aluja-Fabregat, A. (2000). Personality and curiosity about TV and films violence in adolescents. *Personality and Individual Differences, 29,* 379–392.

Anand, V. (2007). A study of time management: The correlation between video game usage and academic performance markers. *CyberPsychology & Behavior, 10,* 552–559.

Anderson, C. A., & Bushman, B. J. (2001). Effects of violent video games on aggressive behavior, aggressive cognition, aggressive affect, physiological arousal, and prosocial behavior: A meta-analytic review of the literature. *Psychological Science, 12,* 353–359.

Anderson, C. A., & Bushman, B. J. (2002). Human aggression. *Annual Review of Psychology, 53,* 27–51.

Anderson, C. A., Carnagey, N. L., Flanagan, M., Benjamin, A. J., Eubanks, J., & Valentino, J. C. (2004). Violent video games: Specific effects of violent content on aggressive thoughts and behavior. *Advances in Experimental Social Psychology, 36,* 199–249.

Anderson, C. A., & Dill, K. E. (2000). Video games and aggressive thoughts, feelings, and behavior in the laboratory and in real life. *Journal of Personality and Social Psychology, 78,* 772–790.

Anderson, C. A., Gentile, D. A., & Buckley, K. E. (2007). *Violent video game effects on children and adolescents: Theory, research, and public policy.* New York: Oxford University Press.

Anderson, C. A., & Huesmann, L. R. (2003). Human aggression: A social-cognitive view. In M. A. Hogg & J. Cooper (Eds.), *Handbook of social psychology* (pp. 296–323). Thousand Oaks, CA: Sage.

Arriaga, P., Esteves, F., Carneiro, P., & Monteiro, M. B. (2006). Violent computer games and their effects on state hostility and physiological arousal. *Aggressive Behavior, 32,* 358–372.

Axelsson, A.-S., & Regan, T. (2006). Playing online. In P. Vorderer & J. Bryant (Eds.), *Playing video games: Motives, responses, and consequences* (pp. 291–306). Mahwah, NJ: Lawrence Erlbaum.

Ballard, M. E., & Wiest, J. R. (1996). Mortal Kombat™: The effects of violent videogame play on males' hostility and cardiovascular responding. *Journal of Applied Social Psychology, 26,* 717–730.

Baranowski, T., Buday, R., Thompson, D. I., & Baranowski, J. (2008). Playing for real: Video games and stories for health-related behavior change. *American Journal of Preventive Medicine, 34,* 74–82.

Barnett, M. A., Vitaglione, G. D., Harper, K. K. G., Quackenbush, S. W., Steadman, L. A., & Valdez, B. S. (1997). Late adolescents' experiences with and attitudes towards videogames. *Journal of Applied Social Psychology, 27,* 1316–1334.

Bartholow, B. D., Bushman, B. J., & Sestir, M. A. (2006). Chronic violent video game exposure and desensitization to violence: Behavioral and event-related brain potential data. *Journal of Experimental Social Psychology, 42,* 532–539.

Bartholow, B. D., Sestir, M. A., & Davis, E. B. (2005). Correlates and consequences of exposure to video game violence: Hostile personality, empathy, and aggressive behavior. *Personality and Social Psychology Bulletin, 31,* 1573–1586.

Bers, M. U., Gonzalez-Heydrich, J., & Demaso, D. R. (2003). Use of a computer-based application in a pediatric hemodialysis unit: A pilot study. *Journal of the American Academy of Child and Adolescent Psychiatry, 42,* 493–496.

Brown, S. J., Lieberman, D. A., Germeny, B. A., Fan, Y. C., Wilson, D. M., & Pasta, D. J. (1997). Educational video game for juvenile diabetes: Results of a controlled trial. *Medical Informatics, 22,* 77–89.

Buchman, D. D., & Funk, J. B. (1996). Video and computer games in the '90s: Children's time commitment and game preference. *Children Today, 24,* 12–15, 31.

Bushman, B. J. (2002). Does venting anger feed or extinguish the flame? Catharsis, rumination, distraction, anger, and aggressive responding. *Personality and Social Psychology Bulletin, 28,* 724–731.

Bushman, B. J., & Huesmann, L. R. (2006). Short-term and long-term effects of violent media on aggression in children. *Archives of Pediatrics and Adolescent Medicine, 160,* 348–352.

Cantor, J. (1998). Children's attraction to violent television programming. In J. H. Goldstein (Ed.), *Why we watch: The attractions of violent entertainment* (pp. 88–115). New York: Oxford University Press.

Carnagey, N. L., & Anderson, C. A. (2003). Theory in the study of media violence: The general aggression model. In D. Gentile (Ed.), *Media violence and children: A complete guide for parents and professionals* (pp. 87–105). Westport, CT: Praeger.

Carnagey, N. L., & Anderson, C. A. (2005). The effects of reward and punishment in violent video games on aggressive affect, cognition, and behavior. *Psychological Science, 16,* 882–889.

Carnagey, N. L., Anderson, C. A., & Bartholow, B. D. (2007). Media violence and social neuroscience: New questions and new opportunities. *Current Directions in Psychological Science, 16,* 178–182.

Carnagey, N. L., Anderson, C. A., & Bushman, B. (2006). The effect of video game violence on physiological desensitization to real-life violence. *Journal of Experimental Social Psychology, 42,* 489–496.

Center for Media Education. (1996). *Web of deception: Threats to children from online marketing.* Washington, DC: Author.

Chan, E., & Vorderer, P. (2006). Massively multiplayer online games. In P. Vorderer & J. Bryant (Eds.), *Playing video games: Motives, responses, and consequences* (pp. 77–90). Mahwah, NJ: Lawrence Erlbaum.

Children Now. (2001). *Fair play? Violence, gender and race in video games.* Oakland, CA: Author.

Chiu, S.-I., Lee, J.-Z., & Huang, D.-H. (2004). Video game addiction in children and teenagers in Taiwan. *CyberPsychology & Behavior, 7,* 571–581.

Choi, D., & Kim, J. (2004). Why people continue to play online games: In search of critical design factors to increase customers' loyalty to online contents. *Cyberpsychology & Behavior, 7,* 11–24.

Chuang, Y.-C., Chang, W.-N., Lin, T.-K., Lu, C.-H., Chen, S.-D., & Huang, C.-R. (2006). Game-related seizures presenting with two types of clinical features. *Seizure, 15,* 98–105.

Chumbley, J., & Griffiths, M. (2006). Affect and the computer game player: The effect of gender, personality, and game reinforcement structure on affective responses to computer game-play. *CyberPsychology and Behavior, 9,* 308–316.

Colwell, J., Grady, C., & Rhaiti, S. (1995). Computer games, self-esteem, and gratification of needs in adolescents. *Journal of Community and Applied Psychology, 5,* 195–206.

Csikszentmihalyi, M., & Csikszentmihalyi, I. S. (1988). *Optimal experience: Psychological studies of flow in consciousness.* Cambridge, UK: Cambridge University Press.

Din, F. S., & Calao, J. (2001). The effects of playing educational video games on kindergarten achievement. *Child Study Journal, 31,* 95–102.

Dorn, L. D., Dahl, R. E., Williamson, D. E., Birmaher B., Axelson, D., Perel, J., et al. (2003). Developmental markers in adolescence: Implications for studies of pubertal processes. *Journal of Youth and Adolescence, 32,* 315–324.

Dowling, N., Smith, D., & Thomas, T. (2005). Electronic gaming machines: Are they the "crack cocaine" of gambling? *Addiction, 100,* 33–45.

Dworak, M., Schierl, T., Bruns, T., & Struder. H. K. (2007). Impact of singular excessive computer game and television exposure on sleep patterns and memory performance of school-aged children. *Pediatrics, 120,* 978–985.

Entertainment Software Rating Board. (2006). *Frequently asked questions.* Retrieved July 24, 2006, from http://www.esrb.org/ratings/faq.jsp

Eron, L. D., Huesmann, L. R., Brice, P., Fischer, P., & Mermelstein, R. (1983). Age trends in the development of aggression, sex typing, and related television habits. *Developmental Psychology, 19,* 71–77.

Federal Trade Commission. (2000). *Marketing violent entertainment to children: A review of self-regulation and industry practices in the motion picture, music recording, and video game industries.* (Available at FTC Consumer Response Center, Room 130, 600 Pennsylvania Avenue, N. W., Washington, DC 20580)

Federal Trade Commission. (2006a). *FTC testifies on marketing of violent and explicit video games.* Retrieved July 31, 2006, from http://www.ftc.gov/opa/2006/06/videogames.htm

Federal Trade Commission. (2006b). *Undercover shop finds decrease in sales of M-rated video games to children.* Retrieved July 31, 2006, from http://www.ftc.gov/opa/2006/03/videogameshop.htm

Fisher, R. S., Harding, G., Erba, G., Barkley, G. L., & Wilkins, A. (2005). Photic- and pattern-induced seizures: A review for the Epilepsy Foundation of America Working Group. *Epilepsia, 46,* 1426–1441.

Freedman, J. L. (2002). *Media violence and its effect on aggression: Assessing the scientific evidence.* Toronto: University of Toronto Press.

Funk, J. B. (2000). Why do we watch? A journey through our dark side. *Contemporary Psychology, 46,* 9–11.

Funk, J. B. (2003). Violent video games: Who's at risk? In D. Ravitch & J. Viteritti (Eds.), *Kid stuff: Marketing violence and vulgarity in the popular culture* (pp. 168–192). Baltimore: Johns Hopkins University Press.

Funk, J. B. (2005a). Children's exposure to violent video games and desensitization to violence. *Child and Adolescent Psychiatry Clinics of North America, 14,* 387–404.

Funk, J. B. (2005b). Video games. *Adolescent Medicine Clinics of North America, 16,* 395–411.

Funk, J. B. (2006). Script development. In J. J. Arnett (Ed.) *Encyclopedia of children, adolescents, and the media.* Thousand Oaks, CA: Sage.

Funk, J. B., Bechtoldt-Baldacci, H., Pasold, T., & Baumgardner, J. (2004). Violence exposure in real-life, video games, television, movies, and the Internet: Is there desensitization? *Journal of Adolescence, 27,* 23–39.

Funk, J. B., Brouwer, J., Curtiss, K., & Leininger, S. (2006, August). *Video game violence ratings by young children, adults, and the ESRB.* Poster presented at the Annual Meeting of the American Psychological Association, New Orleans, LA.

Funk, J. B., Brouwer, J., Curtiss, K., & McBroom, E. (2007, March). *Parents' knowledge and opinions about their young child's media experience.* Paper presented at the Midwestern Psychological Association, Chicago.

Funk, J. B., & Buchman, D. D. (1995). Video game controversies. *Pediatric Annals, 24,* 91–94.

Funk, J. B., & Buchman, D. (1996). Playing violent video and computer games and adolescent self-perception. *Journal of Communication, 46,* 19–32.

Funk, J. B., & Buchman, D. (2006). *Young children's exposure to violent media and desensitization to violence.* Manuscript in review.

Funk, J. B., Buchman, D., Chan, M., & Brouwer, J. (2005, August). *Younger children's exposure to violent media, empathy, and violence attitudes.* Presented at the annual meeting of the American Psychological Association, Washington, DC.

Funk, J. B., Buchman, D. D., Jenks, J., & Bechtoldt, H. (2003). Playing violent video games, desensitization, and moral evaluation in children. *Journal of Applied Developmental Psychology, 24,* 413–436.

Funk, J. B., & Buchman, D. D. , Myers, M., Jenks, J. & Hagan, J. (2000, May). *Contemporary research on children and electronic games.* Paper presented at Summit 2000: Children, Youth and the Media—Beyond the Millennium, Toronto, Ontario.

Funk, J. B., Buchman, D. D., Schimming, J. L., & Hagan, J. D. (1998, August). *Attitudes towards violence, empathy, and violent electronic games.* Paper presented at the annual meeting of the American Psychological Association, San Francisco.

Funk, J. B., Chan, M., Brouwer, J., & Curtiss, K. (2006). A biopsychosocial analysis of the video game-playing experience of children and adults in the United States. *Studies in Media and Information Literacy Education, 6*(3) , 1–15.

Funk, J. B., Flores, G., Buchman, D. D., & Germann, J. N. (1999). Rating video games: Violence is in the eye of the beholder. *Youth and Society, 30,* 283–312.

Funk, J. B., Hagan, J. D., & Schimming, J. L. (1999). Children and electronic games: A comparison of parent and child perceptions of children's habits and preferences in a United States sample. *Psychological Reports, 85,* 883–888.

Funk, J. B., Hagan, J., Schimming, J., Bullock, W. A., Buchman, D. D., & Myers, M. (2002). Aggression and psychopathology in adolescents with a preference for violent electronic games. *Aggressive Behavior, 28,* 134–144.

Gamespot. (2005). *Couples' online gaming causes infant's death.* Retrieved July 30, 2006, from http://www.gamespot.com/news/2005/06/20/news_6127866.html

Geen, R. G. (2001). *Human aggression.* Philadelphia: Open University Press.

Gentile, D. A., Humphrey, J., & Walsh, D. A. (2005). Media ratings for movies, music, video games, and television: A review of the research and recommendations for improvements. *Adolescent Medicine Clinics, 16,* 427–446.

Gentile, D. A., Lynch, P. L., Linder, J. R., & Walsh, D. A. (2004). The effects of violent video game habits on adolescent hostility, aggressive behaviors, and school performance. *Journal of Adolescence, 27,* 5–22.

Gentile, D. A., Saleem, M., & Anderson, C. A. (2007). Public policy and the effects of media violence on children. *Social Issues and Policy Review, 1,* 15–61.

Gentile, D. A., & Walsh, D. A. (2002). A normative study of family media habits. *Journal of Applied Developmental Psychology, 23,* 157–178.

Glickson, J., & Avnon, M. (1997). Explorations in virtual reality: Absorption, cognition, and altered state of consciousness. *Imagination, Cognition, and Personality, 17,* 141–151.

Goldstein, J. H. (Ed.). (1998). *Why we watch: The attractions of violent entertainment.* New York: Oxford University Press.

Graf, W. D., Chatrian, G.-E., Glass, S. T., & Knauss, T. A. (1994). Video game-related seizures: A report on 10 patients and a review of the literature. *Pediatrics, 93,* 551–556.

Greene, J. S., & Asher, I. (1982). Video games. *Journal of the American Medical Association, 248,* 1308.

Griffiths, M. D., Davies, M. N. O., & Chappell, D. (2007). Demographic factors and playing variables in online computer gaming. *CyberPsychology & Behavior, 7,* 479–487.

Griffiths, M. D., & Hunt, N. (1998). Dependency on computer games by adolescents. *Psychological Reports, 82,* 475–480.

Guerra, N. G., Nucci, L., & Huesmann, L. R. (1994). Moral cognition and childhood aggression. In L. R. Huesmann (Ed.), *Aggressive behavior: Current perspectives* (pp. 13–33). New York: Plenum.

Haninger, K., & Thompson, K. M. (2004). Content and ratings of teen-rated video games. *Journal of the American Medical Association, 291,* 856–865.

Hind, P. A. (1995). A study of reported satisfaction with differentially aggressive computer games amongst incarcerated offenders. *Issues in Criminological and Legal Psychology, 22,* 28–36.

Huesmann, L. R., & Miller, L. S. (1994). Long-term effects of repeated exposure to media violence in childhood. In L. R. Huesmann (Ed.), *Aggressive behavior: Current perspectives* (pp. 153–186). New York: Plenum.

Jansz, J. (2005). The emotional appeal of violent video games for adolescent males. *Communication Theory, 15,* 219–241.

Jansz, J., & Tanis, M. (2007). Appeal of playing online first person shooter games. *CyberPsychology & Behavior, 10,* 133–136.

Johnson, J. G., Cohen, P., Smailes, E. M., Kasen, S., & Brook, J. S. (2002). Television viewing and aggressive behavior during adolescence and adulthood. *Science, 295,* 2468–2471.

Kautiainen, S., Koivusilta, L., Lintonen, T., Virtanen, S. M., & Rimpela, A. (2005). Use of information and communication technology and prevalence of overweight and obesity among adolescents. *International Journal of Obesity, 29,* 925–933.

Kirkley, S. E., & Kirkley, J. R. (2005). Creating next generation blended learning environments using mixed reality, video games and simulations. *TechTrends, 49,* 42–53, 89.

Kirsh, S. J. (2002). The effects of violent video games on adolescents: The overlooked influence of development. *Aggression and Violent Behavior, 7,* 1–13.

Kirsh, S. J. (2006). *Children, adolescents, and media violence: A critical look at the research.* Thousand Oaks, CA: Sage.

Klug, G. C., & Schell, J. (2006). Why people play games: An industry perspective. In P. Vorderer & J. Bryant (Eds.), *Playing video games: Motives, responses, and consequences* (pp. 91–100). Mahwah, NJ: Lawrence Erlbaum.

Ko, C.-H., Yen, J.-Y., Yen, C.-F., Lin, H.-C., & Yang, M.-J. (2007). Factors predictive for incidence and remission of Internet addiction in young adolescents: A predictive study. *CyberPsychology and Behavior, 10,* 545–551.

Krahe, B., & Moller, I. (2004). Playing violent electronic games, hostile attributional style, and aggression-related norms in German adolescents. *Journal of Adolescence, 27,* 53–69.

Krichevets, A. N., Sirotkina, E. B., Yevsevicheva, I. V., & Zeldin, L. M. (1995). Computer games as a means of movement rehabilitation. *Disability and Rehabilitation, 17,* 100–105.

Lee, H. (2004). A new case of fatal pulmonary thromboembolism associated with prolonged sitting at a computer in Korea. *Yonsei Medical Journal, 45,* 349–351.

Lee, K. M., & Peng, W. (2006). What do we know about social and psychological effects of computer games? A comprehensive review of the current literature. In P. Vorderer & J. Bryant (Eds.), *Playing video games: Motives, responses, and consequences* (pp. 327–345). Mahwah, NJ: Lawrence Erlbaum.

Mandrid, A. (2006). *Gaming the poor.* Retrieved August 18, 2006, from http://www.msnbc.msn.com/id/13818063/site/newsweek/

Marshall, S. J., Biddle, S. J. H., Gorely, T., Cameron, N., & Murdey, I. (2004). Relationships between media use, body fatness and physical activity in children and youth: A meta-analysis. *International Journal of Obesity, 28,* 1238–1246.

Matthews, K. A., Zhu, S., Tucker, D. C., & Whooley, M. A. (2006). Blood pressure reactivity to psychological stress and coronary calcification in the coronary artery risk development in young adults study. *Hypertension, 47,* 391–395.

McCauley, C. (1998). When screen violence is not attractive. In J. H. Goldstein (Ed.), *Why we watch: The attractions of violent entertainment* (pp. 144–162). London: Oxford University Press.

McMurray, R. G., Harrell, J. S., Deng, S., Bradley, C. B., Cox, L. M., & Bangdiwala, S. I. (2000). The influence of physical activity, socioeconomic status, and ethnicity on the weight status of adolescents. *Obesity Research, 8,* 130–139.

Moneta, G. B., & Csikszentmihalyi, M. (1996). The effect of perceived challenges and skills on the quality of subjective experience. *Journal of Personality, 64,* 275–310.

Moneta, G. B., & Csikszentmihalyi, M. (1999). Models of concentration in natural environments: A comparative approach based on streams of experiential data. *Social Behavior and Personality, 27,* 603–638.

Murphy, J. K., Stoney, C. M., Alpert, B. S., & Walker, S. S. (1995). Gender and ethnicity in children's cardiovascular reactivity: Seven years of study. *Health Psychology, 14,* 48–55.

Murrin, R. J. A. (2004). Is prolonged use of computer games a risk factor for deep venous thrombosis in children? *Clinical Medicine, 4,* 190–191.

Myers, L., Strikmiller, P. K., Webber, L. S., & Berenson, G. S. (1996). Physical and sedentary activity in school children Grades 5–8: The Bogalusa Heart Study. *Medicine and Science in Sports and Exercise, 28,* 852–859.

Ng, S. M., Khurana, R. M., Yeang, H. A., Hughes, U. M., & Manning, D. J. (2003). Is prolonged use of computer games a risk factor for deep venous thrombosis in children? *Clinical Medicine, 3,* 593–594.

Office of Film and Literature Classification. (1999). *Computer games and Australians today.* Sydney, Australia: Author.

Piccioli, M., Vigevano, F., Buttinelli, C., & Trenite, D. G. A. K.-N. (2005). Do video games evoke specific types of epileptic seizures? *Epilepsy & Behavior, 7,* 524–530.

Plowman, L., & Stephen, C. (2003). A "benign addition?" Research on ICT and preschool children. *Journal of Computer Assisted Learning, 19,* 149–164.

Pratchett, R. (2005). *Gamers in the UK: Digital play, digital lifestyles.* London: BBC. Retrieved July 26, 2006, from http://open.bbc.co.uk/newmediaresearch/files/BBC_UK_Games_Research_2005.pdf

Provenzo, E. F. (1991). *Video kids: Making sense of Nintendo.* Cambridge, MA: Harvard University Press.

Ramos, E. M., James, C. A., & Bear-Lehman, J. (2005). Children's computer usage: Are they at risk of developing repetitive strain injury? *Work, 25,* 143–154.

Raney, A. A., Smith, J. K., & Baker, K. (2006). Adolescents and the appeal of video games. In P. Vorderer & J. Bryant (Eds.), *Playing video games: Motives, responses, and consequences* (pp. 165–179). Mahwah, NJ: Lawrence Erlbaum.

Rideout, V. J., & Hamel, E. (2006). *Zero to six: Electronic media in the lives of infants, toddlers, and preschoolers.* Menlo Park, CA: Kaiser Family Foundation.

Rideout, V., Roberts, D. F., & Foehr, U. G. (2005). *Generation M: Media in the lives of 8–18 year olds.* Menlo Park, CA: Kaiser Family Foundation.

Roe, K., & Muijs, D. (1998). Children and computer games: A profile of the heavy user. *European Journal of Communication, 13,* 181–200.

Salisch, M. V., Oppl, C., & Kristen, A. (2006). What attracts children? In P. Vorderer & J. Bryant (Eds.), *Playing video games: Motives, responses, and consequences* (pp. 147–163). Mahwah, NJ: Lawrence Erlbaum.

Schollmeyer, J. (2006). Games get serious. *Bulletin of the Atomic Scientists, 62,* 34–39.

Scott, D. (1995). The effect of video games on feelings of aggression. *Journal of Psychology, 129,* 121–132.

Sherry, J. L., Lucas, K., Greenberg, B. S., & Lachlan, K. (2006). Video game uses and gratifications as predictors of use and game preference. In P. Vorderer & J. Bryant (Eds.), *Playing video games: Motives, responses, and consequences* (pp. 213–224). Mahwah, NJ: Lawrence Erlbaum.

Sik Lanyi, C., Laky, V., Tilinger, A., Pataky, I., Simon, L., Kiss, B., et al. (2004). Developing multimedia software and virtual reality worlds and their use in rehabilitation and psychology. *Studies in Health Technology and Informatics, 105,* 273–284.

Slater, M. D. (2003). Alienation, aggression, and sensation seeking as predictors of adolescent use of violent film, computer, and website content. *Journal of Communication, 53,* 105–121.

Slater, M. D., Henry, K. L., Swaim, R. C., & Anderson, L. L. (2003). Violent media content and aggressiveness in adolescents: A downward spiral model. *Communication Research, 30,* 713–736.

Tamborini, R., & Skalski, P. (2006). The role of presence in the experience of electronic games. In P. Vorderer & J. Bryant (Eds.), *Playing video games: Motives, responses, and consequences* (pp. 225–240). Mahwah, NJ: Lawrence Erlbaum.

Tejeiro Salguero, R. A., & Bersabe Moran, R. M. (2002). Measuring problem video game playing in adolescents. *Addiction, 97,* 1601–1606.

Thomas, S. (2006). Pervasive learning games: Explorations of hybrid educational gamescapes. *Simulation and Gaming, 37,* 41–55.

Thompson, P. M., Giedd, J. N., Woods, R. P., MacDonald, D., Evans, A. C., & Toga, A. W. (2000). Growth patterns in the developing brain detected by using continuum mechanical tensor maps. *Nature, 404,* 190–192.

U.S. Court of Appeals for the Eighth Circuit. (2003). *No. 02–3010.* Retrieved August 4, 2006, from http://caselaw.lp.findlaw.com/data2/circs/8th/023010p.pdf

Vandewater, E. A., Shim, M.-S., & Caplovitz, A. G. (2004). Linking obesity and activity level with children's television and video game use. *Journal of Adolescence, 27,* 71–85.

Wake, M., Hesketh, K., & Waters, E. (2003). Television, computer use and body mass index in Australian primary school children. *Journal of Paediatrics and Child Health, 39,* 130–134.

Walsh, D. A., & Gentile, D. A. (2001). A validity test of movie, television, and video game ratings. *Pediatrics, 107,* 1302–1308.

Wang, X., & Perry, A. C. (2006). Metabolic and physiologic responses to video game play in 7- to 10-year old boys. *Archives of Pediatric and Adolescent Medicine, 160,* 411–415.

Wei, R. (2007). Effects of playing violent videogames on Chinese adolescents' pro-violence attitudes, attitudes toward others, and aggressive behavior. *CyberPsychology and Behavior, 10,* 371–380.

Williams, D., & Skoric, M. (2005). Internet fantasy violence: A test of aggression in an online game. *Communication Monographs, 72,* 217–233.

Wood, S. (2003). Motivating game-based stroke rehabilitation: A brief report. *Topics in Stroke Rehabilitation, 10,* 134–140.

Wood, R. T. A., Griffiths, M. D., & Eatough, V. (2004). Online data collection from video game players: Methodological issues. *CyberPsychology and Behavior, 7,* 511–518.

Yang, Z. (2005). Research on the correlation between life events and video game addiction in junior middle school students. *Chinese Journal of Clinical Psychology, 13,* 182, 192–193.

CHAPTER 11

The Internet

Edward Donnerstein

T hroughout this book, we have discussed the impact that various media have on children's and adolescents' behavior, values, and beliefs. We have seen the enormous ability of the media to transcend the influence of parents and peers in providing information (sometimes correct, but often not) about the world in which they live. The interesting thing about the research and findings we have discussed is that in many ways, it dealt with fairly traditional media forms such as television, film, radio, music, and print. But the media have changed. Newer technologies—in particular, the Internet and interactive video games—have created a new dimension for researchers to consider when they examine the effects of both problematic content (violence and sex) and educational content. Just like the potential effects of video games discussed in Chapter 10, the Internet is highly interactive, suggesting that the effects could be stronger than television or other traditional media (Paik, 2001). There are some researchers (Livingstone & Hargrave, 2006) who consider the Internet as the most interactive of our current media (see Figure 11.1).

Livingstone and Hargrave (2006) see the Internet as an increasing concern with respect to harm on children. They, like many, argue that the Internet now contains content that is on TV or within other media, which, we already know, can influence children. In addition, the Internet often takes the content out of its context, creating more of a problem. Furthermore, the Internet has the "ability" to have more extreme forms of content that can intentionally or unintentionally be accessed by children and adolescents. One reason for this concern is the ability to regulate or control content in traditional media such as TV, but this presents difficulty with respect to the Internet (see Figure 11.2).

Unlike traditional media such as TV, radio, and recorded music, the Internet gives children and adolescents access to just about any form of content they can find. For the first time, these individuals will be able (with some work) to have the ability to view almost any form of sexual behavior, violent content, or advertisement.

"The Internet is cool. I can travel around the world before I'm even allowed to cross the street!"

Figure 11.1

SOURCE: ©WM. Hoest Enterprises. PARADE MAGAZINE, September, 17, 2000, p. 24, the Laugh Parade column by Bunny Hoest and John Reiner.

Unlike years past, this can be done in the privacy of their own room, with little knowledge of their parents.

Are Children and Adolescents Using the Internet?

Much of our discussion on the Internet would be meaningless if its use by children and adolescents was nonexistent. This is not the case, however. According to the U.S. Department of Education (see Kaiser Family Foundation, 2006), almost 25% of children ages 3 to 5 have been online, and by kindergarten, this is almost one third. It seems that the largest group of new users is in the 2 to 5 age range. These findings are similar to those from the Kaiser Family Foundation (2003), which also found that about one third of those younger than 3 had online experience. In a recent national sample of adolescents and adults, the Pew Foundation (2005) found that those in the age range of 12 to 17 had the highest (87%) number of users online. This particular age group also used the Internet differently than adults, preferring games, instant messaging, and other more interactive aspects of the Web.

In a recent presentation at the American Academy of Pediatrics, researchers noted that the Internet apparently is a key source of sex education for U.S. teenagers. About half of teens go online for health information, and they have more

Figure 11.2

SOURCE: Baby Blues by Rick Kirkman and Jerry Scott. Reprinted with permission of King Features Syndicate.

questions about sex than they do about any other topic. According to Borzekowski and Robinson (2005), just over half of teenagers use the Internet daily, according to surveys they cited, and nearly 100% are online at some time.

Think back to other chapters in this book, particularly those that discussed children. We can only wonder how all the issues we have discussed about cognitive processing, reality/fantasy, and early socialization are to be considered in this new medium for children and adolescents. After all, the Internet today carries TV shows, movies, video games, and essentially every medium of media children and adolescents can access. As we have seen throughout this book, the media play a powerful role in the socialization of children and adolescents (Figure 11.3). There is every reason to expect that newer technologies such as the Internet and interactive games (see Chapter 10) will be a significant "player" in their developmental process.

Are Parents Concerned?

For decades, parents and others have been concerned consistently about the potentially "harmful" influences of exposure to sexual and violent media content. A recent survey in Sweden (Carlsson, 2006) asked adults what they perceive to be the factors that lead to violence in their society. While alcohol and drugs were the highest (90%),

Figure 11.3

SOURCE: Baby Blues by Rick Kirkman and Jerry Scott. Reprinted with permission of King Features Syndicate.

it is interesting to note that both TV and the Internet were listed by 60% of respondents as having a strong and significant influence. This was the first time the Internet was used in this ongoing 10-year survey. Furthermore, when respondents were asked their views on the extent of sexual scenes in the media having a negative impact on children, Internet Web sites were considered more harmful than TV or music videos.

These findings seem to also reflect those in the United States. In a national pool of parents (Common Sense Media, 2006), more than 85% considered the Internet more of a risk problem for their children than TV (13%). A majority indicated that their children had found inappropriate material online, and 80% were concerned about sexual predators. For the most part, parents were concerned about content, particularly pornography. Nevertheless, the Internet is seen as the most important medium for children to have access to, particularly with respect to education (see Kaiser, 2007).

The major difference today compared with those concerns in the past is that the Internet is a technology that children and adolescents are often more sophisticated and knowledgeable about than their parents. Too often we hear of computer-phobic adults who possess little knowledge of this expanding technology. Such resistance to the technology, combined with a limited knowledge base, will make solutions to potential problems (such as easy access to sexual images) even more difficult. Furthermore, when policy and advocacy groups attempt to inform parents of the Internet, we would argue it does little good to tell them to contact "www.hereforhelp.com" when they are often ignorant about these terms and World Wide Web usages.

Before discussing this "new" addition to our media world, it is important to point out a few differences in our knowledge base with regard to the Internet and more traditional media. First, the research on effects, both positive and negative, is limited. Not only is the technology new but also so is our research base. Second, content analysis is not only limited but, one may argue, also extremely difficult to conduct due to the problems of determining a proper sample. Finally, the solutions to deal with harmful effects are further complicated by the global nature of this medium. In many ways, this is both a new medium and a new research focus. We can expect in the next edition of this book a wealth of information as to the positive and negative impact on children and adolescents of exposure to the Internet. In the interim, we will look at what we currently know and speculate from past knowledge and theory about what may be the outcomes.

The Internet: What Is It?

Very often we refer to the Internet more generally as the Net. This expanding technology is simply a vast group of computer networks linked around the world. It has a number of various components that are familiar (at least in terminology) to most of us, and they have the ability to deliver an enormous array of information. These include the following:

1. E-mail for electronic communication. Many would agree that this is certainly one of the most popular forms of communication in today's society. Even this simple and everyday form of technology has changed in recent years, with the ability to send voice, video, and other forms of attachments around the world in an almost instantaneous manner.

2. Bulletin board systems for posting of information on almost any topic one could imagine.

3. Chat groups, whether peer-to-peer or in popular sites such as MySpace.com, that can be used for real-time conversations. For many adolescents, it is the global equivalent of a "free" conference call. However, unlike the traditional conference call, you can choose your topic, person, and time in any manner you desire.

4. The World Wide Web, which combines visuals/sound/text together in a manner that allows linkages across many sites that are related to a particular topic. These topics obviously can be those related to sex, violence, drugs, or any other content for which we may have concerns.

And of course, we have blogs and podcasting and other Internet-related activities such as instant messaging that have made the Internet *the* mass media medium of choice.

The introduction of the World Wide Web (WWW) to the Internet increased its popularity and use. Most Web browsers (e.g., Internet Explorer, Netscape) now do more than just surf the Web. Today, these powerful integrated programs deal with e-mail, video streaming, newsgroups, and more.

Many people can now conduct many of their daily activities on the Web. Our banking, airline reservations, weather and news reports, sports scores with live transmissions, and almost anything we can think of can be found, accessed, interacted with, and saved within the World Wide Web.

The popularity and sophistication of the Internet are due to the increase in powerful search engines. A search engine, such as Google, is a server that searches other servers in a systematic manner and indexes its findings in a database. There is basically nothing on the Web that cannot be found by one of these engines. Interested in going to Disney World? Need a hotel? Just go to a search engine such as Google and type in the words *Disney World Hotels* and, as shown in Figure 11.4, you will have in less than a second more than 21 million Web sites where you can access more information than you could ever imagine. Only a few years ago, in the first edition of this book, that number was only 142,000 sites. Take a virtual tour of your selection, book the room, and print out a map with explicit directions on how to

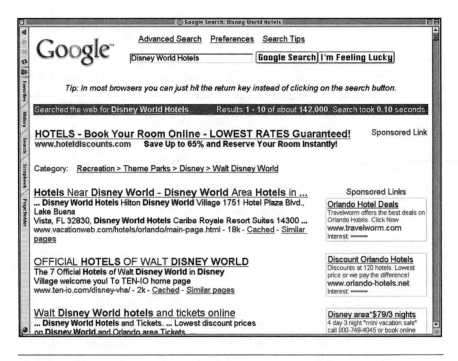

Figure 11.4

get to your hotel from the airport. Of course, you also can book your travel (airline, car rental) with the same ease and speed.

It is important to note that we take the position that the Web and other Internet components are extremely informative and useful. This is one technology that we want our children to have access to and be knowledgeable about. It is exceedingly educational and almost indispensable in today's society. Like any new technological advance, it will have some downsides, but they should in no way be considered a barrier to continued advancement and teaching of children and adults about its vast usefulness and value. We strongly emphasize that in all respects, the Internet is a very powerful information and instruction technology that we must continue to develop. We want the reader to continue to keep this in mind because many of the things we will discuss in this chapter deal with a small part of the Net that we might consider potentially "harmful" to children. This is a small fraction of the materials available, yet they must be discussed because, unlike other technologies, the searching and finding of such materials are much easier than in the past.

Concerns About the Net

We can certainly see that the Internet is increasing in popularity. One of the issues of concern, however, is that this is a medium in which youth are currently not only heavier users than their parents but also more sophisticated in its applications. It is also a medium in which parents often have little control, few rules for use, and minimal supervision. Nevertheless, most parents believe that being online is more positive than watching TV. Perhaps they are unaware of the degree of unsolicited sexual materials on the Net, including violent pornography, which has increased over the years in both newsgroups and Web sites, or of drug advertising, hate groups, and other "risky" content for children and adolescents.

Even if parents were aware of these data, so much of online activities of children and adolescents is done alone, in an anonymous context, and without (as we have already noted) parental supervision. The messages of concern on the Internet do not differ from those of traditional media: concerns of sex, violence, sexual violence, tobacco and alcohol advertisements, and, more recently, advertising of "unhealthy" food products to children. The effects from exposure we would expect to be at least the same, if not enhanced. The interactive nature of the Internet, which can lead to more arousal and more cognitive activity, would suggest that influences such as those found from media violence would be facilitated (see Huesmann, 1998, and Chapter 4, this volume). More important, materials, which should be extremely limited to children's and adolescents' view, are now readily obtainable with the power of search engines and the Internet. Perhaps our discussion of sex on the Internet will make this more apparent.

Sex on the Net: A Primary Concern

One of the most controversial Internet content categories is sexual material, which has raised concerns about child exploitation (see Figure 11.5). Such material ranges from photographs to the Net equivalent of "phone sex," sometimes with a live video connection. Sending of sexual information over e-mail or posting on bulletin boards by those targeting children has been a long-term issue. One of the most comprehensive studies on these issues has come from the Crimes Against Children Research Center (CACRC) at the University of New Hampshire. In some of the best research to date, it notes the following:

> The Internet holds tremendous potential for our nation's youth; however, the misuse of the Internet to prey on them is a serious problem requiring action by legislators, families, communities, and law enforcement. While we have made some strides in helping to prevent such victimization, the results of this survey, Online Victimization of Youth: Five Years Later, show we have not done enough. Exposure to unwanted sexual material, sexual solicitations, and harassment were frequently reported by the youth interviewed for this study. (CACRC, 2006)

This excellent series of studies by the CACRC involved a random national sample of 1,500 children ages 10 to 17 interviewed in 2000 and then an additional sample of 1,500 interviewed in 2005. This procedure allowed the researchers to look at the changes in youths' experiences with the Internet (Mitchell, Wolak, & Finkelhor, 2007).

Figure 11.5

SOURCE: Reprinted with permission of Copley News Service.

The major findings from this study can be summarized as follows:

1. There was an increase over the 5-year period from 25% to 34% of the youth who indicated that they were exposed to unwanted sexual materials. It is interesting to note that this increase occurred despite the fact that more families were using Internet filtering software (more than 50%) during this period.

2. On a positive side, there was a decrease in sexual solicitations (19% vs. 13%). Nevertheless, about 4% of these were considered "aggressive" in that the solicitor attempted to contact the user offline. Although one might consider these small percentages, this represents a lot of children in a time when we should expect zero tolerance. Keep in mind, in this study, 4% of those surveyed were asked for nude or sexually explicit pictures of themselves! Of more concern may be the finding that less than 5% of these contacts were reported to law officials or the Internet provider.

3. There was also a reduction of the percentage of youth who communicated online with people they did not know in person or who formed close relationships (40% vs. 34%) (see Kowalski & Limber, 2007; Williams & Guerra, 2007).

4. Finally, one new disturbing finding is the increase in what has been called online harassment and bullying. Many of these episodes occur from confrontations in school from individuals who know each other. This harassment can take the shape of direct threats, spreading rumors, posting of pictures, or other means of trying to embarrass someone. Most of those who were harassed were females, and usually by other males. Other researchers (Livingstone & Hargrave, 2006) suggest that children and parents are ill equipped to deal with the emotional distress this can cause.

Along a similar line, the Symantec Corporation (2004) recently conducted a national survey of youth ages 7 to 18 on their receipt of spam in e-mails. While 80% said they received spam, the disturbing finding is that almost half of those surveyed indicated that they received e-mails directing them to X-rated Web sites. The survey also found that these youth felt uneasy when seeing this inappropriate content. Often times, they did not even communicate their negative feelings about spam with their parents.

Adult Web sites that feature "hard-core" sexual depictions are of equal concern. One estimate is that such sites are a multi-billion-dollar industry and that half of the spending on the Internet is in this area. Some suggest that it is the "king" of advertising and one of the highest types of sites searched for by users (Griffiths, 2000). In their discussion of the potentially harmful effects of children's exposure to sexual media, Malamuth and Impett (2001) make note of the easy access via the Internet to sexually explicit materials by users ages 9 to 15. This is not to imply that children did not seek out and find sexual content before the Internet. Today, the process is easier, faster, more anonymous, and likely to bring to your computer screen anything you want.

Search engines, such as Google, will allow the user to type in words and word combinations that will ask the computer to search for almost any sexual content. If we take for a moment the curiosity of a 12-year-old and let his or her fingers (and mouse) do the walking, one can see how easy the process can work. For example, if we use our search engine to type in the words *Sex Pictures,* we see in Figure 11.6 that in less than 1 second, we are given a list of 117 million sites that contain these words and most likely the pictures that our 12-year-old is seeking. It is interesting to note that in the first edition of this book, only a few years ago, the number of sites was only 2 million.

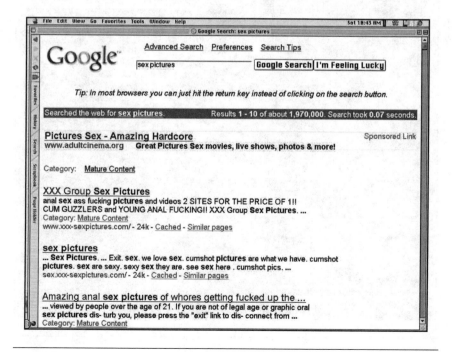

Figure 11.6

If the child then accesses one of these sites, as shown in Figure 11.7, it is not "officially blocked" to minors unless certain blocking software is implemented (and often it is not entirely effective). Most sexually explicit adult sites will merely indicate that the site (a) contains sexually explicit pictures, (b) may be offensive to viewers, and (c) the viewer must be at least 18 years of age; if not, the viewer must exit the site immediately. Needless to say, there are probably a high percentage of sexually curious adolescents, and even children, who will simply click their mouse and indicate they are of age and enter the adult site. Once within one of these sites, the viewer will be able to link into other similar sites offering samples of pictures, text, and video of a "hard-core" sexual nature, as shown in Figures 11.8 and 11.9. The great sophistication of search engines also allows for the searching of Web sites on (a) bestiality, (b) child pornography, (c) rape and bondage, or (d) teen sex.

Search engines exist to help, but the usual Internet user is not going to come in contact with inappropriate content without making a conscious decision to find these sites. However, in recent years, it has become known that certain adult sites have used address codes that are quite similar to popular Internet Web sites, oftentimes leading the user unknowingly into an area he or she did not wish to visit. For example, until a year ago, if children were looking for information about the White House and typed www.whitehouse.com instead of www.whitehouse.gov (not an unlikely mistake in our dotcom world), they would have found themselves linked to an adult site, as shown in Figure 11.10. The site has now been sold and changed. The price of this sale is hard to know, but it is estimated that the Web site Sex.Com sold for more than $10 million. No one can say that sex does not sell.

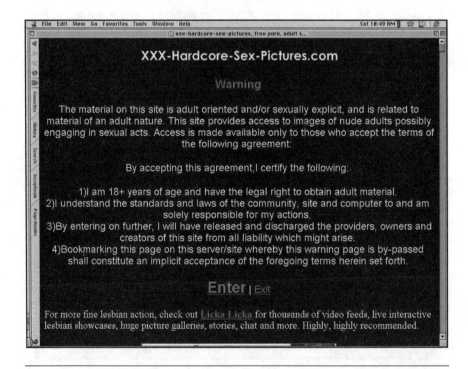

Figure 11.7

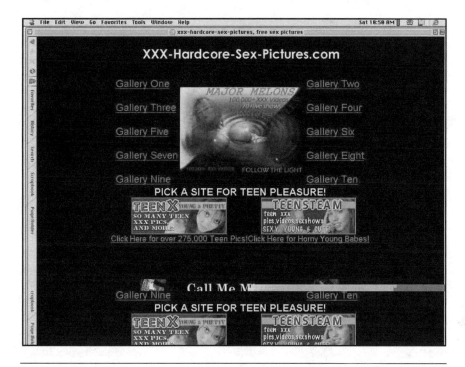

Figure 11.8

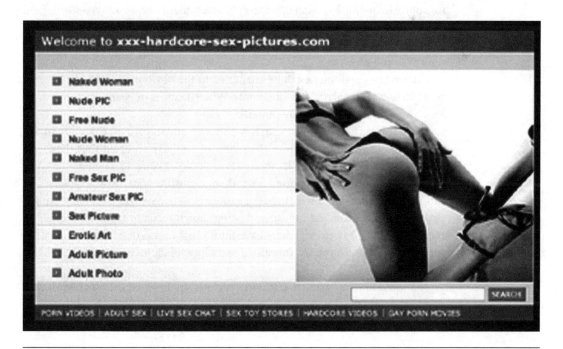

Figure 11.9

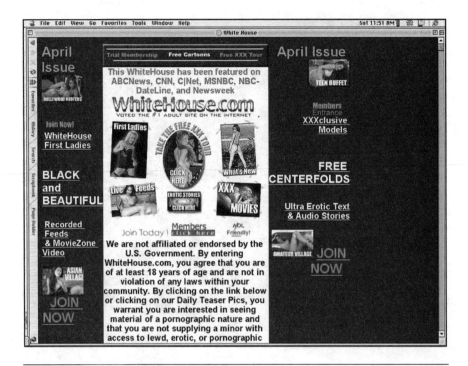

Figure 11.10

In one examination of the scope of the Internet and pornography, Fox (2006) notes that the Internet is a $2.5 billion industry. This research estimates that there are approximately 4.2 million pornographic Web sites (12% of all Web sites). Even with e-mail, it is estimated that Internet users receive 4.5 sexually related e-mails a day. According to Thornburgh and Lin (2002), 70 million different people view an adult Web site each week.

Much of this high usage can be attributed to the obvious fact that the Internet offers its user interactivity and anonymity. When it comes to "wanting" to view sex, these two components are quite powerful.

While it is difficult to do research with those underage, a recent study of 18- to 22-year-olds found that more than 90% of subjects reported that they have seen sexually explicit materials online (Fox, 2006) (Figure 11.11). For the most part, these respondents reported that their exposure was mainly "passive" in nature. The most common methods of exposure were receiving a sexually explicit e-mail, having a sexual ad appear, and being shown sexually explicit materials by another person. Other researchers have found that found that more than half of adolescents had encountered unwanted sexually explicit materials online (Ybarra & Mitchell, 2005).

The speed and anonymity of Internet technology have led users to a variety of ways in which the Internet can now supplement traditional sexual activities. Griffiths (2000) sees five major areas of sex-related use of the Internet:

1. The search for sexual educational materials. Sites related to sex education and healthy sexual interactions are readily available.

Figure 11.11

SOURCE: Copyright Mike Luckovich and Creators Syndicate. Reprinted with permission.

2. The buying or selling of sex-related goods. This can be done in online sex shops in an atmosphere of almost total anonymity. As we noted earlier, the sex industry is one of the most popular types of sites visited by adults and frequented by adolescents. Even the buying of Viagra can be done online.

3. The seeking out of materials for entertainment or masturbatory purposes. The individual can also digitally manipulate images in sophisticated programs. Virtual partners, including children, are now part of the interactive environment. Within a legal context, virtual child pornography will be difficult to manage given the fact that no "real" underage child actually exists.

4. Seeking out sexual partners for long-term or short-term relationships and encounters. Everything from dating or matchmaking services to advertised prostitution is now available with the typing of a few words and the click of a mouse. In recent years, Web sites that provide information and reviews of prostitutes (escorts) have become more popular on the Web.

5. Finally, there is the illegal seeking out of individuals for sexually related Internet crimes (sexual harassment, cyberstalking, children).

There has been the possibility of some form of sexual addiction occurring with the proliferation and use of sexually related Internet sites. One argument is that the anonymity of the Internet could foster such addiction. However, the research does

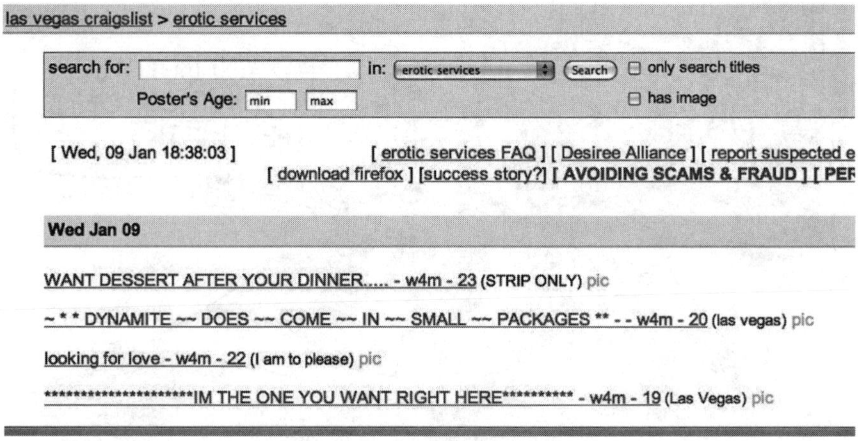

Figure 11.12   Listings of "Escort" Services From the Popular Craigslist Site

not demonstrate that such addiction occurs, and if it does, it is a relatively small minority of users who are affected. There is no question, however, that this is one area that needs further examination. Unlike our knowledge of other media systems, such as TV, we are only beginning to explore the usage, content, and effects of Internet access among children.

Advertising Food Products to Children: The Latest Concern

In a number of chapters in this book, we have discussed the concern of advertising to children and adolescents, particularly with regard to unhealthy food products. Television has been the usual "suspect" in these concerns, and we have seen how federal regulations have helped in reducing both the amount and nature of food advertising to young audiences. But technology has changed, and so has the medium where much of the concerns now reside.

In a recent and comprehensive overview on the Internet and food advertising, the Kaiser Family Foundation (2006) summarized the problem as follows:

> The world in which children encounter advertising is changing rapidly. While television and other more "traditional" forms of marketing to children still dominate, this study makes it clear that food companies are making extensive use of the Internet when it comes to targeting children. There is a vast amount of food related content online, with the potential to significantly expand and deepen children's exposure to food marketing messages. (p. 32)

The findings of this investigation were both fascinating and disturbing. The majority (85%) of companies that advertise to children on TV are also providing children with similar forms of advertising on the Internet. Of these companies, 75% have Web sites specifically created for children, and not surprisingly, many have their Web site URLs on the products package.

Given the interactive nature of the Internet, it was not surprising to find that around 75% of the sites had what are now called "Advergames" in which a company's product or brand characters are featured in an online game format (see Figure 11.13).

The ability of the Internet to have this interactive nature also leads many of the products to taut their "benefits," like taste, fun, and popularity.

With another technology, advertisers have made use of what is now called viral marketing. This innovative technique has the user send e-mails or even e-cards to his or her friends with information about the product in which are contained news and entertainment features related to the product. The Kaiser study found two thirds using a brand character or a link to a game on the company's Web site.

No different than traditional TV or print advertising, these Internet ads also try to attract children through contests, sweepstakes, and other promotional activities. One such promotion in which children can gain points for promotions is to watch what are basically TV ads online and to send the video on to their friends. More than half the sites had TV ads available for viewing, suggesting what we have noted in many places in this book—the "blur" between traditional media and the Internet.

Figure 11.13   Example From the Internet of a Food Products Online Game

Many offer special memberships or clubs within the sites trying to keep children returning to these sites. These memberships may provide access to games, screensavers, or other incentives to maintain the viewer's interest and continual participation. Even without memberships, many sites (75%) offered downloads of logos, screensavers, or wallpaper for their computers. Many sites also offered children the opportunity to "customize" the site (e.g., color, characters) as a means of maintaining their loyalty.

One particular finding stands out in this study (Kaiser Family Foundation, 2006). Almost 40% of the sites offered promotions such as access to awards, games, and other prizes if they or their parents bought the product. This new venture into marketing to children raises a number of regulatory issues. We will discuss these later in this chapter.

Other Areas of Concern

Concerns about children's and adolescents' use of the Internet are not limited to sexual content. Another perceived danger comes from information on satanism and religious proselytizing, as well as drugs and gambling. Religious cults, which only a

Figure 11.14   Example From the Internet of a Food Products Interactive Site

few years ago would have had a limited audience, can now reach out to a worldwide following. Offshore gambling is now a major e-commerce business. We no longer need to go to Las Vegas to place a bet; offshore casinos do the same thing, as well as presenting online slots, craps, and poker. Online poker has become one of the more popular activities for online gamers (see Figure 11.15). According to the Annenberg Public Policy Center (2006), weekly use of online gambling sites among those ages 18 to 22 has doubled from 2005 to 2006. A credit card or a money order (something teenagers can purchase) allows access to any one of hundreds of offshore casinos.

Terrorism is another issue of concern. Some online archives provide instructions for making bombs or other weapons. Since the events of September 11, 2001, terrorist groups have made extensive use of the Internet to recruit and spread propaganda. The proliferation of hate speech and hate groups has also become easily accessible on the Web.

Alcohol and tobacco advertisements and dedicated Web sites to smoking and drinking are another problem. Many of these sites use promotional techniques that are considered quite appealing to adolescents. We have seen in previous chapters the strong appeal of advertising on both children and adolescents. The enforcement of government regulations with respect to tobacco and alcohol has been of significant help with respect to more traditional media such as television. This has not

Figure 11.15   Online Poker

been the case with respect to the Internet and, as we discuss later, is not likely be an effective tool to combat advertising that exists within a global context.

Want to buy drugs? Very easy on the Internet. With a simple money order, you are on your way. In once recent report (NBC, 2006), it was noted that more than 90% of sites that sell prescription drugs do not even require a doctor's note (see Figure 11.16). According to this report,

> Emergency department physicians are reporting an increasing number of adolescents who are overdosing on a bizarre combination of medications. And where are they getting them? More and more often they come from one of the hundreds of online pharmacies where there are no questions asked, no prescription necessary. (NBC, 2006)

Children's privacy is another major issue. In a series of reports from the Center for Media Education (2001), there is growing concern that many Web sites, even those aimed directly at children (younger than age 13), are requesting personal information without asking for parental permission. In fact, less than 25% asked children for their parents' permission to disclose information such as e-mail addresses, phone numbers, home addresses, and information about their parents. According to the Annenberg Public Policy Center (2000), more than 50% of children are willing to give out information about their parents in exchange for a free gift offered on a Web site. The standard advertising techniques discussed in Chapter 2 seem to be just as appealing when children surf the Web. Recent governmental regulations have slowed this steady tide of invading children's privacy, but concerns still exist.

We should not forget that the Internet also has the ability to promote prosocial effects. According to Mares and Woodard (2001), it is a promising medium for three major reasons. First, it is not that expensive for a small prosocial group to reach an audience on a global level. No other medium has this ability at the relative cost of the Internet. Second, it can target a specific narrow audience. The ability of the Web to be selective and to gather information from users allows for the tailoring of specific Web pages to a target audience. Finally, it is interactive, allowing for changes to be made in the site. The major problem is that few children are reaching these sites, and it is a medium that is underused for prosocial purposes.

Figure 11.16   Internet Site to Purchase Drugs

Solutions to Internet Concerns

In thinking about solutions to children's and adolescents' access to inappropriate Net content, there are three major approaches. The first is government regulation restricting the content. The second is technology, including blocking software and some form of rating system. Third, and we believe the most important, is media literacy for both parents and their children as to the benefits and problems of the Internet. The issue of media literacy is discussed more in depth in the next chapter.

Government Regulation

Within the United States, the First Amendment protects offensive speech from censorship, including sexually explicit materials. In general, the U.S. courts have struck down most content restrictions on books, magazines, and films. There are, of course, exceptions such as "obscenity," child pornography, and certain types of indecent material depending on the time, place, and manner of the presentation. In 1996, Congress passed a bill to deal specifically with Internet content regulation primarily in the area of pornography.

The bill took as its premise a number of questions that are to be considered with regard to the issue of protecting children. First, is access to pornography easy for children? The answer is probably yes, if the individual has some computer savvy. As we discussed earlier, sophisticated search engines make the search rapid and extensive. Second, is access to pornography accidental? Except for the typing errors, the answer is probably no. Finally, is access to this type of material harmful? This is difficult to assess and depends on many factors, as discussed in previous chapters. Nevertheless, most of us would agree that we should certainly monitor and protect children from these unwanted sites.

The Supreme Court of the United States ruled on the Communications Decency Act in 1998 and, as expected, held it to be unconstitutional and an infringement on freedom of speech. Likewise, other courts have noted that service providers, such as America Online, could not be held liable for sending pornographic materials over the Internet. It is obvious that the courts are well aware that government regulation in this area would be difficult or near impossible given not only the vastness of materials available but also the global scope of the Internet.

In 2002, the Supreme Court overturned a law that banned virtual images of children, even those sexual in nature. In other words, virtual child pornography is considered legal. These decisions, like many others from the Court, suggest the difficulty of federal legislation in confronting sex on the Internet.

With respect to online food marketing, the Kaiser Family Foundation (2006) notes the following:

> To date, the primary regulatory concern regarding online marketing has been on protecting children's privacy, via the Children's Online Privacy Protection Act (COPPA). At the same time, the advertising industry's self-regulatory body, the Children's Advertising Review Unit (CARU), has instituted a set of

general guidelines to advise advertisers on how to communicate with children in an age appropriate way on the Internet. At the time of this writing (June, 2006), more detailed guidelines regarding online marketing were expected soon from CARU. (p. 30)

Some federal regulations have appeared recently. One is aimed at regulating online gambling. In October 2006, President Bush signed into law new regulations that prohibit people who place bets through their computers from using credit cards, checks, and electronic money transfers. The aim is to make offshore Internet betting a crime. Many believe that given the nature of online gambling, which is for the most part based outside the United States, the ability to enforce such a law is problematic.

Blocking Technology

One solution has been the development of software that is designed to block unwanted sites. This blocking software can block known adult sites, for instance, or any site containing predetermined words such as *sex, gambling,* and other unwanted content. A number of these types of software are available that perform these and other functions.

But none of these blocking systems is completely effective. The Web changes quite rapidly, and software designed for today may not be entirely appropriate tomorrow. In one test of the effectiveness of blocking adult sites (Consumer Reports, 2005), it was found that the "latest tests of filtering software show that while Internet blockers have gotten better at blocking pornography, the best also tend to block many sites they shouldn't. In addition, *Consumer Reports* found the software to be less effective at blocking sites promoting hatred, illegal drugs or violence" (Consumer Reports, 2005). This updated report notes the following:

1. Filters kept out most, but not all, of the pornography. A well-informed teenager could find his or her way around the blocks.

2. Information sites can also be blocked. The best software was also "heavy-handed" against sites about health issues, sex education, civil rights, and politics.

3. Research can be more difficult. These programs may impede older children doing research for school reports.

4. They can regulate more than Web sites. Some can prevent downloading of music and certain e-mail.

Media Literacy

The role of parents in working with their children and becoming familiar with this technology is critical (see Figure 11.17). Children can be taught "critical viewing skills" in their schools so that they learn to better interpret what they encounter on the Web. The same techniques used to mitigate media violence or the appeals of advertisements can also be effective in this area. In addition, a large number of professional organizations concerned with the well-being of children and families have begun to take a more active role in reducing the impact of harmful Internet content (e.g., American Academy of Pediatrics, American Medical Association Alliances). Within this new arena of technology, we should take a lesson from our findings on media violence interventions. Research on intervention programs has indicated that we can reduce some of the impact of media violence by "empowering" parents in their roles as monitors of children's television viewing. These studies indicate that parents who view programs with their children and discuss the realities of violence, as well as alternatives to aggressive behaviors in conflict situations, can actually reduce the negative impact (increased aggressiveness) of media violence (i.e., Donnerstein, Slaby, & Eron, 1994). The same type of positive results could be obtained when parents begin to monitor, supervise, and participate in their children's Internet activities. Chapter 13 examines the possibilities of media literacy in more detail.

On the Positive Side

As we noted at the start of this chapter, the Internet can be extremely beneficial as both an educational teacher and tool for positive development. Although we have alluded to the small fraction of Web sites that can create problems for children and adolescents, we cannot overlook the immense benefit of this technology. We do not

Figure 11.17

SOURCE: Reprinted with permission of Copley News Service.

want to leave the reader with any hesitation about the positive aspects of this technology. The Internet is perhaps the greatest teaching tool we have ever encountered, and its impact on children and adolescents will be to enrich their lives in immeasurable ways. Therefore, it seems appropriate to end this chapter on a more positive note.

The American Academy of Pediatrics (see http://safetynet.aap.org) suggests a number of activities for parents and children that can foster positive interactions and educational experiences. The academy Web site suggests the following:

Find educational resources, including up-to-the-minute news, important documents, photos, and research.

Get help with homework through online encyclopedias, reference materials, and access to experts.

Improve computer skills necessary to find information, solve problems, and communicate with others.

Connect with places around the world to exchange e-mail with online pen pals and learn about other countries and cultures.

Locate parenting information and swap ideas with other families.

Learn and have fun together by sharing interesting and enjoyable experiences.

The whole area of civic engagement for youth has taken on a new excitement because of the Internet. As Montgomery, Gottlieb-Robles, and Larson (2004) note in a recent report on this subject,

Youth engagement in politics and community affairs has quietly been taking on new life and a dynamic new look, thanks to the Internet. Scarcely audible above the hubbub over piracy and pornography and the clamor of the media marketplace, a low-profile civic upsurge—created for and sometimes by young people—has taken root on the Net. Hundreds of websites have been created that encourage and facilitate youth civic engagement, contributing to an emerging genre on the Internet that could loosely be called "youth civic culture." (Montgomery, Gottlieb-Robles, & Larson, 2004)

According to the Kaiser Family Foundation (2004), the Internet is now used by 20% of youth in their decisions regarding political issues. This compares to 13% four years earlier. The popular Rock the Vote Web site (Figure 11.18) is a good example of the Internet interacting with other media to encourage and engage youth.

In the state of Arizona, on a Web site called LawForKids.org, young people can ask questions about anything from child abuse to legal problems such as driving drunk or using drugs (see Figure 11.19). Attorneys within the state of Arizona provide feedback in an attempt to educate children and adolescents about the law, without giving actual advice. Over the past year, the site has had 1.5 million questions submitted and has now expanded into other states.

Figure 11.18   The Rock the Vote Web Site

Figure 11.19   Web Site for Law for Kids

There are Web sites that foster creativity. For instance, MaMaMedia (see Figure 11.20) allows children to create their own digital stories, make digital drawings that include music and animation, and learn word meanings. There are Web sites that focus on social issues. Yo! Youth Outlook (see Figure 11.21) has created a site that discusses current social issues that teens can relate to in their own lives. Sesame Workshop offers children an array of educational opportunities, including games and stories. Among the most popular sites for children are PBS Online, Discovery Online, Nickelodeon, and the child version of Yahoo, Yahooligans (see Figure 11.22).

Figure 11.20

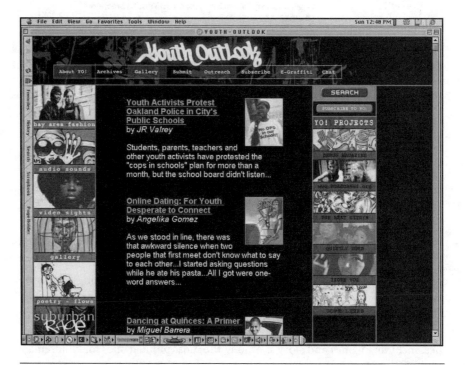

Figure 11.21

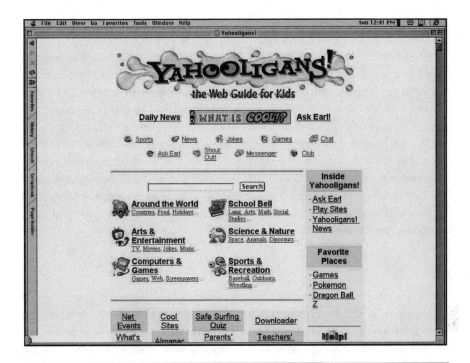

Figure 11.22

The Internet can also be an effective learning tool that can facilitate academic achievement. Roschelle, Pea, Hoaddley, Gordin, and Means (2000) have noted that leaning is most effective when four fundamental characteristics are present. The first is active engagement. There is no question that computer-mediated teaching is highly effective in this area, and the Internet allows students to be anything but passive. The constant interactive nature of the Internet is a highly efficient tool for positively engaging students in the learning process.

A second characteristic is that of learning through group participation. Although on one level, we may think of "surfing the Net" as an individual type of activity, many group-oriented activities are not only possible but highly engaging on the Internet. Many types of learning networks already developed have been shown to be effective teaching models in the classroom.

A third major characteristic is learning through frequent interaction and feedback. There should be no disagreement that computer-mediated learning is ideal for this form of instruction. The research in this area supports the position that children's and adolescents' use of Internet-based activities can increase motivation, a deeper understanding of concepts, and a stronger motivation to engage in difficult assignments.

Finally, the Internet provides an ability to learn through connections to real-world contexts. The vast array of Internet Web sites allows students the ability to explore almost any concept in an interactive multimedia context. Equally important, the Internet allows students the exposure to ideas and experiences that would have normally been inaccessible with more traditional modes of learning.

The Packard report (Packard Foundation, 2000) also found that the Internet could be a positive component in children's lives by enabling them to keep in touch with friends, family, and others to form communities with common interests. Finally, with the advent of media literacy, children should be able to learn and recognize high-quality Web sites that will enhance their leaning and creativity.

There is general agreement that considerably more research is needed in all these areas, but the Internet is a new technology with a rich array of possibilities. Its potential for positive impacts on learning, social and cognitive development, and the overall future of children's and adolescents' lives is just emerging. We need to explore and continue our examination of all these possibilities as more and more children come online and the technology itself changes and expands.

Conclusion

The Internet is without question an innovative and exciting tool for information and education. It is a technology that will become more accessible worldwide over the years and will only improve in its capacity to stimulate and enrich our lives. We need to understand its potential for increasing our children's educational opportunities while recognizing its limitations and dangers. These dangers, however, are not going to be easily remedied through traditional solutions such as governmental regulation. The Internet is a technology that necessitates parental involvement and leadership. With such involvement, it is very likely that both children and parents will experience the Internet as a new and enriching environment in which to interact.

Exercises

1. The Internet can be used for an array of activities, from instructional to entertaining. Consider an activity you normally do in which you have not yet used the Internet, such as taking a trip or buying tickets to a concert. Try doing the same activity with the help of the Internet. Was the process faster? Did you obtain more useful information? Was the Internet a better source for this activity than your normal procedure?

2. If you have blocking software or a service provider (AOL) that allows you to restrict particular content, try the following: Select a topic that might be controversial, such as drugs or gambling. Perform a search on this topic with and without the blocking activated. Is there a significant difference in the quantity and quality of the information you find?

3. One suggestion for restricting children's access to inappropriate material on the Internet is a rating system similar to that applied to TV content. Could a system of this type be effective with the Internet? Given the global nature of the

Internet, would it be possible to define a universal rating system for violence or sex? What might be an appropriate rating system?

4. We indicated in this chapter that the Internet should be used to facilitate learning in the classroom. Design a curriculum for high school students that relies entirely on the Internet. How would it differ from traditional modes of instruction? How might you evaluate its effectiveness?

5. Figures 11.18 through 11.22 illustrate examples of Web sites that are of educational value for children. What other sites can you find? Why would you consider the sites you find to be particularly beneficial for children?

References

Annenberg Public Policy Center. (2000). *The Internet and the family 2000.* Philadelphia: Author.

Annenberg Public Policy Center. (2006). *More than 1 million young people use internet gambling sites each month.* Retrieved August 14, 2006, from http://www.annenberg publicpolicycenter.org

Borzekowski, D. L. G., & Robinson, T. N. (2005). The remote, the mouse, and the #2 pencil: Media and academic achievement among 3rd grade students. *Archives of Pediatrics and Adolescent Medicine, 159,* 607–613.

Carlsson, U. (2006) Violence and pornography in the media: Public views on the influence media violence and pornography exert on young people. In U. Carlsson & C. Feilitzen (Eds.), *In the service of young people? Studies and reflections on media in the digital age* (pp. 288–305). Goteborg, Sweden: UNESCO.

Center for Media Education. (2001). *Children's Online Privacy Protection Act: The first year.* Washington, DC: Center for Media Education.

Common Sense Media. (2006). *9 out of 10 parents think they should have prime responsibility for children's Internet safety.* Retrieved October 15, 2006, from http://www.common sensemedia.org

Consumer Reports. (2005, June). *Filtering software: Better, but still fallible.* Yonkers, NY: Consumer Union of the United States.

Crimes Against Children Research Center (CACRC). (2006). *Second Youth Internet Safety Survey (YISS-2).* Retrieved November 22, 2006, from http://www.unh.edu/ccrc

Donnerstein, E., Slaby, R. G., & Eron, L. D. (1994). The mass media and youth aggression. In L. D. Eron, J. H. Gentry, & P. Schlegel (Eds.), *Reason to hope: A psychosocial perspective on violence and youth* (pp. 219–250). Washington, DC: American Psychological Association.

Fox, J. (2006). *Sex differences in college students' Internet pornography use.* Unpublished MA thesis, University of Arizona.

Griffiths, M. (2000). Sex on the Internet. In C. Feilitzen & U. Carlsson (Eds.), *Children in the new media landscape* (pp. 169–184). Goteborg, Sweden: UNESCO.

Huesmann, L. R. (1998). An information processing model for the development of aggression. *Aggressive Behavior, 14,* 13–24.

Kaiser Family Foundation. (2003). *Zero to six: Electronic media in the lives of infants, toddlers and preschoolers.* Menlo Park, CA: Author.

Kaiser Family Foundation. (2004). *Media, youth, and civic engagement.* Menlo Park, CA: Author.

Kaiser Family Foundation. (2006). *It's child's play: Advergaming and the online marketing of food to children.* Menlo Park, CA: Author.

Kaiser Family Foundation. (2006). *The media family: Electronic media in the lives of infants, toddlers, preshoolers, and their parents.* Menlo Park, CA.

Kaiser Family Foundation. (2007). *Parents, children, and media.* Menlo Park, CA.

Kowalski, R. M., & Limber S. P. (2007) Electronic bullying among middle school students. *Journal of Adolescent Health, 41,* S22–S30.

Livingstone, S., & Millwood Hargrave, A. (2006) Harmful to children? Drawing conclusions from empirical research on media effects. In U. Carlsson (Ed.), *Regulation, awareness, empowerment: Young people and harmful media content in the digital age* (pp. 21–48). Goteborg, Sweden: UNESCO.

Malamuth, N., & Impett, E. A. (2001). Research on sex in the media. In D. Singer & J. Singer (Eds.), *Handbook of children and the media* (pp. 269–287). Thousand Oaks, CA: Sage.

Mares, M., & Woodard, E. H. (2001). Prosocial effects on children's social interactions. In D. Singer & J. Singer (Eds.), *Handbook of children and the media* (pp. 183–205). Thousand Oaks, CA: Sage.

Mitchell, K. J., Wolak, J., & Finkelhor, D. (2007). Trends in youth reports of sexual solicitations, harassment and unwanted exposure to pornography on the Internet. *Journal of Adolescent Health, 40,* 116–126.

Montgomery, K., Gottlieb-Robles, B., & Larson, G. O. (2004). *Youth as e-citizens: Engaging the digital generation.* Retrieved March 21, 2006, from http://www.centerforsocialmedia .org/ecitizens/youthreport.pdf

NBC. (2006). *Teens turn to Internet for prescription drugs.* Retrieved April 17, 2006, from http://www.msnbc.msn.com

Packard Foundation. (Ed.). (2000). *The future of children: Children and computer technology.* Los Altos, CA: Author.

Paik, H. (2001). The history of children's use of electronic media. In D. Singer & J. Singer (Eds.), *Handbook of children and the media* (pp. 7–27). Thousand Oaks, CA: Sage.

Pew Foundation. (2005). *The Pew Internet & American Life Project.* Philadelphia: Pew Charitable Trusts.

Roschelle, J., Pea, R., Hoaddley, C., Gordin, D., & Means, B. (2000). Changing how and what children learn in school with computer-based technologies. In Packard Foundation (Ed.), *The future of children: Children and computer technology* (pp. 145–167). Los Altos, CA: Packard Foundation.

Symantec Corporation. (2004). *Symantec survey shows seniors are the most spam-savvy online demographic.* Retrieved May 8, 2004, from http://www.symantec.com/press/2004

Thornburgh, D., & Lin, H. S. (Eds.). (2002). *Youth, pornography, and the Internet.* Washington, DC: National Academy Press.

Williams, K. R., & Guerra, N. G. (2007). Prevalence and predictors of Internet bullying. *Journal of Adolescent Health, 41,* S14–S21.

Ybarra, M. L., & Mitchell, K. J. (2005). Exposure to Internet pornography among children and adolescents: A national survey. *CyberPsychology & Behavior, 8,* 473–486.

CHAPTER 12

The Family and Media

See, my son's the type you have to drag things out of him as far as what happened in school or, you know, what's going on. He never says anything. Now if we're watching a show or something and something comes up, you know, he may mention, oh, that happened, you know, the other day. So it kind of keeps me abreast of what's going on with that age group, you know.

—African American parent of a 10-year-old boy

It's really a very simple way to just get them to sit down and relax because, you know, my children are very active. [My son is] very active and to me, it's nice, it's very pleasant for me when he's sort of like fed, cleaned, you know, teeth are brushed, and he's going to just sit down for a while and watch TV. It's a calm, nice thing. Now, you know, I could do other things with him at that point.

—White mother of a 12-year-old boy

Oh, it's just a phenomenal babysitter. If everybody in the house needs to be doing things, it's just fabulous.

—White mother of a 9-year-old girl

The above quotes come from a study in which the researchers were exploring how to reduce children's TV time, a study that ultimately found that it would be very hard, given the integral role the medium plays in the lives of both children and parents (Jordan, Hersey, McDivitt, & Heitzler, 2006). Clearly, to truly understand the role of the media in the lives of children and adolescents, we must simultaneously understand what media have come to mean to the family. As these quotes suggest, media are an important part of family life—part of the day-to-day lives of families, part of the resources parents draw on (to baby-sit, to stay connected), and part of the very structure of the modern household (Jordan et al., 2006). Media use not only shapes but also is shaped by what happens in the family setting. What's more, children learn to use media in particular ways based on what they observe their parents and siblings doing with media.

In this chapter, we will (a) offer a picture of the current setup of the home environment as a multiple media environment, (b) examine research on parents' efforts to control children's media use, (c) briefly review four key theories that can help us understand how children make meaning of media in the context of family life, and (d) lay out what research suggests about "best practices" for making the most of media in the home.

The Home as a Multimedia Environment

Children who spend their days in environments that are filled with television sets, computers, and video games have greater opportunity to use media. Saelens et al. (2002) explored home environment factors around TV access and their relation to children's overall TV watching. They followed 169 children from ages 6 to 12. Over time, mothers reported having more TVs and VCRs in the home, a higher frequency of children eating meals in front of the TV, and a higher percentage of children having TVs in their bedrooms (see Figures 12.1 to 12.3). In this study, home environment factors explained a significant amount of children's total TV time. Specifically, as the number of television sets increased in the house, so too did the amount of children's viewing.

Television in the Bedroom

Children's own bedrooms are also replete with media. In part, this is explained by the increased affordability and portability of technologies that are quite popular with children—for example, laptop computers, handheld video game players,

Figure 12.1

SOURCE: Baby Blues by Rick Kirkman and Jerry Scott. Reprinted with permission of King Features Syndicate.

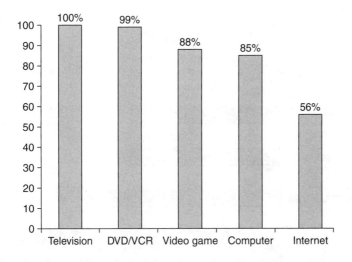

Figure 12.2   Media in the Home

SOURCE: Adapted from Jordan et al. (2006).

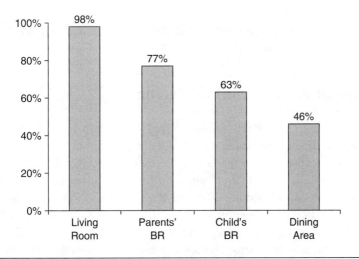

Figure 12.3   Placement of Television Sets in the Home

SOURCE: Adapted from Jordan et al. (2006).

and iPods. Indeed, several studies, including nationally representative studies from the Kaiser Family Foundation (Rideout, Roberts, & Foehr, 2005), suggest that the inclusion of media in children's sleeping space begins at very early ages (see Figure 12.4). However, many experts have expressed concern about consequences of multimedia bedrooms. Does bedroom access limit parents' ability to control media use? Do children spend more time with media as a result? Studies indicate that the answer to both questions is yes. Children with bedroom TVs watch more programs that are

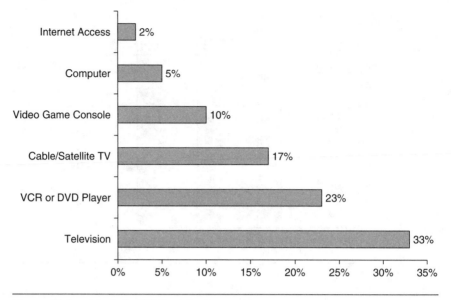

Figure 12.4   Media in Children's Bedrooms

SOURCE: Reprinted with permission of the Kaiser Family Foundation.

inappropriate for their age (Woodard & Gridina, 2000), and they watch significantly more TV (Rideout et al., 2005).

Television Viewing During Mealtime

The Saelens et al. (2002) study described earlier also found that television viewing during mealtime contributed to children's overall TV time, such that children who consume their meals with the TV on spend significantly more time with the medium than children who don't. Eating during meals affects what the family eats as well. Coon, Goldberg, Rogers, and Tucker (2001) argue that "because children learn television-viewing habits, as well as eating habits, primarily from parents, the choices parents make about the use of television during meals may be associated with choices that they make regarding the foods they buy and make available to their children, independently of children's direct requests for advertised foods" (pp. e6–e7). In Coon and colleagues' study—carried out with 91 parent-child pairs—parents were asked whether the television was usually on or off in the presence of children while they ate meals, and they filled out food diaries specifying what children ate and how much. Children from families with high television use during mealtime derived, on average, 6% more of their total daily energy intake from meats; 5% more from pizza, salty snacks, and soda; and nearly 5% less of their energy intake from fruits, vegetables, and juices than did children from families with low television use, and, importantly, these associations hold despite controlling for other variables that might predict this relationship, such as family income.

In addition to affecting what is eaten, mealtime TV might also affect family relationships. Jordan et al. (2006) report that more than half of all families regularly eat dinner with the TV on. As Gentile and Walsh (2002) argue, "This affects family interactions, in that this would be a time when family members would usually talk to one another. . . . Television use may both affect and be affected by family interactions. There is less verbal communication, less looking at each other, but more physical touching among family members when the TV is on" (p. 158). Figure 12.3 suggests that the placement of media may shape the opportunity to eat while viewing. As Jordan et al. (2006) found, 4 in 10 families have a television set in a room normally dedicated to eating (that is, the kitchen and dining room).

The Constant TV Home

A 2005 survey of more than a thousand parents with young children (ages 6 months to 6 years) made national headlines when it was revealed that more than a third of these youngsters lived in homes where the television is on always or most of the time, even if no one is watching (Vandewater et al., 2005). Data from this study suggest that parental beliefs play a significant role in determining the role of television in the home. Children with parents who view educational television as a "very important" contributor to healthy development were more than twice as likely as other children to be from a "constant TV" household. Children whose parents use television as a babysitter and children with no siblings also have greater odds of being in heavy-television households.

But does background TV matter? Dan Anderson, a child development expert at the University of Massachusetts, would suggest that it does (see Kirkorian, Murphy, Pempek, Anderson, & Schmidt, 2005). His research looked at the quality of parent-child interaction with and without the TV on, in an experimental lab setting where trained coders could carefully track parents' engagement with the children and their involvement with the babies' play. He found that in the TV-on experimental condition, parent-child play was of significantly lower quality than in the TV-off condition.

Does the constant TV home environment of very young children affect their later patterns with media? First, children who live in heavy-television households use their time very differently than other children (see Figure 12.5). According to Vandewater et al. (2005), children who live with the television almost constantly on spend more time using electronic media than other children. Children from heavy-television households watch more television and videos than other children. They also spend less time reading books. These patterns appear to persist, moreover. Certain and Kahn's (2002) longitudinal analysis indicates that greater television viewing in early childhood is associated with greater viewing at school age. The persistence of this behavior pattern may reflect continuing environmental influences, the development of child preferences or habits, or, most likely, an interaction between the two.

Figure 12.5

SOURCE: Reprinted with permission.

Socialization to Media Use Within the Family Context

Beyond the media that parents bring into the home, invite to the dinner table, and put into children's bedrooms, families also use media in social ways. The "social uses of media," first described by Lull (1980), means that media are "handy expedients which can be exploited by individuals, coalitions, and family units to serve their personal needs, create practical relationships, and engage the social world" (p. 198). Lull's typology can be a helpful way to think about how socialization to media use occurs within the family context (see Figure 12.6).

The social uses of media generally fall along two dimensions. The first considers how media can structure the space and time of the home. The television set, for example, has been described as a kind of "electronic hearth" (Tichi, 1991) in the home, with furniture in the living room arranged around the set in a way that was once reserved for a fireplace. Others have considered the arrangement of

---

Structural

➤ Environmental (background noise; companionship; entertainment)
➤ Regulative (punctuation of time and activity; talk patterns)

Relational

➤ Communication facilitation (experience illustration; common ground; conversational entrance; anxiety reduction; agenda for talk; value clarification)
➤ Affiliation/avoidance (physical, verbal contact/neglect; family solidarity; family relaxant; conflict reduction; relationship maintenance)
➤ Social learning (decision making; behavior modeling; problem solving; value transmission; legitimation; information dissemination; substitute schooling)
➤ Competence/dominance (role enactment; role reinforcement; substitute role portrayal; intellectual validation; authority exercise; gatekeeping; argument facilitation)

Figure 12.6   The Social Uses Typology

SOURCE: James Lull (1980). The Social Uses of Television. *Human Communication Research 6*(3), 197–209. doi: 10.1111/j.1468-2958.1980.tb00140.x. Blackwell Publishing, copyright 3/17/2006.

media as facilitating multitasking—using several media at the same time or using media while doing chores, homework, or other activities. Media also serve to punctuate family time. Jordan (1992), for example, describes how in some families, books and videotapes are used to transition children from being awake to being asleep (with videotapes or DVDs replacing "story time" in many families). A second dimension to the social uses typology is "relational"—helping families build relationships or helping family members create a psychological distance. Considered in the context of the family, media may be a facilitator of communication (e.g., give family members common fodder for talking), may be a detriment to communication (e.g., a parent trying to talk with a teen while that teen is furiously instant messaging his friends), or may allow for physical connection (e.g., a father snuggling up with his infant daughter while she watches a Baby Einstein video).

Parental Mediation of Children's Media Use

Most parents say they have at least some rules about what media children can use and/or how much time they can devote to watching TV, playing video games, or surfing the Web (Jordan et al., 2006). Indeed, one of the earliest and most important parent-child negotiations that exist could be those in which parents attempt to mediate the flow of media content into the home. Such negotiations give parents an important opportunity not only to set boundaries but also to convey their personal values and cultural beliefs.

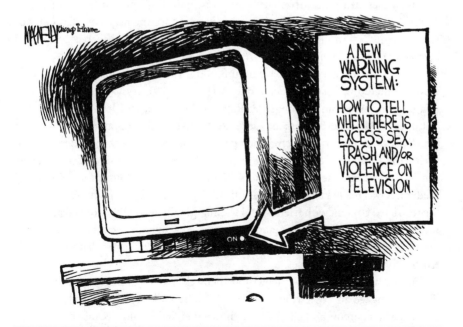

Figure 12.7

SOURCE: Tribune Media Services.

Three types of mediation styles—the ways in which parents try to buffer children's exposure to media content—typically dominate the research literature. First, "active mediation" involves the kinds of conversations that parents (or other adults, such as teachers) have with children about television. Talk about media might be initiated by parents, who aim to assist children in being more critical viewers. Talk might also be initiated by children, who have questions about character motivations or want to understand media conventions. Nathanson (2001) says that the tone of active mediation may be positive or negative, which will have different effects on children's reception of media content and beliefs about the media.

Second, many researchers have described a form of supervision typically labeled "restrictive mediation." This type of parental supervision involves the use of explicit rules about what games can be played, what channels can be watched, or how long a child can be on the Web. For example, parents who use restrictive mediation may use online filtering software to prohibit children from seeing content they feel may be harmful.

Finally, "coviewing" has been explored as a strategy for parents to talk to children about content while watching together. Coviewing has also been used to describe the simple act of sitting in the same room and watching a program with or without conversation.

Do the different mediation styles work to limit children's exposure to the "bad stuff" and enhance the potential benefits of the "good stuff"? Evaluations of media literacy programs, which typically focus on active mediation, suggest that adults can improve children's understanding of television. One way is by involving them in formal media literacy programs. Another opportunity is to explore, clarify, or add to topics introduced by television (Austin & Pinkelton, 1997; Nathanson, 2002). Active mediation has also been shown to reduce the negative effects of violent content in film violence (Grusec, 1973; Hicks, 1968) and increase prosocial behavior (Horton & Santogrossi, 1978).

Many positive correlations have been found for children whose parents restrict viewing, including less product requests (Reid, 1979), less aggressive behavior (Nathanson, 1999; Singer, Singer, & Rapacynski, 1984), and less cultivation-like attitudes (Rothschild & Morgan, 1987). Restrictive mediation appears to be most beneficial for younger children. When parents use this strategy for older children (primarily those in high school), at least with respect to television, restrictiveness can lead to unintended consequences. Nathanson (2002) found that "restrictive mediation was related to less positive attitudes toward parents and more viewing of the restricted content with friends, and was marginally related to more positive attitudes toward the restricted content" (p. 220). She hypothesizes that adolescents interpreted their parents' restrictive mediation efforts as evidence that they are not trusted to make good choices.

Parents who like to watch television themselves have been found to be more likely to engage in coviewing with their children (Austin & Pinkelton, 1997). Indeed, when parents and children watch together, it's usually because children are watching the shows parents want to watch and not because parents are interested in sharing the viewing experience of children's shows (St. Peters, Fitch, Huston,

Wright, & Eakins, 1991). Today, with the average household containing four television sets (Jordan et al., 2006), it is even less likely that parents will coview with their children. Research on parents' coviewing *Sesame Street* with young children suggests that children learn more than children who watch alone (Salomon, 1977). However, it appears that parent/child coviewing of adult programming has potentially detrimental outcomes, particularly if children infer that parents approve of certain kinds of depictions, such as violence (Nathanson, 2001).

Unlike what parents report, about half (53%) of all 8- to 18-year-olds say their families have no rules about TV watching (Rideout et al., 2005). The rest say their families do have some rules, but only 20% say their rules are enforced most of the time. The most common rule parents have is to complete homework or chores before watching TV (36%). Beyond that, parents appear to be most likely to regulate their children's computer use. For example, when it comes to setting rules about the media content their kids consume, 23% have rules about what their kids can do on the computer compared with 16% who set limits about the type of music their kids can listen to, 13% who have rules about which TV shows children can watch, and 12% who restrict the type of video games they can play.

Most research indicates that parents are more concerned about the kind of content to which children are exposed than to the amount of time they spend with a

By Chris Britt. The Morning News Tribune, Tacoma, Wash., Copley News Service

Figure 12.8

SOURCE: Reprinted with permission of Copley News Service.

particular medium (Rideout et al., 2005; Woodard & Gridina, 2000). Concern over content has led lawmakers to insist that media makers provide blocking technology and/or ratings. These regulations have met with only modest success, however. Parents are most likely to avail themselves of the tools to help them monitor their children's computer use: 25% of 7th to 12th graders with a computer at home say it has a filter or parental controls on it. Fewer—only 6%—use the "parental control" technology for the TV (the V-chip or cable provider blocking device). Advisories on music and video games are used by a small minority of parents, just 14% and 10%, respectively.

Given the widespread availability of content indicators and blocking devices, why aren't they more widely used? Studies from the Annenberg Public Policy Center at the University of Pennsylvania and the Kaiser Family Foundation suggest that the industry's efforts to inform and empower parents are often confusing to parents. Very few parents understand that the rating TV-PG-D indicates that the program contains sexual innuendo (Stanger & Gridina, 1998). Similarly, the symbol used to denote educational programming for children on commercial broadcast stations is obtuse and idiosyncratic, as in ABC's light bulb and voiceover that says "illuminating television." Today, most stations use the symbol *ei* to indicate "educational and informational" programming. Moreover, the V-chip device, mandated by the Telecommunications Act of 1996 to be included in all television sets, is generally seen by parents as too complicated to program (Scantlin & Jordan, 2006). And they're right! Figure 12.11 illustrates one of five screens that parents must navigate to block out programs on this television set.

Theoretical Perspectives

To understand how media fit into family life and parenting practices, it is useful to look at family theories for insight. Four family theories are highlighted here, as they are perhaps most relevant to understanding why families use media differently and why parents supervise their children's media diets differently.

Ecological (Systems) Theory

Figure 12.9   TV Ratings

SOURCE: From Kaiser Family Foundation (2000b). Reprinted with permission.

Ecological systems theory, as well as its offshoot, family systems theory, has been used over the past two decades to situate children's media use where it most often occurs: in the home (see, e.g., Atkin, Greenberg, & Baldwin, 1991; Galvin, Dickson, & Marrow, 2006; Jordan, 2004). This theory was born out of the belief that psychologists were not doing a very good job of measuring the many environmental contexts that shape children's development. Bronfenbrenner (1979) proposed that a child can be viewed as growing up in a set of nested systems, and he proposed four distinct subsystems (see Table 12.1). The *microsystem* contains the

All Children

This program is designed to be appropriate for all children. Whether animated or live action, the themes and elements in this program are specifically designed for a very young audience, including children from ages 2-6. This program is not expected to frighten younger children.

What you need to know: *Not all TV-Y shows are violence-free. Some shows with cartoon violence are rated TV-Y, such as the "Road Runner" cartoons. There is no contentrating to let you know if a TV-Y show contains violence.*

Directed to Older Children

This program is designed for children age 7 and above. It may be more appropriate for children who have acquired the developmental skills needed to distinguish between make-believe and reality. Themes and elements in this program may include mild fantasy or comedic violence, or may frighten children under the age of 7. Therefore, parents may wish to consider the suitability of this program for their very young children.

What you need to know: *TV-Y7 shows that contain a lot of fantasy violence are supposed to be labeled with the "FV" rating. But even some TV-Y7 shows with out the FV label may contain fantasy or comedic violence that could be of concern to some parents, although it is usually much milder than in those shows with the FV rating.*

Directed to Older Children-Fantasy Violence

For those programs where fantasy violence may be more intense or more combative than other programs in the TV-Y7 category, such programs will be designated TV-Y7-FV.

What you need to know: *A TV-Y7-FV rating indicates a program that may contain some or all of the following characteristics: violence as a prevalent feature of the program; fighting presented in an exciting–even thrilling–way; villains and superheros valued for their combat abilities; violent acts glorified; and violence depicted as an acceptable and effective solution to a problem. Fantasy violence may be part of an animated cartoon, a live-action show, or a program that combines both animation and live-action.*

General Audience

Most parents would find this program appropriate for all ages. Although this rating does not signify a program designed specifically for children, most parents may let younger children watch this program unattended. It contains little or no violence, no strong language and little or no sexual dialogue or situations.

What you need to know: *Most TV-G shows don't contain any sex, violence or adult language at all. Those that do have such content are usually mild. There are no content ratings used on TV-G shows to let you know if they do contain such content.*

Parental Guidance Suggested

This program contains material that parents may find unsuitable for younger children. Many parents may want to watch it with their younger children. The theme itself may call for parental guidance and/or the program contains one or more of the following: moderate violence (V), some sexual situations (S), infrequent coarse language (L), or some suggestive dialogue (D).

What you need to know: *Many TV-PG shows do contain moderate levels of sexual dialogue or violence, and not all of them are labeled with the content ratings. TV-PG shows with higher levels of sex, violence or adult language are usually labeled with content labels.*

Parents Strongly Cautioned

This program contains some material that parents would find unsuitable for children under 14 years of age. Parents are strongly urged to exercise greater care in monitoring this program and are cautioned against letting children under the age of 14 watch unattended. This program contains one or more of the following: intense violence (V), intense sexual situations (S), strong coarse language (L), or intensely suggestive dialogue (D).

Figure 12.10   Educational Television Symbol

SOURCE: From Kaiser Family Foundation (2000b). Reprinted with permission.

Figure 12.10 (Continued)

What you need to know: Most TV-14 shows contain sex, violence or adult language. Not all of those shows are labeled with the content descriptors. TV-14 shows with the highest levels of sex, violence or adult language are usually labeled with the content ratings. A TV-14 rating without content labels may also indicate a program with a mature theme.

Mature Audience Only
This program is specifically designed to be viewed by adults and therefore may be unsuitable for children under 17. This program contains one or more of the following: graphic violence (V), explicit sexual activity (S), or crude indecent language (L).

What you need to know: Very few shows are labeled TV-MA.

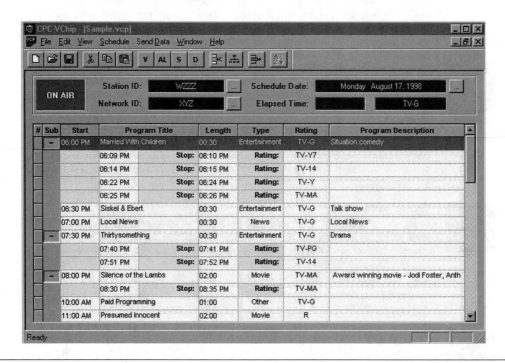

Figure 12.11   V-Chip Screen

people (e.g., family, peers, or teachers) and the settings (e.g., the home, the neighborhood, or the school) that the child comes into contact with on a regular basis. A media-related example of this might be the family's habit of never turning the television set off, a microsystem component that offers children more opportunity to watch. The *mesosystem* lies at the intersection of microsystems and can be thought of as the relationships between them. For example, a mother's and a teacher's instructions to a child regarding which medium to use to research a school project may be contradictory or complementary within the mesosystem. The *exosystems* are those social settings that influence a child's development but in which the child does not

Table 12.1   Bronfenbrenner's Ecological Systems

Context	Definitions/Examples
Microsystems	Child's day-to-day setting: the places they inhabit, the people they live with, the things they do together Examples: family, peers, teachers
Mesosystems	Relationships or intersections between microsystems Examples: the congruence of family orientations and peer orientations
Exosystems	Social settings that influence a child's development but in which the child does not necessarily have a direct role Examples: parents' workplace; media
Macrosystems	The broader cultural context that shapes attitudes, beliefs, and behaviors Examples: ethnicity; historical setting

SOURCE: Jordan (2004).

necessarily have a direct role. For example, parents' educational and occupational experiences shape their beliefs about time (that it is to be filled and is plentiful vs. something that needs to be managed and is a scarce resource). These beliefs then affect parents' rules about children's television viewing. In one study (Jordan, 1992), parents from a higher socioeconomic status (SES) were more likely to limit TV time while lower SES families were more likely to limit content. The likely reason? Parents who had been to college and who worked in higher prestige jobs had to learn to manage their time in ways that parents who lived "by the bell" did not. Finally, the *macrosystem* is the broader cultural context that shapes attitudes, beliefs, and behaviors. If one thinks about the kinds of technological changes this generation of youth have experienced—cell phones with Internet access, handheld screens that play the latest TV shows, just to name a few—it is clear that the macrosystem has dramatically altered media use possibilities. Not only are media more ubiquitous but they are also harder for parents to control.

What role do media play in the functioning of the family system? How do family members assimilate, accommodate, or reject media messages? How do parents or children use media to come together or maintain boundaries? Systems theory would suggest that to answer these questions, media cannot be isolated but rather must be seen as part of what makes up the rich and complex patterns of family life. Critical patterns to understand include how families typically communicate (Chaffee & McLeod's [1972] family communication patterns), the strategies parents typically use to bring up their children (Baumrind's [1978] taxonomy of parenting strategies), and the decisions parents make about whether and how to mediate children's media use. Each of these theories is discussed in more detail below.

Baumrind's Taxonomy of Parenting Strategies

What parents do around children's use of media is likely influenced by their general approaches to parenting and beliefs about how best to raise children. Baumrind (1971, 1978, 1991) identified three parenting styles—authoritarian, authoritative, and permissive. Later, a fourth parenting style, defined as uninvolved or neglectful, was developed out of the permissive parenting group. Two primary components to parenting style are (a) parental responsiveness and (b) parental demandingness. Parental responsiveness, or the warmth and support parents show their children, refers to the "extent to which parents intentionally foster individuality, self-regulation, and self-assertion by being attuned, supportive, and acquiescent to children's special needs and demands" (Baumrind, 1991, p. 62). Parental demandingness, or the control parents exert over their children's behavior, refers to the extent to which parents desire "children to become integrated into the family whole, by their maturity demands, supervision, disciplinary efforts and willingness to confront the child who disobeys" (Baumrind, 1991, p. 1062). Parenting style types are created by assessing parents as high or low on both parental demandingness and responsiveness dimensions (see Table 12.2).

Authoritative parenting, as contrasted with authoritarian, indulgent, or uninvolved styles, has been associated with positive outcomes among adolescents, including higher levels of psychological and cognitive development, mental health, self-esteem, stronger academic performance, greater self-reliance, and greater socialization (Rhee et al., 2006; Steinberg, Elmen, & Mounts, 1989). As might be expected, children with uninvolved parents consistently rate lower than those with parents using all other parenting styles across social, psychological, and behavioral outcomes. Although parenting style has been linked to many developmental and social outcomes within the psychology literature, how parenting styles correlate with parental mediation of media is relatively unknown. One notable exception to the gap is research by Eastin, Greenberg, and Hofschire (2006), who surveyed 520 parents with Internet access and a teenage child living at home and found that, with respect to the Internet, authoritative parents (those who are both warm and demanding) use evaluative and restrictive mediation techniques more often than authoritarian and neglectful parents.

Table 12.2   Parenting Styles

	High Expectation for Self-Control	*Low Expectation for Self-Control*
High Sensitivity	Authoritative Respectful of child's opinions; maintains clear boundaries	Permissive Indulgent without discipline
Low Sensitivity	Authoritarian Strict disciplinarian	Neglectful Emotionally uninvolved, does not set rules

SOURCE: Rhee et al. (2006).

Family Communication Patterns

Chaffee and McLeod (1972, 1973) developed the original model of family communication patterns (FCP) to describe families' tendencies to develop fairly stable and predictable ways of communicating with one another. As communication researchers, they were particularly interested in how information in the form of mass media messages was negotiated by families.

Chaffee and McLeod (1972, 1973) argue that family members typically communicate in two distinct ways. First, they can focus on other family members' evaluations of an object and adopt that evaluation. In other words, they aim for conformity and agreement (even if it isn't genuine) between family members. Because this process emphasizes the relationships between family members, Chaffee and McLeod called this process "socio-orientation." Alternatively, families might focus on the object in the environment by discussing it and its attributes and arrive at a shared perception of the object. Because this process emphasizes how family members conceptualize the object, Chaffee and McLeod called this process "concept-orientation." Consequently, children are socialized differently in regard to the processing of information contained in media messages. Children of families that tend to use socio-orientation rely on others to interpret the meaning of media messages to them, mainly their parents or peers. Conversely, children of families that tend to use concept-orientation elaborate on the concepts and ideas contained in the messages to determine their meanings. In other words, the two strategies to achieve agreement in families are associated with different media uses and interpretations by children.

Several researchers have examined how FCP shapes interactions around media in the home. Krosnick, Anand, and Hartl (2003) and Austin (1993) found that

By Brian Duffy, The Des Moines Register, North America Syndicate

Figure 12.12

SOURCE: Brian Duffy, *The DeMoines Register.* ©North America Syndicate

children whose families emphasize obedience and social harmony (socio-orientation) in discussions are typically unusually heavy viewers, whereas children whose families emphasize open communication and exchange of ideas (concept-orientation) are, by comparison, light viewers.

Krcmar (1996) used FCP to explore children's reactions to parents' attempts to mediate television. Parents and children (in Grades K–1 and 4–5) were given a TV guidebook that described available programs in three time slots. Parent-child pairs were unobtrusively videotaped and observed, and family communication patterns were measured using the FCP inventory. Parent FCP scores were used to predict parents' attitudes and behaviors, and child FCP scores were used to test predictions involving children's attitudes and behaviors. One interesting finding of this study is that communication and control orientation may be perceived differently by parents and children and may differentially affect parents' and children's choices of discourse strategies (Krcmar, 1996, p. 269). The researcher found that children who perceive the family to exercise higher control (socio-orientation) were less likely to be compliant with their parents' wishes.

Social Cognitive Theory

Social cognitive theory (SCT) provides a useful framework for the study of family communication and children's uses of media within the home. Bandura (1977, 1986) believed that social learning occurs in four stages. In the first stage, the individual attends to the behavior of another—either directly via a live model or indirectly via a mediated source such as television. In the second stage, the individual acquires and retains knowledge of the behavior. The third stage occurs when the individual can reproduce what he or she has seen or heard. In the final stage, the individual chooses whether to accept the model's behavior as a guide to performance, a decision that is determined largely by the perceived consequences of the behavior for the model (i.e., will something good or bad happen as a result of the behavior?).

Social cognitive theory has increasingly focused interest in the family as the social unit in which critical social learning occurs (Kunkel, Hummert, & Dennis, 2006). One example of this can be found in the research of James Lull (1990), who wrote extensively about how families provided contexts for learning how to use media (Stages 1 and 2), under what circumstances (Stage 3), and to what ends (Stage 4). From this perspective, it is perhaps not surprising that the best predictor of *children's* heavy television viewing is *parents'* heavy television viewing (see, e.g., Woodard & Gridina, 2000). A recent longitudinal study that tracked the question, "Which comes first: parents' heavy viewing or children's heavy viewing?" found support for the notion that children learn to use television from their parents (rather than parents using more television because their children do) (Davison, Francis, & Birch, 2005).

Reducing Screen Time in the Home

Parents are told that they should limit the amount of time children spend with entertainment screen media to 2 hours per day or less. Recent studies suggest that most parents feel that this is a reasonable recommendation, but because of the integral role of the media in the day-to-day life of children and families, parents have difficulty imagining how they can reduce screen time.

There are, however, several concrete suggestions that might be helpful for families trying to make the most of the media.

1. *Monitor children's time with all screen media.* Children report spending nearly 5 hours a day looking at a television, computer, or video game screen (Rideout et al., 2005; Woodard & Gridina, 2000). Parents, however, report that their children watched significantly less television than the children themselves reported and acknowledged the difficulty of monitoring media time. In one study, parents questioned researchers about what "counted" as media use (e.g., coviewing and background television) (Jordan et al., 2006). One important first step for reducing screen time is to get a clear sense of what that time amounts to and whether it is over the recommended 2 hours per day.

2. *Never put a television set in a child's bedroom.* Children with a television in their bedroom watch more television and have fewer rules about television than children without a television in their bedroom (Dennison, Erb, & Jenkins, 2002). National surveys show that most children have a television in their bedroom. Parents recognize that keeping televisions out of children's bedrooms is a means to control content exposure and time. Yet because of the difficulty the parents would face in trying to remove a bedroom TV, it seems much easier to simply never put it in there.

3. *Eliminate background television.* An easy starting point for many families may be to turn the television off when it is on in the background or when it is not considered the primary activity. As we saw earlier in the chapter, there is a strong correlation between the prevalence of background television in the household and children's time spent viewing. In addition, research by the Kaiser Family Foundation (Rideout & Hamel, 2006) found a negative association between the use of television as "background" and children's time spent reading.

4. *Limit television on school days.* The parents quoted in the Jordan et al. (2006) study at the beginning of the chapter were very focused on their child's school success. Indeed, this priority seemed to drive many of their decisions about television. Some parents restricted television use during the week to encourage homework completion and early bedtimes, and others took away television privileges when children did poorly in school.

5. *Identify nonscreen, in-home activities that are pleasurable to children.* Some parents may have trouble thinking of nonmedia activities that are safe and affordable. Parents may also worry that they will need to be the entertainers if they limit their children's television viewing. However, by restricting television viewing, parents can provide an opportunity for their children to develop their independent play skills. The TV Turnoff Network offers a list of alternatives to screen time that parents can suggest to their children when they sponsor their TV Turnoff Week each April.

Exercises

1. Think about the home in which you grew up. How many television sets were there? Where were they located? Do you think the number and placement of television sets had anything to do with your television viewing habits? In what way?

2. Imagine that you are answering a media use survey. How would you answer the following questions: How much time do you spend watching television on an average day? How much time do you spending using the computer on an average day? What about video games and music? Write your "average" times down. The next day, keep a "media use diary" in which you keep track of each medium you use and how long you use it. Include times when you "multitask." Add up the times at the end of the day. Does the diary show more time spent with media than you thought you were using? If it does, then you're like most American youth!

3. Try this experiment. Invite five friends over for a pizza and salad party. For the first party, just sit around the table, eating and conversing. Notice how much people eat. Wait a few weeks and invite the same people over for pizza, salad, and a movie. Research shows that people eat more when the TV is on than when it's off—families do too. Is this true for your friends?

4. Consider Lull's (1990) contention that media are implicitly and explicitly used to build family closeness and create personal space. Are there ways that family members in your home did this? Did your parents try to find common ground over a shared favorite TV show? Did your brother put up the sports page of the newspaper when he didn't want to talk to anyone?

5. Baumrind (1991) lays out typologies of parenting styles. Go to wikipedia.org or Google and type in *parenting styles* to see the kinds of questions researchers ask to assess whether parents are authoritative, authoritarian, permissive, or neglectful. Where do your parents fall? Do you think it shaped the rules they made (or didn't) about media?

6. Next time you are home for an extended period, try challenging your family members to go "screen free" for 24 hours. See if it changes your family dynamics.

7. One way that parents can supervise their children's TV viewing is with the V-chip. If you have a television set that was manufactured after 2000, you have a V-chip. Locate it on the TV and try to program it. How well does it work? For more information about the ratings parents use to program the V-chip, go to www.tvratings.org.

References

Atkin, D. J., Greenberg, B. S., & Baldwin, T. S. (1991). The home ecology of children's television viewing: Parental mediation and the new video environment. *Journal of Communication, 41*(3), 40–52.

Austin, E. W. (1993). Exploring the effects of active parental mediation of television content. *Journal of Broadcasting and Electronic Media, 37*, 147–158.

Austin, E. W., & Pinkelton, B. E. (1997, May). *Parental mediation as information source use: Political socialization effects.* Paper presented at the annual conference of the International Communication Association, Montreal, Quebec, Canada.

Bandura, A. (1977). *Social learning theory.* Englewood Cliffs, NJ: Prentice Hall.

Bandura, A. (1986). *Social foundations of thought and action: A social cognitive theory.* Englewood Cliffs, NJ: Prentice Hall.

Baumrind, D. (1971). Current patterns of parental authority. *Developmental Psychology Monograph, Part 2, 4*(1), 1–103.

Baumrind, D. (1978). Parental disciplinary patterns and social competence in children. *Youth and Society, 9,* 238–276.

Baumrind, D. (1991). Effective parenting during the early adolescent transition. In P. E. Cowan & E. M. Heatherington (Eds.), *Advances in family research* (Vol. 2, pp. 111–163). Hillsdale, NJ: Lawrence Erlbaum.

Bronfenbrenner, U. (1979). Contexts of child rearing: Problems and prospects. *American Psychologist, 34,* 844–850.

Certain, L. K., & Kahn, R. S. (2002). Prevalence, correlates and trajectory of television viewing among infants and toddlers. *Pediatrics, 109,* 634–642.

Chaffee, S., & McLeod, J. (1972). Adolescent TV use in the family context. In G. A. Comstock & E. A. Rubenstein (Eds.), *Television and social behavior* (Vol. 3). Washington, DC: Government Printing Office.

Chaffee, S., & McLeod, J. (1973). Coorientation variables in family study. *American Behavioral Scientist, 16,* 513–535.

Coon, K. A., Goldberg, J., Rogers, B., & Tucker, K. L. (2001). Relationships between use of television during meals and children's food consumption patterns. *Pediatrics, 107,* e6–e7.

Davison, K. K., Francis, L. A., & Birch, L. L. (2005). Links between parents' and girls' television viewing behaviors: A longitudinal examination. *Journal of Pediatrics, 147,* 436–442.

Dennison, B. A., Erb, T. A., & Jenkins, P. L. (2002). Television viewing and television in bedroom associated with overweight risk among low-income preschoolers. *Pediatrics, 109,* 1028–1035.

Eastin, M. S., Greenberg, B. S., & Hofschire, L. (2006). Parenting the Internet. *Journal of Communication, 56,* 486–504.

Galvin, K. M., Dickson, F. C., & Marrow, S. R. (2006). Systems theory: Patterns and (W)holes in family communication. In D. O. Brathwaite & L. A. Baxter (Eds.), *Engaging theories in family communication: Multiple perspectives* (pp. 309–324). Thousand Oaks, CA: Sage.

Gentile, D., & Walsh, D. (2002). A normative study of family media habits. *Applied Developmental Psychology, 23,* 157–178.

Grusec, J. E. (1973). Effects of co-observer evaluation on imitation: A developmental study. *Developmental Psychology, 8,* 141.

Hicks, D. J. (1968). Effects of co-observer's sanctions and adult presence on imitative aggression. *Child Development, 39,* 303–309.

Horton, R. W., & Santogrossi, D. A. (1978). The effect of adult commentary on reducing the influence of televised violence. *Personality and Social Psychology Bulletin, 4,* 337–340.

Jordan, A. (1992). Social class, temporal orientation and mass media use within the family system. *Critical Studies in Mass Communication, 9,* 374–386.

Jordan, A. (2004). The role of media in children's development: An ecological perspective. *Journal of Developmental and Behavioral Pediatrics, 25*(3), 196–207.

Jordan, A., Hersey, J., McDivitt, J., & Heitzler, C. (2006). Reducing children's television-viewing time: A qualitative study of parents and their children. *Pediatrics, 18,* e1303–e1310.

Kirkorian, H. L., Murphy, L. A., Pempek, T. A., Anderson, D. R., & Schmidt, M. E. (2005, April). *The impact of background television on parent-child interaction.* Poster session presented at the biannual meeting of the Society for Research in Child Development, Atlanta, GA.

Krcmar, M. (1996). Family communication patterns, discourse behavior, and child television viewing. *Human Communication Research, 23*(2), 251–277.

Krosnick, J. A., Anand, S. N., & Hartl, S. P. (2003). Psychosocial predictors of heavy television viewing among preadolescents and adolescents. *Basic and Applied Social Psychology, 25*(2), 87–110.

Kunkel, A., Hummert, M. L., & Dennis, M. R. (2006). Social learning theory: Modeling and communication in the family context. In D. O. Brathwaite & L. A. Baxter (Eds.), *Engaging theories in family communication: Multiple perspectives* (pp. 260–275). Thousand Oaks, CA: Sage.

Lull, J. (1980). The social uses of television. *Human Communication Research, 6*(3), 197–209.

Lull, J. (1990). *Inside family viewing: Ethnographic research on television's audience.* New York: Routledge.

Nathanson, A. (1999). Identifying and explaining the relationship between parental mediation and children's aggression. *Communication Research, 26,* 124–143.

Nathanson, A. I. (2001). Mediation of children's television viewing: Working toward conceptual clarity and common understanding. *Communication Yearbook, 25,* 115–151.

Nathanson, A. I. (2002). The unintended effects of parental mediation of television on adolescents. *Media Psychology, 4,* 207–230.

Reid, L. N. (1979). Viewing rules as mediating factors of children's responses to commercials. *Journal of Broadcasting, 23,* 15–26.

Rhee, K. E., Lumeng, J. C., Appugliese, D. P., Kaciroti, N., & Bradley, R. H. (2006). Parenting styles and overweight status in first grade. *Pediatrics, 117,* 2047–2054.

Rideout, V., & Hamel, E. (2006). *The media family: Electronic media in the lives of infants, toddlers, preschoolers, and their parents.* Menlo Park, CA: Kaiser Family Foundation.

Rideout, V., Roberts, D. F., & Foehr, U. G. (2005). *Generation M: Media in the lives of 8–18 year-olds.* Menlo Park, CA: Kaiser Family Foundation.

Rothschild, N., & Morgan, M. (1987). Cohesion and control: Adolescents' relationships with parents as mediators of television. *Journal of Early Adolescence, 7,* 299–314.

Saelens, B. E., Sallis, J. F., Nader, P. A., Broyles, S. L., Berry, C. C., & Taras, H. L. (2002). Home environment influences on children's television watching from early to middle childhood. *Developmental and Behavioral Pediatrics, 23*(3), 127–132.

Salomon, G. (1977). Effects of encouraging Israeli mothers to co-observe *Sesame Street* with their five-year-olds. *Child Development, 48,* 1146–1151.

Scantlin, R., & Jordan, A (2006). Families' experiences with the V-chip: An exploratory study. *Journal of Family Communication, 6*(2), 139–159.

Singer, J. L., Singer, D. G., & Rapacynski, W. S. (1984). Family patterns and television viewing as predictors of children's beliefs and aggression. *Journal of Communication, 34*(2), 73–89.

St. Peters, M., Fitch, M., Huston, A. C., Wright, J. C., & Eakins, D. J. (1991). Television and families: What do young children watch with their parents? *Child development, 62,* 1409–1423.

Stanger, J., & Gridina, N. (1998). *Media in the home: 1998.* Philadelphia: University of Pennsylvania, Annenberg Public Policy Center.

Steinberg, L., Elman, J., & Mounts, N. (1989). Authoritative parenting, psychosocial maturity, and academic success among adolescents. *Child Development, 60,* 1424–1436.

Tichi, C. (1991). *Electronic hearth: Creating an American television culture.* New York: Oxford University Press.

Vandewater, E. A., Bickham, D. S., Lee, J. H., Cummings, H. M., Wartella, E. A., & Rideout, V. J. (2005). When the television is always on: Heavy television exposure and young children's development. *American Behavioral Scientist, 48,* 562–577.

Woodard, E., & Gridina, N. (2000). *Media in the home 2000.* Philadelphia: University of Pennsylvania, Annenberg Public Policy Center.

CHAPTER 13

Media Literacy/ Media Education

Solution to Big Media?

Robert McCannon

> *The most fascinating thing about dusk is the lack of demarcation. It is one long smooth transition. By contrast, life, especially TV life, seems constantly to insist on more lines, more borders. TV expects you to shift entirely each half hour . . . demanding laughter, fear or sadness. . . . We complain incessantly about the fast pace of modern life, and say that we have* no *time. But we have lots of time, or every study wouldn't show that we watch three or four or five hours of television a day. It's that time the way it really works has come to bore us. Or at least make us nervous, the way that silence does, and so we need to shut it out. We fill time, instead of letting it fill us.*
>
> —Bill McKibben (1992, p. 72)

In today's overwhelmingly mediated culture (hypermediated), media are both good and bad. While the benefits are wonderful, whatever one's job, values, or background, the empirical data on media's probable harms to our children, culture, and government should be a warning, calling into question the enormous increases in centralization, power, and political influence of modern mainstream mass media (Big Media).

Starting with the U.S. Surgeon General's Report of 1971, health professionals, parents, teachers, researchers, and politicians have become increasingly concerned about ever more powerful electronic media. Never before has a society and its children been subjected to so much violence, sex, advertising, materialism, negative role models, and other antisocial messages. Never before has an electorate suffered so many negative and misleading political ads, financed by huge special interests' donations that wind up in media corporations' coffers.

Noted media scholar Robert McChesney (2004) calls today "the age of hyper-commercialism." It is an era in which the world's most dominant organizations are the media cartel and their major advertisers. They drive relentlessly for profit, overwhelming busy parents, teachers, counselors, and preachers. Daily, we create a historic new social experiment with the health of children and democracy. As mainstream media merge into ever larger global conglomerates (Big Media), advertiser-approved content expands to the exclusion of less profitable, prosocial programming for children and quality news for citizens. The resulting union creates the most powerful institution of our time, a combination of Big Media and Big Advertisers that controls society, economy, and politics—the Wal-Martization of the world's information, bigger than governments, loaded with billion-dollar ad budgets and manned by lobbyists galore. Persuasion on such a scale can only be described as a new form of censorship.

Demands for Change

In response, a wide range of reformers and organizations are working for change, demanding (a) *government censorship,* (b) increased *regulation,* (c) *reform* of the media system, and (d) media education or *media literacy* for children and adults. Thousands of organizations and programs dedicated to one or more of these solutions have arrived during the past decade.

Of course, many approve the status quo, especially if they profit from it. Most vested interests prefer the current system of advertiser-provided content and weak media regulation, mostly in the form of an ineffectual rating system. Regarding the aforementioned concerns, Big Media derides critics and commonly suggests that media "effects research" is flawed and that media harm no one. When pressed, Big Media defends its First Amendment rights to artistic expression and suggests that if children or democracy has media-related problems, parents and citizens need to be more responsible in their consumption. It is always the consumers' problem, never the producers' problem.

At this point, a caveat is always necessary. No responsible media critic or educator thinks that media are *completely* responsible for any problem, be it violence, poor grades, eating disorders, sexualized lifestyles, poor self-esteem, drug use, social injustice, lack of faith, materialism, rampant debt, or the weakening of our democracy. Many researchers and critics, however, believe media to be *one of the many causes* of these problems, a cause that could be controlled. Whereas sickness, poverty, racism, poor parenting, genetics, lack of education, and the like have proven difficult to remedy, media could and should be regulated.

Big Media: Part of the Solution?

Ironically, in this era of increasingly powerful global media corporations—an era in which a handful of conglomerates controls most mainstream media—the possibility exists that, with relatively little effort, Big Media could institute prosocial change.

Just one example: An impressive body of research shows that smoking in the movies, especially PG-13 movies, has increased dramatically in the past decade. It is now *the major cause of smoking initiation* in children and adolescents, recruiting 390,000 kids per year (Charlesworth & Glantz, 2005; Sargent et al., 2001, 2002). Interestingly enough, a simple media literacy device, placing an effective antismoking ad (i.e., one not made by a tobacco company) before such a movie, reduces the negative effect of the movie's smoking scenes (Charlesworth & Glantz, 2005).

The anti-ads would portray tobacco and tobacco companies in ways rarely seen in the pro-tobacco, mainstream media. Big Media in concert with Big Tobacco resists such a simple and life-saving innovation. Why? Could it have something to do with the hundreds of nontobacco companies owned by Big Tobacco that spend billions advertising in Big Media?

Thus, the present system of supply and demand, where supply (i.e., information) is controlled by conglomerates, promotes the interests of Big Media and its major advertisers, underreporting what is in the nation's best interests, helping to maintain the status quo (Straubhaar & LaRose, 2004), *even though it hurts children and costs society billions.* This is *censorship by Big Media,* and it is common. Consider just a few of many underreported stories: violence, poverty, food, drink, diets, alcohol, fashion, credit, lobbyists, gambling, and political ads.

In the current political climate controlled by media and advertiser lobbies, solving the media portion of these complex media-related problems will be difficult. It will probably take some measure of all four of the aforementioned solutions. Since the game is loaded in favor of Big Media, changing the rules will require unprecedented citizen knowledge of these options.

Government censorship is controversial and unpopular, although, as mentioned, our current violent, sexualized, and consumerist media are censored *most* by Big Media/Big Advertising in concert with their political allies. Ironically, Big Media protests censorship the loudest, demanding and receiving First Amendment rights, when, in fact, the First Amendment was designed to protect citizens and minorities from more powerful political entities.

Regulation seems to be unpopular, complicated, politicized, and, to some extent, misunderstood. It is typecast by vested interests as "wasteful" and part of "big government." *Reform,* always a loaded term, depends on media education, because *only the media educated perceive the need for media reform.* In a media-educated culture, reform should be a natural process, meeting the needs of the public (Potter, 2004).

So, *media education* and *media literacy* generate the least controversy and seem to be gaining in popularity as a proposed solution to what many perceive as a plethora of pervasive media-related problems.

Defining Media Literacy

The standard definition of media literacy is the ability to access, analyze, evaluate, and communicate messages in a wide variety of forms (Aufderheide, 1992). Because *evaluate* can be confusing, and many believe it to be a subset of *analyze,* a less confusing definition is *the ability to analyze, access, and produce media in a variety of forms and contexts.* A more detailed definition comes from Silverblatt (2001): Media literacy emphasizes the following:

1. A critical thinking skill that allows audiences to develop independent judgments about media content

2. An understanding of the process of mass communication

3. An awareness of the impact of media on the individual and society

4. The development of strategies with which to discuss and analyze media messages

5. An awareness of media content as a text that provides insight into our contemporary culture and ourselves

6. The cultivation of an enhanced enjoyment, understanding, and appreciation of media content

7. In the case of media communicators, the ability to produce effective and responsible media messages

Silverblatt (2001) suggests a *contextual* approach, one that emphasizes issues of production and consumption in addition to content. One can expand this to an analysis of information control and cultural ideologies (Kavoori & Matthews, 2004; Lewis & Jhally, 1998). As Jhally notes, "To appreciate the significance of contemporary media, we need to know why [messages] are produced, under what constraints and conditions, and by whom" (Lewis & Jhally, 1998, p. 111). Another definitive but less recognized element of media literacy is the goal of "purpose" or *activism.* "The purpose of developing media literacy is to give the person greater control of exposures and the construction of meaning from the information encountered in these exposures" (Potter, 2004, p. 63).

Noted author Mary Pipher (2001), in *Reviving Ophelia,* suggests that one of the most valuable activities for an adolescent is to have a *cause.* To this end, a national organization, the Action Coalition for Media Education (ACME), was brought into existence in 2002 to champion a more *independent* view of media education and to provide more *activist* educational solutions to media conglomeration. The keynote speaker at the first ACME conference, Robert McChesney (2002), summed up such a view of media literacy:

The problem we face with a hyper-commercial, profit-obsessed media system is that it does a lousy job of producing citizens in a democracy. A solution is real media literacy education that doesn't just make people more informed consumers of commercial fare, but makes them understand how and why the media system works—so they may be critics, citizens and active participants. This is the type of media education ACME is committed to doing.

Many agreed with McChesney, and ACME was created as the only national media education organization that has a Code of Ethics and refuses to accept funding from Big Media.

So many, in fact, are concerned about commercialization and materialism that the term *commercial literacy* is increasingly being used for media literacy programs that concentrate on the burgeoning forms and content of advertising (Eagle, 2005).

Far more controversial would be to consider representation and the institutional uses of media literacy in its definition. Nonetheless, such a definition seems logical since academic research is used to advise educational policy, particularly in an era of exploding new media technologies. As Livingstone (2004) says about media education, "Crucially, it is the *relationship* among textuality, competence, and power that sets those who see literacy as democratizing, empowering of ordinary people against those who see it as elitist, divisive, a source of inequality" (p. 13).

Thus, while a "best" definition of media literacy is hard to state, it might be *the ability to analyze, access, and produce media in a variety of forms and contexts and a desire to act upon such abilities in a manner that benefits a healthy and democratic citizenship.*

Media Education

What about the term *media education?* Drawing distinctions is difficult, and many use the terms *media education* and *media literacy* interchangeably, but media education should be broader, more diverse, and more targeted toward solutions than media literacy. Media education includes a greater variety of media criticism and scholarship from a greater number of traditional disciplines.

Media literacy draws upon education, communication, media studies, psychology, cultural studies, literature, literacy studies, telecommunications, and library and information science (Hobbs, 2005). Media education adds health, medicine, science, religion, political science, history, and technology. Media literacy tends to emphasize critical thinking for its own sake, whereas *media education is more concerned with using critical thinking methodologies to combat inequities and problems within culture.*

A recent United Nations Educational, Scientific, and Cultural Organization (UNESCO) study sums up the evolving definition of media education with an empowering vision of young media-educated adults: "The emerging new paradigms consider youth as protagonists who are capable of making decisions, exercising choices, and more important, as individuals who are active agents in promoting democratic processes and civic engagement" (Asthana, 2006, p. 6).

This chapter will review most of the literature of programs that use the term *media literacy* and a few that define themselves as media education. Most of these reviewed studies use media literacy methods for targeted purposes, and hence they should probably be termed *media education,* but in terms of actual practice, at this point, it seems to be a distinction without a difference.

After reviewing the results of these programs and curricula, this chapter will provide some of the basics of media literacy methodology, content, skills, and a few examples and exercises.

Uses of Media Literacy

Some see media literacy as purely a subject for teaching media techniques and associated critical thinking skills. Many English teachers view it as another aspect of teaching reading; people should learn how to "read" movie, television, the Internet, and other nontraditional image-based "texts," learning their techniques and strategies, just like one learns to read traditional text-based media (Brown, 2001; Potter, 2004; Tyner, 1998). Such practitioners emphasize "creativity and authentic self-expression" (Hobbs, 2004b, p. 43).

While accepting such purposes, others see media literacy as a way to engage students in "exploring economic, political, social and cultural issues in contemporary society" (Hobbs, 2004b, p. 43). These educators teach the aforementioned techniques and skills but, in addition, use a carefully chosen body of media content to thoroughly and honestly investigate media-related issues and, it is hoped, produce prosocial attitudes, behaviors, and solutions.

Currently, media literacy "interventions" are incorporated into an incredibly wide variety of programs and curricula—everything from standard school disciplines to antidrug programs, smoking prohibition, antipoverty efforts, positive body image, antiviolence, sobriety, nutrition education, and help-the-homeless efforts. Many activists and organizations are attempting to use media literacy to control absenteeism, raise grades, promote self-esteem, reduce teacher/student/parent friction, and more.

Others are involved in a variety of similar "literacies." Eagle (2005) would add *commercial* literacy to the list. *Internet* literacy is the subject of an extensive $1.8 million, 3-year U.S. Department of Education study involving new ways to teach higher level comprehension skills to 1,500 economically disadvantaged youth (Ascione, 2006).

These and other "literacies," such as information literacy, computer literacy, business literacy, technology literacy, and health literacy, seem to have overlapping meanings. The National Forum on Information Literacy, which is supported by more than 90 education organizations, is attempting to provide definitions (see www.infolit.org/definitions/html).[1]

Thus, there are many stakeholders, theories and studies, and some confusion encompassed by this growing wealth of research areas. Nonetheless, one thing is certain: The vast majority of practitioners in these areas want to help youth and citizens become better able to deal with a hypermediated future, and while media literacy is a small part of school curricula and social programs, the use of media literacy is growing rapidly and has contributed content to most of these new literacies.

Media education and media literacy supporters can be found from the PTA to UNESCO (Asthana, 2006) and to all of the major U.S. medical organizations, especially the American Academy of Pediatrics (Committee on Public Education, 1999). Adherents are found in Japan, Canada, Australia, New Zealand, the United Kingdom, Sweden, Finland, Brazil, and every state in the United States (Kaiser Family Foundation, 2003; Yates, 2004). A large number of media literacy programs and media education programs with media literacy components are being funded and implemented. It is symbolic of this growth that Texas has instituted a wide-ranging media literacy program and includes media literacy on its mandatory high school graduation test (Hobbs & Frost, 2003).

Does Media Literacy Work? Reviewing the Literature

In some ways, enthusiasm for media literacy and its resulting expansion is surprising. The empirical data on the effectiveness of media literacy are new, small, and poorly done. Some respected scientists are not convinced of its effectiveness at all. Noted University of Iowa media effects researcher, Craig Anderson, suggests that media literacy, at least in terms of violence reduction, is *not* effective:

> To minimize observational learning, priming, automatization, and desensitization, an intervention must either reduce the child's exposure to violence or reduce the likelihood that the child will identify with the aggressive characters, perceive their actions as realistic and justified, and perceive aggression as acceptable. General media literacy programs do not specifically attempt to accomplish either of these two types of reductions; thus, it is not surprising that there is no valid research demonstrating effectiveness of general media literacy education. (Anderson et al., 2003, p. 103)

There are fewer than a hundred media literacy studies, compared, for example, to the thousands of studies about media effects or smoking effects. The research is weak and mixed, leaving the question of media literacy's efficacy very much up in the air.

As a relatively new field, funding is scarce. Media literacy studies tend to treat small samples. They are frequently survey based, simple in design, nonrandomized, and short term. Replicated treatments are next to impossible to find.

Careful quasi-experimental studies exist, but there are no longitudinal data about changes in *attitude,* and positive results on *behavioral* change are nonexistent or, at best, weak. Many media literacy interventions are done by specially chosen and trained individuals or, worst, by the researchers themselves, rather than day-to-day teachers. Too often, the treatment evaluations are done by the intervening group. Most of the studies are quantitative, despite a need for qualitative studies (Fox, 2005; Potter, 2004).

Nevertheless, there is room for enthusiasm. Many practitioners and researchers find that media literacy programs can successfully change attitudes and, sometimes, behaviors. These studies suggest that the content and skills of media literacy can be taught, and they might be able to enhance childhood, culture, and democracy by leading students and citizens to understand, access, and produce media.

More important, when student media literacy programs include parents, as well as changing students' habits of media consumption to a healthier media "diet," even greater success seems likely.

Teaching Media Literacy Skills

Research strongly suggests that the content and skills of media analysis can be taught. Critical reading and viewing of multiple texts, as well as recognizing point of view, bias, commercial connections, target audience, text and subtexts of messages in multiple forms, construction techniques, and the ability to express the related viewpoints and information omitted from media messages (i.e., the "untold stories" of media), were taught in one form or another and to varying degrees in many of the following studies.

Quin and McMahon (1995) produced one of the first large-scale ($n = 1,500$) measurements of media literacy skills in Australia. Students learned to identify the purpose, target audience, point of view, and qualities of representation of media messages.

Hobbs and Frost (1999) demonstrated similar skills acquisition, as well as showing that media literacy that is integrated into existing curricula can be superior to prepackaged curricular units. Recently, one of the most innovative and carefully done studies of media literacy skills (Hobbs & Frost, 2003) did a quasi-experimental measure of all 11th graders ($n = 293$) in one high school, compared to a random sample of 89 eleventh-grade students in a similar school. The teachers, with some expert aid, designed media literacy interventions that were integrated into a redesigned 11th-grade English curriculum.

The interventions varied somewhat from teacher to teacher and, in total, represent a useful list of the range of innovative possibilities for teaching media literacy, but most emphasized reading, listening, viewing, and writing comprehension, as well as identification of point of view, construction techniques, omissions, purpose, target audience, and comparison-contrast. Treatment students outperformed controls by varying amounts in all areas.

The study had a number of weaknesses: an unusually motivated faculty, an independent faculty who taught the lessons in differing styles, a mostly middle-class suburban student group, a nonrandomized treatment sample, and uncontrolled influences of other courses' media education that were not evaluated or controlled. Nonetheless, it showed that to varying degrees, students can learn media literacy skills and content. Equally interesting were the results concerning traditional English skills.

> This research shows that media-literacy instruction embedded in a secondary-level English language arts course can be effective in meeting traditional academic goals. Teachers need be less fearful of making use of a wider range of multimedia fiction and nonfiction texts as study objects when their primary goal remains the development of students' skills of reading comprehension, interpretation, message analysis, and writing. (Hobbs & Frost, 2003)

Were such results to be replicated, they could influence the inculcation of a wider range of texts and objectives in traditional disciplines without jeopardizing the development of basic skills.

Hobbs (2004a) used a different evaluation of the aforementioned study's data (Hobbs & Frost, 2003) to analyze the effectiveness of a subset treatment of media literacy upon advertising's effect. The treatment resulted in increases in knowledge of advertising preproduction techniques, the students' ability to analyze a print ad, the identification of a target audience and attention manipulation techniques, and the ability to identify ad message subtexts. Livingstone and Helsper (2006) added to the understanding of children's cognitive processing of ads, and they suggest that different treatments are effective for different ages. They use the term *advertising literacy* (another "literacy").

Thus, it is obvious that media literacy encompasses many media-related analytic skills. It is much more than media criticism. Nonetheless, while appreciating increases in students' analytic abilities, many media educators believe that media literacy/media education (ml/me) can accomplish more than analytic skills. Can it make students more knowledgeable and healthier citizens? Can it create a more functional democracy? Might ml/me counter the barrage of advertising that promotes substance abuse, gambling, debt, materialism, eating disorders, obesity, and violence? Perhaps it can create more involved parents. Will ml/me achieve the mythical goal of education, causing students to love education and become lifelong learners, or is it just another educational fad?

Media Literacy and Public Health: Tobacco, Alcohol, and Drugs

Most research has been done in the public health domain because (a) government agencies sponsoring grants see media literacy as a way to counter negative media effects, which the grantors define as health risks (Huston et al., 1992), and (b) it is easy for the public to understand relatively simple problems, such as targeting children with tobacco and alcohol ads, inappropriate sex, and too much violence.

With just a single media literacy session, Austin and Johnson (1997) increased third and fourth graders' understanding of the intent of alcohol advertising and decreased the treatment groups' desire to be like the ads' characters. Even 3 months later, the study decreased their expectation of positive consequences from drinking alcohol and decreased their likelihood of choosing an alcoholic drink ($n = 225$). A small study that used alcohol education and discussion of beer ads among 12- to 18-year-olds predicted cognitive resistance (counterarguing) after the treatment group viewed a 20-minute sports show with four beer ads. The effect lasted months or years after the intervention ($n = 83$) (Slater et al., 1996).

Media literacy has been used in tobacco prevention and cessation efforts (Gonazales, Glik, Davoudi, & Ang, 2004). A large-scale ($n = 1,372$) study by the New Mexico Media Literacy Project used a 6-day intervention with three booster sessions and demonstrated changed attitudes about alcohol and tobacco advertising, anger toward tobacco companies, a greater awareness of advertising, and a desire to live a healthier lifestyle (McCannon, 2002, 2005).

Teen leaders, advised by adults, were effective in developing and teaching an antitobacco curriculum for high school students. The study (Pinkleton, Austin, Cohen, & Miller, 2003) notes that media literacy influenced tobacco use at various stages of the decision-making process. Tobacco users and nontobacco users gained knowledge of tobacco ads' techniques of persuasion, becoming better able to resist them. Nontobacco users gained determination to dissuade peers from smoking. Other students were less likely to identify with people in ads who smoked, and the students felt that they were less susceptible to peer pressure toward smoking.

Use of Emotion

An impressive 6-day quasi-experimental pilot study ($n = 119$) by Austin, Pinkleton, and Hust (2005) was followed by a larger statewide study ($n = 723$) by Austin, Pinkleton, and Funabiki (2007). A precise antitobacco media literacy program combined innovative tobacco information, media literacy skills, analysis, and production with an activation/efficacy element that increased students' comprehension of tobacco advertising methods and students' desire to participate in tobacco prevention advocacy. If one is doing tobacco prevention, this could be a good model.

There is a discussion within the media literacy field about whether media literacy should use emotional activation techniques such as participation in advocacy work, anger at tobacco companies, mistrust of alcohol corporations, and so on. Some think treatments should only teach critical thinking skills. Austin et al.'s (2005, 2007) treatment represented a sophisticated and effective compromise between the two schools of thought.

Regarding activation, Austin et al. (2005) point out that inoculation treatments are effective in promoting resistance to persuasive appeals. As to the more pedagogical approaches to prevention, about which empirical data are rare, such approaches have been more successful at increasing knowledge, especially of media, than changing attitudes or decision-making outcomes (Austin et al., 2005; Graham & Hernandez, 1993).

Further considering the role of activation, media literacy that includes an emotional factor seems to overcome the seductive quality of emotive advertising. Recent media literacy studies have noted an apparent paradox. While media literacy programs can create resistance to persuasive messages, experimental group participations *is often associated with higher levels of participants' perceived desirability of media portrayals* (Austin, Chen, & Grube, 2006; Austin, Chen, Pinkleton, & Johnson, 2006).

Thus, participants need to understand media literacy concepts *and* have the *motivation* to apply this knowledge through logical decision making (Austin et al., 2002). Austin, Chen, Pinkleton, and Johnson (2006) provide an exhaustive analysis of how media-literate students can, for example, enjoy emotion-filled beer advertising yet remain less susceptible to its persuasive subtexts. "Stated more simply, it is possible that participants in the media literacy training have learned to manage their response to enticing media portrayals while still recognizing that message creators produce messages that are highly desirable" (Austin, Chen, Pinkleton, & Johnson, 2006, p. 426).

Returning to tobacco programs, the Centers for Disease Control and Prevention (CDC) and other government entities endorsed media literacy for drug prevention and sponsored a variety of curricula. Few have been seriously evaluated or independently replicated. One, *Media Literacy for Drug Prevention,* done in conjunction with the *New York Times,* reported achieving a number of positive results, but it was only evaluated by teacher surveys (Kaiser Family Foundation, 2003).

A catch-all prevention program with a media education thread, Life Skills Training (LST) by Dr. Gilbert Botvin, takes on important issues and possesses research evaluation, yet it lacks independence from industry support. LST began as an antitobacco program and has expanded to include marijuana and alcohol. It possesses a weak media literacy strand, 1 of 12 lessons, which seems simplistic, watered down, and lacking in the all-important emotive or activation component previously discussed. Programs such as the very successful Florida *Truth* campaign, now the American Legacy Project, have set the standard for activating students against tobacco companies, and they are great models.

Nonetheless, LST was recommended by the CDC in 1997 (Mandel, Bialous, & Glantz, 2006). Recently, LST has been used for the prevention of HIV and even risky driving (Life Skills Training, 2006). The official LST Web site says,

> The results of over 20 studies published in major scientific journals such as the *Journal of the American Medical Association* consistently show that the Life Skills Training program dramatically reduces tobacco, alcohol, and marijuana use. These studies further show that the program works with a diverse range of adolescents, produces results that are long-lasting, and is effective when taught by teachers, peer leaders, or health professionals. (Life Skills Training, 2006, p. 1)

Recent analysis of the research that led to the CDC's approval indicates that LST improved youth knowledge of smoking's physiological effects but did not provide evidence of reduced youth smoking. "In fact, decision-making skills actually moved in the wrong direction" (Mandel et al., 2006).

It is important to note that following CDC approval, Philip Morris (PM) spent millions of dollars to spread the LST program, convincing health professionals, administrators, teachers, and parents of the benefit of LST, including hiring one of the world's largest public relations firms. Philip Morris even used third-party entities to disguise Philip Morris' financial support. Thus, hundreds of thousands of students in more than 20 states have taken or are taking LST.

A standard media education question would be, "Why would Philip Morris go to such extremes to promote tobacco prevention *in a stealthy manner?*" Philip Morris usually publicizes all its supposed prosocial programs. Perhaps, Philip Morris is just a well-intentioned philanthropist, but its history would suggest otherwise.

Mandel et al. (2006) document many industry communications in which PM repeatedly relates its opposition to programs that aggressively lay blame on the tobacco companies' 40 years of deceitful actions. Big Tobacco says such programs demonize them unjustly. Big Tobacco opposes cessation programs that emphasize their irresponsible advertising to youth in magazines, television, and movies.

Also, relatively little of LST is focused on reducing tobacco use *directly,* and there is a controversy about the effectiveness of LST. Almost all of LST's evaluation has been done by LST's creator, Philip Morris' employee, Gilbert Botvin. Whether effective or not, the tobacco companies' documents demonstrate Big Tobacco's concern with public relations *and* suggest that LST *diverts large amounts of resources from other, more proven, more aggressive, and more successful* programs that do attack the tobacco companies' actions and advertising and focus on reducing tobacco use (Mandel et al., 2006).

Many programs avoid the mediocrity and expense of programs such as LST by creating their own *resources.* Over the past decade, Utah's Safe and Drug-Free Schools Program has developed a far more detailed prevention curriculum than LST. Labeled *Prevention Dimensions,* it constantly adds to its media literacy strand. Containing almost 200 lessons, divided K–12, Prevention Dimensions is a comprehensive, age-appropriate health program that features many of LST's techniques and, more important, attacks tobacco companies' advertising in a manner that LST fears to do.

Conundrum: Big Money

The situation presents a conundrum for media literacy/media education (ml/me) scholars. At times, organizations with vested interests see an advantage in working with media education organizations or creating media literacy curricula and research for their own public relations' interests. Such organizations, like Philip Morris, often seek to deflect criticism and, at times, regulation. They will even create "Astroturf" organizations (fake grassroots groups), fake news reports, articles that attack their opponents, and biased studies to aid their public relations campaigns and lobbying for or against legislation. Such industries often fund research that supports their point of view.

More important, the vested interests can produce ml/me curricula that put a positive light on the vested interest, often avoiding legitimate criticism or deflecting attention from criticized activities. *This is not confined to tobacco.* Other examples include Channel One, the cable television industry, the video game industry, alcohol companies, television, movies, toys, and the advertising of food to very young children.

Hence, understanding all types of media education requires vigilance when one encounters industry-supported ml/me curricula. Scrutinize such lessons carefully. Always look for the untold stories in the content. Try to be aware if some "expert" like Dr. Botvin is being paid substantial sums to create the curricula, and, most important, notice if the vested interest is handled with kid gloves.

Media Literacy and Public Health: Nutrition and Obesity

The obesity epidemic seems directly related to the food industry's advertising that targets children as young as preschoolers (Kunkel, 2005; McLellan, 2002). Five-year-olds prefer food that comes in McDonald's wrappers to unbranded packages (Robinson, Borzekowski, Matheson, & Kraemer, 2007). Such data suggest that media literacy would be a natural solution to such food-related problems. Several large industry-sponsored programs exist in this area.

With such media literacy programs, industry hopes to be seen as part of the solution to these problems and, perhaps, avoid advertising restrictions, particularly those aimed at advertising toward young children and toward food products that have little or negative nutritional value (Kleinman, 2003; Teinowitz, 2001). This is acknowledged by the industry itself (Cincotta, 2005). Furthermore, Hobbs (1998) suggests that industry-supported media literacy might reduce criticism of the potential negative effects of the media, which are supported, of course, by much advertising that can be interpreted as unhealthy.

Coca-Cola, McDonald's restaurants, Kellogg's, Nestlé, and others have operated Concerned Children's Advertisers (CCA) as a nonprofit organization in Canada since 1990 and have provided media education for children through public service announcements (PSAs), as well as school and home media literacy resources on drug use, self-esteem, and bullying.

A similar European media education program, Media Smart, is operating in 20% of the United Kingdom. It aims to "help people to understand the distinctions between different media services, to appraise their content critically, to use the tools which are increasingly becoming available to navigate the electronic world, and to become empowered digital citizens. It will also help children to learn how to maintain critical distinctions such as those between fact and fiction (especially in interactive environments) or between reporting and advocacy, as well as how to assess commercial messages" (Media Smart, 2003, p. 1).

Nonetheless, CCA's and Media Smart's stated objectives lack measurable specificity, and these media education programs have been evaluated by relatively superficial means. CCA surveys mass recall, such as 74% of Canadian children believe that the advertisements helped them to better understand television (Eagle, 2005), rather than surveying changes in attitude or behavior (CCA, 2004). Media Smart also uses teacher satisfaction to measure the program (Eagle, 2005; Muto, 2004). Certainly, more rigorous evaluation is needed if the program is to be taken seriously.

And while these efforts may benefit youth, a major question concerns why these industries with their tremendous resources do not subsidize scientific research that systematically evaluates these detailed issues.

Big Media is seldom willing to evaluate the effects of advertising on the health of children and citizens in a democracy. In addition, one wonders why so few advertisers support efforts to create more media-literate consumers (Armstrong & Brucks, 1988; Eagle, 2005), and when considering the value of junk food, industry-sponsored "health programs," and industry motives, one cannot help but recall the feeble efforts of Big Tobacco that continue today, using boring PSAs and dubious educational curricula to "educate" youth to live tobacco-free lives.

A version of Media Smart's 10-lesson program has recently started in several U.S. locations with the support of the National Institute of Child Health and Human Development (NICHD). Media-Smart Youth: Eat, Think and Be Active is for adolescents 11 to 13 years old. It uses hands-on activities to help evaluate complex media messages and teaches media awareness, media production, nutrition, and physical activity ("For Your Information," 2006).[2]

A small Head Start media literacy study (Hindin, Contento, & Gussow, 2004) for parents succeeded in teaching nutrition and diet information, as well as analysis skills and, perhaps most important, changing parents' TV behaviors. Valkenburg (2005) reviews parental mediation techniques, suggesting that exposure to advertising predicts children's materialism and toy requests, which, in turn, affect parent-child conflict. Her study of 360 child-parent pairs found that discussion techniques were more effective than restrictive methods at reducing these effects. This reinforces other research suggesting that media education can work when parents are involved. A weakness of the study was its failure to include a technique of "enlightened" restriction (i.e., leading children to self-regulate and/or reduce their media diets).

Media Literacy and Public Health: Body Image

Several studies hold out potential for media literacy in preventing or treating eating disorders. However, simple treatments are, by no means, guaranteed of success (Irving & Berel, 2001), and changes in *behavior* are hard to produce. A review by Littleton and Ollendick (2003) suggests that school programs have little positive effect on body image satisfaction and disordered eating but can affect self-esteem, life skills, and awareness of media pressures.

A substantial study (Steiner-Adair et al., 2002), organized by the Harvard Eating Disorders Center, evaluated 500 seventh-grade girls who took part in Full of Ourselves: Advancing Girl Power, Health, and Leadership. They were tested before, immediately after the treatment, and 6 months later. The treatment involved 10 sessions, including "Dieting Dilemma," "Claiming Our Strengths," and "The Power of Positive Action" (Giedrys, 1999, p. 1). Improvements in knowledge and weight-related body esteem were significant. Unfortunately, given the extent of dieting in young girls, behavior, such as skipping meals and the subjects' dieting, was unaffected. The lack of behavioral results reflects an unfortunate trend in the results of a number of media literacy studies.

Another study, a randomized control trial with 226 Girl Scouts, found that a six-lesson (90-minute, biweekly) unit

> had a notable positive influence on media-related attitudes and behaviors including internalization of sociocultural ideals, self-efficacy to impact weight-related social norms, and print media habits. A modest program effect on body-related knowledge and attitudes was apparent at post-intervention (i.e., on body size acceptance, puberty knowledge, and perceived weight status)

but not at follow-up. Significant changes were not noted for dieting behaviors, but they were in the hypothesized direction. Satisfaction with the program was high among girls, parents, and leaders. (Neumark-Sztainer, Sherwood, Coller, & Hannan, 2000, p. 1466)

The National Eating Disorders Association's "Go Girls" program of media literacy skills helped high school girls' sense of empowerment and self-esteem regarding media images of women's bodies (Nirva, Levine, & Irving, 2000) and reduced internalization of the slender media-constructed ideal, reduced desire for thinness, and increased a sense of self-acceptance and of empowerment (Piran, Levine, & Irving, 2000).

A small study (Wade, Davidson, & O'Dea, 2003) compared a similar curriculum with a purely self-esteem-focused intervention, and the media literacy intervention had a more positive impact on weight *concern,* although *neither affected dietary restraint.* The authors thought the more collaborative methodology was a factor, but the study was very small.

While these studies evinced many objectives, Neumark-Sztainer, Wall, Story, and Perry (2003) suggest that programs should concentrate only on decreasing weight concerns and improving body image. They gave an exhaustive survey (221 items) to 4,746 students, expecting that weight body concerns, psychological well-being, and health nutrition attitudes would be the major factors in causing unhealthy weight control behaviors. However, *only weight body concerns* correlated significantly with the unhealthy behaviors.

While this research points in some positive directions, especially in the area of self-esteem, much more work remains to be done if such programs are going to affect behavior.

Media Literacy and Violence

As shown in previous chapters, all but a handful of experts, researchers, critics, and medical people accept that media violence can cause aggression, fear, desensitization, and other antisocial effects. Of the few who resist this body of research, most are connected to Big Media (Huesmann & Taylor, 2004). And since media increasingly contain more problematic content and are increasingly marketed toward youth (Anderson & Bushman, 2001), many media researchers are attempting to combat the effects of media violence, which are seen as connected to the high and, once again, rising levels of violence in the United States.

Using media literacy as a vehicle to reduce aggression and promote prosocial behavior is complex. Some commonly implemented media education treatments could be beneficial. Others might be doing harm and accentuating the very effect they try to mitigate. An excellent review of the subject concludes,

Studies show that adults' comments before or during media exposure can reduce the impact of violent programming on children's aggressiveness under some circumstances. Experiments involving more extensive media literacy curricula show that some approaches can alter attitudes toward media violence and, in a few cases, intervene in aggressive behavior. Studies of the impact of antivio-lence media productions reveal that although such efforts can be effective, unanticipated "boomerang" effects are prevalent. Overall, the effectiveness of the 3 types of interventions was highly variable, and age and gender differ-ences were prominent. (Cantor & Wilson, 2003, p. 363)

Violence: Changing the Media Diet

A standard recommendation of media literacy proponents is to limit the media "diet" of youth; indeed, restricting children's media consumption, *if done right*, can be a benefit, but limitations can also boomerang or rebound. One of the most care-ful (if small) studies of media literacy and strategies designed to limit media con-sumption was done by Tom Robinson (see Robinson, 1999; Robinson, Saphir, Kraemer, Varady, & Haydel, 2001; Robinson, Wilde, Navracruz, Haydel, & Varady, 2000). It crystallized the value of this approach by combining elements of limiting television and video games, working with parents, and teaching children to be wiser viewers. *The experimental groups showed decreases in obesity, requests for toys, and, most impressively, aggressive behavior.*

Two months of lessons by regular teachers (trained by the research staff) moti-vated children to monitor and reduce their screen watching habits. Then, a 10-day TV-turnoff period was followed by more lessons and an attempt to *limit viewing to 7 hours per week.* Resources and instruction were provided for parents. After 20 weeks, the researchers achieved significant reductions in self-reported and observed physical aggression and verbal aggression in the experimental school. These studies reveal substantial potential for this combination of media literacy interventions that influence children and parents to recognize the value of limiting their media diet.

A program modeled on Robinson but with a shorter treatment, The 10-Day Challenge, put most emphasis on limiting students' media diet as a form of *strike* against broadcasters, advertisers, and violent entertainment producers. It operated in 20 Quebec and Ontario elementary schools and was evaluated in one high school. Five hundred students participated, and evaluations surveyed students, teachers, and parents.

Fifty percent of the students took the challenge, walking through the streets of their city at lunchtime, just like workers did when the labor movement started organizing. Of the students, 78% participated, and 72% said that the challenge was very or quite useful and they would do it again. Two thirds of parents found the challenge very or quite useful, and 86.2% of staff considered the process very or quite important.

The challenge increased physical activities for half of the students; 45% reported increased time spent with friends, 25% reported increased time spent with parents and increased help for tasks at home, 32% reported decreased physical violence, and 27% reported decreased verbal violence. Verbal and physical violence at home decreased 38%. Sixty-five percent of students reported increased media awareness, and 60% of parents and 90% of teachers reported improvement of children's viewing skills (Brodeur, 2005). The study has a number of statistical and structural flaws, but the details above are presented to show an example of the type of enthusiasm, effect, and evaluation that characterizes many simple media education programs that this review will not be able to consider. Obviously, more comprehensive research is needed in all these areas.

However, media restriction can also produce negative results (Nathanson, 2002), as can rating systems that may increase youth desire to see forbidden programs (Bushman & Cantor, 2003; Bushman & Stack, 1996; Cantor, 1998). More research is needed to discover if the effect outweighs the value of the proscriptions and descriptions.

Thus, it would seem that parents and caregivers need to carefully observe the effects of limitations on children. At this point, it may be obvious but necessary to point out that *giving children other enjoyable and valuable things to do,* especially teaching them to engage in self-directed creative play, rather than banning activities in a vacuum, is always a good strategy.

Violence: Coviewing and Mediation

Another oft-suggested strategy of media literacy is to actively watch with children. Research on giving them information before, during, or after they experience media produces some interesting results. Short media literacy "moments" while experiencing media can influence active cognition, rather than passive absorption, which can empower decision making.

A fascinating study with a fairly large group, 351 second through sixth graders (Nathanson & Cantor, 2000), found that just a brief introduction to a short cartoon clip, asking children to consider the victim and his feelings, caused young children, especially boys, to be more likely to identify with the victim. The children also thought the violence was less justified. Unlike the control group, the intervention changed how children viewed the characters and the violence. The intervention also reduced both boys' and girls' appreciation for the cartoon hero (Woody Woodpecker).

Because parents use cartoons as a babysitter, seeing none or few negative effects of cartoons, this study is important, for as Cantor and Wilson (2003) note,

> Research shows that television violence, especially cartoon violence, typically minimizes the depicted consequences to the victims of violence, and violent cartoons may be especially likely to promote imitation, desensitization, and attitudes accepting of violence (e.g., Wilson et al., 2002). In many so-called classic cartoons (e.g., Tom 'n' Jerry, Woody Woodpecker), the violence is the essence of the plot: The entire story often depicts repeated instances of violence and violent revenge, with the attacks shown to have trivial and comic

consequences and with no attempt to demonstrate real suffering on the part of the victim or to promote empathy with his or her plight. (p. 375)

This study is also valuable in that it suggests that "questioning," a main technique of media literacy, can be effective.

Criticizing violent media content may reduce the inculcation of aggressive attitudes and behaviors. Praise may actually *promote* them (Austin, 2001; Bandura, 1986; Buerkel-Rothfuss & Buerkel, 2001). Perhaps more important, coviewing violence with parents who do not make comments or question the media content may indicate to children and adolescents *that the parents approve of the behavior* (Austin, 2001; Buerkel-Rothfuss & Buerkel, 2001; Hicks, 1968; Horton & Santogrossi, 1978; Nathanson, 1999).

Several researchers report that giving youth information about violence causes them to devalue violence, but the studies give conflicting results, do not measure behavior, or fail to affect behavior when the adult who gave the information is not present (Corder-Bolz, 1980; Hicks, 1968; Horton & Santogrossi, 1978).

A recent study (Nathanson, 2004) compared another media literacy strategy, giving information about production techniques, with giving negative information about violent characters. The former mediation was either ineffective or increased chances for negative effect in children, whereas *giving negative information was more effective, especially with younger children.* This study is also interesting from the standpoint of the value-neutral versus activist/media literacy versus media education debate.

Mediation interventions were also effective in other studies (Nathanson, 2003; Nathanson & Yang, 2003), but it seems that methodology is important. Nathanson and Yang (2003) found satisfactory results of mediation statements placed within violent programming, but somewhat of a rebound effect on older students (ages 9–12). It is possible that younger students (ages 5–8) had a need for the information, but older students found it condescending. Both of these studies were most effective with "heavy" viewers of media violence.

Thus, it would seem that coviewing and mediation that includes censure of violent content by adults can influence the attitudes and opinions of children about violence. One should be careful in the form, method, and age-appropriate nature of the intervention, and heavy viewers of violence should be targeted.

In addition, it would seem that questioning or trying to elicit empathy for victims can also be effective. Perhaps most important is the notion that *making no comment or neutral comments produces an effect similar to praising the violence.* And again, one should recognize the limitations of these studies, which are very diverse and short term, have not been replicated, and, of course, rely on parents and caregivers being present to coview.

Achieving coviewing will also require a substantial change in the culture, as Muto (2004) suggests that up to 85% of children's viewing in multiset households is unsupervised and 58% of children ages 4 to 9 have televisions in their bedrooms. Thus, researchers suggest school programs as a way to promote healthy attitudes.

Media Literacy Programs as a Violence Intervention

Just as some of the aforementioned studies show that students can learn about the techniques and nature of mass media, other larger scale studies show similar results (Dorr, Graves, & Phelps, 1980; Rapaczynski, Singer, & Singer, 1982; Singer, Zuckerman, & Singer, 1980). They usually contain a thread dealing with violence, but it is usually impossible to tease out an independent effect for violence intervention (Cantor & Wilson, 2003). Nonetheless, a few small studies have attempted to ascertain the effectiveness of media literacy as a violence prevention intervention.

Doolittle (1980) showed one group how violent media were created and allowed another group to try producing programming. The former showed no effect, but the latter group self-reported perceived reality, arousal, and *increased aggression,* indicating that media production, especially as an antiviolence method, should be done very carefully and only in conjunction with detailed planning and precise evaluation (Cantor & Wilson, 2003).

Huesmann, Eron, Klein, Brice, and Fischer did two revealing studies in 1983. First, they taught second and fourth graders in three hour-long training sessions over 6 to 8 weeks about the difference between characters in violent shows and real people. They also revealed the production techniques that enabled these characters to do impossible things, and they showed that real people used different strategies to solve problems. The pretest was 9 months before the intervention. The posttest followed it by 3 months and revealed that *the intervention created had no effect* on perceived realism of television shows, peer-assessed aggression, or reported viewing levels of television violence. The study suggests that teaching simple media literacy production techniques alone may not reduce children's vulnerability to violent media.

Huesmann et al. (1983) later modified their intervention. Children made a film depicting students who were deceived, led to break rules, or were harmed by violent media. They wrote papers about the negative violent media, videotaped their reading of the papers, watched the tapes, and discussed the messages. Control group children did the same procedures about an innocuous topic.

The results were significant. While rates of viewing TV violence for the two groups did not differ, treated students devalued television more and believed it less realistic. They were also assessed by peers as less aggressive than the comparison group 4 months after the intervention. Thus, it would seem that *active, carefully planned, and targeted media literacy content and production methodologies can reduce the harmful effects* of watching violent content, whereas *simplistic methods may cause the reverse.*

As we have seen, Robinson et al. (2001) achieved significant reduction in aggression with a comprehensive 18-lesson media literacy curriculum that involved media limitation and parental involvement, suggesting the importance of a comprehensive program or, at the very least, involving the parents.

Vooijs and van der Voort (1993) tested the wisdom of media literacy based on the difference between fantasy and reality. Their 5-week curriculum increased students' perceptions of the seriousness of TV violence and their knowledge of real violence. It reduced their approval of TV violence and their perceptions of TV's realism. Unfortunately, it demonstrated the *importance of continuing media literacy throughout the curriculum,* as some of the significant effects of their study had disappeared at the 2-year follow-up posttest.

An innovative elementary study was undertaken with children in Grades 1 through 3 (*n* = 177) by Rosenkoetter, Rosenkoetter, Ozretich, and Acock (2004). Thirty-one brief lessons revealed the many types of distortion in TV representations of violence. The intervention reduced children's viewing of violent TV and their identification with violent TV characters. While more successful with girls, boys were judged by their classmates to have *reduced their behavioral aggression* after treatment, an unusual result.

More research is needed on matching media literacy treatments, methods, appropriate content, and duration of intervention with different ages and types of students. Some of the preceding studies indicate methods and content that worked with young children and some with older children, helping them deal with media violence more effectively. Some were failures, especially when methods were not age appropriate or precisely thought out. Until more considered, longitudinal studies with larger randomized samples are done with a greater variety of objectives, practitioners need to remain cautious and careful.

> The measurement of aggressive behavior as well as various related attitudes should be encouraged in future studies. In addition, as researchers continue to test various curricula, one useful approach would be to assess other harmful outcomes of exposure to media violence, such as desensitization and fearful reactions.
>
> Although most of the researchers reported cognitive changes in how children interpret violence, the interventions generally failed to modify children's enjoyment of or exposure to violent programming (Huesmann et al., 1983; Rosenkoetter et al., 2002 [boys]; Sprafkin et al., 1987; Vooijs & van der Voort, 1993). Given the potential for desensitization, reducing children's preference for media violence is undoubtedly an important goal of media literacy. The study by Robinson et al. (2001) showed that reducing children's media exposure without targeting violence can reduce antisocial behavior even in the absence of instruction about media violence effects. (Cantor & Wilson, 2003, p. 387)

Using Media Productions

A handful of studies suggest that use of media production can be beneficial. Antirape productions, used in carefully planned curricula, can produce beneficial results among college students and older men (Intons-Peterson, Roskos-Ewoldsen, Thomas, Shirley, & Blut, 1989; Linz, Fuson, & Donnerstein, 1990). However, a similar objective produced mixed results among 15- to 16-year-olds (Winkel & DeKleuver, 1997). Use of a made-for-TV movie about date rape with high school students, *No Means No,* followed by a discussion with two trained college students produced some positive results but led some males (approaching significance) to a rebound effect of less responsibility of the perpetrators and less seriousness of the offense (Filotas, 1993).

In a larger study, Wilson, Linz, Donnerstein, and Stipp (1992) showed a critically acclaimed made-for-TV movie, *She Said No,* to a national sample of 1,038 participants the day before it played nationally. The telephone survey again revealed mixed results: positive feelings about the seriousness of the problem, but a rebound effect occurred among older males who tended to blame the victim.

Antiviolence researchers have used TV programs to suggest alternatives to violent acts, using high-quality antiviolence PSAs with little effect (Biocca et al., 1997). A more carefully planned study used Court TV cases to form the core of a 3-week curriculum that involved active deconstruction and role-playing (Wilson et al., 1999). It showed *significant reductions in 513 randomized middle school students' verbal and physical aggression,* as well as increases in empathic skills and knowledge of the legal system.

These studies suggest that using powerful productions to achieve prosocial results is, at best, a risky business that can result in prosocial effects but can reinforce antisocial attitudes. Obviously, the choice of media content is important, as is getting permission to show controversial media, and it is crucial to create appropriate methodology. Equally important is a carefully constructed strategy of previewing preparation and postviewing activities that *allow the participants to have ownership in the process.*[3]

In a related area, media literacy might be able to help at-risk youth. The New York State Office of Children and Family found there were benefits of media literacy for supporting decision-making skills for young at-risk students (Behson, 2002). The Massachusetts Juvenile Justice System developed Flashpoint, a media literacy program designed to deconstruct media and promote cognition about moments that might lead the students to risky actions (Budelmann, 2002; Moore, DeChillo, Nicholson, Genovese, & Sladen, 2000).

Channel One: The Largest Media Literacy Experiment

Approximately 35 million of the 42 million U.S. students are exposed to corporate advertising, mostly for foods of dubious nutrition (Molnar, Garcia, Boninger, & Merrill, 2006) and ever increasing youth-targeted advertising of a questionable nature. Schools used to be a sanctuary, but are no more. As a Ralph Nader organization notes,

> Our nation is in the grips of a commercial hysteria. Sometimes it seems like everything is for sale. At *Commercial Alert,* we stand up for the idea that some things are too important to be for sale. Not our children. Not our health. Not our minds. Not our *schools.* Not our values. Not the integrity of our governments. Not for sale. Period. (Ruskin, 2006, p. 1, emphasis added)

Commercialism in schools is controversial because students have great buying power and are a captive audience. Many are obviously vulnerable to advertising's effects. In 1980, Consumer Reports counted 234 organizations marketing commercial products in schools, ranging from candy to sponsored educational materials (SEMs). SEMs can be useful or very biased toward the sponsoring company (Consumer Reports).

Clearly, advertisements in schools are an important and separate genre. The American Academy of Pediatrics posits that students may be more receptive to school ads (Brighouse, 2005; Buijzen & Valkenburg, 2003; Reid & Gedissman, 2000). Schools seem to provide a "legitimizing" effect.

Recently, Channel One (C1) has reduced some of its ads for violent and racy movies in favor of ads for candy, gum, video games, skin care products, and the armed forces. The health detriments of candy and gum seem obvious. Some ask if schools should sell video games, which compete for homework time. Skin care products may serve a useful purpose, but they also promote an image of beauty that few girls possess and seem to lead to eating disorders and damaged self-esteem. Glamorizing the armed forces may seem patriotic, but should this be the role of schools?

Research indicates that C1's ads are effective, perhaps more effective than the same ads when seen at home (Infante, Rancer, & Womack, 2003; Palmer & Carpenter, 2006). Interestingly, such corporate advertising adds little to school finances and, if removed, school programs would continue (Molnar et al., 2006).

So, why do schools sign up for C1? The schools receive wiring and small television monitors in classrooms. C1 gets students' eyeballs. Students *must* watch a C1-produced, 12-minute news and advertising program every day. Two minutes consist of four 30-second ads, and the other 10 minutes are supposed to be "current events news." Frequently, the "news" stories feature commercial products. For example, one about Michael Jordan focused on his many Nike products. C1 claims that the hardware "given" to the schools and the value of its "news" programming justify the schools' donation of students' time and attention and the effects of C1's ads.

Since product placement is such a large part of media literacy, it is significant that C1 will not directly say whether it is paid for its product placements, but when questioned, C1's current leader, just like former administrators, artfully dances about the question with sly talk about "advertorials" (Obligation.com, 2006a). Thus, if a parent or school board member wants to know if a guest announcer on C1 who hawks a music CD is paying C1 for the opportunity (and how much), *one simply cannot find out, and this happens in a taxpayer-created environment!*

Approximately 8 million U.S. middle and high school students in 12,000 schools watch C1's show (Business Wire, 2008). Twelve minutes per day equals *one full week of class time annually,* so this would seem to be an important issue.

Critics charge that C1 propagandizes captive students with ads for harmful products. Moreover, they say it legitimizes products, about which the schools are given no choice. Parents, teachers, and administrators have no knowledge of what will be aired until the day of the broadcast, and in reality, few parents ever know what kind of C1 ads are programming their children.

For years, critics have asserted that C1's "news" is simplistic and out of context. Most busy teachers are not trained or motivated to teach current history, and the wide range of issues they are asked to teach is a formula for dubious outcomes and a breach of commonly accepted educational principles.

For example, on October 13, 2006, C1 broadcast a detailed Gatorade "Play of the Day" about a football player who gained a record 648 yards in a football game. Not a negative word escaped the enthusiastic lips of the announcer.

Trained media educators would immediately ask, "What is being left out in this MTV-like sports story?" And, indeed, the day before the story ran on C1, the *Chicago Tribune* castigated the many unsportsmanlike things the record-breaking coach did to pile up his runner's yards, concluding that the coach "embarrassed himself, his players and his school. But he inadvertently provided everyone involved a valuable lesson: When you stop at nothing to succeed, you turn success into a kind of failure" (Obligation.com, 2006b, p. 1).

The story was surely worthwhile and could have provided a teachable moment for C1's captive audience, but the teachable moment about sportsmanship escaped 7 million C1 students because, somehow, it escaped C1's producers . . . or did it? C1's story was exciting and arousing. It probably raised C1's "ratings." Could it be that turning the "record" into a story about sportsmanship and ethics might have lowered C1's appeal (and sold less video games and gum)?

Channel One's Media Literacy Curriculum

C1 suggests that teachers should use their ads and "news" for media education, and C1 provides a media literacy curriculum. Critics charge that C1's media education programs are like Big Tobacco's "education" programs, merely a public relations device to head off criticism. In 2000, Renee Hobbs and Paul Folkemer wrote C1's media literacy curriculum, *Media Mastery* (Business Wire, 2008), which was to use C1's programs for content. It could have been called Media Mystery, because after several years, C1 has removed it from Web sites that used to carry it.

Media Mastery was announced with fanfare and promoted for several years to convince doubtful teachers, parents, and school districts to adopt C1. The theory went like so: "We may have ads that could be bad for your kids, and your teachers may not be trained to do current events, but our media literacy program will fix those problems." Is there some irony here?

Millions of students using media literacy curricula, what an opportunity to study media literacy! People expected surveys and studies, but nothing significant was forthcoming. People who read *Media Mastery* asked questions about why there was *nothing* in *Media Mastery* about junk food, skin care products, rap music, sleazy movies, video games, and the other ads C1 continually sold. In 10 lessons, *Media Mastery* only examined *one product,* and that was the automobile *industry* (not a single automobile, but the industry as a whole), and to this author's knowledge, C1 never advertised automobiles.

Media Mastery is a key piece in the efficacy puzzle that media literacy/media education represents. It taught skills objectives, spending much of its time comparing the use and effect of different media. From this author's point of view, it did not use the important emotive factor, and its level of complexity was over the head of the average high school student (much less millions of middle schoolers). It contained few examples that would have connected the student's concrete media world to the abstractions of media literacy, *which is media education's greatest strength.* And, of course, it avoided any embarrassing questions about media corporations, particularly C1.

Important questions remain unanswered. Huge numbers of U.S. students are affected by C1. This was a perfect opportunity to study media literacy. Could media literacy offset the effect of C1's slick youth programming cues, contexts, sophisticated advertising, Internet tie-ins, and target-keyed news content? Did the school environment add "legitimacy" to the ads? Why was the opportunity to thoroughly evaluate curricula produced by a well-known media literacy expert lost?

The Research on Channel One

There is some research on the use and effectiveness of C1 and media literacy. Interestingly enough, many students seem to enjoy C1 (Bachen, 1998; Johnston & Brzezinski, 1992; Johnston, Brzezinski, & Anderman, 1994). Research on C1's benefits is mixed and of poor quality (Bachen, 1998; Ehman, 1993; Johnston et al., 1994). As expected, students who discuss C1 with parents and older students exhibit a small tendency to improve in knowledge of current events (Anderman & Johnston, 1997; Bachen, 1998; Ehman, 1993; Johnston et al., 1994; Tiene & Whitmore, 1995; Whitmore & Tiene, 1994).

A number of teachers feel they have no role in the adoption of C1 (Barrett, 1995; Knupfer & Hayes, 1994), and others felt unprepared to integrate C1's diverse content into their courses (Bachen, 1998). One study found that C1 increased students' feelings about the truthfulness of ads (Krcmar, 2001)

Perhaps most important, *several studies found that C1 increased the desirability of the products advertised* (Bachen, 1998; Greenberg & Brand, 1993; Krcmar, 2001). As Austin noted in her excellent review (Austin, Pinkleton, Van de Vord, Arganbright, & Chen, 2006), "Bachen (1998) for example, found that >30% of adolescents who viewed *Channel One* believed that '*seeing the ads on Channel One made me want to go out and buy these products,*' and 20% said that *they actually did so.*" And a more recent study has found documented what every parent of young children knows: Seeing ads increases materialism (Buijzen & Valkenburg, 2003).

There are two new studies on C1. Austin, Chen, Pinkleton, and Johnson, (2006) and Austin, Pinkleton, Van de Vord, et al. (2006) created a posttest-only study (n = 239) of randomized seventh and eighth graders who underwent media literacy treatment before or after seeing a C1 episode with somewhat different expectations for the two studies. Both studies appear to have come from the same sample and used similar treatments. While cross-referencing similar factors, they digressed slightly in emphases. The basic treatment was a short media literacy lesson. In each study, the media literacy treatment was divided—one treatment adding an emotive component *designed to make the students angry* at media companies that were "buying them."

Both studies concluded that *the treatment with the emotive component was more effective.* Austin, Pinkleton, Van de Vord, et al. (2006) concentrated on students' preexisting orientations toward relevant media genres. Students responded differently to various measures, depending on their use of media. Heavy users of reality television placed a lower value on measures of materialism after the treatment, and in general, the study supported the value of media literacy for reducing the effects of television advertising. Those students who valued news programming tended to focus more on the news segments. Other students, described as valuing "reality" programming, gravitated more toward the ads. *The treatment seemed to decrease this group's materialistic values,* a hopeful sign for media literacy advocates.

Austin, Chen, Pinkleton, and Johnson (2006) found that the majority of students liked C1's programming, but a significant minority did not. Media literacy training increased recall of both news and advertisements, and the intervention increased skepticism toward advertisers, but the studies were unable to hypothesize about the effect of increased skepticism on future purchases. Those who appreciated C1 were associated with higher values of civic involvement. Students who liked C1 also tended to like the ads, which was associated with materialism. As Austin, Chen, Pinkleton, and Johnson note, "Those who responded positively to the content and presentation style learned more from it *but also tended to want things that they saw in the advertisements*" (p. 429, emphasis added).

Thus, students who liked the program tended to like the ads, and students who liked the ads desired more products. The good news is that education perhaps can buffer C1's ads, but the results also provide justification for concerns about the commercialization of the classroom and the results of showing C1 ads to students, especially without a careful media literacy program directed by trained teachers. This represents a significant pragmatic and ethical problem for practitioners of media literacy.

In addition, only 15% of the students correctly believed that their school "never" approves of Channel One commercials, giving support to the "legitimizing" factor. That C1 is a complex situation is a vast understatement. That it is of critical importance is obvious. Austin, Chen, Pinkleton, and Johnson (2006) conclude,

> This combination of results does confirm that *Channel One* offers the *potential* for positive effects along with the likelihood of effective persuasion by advertisers and the potential for the cultivation of materialism. Positive and protective effects such as current-affairs knowledge, political efficacy, and skepticism toward advertisers were enhanced by media-literacy training. These results therefore suggest that schools that wish to use commercial programming such as *Channel One should include in-service training* for teachers on media-literacy education and should require that media literacy be taught with specific reference to the programming. *Whether schools should use commercial programs such as Channel One at all remains a question of ethics that empirical data such as these cannot resolve.* (p. 431, emphasis added)

Note that the study did not address longitudinal effects or whether teachers actually *use* media literacy, whether they discuss the program, or even if they pay any attention to it at all. Surveys have shown that teachers do not consistently discuss C1 content with their students, perhaps preferring to grade papers while it is shown (Anderman & Johnston, 1997; Barrett, 1995, 1998; Johnston & Anderman, 1993; Knupfer & Hayes, 1994).[4]

None of these studies evaluated the teachers' ability to put "current events" into a historical, social, or issue-based context, something that history and social studies teachers are, it is hoped, trained and able to do, but most other teachers are not.

Thus, there is conflicting news for media literacy and C1. While contradictory and frustrating, the studies reveal a potential for increasing students' knowledge of media but also point strongly to increased commercialization of students. More research is needed in these areas and also on the value of C1's news and, especially, on the ability of non-social studies teachers to create relevant discussion around C1's "news" tidbits.

All stakeholders need to consider the moral implications of annually devoting a *week* of school to C1, which seems to clearly add to the materialistic effects of advertising, thereby placing a *moral burden upon the schools to provide competent media literacy programs to counter the effect of the C1 ads supplied by the schools.*

At this point, one has to wonder again why so little quality research has been done on C1. Millions of students are participating in this huge and mandatory social experiment, and only a handful of studies have evaluated it and media literacy. Why does this multi-billion-dollar corporation fail to research its own profitable work?

Media Literacy and Parents

Many parents are concerned about media's effects on commercialism, addictions, and aggression. As we have pointed out, parental involvement in media literacy programs is important and, probably, essential to success (Anderson et al., 2003; Robinson et al., 2001). Indeed, many parents are trying to mitigate media's effects on their children. A simple survey in pediatric offices of 1,831 parents of children (ages 2–11) from 27 states, Canada, and Puerto Rico indicated that 23% of parents restrict media viewing, 11% use more instructive techniques, and 59% use both of these methods. Only 7% indicated they provided no guidance for their children (Barkin, Ip, Richardson, Klinepeter, Finch, & Krcmar, 2006). As more than half of children have televisions in their bedrooms, one wonders about the quality of these self-reported parental interventions, but nevertheless, many parents seemed concerned about media effects.

We have seen that parents can reduce undesirable media effects, including media-induced aggression (Nathanson, 1999, 2004; Nathanson & Cantor, 2000). Parents can also mitigate children's anxiety (Cantor & Wilson, 2003; Cantor, Sparks, & Hoffner, 1988; Wilson, 1989; Wilson & Weiss, 1991). The effect of ubiquitous alcohol portrayals on television, video games, movies, sports, and music videos can be moderated and may be reduced by parental reinforcement of positive and counter-reinforcement of negative messages (Austin & Johnson, 1997; Austin, Pinkleton, & Fujioka, 2000). Parental actions can also moderate children's materialism and purchase requests (Buijzen & Valkenburg, 2003; Valkenburg, 2005).

Last, it may be obvious, but one should note that parents can increase children's academic performance and learning in a variety of content areas, as indicated by the success of many home-schooled children, so parents could teach media literacy to their children. Some commonsense, pragmatic advice for parents raising children in this hypermediated culture can be found at http://acmecoalition.org/ raising_media_savvy_kids. General resources can be found at http://acmecoalition .org/essential_resources.

Media Literacy and Corporate Funding

Important issues among media literacy practitioners are corporate funding and whether to focus on behavioral/attitudinal outcomes or communication skills outcomes as a measure of the effectiveness of a media literacy intervention (Kubey & Hobbs, 2000). As we have seen, *the latter dichotomy reflects a basic difference in philosophy between media literacy and media education.* Those who want to focus predominantly on value-neutral communication skills tend to favor corporate involvement and funding, and those who distrust corporate aid tend to favor behavioral outcomes as a measure of success. Hobbs (1998) describes the issues from the pro-corporate point of view:

> According to this view, media organizations have a social responsibility to help people develop critical thinking about the media simply as a consumer skill, and the good that media organizations can do by contributing their funding outweighs the potential dangers of its use as part of a public relations campaign, or as a shield against government regulation. Critics of this position point out that the media industry is cleverly taking advantage of educators who are so underfunded and desperate for materials that they will jump at anything that is provided free of charge. Some believe that media organizations are effectively taking the "anti-media" stand out of the media literacy movement to serve their own goals, co-opting the media literacy movement, softening it to make sure that public criticism of the media never gets too loud, abrasive or strident. (Cowrie, 1995, p. 1)

But is teaching basic media skills enough? U.S. education spends more per capita than any other country. Schools teach reading for 12 years, yet love of reading and ability to read are decreasing. We teach history, but knowledge of history is down. Civics is taught, but few vote, and so it goes for health, math, science and so forth.

So, the big question is not what skills of media comprehension does media literacy teach but whether it positively affects behavior. Do we want media education to merely aid in creating more informed but more debt-laden, addicted, aggressive, sexualized, time-wasting, hedonistic consumers? Or do we want media education to help create a culture of more knowledgeable, thoughtful, concerned children and adults? Do we want media education to help produce better citizens or only clever cynics who participate minimally, if at all, in their democracy?

Do we want media literacy to contribute to greater numbers of media-informed parents who will read, play, and talk with their children, or do we want to generate more glib, media-savvy moms and dads who increasingly consume media in one room while their children interact with screens in another?

As we have indicated, powerful and rich conglomerates can take over the media education of our children in order to benefit their reputations and bottom lines.

Should junk food companies, Wal-Mart, Exxon, Channel One, Philip Morris, Budweiser, purveyors of video games, creators of movie violence, and the cable television industries be allowed to dominate the production of media education curricula?

They do now.

The most commonly accepted principle of media literacy is that media create culture. Obviously, corporate media literacy curricula also create culture. Another principle is that all media are commerce. Following the money is important. So, if Renee Hobbs (1998) says, "The good that media organizations can do by contributing their funding outweighs the potential dangers of its use," one needs to ask, why is she saying that? One answer could be that she was paid to write a C1 *Media Mastery* curriculum that was of limited value, used mostly to deflect attention from the negative aspects of a C1 program that is in one of every four U.S. schools.

In today's hypermediated world, Channel One exemplifies the raw political power exerted by a billion-dollar corporation. Corporate entrance to schools is a political process, and today, politics means money and media. *Understanding these intersections should be a main objective of media education.*

We now have e-mails, released by Congress, from the infamous convicted felon and briber of congressional representatives, Jack Abramoff, discussing how to conduct a public relations campaign on behalf of Channel One and how to attack those individuals who dared to fight C1's entry into U.S. schools. The campaign was to involve talk show hosts and tens of thousands of dollars' worth of articles to "bash loonies" and "weasels," such as Commercial Alert's Gary Ruskin and Obligation, Inc.'s Jim Metrock (Committee on Finance, 2006). Thus, it is getting very hard for parents to know what media corporation and what media literacy expert can be trusted with the welfare of their children.

One answer lies in pursuing an *active, independent, and activist* form of media education, one that attempts to lead students to investigate issues and take a position on the media-related problems of the day. That means taking on Big Media, the corporate dominance of our elections, the lawmaking process, and much more. Could this do anything but increase the health, education, and well-being of our children and democracy? Big Media will not support that kind of media literacy, and that is the biggest argument in favor of independent media education.

Teaching Media Literacy

With the exception of complex research interventions that use parents and limit kids' media diets, not much is known about how to use media education to change behavior.

Nonetheless, media education certainly can teach (a) information about the media, (b) skills of analyzing media, (c) techniques of media production, and (d) strategies of active involvement in media-related issues. What follows are some suggestions for teaching ml/me based on the small body of quality research and this author's experience.

Teaching is an art, and despite the empirical data to the contrary, most teachers think they are artists, so giving advice is a risky business that is only attempted by the committed or the foolish. This author probably falls into both categories, but having trained more than a thousand teachers in 4-day media education workshops (limited to 30 attendees) and having seen many successes and failures, here are some tips that come from more than 30 years of experience.

As indicated by the preceding review of literature and radical as it may seem, *affect is more important than content. Emotion is crucial to media education,* hence students must be involved affectively as well as logically (i.e., a media education classroom must be entertaining, and students must feel like they are central to the process of investigation). A multimedia presentation can be exciting and involving or, as so many of us have experienced, deadly. What is more boring than a PowerPoint presentation in which the presenter reads quotations from the screen? Surely, this is as deadly as the plague, killing learning without regard for the educational corpus.

Emotion is primary. Why? Many students are addicted to the most powerful entertainment media our species can produce, so especially when dealing with media, the class must be *involving* and *entertaining.* Great teachers have a sense of drama and a sense of humor. They laugh *with* their students. They move around the room. They are not afraid to be enthusiastic. They notice when students are losing interest, and they are *flexible,* changing lesson plans and examples in mid-class to meet changes in students' levels of interest.

Asking questions about media examples is the key method of media literacy instruction. It is a Socratic process that involves students, honors their judgments and opinions, and creates guided discussion about media. Resonating with the group, listening to students' answers, and, often, letting their responses dictate the direction of the discussion are a must. After all, learning about media is a lifelong process. Creating lovers of media education is one's objective, not pouring a small, finite set of concepts into them.

Insert information into the discussion in a way that seems natural. During discussions, many opportunities for teachable moments arise, and at those times, *one should give students the information they need.* At that time, students will value didactic information. The challenge is to time such moments correctly and avoid the universal tendency of teachers to lecture until all eyes but one glass over.

Credibility is crucial. Media criticism is not media education. One must not seem to be trying to prove that students' media are inferior and that students are passive slaves of media manipulation. When such a perception becomes widespread, the class is doomed. *One's philosophy must be that all media are good and bad.* Only if the facilitator is interested in an investigation of certain principles *with* students will success become possible.

Fascinate students with the reality of media techniques. The teacher has powerful advantages. As many have written, the more students watch, the less they know, so there is a great potential for the teacher being able to interest students. Teaching about the construction and power of images and text can be interesting to the point of inspiration. Make it so, but *avoid continually using examples of what is wrong.* That creates guilt, and no one likes to feel guilty. Nor do students like the person who makes them feel guilty. Encourage students to bring in their own media examples. If they do, they are with the program; if they will not, it is not a good sign.

Challenge students. If the instructor heeds the aforementioned suggestions, students will accept some of the effects research. One should not fear bad news and seek only to entertain. Many media educators do this, and they cannot wait to toss out the video camera and gush about the wonder of their students' videos. This does not equal media education or any kind of education. One should be a responsible and demanding *guide,* a model of intelligent investigation into the media universe.

As the review of the literature clearly shows, when choosing examples to deconstruct, one should always be aware of student interests and appropriateness. What is appropriate for one age or one school may not be appropriate for another. *A good motto is when in doubt, leave it out.* There is no shortage of media examples, and creating a battle with one's administrators and parents is not worth the effort to include some juicy media example in one's curriculum.

The best tool for providing examples in a classroom like this is a multimedia database that can be stored on a computer and projected in the classroom. The database can merely be a variety of examples stored in various folders on the computer's desktop. The objective is to allow one quick access to an appropriate example *in response to the flow of the group's discussion.*

The major goal is to leave the students or group *wanting more media education. The process is more important than the content.* Inspiring students works better than trying to scare them, and positive examples work better than negative. It is hoped that the facilitator will be perceived as a mentor rather than one who is indulging pet media peeves. When deconstructing an example, *accept all honest interpretations as "correct."* If students feel free to disagree with the teacher, the classroom becomes a safe, enjoyable, and rewarding place for media learning. Remember, we spend 12 years teaching kids to read, which is the most valuable media education skill, and as adults, they do not read. Try to beat the odds.

Content of Media Literacy

Media literacy's body of content or the *information* taught varies widely, but some basic principles are fairly standard in all media literacy programs. While wording may vary, there are five traditionally accepted "basic principles" of media literacy:

1. Media messages are constructed.

2. Messages are representations of reality with embedded values and points of view.

3. Each form of media uses a unique set of rules to construct messages.

4. Individuals interpret media messages and create their own meaning based on personal experience.

5. Media are driven by profit within economic and political contexts.

Turning these principles into questions to be asked about a media example makes them into discussion "tools of analysis." For example, in the case of number one (media messages are constructed), one could ask, "How is this message constructed?"

An updated and more precise list of these principles, one that reflects this author's experience, as well as the dramatically changing media problems faced by our culture, would include the following new list of principles of media education.

1. *Media construct impressions of "reality."* An individual's notion of reality is constructed by the deluge of media she or he experiences. As George Gerbner, dean of the Annenberg School of Communication, was famous for saying, children's formative stories used to be told by people—family, friends, teachers, preachers, and so on. Today's storytellers are television, movies, video games, the Internet, iPods, text messages, and magazines, mostly controlled by Gerbner's "handful" of corporations (i.e., Big Media). This is not a Luddite-like position but merely one that recognizes the extent and power of our recent, massive, and imprudent social experiment with our children and democracy.

2. *Media messages affect our decisions, perceptions, and pocketbook decisions.* As Jean Kilbourne is famous for saying and as third-person effect research confirms, people do not think they are affected by advertising, but they are. We all are. The same is true for other forms of media.

3. *Media monopoly, by controlling "reality," threatens democracy.* Decision making in a democracy demands informed citizens. An increasingly small group (five to eight) of huge media-holding companies, Big Media, controls thousands of companies. They, in turn, are dominated by a few global corporations (the Fortune Forty) that pay for most of the advertising sold by Big Media. Hence, less people control more and more mainstream content, including news. This is dangerous, especially since the Supreme Court decision in 1978 (5–4), which now allows these same corporations to exercise political speech rights, radically changes how we elect our representatives. The Constitution's makers sought to avoid this situation, and the First Amendment was actually designed to protect citizen's rights to speech, not big companies.

4. *Monopoly is not capitalism.* Some think media education and media reform are "liberal" issues. On the contrary, fighting monopoly is at the heart of free enterprise, supply, and demand (i.e., capitalism). These have traditionally been concepts that attracted people from all parts of the political spectrum.

5. *Knowing the untold stories is an antidote for propaganda.* All communication is media. Media are always propaganda; that is, they are constructed by someone with a point of view, using techniques of persuasion. Most tell just one side of a story. The side not told, the "untold story," is the related information that is left out of a media message. This can be very subtle or very obvious, but knowing or searching for untold stories is very empowering, and it is a beacon in the search for the truth.

6. *Fantasy differs from reality.* Media can create worlds of imagination that range from nearly real to the totally fantastic, causing people to want to live a particular world's lifestyle. Some lifestyles cause children to strive to be doctors and philanthropists, benefiting humanity. Others are fantasies that can cause time to be

wasted and people to hurt themselves and others. Advertising suggests that our highest calling is to shop. Media literacy tries to help individuals reconcile this spectrum of different worlds.

7. *Vast commercial interests control most media.* As people use media, they should always be alert to the self-interest of media makers, especially Big Media. Is this cute and cuddly radio station, movie, or book created by a huge conglomerate seeking to advance its own economic or political agenda? Often we cannot know the answer to such questions, but asking the question is an important mental exercise in this world of media power that is concentrated in the hands of very few people. Are they concerned about health? Do they care if people are smart or merely buyers? Are they interested in creating active participants in society and culture or merely creating more consumers of their products?

8. *Individuals construct unique meanings from media.* Experiencing media is an active process. People can comprehend different meanings from the same piece of media. Respecting everyone's interpretation is a key strategy for successful media education.

9. *Media teach.* Media can inculcate standards, philosophies, morals, values, ethics, ideals, ideologies, and principles. Budweiser sells drinking beer. Shopping malls whisper that buying stuff solves problems. Church opines that spirituality saves souls. Cadillac repeatedly fuels the notion that status comes with expensive cars. A politician who says, "I refuse to bring up my opponents' troubles with the IRS," has just called his opponent a crook.

10. *It is all about emotion.* Ever wonder why TV ads do not mention the product until the last second of the ad? Emotion is the name of the game. Ads must build emotion to cut through the "clutter" of the thousands of other ads we are exposed to each day. Once emotion is created, it transfers to the product irrespective of any logical connection. This is mostly a subconscious process. Most media seek to engage one's feelings and are wary of one's mind.

11. *Subliminalism exists.* Any part of a media message that one absorbs in an unconscious manner is subliminal. Since one "thinks about" so little of what one experiences, much remains in one's unconscious memory for a time, affecting individuals differently. When a TV ad has 25 scenes in 30 seconds, much stimuli does not reach the level of conscious thought, leaving a good deal to the individual's subconscious. The same can be said for print-based media, but at least one has a greater opportunity to go back and experience it again.

12. *All human communication uses a "language of persuasion."* This is important. All communication is created by someone with a point of view and is biased, sometimes subtle and other times not so subtle, trying to sway people for some purpose, usually to someone's benefit. Truth becomes subjective in a hypermediated culture, whether the medium is fiction or nonfiction or put out by an advertising agency, public relations firm, church, or nonprofit. The good news is that everyone can learn its techniques and "deconstruct" media.

13. *The language of persuasion is created with simple techniques.* All media use specific techniques (like flattery, repetition, fear, and humor). For a number of decades, this author has called these "the language of persuasion." Understanding the language, like these principles, is a survival skill for today's citizens.

14. *Media effects can be obvious or subtle.* Few people believe everything they see and hear in the media, but negative political ads obviously reduce voter turnout, possibly a massive disadvantage for democracy. Few rush to buy beer after a Budweiser ad, and experiencing violence will not turn one into a killer, but it could make it easier for one to lose one's temper, affecting family, friends, and community—a subtle difference. Thus, the effects of media are complex and can be understated or blatant.

15. *Media include "texts" and "subtexts."* What actually happens is the text of a media message. It is objective. The actual impression imparted by the message is the subtext. It is subjective. In Bill McKibben's famous example, the text of a McDonald's television ad showed a sad girl, moving from her hometown and friends; then, it showed her happy with her family in a McDonald's restaurant in her new town (McKibben, 1992). The subtext (which caused the ad to be banned in Sweden) was that McDonald's is just as important and satisfying as friendship.

16. *The brain processes image-based or emotional media differently than text-based media.* As oft lectured by Neil Postman, images evoke emotions in the oldest and most powerful "reptilian" brain. Such reactions are more powerful than written and spoken language, which is processed in the most recently evolved part of the brain, the prefrontal, cerebral cortex. Thus, image-based media, such as movies, TV, and video, are more powerful and more quickly absorbed than text-based media because of their emotional effect, giving rise to much enjoyment but also creating the potential for powerful propaganda and, perhaps, a devaluation of more logic-based communication, for example, books. Reading a book is different than watching a documentary. There are always trade-offs.

17. *Composition techniques add effect.* By using effects, such as camera angles, close-ups, reaction shots, lighting, transitions, framing, graphics, sounds, and music, media increase the emotive and persuasive power of their messages.

18. *Media literacy can create active "deconstuctors" of media.* Constructions of media, especially high-speed electronic media, seek to create spontaneous consumers who accept products, lifestyles, or concepts. "Deconstructing" media is a skill; the more it is practiced, the easier and more automatic the process becomes. Media literacy helps people live life with more freedom, enjoying media, but with critical perspective, thinking of the media's creator and purpose and, it is hoped, with more control over their attitudes and behavior.

19. *Activists can create a better media culture.* Conversation, word of mouth, is valuable, and most of us influence a group of people, be it small or large. We can all make media of one type or another, especially with modern technology. In Russia, the Stalinist system of repression was brought down with word of mouth,

copy machines, and video tapes—a testament to the power and necessity of everyday people telling untold stories.

20. *Media education must precede media reform.* More and more people are realizing how important it is to have a media system that is open to new people and new perspectives, that elevates human values over commercial values, and that serves all human needs in the 21st century. As people better comprehend the information taught by media education, people can take action to reform our media system and create new alternatives, have more justice, and limit the power of those who abuse it by presenting harmful and unbecoming images to so many.

21. *Media education should not be left to Big Media.* As we have seen with curricula produced by Big Tobacco, Channel One, and other industries, conflicts of interests augur against allowing Big Media or their major advertisers to produce or fund media education curricula. It suggests that support for independent media organizations is important.

Unfortunately, most of today's media literacy curricula are financed by the very corporations that control access and censor media content. Groups that take no money from Big Media or big corporate advertisers are necessary.[5]

Student-Produced Anti-Ads

Figure 13.1

An interesting technique that is part of most media education curricula is student-created media education curricula. A common form is the counter-ad or anti-ad. The following pictures are a scan of a real Camel ad (see Figure 13.1), followed by two counter-ads, one by a fifth grader and another by a high school senior (see Figures 13.2 and 13.3).

While these anti-ads vary in sophistication, both are effective at using the *power* of the advertiser's original ad campaign, which cost millions of dollars to create and disseminate, to send a student-created, indeed, reversed and more truthful story, which cost very little.

When it comes to other content that can be investigated in media literacy and media education classes, the sky is the limit. The body of work on media production techniques, media criticism, and media lesson plans encompasses hundreds of books, videos, DVDs, Web sites, podcasts, and more. A good starting place might be the annotated bibliography at http://acmecoalition .org/essential_resources.

Skills of Media Literacy

A plethora of media literacy skills exist, but the basic ones involve being able to deconstruct a media example. To quickly deconstruct any media example, based on the above-cited general principles of media education, one should ask the following commonly accepted questions.

Questions for Deconstructing a Media Example Using the General Principles

1. Who paid for the ad?

2. Why does the company need to do the ad?

3. What group is targeted by the ad?

4. What about the ad leads one to that conclusion?

5. What is the ad's "text" and "subtext?"

6. What kind of culture(s) does the example create?

7. What value(s) are reinforced?

8. What techniques of persuasion are used?

9. What different meanings would different people perceive?

10 What is the connection to the world of commerce?

11. Is this an example of our "monopoly" media system?

12. What is not told? What related stories are missing?

13. How does the example try to move emotions? Is it simple/complex? Is it logical?

14. Is it closer to fantasy or reality?

15. Does it use stereotypes?

16. In what ways does this depict a lifestyle that is healthy and unhealthy?

17. What would a counter-ad based on this advertisement look like?

18. Considering this example, what can you do to help reform our media system?

Figure 13.2

SOURCE: Copyright Bob McCannon.

Figure 13.3

SOURCE: Copyright Bob McCannon.

A Sample Deconstruction

Figure 13.4

SOURCE: ©2008 James B. Beam Distilling Co., Clermont, KY.

The aforementioned "quick deconstruction" develops important critical thinking skills. The following example and possible answers represent the type of deconstruction that students can work toward (see Figure 13.4).

An alcohol company paid for the ad. Why? It is part of a huge industry that sells a cheap product at an expensive price, making great amounts of profit. No one needs the product; in fact, it is usually harmful, and thus all alcohol companies *must* advertise a great deal and tell substantial lies over and over, because if the truth were ever to become mainstream, their industry would die.

The picture indicates that the targets are young males. It is somewhat hard to ascertain, but they are probably Caucasian. The textual message compares relationships with girlfriends, drinking buddies, and Jim Beam whiskey. It shows a picture of the bottle and says, "Real friends. Real bourbon." In very small print, it names the company and alcohol percentage and says, "Real friends drink together responsibly."

The subtext suggests that substituting whiskey for girlfriends is good behavior because girls are frustrating. It suggests a cultural, media, and historical context for male drinking that is often found in our culture and is similar to that of many action movies. The ad's targets are part of that cultural subgroup that participates heavily in drinking as a macho bonding ritual, possibly college men (a big market) or those who see such activities as being cool, possibly young boys.

In this sense, the subtextual message is probably targeted at adolescent-minded males, which can include middle, high school, college, and older males (once a Bud man, always a Bud man . . .). Young adolescents experience the difficulty of relationships. Girls seem to be confusing and, at times, cause pain. Girls cannot be relied on, but Jim Beam will always be a buddy.

Alcohol companies have a problem similar to cigarette companies. They must create a culture that produces brand loyalty by ages 10 to 16 because by then kids decide whether to drink or not, and during this age, they usually develop some degree of brand loyalty. Suggesting that girls don't measure up is a technique that works well with adolescents, as young men have yet to learn how to create satisfying relationships with the female sex in general and dating in particular. In addition, adolescents are near puberty and somewhat insecure, so the psychological ploy (which is similar to tobacco ads) emphasizes the values of rugged independence and macho friendship in an effort to sell an addictive drug.

Jim Beam's other techniques include a variety of male symbols, card stacking, and straw men. The use of a black-and-white photo indicates casual fun and, perhaps, helps to spread the ethnicity a bit. The glass is above the camera and foreshortened to add power to the drink. The dark colors add freshness and reality to the bottle, which is in brilliant color and has phallic power. The picture suggests in powerful terms that alcohol provides status, success, friendship, and dependability; the bottle suggests that such benefits derive from a warm and mystically powerful source.

It is not a healthy lifestyle. Indeed, it glamorizes the fantasy that drinking makes one HAPPY, the life of the party. This lifestyle must be repeated endlessly by alcohol companies and represents Big Media monopoly because we see that message repeatedly in television, movies, magazines, and so on. In fact, reality indicates that those guys have headaches, poor job performance, rocky relationships, and disintegrating livers, not to mention empty wallets.

Media do not tell the untold stories of entertainment media. One often sees a tired movie hero come home and pour a drink or two. How often does one see a tired movie hero come home and take a nap?

How often do you hear such facts as the following: About two thirds of the population drink little or not at all; nondrinkers are just as happy, more successful, and they think big drinkers are uncool, wasteful, and unattractive. Drinkers are poorer, and after the initial drug high wears off, drinkers feel bad because alcohol is a depressant. Other disadvantages include, but are not limited to, headaches, serious medical conditions, sexual mistakes, car accidents, rapes, crimes, and child abuse.

The average person sees 100,000 alcohol ads (in all media) by the time she or he is age 18. That is censorship in a hypermediated commercial culture, the power of which can be seen by asking, "Will the average child have heard 'I love you' a hundred thousand times before he or she is 18?"

Last, the white print at the bottom of the page, which on the original is so small only good eyes can read it, says, "Real friends drink together responsibly." This is a technique called the Big Lie. One could find several reasons for that copy, but it is fun to ask kids to define responsible drinking and then carefully introduce the idea that 10% of the population are alcoholics. Then ask carefully (some parents are alcoholics) if alcoholics drink responsibly. When kids find out that alcoholics consume almost half of the alcohol products produced, many students conclude that Jim Beam makes half its money from irresponsible drinking. The students frequently ask, "Is Jim Beam really serious about responsible drinking?"

The ad is not a healthy message. For those who value loving relationships and friendships based on respect, the ad is an unfortunate addition to youth culture. Binge drinking among high school and college students, particularly among women, is a major problem.

A counter-ad for a product like this might look something like this sixth grader's ad for an alcohol product (see Figure 13.5).

A group of "specific" techniques of media, the "language of persuasion," was mentioned in the deconstruction above. This group of specific techniques generates *valuable skills* of analysis. It is being used by thousands of media education practitioners worldwide, and the *"language of persuasion" is one of the most valuable things to teach students of all ages.*

The general and specific skills are *true* skills. The more students practice, the better they become, and the more automatic the deconstruction process becomes, engendering more critically aware students and citizens. These are genuine and

Figure 13.5

SOURCE: Copyright Bob McCannon.

transferable critical thinking skills. When one asks, "How is this editorial an example of hyperbole?" a student must apply an abstract principle to concrete data, reinforcing both the principle and the process of higher level cognition. The skill can also transfer to other media or media production, and most important, it is *fun*.

The preceding deconstruction concerns what students can *do*. More answers are provided in the next two sections.

Media Literacy Production

Much has been written about how to do media production, but doing it with kids in a media literacy environment can be vastly rewarding or, unfortunately, a waste of time and money. First, one needs to fight the tendency to think that media production equals video production. Students can do much with pencil and paper, art supplies, role-playing, and skits.

Computer word processing, drawing, animation, and music software vastly enhance production, but low tech can also get high marks for media education. In this author's experience, fourth graders making cereal boxes that demonstrate food company sales can accomplish more than many fourth-grade video productions.

Thanks to advances in technology, video is becoming easier and less expensive to produce, but beware the tendency to spend inordinate amounts of time on the production process. One can never compete with what one sees on TV, and attempting to do so can take valuable time that could be spent researching an issue and learning more skills and content. Sometimes, short media education classes leave little time for production. In such cases, simple editing or even *no editing*, when combined with a carefully researched script and storyboard, can produce interesting and valuable video.

A valuable media literacy production technique already mentioned is the anti-ad. Anti-ads or counter-ads can be public service announcements, spoof ads, or ad satires. Creating counter-ads allows students to talk back to deceptive or harmful media messages and to experience some control over these powerful cultural icons.

Counter-ads can be effective educational and motivational devices. They can be parodies of advertisements and deliver untold information, yet they use the same persuasion techniques as real ads. By creating counter-ads, students can apply media literacy analysis skills to production, communicating positive messages in a fun and engaging exercise.

Creating Counter-Ads

The simplest way to create a counter-ad is to alter a real magazine or newspaper ad by changing the text or adding graphic elements; young students can just write or draw over the original ad or paste new materials onto it. Note the examples above. Collage techniques work well. Students can write scripts and read them to the class or record or videotape their counter-ads. Here are some battle-tested tips for making effective counter-ads:

Analyze. Look at several real ads and figure out why they are effective. The best counter-ads use the same techniques to deliver a different message.

Power. Your message has to break through the clutter of all the real ads that people see or hear. Think about what makes an ad memorable. What techniques does it use to grab attention? Use them.

Persuade. Use the same persuasion techniques found in real ads, such as humor, repetition, or flattery (the specific techniques) to deliver an alternative message.

Pictures. Visual images are powerful. People often forget what they read or hear but tend to remember what they see. The best counter-ads, like the best ads, tell their stories through pictures.

Rebellion. Advertising targeted at young people often appeals to a sense of youthful rebellion. Effective counter-ads expose misleading and manipulative advertising methods and turn teens' rebellious spirits against the corporate sponsors who use these methods.

KISS. Keep it short and simple. Use only one idea for your main message. Focus everything on getting this message across.

Plan. Try to think of everything—words, images, and design—before you begin production. Make sketches, storyboards, and rough drafts.

Practice. If you are going to perform a radio or TV script, your cast and crew will need to rehearse until it works.

Teamwork. Working in a team can lighten your workload and spark creativity. Brainstorm ideas as a group. Make sure all members share responsibility.

Revise. When you think you are finished, show your counter-ad to uninvolved people for feedback. Do they understand it? Do they think it is funny? Effective? Use their responses to revise your work for maximum impact.

Distribute. Your ideas were meant to be seen! Make copies of your counter-ads and post them around your school. Get them published in your school newspaper. Show your videotape to other kids and adults. Your counter-ad can stimulate needed discussion and debate around media and health issues that get little coverage.

Have fun! Making a counter-ad is an enjoyable way to learn about media and health, to be creative, and to express your views. Enjoy!

Activism and Media Education

While media literacy purists do not agree, prosocial activities are included in many media education classes and programs. Students and citizens can become active in hundreds of ways. Activism is important for it *changes cynicism, a negative, depressing force, into skepticism,* a positive, uplifting emotion that is based in knowledge of a problem and doing something to try and solve it. *Activist strategies should accompany all media literacy lessons.* What follows are a dozen suggestions for how to create activism. They have been used with students of all ages.

Question by analyzing all media you consume. "Deconstruct" the values promoted by movies, television, magazines, and video games. Do they use flattery, emotion, censorship, or product placements?

Teach by modeling critical media awareness for family and friends. *Share* ideas about media monopoly, media issues, and media reform. Be a "viral" cultural revolutionary; show/send exemplary clips/pictures/ads to friends.

Get busy! Get off the couch! Find activities that make you healthier, wealthier, and smarter. Don't take the flack; strike back!

Boycott by voting with your dollars. Make the worst offenders suffer.

Communicate with others; write letters to editors, sponsors, radio, and TV outlets about things you dislike and like. Look for images that denigrate people and cultures, are dishonest and unhealthy, and target the very young. Express yourself to store managers, billboard companies, advertising companies, politicians, and so on.

Support a position; investigate media's effects, and find out what you believe and develop an opinion. Find and work for a cause!

Volunteer your time and money for independent media, such as community cable, nonprofit campaigns, and so on. Start campaigns about ads, stories, or products. If you don't, who will?

Produce your own media (letters, stories, posters, essays, photos, performance, video, music, murals); encourage others to do so. Make and share counter-ads.

Establish an independent media venue—coffee house, 'zine, Web site, bulletin board—in your classroom or community.

Think about what makes you more feel more alive, more human, more natural, more loyal, more successful—now and (this is hard) in 30 years.

Join a media education/reform organization, such as www.acmecoaliton.org.

Remember that activists established democracy, abolished slavery, got the vote for women, fought for civil rights, and still are fighting for justice everywhere. You can be on a very important team.

Summary

Media literacy should be defined differently than media education. Empirical data on media literacy and media education are immature and mixed. They are especially weak in the area of producing changes in behavior, but the possibility exists if media education is combined with parental cooperation and limiting students' media diets.

Media education holds out much promise for teaching about the media, their access, effects, skills, and techniques of production. Media education skills and content would seem to be genuine critical thinking skills, and they are worth teaching in their own right.

Some basic principles of media literacy are widely agreed upon. Acceptance of media literacy skills is varied.

Techniques for implementing media literacy are varied and complex. They can also be subtle and require skill. Given the wide range of results demonstrated by studies to date, instruction in media education is highly recommended for those embarking upon media education. It is paramount for trainers of teachers to alert them to activities and methods that have been shown to backfire or rebound. Media production could be especially problematic and requires careful preparation and deployment to avoid superficiality, wasting time, and the rebound effect.

Activist strategies are not agreed upon but are numerous and being implemented by many as a crucial part of media education. Freedom of choice and investigation is necessary for activism to be an effective strategy, and an open, media-driven Socratic methodology is most likely to succeed. As shown in the reviewed studies, *many* new and innovative classroom strategies have been developed recently, and media literacy and media education can be part of achieving a long-desired goal of educational reformers—facilitated, active classrooms emphasizing critical thinking and active methodologies that connect to the real world of students, producing the mythical holy grail of education, a lifelong love of learning.

Exercises

1. Read an article or view a video clip. Establish a spectrum of possible opinions about the example by writing down the names of a group of people who would have different reactions to that article. Remember, people negotiate their own meanings from media, and all honest reactions should be honored. An example spectrum might be George W. Bush, Pat Robertson, Al Gore, Ralph Nader, Hillary Clinton, Barack Obama, Eminem, and Bart Simpson. They could be local people or people from your school.

When you have your list, think about the differing viewpoints of your group. If it is a class, assign a name to different students and have them write a paragraph that deconstructs a piece of media *from that person's point of view*. Use Questions for Deconstructing (mentioned earlier in this chapter) as your guide. This is a valuable exercise that circumvents the reluctance of students to express different points of view due to peer pressure. Amazing things can happen when a lover of Comedy Central has to deconstruct *South Park* from the point of view of Pat Robertson or has to role-play Pat in a debate with the student who got Bart Simpson.

2. Select a news article or story. Analyze 10 key words for bias. Then, change the words, and see if you can change the story. Make a list of the related ideas that the story did not mention, the untold stories. Discuss why that might be the case. Write a script for a news story that covers the omitted issues that you think are important.

3. Establish a definition of news (information useful to citizens in our democracy). *View a national network news program.* List the stories. How long was each? How much news fits the definition? How did each story make you feel? How many of the stories cause one to feel anxious? How many were "mayhem" (murders, disasters, typhoons, floods, tornadoes, repeat stories about older mayhem stories, etc.)? How many of these stories were actually useful to the average person? How many of the other stories are? What vital information do the stories leave out? Which were the most "enjoyable"? Were the enjoyable ones valuable for citizens in a democracy? Were any of the stories truly educational? How much of the half hour is advertising? What were the advertisements? (Neil Postman's theory is that bad news makes people anxious, and anxious people buy more pain relievers, medications, insurance, and the other products advertised on the news.) Make lists of the nation's and world's most pressing problems. What did the program leave out? Were any addressed in meaningful detail? What led the news (what the program signaled as the most important story)? Was it the most important issue? If not, why was it first?

4. View a local news program. How many of the questions above also apply? How much of the half hour is local news? How much was repeated national news? Why is there national news on the local news (hint: it's cheaper—why)? How much mayhem? (Why do you have to see every car accident in your town?) How much

was advertising? Was it more than national news? How much was sports? How much was weather? Is all of the weather useful? Did the hosts spend some time in "chitchat"? How much? Were there any "fluff" stories (cute and emotional but useless "kitten rescued from tree" type stories)? Did any stories seem to benefit a corporation (as much as 25% of local news stories are VNRs—video news releases—made by corporations for their benefit)? Make a list of the most important issues in your community for you, your school, or your neighbors. Were any of them addressed? Make your own news program that emphasizes your issues.

5. Visit a local television station. Take a tour. Or have a representative come to your class. Ask the news manager questions about their program. Compare the local television news program to a newspaper for content, detail, variety, depth, and usefulness. Think about the process of reading a newspaper versus watching TV news. In which process do you think the individual consumer has more freedom? Learns more? Has more interest? Why would people rather watch than read? Is it the same for everyone? Which medium is better for voters? Democracy? Seek out some alternative sources of media (broadsheets, the Web, community radio/TV) and apply the same questions, making comparisons between the mainstream and independent media sources.

6. Bill McKibben (1992) insightfully and humorously observes the current explosion of information that has transformed our cultural landscape. He also concludes that, despite our having access to more information than any other culture in history, "we also live in a moment of deep ignorance, when vital knowledge that humans have always possessed about who we are and where we live seems beyond our reach" (p. 9). McKibben refers to this condition as an Unenlightenment, *an age of missing information.* One can test this theory in many ways, but here are a few. Watch a nature program with time-lapse photography of plants exploding before your very eyes or view an SUV commercial that takes place in a natural setting. What meaning is sent about the natural world in these media messages? As the SUV chews its way across fields, climbs mountains, and blasts through forests, what is said about ecology, the delicate balances that maintain life? What message is sent about how to enjoy nature? Or the kind of stimulation that brings pleasure? Or conservation of resources? Or whether there are any limits to man's enjoyment of nature?

Next, grow a plant from a seed. Keep a detailed log. What does growing a plant teach about limits? What happens if the plant does not get enough water or light or nutrients? Or too much? Which teaches the truer lesson about limits, the fantasy world of advertising or the natural world of growing the plant?

Notes

1. *Business literacy:* The ability to use financial and business information to understand and make decisions that help an organization achieve success.

Computer literacy: The ability to use a computer and its software to accomplish practical tasks.

Health literacy: The degree to which individuals have the capacity to obtain, process, and understand basic health information and services needed to make appropriate health decisions.

Information literacy: The ability to know when there is a need for information, to be able to identify, locate, evaluate, and effectively use that information for the issue or problem at hand.

Media literacy: The ability to decode, analyze, evaluate, and produce communication in a variety of forms.

Technology literacy: The ability to use media such as the Internet to effectively access and communicate information.

Visual literacy: The ability, through knowledge of the basic visual elements, to understand the meaning and components of the image.

2. The free program is available at www.nichd.nih.gov/msy.

3. Anecdotally, this author showed the Media Education Foundation film, *DreamWorlds II,* which is about music videos leading to attitudes that can cause rape, to high school juniors and seniors each year for 6 years in a one-semester media literacy course. The first showing was a disaster, with males angry (rebound effect) and females fearful. Parents called, and many of the students criticized use of the film. With the help of a psychologist, a structured previewing preparation and postviewing debriefing were developed that were successful to the point that for the past 2 years, the students' evaluations unanimously rated the video as the number one outside resource used in the course.

4. This writer has provided workshops in hundreds of classrooms where C1 was shown and never saw a teacher-student discussion about C1's news.

5. A gateway to such groups can be found at the Action Coalition for Media Education (ACME) Web site (www.acmecoaliton.org).

References

Anderman, E., & Johnston, J. (1997). Channel One: Television news in the middle school classroom. *Middle School Journal, 28,* 33–36.

Anderson, C., Berkowtiz, L., Donnerstein, E., Huesmann, L., Johnson, J., Linz, D., et al. (2003). The influence of media violence on youth. *Psychological Science in the Public Interest, 4,* 103.

Anderson, C., & Bushman, B. J. (2001). Effects of violent video games on aggressive behavior, aggressive cognition, aggressive affect, physiological arousal, and prosocial behavior: A meta-analytic review of the scientific literature. *Psychological Science, 12,* 353–359.

Armstrong, G. M., & Brucks, M. (1988). Dealing with children's advertising: Public policy issues and alternatives. *Journal of Public Policy & Marketing, 7,* 98–113.

Ascione, L. (2006). *eSchool News.* Retrieved September 10, 2006, from http://www.eschool news.com/news/showStory.cfm?ArticleID=6578

Asthana, S. (2006). *Innovative practices of youth participation in media: A research study on twelve initiatives from around the developing and underdeveloped regions of the world.* Retrieved September 16, 2006, from http://portal.unesco.org/ci/en/ev .php-URL_ID=22831&URL_DO=DO_TOPIC&URL_SECTION=201.htm

Aufderheide, P. (1992). *Media literacy: A report of the national leadership conference on media literacy.* Washington, DC: Aspen Institute.

Austin, E. W. (2001). Effects of family communication on children's interpretation of television. In J. Bryant & J. A. Bryant (Eds.), *Television and the American family* (2nd ed.). Mahwah, NJ: Lawrence Erlbaum.

Austin, E. W., Chen, M., & Grube, J. W. (2006). How does alcohol advertising influence underage drinking? The role of desirability, identification and skepticism. *Journal of Adolescent Health, 38,* 376–384.

Austin, E. W., Chen, Y., Pinkleton, B. E., & Johnson, J. Q. (2006). Benefits and costs of Channel One in a middle school setting and the role of media-literacy training. *Pediatrics, 117,* 423–433.

Austin, E. W., & Johnson, K. K. (1997). Effects of general and alcohol-specific media literacy training on children's decision making model about alcohol. *Journal of Health Communication, 2,* 17–42.

Austin, E. W., Miller, A. C., Silva, J., Guerra, P., Geisler, N., Gamboa, L., et al. (2002). The effects of increased cognitive involvement on college students' interpretations of magazine advertisements for alcohol. *Communication Research, 29,* 155–179.

Austin, E. W., Pinkleton, B. E., & Fujioka, Y. (2000). The role of interpretation processes and parental discussion in the media's effects on adolescents' use of alcohol. *Pediatrics, 105,* 343–349.

Austin, E. W., Pinkleton, B. E., & Funabiki, R. P., (2007). The desirability paradox in the effects of media literacy training. *Communication Research. 34,* 483–506.

Austin, E. W., Pinkleton, B. E., & Hust, S. T. (2005). Evaluation of an American Legacy Foundation/Washington State Department of Health media literacy pilot study. *Health Communications, 18,* 75–79.

Austin, E. W., Pinkleton, B. E., Van de Vord, R., Arganbright, M., & Chen, Y. (2006). Channel One and effectiveness of media literacy. *Academic Exchange Quarterly 10,* 115–120.

Bachen, C. M. (1998). Channel One and the education of American youths. *Annals of the American Academy of Political and Social Science, 557,* 132–145.

Bandura, A. (1986). *Social foundations of thought and action: A social cognitive theory.* Englewood Cliffs, NJ: Prentice Hall.

Barkin, S., Ip, E., Richardson, I., Klinepeter, S., Finch, S., & Krcmar, M. (2006). Parental media mediation styles for children aged 2 to 11 years. *Archives of Pediatric Adolescent Medicine, 160,* 395–401.

Barrett, J. (1995, August). *Student and teacher perspectives on Channel One: A qualitative study of participants in Massachusetts and Florida schools.* Paper presented at the annual meeting of the Association for Education in Journalism and Mass Communication, Washington, DC.

Barrett, J. (1998). Participants provide mixed reports about learning from Channel One. *Journal of Mass Communication in Education, 53,* 54–68.

Behson, J. (2002). Media literacy for high-risk children and youth. *Telemedium: The Journal of Media Literacy, 48,* 38–40.

Biocca, F., Brown, J., Shen, F., Bernhardt, J. M., Batista, L., Kemp, K., et al. (1997). Assessment of television's anti-violence messages: University of North Carolina at Chapel Hill study. In *National television violence study* (Vol. 1, pp. 413–530). Thousand Oaks, CA: Sage.

Brighouse, H. (2005). Channel One, the anti-commercial principle, and the discontinuous ethos. *Educational Policy, 19,* 528–549.

Brodeur, J. (2005). *Preventing youth violence with media education, the 10-Day Challenge (TV and videogame free).* Retrieved August 16, 2006, from http://www.edupax.org/Assets/divers/documentation/1_articles/OCPVE%20Media%20Education%20For%20Violence%20Prevention.htm

Brown, J. A. (2001). Media literacy and critical television viewing in education. In D. G. Singer & J. L. Singer (Eds.), *Handbook of children and the media* (pp. 572–573). Thousand Oaks, CA: Sage.

Budelmann, R. (2002). Substance and flash: Media literacy meets juvenile justice. *Telemedium: The Journal of Media Literacy, 48,* 41–42.

Buerkel-Rothfuss, N. L., & Buerkel, R. A. (2001). Family mediation. In J. Bryant & J. A. Bryant (Eds.), *Television and the American family* (2nd ed., pp. 355–376). Mahwah, NJ: Lawrence Erlbaum.

Buijzen, M., & Valkenburg, P. M. (2003). The unintended effects of television advertising: A parent child survey. *Communication Research, 30,* 483–503.

Bushman, B. J., & Cantor, J. (2003). Media ratings for violence and sex: Implications for policy makers and parents. *American Psychologist, 58,* 130–141.

Bushman, B. J., & Stack, A. D. (1996). Forbidden fruit versus tainted fruit: Effects of warning labels on attraction to television violence. *Journal of Experimental Psychology: Applied, 2,* 207–226.

Business Wire. (2008). *Channel One appoints Dr. Paul Folkemer SVP, director of education.* Retrieved February 2, 2008, from http://biz.yahoo.com/bw/080124/20080124005179 .html?.v=1

Cantor, J. (1998). Ratings for program content: The role of research findings. *Annals of the American Academy of Political and Social Science, 557,* 54–69.

Cantor, J., Sparks, G. G., & Hoffner, C. (1988). Calming children's television fears: Mr. Rogers vs. the Incredible Hulk. *Journal of Broadcasting & Electronic Media, 32,* 271–288.

Cantor, J., & Wilson, B. J. (2003). Media and violence: Intervention strategies for reducing aggression. *Media Psychology, 5,* 363–403.

Charlesworth, A., & Glantz, S. A. (2005). Smoking in the movies increases adolescent smoking: A review. *Pediatrics, 116,* 1516–1528.

Cincotta, K. (2005). Accord gets kids to munch right. *B & T Magazine, 8,* 26. Retrieved April 22, 2005, from www.bandt.com.au

Committee on Finance, U.S. Senate. (2006). *Minority report.* Retrieved October 23, 2006, from http://www.senate.gov/~finance/press/Bpress/2005press/prb101206.pdf

Committee on Public Education. (1999). Policy statement. *Pediatrics, 104,* 341–343.

Concerned Children's Advertisers (CCA). (2004). *2004 annual report.* Toronto: Author.

Corder-Bolz, C. R. (1980). Mediation: The role of significant others. *Journal of Communication, 30,* 106–118.

Cowrie, N. (1995, Fall). Media literacy's new challenge. *Video and Learning,* p. 1.

Doolittle, J. C. (1980). Immunizing children against possible antisocial effects of viewing television violence: A curricular intervention. *Perceptual and Motor Skills, 51,* 498.

Dorr, A., Graves, S. B., & Phelps, E. (1980). Television literacy for young children. *Journal of Communication, 30,* 71–83.

Eagle, L. (2005). *Commercial media literacy: What does it do, to whom—and does it matter?* (Middlesex University Business School Discussion Paper Series). Retrieved August 26, 2006, from http://www.mubs.mdx.ac.uk/research/discussion_papers/marketing/dpap_ mkt_no31.doc

Ehman, L. (1993, November). *Channel One in social studies: Three years later.* Paper presented at the annual meeting of the National Council for the Social Studies, Nashville, TN.

Filotas, D. Y. (1993). *Adolescents' rape attitudes: Effectiveness of rape prevention education in high school classrooms.* Unpublished master's thesis, University of California, Santa Barbara.

For your information: Media Smart youth program. (2006). *AAP News, 27,* 24.

Fox, R. F. (2005). Researching media literacy: Pitfalls and possibilities. *Yearbook of the National Society for the Study of Education, 104,* 251–259.

Giedrys, S. A. (1999). Creating a curriculum to help girls battle eating disorders. *Harvard Gazette Archive*. Retrieved August 6, 2006, from http://www.hno.harvard.edu/gazette/1999/02.11/eating.html

Gonazales, R., Glik, D., Davoudi, M., & Ang, A. (2004). Media literacy and public health: Integrating theory, research and practice for tobacco control. *American Behavioral Scientist, 48*, 189–201.

Graham, J. W., & Hernandez, R. (1993). *A pilot test of the AdSmarts curriculum: A report to the Scott Newman Center*. Los Angeles: Institute for Health Promotion and Disease Prevention Research, Department of Preventive Medicine, University of Southern California.

Greenberg, B. S., & Brand, J. E. (1993). Television news and advertising in schools: "Channel One" controversy. *Journal of Communication, 43*, 143–151.

Hicks, D. J. (1968). Effects of co-observer's sanctions and adult presence on imitative aggression. *Child Development, 39*, 303–309.

Hindin, T. J., Contento, I. R., & Gussow, J. D. (2004). A media literacy nutrition education curriculum for Head Start parents about the effects of television advertising on their children's food requests. *Journal of the American Dietetic Association, 104*, 192–198.

Hobbs, R. (1998). The seven great debates in the media literacy movement. *Journal of Communication, 48*, 16–32.

Hobbs, R. (2004a). Does media literacy work? An empirical study of learning how to analyze advertisements. *Advertising Educational Foundation: Advertising and Society Review, 5*, 4.

Hobbs, R. (2004b). A review of school-based initiatives in media literacy education. *American Behavioral Scientist, 48*, 42–69.

Hobbs, R. (2005). The state of media literacy education. *Journal of Communication, 55*, 865–871.

Hobbs, R., & Frost, R. (1999). Instructional practices in media literacy education and their impact on students' learning. *New Jersey Journal of Communication, 6*, 123–148.

Hobbs, R., & Frost, R. (2003). Measuring the acquisition of media literacy skills. *Reading Research Quarterly, 38*, 330–355.

Horton, R. W., & Santogrossi, D. A. (1978). The effect of adult commentary on reducing the influence of televised violence. *Personality and Social Psychology Bulletin, 4*, 337–340.

Huesmann, L., Eron, L. D., Klein, R., Brice, P., & Fischer, P. (1983). Mitigating the imitation of aggressive behaviors by changing children's attitudes about media violence. *Journal of Personality and Social Psychology, 44*, 899–910.

Huesmann, L., & Taylor, L. (2004). The case against the case against media violence. In D. Gentile (Ed.), *Media violence and children* (pp. 108–130). Westport, CT: Praeger.

Huston, A. C., Donnerstein, E., Fairchild, H. H., Fesbach, N. D., Katz, P. A., Murray, J. P., et al. (1992). *Big world, small screen: The role of television in American society*. Lincoln: University of Nebraska Press.

Infante, D. A., Rancer, A. S., & Womack, D. F. (2003). *Building communication theory*. Prospect Heights, IL: Waveland.

Intons-Peterson, M. J., Roskos-Ewoldsen, B., Thomas, L., Shirley, M., & Blut, D. (1989). Will educational materials reduce negative effects of exposure to sexual violence? *Journal of Social and Clinical Psychology, 8*, 256–275.

Irving, L. M., & Berel, S. R. (2001). Comparison of media-literacy programs to strengthen college women's resistance to media images. *Psychology of Women Quarterly, 25*, 103–111.

Johnston, J., & Anderman, E. (1993). *Channel One: The school factor*. Ann Arbor: University of Michigan Institute for Social Research.

Johnston, J., & Brzezinski, E. (1992). *Taking the measure of Channel One: The first year.* Ann Arbor: University of Michigan, Institute for Social Research.

Johnston, J., Brzezinski, E., & Anderman, E. (1994). *Taking the measure of Channel One: A three year perspective.* Ann Arbor: University of Michigan, Institute for Social Research.

Kaiser Family Foundation. (2003). *Media literacy fact sheet.* Retrieved June 12, 2006, from http://kaiserfamilyfoundation.org/entmedia/upload/Key-Facts-Media-Literacy.pdf

Kavoori, A., & Matthews, D. (2004). Critical media pedagogy: Lessons from the thinking television project. *Howard Journal of Communications, 15,* 99–114.

Kleinman, M. (2003, October). Heinz fights food ad criticism with Media Smart link. *Marketing (UK),* p. 1.

Knupfer, N., & Hayes, P. (1994). The effects of the Channel One broadcast on students' knowledge of current events. In A. De Vaney. (Ed.), *Watching Channel One: The convergence of students, technology and private business* (pp. 42–60). Albany, NY: SUNY Press.

Krcmar, M. (2001, May). *Channel One: The effect of commercials in the classroom—a natural experiment.* Paper presented at the annual meeting of the International Communication Association, Chicago.

Kubey, R., & Hobbs, R. (2000). *Setting research directions for media literacy and health education.* Retrieved September 8, 2006, from http://www.mediastudies.rutgers.edu/mh_conference/index.html

Kunkel, D. (2005). Predicting a renaissance for children and advertising research. *International Journal of Advertising, 24,* 401–405.

Lewis, J., & Jhally, S. (1998). The struggle over media literacy. *Journal of Communication, 48,* 109–120.

Life Skills Training. (2006). *Resource fact sheet.* Retrieved August 23, 2006, from http://www.lifeskillstraining.com/resource_facts.php

Linz, D., Fuson, I. A., & Donnerstein, E. (1990). Mitigating the negative effects of sexually violent mass communications through preexposure briefings. *Communication Research, 17,* 641–674.

Littleton, H., & Ollendick, T. (2003). Negative body image and disordered eating behavior in children and adolescents: What places youth at risk and how can these problems be prevented? *Clinical Child and Family Psychology Review, 6,* 51–66.

Livingstone, S. (2004). Media literacy and the challenge of new information and communication technologies. *Communication Review, 7,* 3–14.

Livingstone, S., & Helsper, E. J. (2006). Does advertising literacy mediate the effects of advertising on children: A critical examination of two linked research literatures in relation to obesity and food choice. *Journal of Communication, 56,* 560–584.

Mandel, L. L., Bialous, S. A., & Glantz, S. A. (2006). Avoiding "Truth": Tobacco industry promotion of life skills training. *Journal of Adolescent Health, 39,* 868–879.

McCannon, R. (2002). Media literacy: What? Why? How? In V. Strasburger & B. Wilson (Eds.), *Children, adolescents & the media* (pp. 322–367). Thousand Oaks, CA: Sage.

McCannon, R. (2005). Adolescents and media literacy. *Adolescent Medicine Clinics, 16,* 463–480.

McChesney R. W. (2002, October). *Keynote.* Presented at the founding conference of the Action Coalition for Media Education, Albuquerque, NM. Recording available at http//www.acmecoalition.org

McChesney, R. W. (2004). *The problem of the media.* New York: Monthly Review Press.

McKibben, B. (1992). *The age of missing information.* New York: Plume.

McLellan, F. (2002). Marketing and advertising: Harmful to children's health. *The Lancet, 360*, 1001.

Media Smart. (2003). *Media Smart overview.* Retrieved August 17, 2006, from http://www.mediasmart.org.uk/media_smart/ofcom.html

Molnar, A., Garcia, D. R., Boninger, F., & Merrill, B. (2006). *A national survey of the types and extent of the marketing of foods of minimal nutritional value in schools.* Arizona State University, Commercialism in Education Research Unit. Retrieved August 15, 2006, from http://www.asu.edu/educ/epsl/CERU/Documents/EPSL-0609-211-CERU-exec.pdf

Moore, J., DeChillo, N., Nicholson, B., Genovese, A., & Sladen, S. (2000, Spring). Flashpoint: An innovative media literacy intervention for high-risk adolescents. *Juvenile and Family Court Journal,* pp. 23–33.

Muto, S. (2004). Children and media. *Young Consumers, 6,* 37–43.

Nathanson, A. I. (1999). Identifying and explaining the relationship between parental mediation and children's aggression. *Communication Research, 26,* 124–143.

Nathanson, A. I. (2002). The unintended effects of parental mediation of television on adolescents. *Media Psychology, 4,* 207–230.

Nathanson, A. I. (2003, October). *The effects of mediation content on children's responses to violent television: Comparing cognitive and affective approaches.* Paper presented at the International Communication Association Convention, San Diego.

Nathanson, A. I. (2004). Factual and evaluative approaches to modifying children's responses to violent television. *Journal of Communication, 54,* 321–336.

Nathanson, A. I., & Cantor, J. (2000). Reducing the aggression-promoting effect of violent cartoons by increasing children's fictional involvement with the victim. *Journal of Broadcasting & Electronic Media, 44,* 125–142.

Nathanson, A. I., & Yang, M. (2003). The effects of mediation content and form on children's responses to violent television. *Human Communication Research, 29,* 111–134.

Neumark-Sztainer, D., Sherwood, N. E., Coller, T., & Hannan, P. J. (2000). Primary prevention of disordered eating among preadolescent girls: Feasibility and short-term effect of a community-based intervention. *Journal of the American Dietetic Association, 100,* 1466–1473.

Neumark-Sztainer, D., Wall, M., Story, M., & Perry, C. (2003). Correlates of unhealthy weight-control behaviors among adolescents: Implications for prevention programs. *Health Psychology, 22,* 88–98.

Nirva, P., Levine, M., & Irving, L. (2000, November/December). Go girls! Media literacy, activism, and advocacy project. *Healthy Weight Journal,* pp. 89–90.

Obligation.com. (2006a). *Deconstructing Judy.* Retrieved August 11, 2006, from http://www.obligation.org/article.php?recordID=44

Obligation.com. (2006b). *Latest news: 2006.* Retrieved October 22, 2006, from http://www.obligation.org/latestnews.php

Palmer, E. L., & Carpenter, C. F. (2006). Food and beverage marketing to children and youth: Trends and issues. *Media Psychology, 8,* 165–290.

Pinkleton, B., Austin, E. W., Cohen, M., & Miller, A. (2003, June). *Media literacy and smoking prevention among adolescents: A year-two evaluation of the American Legacy Foundation/Washington State Department of Health anti-tobacco campaign.* Paper presented at the International Communication Association, Health Communication Division, San Diego.

Pipher, M. (2001). *Reviving Ophelia: Saving the selves of adolescent girls* [Video]. Northhampton, MA: Media Education Foundation.

Piran, N., Levine, M., & Irving, L. (2000). GO GIRLS! Media literacy, activism, and advocacy project. *Healthy Weight Journal, 14,* 89–90.

Potter, W. J. (2004). *Theory of media literacy: A cognitive approach.* Thousand Oaks, CA: Sage.

Quin, R., & McMahon, B. (1995). Evaluating standards in media education. *Canadian Journal of Educational Communication, 22,* 15–25.

Rapaczynski, W., Singer, D. G., & Singer, J. L. (1982). Teaching television: A curriculum for young children. *Journal of Communication, 32,* 46–55.

Reid, L., & Gedissman, A. (2000). Required TV program in schools encourages poor lifestyle choices. *AAP News.* Retrieved July 19, 2006, from www.aap.org/advocacy/reid1100.htm

Robinson, T. N. (1999). Reducing children's television viewing to prevent obesity: A randomized controlled trial. *Journal of the American Medical Association, 282,* 1561–1567.

Robinson, T. N., Borzekowski, D. L. G., Matheson, D. M., & Kraemer, H. C. (2007). Effects of fast food branding on young children's taste preferences. *Archives of Pediatric Adolescent Medicine, 161,* 792–797.

Robinson, T. N., Saphir, M. N., Kraemer, H. C., Varady, A., & Haydel, K. F. (2001). Effects of reducing television viewing on children's requests for toys: A randomized controlled trial. *Journal of Developmental and Behavioral Pediatrics, 22,* 179–184.

Robinson, T. N., Wilde, M. L., Navracruz, L. C., Haydel, K. F., & Varady, A. (2000). Effects of reducing children's television and video game use on aggressive behavior. *Archives of Pediatric and Adolescent Medicine, 156,* 17–23.

Rosenkoetter, L. I., Rosenkoetter, S. E., Ozretich, R. A., & Acock A. C. (2004). Mitigating the harmful effects of violent television. *Journal of Applied Developmental Psychology, 25,* 25–47.

Ruskin, G. (2006). *Executive director of Commercial Alert.* Retrieved August 29, 2006, from http://www.commercialalert.org/issues/

Sargent, J. D., Beach, M. L., Dalton, M. A., Mott, L. A., Tickle, J. J., Ahrens, M. B, et al. (2001). Effect of seeing tobacco use in film on trying smoking among adolescents: Cross sectional study. *Behavior Medicine Journal, 323,* 1–16.

Sargent, J. D., Dalton, M. A., Beach, M. L., Mott, L. A., Tickle, J. J., Ahrens, M. B., et al. (2002). Viewing tobacco use in movies: Does it shape attitudes that mediate adolescent smoking? *American Journal of Preventive Medicine, 22,* 137–145.

Silverblatt, A. (2001). *Media literacy: Keys to interpreting media messages.* Westport, CT: Praeger.

Singer, D. G., Zuckerman, D. M., & Singer, J. L. (1980). Critical TV viewing: Helping elementary school children learn about TV. *Journal of Communication, 30,* 84–93.

Slater, M., Rouner, D., Murphy, K., Beavais, F., Van Leuven, J., & Domenech-Rodriguez, M. (1996). Adolescent counterarguing of TV beer advertisements: Evidence for effectiveness of alcohol education and critical viewing discussions. *Journal of Drug Education, 26,* 143–158.

Steiner-Adair, C., Sjostrom, L., Franko, D., Pai, S., Tucker, R., Becker, A., et al. (2002). Primary prevention of risk factors for eating disorders in adolescent girls: Learning from practice. *International Journal of Eating Disorders, 32,* 401–411.

Straubhaar, J., & LaRose, R. (2004). *Media now: Understanding media, culture, and technology.* Belmont, CA: Wadsworth/Thomson.

Teinowitz, I. (2001). World Ad Federation seeking consistency. *Advertising Age, 72,* 35.

Tiene, E., & Whitmore, D. (1995). Beyond "Channel One": How schools are using schoolwide television networks. *Educational Technology, 33,* 38–42.

Tyner, K. (1998). *Literacy in a digital world.* Mahwah, NJ: Lawrence Erlbaum.

Valkenburg, P. M. (2005, June). Parental mediation of undesired advertising effects. *Journal of Broadcasting & Electronic Media*, p. 1.

Vooijs, M. W., & van der Voort, T. H. A. (1993). Learning about television violence: The impact of a critical viewing curriculum on children's attitudinal judgments of crime series. *Journal of Research and Development in Education, 26,* 133–142.

Wade, T., Davidson, S., & O'Dea, J. (2003). A preliminary controlled evaluation of a school-based media literacy program and self-esteem program for reducing eating disorder risk factors. *International Journal of Eating Disorders, 33,* 371–383.

Whitmore, D., & Tiene, D. (1994). Viewing Channel One: Awareness of current events by teenagers. *Mass Communication Review, 21,* 67–75.

Wilson, B. J. (1989). The effects of two control strategies on children's emotional reactions to a frightening movie scene. *Journal of Broadcasting & Electronic Media, 33,* 397–418.

Wilson, B. J., Linz, D., Donnerstein, E., & Stipp, H. (1992). The impact of social issue television programming on attitudes toward rape. *Human Communication Research, 19,* 179–208.

Wilson, B. J., Linz, D., Federman, J., Smith, S., Paul, B., Nathanson, A., et al. (1999). *The choices and consequences evaluation: A study of Court TV's antiviolence curriculum.* Santa Barbara: Center for Communication and Social Policy, University of California.

Wilson, B. J., & Weiss, A. J. (1991). The effects of two reality explanations on children's reactions to a frightening movie scene. *Communication Monographs, 58,* 307–327.

Winkel, F. W., & DeKleuver, E. (1997). Communication aimed at changing cognitions about sexual intimidation: Comparing the impact of a perpetrator-focused versus a victim-focused persuasive strategy. *Journal of Interpersonal Violence, 12,* 513–529.

Yates, B. L. (2004). Applying diffusion theory: Adoption of media literacy programs in schools. *Studies in Media and Information Literacy Education, 4.* Retrieved August 29, 2006, from http://128.100.205.52/jour.ihtml?lp=simile/issue14/bradfordXfulltext.html

Author Index

Subject Index

ABC, 51, 100, 102
ABCNews.com, 100
Abdul, Paula, 412
Abercrombie, 65
Abortion, 217. *See also* Pregnancy
    (teen and unplanned);
    Sex and sexuality
Absence of resilience, 287
Abstinence-only sex
    education, 226
Academy Awards, 236
Acceptance of diversity, 122–123
Acceptance of others, 122–123
AC/DC, 338
ACME. *See* Action Coalition for
    Media Education (ACME)
ACOG. *See* American College
    of Obstetrics and
    Gynecology (ACOG)
*Acompaname (Accompany
    Me)*, 126
ACT. *See* Action for Children's
    Television (ACT)
Action Coalition for Media
    Education (ACME), 522–523
Action for Children's Television
    (ACT), 82, 100–101
Active mediation, 506
Adolescents:
    anatomical changes to
        brain in, 446
    antisocial peer pressure, 17
    challenges of, 15
    children versus, 14–17
    development transitions
        and, 14–17

hours spent with different
    media, 7–8
impact of advertising of drugs
    on, 287–289
incidence and thoughts of
    suicide among, 186
increased independence and,
    15–16
older children versus, 27–30
peer influence and, 16–17
prosocial media for, 125–126
puberty and sexual
    development, 17
spending power of, 44–45
See also Drugs; Family; Sex and
    sexuality; Young people;
    and entries for specific media
Adults, children versus, 10–13. *See
    also* Parent-child conflict;
    Parents
Adults Only (AO) rating, 444
Adult Web sites, 479–482, 490
Advergames, 76–77, 485
Advertising, 101–102
    advergames as, 76–77, 485
    antismoking, 312–314
    attention to, 53–55
    brand loyalty and, 63–64
    cigarettes, 289–294, 311–314
    cognitive processing of, 53
    comprehension of, 56–63
    comprehension of disclaimers,
        61–63
    content analysis of television,
        49–53
    contraceptive, 248–251

desire for products and, 66–69
digital-age marketing
    techniques, 383
discrimination of, from
    programming, 55–56
drugs and, 289–294
eating disorders and body
    image, 399, 403–404
historical changes in, to
    children, 46–49
impact of, drugs on children
    and adolescents, 287–289
industry self-regulation and,
    84–85
marketing strategies in 21st
    Century, 75–82
media literacy and, 539–544
money spent on, and marketing
    to children, 4–46
music and, 346
"nag factor," 44
nature of, in newer media, 62–63
nonprescription drugs, 308–309
persuasive impact of, 63–73
phases of consumer behavior
    during childhood, 74
prescription drugs, 307–309
recognition of bias, 58
regulation of, targeted to
    youth, 82–85
research on alcohol, 299–304
school billboards, 80–81
sexuality and, 220–224, 241–243
teaching advertising literacy, to
    children, 85–87
television, 44–45, 47–73

About the Authors

Edward Donnerstein is Professor of Communication and Dean of the College of Social and Behavioral Sciences at the University of Arizona. Prior to his appointment at Arizona in 2002, he was the Rupe Chair in the Social Effects of Mass Communication and Dean of Social Sciences at the University of California, Santa Barbara. A social psychologist, he received his PhD in psychology in 1972. He held appointments at the University of Wisconsin, as well as visiting positions at the University of Lethbridge and Beijing University, China.

His major research interests are in mass media violence, as well as mass media policy. He has published more than 220 scientific articles in these general areas and serves on the editorial boards of a number of academic journals in both psychology and communication. He was a member of the American Psychological Association's Commission on Violence and Youth and the APA Task Force on Television and Society. He served on a Surgeon General's panel on youth violence as well as on the Advisory Council of the American Medical Association Alliances violence prevention program. He is Past President of the International Society for Research on Aggression. In addition, he was primary research site director for the National Cable Television Association's 3.5 million-dollar project on TV violence.

He has testified at numerous governmental hearings both in the United States and abroad regarding the effects and policy implications surrounding mass media violence and pornography, including testimony before the U.S. Senate on TV violence. He has served as a member of the U.S. Surgeon General's Panel on Pornography and the National Academy of Sciences Subpanel on Child Pornography and Child Abuse.

Jeanne B. Funk, PhD, is a clinical child psychologist. She is Distinguished University Professor of Psychology and past Director of the Clinical Psychology doctoral training program in the Department of Psychology, University of Toledo in Toledo, Ohio. She is involved in teaching psychology to graduate and undergraduate students and conducting clinical research. She directs a research team that has been investigating relationships between playing violent video games and various personality and behavioral characteristics in children since 1990. In 2005, she was awarded the Outstanding Researcher award at the University of Toledo. Dr. Funk and her team have developed measures of children's attitudes toward violence and empathy that are used in her research projects and by researchers worldwide. She is currently finalizing the development of a measure of engagement in video game playing. At present, the team is focusing on identifying characteristics that may be specific risk factors for negative impact from game playing, including desensitization to violence and deep engagement in game playing. Dr. Funk and her team are also examining parental perception and knowledge of game and other media ratings, particularly among parents of younger children.

Amy B. Jordan is Director of the Media and the Developing Child sector of the Annenberg Public Policy Center at the University of Pennsylvania, where she studies the impact of media policy on children and families. Her children have been valuable sources of information and inspiration.

Bob McCannon is an independent media education consultant and co-founder and Co-President of the Action Coalition for Media Education, the only independent, national media education organization in the United States. He formerly was Executive Director of the New Mexico Media Literacy Project (NMMLP), founded in 1993. From 1993 to 2005, he built NMMLP into the largest and most successful media literacy project in the United States. With an undergraduate degree in psychology and modern German history and a graduate degree in the cognition of education, he has taught propaganda, history, advertising, and media education in middle school, high school, and graduate school. As the only non-pediatrician to be honored by the American Academy of Pediatrics' coveted Holroyd/Sherry award for quality media instruction and concern for the welfare of children, Bob does workshops, keynotes, and presentations each year, having done thousands in every state and many countries. More than 1,000 people have taken his 4-day media education, train-the-trainer workshops. He has authored dozens of nationally recognized media education curricula in the fields of health, history, social studies, English, and civic education.

Dorothy G. Singer, EdD, is Research Scientist in the Department of Psychology at Yale University. She is also Codirector of the Yale University Family Television Research and Consultation Center and a Fellow of Morse College. In addition, she is Research Associate at Yale Child Study Center. Formerly, she was the William Benton Professor of Psychology, University of Bridgeport. She is also a Fellow of the American Psychology Association.

Victor C. Strasburger, MD, is currently Chief of the Division of Adolescent Medicine, Professor of Pediatrics, and Professor of Family & Community Medicine at the University of New Mexico. He graduated from Yale College (summa cum laude and Phi Beta Kappa), where he studied fiction writing with Robert Penn Warren, and from Harvard Medical School. He trained at the Children's Hospital in Seattle, St. Mary's Hospital Medical School in London, and the Boston Children's Hospital.

Dr. Strasburger has authored more than 120 articles and papers and 8 books on the subject of adolescent medicine and the effects of television on children and adolescents, including *Getting Your Kids to Say No in the 1990's When You Said Yes in the 1960's* (1993), which has sold more than 15,000 copies to date; *Adolescent Medicine: A Practical Guide* (1991; 2nd edition, 1998); and *Adolescents and the Media* (1995). In the year 2000, he was named the recipient of the American Academy of Pediatrics' Adele Delenbaugh Hofmann Award for outstanding lifetime achievement in Adolescent Medicine and the Holroyd-Sherry Award for outstanding achievement in public health and the media.

He is a consultant to the American Academy of Pediatrics' Committee on Communications, has served as a consultant to the National PTA and the American Medical Association on the subject of children and television, and lectures frequently throughout the country.

Barbara J. Wilson is Professor in the Department of Speech Communication at the University of Illinois at Urbana-Champaign. She received her PhD from the University of Wisconsin–Madison. Before joining the University of Illinois, she was on the faculty at the University of California, Santa Barbara for 12 years.

Professor Wilson's research focuses on the social and psychological effects of mass media on youth. She is coauthor of three book volumes of the *National Television Violence Study* (1997–1998). In addition, she has published more than 50 scientific articles and chapters on media effects and their implications for public policy. Recent projects include children's emotional reactions to television news and adolescents' interpretations of sexual messages in the media.

Professor Wilson has served as a consultant for Nickelodeon, the National Association of Television Program Executives, and Discovery Channel Pictures. She is Associate Editor of the *Journal of Communication* and serves on the editorial boards of four other academic journals (*Communication Monographs, Communication Reports, Human Communication Research,* and *Media Psychology*).